Searching For Sugar Man II: Rodriguez, Coming From Reality, Heroes & Villains

ROCK N ROLL BOOKS BY HOWARD A. DEWITT

Searching For Sugar Man: Sixto Rodriguez' Mythical Climb To Rock N Roll Fame and Fortune (2015)

Van Morrison: Them and the Bang Era, 1945-1968 (2005)

Stranger In Town: The Musical Life of Del Shannon (with D. DeWitt (2001)

Sun Elvis: Presley In The 1950s (1993)

Paul McCartney: From Liverpool To Let It Be (1992)

Beatle Poems (1987)

The Beatles: Untold Tales (1985, 2nd edition 2001)

Chuck Berry: Rock 'N' Roll Music (1981, 2nd edition1985)

Van Morrison: The Mystic's Music (1983)

Jailhouse Rock: The Bootleg Records of Elvis Presley (with Lee Cotton) (1983)

HISTORY AND POLITICS

Sicily's Secrets: The Mafia, Pizza & Hating Rome (2017)

Meeting Hitler: A Tragicomedy (2016)

The Road to Baghdad (2003)

A Blow To America's Heart: September 11, 2001, The View From England (2002)

Jose Rizal: Philippine Nationalist As Political Scientist (1997)

The Fragmented Dream: Multicultural California (1996)

The California Dream (1996)

Readings In California Civilization (1981, 4th edition revised 2004)

Violence In The Fields: California Filipino Farm Labor Unionization (1980)

California Civilization: An Interpretation (1979)

Anti Filipino Movements in California: A History, Bibliography and Study Guide (1976)

Images of Ethnic and Radical Violence in California Politics, 1917-1930: A Survey (1975)

NOVELS

Stone Murder: A Rock 'N' Roll Mystery (2012)

Salvador Dali Murder (2014)

SPORTS BOOKS

The Phoenix Suns: The View From Section 101 (2013)

"What do we mean here by 'existence precedes essence'? We mean that man first exists: he materializes in the world, encounters himself, and only afterward defines himself. He will not be anything until later, and then he will be what he makes of himself. Thus, there is no human nature since there is no God to conceive of it. Man is not that which he conceives himself to be, but that which he wills himself to be, and since he conceives of himself only after he exists, man is nothing other than what he makes of himself. This is the first principle of existentialism."

~ Jean-Paul Sartre from Existentialism Is Humanism

"We see that Rodriguez, as mysterious and absent as he was, animated these people's lives in a period of despair and isolation. What might have seemed provincial or self-indulgent becomes in Bendjelloul's sensitive hands powerfully life-affirming. He crafts a deeply poignant narrative that's unafraid of personal sentiments but never succumbs to sentimentality. There is no cynicism or back-covering irony. Instead the unusual sincerity of the storytelling casts an enchanting spell over the viewer."

Andrew Anthony, London Guardian, commenting on the Oscar winning documentary Searching For Sugar Man

“This is the best story I’ve ever heard!
It was kind of a fairy tale.”

MALIK BENDJELLOUL

“I was ready for the world. I don’t think
the world was ready for me.”

SIXTO RODRIGUEZ

Searching For Sugar Man II: Rodriguez, Coming From Reality, Heroes & Villains

Howard A. DeWitt

HORIZON BOOKS
PO BOX 4342
SCOTTSDALE, AZ 85261

Horizon Books
P. O. Box 4342
Scottsdale, AZ
85261-4342

E Mail: Howard217@aol.com
First Published 2017

ISBN: 1979310513
ISBN 13: 9781979310512
Library of Congress Catalogue Number: 2017916980
CreateSpace Independent Publishing Platform
North Charleston, South Carolina

Table of Contents

"You either live under a rock or you walk in the sunshine. That's pretty much how it goes."

SIXTO RODRIGUEZ

"I see my path but I don't know where it leads. Not knowing where I'm going is what inspires me to travel it."

SIXTO RODRIGUEZ

"The 'rags to rags' story of Sixto Rodriguez, the 'Latin Bob Dylan,' who is back in the spotlight after forty years in the wilderness."

JAMES DELINGPOLE, LONDON TELEGRAPH
COMMENTING ON A 2009 CONCERT.

Introduction

"But thanks for your time, then you can thank me for mine, forget it."

Sixto Rodriguez

"When I say 'I' it seems hollow to me."

Jean Paul Sartre, Nausea

"All families got secrets, but Joy's had more than their fair share,"

Marsha Hunt's novel Joy (1990)

The Sixto Rodriguez story is well known. He is the singer who came back from the dead in 2012 to become an international star. His two albums **Cold Fact** and **Coming From Reality** failed to sell and he returned to anonymity. Then two South Africans Stephen "Sugar" Segerman and Craig Bartholomew-Strydom brought him back to worldwide acclaim. The tall, portly, bilious South African, Segerman, jiggled when he walked as his baldhead glistened in the sun talking about his brilliance in finding Rodriguez. His partner, Craig Bartholomew-Strydom, was quiet, reserved, a brilliant writer and not prone to overstatement and he didn't trumpet his genius as did Segerman. They told the story of Sixto Rodriguez while appearing in the Oscar winning documentary **Searching For Sugar Man**. Then they wrote an excellent book. They told the story from their perspective. It was convoluted, they twisted the facts, they overemphasized South Africa, they ignored Australia, they diminished London, they didn't understand the American music business and they had a personal agenda bordering on hagiography. They did as much to disrespect Rodriguez as those who cheated him for forty years. Their tale is one of mythmaking, ignoring reality and today Segerman will come to your venue and lecture on the Sugar Man for a four thousand dollar fee plus the perks of a rock star. That is the point of this book. It is to show how an entitled wanker from Cape Town twisted a brilliant story in a morass of unintelligible nonsense. The sub-title to their book tells it all: "The True Story Behind The Award Winning Documentary." This egomaniacal behavior tells one why and how they twisted the story.

This is the second book on Sixto Rodriguez. The first volume, **Searching For Sugar Man: Sixto Rodriguez' Mythical Climb To Rock 'N' Roll Fame and Fortune** concentrated upon the early Detroit influences, his life as a single parent, his failure to find commercial success with **Cold Fact**, and his dramatic comeback as a touring performer as a result of the Oscar winning documentary **Searching For Sugar Man**.

This book covers the background to and the production of Rodriguez' second album **Coming From Reality**. It explains how and why Steve Rowland worked with Rodriguez. It is necessary to examine the inside players, notably Clarence Avant, Harry Balk and Neil Bogart, to understand the story. The fans, Stephen "Sugar" Segerman and Craig Bartholomew-Strydom, are profiled to show how and why their hunt brought the Sugar Man to South African cult audiences.

The rise of Rodriguez' popularity in Australia and the U. K. is also necessary to understanding the story. A record executive, Matt Sullivan at Light In The Attic, is a key to Rodriguez' re-emergence. The re-issues, the concerts, and the drama prior to stardom in 2012 convinced the geeks living in their parent's basement to make the Sugar Man a cult icon.

I faced a structural problem. As I divided the material, I placed it into three categories. The first volume concentrated on **Cold Fact**, the production genius of Mike Theodore and Dennis Coffey and why and how the debut album failed and Sixto Rodriguez fell by the wayside. The mystery that is the Sugar Man ran through the first volume. Rodriguez didn't talk to Malik Bendjelloul for months perhaps even for more than a year. He wasn't interested in a film about his life and his career. He softened his view after almost two years. His daughter, Regan, became close to filmmaker Malik Bendjelloul. Rodriguez was still not impressed. Enter Steve Rowland. He quietly educated Bendjelloul in how to approach and deal with the Rodriguez family. The obstacles Malik Bendjelloul overcame would have defeated most people. Not Malik! He was on his way to an Oscar.

The biographer never approached Rodriguez or his family. Their privacy is respected. But to write the book it was necessary to interview those close to them. This was not a problem. I ambushed some people in Detroit. Others were eager to talk. Many demanded anonymity. The major players talked in numerous interviews but there was a sense of paranoia, suspicion and some attempted to focus the story without historical accuracy. As this book shows Stephen "Sugar" Segerman presented a convoluted view of the Rodriguez phenomenon. In sharp contrast, his research and writing partner Craig Bartholomew Strydom told the story honestly and accurately. The problem is myth continually triumphed reality.

This volume sets the story straight and calls out the misuse of facts, the attempts to focus the story exclusively on South Africa and the personal tales skewing the story beyond reality. The story often was lost in the welter of conflicting opinions and personal angst. The Bartholomew-Strydom book, which he co-wrote with the pompous and the egomaniacal Segerman, is an excellent piece of biography. But it is not about Rodriguez. It concentrates on Bartholomew-Strydom and Segerman's search for the Sugar Man. The sub-title to their book tells one all they need to know about their dilettantish approach.

I did spend an hour backstage with Rodriguez and his family before a concert with Steve Rowland. When Steve said I was writing a book there was a dead silence. They weren't happy. Then the next day, after I left too many of my professor cards around, I received half a dozen phone calls. Suddenly I had people who let me inside the Sugar Man's world. I now had a picture of the mysterious singer-songwriter that emerged as the star of the 2012 Indie documentary. He could still perform with skill. He emerged as a popular concert attraction. The wait was over. Sixto Rodriguez was a star. This complicated the story. Fame and fortune has rewarded Rodriguez while robbing him of his privacy. The documentary brought the Sugar Man to international prominence. This is the story. The back-story is Steve Rowland. He produced Rodriguez' second album **Coming From Reality**, but that is only a small part of the story. Rowland guided Bendjelloul toward completing **Searching For Sugar Man**, extending his advice to Rodriguez on a proposed third album and publicizing the Sugar Man's legend. The difference between Rowland and the South African's is he doesn't have a personal agenda.

Thanks to the documentary, Rodriguez' story is well known. He is the singer who was more popular than Elvis Presley, the Beatles or the Rolling Stones in South Africa. The problem is he didn't know anything about his fame. The rumors of his death, a fake story of a suicide with drugs, his shadowy professional life and his vanishing act after recording two albums made the documentary even more compelling. The truth is Sixto Rodriguez was well and alive living in Detroit's historic Woodbridge neighborhood. He lives in a two-story home on Avery Street. It is a bucolic area lined with trees, students walking to Wayne State University and families strolling with their children. It is a wholesome all American, blue collar neighborhood. Rodriguez would not have it any other way. The notion he was no longer in Detroit was one of many South African myths.

He had not vanished. He performed where and when he could. He did have a career, if a bit under the radar. One of the bogus mysteries perpetuated by the South African detective, Stephen "Sugar" Segerman, is Rodriguez was lost from the general public, missing from the record business, dead or simply his life had taken another direction. None of this was true. Segerman was on a quest. If a mythical one! The beauty of Segerman's obsessive-compulsive search for the Sugar Man is it took on epic proportions. Along with a skilled writer, Craig Bartholomew-Strydom, who lived for a time in Baltimore, the pair described a filmmaker attempting his first full length documentary, and they focused upon him in their book **Sugar Man: The Life, Death And Resurrection of Sixto Rodriguez**. This unknown, but brilliant, young documentary genius, Malik Bendjelloul, brought the story to fruition in **Searching For Sugar Man**.

For a time Bendjelloul lived in Segerman's guesthouse in a Cape Town suburb. They worked on the story flushing out the Sugar Man's mystery, and along the way, Segerman is owed a debt of gratitude by every Sixto Rodriguez fan. He brought the story to the general public. They embraced it. Bendjelloul's documentary **Searching For Sugar Man** won an Oscar as Rodriguez furtively began to tour the world. He had spent forty years off the road. Now it was time to get paid. It is a once in a lifetime tale bringing stardom to Rodriguez forty years after recording two of the finest albums in rock and roll history. When mainstream stardom arrived in 2012, Rodriguez wasn't fully prepared for its impact.

One of the problems with fame and fortune is people want to know everything about the real Sixto Rodriguez. This is not an easy task. He is excessively private. He is eccentric. He has a patterned, defined lifestyle that fame interrupted. His calm Motor City daily rituals remain intact. In Detroit he has a presence. No one bothers him. He is like an existential philosopher sitting at home drinking tea or perhaps smoking the tea to find meaning in his life and the world around him.

The Oscar winning documentary failed to mention his two marriages, his present girl friend, Bonnie, the full lives of his three daughters who were in the story, if only for a moment, but the ultimate sense of privacy Rodriguez demands limited his appearances in **Searching For Sugar Man**. How did Rodriguez react to an Oscar for the documentary?

In numerous interviews the Sugar Man said: "It is Malik's film, let him take the credit." This explains why the shy and reclusive Rodriguez didn't attend the Oscar ceremony. He had more important things on his mind. He also had to recover from a strenuous South African tour. He is the patriarch of a wonderful family.

He loves his family. He does everything he can for them. The Sugar Man is not a complicated person. He is brilliant. He is simple. He wants to be left alone. But he has lost his privacy. Everyone wants to meet him, talk to him and to hear his experiences. It is a burden.

There is an element of myth and reality to Rodriguez' life. One of the critics of my first book, Dr. Goodness, on Amazon, said there was nothing new in the four hundred and forty four page biography. Had Dr. Goodness actually read the book, he would have realized there were hundreds of unknown things about Sixto Rodriguez. It is a story of a career no one has examined in depth. The need to respect the Sugar Man's privacy is paramount. It is also a way of defining his persona.

What is it that drives Sixto Rodriguez' music? What are the elements in Detroit influencing his music? There are fifteen key components shaping Rodriguez' music.

1.) He is the product of his Woodbridge-Cass Corridor neighborhood. This spurred his political activism. It also created the images crafting his songs, as well as the people, instrumental in his life. There is a Wayne State University anti-establishment tone to his politics. The police beat him for his politics. He has conducted numerous political campaigns. He has tirelessly attended meetings of even small groups, like the Detroit Water Board, to support blue-collar politics. He does this quietly. He abhors publicity.

2.) His songwriting brilliance is partially the result of a Bachelor of Arts degree in philosophy from the Wayne State University Honors College. A close friend told me his lyrical talents were in place long before he received his 1981 sheepskin.

3.) The Sugar Man is a high level working musical professional. He didn't retire. The story is after two albums failed to sell he was done with the music business. This is not true. He was never out of the business. He continued to perform in small, local Detroit venues. His desire to share his music never waned.

4.) He is a life long political activist continually running for public office. It wasn't just the Detroit Mayor and City Council positions he coveted, Rodriguez also campaigned for state office. He remains a committed political activist. He has a long record of supporting liberal causes. He is a constant thorn in the police's side due to what Rodriguez said is "disrespect for the average citizen."

5.) He has been a civil rights advocate his entire life. Women's rights are his number one cause. This is followed by attempts to reform Detroit government.

6.) He was an advocate of legalizing marijuana long before it was a popular cause.

7.) He had a cult musical career prior to the release of the award winning **Searching For Sugar Man**. He toured Australia and South Africa prior to the art theater success of Malik Bendjelloul's film.

8.) The question of Rodriguez' royalties were addressed in the first book without a resolution. The various lawsuits remain out of the public eye and in the courts. Word is Rodriguez prevailed in three lawsuits.
9.) Rodriguez' songwriting influence is demonstrated among a wide variety of contemporary musicians including Paolo Nutini, David Holmes, Dave Matthews, Midnight Oil, Petra Jean Phillipson, Nas, The Smoke, a host of reggae musicians and Susan Cowsill among others.
10.) The myths and realities of Sixto Rodriguez examined in the first book remain an integral part of the story.
11.) The business practices and devious nature of the record business was a big part of the first book. That story remains. It will be touched on in this volume without a resolution.
12.) The role of Light In The Attic and Matt Sullivan in re-releasing Rodriguez' two brilliant albums is examined in depth.
13.) Steve Rowland is the catalyst to **Coming From Reality**. Why is this important? It highlights the Sugar Man's creative diversity. The second album was so different from the first one it provides a contrasting commercial style.
14.) **Cold Fact** received virtually no U. S. airplay upon its release in 1970. It had sporadic play on U. K., European, Australian and South African radio. Why is this important? A number of fledgling bands, most of whom who went nowhere, embraced Rodriguez' writing style and vocal nuances. The number of bands that heard the music and were influenced by "Sugar Man" is legendary. A case in point is the English pop group from York, The Smoke. They were excellent songwriters as well as a three-piece dynamite musical group. When they hit the British charts with "My Friend Jack," which rose to number 45 in the U. K. and came in at number two on the German listings, they appeared to be on the

way to stardom. Then the BBC banned airplay of the song over alleged references to drugs. The irony is they listened to Rodriguez' "Sugar Man" and wrote a completely different song using his ideas, musical cadence and lyrical direction. In 1972 The Smoke released a single "Sugar Man" backed with "That's What I Want." It went nowhere but in concert, and in comments to the press, the band talked of how Rodriguez' song defined their sound. The irony continued in 1996 when an anthology of their material was released. The album title was **The Best of Sugar Man**. One wonders how many other obscure, fledgling and perhaps hit bands heard "Sugar Man" and were influenced by it?

15.) How much influence did Sixto Rodriguez have upon fledgling and successful songwriters? No one knows. The question is open to debate. On the surface it would appear he had little, if any, impact upon the creative process of others. Not true! He was an unseen influence upon a host of songwriters from the early 1970s to the present. When The Smoke wrote "Sugar Man" their original song bore his indelible stamp. But in the 1970s others who heard Rodriguez' albums wrote with an elan reminiscent of his lyrical flowering. Since most artists couldn't write like the Sugar Man they recorded his songs. Steve Rowland with his group, The Family Dogg, placed six tracks on an album. Ken Boothe, a Jamaican singer, has made a career of interpreting Rodriguez' music. Paolo Nutini regularly casts Rodriguez' songs into his interpretive mantra. But can others write like Rodriguez? The answer is a resounding "No." He is too original.

The role of legendary producer Steve Rowland is examined in detail. From his Palm Springs home, Steve spent hundreds of hours sitting for interviews, going over the material and recalling his accomplished forty-year plus record-producing career. He was the glue that held the second album, **Coming From Reality**, together. Rowland demanded he be allowed to produce a second Sixto Rodriguez album. The resulting LP brought an intriguing intellectual rock sound to the early 1970s.

Rowland's role producing **Coming From Reality** is a seminal one. He had to lobby for months to produce the second album. He didn't need the job. Rowland saw musical brilliance in Rodriguez. Steve was a multi-platinum producer. Why did he spend months demanding to produce Rodriguez' second album? The answer is a simple one. Rowland had never heard a songwriter of Rodriguez' talent. He was the only person in the industry who believed in the Sugar Man. There were two acclaimed producers who made the first album a masterpiece. The producers, Dennis Coffey and Mike Theodore, were the perfect compliment for the Sugar Man's first song cycle. Why? Coffey and Theodore's production techniques had a pop-psych sense. It worked. That is everywhere but on the charts.

While Dennis Coffey and Mike Theodore produced a brilliant album with **Cold Fact**, there were differences in Rowland's approach. He gave Rodriguez carte blanche studio freedom. Steve would talk in low, reassuring tones to the Sugar Man. He mixed the album for commercial, pop success. It didn't happen. However, more than forty years later, Rowland's producing magic revealed an album that is much like a movie with a beginning story line, a build up to the climax and a theatrical ending. But Rowland's role in Rodriguez' life didn't end with **Coming From Reality**. They connected through the documentary. Rowland remains in constant touch with the Sugar Man. In 2013, he was the musical director for two of Rodriguez' New York shows. They spent a great deal of time together catching up on the past. They had in-depth discussions about Rodriguez' new music. They have been in touch concerning a third album. So far there is no resolution.

As Steve Rowland sat for more than two hundred hours of interviews, his recall is one hundred percent. He has no axes to grind. I found he often downplayed his role in **Searching For Sugar Man**. My joke about Steve is: "The only person who doesn't know Steve Rowland is Steve Rowland is Steve Rowland." He laughs at this joke. In the next breath he tells me I had been a college professor for too many years. He has a point. The extended stardom that the Sugar Man experiences is due to the two albums and a period of forty plus years of commercial gestation. No one is happier for him than Rowland.

There is another person close to the story who received acclaim. Then he committed suicide. That is the filmmaker Malik Bendjelloul. The success of **Searching For Sugar Man** and the Oscar was a double-edged sword. The end result was Bendjelloul's untimely death. The documentary impacted his life in a negative manner. He went to his grave with the dark secrets of how success haunted him. The relationship between Bendjelloul and Rowland was personal, professional and continued until Malik's tragic suicide.

The influence and role of Stephen "Sugar" Segerman and Craig Bartholomew-Strydom remains important in the Rodriguez story. They have a proprietary interest in the Sugar Man and their book, **Sugar Man: The Life, Death And Resurrection of Sixto Rodriguez**, published by Bantam Books in 2015, is an excellent examination of his career in South Africa, Australia and the U. K. There are forces in the U. S. the Bartholomew-Strydom-Segerman book misses.

This book differs from the South African fan tome in many ways. They have a hagiography approach. They seldom take issue with missed concerts, poor business decisions, and they fail to call out those who malign and dehumanize Rodriguez' career. I have attempted to criticize when there is a need to set the record straight, but Rodriguez is above the fray. He is not interested in analysis. Those around him have a protective demeanor. No one is stealing any of his money. He decides where and how it is spent. There are a group of dragons. That is those individuals who want to feed off Rodriguez' incipient stardom and take advantage of the situation either monetarily or personally.

Some, like Stephen "Sugar" Segerman, have attached themselves to Rodriguez' stardom. That is a positive and a negative. Segerman became a distraction in the Sugar Man's career and over time he has been shunted into the background. Bartholomew-Strydom is a professional writer who continues to have Rodriguez' confidence.

When I interviewed people, via telephone and skype, in South Africa there was a great deal of information on how and why Segerman's pompous, imperious and self-aggrandizing posture caused problems. But Rodriguez is unfailingly loyal to friends. Even those who attempt to use him for professional gain.

Over time Rodriguez distanced himself from Segerman. He did so for business-personal reasons. The privacy Sixto Rodriguez demands causes him to run hot and cold on people. Those who have a more professional demeanor remain in his good graces. This is why Craig Bartholomew-Strydom remains close to the Sugar Man.

Craig Bartholomew-Strydom is a serious music journalist, as well as an over the top fan. He likes nothing more than to share a joint with Rodriguez while attending one of his concerts. But Craig never lets his close friendship or admiration for the Sugar Man get in the way of objective writing. He is a fair and impartial observer. For that clearly detached view of the Sixto Rodriguez story read his Bantam Press book. In sharp contract, Stephen "Sugar" Segerman acts like he personally invented Rodriguez. He likes to sign autographs at his record store Mabu Vinyl. From time to time he will hide out in Mabu Vinyl and his business partner, Jacques Vosloo, tells curious sightseers that "Sugar" is not available due to the rigors of fame and fortune. He has a quirky personality as befits a young man who was the longest running Quiz Kid on South African television. He was called the kid who knew everything. He still has that moniker. He is a good guy. He is responsible for convincing Malik Bendjelloul to begin the Oscar winning documentary **Searching For Sugar Man**. But he is also at times, according to friends, an entitled boor. For me, he is seminal to the story.

The problem with Segerman is he believes he is a concert promoter or a music manager. He doesn't understand the first thing about bringing a successful concert to fruition. He brought Rodriguez to South Africa to appear in a record store. He had his daughter open for the Sugar Man. He was involved in a series of London shows that failed financially.

When I briefly interacted twice with Segerman, I found him warm, polite and inviting. Then when I said I was writing a book there was a silence. I sent him a rough copy of my first Rodriguez book, which I rushed out four months before their insipid tome. This was unnecessary as Sugar and Craig's book bears little resemblance to my two volumes. They are good guys. I couldn't have done this volume without their book. When Segerman e-mailed me the statement: "How could I do that without him?" I ended all communication. Then I called a number of people I knew around Cape Town. They told me Segerman was a problem. Over and over people said: "That bald headed son of a bitch is impossible." They said he feels entitled. It is like he owns the Rodriguez story. I did find many others important to the story. In appendix I, in the forthcoming third volume, I have included every person, company, event and circumstance to help understand Sixto Rodriguez. It may be too much information but enjoy it.

The role of music men Harry Balk, Clarence Avant and Neil Bogart needs further study. Bogart was instrumental in Steve Rowland producing the second album. Avant was not the criminal Malik Bendjelloul suggested while interviewing him in **Searching For Sugar Man**. Harry Balk is one of the most respected producers in the music world. At ninety, he was as sharp as in his day when he was one of Detroit's premier record producers. Then he passed away. These music men didn't ruin Rodriguez' career, as some have suggested. They were simply in the mix.

In 1998-1999 I interviewed Harry Balk extensively for the 2001 book **Stranger In Town: The Musical Life of Del Shannon**. What was apparent is Balk did not continue with acts that didn't have an immediate Detroit impact. This is why he named his record label Impact. He tested songs in the local market. If they hit, they received extensive national promotion. Rodriguez didn't have a hit in the Detroit market. Harry told him to get a day job. That said Rodriguez has had only good things to say about Balk. He recognizes he is a Detroit legend.

There is another area of interest in Rodriguez' career. That is the tours and performances since **Searching For Sugar Man**. They took away his privacy while making millions of dollars. It is money he has given away. Financial gain remains of little interest. His family is another matter. They are happy, not just about his artistic recognition, they are equally appreciative of the monetary rewards. The rigors of the road, combined with the whims of the critics, are not the Sugar Man's favorite pastime. He remains on the road for his fans. He loves touring.

The influence of Matt Sullivan and Light In The Attic in producing the reissues of the Sugar Man's two albums is seminal to his developing legend. LITA's role in the concerts he performed, prior to the fame and fortune, brought on by **Searching For Sugar Man** is another key to his career resurgence. How the documentary influenced the lives of all the major players is important to understanding the story. For the **Coming From Reality** album, Steve Rowland's role is critical. What has never been revealed is Rowland was a weekly adviser to Malik Bendjelloul, as he completed the documentary. The Swedish filmmaker called Rowland weekly, sent rushes of the unfinished documentary, and they discussed every aspect of the story line. Steve had a lengthy movie career, and he produced hundreds of hit records. The e-mails between Rowland and Bendjelloul display a warm friendship and professional bond. Rowland never asked for and never wanted credit for the production.

The proof is in the pudding. What this means is the hundreds of in-depth e-mails between Rowland and Bendjelloul provide a road map for the Oscar winning **Searching For Sugar Man**. Malik in an e-mail said Rowland "enhanced the documentary."

Steve Rowland receives inquiries monthly about his producing career, his acting and his in development television series on 1950s Hollywood. It speaks to his current creative muse. Stephen "Sugar' Segerman and Craig Bartholomew-Strydom continue to promote the Sugar Man's legacy. John Battsek, Simon Chinn and Camille Skagerstrom remain active in documentary filmmaking. Sandra Rodriguez Kennedy is a songwriter and a performer with talent. Regan Rodriguez manages her father's career, as well as children and a husband. Eva Rodriguez is retired from the military. She is pursuing her creative interests. She has recently moved back to Detroit and purchased a home in Woodbridge. Sixto Rodriguez continues to delight his fans. He enjoys the notoriety concerning his songwriting.

The comparisons to Bob Dylan are tiring ones. Yet, this is part of Rodriguez' mantra. His use of lyrics, his references to American history, and his hidden meanings cause the critics to make this comparison. The truth is he is an original singer-songwriter.

Where does Rodriguez fit in the realm of biography? This is an important question. His songs reflect Detroit, the broader scope of American history, the woes of the blue-collar, downtrodden worker, as well as the protest minded individual who envisions a need to alter our nation's direction.

These subjects suggest how and why Sixto Rodriguez is an important force in American history. His South African friends, notably Stephen "Sugar" Segerman and Craig Bartholomew-Strydom, talk like they invented the Sugar Man. They didn't. They brought him back. For that we are all thankful. Then they created myths and ignored some of the realities.

The Sugar Man's story could have ended after the failure of **Cold Fact**. It didn't. Why? It was due to one man. That man is Steve

Rowland. Everyone wants to take credit for approving a second album. Until Rowland discovered **Cold Fact,** by accident, in a London music office, no one was interested in Sixto Rodriguez. When he asked to produce a second Rodriguez album, everyone laughed. Rowland persisted. He had to convince skeptical record executives the Sugar Man had a commercial future. He did. He had to convince Clarence Avant. He did. He had to convince Neil Bogart. He did. Industry insiders were not interested in a second album. They wanted hits. What they received was a cult album exploding more than forty years after its production into an international phenomenon.

Rowland produced dozens of chart friendly U. K. hits. Many of his productions crossed over into the American charts. The industry gurus told Steve to do what he needed to produce chart hits. He didn't change the way Rodriguez worked in the studio. Rodriguez laid down his vocals. Steve produced the musical sounds that made the Sugar Man a commercial phenomenon forty-one years later.

What happened to the royalties? This is the $64,000 question. This book takes the available information and makes some basic assumptions. Since 2012 there are reliable figures on Rodriguez' sales figures. How accurate these figures are is open to speculation.

The lawsuits and the threats over royalties remain. When the first book was completed, I attempted to verify some of the royalties paid since 2012. "Mind your fucking business." That was the first response from a major label. Then another caller told me that the lawsuit would reveal who had the money, where it went and who was the culprit in the royalty mess. What I didn't realize is the lawsuit quickly turned into three legal actions.

The last area of interest is the Rodriguez industry. This is the level of sales, concert activity and the ancillary rights from the albums and **Searching For Sugar Man**. For five years there has been speculation, rumor and a few hasty facts concerning a third album. In London, in South Africa and in Australia there is constant demand for a third Sugar Man album. In the U. S. the same anticipation is evident at his concerts. In the American market, he remains a concert favorite. The fervor to read about the Sugar Man is a reflection of strong interest in his continued career. This has prompted Rodriguez' manager, Regan, to cut back on media interviews. After three years of success the Sugar Man and his family are wary of the press. The reporters and industry people I talked to remark: "He is paranoid." They explain so many negative things have happened in his life, he is withdrawn. When Steve Rowland was talking backstage with Rodriguez in 2013, in New York, when he was the master of ceremonies at one show, he complained he couldn't confer privately with the Sugar Man because of industry insiders. They talked continually about deals.

Steve Rowland: "There was a guy from one of the record labels. A big fat, repulsive industry type who told Rodriguez he was the next best thing. We had to go into the bathroom and lock it to have a conversation."

The Sugar Man and his management have limited backstage access. Everyone wants to talk to him. The loss of privacy came with fame and money. The question to ponder: "Is fame and fortune worth the loss of privacy?" The glare of the media and the intrusion of strangers, even ones who write books, is an obstacle. Is it all worth it? Yes!

The question on everyone's mind is: "Who is Rodriguez?" The answer! He is a brilliant songwriter, a seasoned performer and a star. That is a big part of the story as the Oscar for **Searching For Sugar Man** and the money he has made touring is sweet redemption. Is it worth it? This book will answer that question. Listen to the Sugar Man's lyrics. The words create his legacy. He is an ethereal shadow floating in the wilderness.

This is the second of three volumes on Sixto Rodriguez. Why three volumes? The first book dealt with the making of **Cold Fact**, the avarice of the record business, the role of the major players Harry Balk, Clarence Avant, Mike Theodore, Dennis Coffey, Matt Sullivan, Stephen "Sugar" Segerman, Craig Bartholomew-Strydom and Steve

Rowland. This volume concentrates upon the Rowland produced second album **Coming From Reality**, the cascading ride of fame and fortune from the Oscar winning documentary **Searching For Sugar Man**, and how Rodriguez became a cult artist before crashing into mainstream prominence.

Research on this project began in 2012 the afternoon after I left the Scottsdale Camelview Theater. I sat through **Searching For Sugar Man** twice. Then I came back everyday for a week. I realized the Sixto Rodriguez tale was a multi-layered story. By the time the third volume is released the Sugar Man's story will take more than 1300 plus pages and more than 450,000 words to complete the saga. This may seem too long. It is necessary to the story. It is one of the mysteries of rock and roll history. The three volumes on Sixto Rodriguez reach beyond the brilliance of the man and into the deep and dark recesses of a business famous for cheating and destroying its own. Sixto Rodriguez survived in anonymity with his talent intact; miraculously Malik Bendjelloul's documentary gave him a second chance. That is the story. Enjoy it!

The life and art of Sixto Rodriguez tells us a great deal about Detroit, the small record labels like Sussex, and the path artists traverse through the show business milieu. Biography is a path to studying personal humanity. The Sugar Man is a case study in persistence, passion and perseverance. He is quixotic and high-spirited. The Sugar Man's music will live on as it has hit a chord in the American psyche. There is no tragic end to the story. It is one of rediscovery and rebirth. It is also a tale told of myth and a flight from reality.

Prologue

"He is the greatest artist I recorded
and why he didn't have number one
hits for decades still baffles me."

Steve Rowland

"A screaming comes across the sky?"

Thomas Pynchon, *Gravity's Rainbow*

"Never act out words. Never try to leave the floor
when you talk about flying. Never close your eyes
and jerk your head to one side when you talk about
death. Do not fix your burning eyes on me when
you speak about love. If you want to impress me
when you speak about love put your hand in your
pocket or under your dress and play with yourself.
If ambition and the hunger for applause have driven
you to speak about love you should learn how to
do it without disgracing yourself or the material."

Leonard Cohen

**"Cause the sweetest kiss I ever got
is the one I've never tasted."**

Rodriguez

"How much of you is repetition?"

Rodriguez

In the late afternoon on a freezing January day I sat in the Detroit Public Library. I was educating myself on Sixto Rodriguez. The main library branch at 5201 Woodward Avenue had all the materials I needed to understand the Sugar Man's Detroit. As I looked through books, eventually newspapers and magazines the library staff were wary of me. I claimed to be a retired professor. They weren't sure. Then one of them showed up with my **Sun Elvis: Presley In The 1950s** book and another brought over my biography **Chuck Berry: Rock 'N' Roll Music**. They asked me: "How can you write a book about Sixto Rodriguez without hanging out with him?" I explained I was using the Gay Talese approach where I interviewed everyone in the Sugar Man's life. They weren't impressed. Neither was I. But I persisted. Then surprisingly due to Steve Rowland I was taken backstage to the dressing room to meet Rodriguez. It was brief but pleasant. I didn't mention my three books. I shook his hand. I talked to his daughter Regan, watched the baby run around and took in the pre-concert ambiance. It was fun. What did I learn hanging out with the Sugar Man? Plenty. He is simple. He is quiet. He is private. He is a great songwriter. He is a superb entertainer.

The Rodriguez story is also one beset with clichés and contradictions. The story of fame at seventy, the tale of coming in from the creative wilderness, the quiet studious aspects of Sixto Rodriguez are real. What is not real are the clichés. What are the clichés? The tale that he was only popular in South Africa is a fictional one. This is an egregious misstatement of the story, the facts and it besmirches the Sugar Man's life and contributions to the rock and roll culture. The contradictions are many as this book suggests. For a window into Rodriguez's life it is necessary to examine those around him. There is no better place to start than with his second and still current wife Konny Koskos.

Konny Koskos: The Sugar Man's Second Wife

To understand the Sixto Rodriguez story it is necessary to know who Constance Koskos is and how she fits into the Sugar Man's life. Konny is his second wife. He met her in the Wayne State University Library. She is a second generation Greek whose family came to Detroit for a better life. She is Regan's mother. She worked in the magazine and periodicals section of the library handling billing and orders for periodicals and academic journals.

She met the Sugar Man in 1971 when she was twenty-one. She was awe struck by the fact he carried a guitar around campus, and he seemed to have a bevy of friends hanging out with him. He was a charismatic pied piper. She noticed he was handsome and well dressed.

As Konny talked of the Sugar Man she spoke of his love for reading, studying philosophers and having quiet time to read and think. He wasn't famous. He wasn't performing. He was growing as a creative person.

She was with him for the 1979 and 1981 Australian tours, and she came to South Africa in 1998. She was still around in 2009 but by that time for whatever reason she could not live with Rodriguez. She described their Avery Street home as "being stripped" but it soon became livable. And, of course, that's the way he likes it. We eventually put everything in it; things got done. And it eventually became livable."

She didn't want a divorce. She wanted a normal life with some comforts. She was in her mid-fifties. It was the right moment for some Konny time. She moved to the suburbs. There was no way Rodriguez would relocate to St. Clair Shores.

Konny Rodriguez: "It's his home; he's a strong character mentally and ideologically. He will not be pushed out; he's going to stay there. And when he can be part of the city, he'll be part of it. That's his home and that's how he feels."

When Konny talked of Detroit she reaffirmed his love for the Motor City. "He loves getting around Detroit and meeting people, and he's out there right now doing what he loved to do."

The relationship between Konny and her husband is a complicated one. In January 2013 she talked with Eric Lacy who elicited the comment that she was still with him. "He's one of those wiry guys that just isn't going to quit," Konny continued. "He loves it, he absolutely loves it. This whole experience for all of us has been surreal."

When she received her B. A. in psychology from Wayne State University in 1976 it capped a six-year college run that brought her many skills. She is an excellent public speaker.

In 1984 she went to work for the Children's Hospital of Detroit. She spent twenty-one years as an Executive Assistant. In this position she had a wide range of responsibilities. She was the glue that held the place together as three presidents depended upon her expertise. She coordinated the calendar and scheduled hospital events. She arranged travel and handled the confidential and often cumbersome legal issues. She left this position to accept employment in April 2005 with the Presbyterian Villages of Michigan. It appears she is still working in this St. Clair Shores senior living establishment.

In 2013 Konny moved to St. Clair Shores, a Detroit suburb, but her relationship with the Sugar Man remains friendly and by all accounts they are still married. Konny has a professional life suggesting a hard working and responsible family person.

Her life in St. Clair Shores is a bucolic one. She lives on Harper Lake Avenue which is as far away from the Rodriguez' Avery Street home as one can imagine. She remains her husband's best friend in a home that is private, often quirky and the creative mantra of the Rodriguez clan vibrates daily through the greater Detroit area. The family is a complicated one as Malik Bendjelloul discovered when he screened an early copy of **Searching For Sugar Man** for the entire clan. It was a tense moment in the final stages of the documentary.

Malik Screens for the Family: Some Concerns

When Malik Bendjelloul screened **Searching For Sugar Man** for the family, Konny asked to be left out of the film. Malik reluctantly agreed. Eva also requested her son Ethan and her husband Juan be left on the cutting room floor. Her marriage had fallen apart. Malik agreed. He wasn't happy about it. The volatile nature of Rodriguez and his family threatened the documentaries completion but somehow Malik avoided the pitfalls that could have derailed the film. When I was backstage with Rodriguez and his daughter Regan, I observed the pressures of fame and fortune on the Sugar Man.

Malik Bendjelloul: "They told me they wanted their privacy protected. This took place while collaborating on a movie." This comment is only one of many Malik made to different people while frustrated with the progress of the movie. It was not easy working with the Rodriguez family.

California State University Hanging Out with The Sugar Man

California State University Luckman Auditorium is a concert hall on a beautiful grassy knoll in East Los Angeles, just off Interstate Highway 10. The grassy knoll in front of the auditorium projects serenity. It is the perfect setting for a Sixto Rodriguez concert. It is a fitting tribute to the money the Golden State spends on education and culture. The sign outside the concert hall simply reads "Rodriguez." The Sugar Man is in the midst of a West Coast tour with his daughter Regan, her husband and a young child running around during the show. Nearby the Sugar Man's other daughter, Sandra, who writes her original songs as SK, is standing around getting ready to perform a couple of her wonderfully written tunes at the end of the intermission.

Rodriguez sits in a corner. He is dressed in cool rock and roll clothes. Black pants, a shimmering black shirt and gold-rimmed sunglasses. He is talking to producer Steve Rowland. The Sugar Man looks drawn, tired and ready to go back home to Woodbridge. It is May 31, 2014 and Rodriguez' success since the January 2012 screening of **Searching For Sugar Man** shows no signs of ending. He is a rock star. He is a cultural phenomenon. He is still able to perform at seventy-two. He loves the chance to play his poetic songs that have been ignored for forty years. He is tired. The road is a grind. Stardom arrived. It is a mixed blessing. He lost his privacy. The money is great. The acclaim continues. The problem is he doesn't have time to record a third album.

By May 2017 rumor has it Rodriguez finished a fresh batch of songs for a third album. He had been in touch for months with different producers. His plan is to pay for the session musicians, the producer and the studio to record his third album. He will own the master tapes. Like Van Morrison or Bob Dylan, he will control his product. If not there will not be a product. He has nine new songs crafted with care and precision. The time is ripe for a third album.

In the aftermath of **Searching For Sugar Man's** commercial gold rush, Rodriguez has been in a recording studio at least half a dozen times. At various times he has contacted Steve Rowland, Paolo Nutini, Mike Theodore, Dennis Coffey and David Holmes about producing a new album.

The Luckman Crowd Keeps The Sugar Man in a Cocoon: The Perils of Fame

The night Rowland and Rodriguez talked in a small, makeshift dressing room the perils of fame were obvious. They had to literally hide out from the large concert audience, the assorted hangers on and those who told the Sugar Man he was the next big thing. Everyone wanted a piece of him. Everyone wanted to make a deal.

I stood in the background talking to the Sugar Man's daughter, Regan, as she deftly managed the intricate planning for the Luckman Center show. It was a family friendly atmosphere with a calm and relaxed ambiance. When the Sugar Man appears on stage his mellow presence owes a great deal to Regan's management skills.

Rodriguez and Rowland were in deep discussion about a third album. He has songs. Steve has musicians ready to go into the studio. The only problem is time. It is difficult for either of them to find the time. This is one of the supreme ironies of the comeback story. Both men have more on their plate than they have time for in the musical universe.

The crowd outside his dressing room was eager to see him. The lines were long and young female fans brought flowers. Rodriguez' companion, Bonnie, scurried around making last minute preparations. The show was opened by a local musician with a marvelous voice, LP, and she was from the first note the right opening act as her hip, fresh songs displayed not only her talent but she is in fact a Rodriguez type performer. She is a songwriter who only recently began performing and her connection to the Luckman Center audience was immediate.

Laura Peregolizi is now in her early thirties and her stage name, LP, is perfect. In 2010 she relocated to Los Angeles to showcase her songs to the music business. To make ends meet she began to perform. She quickly became a sought after club act. She has released three albums and an EP. She has written songs for Rihanna, Christina Aguilera and Cher. She has a cult Los Angeles following. She wowed the crowd. Now the audience was ready for the Sugar Man. LP is much like Rodriguez, she is a performer who spent a decade plus getting into the music mainstream. Now she is there and her opening for the Sugar Man energized the audience.

What Has Touring Done to Change Rodriguez?

He loves to tour, but he is tiring of it. The first class tour bus, premier hotel accommodations, an experienced tour manager, and the skilled management of his daughter Regan leads to tours that are a joy. They are also a profitable enterprise. The support of Sony Records helps to navigate the problems the road presents. But he is in his mid-seventies. So every precaution is taken to maximize his comfort level.

The truth is Rodriguez' failing eyesight, the grind of the road and the mercurial nature of the critics wears on him. He toured less in 2015-2017, but he still loves the road. He enjoys stardom. It has been a lengthy and brutal forty plus years to performing when and where the Sugar Man desires for a lucrative guarantee. This validated his performing life. His private life was, as it always has been, quiet and fulfilling.

Rodriguez' life was less complicated before the success of **Searching For Sugar Man**. When Malik Bendjelloul was presented an Oscar, Rodriguez had been on the road steadily for three years to small audiences. Then all hell broke lose as the Oscar impacted the story with an international audience for the Sugar Man.

How the Oscar for Searching for Sugar Man Impacted the Story

This first part of this book is about Rodriguez' second album, **Coming From Reality**, as well as the roles of Steve Rowland, Matt Sullivan,

Clarence Avant, Stephen "Sugar" Segerman and Craig Bartholomew-Strydom among others. The second part deals with stardom, money, and a loss of privacy. How did the trappings of international prestige change his life? What impact did it have on his family? There was no one who wasn't impacted by the Hollywood Oscar.

When the 2012 Sundance Film Festival opened it was snowy, brutally frigid, and there was a dreary countenance from those longing for their Hollywood pools. Park City Utah is not Beverly Hills. But Sundance is too prestigious to ignore.

On opening night Tom Bernard of Sony Pictures Classics told everyone it was a blockbuster. Most people laughed. The story of a Mexican American singer who didn't make it in 1970-1971 was a piece of cinema that hardly sounded like a blockbuster. The times were changing. Of the 114 films selected for the 2012 Sundance Festival an amazing thirty-nine were documentaries.

Sony knew it had a hit. They quietly supported the project for almost two years. They devised elaborate marketing plans before its initial screening. The Sony Executives, Tom Bernard and Michael Barker, who were co-Presidents of the Sony Art House Film Division, were responsible for making the documentary a word of mouth hit. Before working for Sony they were in charge of the United Artists Classics and then Orion Classics. Bankruptcies, bad bosses and their ambition prompted Sony to hire them. They were brilliant in placing **Searching For Sugar Man** in the public eye.

The Barker-Bernard team had a detailed plan. It was to bring art movies to the attention of critics, whose favorable reviews found an eager and ready audience. They had to over publicize to place the documentary into the art houses. American art houses are notoriously selective in the films they show. The Sony publicity machine began the drum roll for the story in December 2011. A month later, at the Sundance Festival, word of mouth publicity was like a whirlwind. When Sixto Rodriguez appeared on a Sundance stage to sing "Sugar Man" the crowd was ecstatic. The cheering and applause cut into the cold Utah air. There is no reliable figure on how much the documentary cost. The rumor is the Malik Bendjelloul film came in at less than a million dollars. It grossed 3.7 million dollars in American domestic video sales, while it grossed almost four million at the American box office and almost nine million in the European market. The worldwide box office was approximately thirteen million dollars. In DVD and Blue Ray sales there was 3.6 million dollars reported. It was a highly profitable documentary. As of June 2017 almost seventeen million dollars came into Sony's coffers.

On opening night at Sundance **Searching For Sugar Man** was selected for the World Cinema Documentary Audience Award and a special world cinema documentary jury prize. The stage was set for a rush of awards. Rodriguez found his quiet life suddenly in the midst of the **Searching For Sugar Man** phenomenon.

Once the movie became a hit Steve Rowland had his quiet Palm Springs California retirement life upset by the demand for interviews. Steve acquiesced. He doesn't like to do interviews. He has an active California fun in the sun social life. Many of his friends had no idea about his film career, his musical performing days, or his time as a hit record producer. Steve is quiet. He is laid back. He would produce records if things were right. He has money. He will pick and choose what he wants. In many ways Steve Rowland and Sixto Rodriguez have led parallel lives.

What to Remember About Rodriguez and His Body of Work

When Sixto Rodriguez was re-discovered in 2012 forty-two years after his debut album, he had a small body of work. There were two LPs **Cold Fact** and **Coming From Reality**. There were three new songs added to the reissues. The modesty of scale did not hide the ambition in the Sugar Man's writing. His work was praised before the thunderstorm of acclaim for **Searching For Sugar Man**. There were many questions about Rodriguez' minimalistic level of production. There was little biographical information.

In the first volume, of what will be a trilogy, on Rodriguez, I asked the question: "Who influenced him and what impact did Detroit have on the Sugar Man?" I answered that question in depth with a look at the Motor City and the local musical scene. I found Sixto Rodriguez is private, shy, demonstratively intellectual, paranoid, suspicious and wary of strangers. There are people who protect him from the press. It is generally his family. The general public and the hangers on who permeate the lower rungs of the rock music world surround him daily. This has caused Rodriguez' daughter, Regan, to impose a hands off policy. He is no longer freely available for interviews. Why? It is a combination of the pressures of celebrity, the need to scrutinize the multiple offers for concerts, the images of business decisions and the necessity to maintain a balanced life. It is not an easy task.

The flurry of interviews from 2012 through 2014 has slowed to a trickle. By 2017 there were virtually no interviews. There was also little press coverage. This is a plus and minus. It is a plus for Rodriguez who is free to pursue songwriting, concentrate upon performing and spend time with his family. For the biographer it poses a problem. The way around it is to do what Gay Talese did when he wrote about Frank Sinatra. The crooner would not talk to Talese, so he interviewed everyone around Sinatra. The result was the 1966 **Esquire** "story "Frank Sinatra Has A Cold" which is a hallmark of the new journalism. This book follows that pattern.

There are many ways to describe Rodriguez. Some say he is a poor man's poet. That is simplistic. It fails to recognize his B. A. with honors in philosophy. The power of Rodriguez' songs is a window into his life. The power of his imagination is a key to his intellectual prowess.

The Sixto Rodriguez story is one about a reticent poet. He has attempted to keep his life story away from the public. Now there are two books on Rodriguez. My volume was the first in 2015. In

Searching For Sugar Man: Sixto Rodriguez' Improbable Rise to Rock N Roll Fame and Fortune I told the story of the **Cold Fact** album, the background to it, the controversy over royalties and the phenomenon in the **Searching For Sugar Man** documentary.

I wasn't going to write another book. Then six months after my book sold well, the Bartholomew-Strydom-Segerman book came out. Except for the portions on South Africa, the remainder of the book combined fiction with hagiography. Myth triumphed reality. To add perspective I spent two and a half years on this book. Compare it to the Bartholomew-Strydom-Segerman tome. Then draw your own conclusions.

There is an aura of mystery to Rodriguez. That is unfortunate. The real Sixto Rodriguez is a quiet, self-effacing, normal family man who has a woman by his side to take care of him. There is no mystery to the Sugar Man. The mystery provided by **Searching For Sugar Man** is important to the story. It obscures the real Sixto Rodriguez. When I interviewed Harry Balk before his death, Harry asked: "Is there a real Sixto Rodriguez?" The answer is an unequivocal: "Yes."

Is There A Real Rodriguez?

Is there a real Rodriguez? That is the question! The answer is there is an elusive Sugar Man. He has a knack for using Detroit themes, the civil rights conflicts of the 1960s, the boy-girl relationships that he experienced growing up and the imagery of the hip, jazz, rock subculture to craft his songs. He has a long history with two wives and a large number of beautiful girlfriends. He never discusses his marriages, his lady friends and his social attitudes. He has never compromised his view of life. He has a defined lifestyle. Simple! Pragmatic! There are no frills in his home. This is the reason for the two wives living elsewhere and the present girl friend remaining just that a girl friend. His defined hippie lifestyle is devoid of modern conveniences like a telephone, a television set, central heating, air conditioning and the appliances necessary to suburbanization. He abhors the thought of suburbanization. He resists anything middle class. He remains a Catholic. Shy! Quiet! Humble! This is how his friends describe the real Sixto Rodriguez.

Not much is heard from his first wife, Rayma. And his second wife, Konny Koskos, has not divorced him. He does live with Bonnie. Other than that little is known about his amorous life. One suspects it is a rich and private life that nourishes his art. He maintains a discrete privacy. More on that in volume three.

In his creativity Rodriguez displays the real Sugar Man. He has a passion for music and literature that evolves into lyrical beauty. It is a shadowy life. His daily life, however, defines his working patterns. He reads. He writes. He thinks. He is politically active. He is always under the radar. This is the real Sixto Rodriguez.

Rodriguez is a towering figure in comeback rock and roll music circles. One way to understand the real Rodriguez is to compare his life to that of the producer of his second album **Coming From Reality**. That producer, Steve Rowland, highlights another side of the Sugar Man, and his musical journey. Rodriguez and Rowland lived parallel lives. This is a key to understanding the man and his music.

The barometer of how things have changed for Sixto Rodriguez is shown by the fact he was booked for a time by the Richard De La Font Agency Inc. This agency books everyone of any significance in the rock and roll world. You name it. They book it. The concert guarantees vary but into 2017 Rodriguez received prominent fees and top billing. The exceptions were when he opened for Beach Boy major domo Brian Wilson and when he appeared in festivals. But money was no longer a question.

The Richard De La Font Agency is the Cadillac booking service that makes it easier for Rodriguez to go on the road.

The Symbiotic Connection to Steve Rowland

From the time Steve Rowland met Sixto Rodriguez, they developed a personal connection that evolved into a lifetime friendship. After producing **Coming From Reality**, Steve and the Sugar Man went their separate ways. The irony is they didn't talk again until 2009 after Rodriguez' second album failed to chart. In that time they both were married, they were family oriented, they experienced financial difficulties, they had financial successes and they continued to be creative.

In 1970-1971 Steve and Sixto lived parallel lives but they didn't know it. Why is this important? Their parallel lives is a key to their combined creativity. Without these intellectual parallels there would not have been the brilliance of **Coming From Reality**.

Although Rowland and Rodriguez came from different backgrounds they were amazingly alike. They are quiet. They don't like to sit for interviews. They work slowly and diligently creating perfection.

The Sugar Man and Multiple Sources

Sixto Rodriguez is known as the Sugar Man. The name comes from a song he wrote in 1969 "Sugar Man." He wrote this tune in the late 1960s. The term is one identifying the urban drug dealer. What is the genesis of "Sugar Man?" Rodriguez has never talked about why he wrote the song or the circumstances behind it. There were other "Sugar Man" songs before his gem, but there is no evidence they influenced his writing. Still there is some interesting conjecture.

There are two mainstream artists who wrote different songs with the title "Sugar Man." Roy Orbison's **Focus On Roy Orbison** two-vinyl disc in 1965 album contained a song he wrote with the title "Sugar Man." It is not the same as the Rodriguez song but one wonders if the Detroit singer heard it. Orbison's 45 release of "Sugar Man" received little in the way of promotion. In the U. K. it was released on the London label in 1968 and the Wesley Roe and Jim Vienneau song had sporadic airplay and solid sales. In the U. S. the single and album sang from sight. The twenty-four track London Record release **Focus On Roy Orbison** was quickly in the budget bins. The album included covers of "Land of A Thousand Dances," "Memphis, Tennessee" and "I Fought the Law" with some of the more over the top guitar solos from Orbison on "Sugar Man."

The Orbison song has no reference to drugs. It is a tune in which a young man says to a woman: "I'll make your dreams come true, I'll do what I can. Baby when I do, you can say you knew the sugar man." If he heard Orbison's lyrics they would appeal to Rodriguez. He has never talked about these songs but they were in a time frame when Rodriguez was a regular buyer at the cut out bin for 45s. Orbison's record was in those bins.

Bobby Darin's "Sugar Man" was a 1969 single from his own label Direction. A 45 "Sugar Man" backed with "Jive" was a Direction 45 single in 1969. Again, like Orbison's song, this is not the same as Rodriguez' but there are elements in the lyrics and music that may have influenced him. He has never discussed it.

While the Darin song is faster, more pop and less psychedelic there is an eerie sense of the drug dealer. "Sugar Man you are the only one who understands," Darin sings. This is like a sentence from the Rodriguez portfolio. He sings of being without a drink or a song. It is a poignant reminder that in two years Rodriguez would record a similar song. While the Orbison, Darin and Rodriguez songs are all different, they convey the local neighborhood drug dealer of the late 1960s.

In 1967 the Philly singer James Barry Keefer, who recorded as Keith, had a hit with "98.6." He recorded a bubblegum song written by D. Randell and S. Linzer, "Sugar Man." It charted at number 103 according to **Record World's** September 1967 issue. Then Keith joined Frank Zappa's band and faded into the background. The Monkees were approached to record this version of "Sugar Man" and they wisely refused. The song was a pop, bubble gum disaster. The songwriters Linzer and Randall were songwriters and performers who had close connections to the Monkees. They issued a single in 1966 "Sugar Man" backed with "I Wanna Be Your Puppy Dog" but the songs were too lame even for the Monkees. Both sides make fun of the Beatles and bubble gum pop. This is one reason Don Kirshner couldn't convince the Monkees to record the song.

Fortunately, Sixto Rodriguez lived in a world where he wrote marvelous lyrics and wonderful music. The point is "Sugar Man" was a common theme for mid to late 1960s songwriters and this didn't help his connection to the industry.

One

Sixto Rodriguez and Steve Rowland: Parallel Lives in 1970 and they didn't Know It

"I was trying to find an artist that would make me credible. I wanted to get away from pop music."

Steve Rowland

"I've always gravitated more to the edgy people."

Steve Rowland

"This is a lesson to anybody who has a dream. Never give up on your dream."

Steve Rowland

"Everything great in the world comes from neurotics. They alone have composed our masterpieces."

Proust

In 1970 Sixto Rodriguez and Steve Rowland were leading parallel lives. They didn't know it. In the spring of 1970 Sussex Records released **Cold Fact**. It went nowhere. Despite a 4 Star review in the April 19, 1970 **Billboard**, Rodriguez went back to work while performing on weekends around Detroit. The Sugar Man had new songs. He was eager to cut a second album. He possessed a mainstream creativity despite his lack of success. He was eager to get on with his second set of songs. There was a desire for creative credibility. Rodriguez didn't care about hitting the **Billboard** Hot 100. He wanted his songs heard and reviewed. No one listened.

In sharp contrast, Rowland was a noted London-based record producer with a bevy of hits. Rodriguez was broke. Rowland had money. But Steve wasn't satisfied with what he produced. He was proud of his hits. He brought bands back that had no hits. He made them stars. There was something missing in Rowland's creative psyche. Like Rodriguez, he wanted a larger stage, more recognition, and he despised the pompous attitude of the London based music industry.

Rowland was stifled. He produced thirteen hits for Dave Dee, Dozy, Beaky, Mick and Tich. He reformed the Herd in the studio bringing Peter Frampton's voice, as well as his guitar, to the forefront of their records. Rowland also had his designs on more in-depth personal creativity. He had a vision for a California sound in London. This led him to form the Family Dogg. When he talked to those in the record business many of them gave his ideas short shrift. He ignored them.

The Sugar Man had the same problem. He approached Detroit producer Harry Balk with new songs. Balk said: "Kid, a Mexican is not cutting it in the pop market. It's the blonde haired, blue-eyed guys who write syrupy pop. Your day with the protest song is done." Rodriguez ignored him. What did Rowland and Rodriguez experience in a parallel creative universe? Like Rowland, the Sugar Man wanted no part of the pretty boys and their sound. He would make a pop sound with meaning, a flair for instrumentation, and a sense of the social environment.

Parallel Creativity and What it Meant?

As the 1970s dawned, Steve Rowland branched out with his newly formed group, the Family Dogg. He was a Californian who grew up with hot rod and surf music. He also loved the blues. Steve had a knack for hit records. His commercial instincts were exceptional. He looked at the Mamas and Papas, the 5th Dimension and the pop songsmiths of the late 1960s and early 1970s. He believed he had better songs, and he had a more defined commercial direction. He understood how to produce records to top the charts.

Much like Rowland, Rodriguez put together a series of chart friendly tunes. He played these songs in his Detroit bar room shows. Like Rowland, the Sugar Man had a keen ear for what was and what wasn't commercial. He could never find anyone to share his vision. As the 1970s brought in the singer-songwriter, Rodriguez crafted half a dozen potential hits. He was a slow writer. It took him months to complete a song. The constant rewriting and the changes in tenor and tone reflected the times as well as the Sugar Man's precision.

Rowland shared the same attention to detail. He was a perfectionist carefully crafting hit records while he put together a group that became a U. K. and European mainstream act. That group, the Family Dogg, never broke out in the U. S. market.

Creativity in the Coffee Shops

There was another sign of parallel creativity that came from hanging out in the local coffee shops. Rowland met Ronnie Oppenheimer at London's Kenco Coffee Shop on King's Road in Chelsea. Who was Oppenheimer? He was an accountant with an eye for the ladies.

They talked about the London music scene. Oppenheimer was a businessman with a desire to enter the music business. In time, he became Rowland's partner.

Steve Rowland: "Ronnie told me he was bored. He liked the ladies. That was his full time interest."

After they sat drinking coffee, Steve suggested they set up a production company. They did. It was known as Double R Productions. Oppenheimer checked Rowland out to see if he was a bullshitter. He wasn't. After looking at record sales figures, Ronnie was impressed. Steve produced Dave Dee, Dozy, Beaky, Mick and Tich's "Hold Tight" selling more than a quarter of a million copies. But that was three and a half years ago. Steve was ready to move on from being a strictly pop music producer into new creative directions.

As an observer of people and styles, Rowland crafted songs and productions from his surroundings. Steve has the ability to see inside people's psyche. He has an intuitive mind. A good example of Rowland's early songwriting talent is Wanda Jackson's "You're The One For Me," which was released on her 1962 album **Rockin' With Wanda**. When Steve saw Wanda in concert, he realized that her country-rockabilly audience was a hybrid. She fit into two popular music categories and "You're The One For Me" was a crossover song exploiting all of Jackson's formidable vocals talents. When he wrote the song for Jackson he crafted it for her fans.

The key to Rowland's early songwriting and later studio brilliance came in the hundreds of hours he studied an artist, the hundreds of hours he spent crafting songs and his intuitive understanding of the marketplace. Not all of his songwriting was successful. But for collectors Steve has many tunes that remain cult collector items. This is the example of parallel lives Rowland and Rodriguez lived without realizing it. They are both creative spirits fitting into a cult mold. They both, at different times, achieved ultimate stardom.

Steve also wrote a 1961 tune "Hide And Seek" for Marc Cavell on Candix. This is a good example of a marvelous song that didn't hit the charts. He also composed two songs for the 1967 movie soundtrack for **Hallucination Generation**. His best selling American song is "Riker's Island" on The Family Dogg album. "Riker's Island" was a b-side released by Bell Records in the U. S. with "This Unhappy Heart of Mine" (B-939) as the A side. Neil Bogart told Bell Records "Rikers Island" was a top 40 hit. His recommendation for it as an A-side was lost in the mix. Bogart did a great deal of promotional work on "Rikers Island." It charted regionally. Bogart believed Rowland was an accomplished songwriter. He thought Steve needed a push in that direction.

The songwriting side to Rowland's life is one he doesn't like to talk about. Why? It is simply Steve's way. He doesn't consider himself a songwriter. He was also busy producing and promoting his material. This put songwriting into the background. Bogart hoped to bring it to the foreground.

To understand Rowland and Rodriguez it is necessary to examine how and why they perpetuated their creativity in local coffee shops. Rowland did it in London. Rodriguez was a political-coffee shop regular in Detroit's Cass Corridor.

Rodriguez in Detroit and the Amsterdam Espresso

In Detroit Rodriguez frequented a number of local coffee shops near Wayne State University. This was at the same time Rowland spent part of every morning in a trendy London coffee emporium. They were looking for new song themes, reading **Billboard** and keeping in touch with student life. At this point Rodriguez didn't have a large family. He had one daughter and plenty of time to read and write. While Rowland was social and outgoing, the Sugar Man kept to a small coterie of friends. He was more interested in social causes. He was attuned to what he labeled the "Three P's." They were the politicians, the police and the punks.

It was in Amsterdam Espresso that Rodriguez hung out and found much of his early inspiration. At this Detroit coffee shop, he spent hours talking with John Sinclair, the well-known political activist, poet and itinerant musician. They plotted out political intrigue and literary masterpieces. Much of this intrigue wound up in the Sugar Man's songs. They both liked to talk about how the 1970s were poised to end the counterculture. This coffee shop, near Prentis Street, was one of Rodriguez' writing hangouts. The Amsterdam Espresso burned down in 2008.

The Amsterdam Espresso had a midtown Detroit flower power reputation. It was located in the Forest Arms a business housing complex a good walk from Rodriguez' apartment. The sight of the Sugar Man, with a guitar on his back, walking down Cass Avenue with a shortcut down Prentis Street filled with leaves over to Second Avenue was a familiar sight in 1969-1970.

Rodriguez' community activism was demonstrated in the years after the Amsterdam Espresso burned down, when he volunteered with others to clean up the area. This took place after the 2008 Forest Arms fire, as Rodriguez' career was slowly starting to heat up. He still made time for community service. Why? He told a friend part of his creativity was due to the atmosphere at the Amsterdam Espresso.

What made the Amsterdam Espresso unique? It was near the Graphic Arts Building, which was a place for artists and literary types. They frequented the coffee shop. It was at the Amsterdam Espresso that Rodriguez met Rainy M. Moore. His marriage to Rayma was on the skids. Rainy became his girlfriend and manager. She was a local girl with a zest for the Motown sound and creative musicians.

Rainy M. Moore Comes into the Picture in a Local Coffee Shop

Who was Rainy M. Moore? Her friends knew her as Margaret Moore. She was musically sophisticated, creative and business minded.

Moore persuaded Mike Theodore and Dennis Coffey to come to the Sewer By The Sea to see Rodriguez perform. They weren't impressed with the Sewer. The pop, commercial sound coming from the stage intrigued them. They realized the Sugar Man was quiet, private, quirky and enormously talented. From 1969 into early 1972 Rainy was a part of the Rodriguez story.

By the time she came into Rodriguez' life, Rainy had a young son from a relationship with Temptations singer Dennis Edwards. Her son, Kelly Moore, was four years old when she began dating the Sugar Man.

Kelly Moore, told Craig Bartholomew Strydom, his mom's parents said: "If the baby came out black there will be consequences." There were. She was placed in a mental hospital. She also endured electroshock therapy. Kelly said: "I recall Dennis as mom's friend not as my father."

Her parents had a fit. She had a baby with a black man. Now she was dating a Mexican. Her parents couldn't believe it. In the end the Rainy M. Moore story is a tragic one. Her life long physical-mental problems were due to a family unable to accept the changes in America in the 1960s. It is a tragic tale influencing the Sugar Man's life. His songwriting and the conflicts with Rainy's parents exacerbated the flow of his existential writing. Rodriguez stared evil in the face and overcame it. But there were normal, wonderful family times as Rodriguez had a child living with him and Rainy's son was the love of her life. It was a normal life with complications. The normal times she had with Sixto Rodriguez was the best part of her life. She lived with him in a downtown Detroit apartment, and her son remembers Eva as a child.

Rainy M. Moore took the role the Sugar Man's wives and lovers have played in his life. They support him. They take care of him. They encourage him. When he went into the studio with Mike Theodore and Dennis Coffey, Moore was at Rodriguez' side. He lacked confidence. She provided the support to get him through the **Cold Fact** sessions.

When Rodriguez traveled to London to record **Coming From Reality**, Moore was with him. Rowland remembers her as smart, plain, charming and protective of the Sugar Man. She sat quietly in the studio. During his month planning and recording the album in London Rainy and the Sugar Man toured Europe with stops in Paris and a longer stay in Amsterdam. The Sugar Man was writing during the trip. One wonders if there are some songs in his notebooks we haven't heard.

As Rodriguez and Moore arrived in London, they were impressed with the setting. Their apartment was in one of the plushest areas of London. Steve Rowland made the couple comfortable in and out of the studio. There was free time to explore the shopping on Oxford Street, the theater in the West End and the clubs in and around Soho. Rodriguez was not a club or nighttime guy. He wanted to cook in and enjoy the tranquility of the plush apartment. The calm relaxed nature of the London visit contributed to the mellow sound making **Coming From Reality** a pop album with enough hits to fill the charts. It didn't happen until 2012.

When Moore and Rodriguez returned to Detroit, they believed it was a short time until he was permanently on the road. It didn't happen. They were devastated. She died early and much of her story vanished. She was an important muse to Rodriguez. After Rodriguez recorded two albums, Rainy was no longer in the picture. Her early death was a tragedy.

Steve Rowland Looking Back on 1970

Steve Rowland: "In 1970, the main reason I got the Rodriguez gig was because I had had many hits with Dave Dee. At the time I had a record in the charts with Dave Dee, the Pretty Things' 'Progress' and my own band the Family Dogg's 'A Way of Life.' That's why they agreed to have me produce Rodriguez' album. Neil Bogart picked up 'Riker's Island.' He loved it. That is why Clarence Avant let me have a go."

Did you feel respect with all the hits?

Steve Rowland: "Nope! I wanted to be credible. I wanted to do what I felt was a pop act which would take me from being just a pop producer. I didn't get the respect that I would like to have as they all thought I was just a pop producer. Records with no depth were what I felt. You get labeled a pop producer, therefore you have no credibility."

In 1970 what acts do you think were taking away from you thereby preventing this credibility?

Steve Rowland: "Even though I had a minor hit with the Pretty Things. I received no credibility for 'Progress.' I wanted to be able to do credible productions. It was the kind of groups I was making hits with that caused people to dismiss those chart songs. I was viewed as a simplistic producer that only did pop stuff. I used to say it worked for Mickie Most."

When you met Neil Bogart what do you remember?

Steve Rowland: "He came to my house on Chester Street. The inside was like a movie studio. You entered into a room that was forty feet long with a twenty-foot ceiling. I had five foot pseudo oak, dado oak panels that went around the room."

Did you know about Rodriguez the first time you met Bogart?

Steve Rowland: "He came to see me about releasing 'Riker's Island.' He asked me if it was about personal experience. I had no idea about Sixto Rodriguez."

Did he mention Rodriguez to you?

Steve Rowland: "No."

Had you listened to Rodriguez' **Cold Fact** album?

Steve Rowland: "Yes, I told him I would like to get an artist like Rodriguez."

So Bogart never told you he had listened to **Cold Fact**, he liked the album and he petitioned Clarence Avant to do a second album with a known hit maker.

Steve Rowland: "I didn't know any of this. This is all news to me."

Bogart was acting as a talent scout. At least in his mind! People around the Detroit music scene remember Bogart lurking around the edges of the clubs seeking out new talent. He talked to many of the local music people about the eccentric Sixto Rodriguez. He saw talent in the Sugar Man. He also envisioned talent in Steve Rowland's production skills. He wondered how the two would mesh in the studio? How much he influenced Rowland producing the second album is open to debate.

For whatever unexplained reason Bogart and Rowland never talked about Rodriguez's career, an album or what he might have had in the way of a career. Those around the Detroit club scene remembered Bogart wanted to sign, perhaps have a hand in the production of a Rodriguez album and Bogart was putting together a record label. Why didn't he sign the Sugar Man? The answer is a simple one. Musical tastes changed. The direction of hit records was altered. Bogart was a shrewd music man. He realized Rodriguez would have difficulty charting hits. As Bogart talked to studio musicians, local managers and those who ran the small Detroit labels he was told Rodriguez was "quirky," "non-commercial" but a "brilliant songwriter." This scared Bogart off the Sugar Man's trail.

Neil Bogart is an elusive, yet important, character in the Rodriguez tale. He did his best to recommend a second Sugar Man album but his full influence has been lost in the conflicting tales surrounding Rodriguez' early life. One thing is certain. Bogart recommended to Clarence Avant that Sussex hire Rowland to produce the second album.

The Symbiosis Continues in 2016

By 2016 Sixto Rodriguez and Steve Rowland achieved new levels of success. The symbiosis continued. Their careers in late middle age persisted and prospered. Rodriguez toured Australia in late 2016 approving the release of a new album from of all places an Aussie Hi Fi store. Rowland finished developing a television series based on his book. He remains socially active with a wide-ranging group of friends including his old mate Budd Albright. He had one of his former girl friends into his Palm Springs home for a Christmas visit. The Sugar Man returned to Detroit to have a quiet holiday with his family.

After they reconnected in 2009 at Los Angeles' El Rey Theater, the backstage reunion saw the two old friends catch up with each other's projects. They talked briefly about a third album. They were busy with their lives. They were both pissed. Not at each other, but with the creative world and what it failed to provide. Rodriguez hoped to complete a third album. Perhaps Rowland would produce it. Maybe! Maybe not! Rowland finished his scripts for his proposed television series. It was going to be ready to circulate and various cable TV channels showed interest. They are perfectionists. Both were fiddling with their product as they celebrated Christmas 2009.

It was three years before **Searching For Sugar Man** hit the big screen. Steve Rowland predicted Oscar consideration. He was working with Malik Bendjelloul. The future was bright. But, like Rodriguez, Rowland was skeptical of the media and the entertainment industry. They had that in common.

There were other common areas of concern. Rodriguez and Rowland ignored the continued media attention and the requests for interviews. Rowland completed a series of interviews with a German film company working on a documentary of his father, producer Roy Rowland. Rodriguez gave very few interviews in 2016. Both men had their fill of media nonsense. They were polite to the press. They were cooperative. They did their best to avoid the media glare. They were creative artists working in late middle age. There was no time for wasted press.

Rodriguez needed people to talk with about music. In 2013, when Rowland was the musical director for the Sugar Man's two shows at New York's Radio City Music Hall and the Brooklyn Barclays Arena, they talked music night and day. Without these discussions Rodriguez had little, if any interest, in recording new music. By January 2017 those close to the Sugar Man privately and quietly doubted there would be a third album. Then Rodriguez reached out to Rowland. One of the Sugar Man's close friends at the Motor City Brewing Company listened as Rodriguez called his daughter, Sandra, and told her to approach Rowland about producing a third album. His creativity continued. Some close to the Sugar Man view Rowland as the only viable producer for a third album. They also liked the idea of bringing David Holmes in to produce some remix singles.

In 2017 Sandra called Steve about a proposed third album and later Rodriguez talked with Rowland. No decisions were made on a proposed album, but gossip over what he had written circulated among his fans.

Word leaked out in early 2017 that Rodriguez had written seven or nine songs according to two close friends. But they are not fully finished. An Australian record storeowner told me Rodriguez not only had new material, he was taping live songs he covered for an Australian small label album release. Every indication in June 2017 was a new album was in the works. But it was nothing more than rumor.

Why did you have such excellent results producing **Coming From Reality**?

Steve Rowland: "I paid specific attention to every syllable of his words without losing the background music. I made sure the musical arrangements nourished and enhanced his lyrics."

When I asked Steve Rowland if he was going to produce the third album, he replied: "I don't talk about that and I am not going to reply to questions about Rodriguez' third album or about anything personal. Do you understand Howard?" Steve is sometimes testy. I pushed the wrong button. He does not discuss the personal Sugar Man.

In 2013 when Rowland, arranger Richard Niles and Manny Elias, who managed the group Imagination, met with Rodriguez in New York there was discussion about producing a third album. Steve and Richard would lineup the top Los Angeles studio musicians. They would generally be a contingent of jazz session artists. Particularly, if Rodriguez covered Frank Sinatra songs.

Why is Richard Niles important? Why did Steve Rowland bring him into the mix? Steve said: “He is a fantastic musician, a great arranger, he is knowledgeable and intuitive. He leans toward jazz productions. He is astute in the jazz vernacular. He is a friend. I wanted to use him. I know he would do a good job arranging Rodriguez’ new songs and the covers.” Niles worked with Ray Charles, the Pet Shop Boys, and Paul McCartney among others. He has the pedigree, along with Rowland, to produce a third album. Nothing has come of these talks. Rodriguez has been on the road non-stop since the success of **Searching For Sugar Man.** A third album will happen. When? No one knows!

Steve Rowland: “Everything is for Rodriguez, it is not for the musicians. Obviously, the musicians are considered. What does go down is the tracks are the best I can get for the artist Rodriguez. If I do a third album I am not compromising. When I work it is all for the artist. Period. Got it Howard?” I did.

I asked Steve: “Did psychedelic music influence his production?”

Steve Rowland: “There was no psychedelic in **Coming From Reality**. If you look at the songs there was a dreamscape fantasy as in “Sandrevan Lullaby-Lifestyles.” It was fantasy, soul searching. ‘Cause’ is soul searching. I didn’t use any of the psychedelic sounds. I was looking toward Leonard Cohen more than anybody else.”

He will line up top musicians for a small, comfortable West Coast studio if a third album is to take place. Rodriguez liked the idea. They talked at length backstage when the Sugar Man appeared at the Luckman Center at California State University, Los Angeles in 2014. That wasn’t the last time they spoke of a third album.

Malik Bendjelloul Explains How and Why He Made Searching for Sugar Man

The road to completing **Searching For Sugar Man** would have been impossible without the advice, constant e-mails and phone calls between Malik Bendjelloul and Steve Rowland. Along the way Sixto Rodriguez didn’t want to be a part of the documentary. His daughter,

Regan, talked him into appearing for a few minutes. Much like Rowland, Rodriguez wanted the film to be Bendjelloul's. It was a tribute to the fledgling filmmakers life. It was a constant battle to maintain Rodriguez' interest. His girls were the guiding force. Regan, who was close to Malik, provided a day-to-day look into Detroit, her life concerns, and the family dynamics provide a personal window into her father's life? As Malik planned and executed the film, Rowland and Rodriguez were with him every step of the way. Their creativity took place in a parallel universe.

Malik Bendjelloul: "In 2006, after five years making TV documentaries in Sweden, I spent six months traveling around Africa and South America looking for good stories. In Cape Town I met Stephen 'Sugar' Segerman, who told me about Rodriguez and his involvement in Rodriguez's rediscovery. I visited 16 countries in that trip; in each country I searched after good stories by reading newspapers and books and asking fellow travelers. This was by far the best. I was completely speechless – I hadn't heard a better story in my life. I had never heard Rodriguez's music when Stephen Segerman first told me about him. I fell so totally in love with his story that I was almost afraid to listen to his work – I thought the chances were very slim that the music would be as good as the story; that I'd be disappointed and lose momentum. I started to listen to it when I came back to Europe, and I couldn't believe my ears – literally. I thought my feelings for the story might have influenced my judgment, and I needed to play it to other people to see if they agreed. Their reactions convinced me – these really were songs on a level equal to the best work of Bob Dylan, even the Beatles."

Parallel Creativity and Searching for Sugar Man

The combined creativity of Steve Rowland, Sixto Rodriguez and Malik Bendjelloul made **Searching For Sugar Man** a rare documentary. It integrated original music with breathtaking filmmaking, a rags to riches tale of an underdog, and an insider's look at the record business. The documentary is unprecedented in its honesty.

Along the way it also created a strong interest in why and how Sixto Rodriguez's career was derailed. When his second album arrived, **Coming From Reality**, it demonstrated the breadth of his creative mind. It didn't chart. But forty years later everyone is lining up to cheer for the Sugar Man. The parallel universe of creativity brought everyone to the Oscar ceremony and to the realization the story was a once in a lifetime tale.

Rowland and Rodriguez work in the same way. They keep their projects to themselves until completion. It is ultimately perfect. They continually rewrite, rethink and recast their ideas until ultimate perfection is reached. There are never accidental creations; they spend hundreds of hours in the creative wilderness to bring their product to the market.

The Music Managers Who Hampered Rowland and Rodriguez' Career: Robert Mellin and Harry Balk

Robert Mellin was a publisher in London. He was born in 1902 in the Ukraine and immigrated to England and then to Chicago where he began working as a song plugger in 1939. By the time rock and roll became a commercial phenomena, Mellin was in the midst of the record industry as a manager. In 1947, now living in New York, he formed a company Robert Mellin Inc. and he began a career of one-sided business deals failing to benefit his performers.

Mellin was also a writer. He penned the lyrics to Acker Bilk's 1952 British hit "My One And Only Love." He wrote 608 songs, and he made millions garnering the musical rights to spaghetti westerns and European films. His foray into rock and roll music did not produce any artists of note, because he was the stereotypical manager who cheated you out of the gate. Steve saw that trait. But he knew he could deal with it. Mellin was a major figure in the London music publishing industry. Although Steve hoped to be a performer, he was an excellent songwriter. He knew enough about the music business to handle Mellin's nefarious business deals.

Mellin was an industry heavyweight who had a financial connection to Led Zeppelin's **Coda** album through his musical publishing firm. To Rowland and other fledgling acts he appeared to be a conduit to the music business. The truth is he was a conduit to his bank account.

Steve Rowland: "I made a film in Spain, 'Hallucination Generation', I wrote four songs, one of the songs I sang live in the film. I had my band Los Flaps and I sang the song. I said that to my father, as he was preparing to leave for London. He said: 'I know someone in London who can help you get your songs published.' I came to London. I wanted to see Mellin. I called up. I made an appointment and went to see him. The first thing he said was 'take off your fucking sunglasses." This startled Steve. He looked at Mellin. What did he see? "He was a fat little guy who sat behind a big desk," Steve recalled. Mellin glared at Steve puffed on his cigar and said: "I know your father so let me see what you got. I want to sign you up I can get you a deal." Then Mellin went on about how important he was in the record business. Like Phil Solomon, Mellin took advantage of young artists by signing them to unbreakable contracts. The result was little in the way of royalties. Steve was not the typical starry-eyed young singer. He was an astute businessman ready to set up a production company. Steve signed a contract with Mellin and abruptly broke the agreement. Mellin didn't challenge Rowland. I asked Steve: "Did you use your mob connections to get out of this one sided deal?" Rowland said: "Next question."

After Steve broke the contract with Mellin, the industry insider threatened to blackball him, to make sure he never recorded for another label and he said he would never produce. Steve ignored him. He continued to pursue a solo singing career. He continued to send his demos to other managers.

Steve Rowland: “I sent those same songs to Phil Solomon, he played the songs, he had the record, he took the record and dropped it in front of me. Phil said: ‘That’s crap.”

This was Rowland’s first lesson in the ways of the London music business. He had seen similar behavior in Los Angeles. He knew how to deal with it. What did Rowland learn from talking with Bobby Mellin and others like Phil Solomon? He realized he was in a competitive, corporate jungle, and he had been there before. It was at this point with no records produced of any significance, no real place in the music business and what looked like an uncertain future, he took a giant step. He formed a production company. He was the boss. He was the sole decision maker. He would take on new projects. He would bring hits to the charts. It was this decision that prompted Clarence Avant to examine the hits Rowland produced from 1966 to 1970. When he did so, he gave the green light for a second Sixto Rodriguez album.

Everyone in he industry asked: “Why a second Rodriguez album?”

Two

Why A Second Album?

"I've been working on my consciousness for the past twenty years."

Sixto Rodriguez

"For the truth is a terrible thing. You dabble your foot in it and it is nothing. But you walk a little further and you feel it pull you like an undertow or a whirlpool."

Robert Penn Warren, All The King's Men

The question of Sixto Rodriguez' consciousness is addressed frequently. He tells anyone who will listen he channels songs from another dimension. This is his humble way of shying away from the constant barrage of praise for his songwriting. He also doesn't like to speculate on what his songs mean. They are personal tales from a rich and full life. Why did he write them? Who knows! What describes the Sugar Man? Integrity! Honesty! Observational skills! Existential thinker! Perseverance! There is another word that describes Rodriguez. Private! That is the key word in a personality fluctuating from effervescent to stoic.

Rodriguez' Emergence: The David Letterman Show

There is a pronounced paranoia to Rodriguez' persona. Why? The various record labels from 1967 through 1971 manipulated him, and ignored his musical genius, as he fell off the commercial radar. Neither of his albums sold. No one cared. He was marginalized in the commercial marketplace. That changed in 2012-2013 when **Searching For Sugar Man** became a phenomenon winning an Oscar in the documentary film category.

When he appeared on the David Letterman Show in August 2012, a whirlwind of fame and fortune was bestowed upon the Sugar Man. From the time he left the Cadillac SUV in the front of the legendary Ed Sullivan Theater at the corner of Broadway and 53rd Street there was a large crowd shouting his name and asking him to turn for photos. He smiled in a stylish black suit as his daughter Sandra Rodriquez Kennedy had one of her children grab a guitar. That made for a long day as a rehearsal session with a twenty-five-piece violin section, a horn section and Letterman's band created a masterful sound when he performed later that night. The practice and patience paid off in a stunning performance. With three minutes left in the show, David Letterman said he didn't know where to begin, and he explained the power of **Searching For Sugar Man**. Rodriguez stood in front of the microphone performing "Crucify Your Mind." He wore a black hat, shimmering sunglasses, and he played a stylish acoustic guitar. Sixto Rodriguez is the personification of cool. Finally, after more than forty plus years in the creative wilderness, he was a star. It was surreal.

The Letterman audience sat in stunned silence. "Crucify Your Mind" contained lyrics that were so original and so close to the poetry Bob Dylan wrote in song form that the bursting applause announced a new singer-songwriter on the horizon. The problem was the new songwriter spent forty plus years writing, performing and leading a normal family life in Detroit before his discovery.

The afternoon when Rodriguez arrived for the Letterman taping, as he exits the Sony sponsored Cadillac Escalade SUV, he remarks: "Uncle Sony's been good to us." His oblique comment suggests **Searching For Sugar Man** was responsible for his emergence as a major music act. He was finally receiving the necessary promotion. In 1971, when his second album, **Coming From Reality**, was released, he had high hopes for his well-written, commercial songs. There was a chart friendly tone to the album, thanks to Steve Rowland's production. The LP quickly sank from sight. Rodriguez went back to work rehabbing Detroit homes. Rowland continued to produce gold and platinum albums. But the Sugar Man was never far from his mind.

In 1971, when Sixto Rodriguez' **Coming From Reality** was released on the Sussex label, no one was interested. His debut LP, **Cold Fact**, failed to sell and had trouble finding a distributor. The Sugar Man's songs did not receive airplay. Then something unexpected took place. In 1972 South African's not only listened to the Sugar Man's two albums, they made taped copies, and they passed the tapes around to those who didn't know Rodriguez' music. He was a cult artist in a nation undergoing political change. Why is this important? It gave words like "anti-establishment" a new meaning for those who hoped to end apartheid.

Nelson Mandela was challenging the repressive white South African government. His South African based popular democracy movement to end apartheid slowly but surely marched to a final triumph. The apartheid system separated the races. The result was black South Africans living in poverty were prevented from education and employment. There was brutal repression. The white Dutch settlers enjoyed the fruits of a robust local economy while incarcerating native leaders, practicing genocide on those who opposed white rule and the result was an international boycott on all things South African. In this political morass, Rodriguez' lyrics spoke to the need for freedom. The rights of the common person were intertwined with the local counterculture and the Sugar Man's lyrical brilliance.

In 1976, because of Rodriguez' legendary South African popularity, the second album, **Coming From Reality**, was re-released with the ubiquitous title **After The Fact**. This was an attempt to cash in commercially on the best selling South African debut **Cold Fact**. In this scenario there was an unlikely early hero. He was a champion of the Sugar Man's music, and his personal vendetta was to make Sixto Rodriguez a household name. In time he would arrange for Rodriguez' South African concerts. His name was Stephen "Sugar" Segerman. He worked indefatigable to popularize Rodriguez. He told anyone who would listen about the Sugar Man's lyrical-songwriting brilliance. Everyone believed Rodriguez was dead. That is everyone except the man called Sugar. He quickly became an expert on all things Sixto Rodriguez.

Stephen "Sugar" Segerman co-wrote the liner notes for the South African release of Rodriguez' second album. He also provided the record label with a pristine copy of **Coming From Reality**. The label was ecstatic. The result was another best selling South African Rodriguez album. He was working in Detroit unaware of his South African stardom. The mystery and myth surrounding Rodriguez was taking shape. It would continue to grow until he appeared in South Africa in concert in 1998.

How Rodriguez re-emerged and continued his career is a story in persistence. The Sugar Man's comeback also had a great deal to do with Steve Rowland's vision. When he produced **Coming From Reality**, he asked a simply question. Why a second album? Steve Rowland believed a second Rodriguez album would break his original songs. But the record business is a tough one. Success is based on records sold not original talent.

No one supported a second Rodriguez album. That is until Steve Rowland heard **Cold Fact**. He told everyone he found America's best singer-songwriter. I wasn't sure what Rowland saw in Rodriguez' debut album. I sat down for a series of interviews with Rowland. He spun a tale of recording an artist so talented and so unique he believed he would have a hit record each year until the Sugar Man retired.

Steve Rowland spent hundreds of hours talking to me about his career prior to Rodriguez, how he made **Coming From Reality** such a brilliant second album, and how and why the Sugar Man was able to achieve stardom forty years after the fact.

This book details Steve Rowland's seminal role not only in producing **Coming From Reality**, but his championing of the Sugar Man's career since fame arrived. The continued support of Matt Sullivan's Light In The Attic label, the role of the Oscar winning documentary and the rigorous touring that brought Rodriguez a large audience, as well as fame and fortune, is another aspect of the story.

By 2012 Rodriguez was no longer a forgotten item. He was a Cinderella story. The rumors the Sugar Man was dead helped the myths encircling his career. When the **London Times**,' Jonathan Dean, interviewed Rodriguez about his strange journey to fame and fortune, the Sugar Man commented: "It was a surprise." That said it all. Rodriguez' understated personality and humility caused him to ponder the future.

When Jonathan Dean described Rodriguez as "a hippie taken out of the deep freeze," he missed the essence of the Sugar Man. Rodriguez is humble, laid back, and he has little concern with money. There is one thing that drives him. That is his music. He wants to share it. The result has been some of the most extraordinary concerts around the world since 2012.

There is another part of Rodriguez that flummoxes the critics. That is his references to Aldous Huxley, Karl Marx or perhaps a literary figure like William Blake. Then he will use a term like "young bloods" to describe the current musicians. He often refers to people as "cats." He is the ultimate hipster with an intellectual persona.

Matt Lucas, who played Detroit clubs, described Rodriguez as "a jazz guy." "He was more than just a rocker," Lucas said. When he played in and around the Motor City in the early 1970s, Lucas recalled the Sugar Man was a fixture in the small clubs.

One of the strange aspects of the Sixto Rodriguez story is the journey of Stephen "Sugar" Segerman who discovered Rodriguez' music in 1972 while serving his year of compulsory military service in South Africa. Segerman's journey to bringing Sixto Rodriguez to South Africa in 1998 began in a Johannesburg suburb. Once he heard the lilting strains of **Cold Fact** in the early 1970s, he was on a mission to find Sixto Rodriguez. He told anyone who would listen Rodriguez was the best singer-songwriter of his generation.

The Three Decades Segerman Devoted to Hunting Rodriguez

After he listened to **Cold Fact**, Segerman devoted more than three decades to bring Rodriguez' music into the mainstream. After the 1998 South African Rodriguez concerts, Segerman kept after the story until 2006 when he convinced Swedish filmmaker Malik Bendjelloul to begin and eventually complete the Oscar winning **Searching For Sugar Man**. That wasn't the end of the story. Segerman took a proprietary interest in Rodriguez' post documentary career. The result is **Sugar Man- The Life, Death And Resurrection of Sixto Rodriguez**. This September 10, 2015 release of Craig Bartholomew-Strydom and Segerman's 382-page inside look at Rodriguez' career is a masterpiece. It emphasizes their role in the Sugar Man's resurgent career. It is a marvelous piece of journalism. Rodriguez penchant for smoking marijuana is all over the Segerman-Bartholomew-Strydom book. That is unfortunate. His privacy is compromised. Stephen "Sugar"

Segerman's disruptive behavior in parts of the Rodriguez story suggests why they are no longer close friends. He was considered a bad influence on the Sugar Man, as he asked for smoking rooms. He also posted pictures on the Internet that upset Rodriguez' daughter Eva. He also told anyone who would listen he invented the Rodriguez story. His critics have been a bit harsh. Segerman is a good guy. He is just full of himself.

Cape Town is filled with people who describe Segerman as seeking fame and fortune. He is at times cranky and at other times sweet as well as accessible. He had nothing to do with any of the Sugar Man's recordings. He has opinions often contrary to the facts. It is important to examine Rodriguez's career in its second phase. He recorded with Steve Rowland and the result was **Coming From Reality**. When one listens to Segerman, he sounds like it was **Cold Fact** that was the beginning and end of Rodriguez' recording career. The reason? He has made a career out of being Mr. Cold Fact.

The Second Phase of Rodriguez' Career: Coming From Reality

The second phase of the Rodriguez story centers around Steve Rowland's magnificently produced album **Coming From Reality**. This LP quickly fell by the commercial wayside. It is a perfect reminder of what is wrong with the music industry. It also tells one a great deal about the integrity and perseverance that made Sixto Rodriguez an international superstar after **Searching For Sugar Man** stormed the world stage in 2012.

It also tells one a great deal about Rowland's perseverance. Without Steve Rowland's demands there would not have been a second Rodriguez album. He saw a commercial side to the Sugar Man Sussex Records missed. As a consistent producer of London based hits, it was not uncommon for Rowland's records to chart on both sides of the Atlantic. This is one of many reasons he was selected to produce **Coming From Reality**. If there was a producer who could bring Rodriguez to the charts, it was Rowland.

The question persisted: Why a second album? The answer is a simple one. One producer (Steve Rowland), one inside industry figure (Neil Bogart), and a legendary American music man (Clarence Avant) paved the way for the second album. There wasn't anyone who thought Sixto Rodriguez would record a second album. There was, however, one person who was Rodriguez' strongest supporter. His name was Steve Rowland. He was an industry insider. He was a mega-hit producer. He was a seasoned performer with his group The Family Dogg. He had an ear for songwriting talent. He developed a legendary career in London as a gold and platinum record producer. After Rowland insisted on a second Rodriguez LP, he staked his future reputation on **Coming From Reality**. Like Rodriguez, he had to wait forty years to have his producing vision vindicated. Why a second album? The question persisted.

That is the question everyone in the industry posed when Clarence Avant gave Steve Rowland the green light to produce **Coming From Reality**. That began the resurrection and legendary journey of Sixto Rodriguez.

The imperious nature of those around the Sugar Man is a strange phenomenon. He is his own person. The problem is fame and fortune in 2012 brought him more would be advisers and even more hangers on. He didn't sign up for this intense level of fame.

The personal Sixto Rodriguez is quiet, shy, and he prefers walking the Detroit streets than hanging out in Beverly Hills. His lifestyle remains the same as when he was a day worker raising a family. Despite his newfound wealth, he lives an existential life. His family is his most important concern. He avoids publicity. Since the initial press onslaught arrived with **Searching For Sugar Man**, Rodriguez has granted fewer interviews. There is an aura of paranoia in and around his management team. Despite his international successes, he remains a blue collar Detroit native with a strong presence in the

Motor City. He prefers a drink, a dinner, and a bit of conversation in the Cass Corridor. He still hangs around the Wayne State University campus. The journey to fame and fortune didn't change Rodriguez. It impacted everyone else.

One of the curious reactions to **Searching For Sugar Man** is it is a fairy tale. That is a rags to riches story that took place forty years after his two albums failed. Rodriguez was another casualty of the record business. His story is one told a thousand times over with many artists who experienced a lack of promotion, a bastardization of their music, an inability to find out if there were royalties and a disdain for their product. Sixto Rodriguez was given a second chance thanks to the Oscar winning documentary. Now everyone wants to be the Sugar Man's best friend. There are those who tell the "true story." This has clouded the real tale and muddied his reputation. The best way to look at Sixto Rodriguez is to remember he is shy, private and there is a back-story. He is one of the most accomplished songwriters in the folk-rock idiom. His story is one that tells us what is wrong with the record business and what is right with Sixto Rodriguez.

It appeared Rodriguez' career was over when **Cold Fact** didn't sell. But in London an American expatriate record producer, Steve Rowland, picked up the Sugar Man's first record. He took it home. He listened to it for a week. He couldn't believe Rodriguez wasn't as popular or didn't sell as well as Bob Dylan. He volunteered to produce the Sugar Man's second album. The suits agreed. The plans were made for **Coming From Reality**.

The improbable journey to fame and fortune is a tale that will not be repeated. But it demonstrates how the visual media created Rodriguez' re-emergence. When **Searching For Sugar Man** burst onto the big screen it brought Rodriguez' music back with a roar. He can tour as long as he likes. The journey to fame tells us more about the record industry than we care to know. It also highlights there were elements other than South Africa bringing Rodriguez into the commercial mainstream.

Sixto Rodriguez and Steve Rowland, New York, 2013

Three

The Sugar Man's Journey to Fame

"Madness passed me by, she smiled Hi. I nodded."

Sixto Rodriguez "Inner City Blues"

"It is impossible to overlook the extent to which civilization is built upon a renunciation of instinct."

Sigmund Freud

Learn as if you will live forever; live as if you will die tomorrow."

**Miss Maria Mitchell, Astronomer
Vasser, late 1870s.**

In 1998, when Sixto Rodriguez appeared in his first series of South African concerts, the local media referred to the shows as "Dead Man Walking." Since 1970-1971, when a small cult of Rodriguez collectors began to tell anyone who would listen Sixto Rodriguez was the world's greatest singer-songwriter, he quietly became a superstar. He rivaled Elvis Presley, the Beatles and the Rolling Stones for South African popularity. No one knew anything about Rodriguez. The rumor was he was dead. He had no sales in America. No one had heard of him.

In the most unlikely story in the rock and roll world, it took Sixto Rodriguez twenty-seven years to achieve South African fame. There wasn't much fortune, in South Africa, and then he simply fell off the record business grid. When he stood in the auditorium in Park City, Utah for the premier of **Searching For Sugar Man** he envisioned a few months of fame. That was in January 2012. Now more than five years later the fame that eluded him is back. It is permanent. He is a musical icon who can tour as long as he is healthy. That is the beauty of the Sugar Man's journey.

South Africa Piques the Early Sugar Man's Resurgence

Rodriguez' road to fame in South Africa came as the nation suffered world isolation. The apartheid government, which excluded native South Africans, had a color line that made rock music a watered down pop sound. The censors were out, and those who listened to the Sugar Man had a special sense of his music breaking the law. The P. W. Botha government was racist and repressive. It was impossible for the black population to live a normal life. Then in 1948 freedom minded musicians, writers and politicians began the slow revolution that led to the end of apartheid in 1994. From 1970 onward Rodriguez' songs were one of the bulwarks of the anti-apartheid movement. The South African population grew from 3.8 million to 4.8 million in the 1970s and 1980s. A disposable income was one of the byproducts of this growth. South Africans had more money to spend on consumer goods. Rodriguez' albums continued to sell in South Africa. He was on an improbable journey to fame that began in 1998 in a series of South African concerts. His dream of stardom didn't materialize after these concerts. He continued to perform sporadically in South Africa as well as Australia, the U. S. and England. When an American record label, Light In The Attic, re-released **Cold Fact** and **Coming From Reality** the stage was set for his comeback.

When Matt Sullivan, the LITA label head, showed up at Rodriguez' Detroit house on Avery Street, he was greeted warmly. The Sugar Man was feeding firewood into a stove. Next to the wood-burning stove was a neatly made bed where Rodriguez slept. It was Spartan. This impressed those who came into the house. LITA regularly sent Rodriguez firewood. Why is this important? He had no central heating or air conditioning. He lives close to the earth. His wife, Rayma, has said repeatedly that she loves her husband. She simply couldn't live with him. He is too close to nature and so uncomplicated. He is the primary example of an urban existentialist.

The LITA re-releases and concerts they promoted featured his music from 2007 through 2011. This paved the way for future success. The five years that LITA spent promoting, booking and extolling Rodriguez' musical greatness did a great deal to set in motion the hurricane of publicity that made him an international star.

While Stephen "Sugar" Segerman was instrumental in Rodriguez' 1998 South African tour, it was a shy, little known alternative musician, Tonia Selley, who filmed the musicians, the atmosphere and the credibility convincing skeptical South African audiences that the "dead man walking" was alive. Some critics believed his concerts were a hoax. Still they sold out. A TV show of his 1998 shows, **Dead Men Don't Tour**, set up by Selley ended the erroneous speculation a Rodriguez impersonator was bilking the South African audiences. The **Dead Men Don't Tour** documentary is on You Tube.

Who was Tonia Selley? She worked in the 1980s South African alternative music scene when she was known as Karla Krimpalien. She is a talented multi-instrumental percussionist and a statuesque beauty. Her creative credentials are superb. In addition to being an accomplished performer, she is a songwriter, producer and filmmaker.

Selley's importance is she videotaped the 1998 shows and her film became an integral part of **Searching For Sugar Man**.

In 2012, the whirlwind interviews, after the success of the Oscar winning documentary **Searching For Sugar Man,** prompted interviewers to marvel at Rodriguez' composure and understated wisdom. When asked what he felt over the last forty years, Rodriguez replied: "I didn't feel lost, I knew exactly where I was." That is typical Sixto Rodriguez.

The interviewers were amazed. He was forthcoming and intelligent. Most of the rock and roll press hadn't done their homework. They had no idea the Sugar Man earned a BA with honors in philosophy. He seldom mentioned it. He was too humble. They also had little notion of his family ties, his wives or his liberal political interests. It was as if he had just arrived from Mars. The questions from those who interviewed him were often disjointed, imperious or simply lacking in intelligence. He bore this burden with his usual eland. He is an existential gentleman.

What Separates Rodriguez from others and Why: The Detroit Water Board Speech Tells Why

What separates Rodriguez from those who practice the craft of rock and roll music? It is his stoic personality with an existentialist's touch. In June 2014 the **Hollywood Reporter** asked: "Searching For Sugar Man: Where Is Sixto Rodriguez Today?" It had been two and a half years since the success of the Oscar winning documentary. The **Hollywood Reporter** wrote: "He still lives in the same rundown Detroit neighborhood and even plays his trusty old guitar." That observation is nonsense. He lives in a bucolic tree lined street with young families, college students, artists, writers and intellectuals. It is not Beverly Hills, but it is not the hood.

In March 2014, Rodriguez and his family rested at home in Detroit preparing for a May tour of England and Italy. He returned to Detroit and prepared for a two-month tour opening for Beach Boy major domo Brian Wilson. Rodriguez was busy, but he didn't ignore his constituency. Few people outside of Detroit realized the Sugar Man was a committed political activist. He remains a voice for the poor, the blue-collar worker and those the city of Detroit ignores. When the Detroit Water Board held a public hearing in March 2015 Rodriguez was front and center complaining about the anticipated water increase rate.

When he appeared at the Detroit Water Board meeting on March 11, 2015, the Sugar Man spoke of the need to maintain the present water rate. He said people living on fixed incomes, below the poverty line, and renting with barely enough money to pay the water bill would be homeless if an increase took place. He was elegant, well reasoned and quietly passionate in his plea for Detroit's poor. The next speaker was Rodriguez' middle daughter, Sandra Kennedy Rodriguez, she pointed out health conditions were imperiled if people couldn't afford water. If he had a choice between political activism and music, he would select politics. His sense of community improvement remains his driving force.

Back in 1970-1971, he had dreams of mainstream musical success. So did his producers Dennis Coffey and Mike Theodore for **Cold Fact** and Steve Rowland for **Coming From Reality**. Neither album sold. He wasn't upset. Disappointed? Yes! He went on with his life with brief stops in Australia to tour in 1979 and 1981 and the comeback in 1998 in South Africa. He wasn't mainstream. He remained a cult artist. He had a fan following. It was a small, niche base.

Searching for Sugar Man Brings Him Back

Although Rodriguez' second album was ignored, he created a set of songs that were highly commercial. He didn't have commercial success. He vanished into a normal life. He wasn't concerned about his future. He had a full life. It was also a private life. Rodriguez was unaware South Africans continued to listen to and popularize his music.

The coup de grace to his career came in late February 2013 when **Searching For Sugar Man** won the Oscar for best documentary at the 85th Annual Academy Awards. The **Huffington Post** called the Sugar Man's music "Medicine For Salty Wounds." The ensuing story labeled him a cultural healer. What did this mean? It was an early indication of how his music crossed over into the intellectual, contrarian mainstream. That praise came as Rodriguez prepared for his first post Oscar Detroit show. Suddenly, he was a star. He was more than an itinerant walking in the Cass Corridor. This turned out to be a mixed blessing. Fame and fortune impacted his private life. It was worth it. The Sugar Man was onboard for the newfound touring and public acclaim. He had waited more than forty years for recognition.

The Sixto Rodriguez story has a never-ending sense of drama. In July 2013, he walked out on stage at the Wayne State University graduation to receive an honorary Doctor of Humane Letters. It was a nostalgic moment for Rodriguez who spent a decade earning an honors degree in philosophy. The ceremony at Ford Field prompted a university official to remark Rodriguez was being honored for his "musical genius and commitment to social justice." It was a special interlude. One he worked on for forty years. Artistic praise and being ignored commercially is not a recipe for happiness. Ironically, the Sugar Man was happy. Music and family took up his time. Money! He could care less.

Sixto Rodriguez: "I'm a solid seventy. I just received a doctorate from Wayne State University. I hear that I am going to receive the Legion of Honour from France," Rodriguez remarked when he opened the Montreux Jazz Festival in July 2013. He seldom talks about his musical accomplishments. He is a prickly character. He doesn't like his picture taken. He doesn't like to do interviews. He didn't want to appear in **Searching For Sugar Man**. He did! Why? It restarted his dormant career and put him on the road to making a million dollars a year. But the prickly behavior remains. He is moody. He is private. The mood swings and the desire for anonymity make it difficult for the biographer. But that is the challenge.

The hundreds of people who surround Rodriguez are free with their praise, their observations and universally their admiration. From the stage manager, to the bus driver, to the booking agent, to the musicians, to the promoters, to the friends and family there is a story that emerges much like the Sugar Man that Malik Bendjelloul portrays in **Searching For Sugar Man**. It is a once in a lifetime story.

There is a great deal of irony in this second book on Rodriguez. He is a new person. He took aggressive control of his career. He hired a battery of lawyers. He has at least eight bands throughout the world ready to back him in concert. His daughter, Regan, provides excellent management.

Sony regularly sends royalty payments, as does Clarence Avant. The Sugar Man receives other royalties in a timely manner. For the first time foreign royalties streamed into the family coffers. His daughter Regan takes care of the taxes. He may not have cared about money but there is a financial responsibility. The Sugar Man is all business.

Rodriguez cares about justice for his music. He prioritizes his life. There is no mystery to Sixto Rodriguez. He is a natural performer. He remains a brilliant writer. He continues to be political. He works daily as a social advocate. He supports everything from women's rights, to green peace, to international peace, to environmental issues, and he continues to argue reform is possible in this fractured world. He is not happy Donald J. Trump is president. But he has not commented on the Donald. He has been too busy with his recharged music career.

Rodriguez' Royal Albert Hall Debut: What It Meant

On May 7, 2015 Rodriguez made his debut at London's Royal Albert Hall. This is the pinnacle of the U. K. entertainment world. The recognition for **Searching For Sugar Man** began when the prestigious British award, the BAFTA, praised Rodriguez' music and honored the documentary. This iconic British entertainment venue is not only a world-class venue; it provided recognition of his rise to stardom. It was a bittersweet triumph. After forty years in the musical wilderness, he was an overnight star.

After the Royal Albert Hall show and a brief European tour, Rodriguez' high profile concerts continued. He opened for Brian Wilson in the summer of 2015. It was a heady time for the Sugar Man. How did he get there? Stay tuned. The **Coming From Reality** album, the Oscar winning **Searching For Sugar Man** and the subsequent roller coaster touring schedule indicated another chapter in Rodriquez's late in life rise to stardom.

The Royal Albert Hall show was a brilliant one. The London audience appreciated and cheered for covers of "La Bamba," a Platters influenced "Only You," a B. B. King influenced "The Thrill is Gone," (Rodriguez dedicated the song to King) a Jefferson Airplane tribute to "Somebody to Love" and to show that he was still fond of the classic rockers a version of "Blue Suede Shoes" owed its inspiration to Carl Perkins. He performed three other covers in his show but raucous applause and after a spellbinding version of "Forget It," Rodriguez left the stage to rapturous applause. He returned with three encores including a lilting version of "Street Boy." The reception was over the top and Rodriguez now played the larger, more prestigious London venues. The days of performing in Camden Town were in the past. He was now a major U. K. concert attraction. This was sweet considering the betrayal and fraud early in his career.

The Sugar Man's Story is One of Betrayal and Fraud

The Sugar Man's story is much more than a singer who failed to achieve commercial success. The Sixto Rodriguez tale is one of betrayal, outright fraud by those around him, his successes as a family man, and his eventual emergence as an international superstar. Much of the Sugar Man's success is due to the Oscar winning **Searching**

For Sugar Man. Malik Bendjelloul's documentary is a beautifully scripted, musically brilliant, cinematic masterpiece. It is only a small part of the story. The remainder of the story results from the Steve Rowland produced album **Coming From Reality**. It offers a tale of personal and musical redemption.

As Rodriguez said in "Ill Slip Away," "I'll forget about your lies and deceit and your attempts to be so discreet. Maybe today, yeah. I'll slip away." He did. When he began performing in mainstream, well paying venues in the summer of 2012, he was the same old Sixto Rodriguez. He was now, as he said, "a solid seventy." It was sweet redemption. He is enjoying every minute of it.

Rodriguez' "Climb Up On My Music," from Steve Rowland's brilliantly produced **Coming From Reality,** summed up his attitude toward his music. "Well, just climb up on my music, and my songs will set you free." That says it all. It just took forty years for the message to resonate with the listening public. Sixto Rodriguez' resurrection is a multi-layered story. It is much more than his triumphant series of concerts in South Africa in 1998 or the **Searching For Sugar Man** Oscar.

There are many misconceptions about Sixto Rodriguez. The team of Stephen "Sugar" Segerman and Craig Bartholomew-Strydom brought him back. However, they ignored a large portion of the story. They became not only protectors but also progenitors of many of the Sugar Man's myths. The notion he recorded his last song with Steve Rowland, "Cause," for the **Coming From Reality** LP is a correct one. It is the last released tune. He continued to record sporadically. The finished product never satisfied the Sugar Man. He was in the studio with Mike Theodore in the mid-1970s and again in 1997-1998. He was also into various studios sporadically from 2012 to 2016. But there are no concrete facts other than cutting some songs in a London studio and others at a Los Angeles area radio station.

Once thing is certain, Rodriguez has worked on new material for more than forty years. He performed sporadically when and where he could and then in 2008 the Seattle based Light In The Attic label brought out **Cold Fact** and Rodriguez' second career advanced slowly, but quietly, until **Searching For Sugar Man** created a commercial avalanche. Matt Sullivan's Light In the Attic imprint was the perfect place to bring Rodriguez into commercial prominence.

What did the Journey to Fame Do to Rodriguez?

What did fame do to Rodriguez? The best way to understand fame is to let the Sugar Man describe his rise to performing prominence. He sat down with a South African TV show in February 2013, and he explained what the last year had been like. He went into detail about how and why the documentary impacted his life. He spoke of his reluctance to be involved in the project. The conclusion was obvious. He had been disappointed too many times.

He also did a lengthy interview with the **Hollywood Reporter** in February 2013. This is a window into his creative genius. The Sugar Man opened stating: "I've been chasing music since I was sixteen." When asked if he knows how talented he is, Rodriguez replied with characteristic humility: "It is all practice." For some reason, he felt comfortable with the **Hollywood Reporter** and the saga of the Sugar Man was laid out to the general public.

To understand why and how Rodriguez developed from a pop-psych act in **Cold Fact** to a more mature pop oriented artist it is necessary to examine Steve Rowland's career. He did more than produce **Coming From Reality**. Steve was able to help the Sugar Man craft his music into a more commercial direction. Whether you like **Cold Fact** better than **Coming From Reality** it was as Mike Theodore said: "a matter of apples and oranges." Both albums are superb. The difference is that there is less of a cutting edge, less of the biting political satire and less of the hard driving psychedelic sound in **Coming From Reality**. Clearly, Rowland produced a pop album.

Rodriguez was with him every step of the way. The songs were chart friendly. The tragedy is they didn't chart. The personal and professional side to Rowland's life provides a window into how **Coming From Reality** was produced and why it came roaring back to critical acclaim in 2012.

The journey to fame had a minimal impact upon Rodriguez. It did give him a chance to share his music with the world. He had a vision. He never gave up on the belief that his lyrics were mind altering in a philosophical sense. In 2012 the world agreed. The fairy tale ended and happiness was assured.

In February 2013 Rodriguez appeared on EWN in South Africa, after a year of fame, he discussed the changes in his life. He found touring rigorous, but he loved it. He talked about working on new material. He left no doubt he was happy to be in the music business mainstream. EWN, known as Eye Witness News, was the perfect vehicle for Rodriguez to explain his life, his music and his concerns for the future.

Sixto Rodriguez is an enigma. He has maintained a private face. There is no rage, no humiliation, no shame and no guilt in a tough life that should have elicited those feelings. It didn't! His personality is preserved under an obsidian veneer.

Rodriguez and the Spell His Casts Over His Fans

The Sugar Man has always cast a spell over his music fans. The reverence for his songwriting is buttressed with unwavering support for his lilting vocals. "Sugar Man" is a song most critics consider his masterpiece. He translates his emotions, the images surrounding Detroit and his personal life into music that connects with his audience. He translates his personal life into songs with as Rodriguez says employing the writer's gift for fiction. In his early life Rodriguez set the stage for a heroes life. He saw, described and wrote about a time in

America that captured with such rare insight his songs sound more like novels than rock an roll tales. The villains who arrived failed to derail the Sugar Man's career and the story is more than about Sixto Rodriguez. It is a tale of betrayal, outright fraud, deception, over the top manipulation and the music industries nefarious activities. Rodriguez is almost a minor character in his own biography.

This book is not about everything you want to know about Rodriguez. It is a tour de force of how the music business almost destroyed one of the greatest singer-songwriter's to embrace the industry. Rodriguez was resilient, had personal strength, turned angst into positive thoughts and celebrated romantic love. He had courage. He was vulnerable in lyrical form and tough as nails in life. That is the Sugar Man. There will not be another one in the music industry. Think of this book as "My Dinner With Sixto Rodriguez." You will find out he is a moody, irascible, complex individual that you will come to love.

When the second album **Coming From Reality** arrived there was no interest. Zero! Steve Rowland made sure no one forgot Sixto Rodriguez. He wasn't out there promoting the Sugar Man after the release of the seminal album. But when asked Rowland said the Sugar Man was the greatest singer songwriter he produced. There is a symbiotic relationship between Rodriguez and Rowland. This is the reason they complete each other's sentences to the present day. Rodriguez is the hero of his life. Rowland is along for the ride describing the brilliance and humility of his friend.

Four

The Genius of Steve Rowland: The Personal and Professional Side

"For though the artist may all his life remain closer, not to say truer, to his childhood than the man trained for practical life-although one may say that he, unlike the latter, abides in the dreamy purely human and playful childlike state…."

Thomas Mann, Doctor Faustus

"If you're not living on the edge you're taking up too much room,"

Steve Rowland

"It is in self-limitation that a master first shows himself."

Goethe

"Everybody thought I had it easy. I didn't have it easy. Nepotism was the big killer. Because I was the son of a top MGM film director no one took me seriously. Nepotism always put the breaks on."

Steve Rowland

Steve Rowland is enjoying a well-deserved retirement in Palm Springs, California. The problem is Rowland is not retired. He is working on a television series based on his book **Hollywood Heat**. He is putting together documentary material on his life as an actor, singer, performer and producer. He is considering going back into the studio. He is also outlining another book. The indefatigable energy that is Steve Rowland is well and alive.

As he eases into semi-retirement, Rowland looks fifty and acts thirty. It is with his good looks and winning personality he remains a strong spokesperson for the Rodriguez documentary. He is also an emphatic supporter of Rodriguez' musical career. For years, Rowland told anyone who would listen the Sugar Man was his best act. No one listened. Then Malik Bendjelloul's **Searching For Sugar Man** won an Oscar for best documentary. Suddenly Steve Rowland's opinions mattered. He is constantly called for interviews. He works these into his busy schedule.

The legendary producer is quiet, self-effacing, and he is one of the few industry insiders who never took advantage of Rodriguez' talent. "I want the best for him," Rowland continued. "I consider Rodriguez the most brilliant songwriter of this generation." Until Steve Rowland came along no one allowed Rodriguez proper freedom in the recording studio.

When he produced **Coming From Reality**, it was with an eye to Rodriguez' inner creativity. The album failed to sell. Rodriguez vanished to Detroit. Rowland continued his production and performing career in London.

After a lengthy and acclaimed career, Rowland retired to Palm Springs. He was looking to slow down and enjoy himself. He did for a while. Then the Rodriguez phenomenon burst on the scene. Suddenly, tranquility was not an option. Rowland was bombarded with questions about the legendary Detroit musician.

The Tranquility Ends for Steve Rowland

The tranquility of Palm Springs ended in 2012 when Rowland appeared at a local art theater to talk about and preview **Searching For Sugar Man**. He was featured in Malik Bendjelloul's film for producing Rodriguez' second album **Coming From Reality**.

On August 31, 2012, Rowland climbed up on the Palme D'Or stage in Palm Desert to discuss Rodriguez and his musical career. This luxurious theater is known as the Grand Prix of Cinema. It was the perfect place for Rowland to explain the Rodriguez phenomena. As an accomplished actor, musician, writer and record producer, Rowland's sixty years of in-depth experience sparkled in his explanations. He mesmerized the Palm Desert crowd with his tales of Rodriguez' lyrical beauty and charismatic stage presence. As always, Rowland downplayed his role.

As Rowland told his story of producing the album for an unknown Mexican American singer from Detroit, the documentary **Searching For Sugar Man** exploded in art theaters. Soon it was a first run documentary with an Oscar buzz. When it won an Oscar, there was so much attention focused on Rodriguez' music that he talked of a third LP.

By January 2013 Rodriguez told **Rolling Stone** he wanted to make a third album with Rowland producing. Rodriguez said of Rowland:

"He told me to send him a couple of tapes, so I'm gonna do that. I certainly want to look him up, because now he's full of ideas."

Rodriguez implied Rowland would bring out all facets of his songwriting and performing on record. Rodriguez' desire to work with Rowland is one indication of Steve's lengthy and legendary career in the entertainment business.

Who is Steve Rowland? How did he come to produce Sixto Rodriguez? It is in the first thirty-five years of Rowland's life that he evolved into a multi-faceted entertainment icon.

Rowland Growing Up in Beverly Hills Royalty: Wild in the Streets

On September 3, as the Great Depression raged, Steve Rowland was born in Los Angeles. He grew up in Beverley Hills amongst Hollywood royalty. He is the great nephew of Louis B. Mayer who never came to the Rowland home. "I was pleased with his absence," Rowland said. It was after all Hollywood and Rowland considered Mayer a despot.

Rowland has fond memories of tinseltown. He made many friends while being cast in movies and television shows like the Rifleman, Bonanza, Wanted Dead or Alive and Wagon Train among others. He was a featured columnist in various fan magazines. Rowland's writing style was in the vein of the 1950s. He was a much sought after writer on inside Hollywood.

He had a full life that also included performing as a rock musician up and down Hollywood's Sunset Strip. One well-known entertainer remarked: "Steve was the first Johnny Rivers." This was a comment about his appearances in local clubs.

His father, a film director, Roy Rowland was well known from 1934 into the mid-1960s. For film aficionados there are eleven of Roy's cult movies including "Affair With A Stranger" starring Jean Simmons and Victor Mature and "The 5,000 Fingers of Dr. T," starring Hans Conreid that cemented his reputation. "The 5000 Fingers of Dr. T." is a cult classic featuring a character known as Dr. Terwiliken who captures five hundred boys and forces them to play the piano around the clock. What made the movie unique is Dr. Seuss did the sets. Dr. Theodor Seuss Geisel was famous for his forty-eight Dr. Seuss books. He collaborated with Rowland on one of the most unique cult movies in American cinema.

"Our Vines Have Tender Grapes" is perhaps Rowland's most controversial movie. This 1945 film featured Edward G. Robinson and Margaret O'Brien in a movie based on the 1940 novel by George Victor Martin, a Norwegian-American, who lived in a small Wisconsin dairy town. It is a heartwarming story featuring a Norwegian immigrant farmer whose greatest hope is to build a new barn. He is a loving husband. The story is about how a rural American family copes with the tough ways of the farming life. It is a wonderful tale of a hard working immigrant who is a proud American. The film was hampered by the revelation that Dalton Trumbo wrote the script.

In Hollywood in the 1940s Trumbo was a blacklisted writer due to his left wing political views. This was Trumbo's last script before he appeared before the House Un-American Activities Committee. Margaret O'Brien remarked the movie was ignored for decades because of Trumbo's radical political reputation. Roy Rowland defended Trumbo, used his scripts and did his best to support him.

Steve Rowland: "The best cult movie that my father made was 'The Five Thousand Fingers of Dr. T.' It was a musical masterpiece. They tried to get it on Broadway. They are still trying to get it on Broadway. I get contacted about it all the time."

Roy Rowland was an accomplished mainstream director. He did much more than cult films. While many of Rowland's movies were exploitive ones, he was always able to attract well-known actors. A good example is the 1956 classic James Cagney-Barbara Stanwyck "These Wilder Years," which was not well reviewed, but went on to become a cult classic. When he directed "Meet Me In Las Vegas" starring Cyd Charisse, Dan Dailey, Agnes Moorhead and Jim Backus,

Rowland was in the mainstream of A list directors. Cameo appearances by Frank Sinatra, Debbie Reynolds, Pier Angeli, Peter Lorre and Tony Martin helped the box office. Near the end of the movie Sammy Davis, Jr. sings “Frankie and Johnny” with Cyd Charisse dancing. It was a stupendous piece of cinema.

”Witness to Murder” is another Roy Rowland masterpiece starring Barbara Stanwyck that didn’t do well at the box office. The reason Alfred Hitchcock’s “Rear Window” opened a month later. By the mid-1960s Rowland retired after directing three spaghetti westerns.

Steve’s mother, Ruth Rowland, was a screenwriter at MGM Studios. She also wrote fiction. When asked about Louis B. Mayer, Rowland commented: “He and I never got on. If things didn’t go his way, he didn’t like it.” The critics often said Rowland came from “Hollywood royalty.” Comments like this often blocked Steve’s multiple talents. He was a singer, a songwriter, an actor, a columnist and a talented producer. In Hollywood the powers that be wanted the talent to wear one hat. Steve was a renaissance man. He was blocked by nepotism and his penchant for multiple talents at every turn.

One of the ironies of Steve’s early career is he was told he was too accomplished. He wrote movie columns read by more than a million readers. There were a number of different columns for movie or fan magazines. He was also a car enthusiast who raced. He acted. He wrote songs. He played in a band. He had a business knowledge of and working relationship with record label owners, song publishers and anyone associated with the music industry. At some auditions he was turned down for being too accomplished. Steve had trouble with the people who drew these conclusions. It is one of the reasons he relocated to London to produce records.

Steve Rowland on Hollywood

Steve Rowland’s independent minded personality, and writing skills, made him one of Hollywood’s shrewdest observers. Steve’s greatest trait is his honesty. That trait at times hindered his career.

"He was a benevolent despot," Rowland remarked of Louis B. Mayer. When the Rowland family went to Mayer's massive mansion for dinner in Bel Air, Mayer complained Rowland's parents bought him a Corvette after graduation, and that this gracious gesture for his academic achievements was a mistake. Rowland said: "I am lucky that you are not one of my parents." From an early age Steve Rowland was his own man. In Hollywood this is not a good thing. He survived the pitfalls of the Hollywood life and made a name for himself in movies and television.

From the age of eleven to twenty one, young Steve was an observer to Hollywood royalty. By the early 1950s, Rowland was cruising Hollywood and Sunset Boulevard in his black leather jacket and new Corvette. He went on to become an actor, a columnist, fronting a rock band, and he evolved into a legendary music producer. His drop-dead good looks and personable nature led to success in a number of fields.

Rowland's ability to hire musicians, to function as a band's lead singer and to write and arrange songs brought him engagements at some of Hollywood's premier clubs. He learned the first steps on how to become one of the best pop-rock music producers from the 1960s until he left London in 2007. The best way to understand Rowland is to analyze his comments on Hollywood.

Steve Rowland's Book on Hollywood

When Steve Rowland goes to dinner in Palm Springs, he is just another local resident. He doesn't talk about his multi-faceted career. There is a refreshing humility to Rowland.

In 2008 Rowland's **Hollywood Heat: Untold Stories of 1950s Hollywood** was released in the U. K. to positive reviews. The beautifully designed, picture-laden volume contains some of the best stories from Rowland's personal archives. Along with his friend, Budd Albright, they cut a suave path through Hollywood. The book includes Rowland's columns for **Dig** and other popular fan magazines, which were written in the hipster lingo of the day. His sense of drama and self-deprecating humor make his book a must read for Hollywood aficionados.

Rowland's writes of nights out with Elvis Presley, meeting Marilyn Monroe in the doctor's office and the likes of encounters with Marlon Brando, James Dean, Natalie Wood and Steve McQueen. He recalls these stories of Hollywood's coming of age with insights into what made these years the Golden Age of Tinseltown. During his Hollywood years, James Dean was one of his closest friends. They shared a passion for racing. They also had common acting interests and much of Steve's early life provides the foundation for his Hollywood book.

Hollywood Heat: Untold Stories of 1950s Hollywood, published in London in 2008, is a fascinating look inside tinsel town. There are stories of many celebrities but the most interesting one involves Elvis Presley. One night Steve was feeling down. He called Elvis who was staying with the Memphis Mafia at the Beverly Wilshire Hotel. They hung out and Rowland had one of the best nights of his career riding around in a long black Cadillac limousine with Elvis at the wheel.

Few people realized Rowland was a local rock and roll star in Hollywood before he went off to England to produce and form his group, the Family Dogg. He was training in Hollywood for a career in London.

Steve Rowland's Family Dogg: The Mission

The Family Dogg was a rock group providing interesting insights into Steve Rowland. When the London based Cherry Red label released the double CD **The Family Dogg, A Way of Life: Anthology 1967 To 1976**, it provided a window into Rowland's creative genius. The CD title is taken from the band's first U. K. top ten hit.

When Rowland put together the idea for the Family Dogg, he was living in Spain. At the time he was making movies in the daytime and singing with the Los Flaps at night. He listened to the Mamas and Papas and the Fifth Dimension, and he realized these groups had not only a pop, hit sound; it was one that could be taken to another level.

Rowland hired two female singers and made them the centerpiece of the Family Dogg. He worked with the songwriting team of Albert Hammond and Mike Hazlewood. They wrote chart friendly commercial pop songs. Rowland also selected Jimmy Webb's "Pattern People," Bob Dylan's "Love Minus Zero-No Limit," Paul Simon's "Save The Life Of My Child" and Stevie Wonder's "A Place In the Sun" for inclusion in the album.

It was Rowland who hired the studio musicians, paid for the sessions and publicized the group. Although there was some chart success in Europe and the U. K., the Family Dogg didn't become the hit-making machine Rowland envisioned. There was, however, a place for the Family Dogg unwittingly in the Sixto Rodriguez story.

When Albert Hammond and Mike Hazlewood left for America, searching for greener commercial pastures, Rowland reconfigured the group. He changed the group's name to Steve Rowland And The Family Dogg. He began searching for new songs. It didn't take long. He found Sixto Rodriguez' amazing songwriting.

Initially, Rowland didn't envision recording Rodriguez' material. "He was such a great songwriter, I didn't think that I could cover his material. Then I realized that Sussex wasn't promoting **Coming From Reality**," Steve said. Rowland is a humble man. He wouldn't criticize Clarence Avant, Neil Bogart or anyone else involved in the Rodriguez story. "I think a lot of people believed in Rodriguez' talent," Rowland continued. "It just didn't work out. Why? I don't know."

The Family Dogg anthology highlights Rowland's production brilliance. In his spare time, if he had any, Rowland wrote songs.

He also produced solo singles. Such Rowland singles as "So Sad," "I See Red," and "We Stand Closer Together" are included in this anthology. His collaborations with Albert Hammond on "Follow The Bouncing Ball" and "I Don't Wanna Go To Sleep Again" are a sheer delight. Rowland and Hammond created the Pancho and Cisco records.

At times the publicity was not positive. When John Peel labeled the Pancho and Cisco songs amongst the worst in English rock history, there was enough publicity to sell the solo singles. Rowland found bad publicity sold records as well as good publicity.

Steve Rowland learned from his Family Dogg experiences. What is obvious is he honed his studio talents to a higher level. He emerged as one of rock music's top pop producers. But there is another side to Rowland's talent. He is an exceptional writer.

Rowland the Writer

Steve Rowland has many talents. One of the hidden ones is his ability to capture a scene, an atmosphere, a trend or a cultural direction. He has done this in his writing career. He has chronicled Hollywood in deep, penetrating tales of Tinseltown's underbelly. While writing songs, producing music, performing and appearing on television and in the movies, Rowland established an extensive journalism career.

His articles have appeared in **Screen Life**, **Movie Stars**, **Dig**, **Movie World** and **Movie Play** among others. His most popular column "The View From Rowland's Head," had a multi-million readership. He also wrote record reviews, and he appeared on a weekly radio show on Hollywood's KGIL. There is an urban hipster tone to Rowland's early writing. His early reviews on jazz are among his most interesting articles. As a writer Rowland captures the mood, the character and the people in the Hollywood of the 1950s, and you feel like you have dropped into this time in history.

Rowland on Rowland

The popularity of **Searching For Sugar Man** prompted Rowland to do three telephone interviews with movie critic Rhett Bartlett. Rowland discussed Rodriguez and Bendjelloul's production techniques on **Coming From Reality**. He also talked about the present state of the Sugar Man's career. The interview was more about Rodriguez and less about Rowland. The best comment on Steve Rowland comes from Sixto Rodriguez. The singer remarked it was Rowland who deserves enormous credit for his production of the second album. What Rodriguez meant is Rowland took him into a new and successful creative direction. Rowland was also significant for his cooperation in the documentary. In just a few minutes on screen, Rowland explained Rodriguez' creative genius.

"In 1970 I had two or three records in the charts," Rowland continued. "I picked up an album **Cold Fact**, by an artist called Rodriguez. I went absolutely crazy." Then Steve Rowland observed no one was interested in promoting him. They called him a poor man's Dylan. "How are you going to sell that material?" an executive asked him. While listening to the songs on **Cold Fact**, Rowland realized Rodriguez' unique talent. He wanted to produce his second album. No one else was interested. Rowland maintained there was commercial gold in his voice and songs.

There was a problem. Rodriguez was signed to a fledgling label, Sussex, and there were no guarantees of future success. They didn't have a lot of money. The front man, Clarence Avant, depended upon two hits by Bill Withers to fund the label. Money for promotion was simply not in the cards. But Steve Rowland persisted.

Rowland got Sussex to front the money. Clarence Avant sent Rodriguez to London, Avant rented a small apartment in a posh London area. This allowed Rodriguez and Rowland to spend a month thinking, planning and producing his second album. After Rowland finished **Coming From Reality**, it was a complete flop.

In 2007 Rowland got a call from a Swedish director. The person on the phone was Malik Bendjelloul who asked if he was the Steve Rowland that produced the album **Coming From Realty**? He told Rowland he was making a film on Rodriguez. He asked if he could come and interview him. Rowland said that would be fine. They vowed to remain in touch via e-mail. They did.

There were two problems. Steve was moving to Palm Springs. He also had a book coming out. After spending some time in America, he would have to fly back to London for his book launch.

Rowland remembered Malik said not to worry. He wasn't ready at the moment to film. He would be in touch.

Steve Rowland In His Palm Springs Home

On September 21 2007, Steve flew into Los Angeles. He drove over to Palm Springs and began the lengthy, sometimes cumbersome, task of purchasing a home. He moved his furniture in, he arranged his nineteen gold records on the wall in the television room, and the rest of the home was furnished with advertisements for his movies. He hung a number of celebrity pictures. Just as he was finishing arranging his Palm Springs home, Malik Bendjelloul called. He was in Los Angeles. By now Steve was settled comfortably into the Palm Springs lifestyle. He almost forgot about Bendjelloul's earlier phone call. When the Swedish director called from Los Angeles, he said he was filming a commercial. He was ready for the interview.

He drove to Rowland's Palm Springs home. "I remember how committed he was to the project," Rowland continued. "He knew Rodriguez' music inside out. I was impressed."

It is unusual for Rowland to give lengthy interviews. He is busy. But there was never a question. If Rodriguez was the subject, Steve was on board. Steve would make the world aware of the Sugar Man's talent. He had a mission. For more than forty years he told anyone who would listen Sixto Rodriguez was the best songwriter and the most talented artist he produced.

Steve Rowland: "They filmed me and we became pretty friendly, he found out about all the films I had been in."

This fascination with Steve's movie career was the driving force behind Bendjelloul's curiosity about Steve and his father, producer Roy Rowland, and they spent hundreds of hours discussing how to frame the documentary. Perhaps Rowland's greatest contribution was to extol, explain and reinforce the genius of Bendjelloul's cinematographer Camille Skagerstrom. Steve described her as an artist who painted a cinematic picture emphasizing tranquility, beauty and a clear vision of the project. She certainly did this filming Rowland.

Camille Skagerstrom caught the essence of Rowland sitting in a chair listening to Rodriguez' music in his front room, as he reminisced about his days producing **Coming From Reality**. It was a heartfelt moment early in the production of **Searching For Sugar Man**. After Bendjelloul and Rowland talked, they realized the project had not only creative possibilities, but there was a commercial tone.

There were two separate filming sessions in Rowland's home. The first was in the listening room where Steve talked about "Cause" and how Rodriguez lost his job two weeks before Christmas. Clarence Avant and Sussex Records terminated his contract. He was out of show business. It was a poignant moment. Steve showed obvious emotion in the documentary. He shook his head. He looked frustrated. He couldn't understand why the Sugar Man wasn't a major star.

I asked Steve about this moment in the film. He didn't answer the question. He looked out the back of his house to the mountains. He got up and poured a cup of coffee. He sat down. He looked at me. Steve said: "I don't want to talk about it." That is Rowland. He has memories of the Sugar Man that he has difficulty describing without becoming emotional. Steve is still angry Rodriguez' talent went unrecognized for more than forty years. Rodriguez has forgiven people. Rowland hasn't although his anger is private.

After Malik left he said he wanted to return for another filming session. He loved Rowland's front gate. He envisioned it as a prop in the documentary. Malik filed the idea away. The second time when Bendjelloul arrived without Skagerstrom he had visual images of Palm Springs that contrasted beautifully with Cape Town and Detroit.

Then sometime later Malik called again. He told Steve he wanted to come back and film the front gate. This was a moment in the film that highlighted Rowland's home, and his demeanor as a Svengali producer. The front gate became a symbol of moving into the Sugar Man's legend and unfolding the real Sixto Rodriguez. It was an existential moment befitting a gifted filmmaker, an actor-producer advising Bendjelloul and the Sugar Man. The ability to define, categorize and display Rodriguez' talent was the result of these early production decisions.

After the movie opened, Rowland observed the cinematography was brilliant. Skagerstrom had great lighting ideas. It showed. He loved the story. Like everyone, Rowland wondered how Rodriguez had slipped under the commercial radar. How was it possible?

When Rowland attended the Los Angeles Film Festival, he was mobbed. He did a question and answer session with Rodriguez and Bendjelloul. "I had the feeling that this was going to be big," Rowland observed. At the Q and A, Rowland remarked Rodriguez wrote his songs when things were changing culturally. "The irony is these tunes still sounded fresh after more than forty years," Rowland continued: "This guy Rodriguez wrote songs that made you think, I feel it came at the wrong time. I think people didn't want to hear it, they wanted to have a good time. Disco was in." Rowland was right. The early 1970s left the protest songs of the 1960s in the past.

It was September 28, 2012 when the two sat down for a second time once again backstage at Los Angeles' El Rey Theater reminiscing about the old days. "He's a wonderful person, he is the real deal. This is a lesson for anyone who has a dream, never give up your dream," Rowland concluded.

This interview was an important one. It demonstrated Rowland was as humble as Rodriguez. As a writer, actor and musician, Rowland is a multi-faceted talent. It is as a music producer that he excels.

Steve Rowland Explains Some Hollywood Influences

Steve Rowland's influences from his early Hollywood life were important ones. His talent is multi-faceted. He is a singer. He is a songwriter. He is an actor. He is a writer. He put together music groups. Rowland was never able to establish a mainstream career that satisfied him. That is until he became a record producer. Then his past talents blended into a platinum-producing career.

Sitting down with Steve in his comfortable Palm Springs home, he sips a coffee and reflects on his Hollywood influences.

You were a popular Los Angeles disc jockey. Why have you not talked about this aspect of your career? There was a long silence.

Steve Rowland: "I had not only an interest in rock and roll but I collected records. It was natural for me to go on the radio."

What Steve fails to mention is he was a regular guest commentator, record rater and a fountain of knowledge on numerous rock and roll radio stations throughout the Valley? He was in demand as an insider on the Hollywood record scene. It was acting that remained his first love. He pursued an acting career with a determined vengeance.

Were there any roadblocks in your early acting career?

Steve Rowland: "One time early on I had a small part in one of my father's films. I realized I had to prove myself because my father was a director. Nobody took me seriously as an actor. That was frustrating."

What did you want to accomplish in your early Hollywood career?

Steve Rowland: "I wanted to be an actor, because I wanted to have the experience of other lives. I was so frustrated with the nepotism in Hollywood. As an actor I would be credible."

What happened due to the early acting experiences? How did this shape your career?

Steve Rowland: "I got fan mail from my early acting career that said I was a pretty boy. I hated that. I always worried about credibility."

Was it difficult during your early acting career?

Steve Rowland: "I was struggling like hell to get a break. I studied at the Actor's Studio, and I took a great deal of time with my acting studies."

What did this do for you?

Steve Rowland: "I did a play 'Grapes of Wrath' with John Carradine. The reviews for the John Steinbeck classic were exceptional."

But as Rowland talked there was no doubt he was frustrated with Hollywood. He was the son of a famous director, Roy Rowland, and his parents were determined to have him find his own way in the industry. That became a source of abject frustration. Steve was out daily doing auditions, practicing with his band, writing songs, studying acting and directing. In his spare time, he learned how to produce and edit rock and roll music. He was a one-man band. He could do everything.

To understand how and why Rowland became an acclaimed record producer it is necessary to examine the influence of his lengthy acting career, his time as a writer for Hollywood movie magazines and how Hollywood rock and roll was an educational tool for his future productions. Acting and writing were the glue holding Rowland's creative personality together. The magazines were an important influence. He called his column: "The First View From Rowland's Head." The column established his writing credentials.

The First View from Rowland's Head

He had a photogenic face perfect for movie magazines. During his acting days Steve's appearances on the screen and TV spurred his creative energies. He wrote eight columns for fan magazines with "The View From Rowland's Head" being the most famous. It had a readership in the millions each month.

"The View From Rowland's Head" inspired his musical vision. He also recorded an album of the same name with his London based group, the Family Dogg. He was a renaissance man with intellect, charm and driving ambition. The Los Angeles radio station, KGIL, featured a weekly broadcast on the latest rock music with Rowland commenting. That show made Steve a rock and roll icon. It led him to bookings in local Hollywood clubs.

The KGIL rock and roll show broadcast from the original Hamburger Hamlet, which was a little hut on Sunset Boulevard, came on once a week at ten at night. In between spinning the latest rock hits, Rowland had guests like actress Sherry Jackson. As he wrote about the latest rock albums for a wide variety of publications his popularity as a featured columnist brought out fans to his films and rock and roll shows. He was a multi-talented performer. This proved to be a detriment rather than an asset to his fledgling career.

Steve Rowland: "I always wanted to prove I was sensitive. I wanted to write like Raymond Chandler, Mickey Spillane and I wanted to act like Robert Mitchum."

What did this do for you in your record-producing career?

Steve Rowland: "This is why I was attracted to Rodriguez' music. He had that gritty, street-smart feel to his songs. He was authentic. He was one of a kind. He reflected Detroit."

Rowland's brilliant writing reflected the times. This made him a perfect match to produce Sixto Rodriguez. There was a hip, cool vernacular to his persona. He used his talent to describe the soda fountains, the nightclubs, the street cruising and the gossip that was part of the Hollywood subculture. He reflected the beat movement. His writing had the subtle nuance of Jack Kerouac's slang. As the music changed, the cultural scene moved into new directions, and the nation turned its attention to new ideas, Steve Rowland interpreted it. He had a knack for visualizing musical trends. He was a friend to many Hollywood icons. This helped him avoid the pitfalls of Hollywood celebrity.

Rowland and Elvis in Hollywood

When Elvis Presley came to Hollywood to make his early films, Rowland was in the car with him as the King of Rock And Roll negotiated a date with a buxom starlet with the personality of a barracuda. As Rowland watched the Hollywood beauties work Presley, he was intrigued by the King's persona.

George Klein introduced Steve to Elvis. They became instant friends. Both liked custom cars. Both liked the ladies. Both liked cheeseburgers. Both liked the blues. Elvis and Steve were frequently seen about town.

Rowland was on the set of the movie Viva Las Vegas. It was on this movie set that they cemented their friendship with observations about Hollywood. "I always gravitated toward the more edgy people," Rowland observed. "Elvis was one of these regular guys, he liked going out and having a good time," Rowland continued. "Once you got over who he was you relaxed and you had a great time."

Rowland and Jazz Influences

The jazz clubs in and around Hollywood were his haunts. He loved to hang out at the Lighthouse in Redondo Beach and the Haig on Wilshire Boulevard in Hollywood. The Haig, a small Hollywood jazz club, featured Chet Baker on Monday nights. There was another influence from the Haig. When Laurindo Almeida came to play the small club he had a unique guitar sound. Rowland was a young rock and roll guy. He had never heard anything like Almeida. He immediately perfected the sound. Clubs like the Haig brought out Rowland's rock and roll side. He had no idea he was to evolve into a legendary producer. The diverse music he heard at the Haig blended into a rock sound with jazz and pop overtones. Rowland was in producing school. He just didn't know it.

While growing up in the plush and socially active Beverly Hills milieu, Rowland hung around and partied with James Dean, Robert Wagner and Tony Curtis. He tried to date Natalie Wood. He also partied with Tuesday Weld and Sandra Dee.

Steve Rowland: "One day I went to my doctor for a quick physical. While I was waiting in the reception room, I started talking to a young blonde with a scarf over her head. We got on quite well and I asked her if she was available for coffee. She said yes if her doctor's appointment didn't go on too long. My doctor called me in. I asked him who the young lady was? He laughed. It was Marilyn Monroe. I told him she didn't look like Marilyn. He replied that she only did so in the movies." That is the kind of great life that Rowland experienced hanging out in Hollywood.

It was while appearing in thirty-five different television roles that Rowland became uncomfortable with Hollywood. He was Roy Rowland's kid. He was related to Louis B. Mayer. His privacy was invaded constantly. He was never fully recognized for his acting talent. This bothered him despite his wide-ranging acting roles. He did have great success on television.

While working in television he appeared in "Bonanza," "Wanted Dead Or Alive," "The Rifleman" and he had a recurring role in "The Legend of Wyatt Earp." He was always the subject of Hollywood gossip magazines.

"There was so much false publicity about me I couldn't believe it." Steve continued. "They even had me dating Jean Seberg. Which is the one rumor that I loved." But his social side was only one part of Rowland's personality.

He was also a champion athlete. He had an Olympic quality score as a diver. While at Flintridge Prep High School, Rowland was the diving champion of that school. He was also a California Interscholastic champion diver. He qualified to attend the trials for the 1956 Olympic diving team, but he failed to make it. He lost out to Gary Tobian who won the silver medal in the 1956 Melbourne Olympics and silver and gold in the 1960 Olympics.

He was polite to a fault, extremely well read and educated. He was handsome, as well as a great athlete. This led to parts in television and Hollywood films. He had a solid career. When mega-stardom didn't materialize there was one reason. He was less than six feet tall and before James Dean and Tom Cruise broke the mold for short actors, he realized he would not be a leading man. This fact guided his career toward music. He was still an accomplished actor. He also had other interests.

Rowland was a pretty fair racecar driver. He was a good friend to James Dean who was an excellent racecar driver. "James Dean could have been a world champion race car driver, he had no fear and he was an intelligent driver," Rowland continued. "I didn't race against or with James Dean, I admired Jimmy so much as an actor. It was him that inspired me to start sports car racing." Rowland also raced go-karts. He dabbled with motor cross racing. "I was only fair, I realized that I wanted to be an actor or a singer. I kept thinking, caution bombarded my brain." In the go-cart world, Rowland was in the middle of the pack, but he was recognized as a serious competitor. The music bug was Rowland's initial passion.

Steve Rowlands' Movie High Points

The lack of height didn't deter Rowland. He became a well-regarded television actor who eventually became a busy movie actor. He had a co-starring role with Henry Fonda in **The Battle of the Bulge**. He appeared in **Gun Glory** with Stewart Granger, **Crime In The Streets** with Sal Mineo and John Cassavetes and the **Thin Red Line** with Kier Dullea and Jack Warden.

He was the youthful lead in a cult western, **Gun Glory**, in which he was the featured actor alongside Stewart Granger. **Gun Glory** is the story of the American West in the 1880s. Stewart Granger plays a gunman and gambler, Tom Early, who returns home to settle down. Rowland is cast as his son Tom Early Jr. The plot involves an evil cattleman who is put in his place by Tom Early Jr. Steve Rowland is the hero of this cult classic. The cast also included Rhonda Fleming and Chill Wills. The movie, directed by Steve' father, Roy Rowland, came out in 1957 with a two and a half million dollar world wide box office. In France the film attracted a strong cult audience and foreign earnings exceeded the American box office. It looked like Steve Rowland's' movie career was on the up swing.

His social life included playing touch football with Elvis Presley, drinking with Robert Mitchum and hanging out with Debbie Reynolds, Harry Belafonte, Jayne Powell, Ed "Kookie" Byrnes, Clint Eastwood, Charles Bronson and Tony Curtis. He had the best of all worlds. He was an established actor. He was an integral part of Hollywood royalty. His father was a famous director. His drop-dead good looks and winning personality made him a celebrity. But there was something missing in Rowland's life. He was competitive. He was determined to be a superstar. It wasn't happening in television or the movies. It did happen in the music business. He went on to become one of the industries most celebrated record producers. But movies remained his first love. His current in-development television series, **Hollywood Heat**, is ready for prime time. The years observing, playing in and analyzing the Hollywood scene comes through in this series.

There are other high points in his movie career. In 1961 his role in **Wild Youth** centered around a story featuring a good looking young man, Arthur, who gets involved in a web of intrigue and crime. Rowland plays a character, Switch, and Robert Arthur plays Arthur. For fans of schlocky movies about juvenile delinquents this one is a winner. Then came two big time movies, **The Thin Red Line**, where he played Pvt. Mazzi and **Battle of the Bulge** where he had a top featured rule with Charles Bronson, Pier Angeli, Robert Ryan, Dana Andrews, Robert Shaw, Telly Savalas and Henry Fonda. Looking back on the **Battle of the Bulge** Rowland reflected: "I was absolutely overwhelmed to work with Henry Fonda and everyone else. At Easter and Christmas on television I watch this classic and my friends ask me about the good old Hollywood days. I laugh and tell them the film was made in Spain."

His youthful good looks persisted into his thirties keeping Rowland working steadily. In 1965, he played the Kid in **Gun Fighters of Casa Grande**. His youth and acting ability landed Rowland the part of Stan in the 1966 low budget classic **Hallucination Generation**. One reviewer said of Rowland that he was "a promising young actor who doubles as a singer-composer, and he has had several rock 'n' roll hit records to his credit." **Hallucination Generation** is a classic anti-drug movie centering on the dangers of pill popping and the sexual liberation of the 1960s. It is a sequel of sorts to the 1936 cult film **Reefer Madness**.

Why is it important to Rowland's career? He filmed **Hallucination Generation** in Spain, and it was here his musical career took a mainstream turn. He became the lead singer in a cult band, Los Flaps, while making movies in Spain. As a popular lead vocalist, Rowland decided to take his talent to London. It was the mid-1960s, and the rock and roll revolution in London provided opportunities for new singers and bands. Steve Rowland heard this call and left for London. It was the first step in his road to worldwide prominence in the record industry.

Rowland's Record Production

Steve reflected on his record production: "When I produced Sarah Brightman and Dave Dee, Dozy, Beaky, Mick and Tich's 'The Legend of Xanadu' in 1968 I knew what made a hit record." Why was Rowland different from other producers? I asked him the question. He thought for a long time. Rowland said: "I made the records much like I envisioned a movie. It was a story that I wanted to tell." To Rowland record production is an art form. He views it as telling and selling an interesting vignette with a compelling beat.

The career of Dave Dee, Dozy, Beaky, Mick and Tich is a case study in Rowland's producing genius. By all accounts the group was little more than a novelty pop/rock group when Rowland produced their first thirteen 45s. He saw two of their records sell in excess of a million copies. Due to Rowland's' production from 1965 to 1969 the group spent more weeks on the U. K. singles chart than most pop acts.

He helped to write, produce or advise the group on such U. K. hits as "Hideaway," "Hold Tight," "Bend It," "Save Me," "Touch Me, Touch Me," 'Okay," "Zabadak," "Legend of Xanadu and "Last Night In Soho." Even when the group moved on to another producer, they kept in touch with Rowland and asked his opinion on their material.

"The Legend of Xanadau" was the song establishing Rowland's producing credentials. It was a number one U. K. chart hit in 1968.

It was the special effects, a whip cracking and a marvelous trumpet section, that made Rowland's production unique. There is a humility to Rowland. He praises others for his successes and effusively pays tribute to their talents. His arrangers, the studio musicians, those who helped him mix his records were to a person happy to be working with Rowland.

Steve Rowland: "Without the superb writing talent of Ken Howard and Alan Blakley and their intelligent management skills the group might have languished in a local pub." This comment is typical of Steve Rowland. He refuses to take the credit for Dave Dee, Dozy, Beaky, Mick and Tich's success.

The many songs Rowland produced for the group is the hallmark of their career in terms of sales and critical acclaim. Like many rock groups they became full of themselves and they took over the production tasks. Fontana Records was delighted with Rowland's studio efforts. He was also a big part of the packaging of their early albums. The first LP simply entitled **Dave Dee, Dozy, Beaky, Mick and Tich** (Fontana 5350) was released in June 1966; it was followed by **If Music Be The Food Of Love...Prepare For Indigestion** (Fontana 5388) in November 1966, followed by **If No-One Sang** (Fontana 5471) in May 1968. When Dave Dee, Dozy, Beaky, Mick and Tich moved on to another producer, they never had another hit.

The years producing a wide variety of U. K. artists honed Rowland's production skills. He was ready for the album that would define his career. He viewed Sixto Rodriguez' second album as his defining moment. Steve's movie career, his work in Los Angeles and Madrid recording studios, his time hanging out with Sam Cooke, Earl Palmer, the Mesner brothers at Aladdin Records and a host of other Los Angeles musicians, producers, record label owners and assorted musical types created a producer with a vision. But what was the vision for **Coming From Reality**?

I asked Steve about the Rodriguez album. Did you envision **Coming From Reality** much like it was a movie? I was surprised at his answer.

"No," Steve said. "I wanted to produce an album that was lyrically beautiful and clearly understood. I wanted the listener to feel every word."

There are some unique records as a performing artist in Rowland's career. In April 1963, he cut what is now a collectible 45 with the A side featuring "Out Ridin" backed with "Here Kum the Karts" (Cross Country 1-1818-9) featuring saxophone player Earl Bostic of "Flamingo" fame. It is a b-side that collector's covet. He put together a group Steve Rowland and the Ringleaders using Bostic's saxophone sound. A motorcycle engine starts the record as Steve says: "Are you ready baby, hang on." Then a blues-jazz sound dominates the record. This song was a regional hit throughout the U. S. on jazz and blues stations. However, in Spain and Mexico, it was surprisingly a staple of dance radio stations. The picture sleeve for the 45 shows Rowland in a small go-kart with three beautiful young ladies looking on. How did an accomplished actor become a record producer? How did Rowland get into the record business? You have to go back to Hollywood in the 1950s to find Rowland's initial influences. Rowland never expected "Here Kum The Karts" to have a second life. It did.

Here Kum The Karts in Holland in the 1970S

In Holland, Joost den Draaljer (Willem van Kooten) was a Dutch Radio personality and DJ at Radio Veronica. He loved The Family Dogg. He was also a racecar fan. In the 1970s his label, Pink Elephant, released a 45 of "Out Ridin" and "Here Kum The Karts." They also released a Family Dogg 45 "Sweet America" and "Rikers Island."

The Rowland U. S. 45 sold well enough due to a brilliant 45 cover with three beautiful young ladies standing over Steve as he smiles sitting in a go-cart. The 45 with the picture sleeve cover now sells for more than a hundred dollars on e-bay. But there were earlier musical influences shaping Rowland's musical direction and inevitably his future productions.

As Steve sat in his Palm Springs home, he recalled some of the blues, rhythm and blues and soul pioneers, as well as the classic rockers, who influenced his music career. "There was no one I admired more than Sam Cooke," Rowland continued. "He was a great musical talent, a gentleman and his approach to the music intrigued me." Cooke became an early mentor to Rowland during the heyday of rock music in the 1950s. It was Cooke and the Champs, as well as the Mesner Brothers at Aladdin Records that helped to form the producing persona that became Steve Rowland.

On to a Music Career: Sam Cooke's Influence: The 1950S

It was a chance meeting with soul singer Sam Cooke that encouraged Rowland to enter the music business. One day Steve wandered into Bob Keene's office at Keene Records. He met Sam Cooke and they talked for a couple of hours. Steve impressed Sam when they talked about the 5-4 Ballroom and gospel music. The Soul Stirrers records were a big part of Steve's record collection. He also had aspirations, which he kept to himself, to become a gospel vocalist.

Why did Steve regularly go to the 5-4 Ballroom? It was in the heart of Los Angeles's Central District and it was a dangerous place for a young white guy. The reason was a simple one. Rowland was a stone B. B. King fan. He had all his records. He went to every show in the greater Los Angeles area often driving as far as San Diego to catch King's act in the gutbucket blues clubs of the 1950s. Personally, Steve was repulsed by the attitudes toward and treatment of African American artists.

When Steve met and talked with B. B. King the discussion was invariably about how to blend the blues with rock music. At this point Steve wanted desperately to be a blues singer or perhaps a gospel performer.

After meeting Cooke and J. W. Alexander, the Soul Stirrers leader, he intensified his study of gospel music. The records, the artists and the history of gospel quickly became Rowland's forte. When Sam and J. W. Alexander came over to the Rowland's Beverly Hills home they talked music for hours. Alexander, who led the Soul Stirrers, helped Steve with his proposed gospel vocals. "J. W. Alexander took me under his wing and mentored me," Steve recalled.

The idea of becoming a gospel singer was not a good one. Rowland didn't have the voice, he didn't have the church experience but he continued to work on a gospel tone. This is important! Why? It was a training ground for his future rock and roll vocals. But, as far as gospel music was concerned, Steve came to his senses.

Steve Rowland: "I realized I couldn't do it like they did it."

Steve does not like to discuss his songwriting. He is an accomplished songwriter. The only person who doesn't think so is Steve Rowland.

Steve Rowland: "I meet Sam Cooke at Keene Records. I loved 'You Send Me." That was the biggest influence on my career. I wanted to be a gospel singer. I was too naïve to realize I was never going to be a gospel singer."

I asked Steve if his gospel background influenced **Coming From Reality**?

Steve Rowland: "I added a couple of back up vocal people when we recorded 'I Wonder' and it had that gospel tinge I recalled from my early Hollywood days."

This is how gospel music influenced Steve's rock and roll productions. On "I Wonder" there wasn't a gospel choir but there was a hint of it.

One of the stories Bob Keene loved to tell is when Sam Cooke wrote "Only Sixteen," he had Steve Rowland in mind. Keene told a number of people that Rowland, now in his early twenties, still looked sixteen. I asked Steve about it.

Steve Rowland: "Sam gave me the demo of 'Only Sixteen,' I loved it."

I asked Steve if the rumor was true Cooke wrote it for him?

Steve Rowland: "You are the professor. You are the writer. You figure it out. Sam gave me a demo copy. That's it! Is there something wrong with you? It's a demo copy where in the hell did you get the story that Cooke wrote the song for me?"

I switched to another line of questioning. Steve can be a cranky guy at times.

Chuck Rio of The Champs and Rowland's Musical Education

When he became a musician in the 1950s, Rowland befriended the sax playing Chuck Rio of the Champs. He was not in the studio when they cut the mega hit "Tequila," but Rowland knew and hung out with every member of the Champs. This led to sax player Chuck Rio coming aboard on Rowland's twist band. Soon Rowland put together a musical group, the Exciters, and they opened at the Encore Room on Hollywood's La Cienega Boulevard.

While performing in local clubs, Steve saw first hand how African American rock and roll crossed over into a white audience. Sam Cooke was an example of a black singer who early on played New York's Copacabana and all the top nightclubs. He was more than an African American singer, Cooke crossed over into the commercial mainstream with a management company, a publishing business and his own record label. This was a lesson that made an indelible impression on Rowland. Pop records sell. Steve trained himself to sell them by 1963 when he left for Spain.

He didn't realize when he produced hundreds of hits in London that his critics would cry out: "You are so American." That attitude prompted Steve eventually to leave London. In the 1950s in Hollywood he watched and learned from Sam Cooke. In London, Rowland established the same triangle of businesses. But that was all in the future. Playing music. Chasing the ladies. Figuring out the rock and roll life. That was Steve Rowland in the 1950s. His band, the Exciters, was the beginning of a musical education taking Rowland into legendary producing country. If the Exciters weren't the beginning, they were certainly an early start to a life on stage and in the studio.

The Exciters were short lived but quickly emerged as one of the most popular Hollywood club bands. Their popularity was due to having two unique lead singers. Steve Rowland was one and his actor friend Budd Albright was the other. Together they formed a dynamic duo with great stage presence. Albright was incredibly handsome. He continued on in the movies making cameo appearances in major movies like Ocean's 11. With Steve's drop-dead good looks, they had a ball. When Rowland's roommate, Jim Mitchum, showed up the ladies flocked to them.

Why did the Exciters exit the Los Angeles music scene? They never left. In 1962 a New York based girl group, the Exciters, had a number four **Billboard** hit with "Tell Him." Rowland changed the band's name to the Twist Kings.

"We were mobbed by the girls. We weren't that great as singers. The club owners loved us because guys came in to buy the girls drinks," Rowland said. He paused and remarked: "We did such a great job drawing the guys to meeting the girls and buying them drinks that we most of the time went home alone."

When the club owners found out major Hollywood stars came to see Rowland and Albright, they hired them on the spot. The problem was at times they weren't paid. So Steve went to see one of his friends who talked to the club owners about getting paid. I asked Steve who his friend was? Steve said: "You can call him Tony, Bruno, Gino, Paulie or Charlie." Rowland looked at me and asked:

"Do you understand?" I said: "Charlie sounds like your insurance man." Rowland laughed. "I guess you could say that. An Italian insurance man with a strong arm." I understood. But I didn't want to use the word mob? Steve doesn't' like to talk about gangsters or their Hollywood influences. He does like to write about them.

For Rowland the late 1950s and early 1960s was a time of growth, experimentation and education in the music business. He experienced the ups and downs of the various record labels attempting to cash in on his drop-dead good looks and singing-acting talent.

In 1956 a picture of Natalie Wood on Steve's shoulders was all over fan magazines and the newspapers. This picture was for a fan magazine layout shot by Earl Leaf at State Beach, Santa Monica. The picture was in the home of Elaine Stewart who showed it to everyone at her July 15, 1956 Thalians Beach Ball. This charity event in her home cast Rowland into the celebrity fish bowl. He was not happy about it. Rowland now had a public life. The record labels came calling when they heard he could sing.

There were a number of record labels hoping to sign young Rowland. Despite his youth, he had in-depth knowledge of the industry. Rather than inking a contract with one of the smaller black owned or rhythm and blues labels, he selected the industry giant, Liberty, to advance his recording career. He thought they had the best chance of breaking him in the pop market.

Rowland's first record on Liberty "How Many Miles" backed with "Flat Wheel Train" (Liberty 55030), didn't sell well. Liberty released him from his contract. It turned out to be a blessing. He found a label, an owner and musicians who understood his direction.

Rowland's musical career finally got off the ground in 1957 when Intro Records signed him to a three-year recording contract. This label was the country-rock music subsidiary of Eddie and Leo Mesner's Aladdin label. The reasoning behind signing Rowland was to tie in his television and movie westerns with his records.

Aladdin was a small African American label owned by two Jewish brothers who were honest and actually paid royalties. They envisioned a bright future for Rowland who set the template for Johnny Crawford's hits when he co-starred in "The Rifleman." Crawford's hit "Cindy's Birthday" in 1962 was written with Rowland in mind. By that time Steve moved on to more important acting parts.

When Rowland spent time in the studio, he learned from an experienced producer Earl Palmer. What did Rowland pick up from Palmer? It appears plenty. Steve easily found his way around Los Angeles, Madrid and London recording studios.

Palmer is an unsung hero. He taught Steve a great deal about the recording process. This helped his debut Intro single.

The debut Intro 45 was reviewed in **Billboard**. In July 1957. The review of Rowland's "Say The Word" and "Gonna Sit Right Down and Cry" (Intro 6098) was a positive one. He covered a song that Roy Hamilton recorded for Epic Records in 1954. **Billboard** envisioned a bright musical career for him. Steve Rowland, with the Earl Palmer Band, was how the record was advertised. It was a strange product as an African American blues group provided the musical background.

Steve Rowland: "I loved Roy Hamilton, I had all his records, I tried to sound like Roy and I failed. When I recorded with the Earl Palmer band I thought all my Christmas's and birthday's had come at once. The result certainly didn't bring me any presents."

The Intro label, headed by Leo Mesner, recognized Rowland's television and movie appearances and his immersion in the Los Angeles music scene made him a possible recording star. The Mesner brothers saw Rowland as the next Frankie Avalon or Fabian. They concentrated on local radio. The results were impressive publicity wise. Record sales were another matter.

Steve Rowland: "They thought that I could be made into a teen idol. They took teenage photos, put out a great deal of publicity and fan magazines picked it up. I can still hear the sound of the mighty flop that the record was."

The Intro contract was for eight sides a year. The first promotional activity was tied to Rowland's role in the MGM movie **Gun Glory**. It was scheduled for an August 1958 release. Nothing came of these early releases. Rowland left Intro and signed with Virgo.

In 1959, the Virgo label released "How Would You Like It," backed with "Dear Little Pen Pal" (Virgo D-1003). This 45 sounded like Ral Donner or Curtis Lee. It is a fast paced vocal with a teen idol sound. The A side was co-written by Tommy Boyce. The 45 failed to chart. Rowland concentrated upon television and the movies. He still had the itch to perform. He put together a band to play the rapidly multiplying Los Angeles rock and roll clubs. He did it at the right time as the era of classic rock and roll was fading as the twist dominated the clubs.

Looking back on his early songs, Rowland is upset with the covers he was forced to sing. "I wanted to be a blues singer who sounded like a combination of Roy Hamilton and B.B. King. It didn't work out." I asked Steve why? He said: "I was put into a teen idol mode with bad songs like 'Flat Wheel Train' and when it turned out to be crap they blamed me."

On to the Los Angeles Club Circuit

The Los Angeles club scene was changing. The jazz groups were fading, folk music was not for the drinkers and rock and roll began appearing in the major Hollywood clubs. The rockers brought in girls, drinkers and a party atmosphere. It didn't take long for a host of bands to form up and down the Sunset Strip.

Steve Rowland: "I look back at our appearance at P. J.'s on Santa Monica and Crescent Heights, Budd and I went around the bar where Trini Lopez was singing. We knew Trini and we asked him if we could sing a number. He said sure. We sang, Trini's band backed us, and the crowd went nuts. It was from that casual appearance that we got the idea to sing and form a band."

There were so many talented musicians looking for work Rowland had no trouble hiring excellent band mates. It was the day of the young musician coming to Hollywood looking for fame and fortune. The local bars opened their rooms to bands that played for a small fee.

Steve Rowland: "When we set up at the Encore Room for our opening night, the manager, Jack Chambers, started hollering at us as only a few bar fly's were sitting at the long wooden bar. It was a quarter to ten. Chambers threatened to fire us. Then at ten o'clock on the dot Robert Mitchum, Mitzi Gaynor, Martha Hyer and many other stars walked in to fill the place. We did rock and roll numbers, and it turned into a two hour show."

They played there three nights a week to sold out crowds. The large crowds at the Encore prompted talent scouts from Las Vegas' Thunderbird Hotel to waive a lucrative contract at Rowland's group. Steve had no idea the Thunderbird was a mob hotel. He didn't sign the contract. The Encore Room was too sweet a deal. He could act in the day and play music at night. His pocketbook was full.

There were a number of local mobsters who loved to listen to Rowland's bands, hang out at the clubs and make sure Steve and Budd got paid. The local mobsters didn't like traveling all over the valley to see Steve and Budd's lounge act. That ended when the Encore Club discovered their small bar brought in more money than the restaurant. The Mafia enforcer, Charlie Capresse, may have been responsible for helping the pair but their music paved the way for their classic rock and roll lounge shows.

How The Encore Club Cashed in with Steve and Budd's Good Looks and Musical Chicanery

Los Angeles' Encore Club was primarily a restaurant that cashed in on rock and roll music. In March 1953 the Encore cocktail lounge began as a jazz venue featuring the Walter Gross Trio nightly. This increased the bar business and the few hundred dollars paid to the band was recouped ten times over with the bar having standing room only. The Encore attracted Hollywood's most notorious gangsters. Charlie Capresse, a known hit man, sat at the bar and became a friend to Steve and Budd. When they had trouble collecting their money, Charlie spoke quietly to the owner. Within fifteen minutes the money arrived, Charlie lit a cigarette and tilted his straight scotch glass at the band. He was a regular. He loved the early rock and roll sound.

The Encore had the distinction of not one, but two, prominent businessmen killed while in the bar-restaurant. As Steve and Budd played their rock music with a widely changing assortment of sidemen they were baptized into the rock and roll world. There were no drugs. But sex, gangsters, booze and good times prevailed. I asked Steve about the sex, gangsters and booze. He said: "Next question."

The mob was all over the Los Angeles music scene. They haunted the Sunset Strip clubs looking for potential new Las Vegas acts. They approached Rowland. He wasn't interested. The Twist Kings were a forerunner of things to come. Soon the San Fernando Valley would have more bands than the clubs could accommodate.

The Tale of the Twist Kings: Las Vegas and The Carolina Lanes

The Twist Kings drew talent scouts, record company executives, television bookers and a wide range of journalists. The Las Vegas entertainment scouts set up an audition at the Mocambo Night Club on Hollywood's Sunset Boulevard. The Twist Kings were thinking of accepting a lengthy Las Vegas residency. As the Las Vegas talent scouts smoked their cigars, Steve and Budd went into a blistering rock and roll set. The audition was a successful one and they were told a contract would come within a few days. Rowland didn't sign it.

Steve Rowland: "In 1962-1963 the Thunderbird Hotel wanted us to give us a long term residency. We had problems and just couldn't get out of Hollywood. David Gates, Leon Russell and Chuck Rio were in the group and we became a much sought after twist band."

Why couldn't the Twist Kings get out of Hollywood? Rowland got sick. He had strep throat. He was prescribed penicillin. He went into anaphylactic shock. The reaction to strep throat came at a time Steve and Budd were in demand for club performances.

He and Budd moved into an apartment at the Sunset Towers West so they could continue performing in local clubs. Las Vegas was ruled out. In the greater Los Angeles area they remained one of the most popular bands in half a dozen clubs. They quickly became a featured act at the Carolina Lanes.

The Twist Kings ruled the club circuit. They had a bit of a rivalry with the Whiskey A Go Go but all the clubs made money. The clubs the Twist Kings played were all over Los Angeles and the San Fernando Valley.

When they played Carolina Lanes at the L. A. Airport, they drew huge crowds. In 1959 the Carolina Lanes opened as a bowling alley, it was just a few blocks from the Los Angeles International Airport. Like most bowling alleys, it had a bar and a dance floor. The bar was not well lit, it was new, modern and it had a sleek, well-equipped small stage. The sound system was state of the art. Soon the club was filled with drinkers. Then the ladies showed up. The club owners quickly looked for musical acts. They found one in Steve Rowland's band. But that was at the beginning. Eventually, the Carolina Lanes attracted big name entertainment. Delaney and Bonnie played part time in the Shindogs, which was a TV band on the Shindig TV Show and one of their last appearances was playing at the Carolina Lanes. It became a home for musicians who needed a small payday to survive in the cutthroat music business. Rent money and playing at the Carolina Lanes was synonymous with the times. The early 1960s was a magic time for Rowland. He was still busy acting. The Twist Kings gave him an outlet for his musical creativity. He also expanded his already formidable musical knowledge. He was also learning about the business side of the music industry.

Marshall Edson, Ye Little Club and Educating Rowland

If there was a college for training musicians in the business it was Marshall Edson's Ye Little Club. The club was an architectural masterpiece with a long, narrow, deep and relaxed bar area. The location at 455 North Canon Drive in Beverly Hills had the illusion of going into someone's home.

You had to get there early to find a barstool. Young girls showed up to crowd the bandstand. Before Steve Rowland and Budd Albright rocked the club with their Little Richard covers jazz singers like Ruth Olay filled the place. Why replace Olay or Chet Baker who appeared on Monday nights? The answer was a simple one. Rock and rollers drank hard, spent more money, and they were still drinking as the bar closed. Sometimes the bar didn't close. Edson simply greased the palms of the local gendarmes. The wild atmosphere spread, and the club had lines down the street. The **Los Angeles Times** took note and the lines increased.

Marshall Edson was one of a few Los Angeles club owners in the forefront of civil rights. He never discriminated at a time when there was a de facto color line in many Hollywood clubs. Edson's list of non-white performers was a lengthy one.

On Sunday nights Edson brought in Rudy Render to sing his plaintive ballads. Render was a well-known African American balladeer who drew large crowds and a nightly appearance by Marlene Dietrich. It was common to see Render climbing into Dietrich's limousine for a late night round of drinks and fun at her hotel. Render had a day job. One wonders if he went to work after a night with Marlene Dietrich.

What the Hell is Marlene Dietrich Doing Coming to Ye Little Club?

When Marshall Edson saw Marlene Dietrich walk into his Ye Little Club, he remarked: "What the hell is Marlene Dietrich doing coming into Ye Little Club?" No one gave him an answer. She was in her late fifties and her best days were long gone. But Dietrich had a plan. She was now a major nightclub act performing with adoring gangsters at ringside in Las Vegas. She also recorded a number of record albums. Steve and Budd were young guys with sex appeal, and their music brought out the crowds.

Dietrich hired a young songwriter, Burt Bacharach, to refine the music in her nightclub act. She only was in Ye Little Club a few times. But she never forgot the atmosphere, the music and the young bands as they pranced on the small stage mesmerizing the youthful audience. She may have been ready to turn sixty but she had another thirty years of show business success in her finely tuned body. She also loved the liberal, racially free atmosphere Steve and Budd promoted in Ye Little Club.

The bisexual Dietrich had a great time at Ye Little Club as her fame allowed for a smorgasbord of lovers. Marshall Edson couldn't have asked for anything better than continual gossip about Marlene Dietrich at Ye Little Club. The multicultural showcase that was the Ye Little Club remains a legendary part of Hollywood lore.

Ye Little Club and How it Impacted Los Angeles

Ye Little Club audiences were racially mixed. The atmosphere was a festive one. But Edson was a businessman. He wanted to maximize the profits. Rock and folk music brought in the drinkers. When the Twist came in to dominate the early 1960s he hired Rowland's band The Twist Kings. When folk rock emerged, he booked Barry McGuire when he was transitioning from the New Christy Minstrels to a solo career. After a brief time at Ye Little Club, McGuire was let go. When "Eve of Destruction" hit the top of the **Billboard** pop chart in September 1965 Edson was outraged that McGuire wouldn't play the club. So he hired a look a like for a week until Dunhill Records served Edson with a cease and desist order. He burned it. He called Dunhill. He told them to go "fuck themselves." He threatened to send over one of his mobster friends. He never heard another word from Dunhill. The Barry McGuire look a like continued to perform "Eve of Destruction" nightly in Ye Little club. Charlie Capresse relaxed at the bar smoking a cigar and throwing back scotch.

A young P. F. Sloan was a regular. He loved the small club and it was amusing for the person who wrote "Eve of Destruction" to sit at the bar watching a fake Barry McGuire. He told Capresse the look a like had a better voice and looked younger than McGuire. One of the ironies was Sloan at twenty wasn't carded. He was underage but looked as old as anyone at the bar.

Folk music brought a crowd that listened to the music and didn't imbibe large amounts of alcohol. When Ethel Azama, a Hawaiian Japanese jazz artist, made her California debut, it was at Ye Little Club. She was a Hawaiian performer who opened for folk legend Josh White and singer-actor Herb Jeffries. Like Sixto Rodriguez, many of the performers at Ye Little Club were talented artists who didn't hit mainstream stardom. Artists like Render and Azama were destined to performing obscurity.

Steve Rowland: "The guy who managed us, Marshall Edson, owned Ye Little club in Beverly Hills, and it was a major jazz venue. It was always a jazz club but rock and roll was seeping into the mix. Edson saw the dollars in rock and roll and immediately turned his club into a gold mine. In doing so, he launched our career."

How did Rowland and Albright Get Hired at Ye Little Club?

When Rowland and Albright went into the Ye Little Club for the first time there was a small stage in the back. One night a trio with Jack

Nietzsche was playing in the small room. They asked Nietzsche if they could sing a couple of songs. He agreed. Steve and Budd began singing and the crowd rushed the small stage. They covered Chuck Berry's "Sweet Littler Sixteen," a Larry Williams inspired "Bony Maronie" and a Little Richard influenced "Long Tall Sally." The crowd went nuts. The club manger took note as the drinks flowed.

Steve Rowland: "After that night at Ye Little Club we came to the house. My roommate, Jim Mitchum, said: 'You guys should form a band." They did. The reception brought in capacity crowds. Steve decided to put together a classic rock band.

This led Rowland's band to cover "Whole Lot of Shaking," "Good Golly Miss Molly," "Linda Lu," "Johnny B. Goode," "Sweet Little Sixteen" and "Roll Over Beethoven." Edson told Rowland and Albright they had a future in rock and roll music. Rowland watched the financial end of the music business closely. He quietly educated himself in the ways of the industry.

The club scene soon got out of hand. Standing room only led to people milling around outside. From time to time the Los Angeles Police Department showed up to see if something was wrong. There was. Underage drinkers were everywhere. If you wore a suit, had a fake id or simply looked twenty-one you were in the Encore Room. The LAPD looked the other way. Edson was connected. He also had gratuities ready for the police.

In 1963 Rowland left Los Angeles for Spain and signed a five-picture movie deal. It was when he arrived in Madrid the music bug germinated into a defined career direction. Steve would find a band to front as his success in the Los Angeles clubs gave him confidence. He entered the Spanish music business when he became the lead singer of the Madrid group Los Flaps.

The band was well known for an instrumental cover of "Washington Square." The popular You Tube version displays their instrumental talent and performing skill. See https://www.youtube.com/watch?v=dEUuD8HkJQI

The "Washington Square" cover on RCA was a record that sold in Spain on compilations into the 1980s. They also had surf music instrumental "Quizas, Quizas Quizas" which was released on a four song EP **Yenka** in 1965 with a mysterious cover. See it at https://www.youtube.com/watch?v=tnjzZJCkNc8.

The Los Flaps instrumental success prompted them to advertise for a lead singer and bring Steve Rowland in to front the band. It was a partnership mutually beneficial to everyone.

In 2012 a reformed Los Flaps covered Elvis Presley's "All Shook Up" with a surf instrumental sound to commemorate the King's lyrics. There is also a You Tube clip of the band performing "Atlantis" https://www.youtube.com/watch?v=2MKtF9zQRaA. It was a rare moment in Spanish rock and roll history when Los Flaps once again graced the stage. See. https://www.youtube.com/watch?v=lBjCRjFLgu8

Steve Rowland stood out as the lead singer in Los Flaps. Polydor signed him in 1964 to a contract as a solo artist. They released a four song EP with covers of a Ray Sharpe inspired "Linda Lu," a Ray Charles influenced "I Got A Woman," an original written by Joe Bennett of the Sparkletones "She's Gone" and a Cliff Richards cover "Dancing Shoes." Richards' cover caught the attention of labels, record scouts, managers and those in the production side of the industry. While Steve's Spanish records sold well in Spain, it was a limited market. He wanted more exposure. So he left for England in 1966. The music moguls in the U. K. wanted him as a lead-singer. There was no interest in Rowland as a producer. When he was labeled a producer, it was to circumvent British immigration law.

Steve Rowland: "I was making films. I wanted to supplement my income. I saw an ad in a free American magazine to audition for a Spanish rock group. My audition was successful. I became the lead singer in Los Flaps, we were successful. Since we were a hit band, I decided to go to England to try to make it in the music business over there." The time with Los Flaps began his early mainstream musical career.

Steve's Los Flaps interlude was an interesting one. The group was organized by a group of aeronautical engineering students who loved American rock and roll. Los Flaps was a Madrid based group in 1964-1965 who charted five hits thanks to Steve Rowland's production and lead singing skills. They also served as Rowland's backing band, as he performed in and around Spain while making movies. Mickey Hart, the future Grateful Dead drummer, was in a rival group, the Jaguars. Rowland loved their sound. From time to time he joined them as the lead singer. This is only one of the many bands that Rowland's superb vocals graced.

Los Flaps and the Jaguars provided Rowland with another notch for his rock and roll experiences. He realized both bands needed to have their songs crafted in a more professional manner. He was becoming a producer. He didn't realize it.

The Los Flaps were a legendary band prompting Hispovok to sign the group. As a subsidiary of Polydor, Hispovok had tremendous promotion. The result is the Los Flaps evolved into a legendary Spanish rock band. Even after they disbanded, the group had 45s released by RCA. This brief period of success on the Spanish charts turned into long-term cult record success.

Did The Beatles-British Invasion Influence Rowland?

From 1963-1966 Steve Rowland made five movies in Spain. He also kept in touch with American television. Not surprisingly, he glimpsed a musical revolution one night as a British band appeared on America's premier variety spot, the Ed Sullivan TV Show. What struck Rowland about the new music was its visual imagery. He never forgot the image of the Beatles that night as it flashed all over the U. S. and Beatlemania took root internationally.

When the Beatles appeared on the Ed Sullivan TV show in February 1964, Rowland saw his future. He relocated to London. He formed a band, the Family Dogg, with Albert Hammond and Mike Hazlewood. He also attracted the attention of a number of industry people. Rowland was a one-man band. He could write. He could produce. He could sing. He could arrange. He could hire the session musicians. He could promote the albums and 45s. These multiple talents were rare in the music business.

Steve Rowland: "Jack Baverstock was the head of Fontana Records in England. He wanted to sign me as an artist, but I was deported to Spain. He said that the deal was no longer on the table."

Baverstock didn't abandon Rowland. He wanted him back in London as a singer and as a producer. Steve had never produced. Baverstock saw something in him during studio sessions. What Baverstock had in mind was to place Fontana's 45s and albums into the lucrative American market. He envisioned Rowland as the conduit to that market.

When he was deported from England and Fontana Records brought him back to London as a producer, it was a ruse. The British government wasn't fooled. The Home Office showed up at Fontana Records and inquired about Rowland: "What is he producing?" A demure Englishman with a sense of the music business, Baverstock decided to assign Rowland a producing project that would allow him to quickly turn out a record. Then Baverstock would record a Rowland 45 and begin the process of making him a U. K. teen idol. The same formula that brought P. J. Proby stardom is the one Baverstock favored. The record mogul would find a band that had no chance of producing a hit and get them in and out of the studio. The only problem is that this band, Dave Dee, Dozy, Beaky, Mick and Tich had thirteen hits with Steve Rowland acting as the producer. No one could believe it. Baverstock had no idea that Rowland had a long rock and roll pedigree in Hollywood and Madrid. He was ready to be a major producer.

Steve Rowland: "Jack Baverstock brought me back from a temporary exile in Spain as a record producer." Rowland paused and laughed. "What he wanted was a singer." No one realized Rowland had a decade of experience in the studio. He knew how to produce records.

Steve Rowland: "The initial idea was that I was going to produce English artists for better sales in America. The Home Office said that we will check this. If this doesn't come to reality, he will be deported."

His first record for Dave Dee, Dozy, Beaky, Mick and Tich, "Hold Tight," went Top Ten in the U. K. He quickly produced thirteen hits for the group. The biggest hit "The Legend of Xanadu," sold a million in the U. K. and reached number one on the charts. "I had to create a whip sound by taking a mandolin player and a guitar player to make the whip sound. Then I would bang a piece of wood to complete the whip sound," Rowland said. But Rowland didn't exclusively produce U. K. hits. He had chart records all over the world.

Steve Rowland: "We had five records number one in both Germany and Japan."

The rock and roll world offered Rowland a chance to employ his talents. He was a writer. He had an eye for commercial music. He could produce. He intuitively understood excellent songwriting. This allowed him to appreciate and produce Sixto Rodriguez.

Rowland's British Rock Discoveries and Production

He discovered a side of Peter Frampton and the Herd no one recognized. That is he put Frampton's pretty face up front. It was a marketing device that worked. Rowland produced the Herd's "I Don't Want Our Lovin' To Die," which reached number two on the British charts. He also produced "From The Underworld" and "Paradise Lost" with the Herd. The lead vocals by Peter Frampton were the first time he charted as a singer.

Steve Rowland: "Peter Frampton didn't want to sing on the record. Gary Taylor was a good singer. We wanted Frampton to sing because the **New Musical Express** made him the 'Face of 1967." **Disc** and **Melody Maker** also praised Rowland's work with the Herd as well as a wide variety of U. K. hit acts. He was in demand. One of the icons of American rock and roll, Jerry Lee Lewis, showed up to have Rowland produce a hit album.

How Steve Rowland Got to Produce Jerry Lee Lewis

How did Steve Rowland get to produce Jerry Lee Lewis? There were many reasons. Rowland had a knack for picking the right session musicians. He had a track record of hits. He came in on or under budget.

Steve Rowland: "Mercury Records called Jack Baverstock and asked if they could meet me. Charlie Fach came over from Chicago and interviewed me. He told me that he would fly me to Chicago to set up the deal. Then we went to Memphis to meet Jerry Lee Lewis. He told me that Jerry Lee had to approve it. We met Jerry Lee at a club in Memphis. I sat down. Charlie Fach left. The first thing Jerry Lee said to me 'Hey limey boy you are going to work with the killer and it better god damned be good.' He thought I was English, but the evening still went well. I went back to London and he flew over with his group. We had to do the whole album at Advision Studios on Gower Street in London in one week. Mercury gave me one week to do twenty-nine songs, a double album. Luckily I talked with Jerry Lee and made a list of twenty-nine songs. I called the top British musicians, like Stevie Winwood, Gary Wright, Klaus Voorman; they all loved the idea of recording with Jerry Lee and they all agreed to play for scale. Stevie Winwood said that he was busy. I called Barry Gibb but the Bee Gees were recording."

Steve hired the musicians he wanted for the Lewis album. Some were upset by not being asked. One was Elton John. I asked Steve how come Elton John wasn't asked to back Jerry Lee Lewis? Steve looked at me like I was nuts. "You really want an answer to that question? I didn't know how to get hold of John. Enough with the stupid questions." Steve can be a prickly guy.

John complained to **Rolling Stone** wondering why he was not asked to play on the record. But Rowland had other things on his mind than the musicians who weren't asked to back Lewis. He had twenty-nine songs to record in a week.

Rowland went on to organize, hire and get the studio ready for Jerry Lee and the musicians. As he did this, he thought about his early years in Los Angeles. It was here in the African American clubs he found some of the music he knew Lewis could cover.

Steve Rowland: "I used to go to the 5-4 Ballroom to see Wynonie Harris sing 'Drinkin' Wine Spo-Dee-O-Dee,' I thought that this would be a great song for Lewis. Jerry Lee did it in one take."

Jerry Lee Lewis: The London Sessions was cut live and the production costs were low. The profits were huge. Everyone was happy. But there was controversy. Rowland is a quiet, often understated person, who doesn't talk about his productions. As a result the engineer on the project, Martin Reshent, told the **New Musical Express** that he produced the Lewis album. Not even **NME** gave this preposterous claim credence. It was a Steve Rowland production that brought rave reviews from executive producer Charlie Fach. He remarked Steve did everything including bringing Jerry Lee his cigars, and he arranged for the staff to have snacks, coffee and tea. The musicians received what they needed to make the album a success. Most important to Fach was the song selection Rowland set up for Lewis. He made the album not only successful but one Jerry Lee loved recording.

What the critics missed is Rowland supervised the Jerry Lee Lewis sessions while bringing out the best in the Killer. He did this by running a tight studio, on a schedule and bringing in brilliant musicians who could cover Lewis's songs without session sheets. There were six songs recorded each day. Mercury was ecstatic. Rowland was not just a brilliant London producer; he was one who came in on and under budget.

Jerry Lee Lewis commented many times the musicians were serious, no one was drinking or smoking dope and they knew the songs inside out. He considered it the finest group of musicians he had been in the studio with to that point in his career. Later during interviews the Killer would embellish the sessions with anecdotes that sounded good but lacked truth. From day one Lewis recognized Rowland's ability to catch his piano magic on vinyl. He was in the studio early and worked as late as needed to cut the twenty-nine songs. It was a workable partnership with wonderful results.

American artists recognized Rowland's' talents and piano wild man Jerry Lee Lewis has spoken highly over the years about Rowland's production on **Jerry Lee Lewis: The London Sessions**. Not only did the Lewis LP go gold, it led to Rowland winning an ASCAP award for producing Lewis' cover of Charlie Rich's "No Headstone On My Grave."

Steve Rowland: "I had no trouble with Jerry Lee. The only problem is that he broke the Beckstein piano because he played it so hard. It has an extra octave."

Rowland with P. J. Proby and The Pretty Things

He also produced albums for P. J. Proby and The Pretty Things. As the music changed, he was an in demand producer. His skills weren't limited to one style of music. He could do it all.

Steve Rowland: "James Marcus Smith was a friend of mine. He had a house built on the side of a hill in Hollywood. He and I used to run around a lot. Dotty Harmony was a girl that went out with Elvis. She brought Jim to my house. He walked in with torn jeans. Dotty was in shorts with great legs. Jet Powers was the name he used. He came along with Dotty showing the best legs in town and I knew we were all ready to have some fun. I sang with Jett Powers at the Sea Witch on Sunset Blvd near La Cienega. Jett Powers was now the stage name of Jim Smith, and he would soon be P. J. Proby."

Dotty Harmony was one of Elvis Presley's many girl friends. For a time Harmony was a Las Vegas showgirl who went home with Elvis to Memphis for a 1956 Christmas celebration. By the time Rowland produced Proby's album in London he had known the Texas transplant for a decade. As Rowland observed Dotty Harmony's legs opened a lot of doors. When he reconnected with Proby in London, he was ready to produce a great album. He did.

The P. J. Proby 1969 album **Three Week Hero** is one of Rowland's most interesting productions. One reason is Led Zeppelin's bass player John Paul Jones was brought in to help arrange the songs. He also played some piano and organ on the album. Jimmy Page's acoustic and electric guitar make this LP a cult favorite. John Bonham played drums. Robert Plant performed some key harmonica riffs. The album provided the future mega star Led Zeppelin with new song ideas.

Rowland brought in his group, the Family Dogg, to provide back up vocals. It proved to be an LP unlike any in Proby's career. It gave him a different sound and a wider fan base. There are two weak songs on the LP that don't seem to belong, Albert Hammond's "Empty Bottle" and "New Directions" which sounds like they were written for Petula Clark. Why were they included on the album? This remains a mystery.

The most interesting song on **Three Week Hero** is one Rowland arranged. It is a medley "It's So Hard To Be A Nigger-Jim's Blues-George Wallace Is Rollin-In This Mornin." These were traditional and politically explosive songs woven into a beautifully produced medley. It was Rowland's way of making a statement on American race relations. Rowland and Proby were making a strong statement against racism. No one seemed to get it. The major London music magazines were flummoxed by the medley. **Melody Maker** and the

New Musical Express ignored the song while praising Proby's album. This didn't translate into sales.

What Rowland had in mind for Proby was to mix dramatic pop songs, some blues, some country tunes and a bit of rock into an eclectic package! The title song, written by former Kingston Trio member John Stewart was a strong lead. It had the country flair typical of the bard of the west.

Steve Rowland: "I heard the John Stewart song and loved it."

Steve also worked as a talent scout discovering, signing and producing the Cure, Japan, the Thompson Twins, and he helped in the London Studio with the songs Boney M cut for the Top of The Pops. He also produced the first Japan record. Steve is a renaissance man who is a singer-songwriter and producer. He evolved into a consummate musical production machine turning out one hit record after another.

Eventually, he became a top disco producer. His eye for new talent was infallible. He produced and helped arrange Sarah Brightman's "I Lost My Heart to A Starship Trooper." Brightman was a soprano, actress, dancer and songwriter. When she married Andrew Lloyd Webber, he took over the production tasks. Her song was a 1978 disco hit with the teen age Brightman cashing in on the hype surrounding Star Wars. Rowland understood how to produce the sound for maximum chart success. "I Lost My Heart To A Starship Trooper" reached number six on the U. K. singles chart.

The breadth of Rowland's musical interests is suggested by the diversity of artists he produced. He worked with jazz piano diva Blossom Dearie, 1950s pop legend Theresa Brewer, model turned singer Marsha Hunt, dancer Marsha Raven, disco pioneer Gloria Gaynor, and the British rock group Babe Ruth. The r and b and dance music singer Jocelyn Brown, among others, benefitted from Rowland's production. His wide and varied musical interests were so sophisticated, he could move with ease between musical genres and place-hit records on charts all over the world.

Rowland's Cult and Classic Productions

Steve Rowland produced so many artists and groups, it is difficult to keep track of them. Fontana said Steve Rowland worked with the cerebral artists. He also had some great cult acts.

In the late 1960s, an English cult band, The Magic Lanterns emerged on the U. K. music scene. The Magic Lanterns originally signed to CBS Records didn't have a commercial focus. They had little success. They didn't have the right producer, enter Steve Rowland. He produced the English cult band's hits "Shame, Shame," "One Night Stand," "Let The Sun Shine In" and "Country Woman." All were significant chart hits. Along the way, the Magic Lanterns achieved cult status in the U. K. and U. S.

Rowland was brought in by Atlantic Records to get the Magic Lanterns a hit. He did. "Shame, Shame" was their first American hit charting at twenty-nine on **Billboard** and ten on **Cashbox**. Then "One Night Stand" came in at seventy-four and "Country Girl" ended their U. S. run at eighty-eight in 1972. The Magic Lanterns' success was due solely to Rowland. The first two Magic Lanterns' albums **Lit Up-With the Magic Lanterns** and **Shame, Shame** bear Rowland's unmistakable producing touch. The problem with the **Lit Up-With The Magic Lanterns** is that Rowland's song arrangements and mixing, his producing touch and his advice had a lasting impact on the band. When CBS released the LP, Mike Collier was listed as the producer. He was only the producer in the final stages. It was a Steve Rowland produced album. The credit was taken away from him. Collier built the album upon a foundation that Rowland laid with the band. This happened to Rowland because of a lack of integrity in the record business. There was one artist who wasn't a singer that Rowland turned into a hit recording phenomenon. She was a model and dancer as well as Mick Jagger's sleep over girl friend. Her name was Marsha Hunt. Her brother, Dennis, was also a well-known rock critic, and the British press treated her like a rock star. Steve Rowland made her into a rock and roll icon.

Producing Mick Jagger's Girl Friend: Marsha Hunt, is She Another Rodriguez?

When Rowland went into the studio with Marsha Hunt, he had an American singer who was also a famed model. Under Steve's interpretive guidance and creative mantra, she evolved into a recording artist eventually going on to become a best selling author. She is best known as the inspiration for the Rolling Stones' "Brown Sugar." Her time sleeping with Mick Jagger inspired the song.

By coincidence, Hunt arrived in London at the same time as Rowland. She had trouble obtaining a visa. So she married Soft Machine's Mike Ratledge. She viewed it as a quickie marriage. After forty years they were still married. Then she moved to France where she lives to the present day. Her musical talent was much greater than the media recognized.

Hunt has said in numerous interviewers she is not much of a singer. This is not correct. She is one hell of a performer and a fine singer. Her video of a cover of Simon and Garfunkel's "Keep The Customers Satisfied" on an Italian television show is testimony to her talent, and it bears some of Rowland's trademark teaching skills. She is a great performer with a long and varied music career.

When Hunt joined the Alexis Korner Trio, her well-publicized relationship with Stones lead singer, Mick Jagger, got her a recording contract. She had the talent, but the sensational minded London press never recognized her vocal gifts. She recorded a large number of songs and they show her vocal nuances and a voice that is unique. When she joined the Korner band it was with the idea of earning enough money to return to the San Francisco Bay Area.

The idea of returning to the U. S. ended when she met Marc Bolan in 1969. They quickly became a couple and Bolan was a catalyst to her developing musical career. She had attended the University of California in 1964 marching in protest with Jerry Rubin. In Pat Thomas' book **Did It From Yippie to Yuppie: Jerry Rubin, An American Revolutionary** he describes the excitement the Free

Speech Movement provided for Hunt. When she arrived in London, she found many of the musicians dull by comparison with her San Francisco Bay Area radical political cohorts. She had trouble accepting the role of Mick Jagger and later Marc Bolan's girl friend. She was a feminist. The London press refused to recognize this aspect of her personality. It was frustrating. But she did have a music career.

In 1973 the Vertigo label signed Hunt and she cut a cover of the Jefferson Airplane's "Somebody To Love" backed with the traditional "(Oh, No! Not) The Beast Day" with Steve Rowland producing and arranging. It quickly became a cult 45. There was an immense amount of publicity from the London trade magazines **Disc**, **Melody Maker** and the **New Musical Express**. The strong press did not translate into sales.

When Steve Rowland produced "Somebody To Love" Hunt's voice had a soul sound that was extraordinary. Mercury in the U. S. and Philips in the U. K. distributed the Vertigo label and Hunt looked for a time looked like a break out star. It didn't happen. A follow up "Black Flower" was a great song and was a Marc Bolan composition. There were other songs including "Hot Rod Poppa." and "Hippy Gumbo" that gave the T-Rex songwriter a great deal of publicity. Almost no one mentioned Marsha Hunt was the vocalist. The 1969 song "Desdemona" should have been a hit. It wasn't!

In 1969 Hunt was a festival regular appearing with Deep Purple's Nick Simper at the Belgium Blitzen Festival when he stepped in to back her when Hunt's drummer didn't show up. Her album **Woman Child** contained thirteen songs including a cover of "Wild Thing." She displayed her full vocal talents. The cover of "Let the Sunshine In" highlighted her time on the London stage in **Hair**.

From 1969 until 1973 Hunt frequently appeared on the German TV show "Beat Club" performing "Keep the Customers Satisfied." In the last stages of her performing career she was a cult star. Her vocal styling is evident in a cover of Traffic's "No Face, No Name, No Number."

The Vertigo release of "(Oh No! Not) The Beast Day" was a children's traditional song they made an original arrangement of. Since there was no music to the song they wrote the music and completed the arrangement. It was Hugh Burns, Marsha Hunt and Rowland who composed the music. It became a collectible cult 45. When Hunt appeared on the cover of **Vogue** with her stylish Afro and later in the London cast of Hair, she established a strong fan base. This helped her to sell cult 45s.The Rowland produced 45 is one that has brought Hunt a cult music audience. When the movie **The F Word** was released in 2013 the song was in the film in its entirety. When Rowland received a royalty check for the music used on the soundtrack, he felt vindicated. He shared the royalties with Burns and Hunt. It had been a long time but Rowland did get it right.

Steve Rowland: "I was one of the arrangers on '(Oh No! Not) The Beast Day.' I said how about if we do it in the direction of Dr. John. We were after creating a New Orleans voodoo effect."

Marsha Hunt left the rock and roll world, overcame breast cancer and went on to a successful writing career. Her debut novel, **Joy**, in 1990 is a heart-wrenching story of a young girl in a group like the Supremes who dies early. **Joy** is a no holds barred look at the music business. The impact of stardom and the difficulty of an African American performer are set in a million dollar New York apartment with flashbacks to a poor black neighborhood. Her second novel, **Free**, published in 1992, is a departure as it examines freed slaves in Germantown Pennsylvania in 1913. In both novels the acceptance of light skinned African American women versus their darker compatriots is an indictment of American society. She followed this with the 1998 **Like Venus Fading**, which is a fictionalized account of light skinned black women inspired by the lives of Adelaide Hall, Josephine Baker and Dorothy Dandridge. By the time she was writing her novels she lived in isolation in a remote house in the French countryside. Like Rodriguez, Marsha Hunt's intellectual fame came late in life. Her earlier fame was an indication of multiple talents. Like Steve Rowland, she was multi-talented. It was in many ways a detriment to her career. She has also remained in Europe living in Ireland and France for decades.

Steve Rowland: "As far as I am concerned Marsha Hunt is a complete class act. It was an honor to know her and to have worked with her." At the time Hunt lived in London's St. John's Wood and Maida Vale was where Steve lived. They saw each other infrequently as Steve conducted to produce and Hunt moved along quickly with a storied career.

Steve Produces Babe Ruth and Other Acts with a Hit Flair Even for Minimally Talented Bands and Gangsters

In the 1970s Rowland produced two singles from Babe Ruth's album, **Private Number** (Harvest 5090), which had a progressive rock direction and **Those People (Who Are Darker than Blue)**, which had a soul, funk sound. The lead vocals by Jenny Haan, who left the group in 1975 only to return in 2005, are incredible. Rowland was able to showcase her vocal sounds creating another cult vocalist.

In the 1980s Rowland demonstrated the breadth of his production skills. He produced "I Like Plastic" for Martha Raven for Red Bus Records. Raven began her career as a Tina Turner imitator and with her good looks and dancing ability became something of a U. K. dance star. She couldn't sing a lick. Rowland's production disguised her weak vocals. After Rowland got her on the charts, he helped her refine her stage act. She took a one-dimensional talent to the bank with Steve's mentoring. She signed with another producer and a new label. That was the end of her career. She never had another hit. Raven came from a wealthy family. She receded into the abyss of celebrity life.

In the 1980s, Rowland was a mover and shaker in the French recording industry. He produced "The Lost Opera" with Kimera and the L. S. O. It was a Top 5 French chart hit for twenty weeks selling almost two million albums. Kimera and the L. S. O. was produced for an allegedly disreputable international businessman. His wife had a five octave vocal range. She was the daughter of the last King of Korea. Her name was Kim Hong Hee.

Steve Rowland: "In the middle of mixing the control room door opened and the boss walked in with a bunch of his friends and sat down in the back. As I was mixing I needed complete quiet but the boss and his friends started talking. I asked everyone to be quiet but thy kept talking. After about two or three minutes I couldn't concentrate. I turned around and said 'please stop talking I have to be able to focus.' They kept talking. I stopped in the middle of what I was doing and said everybody has to leave the control room. The boss didn't take kindly to my words. He said: 'I'm the fucking producer, I pay for this if I want my friends in the studio I will have them in the studio.' I called the session and shut it down. We had a meeting and sorted out the problem."

The Kimera production was a nightmare. Steve worked with a ruthless boss. There is another weasel in the mix. His name is John Fiddy. He was hired by Steve to arrange the album as they were using the London Symphony Orchestra. He went behind Steve's back attempting to take credit for producing the album. He didn't receive the credit but after the gangster refused to pay Steve, Fiddy was given a contract to produce the second album. He did. The second album was a mess. Steve was hired to remix the second album. "If you want me to do it, you will have to ship it here and I will mix it in London." Steve did. The second album didn't sell.

The payment came in for his work only after they screwed up the production on a second album. They called Steve in to fix it. In France it was not only a mammoth hit but continues to sell to the present day. Why? It is a record Rowland produced with the London Symphony Orchestra that has had nineteen separate releases in the U. K. and Europe. The 1984 release is described as "the lost opera" and the electronic classical album had a semi-disco style including compositions by Verdi, Puccini, Strauss, Bizet and Mozart among others. Steve was lucky to escape this production with his life and the money was a secondary concern to staying alive. It is his strangest production, but it also went platinum. Current statistics suggest Kimera and the L. S. O. has sold over ten million copies. Steve received two payments from the alleged gangster. He has never received a royalty statement.

What is the importance of the Kimera story? It is an example of the various influences, roadblocks and nonsense that Rowland put up with in his forty plus year recording career. The people who hired him referred to the headman as "the boss." His name is Raymond Nakachian, and he was listed as the executive producer. There were rumors of alleged ties to the Russian Mafia, the notorious London based gangsters the Kray Brothers were his lunch mates, and when it got time to get paid for an album selling two million copies in France and staying on the charts for months, Steve wasn't paid. There is no evidence Nakachian is a criminal. He has never been convicted of a crime. He was allegedly tied to crime. The London press reported his activity with innuendo and a lack of facts. He was an over the top London-Paris businessman with an idea for his wife, Kim Hong Hee, to perform classical music in a medley of operatic arias set to a mid-1980s disco beat. Enter Steve Rowland who produced the Kimera album. It was a cross pollination between disco and classical music. It was the same beat all the way through.

The last point in the Kimera story is Rowland produced her hit album despite threats, interference from Nakachian and a cast of gangster types who had watched the Godfather too many times. All Steve wanted to do was to produce hit records. But in the music business the bullshit, the wannabes and the assholes provided him with a daily challenge. After forty years he fled to Palm Springs. There were some pleasant discoveries.

The Mel and Kim Story Begins Rowland's Negative Feelings on the Record Business

As he made one hit after another for various artists and record labels, Rowland grew tired of hearing the phrase: "cred man, we need cred." The producers and publicists for record labels were self important and pompous. They screamed "cred" day and night. What they said was the truth. At least that's what they thought. Of Rowland they commented: "You're so American." After twenty years of producing one hit after another on both sides of the Atlantic, he ignored the naysayers. It did bother him.

Because of his brilliance as a producer, he was allowed to carry out a Monday audition night at London's Valbon Club. Steve Rowland: "One night a friend came in with Mel and he was running a night club that had almost porn dancers. I began talking to Mel and I asked her: 'Can you sing?' She said: 'Yes, that's all I ever wanted to do." Steve asked her if she knew someone else who could sing. Mel responded: "My sister."

It was in a small recording studio about seventy-five miles outside of London that Mel and Kim cut demos of four Trevor Cummings songs. The demos, according to those inside the London record business, were superior to the product Mel and Kim released. It was Steve Rowland who got them into the recording business and set the stage for their career.

Steve contacted their manager Alan Whitehead and spent many hours on the four demo tracks.

Steve Rowland: "I went out with their manager and I negotiated the deal. I sent the demos to Supreme Records and they got a recording contract. I went in and told him I want you to listen to these four demos." Then a Supreme Record executive asked Steve if he had pictures of the girls? Rowland responded: "I am not going to show you pictures. I played the demos. He loved them. I showed him the pictures and we had a deal."

Then Steve got screwed. Their manager wanted Pete Waterman and his three-person production crew to take over making the dance records. Rowland agreed. Mel and Kim's manager, Alan Whitehead, didn't have a sterling reputation in the industry. Mervyn Solomon told me Whitehead was "a rascal who belonged in Soho."

For his efforts Rowland received neither thanks nor financial compensation. What the Mel and Kim discovery did was to make Rowland credible as dance music overtook London and the U. S. I asked Steve Rowland how he felt about the Mel and Kim interlude. He smiled: "No comment." Then I asked him: "Wasn't Alan Whitehead the asshole that cheated you out of millions?" Steve smiled. "No comment." I took his look for a "Yes."

The Dance Craze Proves Rowland's Versatility and Continued Hit Record Production

The dance craze prompted Rowland to establish his own record label, Dr. Beat. He also served as a creative director for Wham Records. By 1993, Rowland was winding down his career as a creative director for Pavilion Studios, where he worked with young D. J's, fledgling producers, new artists and programmers. He auditioned and attempted to sign the then unknown Spice girl Geri Halliwell. By 1995 Rowland was a Managing Director for the Media Bank U.K. a Hong Kong based international production company. Media Bank is a subsidiary of City Telecom HK Ltd. They are primarily a media production and distribution corporation. It was a perfect fit for Rowland's talents.

Steve Rowland is not only a brilliant producer-arranger-musician; he is an experienced and accomplished singer. He has had movie-television success. He remains a first rate writer. There isn't much that he can't do.

The big change in Rowland's life took place when he connected with Malik Bendjelloul. He helped Bendjelloul complete the Oscar winning documentary **Searching For Sugar Man**.

Catching Up with Rodriguez at the L. A. Film Festival

When Malik Bendjelloul showed up at Steve Rowland's Palm Springs home, Steve pulled out some pictures of Rodriguez. He gave a heart felt and in-depth interview. Steve remarked of all the people he produced Rodriguez was the best. This was a heady compliment. Rowland produced some of the most commercial music acts from the 1960s until the early 2000s. Then **Searching For Sugar Man** came out and Rowland was in demand for interviews, his past productions drew interest, and he was busy putting his Hollywood based TV series together. It is ready for prime time.

He appeared at the documentaries opening at the Palm Spring Palme d'Or Theater. He talked at length and in-depth with Rodriguez in June 2012 at the Los Angeles Film Festival in the aftermath of **Searching For Sugar Man's** success, and they appeared to be plotting for the future. There is a great picture of Rowland holding a beer sitting next to Rodriguez after more than forty years. It looks like they are still fast friends. They are! Rodriguez said to **Rolling Stone** Rowland will produce his new album.

It was at the after party at the Los Angeles Film Festival that Rodriguez and Rowland talked of a new album. As Rowland said of Rodriguez: "This is a lesson to anybody who has a dream. Never give up on your dream." Steve Rowland is ready to make Rodriguez a household word with a third album. Stay tuned.

Steve Rowland and Matt Sullivan Discuss Searching for Sugar Man

When Steve Rowland stepped up on the Cinema Palme D'Or Stage in Palm Desert on August 31, 2012, along with Light In The Attic chief, Matt Sullivan, he provided the best description of why the Rodriguez phenomenon was taking place and what the future held. In a question and answer session, Rowland made it clear Rodriguez was one of his top five favorite artists. He also said Rodriguez was among the most original talents in rock music. He was talking as a music producer with an eye to the sound and its commercial possibilities.

Steve Rowland: "There are some great artists, but to me, he's the best. The fact that nobody recognized it, to me, is insane."

The beauty of Rowland's remarks is he produced gold and platinum albums. Often these artists had half as much talent as Rodriguez. But he has never faltered in his admiration or praise for Sixto Rodriguez' music.

The Steve Rowland Factor

The second Rodriguez album had a definite hit or pop edge **Cold Fact** lacked. This is not surprising as Steve Rowland and Sixto Rodriguez were on the same page. They were intent upon pop, romantic songs. They were resisting the changes that rock music brought into the popular culture arena. If there is a crowning achievement, it is Rowland's tribute to Rodriguez in the Family Dogg album **The View From Rowland's Head**. Why? Because the album contains a marvelous original version of Rodriguez' "Advice To Smokey Robinson" and a cover of "I Wonder" with a gospel choir. In these covers there is a sense of Detroit's mysterious past. It is a window into how the Sugar Man's songs translate to other artists, and how he used incidents in his life to craft his songwriting genius. The critics took note praising both covers. The Family Dogg received more publicity than the Sugar Man. There were six Rodriguez songs covered in the album. Rodriguez never recorded "Advice To Smokey Robinson." Rowland's version does it justice. Steve took the Sugar Man's songs and made them his own.

Revisiting the Coming From Reality Album

In 2009 Matt Sullivan and Light in the Attic re-released **Coming From Reality** with marvelous new liner notes by Kevin "Sipreano"

Howes. Since the release of **Cold Fact** in March 1970, Rodriguez was a dead letter in the American music scene. Matt Sullivan and Light In The Attic brought the Sugar Man back as a cult artist. The visual imagery in the LITA albums presents a new, sensitive singer and his talent built from this base.

On **Coming From Reality** the photos of Rodriguez are superb. They tell a great deal about his personality. With London's Big Ben in the background, he sits on a ledge the ultimate, cool persona of a rocker. He is shown with young kids at Glasshouse Walk. What is Glasshouse Walk? It is a place that interested Rodriguez. Glasshouse Walk, formerly known as Glasshouse Street, contained the last remnants of London's glass making industry. The small cafés and coffee shops in and around Glasshouse Walk appealed to Rodriguez. He spent hours there drinking coffee, writing in a journal and talking to the locals.

The ten original tracks in **Coming From Reality** were remastered and three bonus songs "Can't Get Away," "Street Boy" and "I'll Slip Away" were included in the LITA release. The packaging is spectacular. The liner notes first rate. Light In The Attic released the CD when there was only a small Rodriguez market. How times have changed.

Why Steve Rowland was Right for Rodriguez

When Steve Rowland was assigned to produce Rodriguez' **Coming From Reality**, he was the right person for the project. The reasons are many and varied. He loved Rodriguez' songwriting. He felt he shouldn't tamper with the lyrics or music. When Rodriguez wrote the haunting instrumental "Sandrevan Lullaby-Lifestyles," Rowland encouraged him to use it as a break in the mood of the album. It worked perfectly. It set a mellow mood for the remainder of the LP.

Steve Rowland: "I realized that Rodriguez' writing was something special. I simply wanted to bring the best sound from him in the studio."

There are a number of reasons Rowland produced a masterpiece with **Coming From Reality**. He didn't pressure the Sugar Man for any type of sound. He told him he wanted his original tunes with an equally original production. The years of experience producing U. K. hits made Rowland's advice indispensible. He recorded at hours convenient to the Sugar Man. "I had never heard a songwriter with such original talent. I just wanted his album perfect," Rowland concluded. What was it that drove the inner Rowland? As Steve looked back on his career, he continually referred to nepotism and how it hurt his drive toward mainstream stardom.

Nepotism is What Drove Steve Rowland

Steve Rowland was driven by the negative impact of nepotism. He had to scrap for acting jobs and more often he didn't get an acting job because his father was a famous and well-respected director. During the 1950s and 1960s Steve appeared in a number of movies and even more television series. He never had it easy. He had to prove his acting chops. When he was between acting jobs, his music kept food on the table. He never had the pampered, Hollywood lifestyle that some writers have suggested. From day one, Steve had to scratch for a living. In the process he became an actor with a wide resume. He realized he would never be a superstar.

The next step was music where he excelled. He had a large number of 45 record releases in Hollywood and Madrid. In the process, he educated himself on how to work in the studio. When he left for London, he had the knowledge to produce a wide variety of artists.

The next phase of his creative career led Rowland to produce hundreds of hit records. He revolutionized how music was produced using his acting background to craft hit records that were extended stories.

Nepotism drove Rowland from the movies and television, to a brief music career as a recording artist, and this set the stage for his lengthy time in London studios producing hit records. He always searched for credibility. He was driven by the charge of nepotism that made his Hollywood acting career difficult. He moved on to record production as a result of the constant roadblocks.

For some aspiring film makers and actors nepotism is an aid to establishing their career. For Rowland it was the constant complaints he was Roy Rowland's son that prompted him to relocate to London and become a record producer. If that had not happened there would not have been **Coming From Reality**.

Malik Bendjelloul And Sixto Rodriguez

Five

Coming From Reality and Steve Rowland's Producing Genius: How He Got It Made

"I've produced a lot of big-name artists with big hits, like Peter Frampton and Jerry Lee Lewis, but I've never worked with anyone as talented as Rodriguez."

Steve Rowland, who produced the singer's second album, "Coming From Reality."

"We spent thirty wonderful days recording the Coming From Reality album, we stayed in Belgravia, London."

Sixto Rodriguez

" I wanted to make sure that every syllable was heard."

Steve Rowland on producing Coming From Reality

"The conversations between myself and Rodriguez will always remain private. I don't talk about him personally. Ask me about the music."

Steve Rowland

There wasn't going to be a second Sixto Rodriguez album. Sussex Records was looking to maximize its investments. That is getting rid of Rodriguez. He had a three album record deal. His sales were dismal. What happened? It was the rise of soul music, disco and television that alerted Sussex to another investment opportunity. One that would pay dividends and help recoup some of the money Sussex Records was losing. That money would be recouped from an African American television show.

Clarence Avant was quietly backing Don Cornelius as he set up the future mega hit TV show Soul Train. Avant's distribution partner, Neil Bogart, was planning a disco label Casablanca Records. Freddy Bienstock, the founder of Carlin Music, was in London looking for the next big act. None of these music giants believed a second Rodriguez album was feasible. **Cold Fact** hadn't sold well. That was it for Sixto Rodriguez.

Steve Rowland came to a producing career almost by accident and he came to producing **Coming From Reality** by picking up **Cold Fact** and listening to it. He was floored by Rodriguez' songwriting and vocal styling.

There was a long and circuitous road Rowland took to becoming a respected platinum record producer. He understood how to make hit records. Had it not been for Jack Baverstock at Fontana Records he might have ended up as a solo artist. It was Baverstock who signed him as a producer. The story of how Rowland became a record producer tells one a great deal about the music industry.

How Steve Rowland Set Up His London Production Career

When Steve Rowland arrived in London in the mid-1960s it was to pursue a career as a lead singer. Jack Baverstock, the CEO of Fontana Records, had high hopes for promoting Rowland as a teen idol. His background in the Hollywood and Madrid music scenes indicated his popularity with a teen audience. The plan to make him a pop star was thwarted when the Home Office deported Rowland back to Spain. When he returned to London, Jack Baverstock signed him on to Fontana Records as a producer. The Home Office didn't believe this ruse. They showed up at Baverstock's office and asked whom Rowland was producing. This led to the hits with Dave Dee, Dozy, Beaky, Mick and Tich.

Because he had business expertise, Rowland set up a production company. He was an independent producer. This allowed him to control his product. This was the reason he was able to convince the skeptical powers he could produce hits for Sixto Rodriguez. They told Rowland to record the acts that gave him "cred." He hated the word. He hated the people who continually screamed: "cred." This attitude eventually drove him out of London. But he didn't leave London until September 21, 2007 after he had produced hundreds of chart records. The road to discovering Sixto Rodriguez was a strange one. It tells one a great deal about how and why Steve Rowland selects his musical acts. He won't just record anyone. He picks and chooses. He is also a person with strong convictions. You do it his way. Or it is the highway. As one of Steve's friends said: "He is a study in persistence."

Jack Baverstock was the first person to give Rowland a chance to produce. Steve has only positive things to say about Baverstock. But there is another industry giant who was in the midst of Rowland's career. His name was Freddy Bienstock. He founded Carlin Music in London. Between Baverstock and Bienstock they provided Rowland with the foundation and platform for his productions.

Freddy Bienstock and Carlin Music in London

While producing records in London, Rowland from time to time had dealings with Freddy Bienstock and his Carlin Music Company. Ironically, Bienstock and Rowland arrived simultaneously in London in 1966. Who was Freddy Bienstock? He began in the music industry as a song plugger who didn't care for rock and roll. His cousins Jean and Julian Aberbach had an office in New York's Brill Building. Bienstock worked in the mailroom. When the Aberbach's were commissioned to find songs for Elvis Presley they came up with "Don't" and "Jailhouse Rock." They handed off much of this work to Bienstock. Freddy went to Mike Lieber and Jerry Stoller telling them they had until the next morning to write a hit song for Elvis Presley.

Jerry Lieber: "Mike and I would stay up all night and write." Then Bienstock would take the song to Elvis and Colonel Tom Parker. They approved. Bienstock's fortune began to accumulate when he copyrighted the songs. It was through this experience with Presley that Bienstock realized there was gold in publishing. He also realized the American music publishing game was filled with gangsters, crooks, dishonest companies, assholes and nefarious business people. They would steal everything from you. He headed to London where he purchased Hill and Range's British subsidiary Belinda Music renaming it Carlin Music to honor his daughter Caroline.

Carlin Music published some of the Family Dogg's best songs including "Sympathy." The artists Rowland produced were often published by Carlin including P. J. Proby and his connection to Carlin Music gave Steve full run of their office. The music business is a closed corporation. Rowland was in the middle of it. This is how and why he eventually was able to convince the powers to let him produce Rodriguez' **Coming From Reality**.

Baverstock and Bienstock were heavyweights on the London music scene. They were consulted on the Rodriguez project, as was everyone else. No one was interested!

Rowland's Persistence in Producing Coming From Reality

They didn't count on Steve Rowland's persistence. How did Rowland discover Rodriguez? It was by accident. He picked up the **Cold Fact** album in a London music office. He had no idea who the Sugar Man was, or where his career was going. He came into the Carlin Music office. He saw a picture with an interesting looking young guy. He picked up **Cold Fact** on top of a pile of promotional albums sent to Carlin. That simple act began the road to producing **Coming From Reality**. That was only the beginning. The story took twists and turns necessary to convince the skeptics in the music business to allow Sixto Rodriguez to record a second album.

What was Rowland looking for? Every band looked and sounded the same. Steve was an innovator not a follower. The day he headed down to Carlin Music, he thought about finding a singer-songwriter. It was the Fall of 1970. He loved the singer-songwriters who could also perform. Steve Rowland had a vision. He was making records like the movies he starred in during the 1950s and 1960s. Rowland envisioned records as having a beginning to grab your attention, to have the story expand in the middle and finally a dramatic climax taking the song to a thundering conclusion.

A good example of recognizing new talent came when he discovered the Cure. He do so half a decade after working with Rodriguez. The story behind the Cure suggests how and why Rowland had success in the music business. He had an ear for new musical talent and innovative sounds. He also liked the look and concert flow of some new artists. The Cure had great original songs, a distinctive sound and a great stage presence. He discovered them while working with the German label Hansa in their London office.

When Rowland reported to the Hansa label on the Cure he said their primary songwriting was highly commercial. Their abilities in the studio were unparalleled. They had something different. The owners at Hansa and the major executives disagreed. It was a costly mistake but the story of how and why Peter and Irmtrud "Trudy" Meisel turned down the Cure suggests more about the record business than it does about Rowland's eye for talent. The Meisel's worked or signed such American and English artists as Albert Hammond, Elton John, Otis Redding, Sonny and Cher, Paul Anka and Neil Sedaka. They depended upon Rowland for advice on these acts, and he was instrumental in their working with Boney M. and Sarah Brightman. The Meisel's made a fortune beginning in 1973 when Meisel's publishing administered the Beatles songs in Germany, Austria and Switzerland for a decade. They were great business people who parlayed Rowland's ear for hits into a multi-million dollar company.

Steve Rowland Discovers The Cure and Japan: Almost A Decade After Rodriguez

Peter and Trudy Meisel, the owners of Hansa Records, decided to take a two-week vacation from their London office. They placed Steve Rowland in charge. His task was to help sort out thousands of tapes that arrived at the label when they put out a call for new artists.

Hansa placed ads in **The New Musical Express**, **Disc** and **Melody Maker** requesting audition tapes. The German based label hoped to use London as a base to expand its product line. There were thousands of tapes sent in and a crew was assigned to put the acceptable ones in a special bin. Eventually, ten tapes made the final cut. They were placed in the special bin. The Cure and Japan were the two of the finalists.

Steve sat in the Hansa London office with the ten final tapes. When he came across the Cure tape, he was smitten by Robert Smith's songwriting. Hansa was a pop label. Steve told the Meisel's they needed to expand their musical base. They had Donna Summer, Georgio Moroder, Boney M and Tangerine Dream. They were doing fine with these artists. But Rowland saw new sounds on the horizon.

Steve Rowland: "I had been with Hansa five years earlier. We had a little office on Denmark Street. They were trying to get established in London. They got me because I produced the debut records for a number of artists that went number one in Germany. I formed the foundation for Family Dogg in that Denmark Street office."

He realized this unknown band, the Cure, from Crawley West Sussex in England had an enormous hit potential. After listening to the Cure's tape, Steve took the band to the Morgan studios in London to video them doing their material.

Steve Rowland: "We had thousands of tapes and we put them in bins. Peter was in Germany. His wife Trudy was in charge. We auditioned the tapes and created an acceptable bin. The tapes that were in the acceptable bin and sounded good we took to the Morgan Studio to videotape the bands to see how they looked. Then Peter and Trudy went away for two weeks and left me in charge. They said offer the acts you think are good a contract. They were known as the Easy Cure at the time. I gave them a contract not signed by Peter Meisel. I had recorded a version of 'Killing An Arab' and because the Cure was so angry at Hansa's remarks on their hair they wrote and christened the b-side 'Do The Hansa."

When Steve played the video for Meisel he exploded with anger.

Peter Meisel: "But Steve I don't like boys with lipstick."

The operative word on the Cure is they won a talent competition with the German record label Hansa. Rowland says this story is complete nonsense. The truth is he took a tape of the band and listened to it. He went to Hansa label management. He told the suits that the Cure were a million dollar act. Robert Smith's demo tape was what made Rowland lobby for the group. It was songwriting brilliance par excellence. The management at Hansa couldn't believe the Cure had a commercial future. Rowland argued long and hard to release their demos. Hansa signed the Cure. They voided their contract without releasing their material. Why? The suits didn't like the way they looked, the way they dressed and their insolent manner. It was punk music. Hansa Record's didn't have a clue. Steve pointed out Hansa missed a name act and a lot of money.

Steve Rowland: "Peter wanted pop hits. I wanted a more credible musical territory."

When the Cure released their debut single "Killing An Arab" in December 1978 they had Steve Rowland to thank for their place in the recording industry. Although this took place seven years after he finished producing **Coming From Reality**, it is an example of his continual ability to recognize highly commercial hits. Rowland was first and foremost interested in developing new and undiscovered talent. Rowland remembered eight years earlier when he had taken a hard line with the industry suits who failed to recognize new talent. He told the powers that be at Hansa his story of finding and recording Sixto Rodriguez' **Coming From Reality**. They told him it didn't sell. He told them it should have sold. The Cure story is an example of how over decades Rowland continually discovered new talent. Some he nurtured. Others he couldn't get in the front door. It's the record business. It frustrated him.

But 1970-1971 was a different time and Rowland prevailed in the great Rodriguez battle for a second album. He recognized he was also a gifted performer. He told anyone who would listen, he had to record Rodriguez' second album. It became an obsession. It was all due to listening to **Cold Fact**. But Rowland didn't know anything about Rodriguez or his place in the Sussex Record hierarchy. In 1970 Rodriguez was not on the industries commercial radar. Only Steve Rowland saw his potential.

Where Rodriguez Stood with Sussex Records

Clarence Avant and Sussex Records were not able to adequately promote **Cold Fact**. The music world was heading toward disco. No one cared about an obscure Detroit singer-songwriter. Enter Steve Rowland. The legendary producer was looking for new material. He found **Cold Fact**. He listened to it. He demanded Sussex Records honor the contract for a second album. They had lost money on Rodriguez. They eventually acquiesced to Rowland's demands. Thus, the **Coming From Reality** LP was born.

It took almost a month for Rowland to convince Clarence Avant Rodriguez was the next Bob Dylan. He also had the potential talent for a lucrative songwriting career. Avant thought about it for almost a month. Then he gave the go ahead signal.

Whether or not Avant realized the material in **Cold Fact** was as good as anything on the market remains an unanswered question. Was the protest song era waning? "Yes." Did Rowland have other pop, mainstream ideas for the second Rodriguez album: "Yes." There was little demand for anti-establishment music, but Rowland saw a romantic pop side to the Sugar Man's writing. That said, Steve viewed Rodriguez' writing as that of a pop philosopher.

Rowland remarked of Rodriguez: "After I listened to **Cold Fact**, I realized that Rodriguez' songwriting was more than anti-establishment." Steve saw the mellow, romantic side to Rodriguez' music. Everyone else in the music business missed it. He envisioned a wider market for Rodriguez as a romantic pop singer with an at times hard edge.

No one realized Rodriguez listened to Frank Sinatra, Lou Rawls or Cole Porter. He had a wide range of cover songs he loved to perform and for Rodriguez nothing was better than covering Frank Sinatra. He was more than a hippie oriented singer-songwriter dealing with peace and love. He was a consummate songwriter with varied themes. The road to **Coming From Reality** was a long and twisted one. It all began in Rowland's London apartment.

Steve Rowland in London: The Accidental Discovery of Rodriguez

At number two Chester Street in Belgravia London, Steve Rowland got up one morning to make coffee for his live in girl friend, Sally Farmiloe. He told her he needed to find new songs. He remarked he had an itch to produce a new artist. The career driven Rowland walked up to his second floor home office. He greeted his assistant. He was ready for another day's work. This would be the day he discovered Sixto Rodriguez. It was an overcast September morning. Rowland needed to catch up on some business before he went into his main downtown office. Steve liked to work part of the time at home where he had fewer distractions, and he didn't have to listen to the constant blather of those who talked about "the next big thing." "I had an assistant, Sandee Thong, who came to help me with the day's business," Rowland said. This is an insight into how many hours Rowland spent publicizing and promoting his record productions.

As he got his publicity releases in order, Rowland thought about the Family Dogg's future. Steve was career driven, as was Farmiloe. She was an actress, model and TV presenter. They were both driven, hard working personalities.

As the cold early autumn day broke Rowland left his apartment for the Carlin Music Office on Savile Row. It was the day he discovered Sixto Rodriguez. This accidental glance at an album cover began Rowland's infatuation with the Sugar Man's music.

Steve Rowland; "I went down to the Carlin office on the tube, I was looking for songs." His rock group, the Family Dogg, was going through personnel changes. Albert Hammond and Mike Hazlewood left for California. "I wanted to carry the Family Dogg on to hit records," Rowland continued. "I was looking for new songs for my group." It was this search for Family Dogg material that led Rowland to cover six Rodriguez' songs on the Family Dogg's second album.

When Rowland walked into the mammoth building where Carlin Music had offices on the second floor, he had business to discuss.

There was a lot on his mind. The Family Dogg had hits in the U. K. and Europe. But the group was unraveling. Rowland was upset he had to reconfigure the band. He also wanted a new producing project. Albert Hammond's defection to Los Angeles hurt the group's cohesion. The distractions of the Family Dogg didn't prevent Steve from continuing his quest for new hit makers.

Steve Rowland: "I went into Freddy Bienstock's office and on the corner of a table outside his office my eye caught an album cover with the picture of a strange looking guy with sunglasses sitting cross-legged on the floor. You couldn't tell who in the hell he was." This intrigued Rowland. He thought that he looked interesting. "I asked who is this?" Bienstock replied: "It's some American singer-songwriter, I haven't listened to it." Bienstock indicated there was little interest in Rodriguez' **Cold Fact**. One song made Rowland sit up and take notice. That song, "Like Janis," played a pivotal role in Rowland's resolve to record Rodriguez. But initially, the album cover to **Cold Fact** mesmerized Rowland.

Like Janis Does it for Rowland

He left Bienstock's office and went to a small room with a record player. He played one cut. "I always liked Janis Joplin and I saw a song that I thought was about her. Why not listen to it?" Rowland concluded.

When Rowland heard "Like Janis," he couldn't believe the song. He wanted to hear more of **Cold Fact**. He took the album home and listened to it over and over. "The first track I heard convinced me that this guy was a great writer," Rowland continued. "I couldn't believe the quality of the songs, the depth of the lyrics and the commercial possibilities." Rowland went back into the Carlin Music for the next couple of days to chat them up about Rodriguez. They looked at him like he was nuts. No one listened to **Cold Fact**. No one was interested. Rodriguez was not in Carlin Music's future plans.

Steve Rowland: "I went back into Freddy's office, I said I would love to get the chance to produce Rodriguez. There seemed to be total disinterest in a second album." Rowland realized that he would have to sell the idea of a second Rodriguez LP.

"They wanted the next big thing and that was not Rodriguez," Rowland concluded. Rowland was a major producer with a proven track record. He had some clout. A call went out to Clarence Avant. He was asked his opinion about a second Rodriguez album. Initially, Avant wasn't interested. Rowland was forceful about his desire to make a Rodriguez album. Avant and Bienstock talked. Most of the discussion was about Steve Rowland's producing talent.

"During the week that I was talking to Freddy, I had three charts hits with the Pretty Things, Dave Dee, Dozy, Beaky, Mick and Tich and the Family Dogg in one week at the same time on the U. K. charts. I waited to see if I got the gig." At the time Rowland was one of the hottest producers on the **New Musical Express**, the **Melody Maker** and the **Disc** charts.

It took almost a month to hear he would produce Rodriguez. One day Rowland was at home working with his assistant Sandee Thong on the next Family Dogg project. Then he got a phone call. Thong answered. She screamed.

"Steve! You got the deal."

"What deal?" Rowland asked. He looked bewildered.

"You are going to produce Rodriguez' second album."

"Great." Rowland was elated. He had listened to **Cold Fact** dozens of times. He had a commercial vision for Rodriguez. Rowland believed he would spend the next decade producing a Rodriguez album each year. One hit after another, Rowland thought.

It was this commercial vision that prompted Clarence Avant to approve a second album. They agreed that if anyone could break Rodriguez, it would be Rowland. Steve labeled Rodriguez "an undiscovered songwriting genius." He kept pressing to do the album.

"He's the next big thing," Rowland told anyone and everyone. Steve single handedly changed their minds.

Things looked good. But then disaster struck. Avant made a disastrous business deal with Neil Bogart of Buddah Records. It was a simple distribution agreement. It sunk Sussex Records. It appears Bogart never paid Sussex proper distribution royalties. Avant survived. Rodriguez didn't. This agreement torpedoed Rodriguez' career. Clarence Avant was one of the shrewdest businessmen in the music industry. He met his match in Neil Bogart.

Rowland Producing the Second Rodriguez Album

When Steve Rowland received the green light to produce Rodriguez' second album, he made himself a promise. He would allow the artist to interpret his material. No roadblocks! No restrictions! Rowland saw his job as one of providing the best musicians and production. He told the musicians: "Rodriguez will be the next best thing." He made sure that there was a hit, pop sound to **Coming From Reality**.

"I was making one hit after another, I thought this was a massive world wide hit artist who would be far bigger than any of the records I had produced," Rowland continued. "I was hoping that I would work solely with Rodriguez as I loved everything that he was writing. When **Coming From Reality** came out I was ecstatic, the packaging was so good."

Rowland took the album around for the people at Carlin Music to hear. They could have cared less. He was crestfallen. "Rodriguez' poetic influence is more like Leonard Cohen's, I knew it would sell," Rowland continued. "When it wasn't a hit I tried to forget about it, so did Rodriguez, he went back to Detroit and obscurity." Rowland didn't realize there were other forces in play.

There were circumstances that doomed Rodriguez' second album before it's release. Avant's distribution partnership with Bogart shifted marketing away from pop toward disco. This led to completely ignoring Rodriguez' music. Avant and Bogart were old style record marketing pros. When **Coming From Realty** was released in 1971 the singer-songwriter syndrome was waning. Disco was poised to take over the record business. For whatever reason, Rodriguez didn't fit into company marketing plans.

The irony is Rowland and Bogart became good friends. At the time, Bogart didn't talk about Rodriguez' music. "If I had known that Neil had knowledge of Rodriguez' songs, I would have said something." Rowland continued. "I still feel terrible I didn't recognize that fact."

Steve Rowland and Neil Bogart: Opposite Ends of The Muscial Spectrum

Steve Rowland got to know Neil Bogart when Buddah released the Family Dogg's 45 of "Riker's Island," which was the b-side of "Sweet America" (Buddah 2011143). It was released to sporadic play in New York and the Carolina Beach scene. It was 1972, and the dance music craze was taking over the Beach Music scene. It was not uncommon to hear Bill Deal and the Rhondels "I've Been Hurt" on the radio followed by the Family Dogg's "Rikers Island." The heavy radio airplay caught Bogart's attention. He liked everything about the Family Dogg. He began asking around. Soon he found out Hammond and Hazlewood had left the group. It was now the work of Steve Rowland. Bogart smelled hit records.

After Neil Bogart listened to "Rikers Island," he met Steve Rowland in London. It was 1972. Bogart was aware of Rowland's impressive producing talent. After he listened to the Family Dogg LP **The View From Rowland's Head**, he loved all the songs. Bogart realized the album contained six Rodriguez songs. One song caught his attention, "Advice To Smokey Robinson," which had not been recorded by Rodriguez.

Steve Rowland: "Rodriguez gave me his blessing to record it, he had no plans to record it." Bogart loved Rowland's version. He spent a great deal of time sitting in Steve's London home and hanging out in the coffee shops arguing "Rikers Island" was a sure hit. Steve was excited. The irony is they never talked about Sixto Rodriguez.

After Rowland spent some time talking with Rodriguez about his new Family Dogg album, they agreed Steve and his group might be able to garner commercial popularity for the Sugar Man's original songs. After Rowland finished **Coming From Reality**, Rodriguez suggested that he record, "Advice to Smokey Robinson." Rowland loved the idea. He had plans to record five other Rodriguez tunes.

The Family Dogg had popularity in the U. K., in Germany and in the Netherlands. The road to this popularity began in Spain when Rowland was making movies by day and playing music at night. When Steve Rowland conceived the Family Dogg in Madrid in 1964, he worked on perfecting the concept with Albert Hammond. It was the Mamas and Papas European style. In 1967, the Family Dogg came together in England. After Rowland worked extensively with vocalists Albert Hammond, Mike Hazlewood and Kristine Sparkle, the Family Dogg released its first solo LP in 1968, **Way of Life**. They had a number six hit on the UK Singles Chart as Jimmy Page, John Paul Jones, Robert Plant and John Bonham of Led Zeppelin fame teamed up with Elton John to add the hit studio sound. Although they only performed sporadically, the Family Dogg was a well-known U. K. and European band. They scored a number two hit in the Netherlands with "Sympathy."

Rowland worked on his breakthrough album for some time. The 1972 Family Dogg LP **The View From Rowland's Head** was to be their hit American LP. Neil Bogart was sure of it.

Steve Rowland: "I had already recorded Rodriguez and I had no idea that Neil Bogart was involved in distributing Rodriguez' albums. I met and hung out with Neil. He liked the songs on **The View From**

Rowland's Head. He wanted to meet me based on 'Riker's Island.' He loved the 45."

When Rowland and Bogart hung out in London. They had two things in common. They were career minded. They loved the ladies. "At that time," Rowland said. "Bogart had little interest in drugs. He was a label head intent on making money. That's it!"

Neil Bogart was working on a fledgling record label Casablanca, as well as a new act KISS. He displayed no interest in Rodriguez. His interest in talking with Rowland was as much to find out how to promote his new label and his new acts.

Steve Rowland: "Neil and I hung out a lot. He was a straight-ahead businessman doing a great job. He would come over to my Belgravia house we would have some tea or a glass of wine and talk musical changes."

Bogart believed he could break the Family Dogg in the American market. He told Rowland they were the "new Mamas and Papas." For the better part of a year they hung out when Bogart came to London.

After **The View From Rowland's Head** was released Rowland went on with his career. Rodriguez vanished to Detroit. Neil Bogart also vanished from Rowland's life. Bogart was the kind of guy who wanted to take business advantage of people. Steve knew the business end cold. Bogart quickly left London.

Rodriguez on Meeting Steve Rowland: A Friendship Develops

On meeting Steve Rowland, Rodriguez said: "I was recommended to work under him by a person named Neil Bogart." It appears that Rodriguez didn't realize that Bogart had one of the worst reputations in the music business. As a Buddah employee remarked: "It took Neil three dollars to make two dollars." He wasn't known allegedly for paying royalties. Bogart always said the expenses were too great. After all hookers and drugs didn't come cheap.

Meeting Steve Rowland was like the inner city meets the Hollywood hipster in London. "Steve Rowland is sensitive...he's a Hollywood cultured person," Rodriguez said. From day one Rodriguez loved working with Rowland. He continues to hold him in high esteem. He appreciated Rowland understood his songwriting and he was not attempting to change it.

Everyone agreed Rodriguez was an enormous talent. No one had a clue how to break him. Sussex Records had success with Bill Withers and the SOS Band. Most of their energy was placed behind promoting these artists. Dennis Coffey also had a top ten hit with the instrumental "Scorpio." This further took attention away from promoting Rodriguez.

In London with Rodriguez

Steve Rowland has great respect for Rodriguez' songwriting. He also believed his music needed the best sessions players. He brought in some of the finest session musicians for **Coming From Reality**. Chris Spedding was on guitar, Tony Carr on percussion, Phil Denny on keyboards and Colin Blunstone's guitar helped to craft the Rodriguez sound. The Herd's, Gary Taylor, added his unique bass. The backing musicians were arrangers, songwriters and multi-instrumentalists who worked with hundreds of hit acts. Rodriguez was in good hands. Steve Rowland hired and oversaw the process.

When Rodriguez arrived in London, Rowland took him to his apartment in the posh Chelsea area. He made sure Rodriguez was comfortable. They talked about songs, recording techniques and life in general. "I told Rodriguez that I loved his sound," Rowland continued. "He was modest."

The songs were recorded with Rodriguez and his guitar. Later, other instruments were added. "He was such a pro," Rowland recalled. "We did everything in one or two takes."

In the studio, Spedding's guitar and Carr's percussion translated Rodriguez's lyrical magic into a lilting musical opera. There is a sophisticated sound in the second album. Rowland employed instrumental breaks that were pop and romantic. There was less politics and more AOR radio friendly tunes. The Adult Oriented Radio sound took over the airwaves in the early 1970s. Rowland was one of this sound's best producers.

Rowland asked Rainy M. Moore where Rodriguez got his writing ideas? She replied: "He's coming from reality." This became the LPs title.

The Unique Sound from Lansdowne Studio

The Lansdowne Studio was one of the best in the U. K. It had a Cadac twenty-four-channel console board. Up to 1970 Lansdowne's EMI 12:2 tube desk was favored by English acts looking for a hit record. What interested Steve Rowland was the sixteen track Ampex-Telefunken M10. He wanted to record Rodriguez with a basic sound.

The key to Rowland's production genius was organization. He had everything ready for the musicians. There was a precise production schedule. There was never a question of too many takes. Rodriguez had a knack to lay down his songs quickly with little need for post-production.

Steve Rowland decided to record Rodriguez on sixteen tracks. "I wanted to preserve his original sound," Rowland recalled. He was successful. The sound on **Coming From Reality** is like Rodriguez is playing in your living room. After he arrived in London, Rodriguez met Rowland, and they went through acoustic versions of his songs. Rowland sat stunned. He had found a million dollar artist.

Steve Rowland: "The main thing that I wanted to do was to get the clarity of the voice right." That was more important than anything to Rowland. He believed this could cement the Sugar Man's songwriting reputation. "In 'Cause," Rowland remarked, "Rodriguez' songwriting brilliance is obvious." Rowland said Rodriguez was a minimalist. "There was no overproduction," Rowland continued. "I hated the bells and whistles that some producers employed. So did Sixto."

While in London, Rodriguez kept a low profile. He was invited to all the hip clubs, to the parties and to meet the Beatles and the Rolling Stones. He preferred a quiet night in the small flat off Eaton Square. "He was very private," Rowland continued. "He is a reflective intellectual."

In the Studio with Steve Rowland

"I looked at the songs that Rodriguez was about to record," Rowland continued. "They were all about his life. Then we talked about 'Climb Up On My Music' as the initial single. Rodriguez had a clear picture of where his music was going." Rowland loved the stories and the romantic direction. He was determined to make it right.

The Lansdowne Studio, which was established in 1957, was booked for Rodriguez' sessions. When it opened Lansdowne was London's premier jazz recording venue. As rock and roll emerged, it became the technologically most advanced London studio. The early equipment was built to specification with advice from legendary producer Joe Meek. In 1957, Meek engineered Lonnie Donegan's "Cumberland Gap," and it reached number one on the U. K. charts. The hits just kept coming.

The studio was constructed in an apartment building with the recording equipment in the basement. The area had once been an indoor swimming pool. When legendary British producer, Joe Meek, supervised the early set up of the recording equipment, he was excited about the potential echo.

The clarity of sound was the reason Rowland selected Lansdowne Studio. He hoped to achieve the same pop sound his fellow producer Mickey Most was using to dominate the U. K. charts. As Rodriguez prepared to go into the studio in 1970, Lansdowne Studio began a major remodeling. This not only made production easier, the sound was even more magnificent.

Steve Rowland Talks About the Tracks on Coming From Reality

When Rowland finished mixing **Coming From Reality**, he sat in a chair in the Lansdowne office. He smiled. He had a hit album. There would be more to come with Rodriguez. He envisioned a decade of hits.

As he cut the Rodriguez album, there was one track in retrospect that stood out. It was "Cause." The reason is a simple one. Sussex Records dropped Rodriguez from the label two weeks before Christmas. "Cause I lost my job two weeks before Christmas," Rodriguez sang. "And I talked to Jesus at the Sewer...While the rain drank champagne." The imagery is one where Rodriguez predicts the end of his recording career. "For me, 'Cause' had a special meaning. It ended Rodriguez' career. I couldn't believe it," Rowland said. As he looked back upon the Sugar Man's songs in **Coming From Reality**, he had an epiphany. He had a feeling the LP presented a stark realism. Rowland thought it would take some time to connect with the general public. He was right. It took forty plus years.

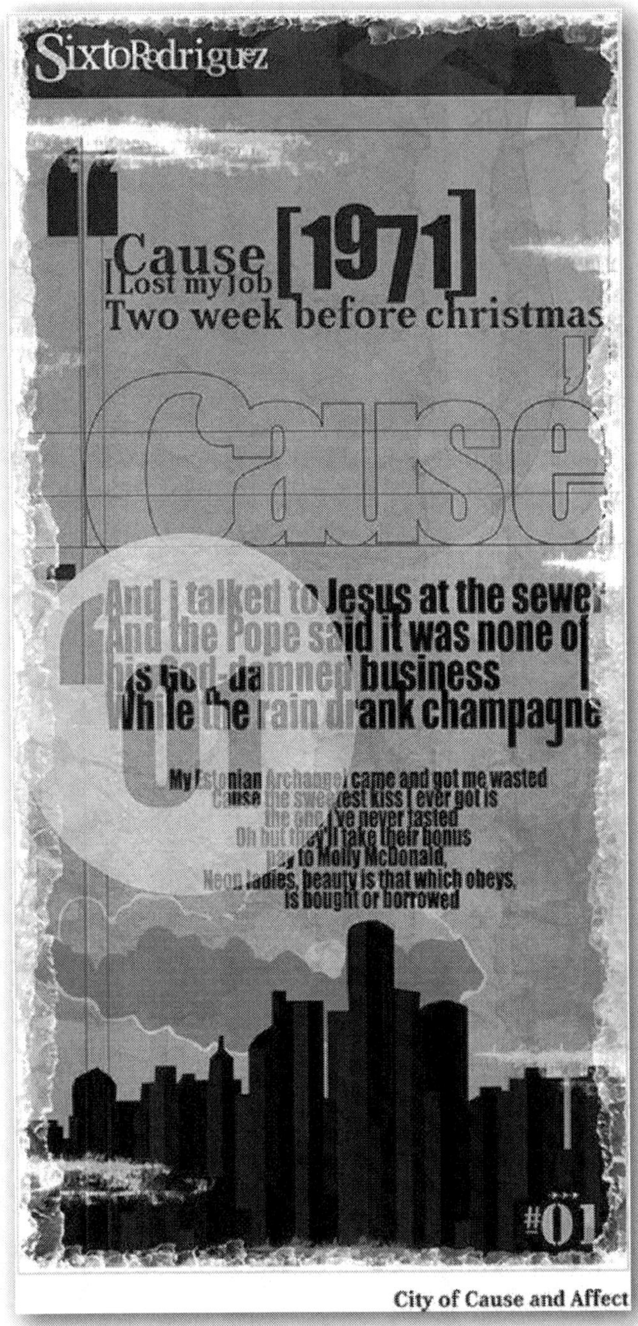

City of Cause and Affect

The Coming From Reality Album Covers in South Africa

Coming From Reality has had more releases than anyone imagined. They all came without royalties. There are seven different releases with a variation of the original cover. The original American release **Coming From Reality** in November 1971 led to a 1972 release in South Africa. Those two LPs are exactly the same. Then the funny business began. This is where the lost royalty trail begins. The end! That is to be determined.

In 1978, **Coming From Reality** was re-titled **After The Fact**. This obvious ploy was to cash in on **Cold Fact's** popularity. Then in 1996 the two albums were bundled for a South African release using the **Coming From Reality** cover. In 2002 it was released once again. In 2005, the two albums were remastered for release. Someone was making money. It wasn't Rodriguez. It wasn't Steve Rowland. It wasn't Clarence Avant.

Finally, in 2009, the Light In The Attic version of **Coming From Reality** ended the bogus releases. Rodriguez and Rowland received royalties from this LP. "My royalties came quickly and on time twice a year," Steve Rowland observed. "It was the first time I was paid for producing **Coming From Reality**."

The Lyrical Beauty of Coming From Reality

When **Coming From Reality** was released in November 1971, it had stupefying lyrical beauty. When he begins with "Climb Up On My Music," Rodriguez preaches: "Just climb up on my music." The message came through as a clear one. "My songs will set you free" was the Sugar Man's message. The guitar solo provided by Chris Spedding brings an ethereal dreamy tone to the song and the sound is complimented by Phil Dennys' jazz piano. The ride is an exciting one.

The songs, all originals, differ in themes. Rodriguez surprises the listener with an autobiographical “A Most Disgusting Song,” in which he traces the early Detroit venues where he developed his music. The lyrical imagery is brilliant as Rodriguez croons “The local diddy bop pimp comes in…Acting limber he sits down with a grin… Next to a girl that has never been chaste…the bartender wipes a smile off his face.” That says it all about playing in, drinking in and hanging out in Detroit’s nastiest clubs. There are Dylanesque images when he writes: “The delegates cross the floor. Curtsy and promenade through the doors.”

Then he lapses into a romantic song “I Think of You,” which tells the story of a lost love. “Of the dreams, we dreamt together, Of the love we vowed would never melt like snowflakes in the sun” tells the story in brilliant lyrics. The romantic side of Rodriguez’ songwriting takes over in “I Think of You.” The lyrics suggest: “The change you have made in me defines love.” This is a reflection on his life. This song also is a comment on fledgling love and a young woman who made changes in Rodriguez. Only Rainy M. Moore can tell us the real story. No one else knows.

“Heikki’s Suburbia Bus Tour,” which is not only a parody of the Beatles “Magical Mystery Tour,” follows this song but it is also a tale of suburban Detroit. “Heikki’s Suburbia Bus Tour” is about a wild group of motorcycle riders touring and pointing fingers at suburban squares. Eva Rodriguez said the motorcycle club known as the Penetrators was responsible for this suburban jaunt.

Steve Rowland wanted a sense of romance, a break in the production and some ethereal music to calm the listener. He took Jimmy Horowitz aside to sketch out in word form what he wanted.

“Sandrevan Lullaby-Lifestyles” demonstrates how far Rodriguez’ lyrical and musical maturity had grown since his first album. Rodriguez incorporates his daughter’s names in the song. Jimmy Horowitz’ violin sets the song apart.

"To Whom It May Concern" is a brilliant Top 40 song. When it was released as a 45 backed with "I Think Of You" (Sussex 234) it failed to chart. This songs biting commentary on America's social-economic failures make the "Lifestyles" segment of the LP special. No one seemed to notice.

The next song, "It Started Out So Nice" continues the lyrical strength of Rodriguez' writing. It weaves a plaintive tale of finding happiness. Such phrases as a "pumpkin oval moon" and "celestial canopy" highlight Rodriguez' sophisticated use of language.

Rodriguez is a master at writing pop, Top 40 hits. It is ironic that none of these songs charted. "Halfway Up The Stairs" is a sure hit record; no one knew how to promote it. **Coming From Reality** evokes the disappointment and despair that went with Rodriguez' lack of sales and chart success. Thank God, LITA's Matt Sullivan found **Cold Fact** used.

Why Coming From Reality Didn't Sell

The themes and direction in **Coming From Reality** were different from **Cold Fact**. Why didn't the second album sell? There are two reasons. First, Neil Bogart wanted Rodriguez to change a line in one song "And the Pope said it was none of his God damned business." When Bogart listened to this line, he demanded Rodriguez change it. He refused. Bogart pulled the publicity stops out. Second, Clarence Avant and Sussex Records had serious financial problems. The royalties from Bill Withers' "Lean On Me" kept the label alive for some time. Avant clearly was out of his depths with new artists. The IRS closed Sussex. After **Coming From Reality** was released, Avant kept the copyright to Rodriguez' material just in case it ever sold. It did!

At the time **Coming From Reality** was prepared for release Bill Withers was taking up most of Sussex's promotional budget. So Clarence Avant told his cover photographer to shoot the LP photos quickly and spend as little money as possible. Ironically, the cover for **Coming From Reality** is a masterpiece.

Shooting the Album Cover: Coming From Reality

It was a well-known photographer, Hal Wilson, who traveled to Detroit to shoot the album cover. As Wilson and Rodriguez walked around the city they came upon some tenements. These run down houses looked like the perfect backdrop for an LP cover.

Some critics have asked: "Did the shoe on the album cover have some deeper meaning?" The press was all over the story. Rodriguez observed: "We walked around Detroit and saw the house. Debris was lying around and the shoe was nearby. I took it and placed it beside mine." Then Wilson shot seven different pictures of Rodriguez and the album cover was complete.

Rodriguez loved to show the inner workings of the Motor City to visitors. This trait persists to the present day. The Sugar Man is a born and bred Detroit icon. When Milton Sincoff received the pictures he put together the LP cover at Buddah Records.

The Critics Weigh in on Coming From Reality and One Release after Another

On September 6, 1971 **Billboard** recommended, "Cause," "Climb Up On My Music" and "To Whom It May Concern" for airplay. **Cash Box** on January 1, 1972 said Rodriguez was an original artist with vocal hints of Jose Feliciano, Donovan and Cat Stevens. The **Cash Box** review observed Rodriguez had a sound perfect for FM radio. The review commented "Heikki's Suburbia Bus Tour" was a striking touch of Donovan's "Season of the Witch." **Cash Box** called "A Most Disgusting Song," a "long FM narrative."

In 1972, A & M Records released **Coming From Reality** in South Africa with a great deal of publicity. The result was strong sales. It was also released in Australia on A & M. In 1979 the Australian Blue Goose Music label released the album. It charted immediately at twenty-four in Australia's album listing.

Coming From Reality had a long life, as the 1996 Polygram release suggests. One wonders where the royalties went. The liner notes to the South African **Coming From Reality** release are particularly interesting. Stephen "Sugar" Segerman and Mad Andy Harrod wrote brilliant liner notes. They speculated: "If ever there is an air of intrigue and mystery around a pop artist, it is around the artist known as Rodriguez." Not only did these carefully crafted 1996 liner notes to Rodriguez' reissue correct past mistakes, the information was the first accurate account of the Sugar Man. "So a mystery was born and a mysterious lost album was sought after," Segerman concluded. This ended the liner notes but the story was just beginning. It was April 1996 when Mad Andy and Segerman wrote the liner notes, they had no idea they had taken the first step in igniting the Rodriguez phenomena.

As the World Ignored Rodriguez: The Phenomena Builds Slowly

After Rodriguez arrived in South Africa for his triumphant 1998 concerts the music industry continued to release his material. Someone was making a lot of money. It wasn't Rodriguez. Clarence Avant's name came up only when a record label mailed a check. There were rumors the money was sent to London. There were rumors the money was sent to Los Angeles. No one knows the truth. When Craig Bartholomew-Strydom called a London office the telephone had been disconnected. It was a weird time. The Rodriguez material continued to sell. He received nothing in the way of royalties. There were rumors not concrete facts. That is the problem with the story. Unconfirmed rumors and misleading facts dominate. No wonder Rodriguez is a bit skeptical of the music business.

In October 2002, PT Music South Africa re-released **Coming From Reality**. It was a rush job. The CD sounded like it was re-mastered in a toilet. The sound was dreadful and the packaging atrocious. But PT Music was a legitimate label. PT Music continued to release Rodriguez' material. In 2005, **Coming From Reality** was re-mastered, the sound dramatically improved, and it was released with extensive liner notes.

The best re-release of **Coming From Reality** came from the Seattle based Light In The Attic label. On May 5, 2009 Light In The Attic released the CD with bonus cuts. The bonus tracks were "Can't Get Away," "Street Boy" and "I'll Slip Away." The sound was beautifully re-mastered, the liner notes were excellent and Rodriguez was paid. As the Light In The Attic publicity release suggested: "Sixto Rodriguez....Still coming from reality and bigger than ever before."

In 2012, as the **Searching For Sugar Man** documentary created the Rodriguez cult and his commercial re-emergence, Sony Music in South Africa released **Coming From Reality**. Sony was determined to pay royalties. The question of future royalties was no longer an issue. Past royalties continued to be a problem. But, as Clarence Avant said to Malik Bendjelloul: "As far as I am concerned Rodriguez never happened."

Steve Rowland's Secret Weapon

Everyone describes Rodriguez as the next Bob Dylan. Rowland realized this, but he also saw another window into the Michigan singer's repertoire. There was a Frank Sinatra side to Rodriguez. Rowland brought it out beautifully in "I Think Of You." It is Rodriguez' ability to cover a ballad with precision and purity that paid tribute to

Rowland's producing talent. Not surprisingly, when Rodriguez re-emerged as a concert artist, he covered Frank Sinatra songs.

What Rowland accomplished in **Coming From Realty** was to blend the rough edged contemporary political criticism in Rodriguez' original songs with the lyrical beauty that makes him a pop crooner. It was a balancing act in **Coming From Reality** tied together with the song "Sandrevan Lullaby-Lifestyles."

"I tried to show both sides of Rodriguez when he recorded the album, I think we succeeded," Rowland concluded.

The Hidden Factors in Coming From Reality

There are influences on **Coming From Reality** that have gone unrecognized. Jimmy Horowitz put together the instrumental interlude in "Sandrevan Lullaby-Lifestyles." His violin makes this smooth, soft interlude a romantic break in the music that is dreamy and breathtaking. Phil Dennys completed some of the key arrangements. The twenty-six year old English guitarist Chris Spedding is not only a versatile guitarist, he has a vision for what the artist is attempting in the studio. Spedding's guitar was the glue holding Rodriguez' songs together. **Coming From Reality** is not only highlighted by Spedding's guitar genius that made the songs stand out, but his lush, pop direction made for chart friendly songs. Ironically, Spedding released his debut solo album **Song Without Words** in 1970 with great anticipation. Like Rodriguez, Spedding's debut album didn't sell. It did, however, begin his legendary solo career.

The hidden factors in **Coming From Reality** include the musicians, the studio comfort, the arrangements, the freedom given to Rodriguez and the time spent layering the music behind the lyrical beauty that is the Sugar Man. These factors highlight Steve Rowland's producing genius.

Coming From Reality provided another window into Rodriguez' unique talents. But he wasn't through in the studio. In the mid-1970s he continued to record sporadically. He wanted to record a third album. Fast-forward to 2017 and word in the Rodriguez camp is he has nine new songs and he is ready to finally place that third album in the can. Hopefully!

Steve Rowland, Malik Bendjelloul and Britanny Huckabee

Six

How 1971 Prevented Coming From Reality from Charting: Steve Rowland and Producer Cred

"All the English ever talked about was 'cred, cred, cred.' It drove me crazy. I never talked about it but everything I did had credibility. This drove the snobby producers who were little more than errand boy's nuts. I was independent and I did it my way."

Steve Rowland

"Best be yourself, imperial, plain and true."

Elizabeth Barrett Browning

"Everybody thought I had it easy. I didn't have it easy. Nepotism was the big killer. Because I was the son of a top MGM film director no one took me seriously. Nepotism always put the breaks on."

Steve Rowland

When Steve Rowland outlined how he would produce **Coming From Reality**, he had a plan. He would tell a story much like the movies he acted in and his dad directed. Why is this important? In 1971 most producers worked for record companies who dictated the album's direction. Rowland refused these assignments. He was an independent contractor. If he did not like the way a session was planned, if the session became oppressive, or if there was a problem, he walked away from the project. The major labels didn't want him to walk away. As he produced one hit after another in a variety of genres, his producing touch was gold. He also had an excellent grasp of the business. His projects came in under budget or on the dime.

In London many producers worked as little more than session set up people. Others like George Martin with the Beatles, Rodger Bain with Black Sabbath, Americans like Shel Talmy producing the Kinks and the Who among others and Richard Perry who produced Harry Nilsson in London were equally creative and independent minded. Although the twenty-nine year old Glyn Johns was a record company employee, he was one of the respected in-house producers. All of these talented people produced hits independent of the labels. But they were the exception not the rule. Steve Rowland was in this school of producers. The record companies often didn't publicize artists with independent producers.

What made the London music scene exciting in 1971 is it was a crossroads for excellent studio musicians who would work for the minimal studio fee. Chris Spedding is a good example of a guitarist on **Coming From Reality**. He was a much in demand session musician who played on Rodriguez' second album. Why? Because he believed in Rowland's production techniques. He also began a storied solo career.

What role did the session musicians play? This was a key to Rodriguez' album. They translated his music and lyrics into a defined commercial package. There was another factor impacting the second Rodriguez album. The music was changing. No one was more aware of this than Steve Rowland. He watched the trends and crafted Rodriguez' music into a pop commercial direction.

What changed in the music industry? It was the emergence of new artists, new sounds and new directions. Rowland took all this in as he produced **Coming From Reality**. One barometer of musical change was David Bowie's **Hunky Dory** album. It wasn't a blockbuster, but it was a portent of things to come artistically and commercially.

Why David Bowie's Hunky Dory Indicated Change

Hunky Dory is not one of David Bowie' best selling albums. But it is important as a forecaster of musical change making it difficult for Rodriguez' songs in **Coming From Reality** to hit the top of the charts. But Rodriguez was more than aware of Bowie's impact.

How did Bowie change the rock and roll culture? There was a reference to space travel in "Life On Mars." There was an oblique Andy Warhol reference. Bowie had been to America and the experience created songs with a view of the newly emerging club life.

When RCA completed Bowie's **Hunky Dory** in mid-November 1971 the music world changed. Bowie, according to **the New York Times**, was "the most intellectually brilliant man yet to choose the long-playing record." That, of course, was sheer nonsense. There is no doubt Bowie was a gifted performer and songwriter. He couldn't hold a candle to Rodriguez' lyrical beauty. But RCA had money to burn and Clarence Avant burned up the road relocating to Los Angeles.

It wasn't until the middle of December 1971 that **Hunky Dory** was released, but for Rodriguez and others like him it killed his record. **Rock Magazine** labeled Bowie "the most singularly gifted artist creating music today." This quote was along side a page ad from RCA boosting Bowie's new album.

Hunky Dory wasn't a massive chart hit. In fact, earlier in his career, Mercury let Bowie loose from his contract, and he was signed by RCA. The album didn't sell in America. So how did this influence Rodriguez? What Bowie did was to change the landscape of commercial rock music. The singer-songwriters weren't gone but they were on their last legs. RCA had the worst reputation and the sorriest roster of rock stars. They put everything behind Bowie. The self-promotion and self-awareness Bowie demonstrated should have been a lesson to every fledgling rock star.

When Bowie paid tribute to Bob Dylan, Andy Warhol and the Velvet Underground, he altered the landscape of rock and roll music. The fantasy world replaced the political song. Rodriguez' "The Establishment Blues" was as dated as a Glenn Miller record.

Steve Rowland Finished Coming From Reality and Why it Didn't Chart Remains A Mystery

Steve Rowland finished **Coming From Reality**. He did some mixing. There were others involved, but Steve had no doubt this was a gold record. He told a close friend he would produce a new Sugar Man album each year. In thirty years they would retire. They would both be rich. Respect! Acclaim! Historical veracity! These were the words Rowland and Rodriguez were ready to hear. It didn't happen. No one knows why. The answer is a simple one. It was 1971. The time was over for a Bob Dylan type songwriter who wrote more like Leonard Cohen and sounded like Jose Feliciano.

How did 1971 differ from previous musical years? It appeared Sixto Rodriguez would have a clear path to stardom. In 1971 David Bowie, Rod Stewart, Led Zeppelin, Pink Floyd, Van Morrison, Elton John and Joni Mitchell became mega stars. They all had worked some years in the industry. The forces of the marketplace blessed them in 1971 as musical trends changed. These trends spelled doom for the Sugar Man.

Sixto Rodriguez didn't change. His talent was obvious. It was the industry, shifting public taste, the fickle fate of history, and the rise of other cult artists that derailed his embryo career. The major labels torpedoed Rodriguez' path to stardom. How? They created promotional campaigns to develop "creative artists." This was a category Sussex did not use for the Sugar Man. Warner Brothers placed its artists in a creative box. They employed the "cult artist" label to describe Van Morrison. The term allowed them to forgo heavy promotion on Van The Man. He left the label. It was demeaning to Morrison. It diminished his original talent. No one fought Warner Brothers harder than Van Morrison. When Van Morrison's album **His Band And Street Choir** burst upon the scene the hit record attached to it, "Domino," made him seem like a new artist. He had sold consistently since 1967 with Them and as a solo artist. The term or tag cult artist prompted Morrison to leave Warner Brothers with bad feelings. He also had an empty pocket book. The majority of artists left with an empty pocketbook. The justification from the record companies for their mistreatment of artists, stealing their songs and cheating them out of royalties is an old story. But it is a never-ending one.

When Bobbie Gentry threw up her middle finger at her label and fled into obscurity, it was as much a protest of conditions in the business, as it was to protect her artistic integrity. It wasn't just the artist who complained. The managers, the roadies, the record distributors and those who owned the record stores bitched constantly about a business that made the Mafia look honest. Criminals, assholes and wannabes ran the record business. This is what the private, mild mannered, non-assuming Sixto Rodriguez faced in 1970-1971.

This was not the case with Steve Rowland. He was a tiger. He wouldn't allow the industry to abuse him. A good example of his expertise is seen in his production company, which collected his royalties in a timely manner. Even with Rowland's business expertise he was from time to time cheated. He produced the gold record **Jerry Lee Lewis: Live In London** in 1973, and he didn't receive a royalty statement. Mercury told him the album didn't sell. It went gold in the U.S., silver in the U. K. and gold in Europe. Rowland persisted. In 2017 he received a seven hundred dollar royalty check. The industry told anyone and everyone to make their money in concert. As Rowland pointed out, this was not possible for the producer. This was the industry Sixto Rodriguez fought with and lost the early battle. He has won the war. Royalties now come in on a timely manner.

What the Billboard Review Tells us About Coming From Reality

On November 6, 1971 **Billboard** reviewed **Coming From Reality**. While the review was a positive one, the comments comparing the Sugar Man to Jose Feliciano and Bill Withers killed his chances for commercial success. He wasn't a Mexican American Feliciano, and he certainly wasn't an African American balladeer like Withers. His songs were unique. His vocal style was different. His performing mantra was exciting. What happened? The answer is a simple one. The changes in rock music, the industry business standards, the marketing of new and diverse styles and the slow but steady decline of the singer-songwriter spelled doom for **Coming From Reality**. There was another problem. That was the release in November 1971 of Harry Nilsson's **Nilsson Schmilsson**, which captivated the Beatles and much of hip London.

There was another trend that hurt Rodriguez. It was album sales. They declined. In 1971-1972 there was a lull in vinyl sales. In the cinema it was the year of what film critic Vincent Camby labeled the "blank gaze." With movies like "A Clock Work Orange," "The French Connection" and "Carnal Knowledge," there was no room for the Sugar Man's post hippie dream songs. It was a new day commercially. Rodriguez didn't fit into the mold. Frank Zappa's Mother's of

Invention were on the road selling their version of the counter culture. This was another competitor that might have been from Mars compared to Rodriguez' plaintive ballads. The Fillmore East and West in New York and San Francisco featured three hard rocking bands most nights. None of this was close to the Sugar Man's sound. He might as well have been playing on Mars.

When the Velvet Underground, Lou Reed and Detroit's Iggy Pop and The Stooges worked the concert circuit there was no room for Sixto Rodriguez. He appeared to be from another time. Trends, hip attitudes, the disinterested record labels and the lack of an impact rock and roll press hurt Rodriguez' chances for commercial success.

Then the world came to an end in late 1971 when Don McLean's "American Pie" said that rock and roll died with Buddy Holly. When he opened for Laura Nyro at a college show in Philadelphia, McLean played "American Pie" for the first time in concert. He hadn't recorded it. He was brought into the studio and after a great deal of production "American Pie" was released in November 1971, as **Coming From Reality** had strong critical praise and minimal sales. "American Pie" was an eight-minute single looking back on rock and roll history. The Sugar Man was once again left out in the cold. The Rolling Stones benefitted from the McLean song as the Stones compilation album **Hot Rocks, 1964-1971** went platinum. Elvis Presley was also back performing in Las Vegas. He also was touring the country re-establishing his brilliant concert legacy. The changes in the music industry from 1969, when Rodriguez began planning and recording **Cold Fact**, until **Coming From Reality** was released in 1971, made it difficult for him to publicize, promote and take his music to the next level. He still wanted time in the studio. He would have one last gasp, but the two albums were the beginning and end of his recording career. The changes in 1971 placed him in a strange position. He wasn't a new artist. He wasn't an old artist. He was in an artistic limbo.

Most of the musicians who became superstars in 1971 didn't measure up as songwriters to Sixto Rodriguez. They were mostly in their twenties to early thirties when the Rod Stewart's, the Led Zeppelin's and the David Bowie's created a second generation of rock and roll. Sixto Rodriguez was caught in the middle. He was the child of both eras. That was not good for commercial purposes.

What Did 1971 in Rock Music do to Rodriguez' Career

Everyone who has viewed **Searching For Sugar Man** shakes his or her head about one vexing question. Why didn't Rodriguez become a major rock star? The answer is 1971 produced more classic rock albums than at any time in history. Carol King's **Tapestry** set a record for number of weeks on the **Billboard** chart. The Rolling Stones **Sticky Fingers** and Santana's two albums brought a cavalcade of press for their sounds. The Who's LP, **Who's Next** was praised as the influx of albums exploded in the marketplace.

As the Beatles split up, the Doors **LA Woman** album topped the charts, and artists like Marvin Gaye, thanks to Harry Balk, went platinum with "What's Going On." Balk printed up thousands of extra copies. Berry Gordy was in Europe. He told Balk he would be fired. The Gaye record went to number one on the **Billboard** pop chart. Balk was promoted and given a six-figure bonus. These records created a diverse musical audience and it was one far from the Sugar Man. In Rodriguez' hometown Iggy Pop and the Stooges won the buzz guitar sound sweepstakes. They became a big concert draw without hits. Joni Mitchell kept the singer songwriter concept alive. George Harrison broke away from the Beatles for "The Concert For Bengla Desh." The new albums, the publicity for the rock aristocracy centered on former Beatle Paul McCartney and the global popularity of Led Zeppelin created too many musical choices. In 1971 the rock and roll world submerged the obscure Mexican American singer. His stardom arrived forty-one years later.

Sixto Rodriguez and Steve Rowland

Seven

The Last Gasp in the Studio and Touring Australia: Why Zev Eizik is a Hero

"Music is a living art. The thing is, we recreated that night. The thing is, the last night is the best night, too. Like you do with the David Letterman show, a 25-piece orchestra. I did the Jay Leno Show with a 20-piece orchestra and they again take it apart say, and put a piccolo there...so again, it's a moving kind of manageable art. It's living. It's moveable."

Rodriguez

"Try not to be one of the people on whom nothing is lost!"

Henry James, The Art of Fiction

By the mid-1970s, Rodriguez' career was on hold. The irony is as Sussex released him from his contract, other musicians were discovering his songs. In 1975, Delroy Wilson, a Jamaican ska and reggae singer, covered Rodriguez' "Halfway Up the Stairs." Another Jamaican vocalist, Ken Boothe, covered "Silver Words." Both artists were big in the U. K. as a small group of record collectors began searching out Rodriguez' albums.

The reggae singers loved the lilting vocals and Rodriguez' smooth musical accompaniment. It was symptomatic with the reggae tradition. When Trojan Records released a compilation CD, **Blood And Fire-Niney And Friends, 1971-1972**, one reviewer mentioned Rodriguez' songs. That began the earliest underground movement in the U. K. for Rodriguez' embryo fans. Steve Barrow, who wrote the liner notes, observed that Ken Boothe's hit "Silver Words" was a Rodriguez composition. That reference led to other performers and fans establishing the Sugar Man's small, but committed, fan base.

The irony is reggae artists took credit for the songwriting. When "Silver Words" was released the songwriting credits were Boothe/ Brown. Dennis Browne and Ken Boothe said they copyrighted the song and when they were challenged about their dubious songwriting credits, they backed off and evaded questions. The operative word is they could not write their names. The question they were asked was did Sixto Rodriguez write the song? "Man it be possible," Ken Boothe told a London journalist. This is another royalty issue that no one has addressed. It creates another set of questions.

Although he no longer had a record contract, Rodriguez continued to perform where and when he could. At times the various Detroit bars advertised Rodriguez as signed to a major label. The ads for these shows drew a large Detroit crowd. As 1975 ended, Rodriguez played fewer of the Detroit dive bars. He remarried. He continued to raise a family. He regularly purchased **Billboard**. He read it voraciously. He was still interested in and kept up with the music business.

Rodriguez: The Last Gasp in the Studio, 1972-1976

For all the criticism and vitriolic comments directed at Sussex label head Clarence Avant, he had Rodriguez' best interest at heart. He believed the Sugar Man had a future. He decided to bankroll one more mini-recording session. What was the importance of the Pampa Studio recording sessions? The main significance is the Sugar Man cut his last three songs.

At the Pampa sessions Mike Theodore experimented with flutes, a steel guitar and he had a vision for pop, chart friendly tunes. "Street Boy" with its plaintive wail into the inner city, is lyrically and emotionally a window into the Sugar Man's early life. Theodore's string arrangement makes "Street Boy" a confessional Top 40 hit. It didn't happen. It is the only Rodriguez song containing a back up voice, that of Jim Gold of Gallery fame, and the sessions producing the three songs say as much of Theodore's ability to produce Rodriguez as it does about his songwriting.

Avant hired Theo-Coff to produce Rodriguez's songs. Mike Theodore was in the forefront of the Pampa Studio sessions. The records are not clear on what Rodriguez recorded. Nor is there any mention of how many times he went into the studio. The date for the first sessions was in the spring or early summer of 1972, and there is mention of an abortive 1975 session. There is also anecdotal evidence the Sugar Man was in the studio in 1976 with new songs. But again the records are sketchy and nothing can be confirmed. Rodriguez was in and out of local Detroit studios from 1972 to 1976. That's it! There is a smattering of new songs. Nothing was finalized.

One thing is certain. Mike Theodore produced the last gasp in the studio. He booked the studio making sure it fit into the Sugar Man's nighttime schedule. He made sure Rodriguez had a slow and easy session. It worked. The Pampa recordings produced three classic Sugar Man songs. Theodore and Rodriguez worked very well together. He understood how the Sugar Man operated in the studio. The experience was a pleasant one for both of them. Rodriguez continued to think of a full time musical career. He saw the odds. The Sugar Man retreated to day jobs.

This last gasp in the studio convinced Rodriguez to consider putting his musical career on hold. He had a family. He had responsibility. He hated the teen dances that Harry Balk and Clarence Avant wanted him to frequent to sell his records. He was a grown man with interests in philosophy and literature. He was not interested in teenage nonsense. He was committed to writing songs and recording his material. From 1972 to 1976, he didn't give up his musical dreams; he pursued them at the dive bar level. He went into the studio playing low-level Detroit gigs to record his last songs. The streets and his nascent career influenced his writing. When he cut "Street Boy" and "Can't Get Away" the songs told his story in detail.

In July 1975, when Rodriguez walked into Detroit's Pampa Studio with Mike Theodore, he was ready to give it one more shot. In "Can't Get Away" the Sugar Man sings, "I vowed I would break away. Listened to the Sunday actors. But all they would ever say. That you can't get away from it." That said it all. He wanted out of the commercial mainstream. He left for a normal life.

Rodriguez remarked Pampa Lanes was a strange recording studio. It was located in the Pampa Lanes Bowling Alley. Bob Seger recorded **Smokin Ops** at Pampa. Gladys Knight and the Pips and Burt Bacharach, among other artists, cut songs important to advancing their early careers in this primitive studio.

It is unclear what Rodriguez recorded at Pampa other than the three songs "Street Boy," "Can't Get Away" and a remake of "I'll Slip Away." The Pampa Lanes sessions provided a strange ending to Rodriguez' recording career. The first song he cut for Harry Balk's Impact label "I'll Slip Away" was the last he cut for Mike Theodore. The three Pampa

Lane tunes made it to the market. They were included on the **Coming From Reality** reissue from Light In The Attic. This made the album a special one for collectors and Sugar Man aficionados.

Australia and at His Best

In 1977, Rodriguez' album **At His Best** was released in Australia with the bonus cuts. They were not re-mastered very well. They sounded terrible. Then the Blue Goose label licensed the rights to his back catalogue from Clarence Avant. Phil Birnbaum at Blue Goose claimed Clarence Avant agreed to license Rodriguez in South Africa. I found just the opposite. Avant wasn't interested in licensing to an area with relatively small sales. It was a waste of his time. Birnbaum eventually secured a contract. It didn't come easily.

There is no doubt Rodriguez was a bankable act in Australia. Zev Eizik also was in the mix negotiating in May 1978 to release **Cold Fact** through RCA. The next year Eizik licensed **Coming From Reality** to Blue Goose. In 1978 Rodriguez sued Eizik in an Eastern Michigan Court. The case is sealed. It may have been a lawsuit over the record released and it may have been for promotion. There is no evidence to support either conclusion.

At His Best mixed eleven tracks from Rodriguez's two albums. "I'll Slip Away" was a re-recording of the 1967 single. The album also contained the two previously unreleased bonus tracks "Can't Get Away" and "Street Boy." These rarities prompted early Rodriguez collectors to praise the reissue. The Sugar Man's legend was building.

When the material was released in South Africa it went platinum. By 1978, Rodriguez was an established music figure in Australia and South Africa. America was still waiting to discover the Sugar Man. He went off each day to work in the slowly declining Motor City. There is anecdotal evidence he collected small royalties.

The reviews for **At His Best** were excellent ones. The references to the Sugar Man's cynicism and insights blended with his high tenor voice to create an aura much like Bob Dylan's music. The curious aspect of **At His Best** is the songs were credited to Jesus Rodriguez. No one explained why.

When Zev Eizik released **Coming From Reality** in Australia for Blue Goose one reviewer wrote: "Something in between the two albums obviously changed his point of view because **Coming From Reality** consists mainly of love songs." Roger Crosthwaite's review predicted big things for Rodriguez. No one else paid attention. The Sugar Man continued to have a career. No one realized it.

Rodriguez Did Have A Career After He Retired

Rodriguez is fond of telling people he left the music business in 1975. The only problem is he continued to perform around Detroit. One of Rodriguez' favorite performing venues was the Ann Arbor bar Mr. Flood's Party. It was a mainstay of the University of Michigan 1970s and 1980s drinking, dancing and music scene. The vintage Wurlitzer jukebox and the seven nights a week music schedule made the bar a rock music emporium. Drunken students could walk across the street and eat a cheap breakfast at the twenty-four hour Fleetwood Diner. Rodriguez played there regularly. He finished most nights eating at the Fleetwood Diner.

There was a seedy ambiance to Mr. Flood's Party. The Sugar Man loved the club as he climbed the three cement steps into the dance club with memorabilia all over the walls. The bar was filled day and night. The 120 W. Liberty street location was in the middle of student-frequented bars, coffee shops, head shops, record stores and cheap housing.

Who played at Mr. Flood's Party besides Sixto Rodriguez? It was largely local blues and rock legends. The performers and bands, like Rodriguez, that failed to achieve stardom. Dr. Ross was the most popular act at Mr. Flood's Party. He was an older one-man blues band, and he worked at either the Chevy or GM plant in Detroit. It was Dr. Ross, the Harmonica Boss, that brought the blues to Mr. Flood's Party in the early 1970s. When Rodriguez wasn't performing at the venue he showed up to hear the music.

Another bar, the Blind Pig, was even more blues oriented. The Sugar Man has never talked about how the Ann Arbor college blues scene impacted his music. But there is no doubt he was influenced by it.

In 1971 the Blind Pig's founder, Tom Isaia, brought the first cappuccino machine to Ann Arbor. Not just Rodriguez but his buddy John Sinclair was seen in and around the University of Michigan campus. It was a time of political ferment and social change. The Sugar Man preferred the blue-collar life in and around Wayne State University.

In addition to local bands, touring acts included Asleep At the Wheel with Ray Benson loving the wide-open atmosphere. Blues legend Alberta Adams regularly played the club into the early 1970s. Rodriguez in "A Most Disgusting Song" talks about the atmosphere at the club. Many small time Chicago blues bands loved Mr. Flood's Party. The local music scene was a vibrant one with blues bands dominating.

Alberta Adams performed at times in Detroit with the T. J. Fowler band. She was a regular performing as a tap dancer in Detroit's Hastings Street clubs and she went on to appear in Detroit as a singer performing alongside John Lee Hooker, Eddie Burns and Eddie

Kirkland. She was not a mainstream music performer in the 1970s as she was in her mid-fifties and she had a normal family life. But to Detroit's musical aficionados she was a brilliant performer. Phil and Leonard Chess saw her perform in the Hastings Street clubs and they signed her to the Chess label. She also recorded for Savoy Records and toured with Louis Jordan, T-Bone Walker, Duke Ellington and Lionel Hampton. How did this impact Rodriguez? It is hard to say as he has talked about seeing T. J. Fowler in the clubs. If he did, he probably witnessed Alberta Adams amazing talent. Like Rodriguez she had late in life success and at age ninety-one in 2008 her album **Detroit Is My Home** highlighted her love for the Motor City. It is probable Rodriguez saw her rising career and he certainly knew of her popularity at Mr. Flood's Party. Adams passed on December 25, 2014 at the age of ninety-seven, and she was called "the personification of the Detroit blues scene."

In the 1990s Rodriguez had a fan base. It was an international fan base in Australia and South Africa. In the U. K. there was sporadic interest in Rodriguez' songwriting. The key to Rodriguez' popularity came from hit groups like Australia's Midnight Oil, South African record collectors and London critics who extolled his songwriting as a lost art.

Cold Fact continued to sell in used record stores in Australia from the late 1970s well into 2000. This was the reason Rodriguez' **At His Best** was released by Blue Goose. It is impossible to find accurate sales figures on any of Rodriguez' albums. The various industry heads interviewed in **Searching For Sugar Man** admit they were guessing on sales figures. But a common guess is more than half a million albums sold in South Africa. There is another mystery associated with royalties. That is where the royalties were paid. To this day there is no reliable information on what happened to his royalties. That seems impossible in this Internet age. But it is what happened.

What did Australia do for Rodriguez' Career?

There was a hidden side to the Sugar Man's story. Neil Bogart, acting as Sussex Record's distributor, stored four hundred copies of **Cold Fact** in a New York warehouse. He had no intention of distributing them. One night in New York an Australian representative of Blue Goose went out on the town with Bogart. They got stinking drunk. The Australian, who was also an obsessive-compulsive collector, convinced Bogart to take a taxi to the distribution warehouse. He wanted to take some albums home.

Almost by accident the Blue Goose executive picked up a copy of **Cold Fact**. Bogart said: "Take it." The collector did. Then they made a deal to ship the rest to Sydney. Bogart sold the four hundred remaining copies of **Cold Fact** for twenty-five cents or one hundred dollars. It was December 1971. This began **Cold Fact's** odyssey down under leading to local stardom.

Why did this record executive pick up **Cold Fact**? It was the cover. Or perhaps it was too much cocaine. Who knows?

For the next eight years **Cold Fact** became a cult favorite. It was 1978 when Blue Goose Music released a vinyl version of **Cold Fact**. There were bootlegs and crude pirated editions attesting to his never-ending popularity and constant radio airplay. Radio airplay was extensive. This eventually led to Australians searching for and finding the Sugar Man. It was 1979. He was not lost. He was not dead. He was well and alive. He was working in Detroit. He had a full family life. He was a dedicated political activist. He was offered a contract to appear down under. He accepted. He was ready to tour Australia. It was easy to contact him. This paved the way for two early Australian tours.

What Australia did for Rodriguez' career was obvious. The 1979 and 1981 concert tours revived his dormant career. He primarily played medium sized concert halls during his two Australian tours.

His records were re-released down under. He also completed an arena tour with the Australian mega hit act Midnight Oil in 1981. Then, thirty-two years later, Rodriguez stood on the stage of the Sundance Film Festival the subject of an award-winning documentary. It wasn't a dream. It was, as Rodriguez said, "coming from reality." When asked if he was disappointed being a forgotten artist? The Sugar Man responded: "Nothing beats reality."

In 2012, Rodriguez appeared at the Sundance Festival to the acclaim of critics celebrating the brilliance of **Searching For Sugar Man**. He performed a cover of Midnight Oil's "Redneck Wonderland" to demonstrate his thanks for their support. But it wasn't just Australia where Rodriguez had a following. He had a cult audience in the U. K. and Europe. South Africa remained his hottest record selling spot.

What was evident in the mid-to-late 1970s was Rodriguez' music sold well. The albums were either used or bootlegged. He didn't receive royalties. He was also an icon to black, as well as to white, South Africans and ethnic Australians. It wasn't just that he was a counterculture musician; he was a political lightning rod for civil rights.

The South African release of Rodriguez' **At His Best** was a favorite of anti-apartheid activist Steve Biko. It was in Australia that he made money touring. Because of his popularity down under, Rodriguez recorded a live LP during his 1979 Australian tour. It came out in 1981 on the Blue Goose imprint as **Rodriguez Alive**. It remains his most collectible and obscure LP. The songs were selected from the first two LPs. It was recorded at the Regent Theater in Sydney on March 17-18, 1979. The most unusual song on the album "To Whom It May Concern," was a completely different arrangement including a bass solo and a jazz flute.

The deal between Rodriguez and the label was for one year. The Mark Gillespie band provided back up. The live LP never touched the U. S. shores. It sold well in South Africa and Australia.

The esoteric album releases kept Rodriguez' career alive outside the U. S. He was happy to tour sporadically. He didn't care about money. It wasn't until he met Stephen "Sugar" Segerman that Rodriguez learned just how much money he was owed. He became concerned. He hired a lawyer. He is still attempting to collect back royalties.

Rodriguez is on the Road 1979-2007

Although he remained a relatively obscure American artist, Rodriguez was busy at times performing. He continued to appear outside the U. S. From 1979 to 2007 he completed thirteen tours. His music was an international cult favorite. In Australia, he toured at times with the Mark Gillespie Band. This is an accomplished Australian band led by one of the most creative and original artists down under. Gillespie is an enigmatic Australian musician who developed a cult following for an original talent not unlike Rodriguez.'

Because South Africa wasn't the only place Rodriguez was a cult favorite, there was a great deal of press. Much of it misguided and incorrect. No one picked up on the fact Rodriguez was working in housing remodeling or doing anything he could to feed his family. The irony is after his triumphant 1998 South African re-emergence, he returned home to Detroit to continue the backbreaking work that compromised his health, deteriorated his eyesight and tugged at his creative genius. His talent never wavered. He was quiet, quirky, and he never bragged. When he drank a beer with his fellow home reconstruction colleagues after work, he never mentioned his albums, his tours or his musical background. When **Searching For Sugar Man** became an international success, his neighbors were shocked. The reason! Sixto Rodriguez was humble. He continued to pursue his music. He just didn't talk about it.

Festival Records Licensing Rodriguez in Australia

The story of the partnership between Australia's Festival Records and Sixto Rodriguez' music tells one all they need to know about the nefarious record industry. The story begins when Festival purchased the four hundred vinyl **Cold Fact** albums from a New York warehouse. The intention was to sell the LPs, thereby testing the market. The results were amazing. It took less than a month to sell out **Cold Fact**.

In Australia, Festival Records licensed **Cold Fact** from Clarence Avant. Then Festival licensed the material to other labels and other countries. In 1972, in the Philippines, A & M released a seven-inch single "I Think Of You" backed with "Halfway Up The Stairs." In the convoluted music world, Clarence Avant licensed the material to Festival. In return they licensed it to A & M. This began a pattern for Rodriguez' music. He was licensed outside the U. S. market. No one kept track of what was going on. The royalties were lost in the commercial shuffle.

The New Zealand Interfusion Festival label released a **Cold Fact** album in a clear vinyl numbered edition. It remains a rarity. Festival made a lot of money licensing Sixto Rodriguez. The Sugar Man allegedly never saw a dime.

The trail is murky and imprecise on Rodriguez' Australian rereleases. The only reliable information is BMG Arista and RCA Australia released albums. BMG did the distribution. It gets convoluted. **At His Best** was released by Blue Goose Music and distributed by Festival Records in New Zealand. The murky business deals have never been fully disclosed. Royalties? No information!

When asked about royalties, a Festival Records spokesperson said they were sent to Clarence Avant's production company. The company spokesman said that after expenses for shipment, storage and promotion, there were no royalties. This familiar story rang true time and time again.

Festival Records is typical of companies releasing Rodriguez' material. News Limited owned the label from 1961 to 2005. They released albums for profit without promotion. In other words, Festival hopped on the next big thing. In the Rodriguez story this suggests he had a large Australian fan base. Rupert Murdoch, who siphoned off the profits, owned Festival. He had a hissy fit over any money spent on promotion. None was spent. The label was successful. They didn't break new acts. They sold a product with guaranteed sales. Rodriguez' re-releases is one indication of his popularity down under.

Festival Records was a poor choice for the Sugar Man's releases. The Rupert Murdoch owned company had little, if any, knowledge of how to promote a rock music artist. The irony is Festival's Mushroom offshoot label sold its product extremely well in the early 1970s. The label didn't need promotion as they had albums by such international Australian stars as the Bee Gees, Olivia Newton John and every other important local act. Somewhere Johnny O'Keefe was looking on enviously.

The Mixed Bag 1979 Australian Shows

The 1979 Australian tour was a mixed bag. Some shows were spectacular. Others were not so well received. An Australian disc jockey, Holger Brockman, was the catalyst to Rodriguez' popularity down under. His various radio shows were a veritable Rodriguez showcase. The disc jockey's popularity in the early 1970s on 2SM made him a music power broker. He played the Sugar Man's music so often, the station threatened to fire him. He brought the radio station so many new listeners, his job was safe.

In 1975, Brockman became a progressive disc jockey. This began Rodriguez' elevation to cult status. When Brockman worked with the Triple J network in Australia it broadcast rock and roll to people eighteen to thirty. This created a new, vibrant record audience. The Rodriguez Australian fan base remains with him to the present day.

On his 1979 Australia tour Rodriguez' wife, Konny, and two of his children, Eva and Sandra, accompanied him. The family atmosphere was important to Rodriguez. He used this tour to educate his children on such diverse subjects as Australia's aborigine population; it's colonial past, and the manner in which Australia evolved historically. He also needs family support to overcome his natural shyness on stage.

The Magic of the Australian Shows: Album Demands are Greater Than Ever

From Rodriguez' first show at Sydney's Regent Theater there was a buzz about his music and universal praise for his concert appearances. For a decade Rodriguez' records sold well in Australia. He had an established fan base. Now it was time for his fans to connect. They did!

On stage in Australia the thirty-seven year old Rodriguez looked like a college professor in his stylish beige suit replete with a blue shirt. He carried a brief case with sheet music. He appeared nervous. Getting over stage fright was a continual concern. That ended when he began his concerts with the lilting words to "Street Boy." The crowd quieted at the Regent Theater, as they were one and the same with his music. One fan described the Sydney shows as "kind of a holy communion." That reaction did not go unrecognized by the record labels. They showed up to make a pitch for a new album. The Sugar Man had new songs. What he didn't have was confidence that the limited Australian market could properly showcase his music. That was his main concern. Rodriguez came up with a compromise. He would sign for a limited live album. This was a smart decision. The album **Rodriguez Alive** evolved into a rare release further enhancing his legend down under. The Blue Goose label was the one Rodriguez selected to further his already growing legend down under.

Rodriguez Alive: The Legend Grows

What is the importance of **Rodriguez Alive**? The answer is a simple one. When two concerts were recorded on March 17-18, 1979 the stage was set to create a vehicle highlighting his talent. For forty plus minutes the soft, lilting sounds of the Sugar Man are highlighted with a flute that floats through his music.

The live album opens with "Can't Get Away" and then in a very soft, plaintive, almost dreamlike visage Rodriguez begins singing "Street Boy" with a flute adding an extended jazz sound. The extended breaks by the musicians adds to Rodriguez' soft, but always present, guitar sound that comes in behind his vocals.

There is a beautiful change of pace as Rodriguez begins an acceppella version of "Like Janis" in which the musicians join him about thirty seconds into the song. The arrangement is a crowd pleaser attesting to the Sugar Man's performing karma. The romantic side of his music continued with "I Think of You." Rodriguez never forgot Steve Rowland's advice to give the audiences his soft, romantic side. He did in the early songs on this live album.

A burst of polite applause greets Rodriguez as he begins "I'll Slip Away." His voice has matured. The Blue Goose live album captures his rapturous vocals. Australia couldn't get enough of the Sugar Man.

Holger Brockman Infuses the Rodriguez Legend

After Brockman played the entire **Cold Fact** album every night for months on Australian radio there was a huge demand for his debut record. No one could find it. Brockman's on air tirade about the beauty of Rodriguez' music, while playing it repeatedly, spread the news about the Sugar Man. He also skewered the music business for overlooking Rodriguez. Soon a number of Australian record labels searched out the copyrights. They found they belonged not to Rodriguez but to Clarence Avant and Harry Balk. The Blue Goose label realized there was money to be made from releasing Rodriguez' material. Clarence Avant was cautious about granting reprint rights to Rodriguez' LPs. He didn't like the small Australian labels. He believed they were wasting his time. The market was too small. But South African and Australian labels wouldn't give up.

This prompted Zev Eizik and Michael Coppel to contact Clarence Avant in Los Angeles about licensing Rodriguez' music for the Australia and New Zealand markets. A contract with the Australian based Blue Goose label led to the release of **Rodriguez At His Best** (Blue Goose VPCD 6748). There was a good reason for Avant allowing Blue Goose to release Rodriguez' albums. Blue Goose was affiliated with RCA. Clarence Avant knew he would make some money.

It appears Rodriguez was left out in the fiscal cold. The Blue Goose LP contained eleven songs and among these were the previously unreleased "Street Boy" and a re-recording of "I'll Slip Away." There were six songs from **Cold Fact**, and three tunes from **Coming From Reality**.

When **Rodriguez: At His Best** went gold in Australia, Avant licensed **Cold Fact**. It quickly became another gold record. The royalties bypassed Rodriguez. The music, however, continued to draw rave reviews. If things were not going well commercially for Rodriguez, his music and performances were an artistic success.

One of the by-products of the music industry is record labels often tell artists they can make their money in concert, not on album sales. Whether or not Avant told Rodriguez this is unknown. What is known is the Australian 1979 tour was an unqualified success. Then Rodriguez returned home to back breaking work in the crumbling Detroit housing industry.

From Australian superstar to remodeling guru seemed to be Rodriguez' future.

The 1979 Austalian Tour Dates

March 15
Dallas Brooks Hall, Melbourne
March 17
Regent Theatre, Sydney (Saturday)
March 18
Regent Theatre, Sydney
March 20
Festival Hall, Brisbane
March 23
Regent Theatre, Sydney
March 24
Canberra Theatre, Canberra
March 26
Festival Theatre, Adelaide
March 28 Majesty's Theater, Concert Hall, Perth. His show was simulcast on 96FM. This began radio airplay for Rodriguez that continues in heavy rotation to the present day. What made the Australian tour an important one? The reason is Rodriguez hadn't played to large crowds in his career. It was the first time. He was understandable nervous. It didn't matter as everything worked out.

The 1979 Australian Tour Continued After A Holiday

April 3
Dallas Brooks Hall, Melbourne
April 7
Civic Theatre, Newcastle (2 shows)

April 8
Regent Theatre, Sydney

Musicians on the 1979 Australian Tour

Rodriguez: Vocals, Acoustic guitar
Steve Cooney: Guitar, mandolin (from Australia)
Doug McDonald: Drums (from New Zealand)
Jake Salazar: Bass
José Guadiana (*or* Guadiama): Flute

Jake and José were Americans who left three-quarters of the way through the tour. An Australian, Joe Creighton, on bass, replaced them. The local boys all came from the Mark Gillespie Band who was the supporting act. Gillespie was an Australian cult musician some compared to the U. K.'s Nick Drake.

When he toured with the Mark Gillespie Band, there were calls from the audience for Gillespie's "Small Mercies." Rodriguez loved it. The audience wanted a Gillespie song. He moved smiling to the background. Gillespie performed his Australian favorites to adoring crowds. Gillespie was a pub favorite in Australia. He remains a critical acclaimed performer with little commercial success. He retired and became reclusive. Mark Gillespie is a story still awaiting presentation.

The Critical Reaction to the 1979 Australian Tour

When Rodriguez wandered out on stage at Sydney's Regent Theater, he was excited. He was ready to cut a live album. The first two nights of the Australian tour were special as journalists raved about his music and stage show. It was cathartic to a musician who had given up any thoughts of acclaim or monetary reward.

The question of stage fright continued. How Rodriguez overcame it is not known. But he was terrified of large performing venues. His family, the promoter and his Zen like character allowed him to put stage fright into the past.

On stage in Sydney, Rodriguez came out from the wing in a stylish suit carrying a briefcase. The rapt audience was silent. They anticipated his signature song "Sugar Man." He pulled some music sheets out of his brief case. He smiled. The audience looked on with anticipation. They weren't disappointed as Rodriguez, although appearing nervous, delivered a stunning show.

When he opened with "Street Boy" there was thunderous applause. After he finished his Sydney concerts, Rodriguez remarked of the heady applause: "After ten years you gotta be kidding…I'm just an everyday person." While living in obscurity in Detroit and tasting a moment of fame in Australia, Rodriguez remained true to his personal vision. He had no regrets. When he was asked about the lack of royalties, he gave his stock answer: "It's the music business."

Not everything was perfect during the 1979 Australian tour. There were some disputes with his backing band. For some reason Rodriguez fired Jose Guadiana and Jake Salazar in the middle of the tour. There was no explanation for the parting of the ways. Jake Salazar returned to the U. S. He received three Grammy nominations for production.

The 1979 Australian tour made Rodriguez comfortable and seasoned as a concert act. This was due in part to his family enjoying the trip and supporting him.

Returning to Australia in 1981

In 1981, Rodriguez returned to Australia to tour with Midnight Oil. He also performed some solo shows. Midnight Oil was on the cusp of becoming a world-class mega hit act. Their international hits began in 1982 as they stormed into the commercial mainstream. They had been together in one form or another for almost a decade. They were also Rodriguez fans.

Although Midnight Oil was on the verge of mega stardom, they let the crowds know the Sugar Man was a mentor. Like Rodriguez, they spent years performing at small clubs or before disinterested bar patrons. They never wavered from their musical direction. Their dreams became reality in the 1980s.

Midnight Oil was an alternative, punk rock band whose fourth album went platinum in 1982. As Rodriguez opened for Midnight Oil, on select shows, the band made references to his songs and his performing influence.

The first two nights on September 9-10, 1981 in NSW Country, Rodriguez' music was eclipsed by the excitement over "The Scorching of the Earth" tour that Midnight Oil christened to enter the musical big time.

After the success of **Searching For Sugar Man**, Midnight Oil told reporters they had no trouble finding Rodriguez. They couldn't imagine America had no clue about his talent. They wondered why the South African's couldn't find the Sugar Man.

Rodriguez loved opening for the band. He wrote of Midnight Oil's lead singer: "For me, Mick Jagger is King, but Peter Garrett is also high on the list of music aristocracy."

When Midnight Oil toured the U. S. in 1984, they hung out with him. Rodriguez loved Midnight Oil's message that nuclear power, American foreign policy and military spending were killing the U. S. Rodriguez believed the band were his political-musical stepchildren. Midnight Oil's lyrics raged against U. S. influence in El Salvador, and the silence over the inhumanity of the Hiroshima atomic blasts. There was a song criticizing the U. S. spy satellite station in Australia. They talked on and off stage about political activism. When they donated half a million dollars to anti-nuclear organizations and Green Peace there was a smile on Rodriguez' face. He was a mentor.

His most memorable concert at the Canberra Theater on October 20, 1981 was a solo show. Rodriguez and a back up guitarist mesmerized a sold out crowd. When Rodriguez came out for his portion of the show the audience called out for songs from **Cold Fact** and **Coming From Reality**. But the Australian shows were only a temporary shot in the arm. He returned to his day job. He also continued campaigning for political office. He was a community activist. The blue collar, working person was his focus.

The 1981 Australia tour was one where Rodriguez received more applause at the Tanelorn Festival than the headliners Midnight Oil, Men At Work, Billy Thorpe and the Split Enz. Rodriguez arrived at the Tanelorn Festival in a helicopter after Redgum came off stage As Rodriguez landed and left the helicopter, his scarf was flying in the wind, and his guitar hanging on his back. He looked tired. He delivered a brilliant set if at times an uneven one. The cheers for "Sugar Man" indicated he was well received. The shouts from the audience were for songs from **Cold Fact**.

It would be another seventeen years before he went on an extended tour. Some years later, Rodriguez remembered these shows fondly: "I saw Billy Thorpe, may he rest in peace...." This reference to Thorpe tells a great deal about Rodriguez. When he died at age sixty in 2007, Thorpe had a successful, if under the commercial radar, career that began with the pub rock band, the Aztecs and continued with cult solo albums. Like Rodriguez, Thorpe was talented and musically prolific. He is described as Australia's "wildest and heaviest blues rocker." Rodriguez loved his music. Rodriguez retains a warm spot in his heart for Australia as well as for the memory of Billy Thorpe. Sharing a smoke with Thorpe was a fond memory that never vanished.

When he toured with Midnight Oil, the band considered him the star. As the **Searching For Sugar Man** documentary opened and became a hit, Jim Moginie remarked he couldn't believe Australia was not in the film. "It's funny that no one knew where he was...we knew where he was all the time!" That comment ignores the fact few in the U. S. had heard of Rodriguez. It took Stephen "Sugar" Segerman and Craig Bartholomew-Strydom two plus decades to achieve that goal. Why? This is the question!

Rodriguez: What Australia Meant

Australia was an important part of Rodriguez' career prior to the success of **Searching For Sugar Man**. His albums continued to sell down under and his cult audience turned out in large numbers for his two tours.

Sixto Rodriguez: "I thought that my high point in my life had been Australia." This comment, in an interview with Andrew Watt, is typical of the Sugar Man. There is an endearing honesty to Rodriguez. He went on to observe he loved everything Australian. "I even went to the Brisbane Ballet when it came to Detroit," Rodriguez concluded.

Fast forward to 2013. When Rodriguez toured Australia, after the success of **Searching For Sugar Man**, Midnight Oil's Jim Moginie formed a band with his mates Martin Rotsey and Rob Hirst, and they convinced Violent Femmes bassist Brian Ritchie to join a group they called the Break. It was a surf instrumental band that opened for Rodriguez. They also backed him in concert.

Rob Hirst, Midnight Oil's drummer, told **Rolling Stone** everyone in Australia had the **Cold Fact** album and since 1972 Rodriguez was well known down under. Hirst couldn't understand why no one knew Rodriguez. Midnight Oil hung out with him on every American tour.

"Midnight Oil was a magic band," Rodriguez remarked. "They were a high-powered band, so they are toning down for my performances. It's a living art...."

Rodriguez Reflects on Australia

As he looked back upon his two Australian tours, Rodriguez believed it was the apex of his career. He had played for the first time in stadiums to large crowds. He was a revered figure among the musicians. Michael Coppel, the Australian promoter, told **Billboard** the large crowds, as well as the loud vocal reception, stunned Rodriguez. The constant cries for "Sugar Man" and "Crucify Your Mind" indicated the favorite Australian tunes. He gave such strong shows the press pointed out he was as popular a draw as Rod Stewart who was also touring Australia.

"I thought it was the highlight of my career," Rodriguez continued. "I had achieved my epic mission. Not much happened after that. No calls or anything." There were no calls because he didn't have a phone or management. He never said a word about his future. The dream of musical stardom persisted.

Each week Rodriguez took his young daughters to the Detroit Public Library where he read **Billboard**. He continued to dream of rock and roll stardom. It was still more than thirty years before legitimate stardom came in like a rushing wind.

When Rodriguez returned to Australia in 2013 the local press was upset with **Searching For Sugar Man**. The Sydney media was incensed his 1979 and 1981 Australia tours were excluded from the documentary. Australian critic, Paul Byrnes, called the documentary "romantic." He alleged the thesis of redemption and discovery after years in the creative wilderness, would have been weakened by the inclusion of the Sugar Man's popularity down under.

Paul Byrnes: "I saw Rodriguez perform at the East Coast Blues and Roots Music Festival in Byron Bay in 2007. He was frail, confused and weak of voice. That may be because he is now seventy years old. The story of his reemergence is fascinating and moving. I just wish it was more complete and trustworthy."

Byrnes should be reminded Rodriguez was sixty-five and, according to the reviews, he was at the top of his game. What Byrnes reacted to was the exclusion of Australia from **Searching For Sugar Man**. He didn't care for the Rodriguez shows solely due to this reason.

That is a comment on the Sugar Man not shared by other observers. By 2017 his health was excellent, his energy on stage at a high level, and his concerts drew rapturous applause. There is nothing aged about the Sugar Man.

The Cold Hard Facts About Rodriguez in Australia: There Were Lawsuits Before Searching for Sugar Man

The cold hard facts about Rodriguez in Australia are that his Blue Goose live album went platinum. **Cold Fact** sold out when it was in print. He filled stadiums. He filled small clubs. He filled medium venues. His radio airplay was constant. The classic rock stations featured his music.

What does this mean? It leads to another mystery. After touring South Africa, Australia and sporadically London from 1979 to 2007, Rodriguez filed a lawsuit in 2007 in Michigan. The suit was against Zev Eizik. There is no information on why Rodriguez sued or the outcome. Those close to him told me it was a dispute over money matters. I have no way of verifying the outcome. It appears Rodriguez had money for legal fees, and he had a complaint about bookings, concert fees and equitable royalties.

To quote Rodriguez it is "a concrete cold fact" he made someone a lot of money. Where the money from Australian record sales is stashed remains a mystery. There is a pile of money somewhere. There were some other constants from his Australian tours. He doesn't like to do press interviews. He is polite but shy. He will tell reporters his social conscience remains active.

Sixto Rodriguez: "These are new times and there are different answers that we're trying to seek out. There has to be an end to violence but the answers are not as easy as they were ten years ago." He made this comment to reporters upon landing in Sydney in 1981.

When he arrived in Australia, Rodriguez was nervous. He doesn't like crowds. He doesn't like his solitude interrupted. As he prepared to go on stage during his first night in Australia, he sat outside the concert hall in a taxi for fifteen minutes. He was composing himself. He did. He went onstage and gave a dynamite show. Whatever else Rodriguez is, he remains a legendary performer. **Searching for Sugar Man** made him famous. Rodriguez simply shakes his head. He can't understand what the fuss is about. Rodriguez wrote: "Just climb up on my music and my songs will set you free."

The 1981 Australian tour came at an early crossroads in his career. He was down. He never thought he would come back. The second Australian tour convinced him he had something to offer to larger audiences. He continued to make music when he returned to Detroit. It would be another seventeen years before he re-emerged in South Africa. He didn't know that Stephen "Sugar" Segerman and Craig Bartholomew-Strydom were lurking in the shadows waiting to bring the Sugar Man back from obscurity.

Why Zev Eizik is a Hero in Australia to The Sugar Man's Story

The 1979 and 1981 Australian tours kept Rodriguez in the music business. Since 1972 when Festival Records released his material his audience grew yearly. He learned his lyrics had as much of an impact as his music. The unintended influence of the two Australia tours was to convince Rodriguez to finish his honors degree in philosophy at Wayne State University. He did. The wordsmith now had a B. A.

Zev Eizik is the hero in the early Australian Rodriguez story. He was a young man much like Matt Sullivan who wanted stardom for the Sugar Man. No one could tell Eizik no. He was a persistent and continual supporter of Rodriguez. But he wasn't a media person. It turned out Australia's most respected journalist was on the Rodriguez train headed for local stardom.

Glenn Baker, the Australian factotum for **Billboard**, was a Rodriguez booster. He was also the most respected music critic down under and his constant praise for Rodriguez' music was a contributing factor to his elevation to cult status.

There was censorship in Australia much like that in South Africa. The Sugar Man's music overcame it but the stories are hilarious. When Holger Brockman broke "Sugar Man" he worked for a Catholic owned radio station and he had to use the name Bill Drake because it sound more Australian. The station censor warned him about playing Rodriguez' music and they complained about a derogatory remark directed to the Pope. Peterson left the Catholic owned radio station and moved on to friendlier and more progressive radio.

Baker pointed out the demand for Rodriguez' records was constant throughout the 1970s. When record stores no longer had access to **Cold Fact** or **Coming From Reality** the Festival Record printings were purchased even though the sound was poor, there were no liner notes and the aura of mystery intrigued the listener. Why was Australia excluded from **Searching For Sugar Man**? The operative answer from those close to the documentary is Stephen "Sugar" Segerman convinced Malik Bendjelloul it wasn't an important part of the story. Interesting!

In Melbourne a young man who had immigrated to Australia, Zev Eizik, learned of Sixto Rodriguez while in college. He was intrigued by the constant questions about the Sugar Man. Who was he? Where did he live? Why have there not been more albums? These questions interested and perplexed Eizik. The young man, who had recently arrived from Israel, was a businessman beginning what would become a legendary entrepreneurial career. He started out small in a flea market stall selling a number of things including vinyl records. The more he heard about the Sugar Man the more he realized there was money in the promotion business. He cast a careful eye on many promoters and he decided he understood how to promote rock and roll acts.

Eizik began his foray into the record business contacting Jack Baverstock's Fontana Record office in London. By this time Manfred Mann had hits in Australia and other Fontana acts including Wayne Fontana were on the charts. Nothing resulted from the Fontana connection and he attempted to look up Sussex Record impresario Clarence Avant. That attempt met with success.

By the time he found Avant, Eizik owned a share in Blue Goose Records. He flew to Los Angeles and made a deal to release Rodriguez' material down under. The Blue Goose subsidiary label, Blue Beat, released **Rodriguez: At His Best**. It was 1977 and Eizik envisioned a bright future for the Sugar Man's music. The following year in 1978 Eizik was instrumental in RCA releasing **Cold Fact** to a highly receptive audience. When asked what the Rodriguez RCA albums sold, he responded with a sales figure in excess of 100,000 copies. Maybe! Maybe not!

By the late 1970s Eizik was a prime mover in the Australian music industry. He is for all purposes one of the Australian heroes bringing the Sugar Man to mainstream audiences. There are other Eizik business deals adding to his wealth and acclaim. He promoted concerts with Midnight Oil as they headed to international stardom. His company, Australian Concert Entertainment, had a reputation that brought many top-flight bands into his office to have Australian tours put together.

When Rodriguez was approached by ACE for the 1979 tour, there was a considerable amount of time before the Sugar Man agreed. He negotiated to have his wife Konny, who was pregnant with Regan, and his daughters Eva and Sandra join him on the tour. Eizik readily agreed. When the Sugar Man and his family flew in March 1979 to Australia there was a great deal of uncertainty. He had been disappointed too many times. He wasn't sure what to expect. The reception was an astonishing one. It was more than Rodriguez expected, and he began the tour in a positive way. Again Zev Eizik is the hero putting this together.

Rodriguez questioned at thirty-seven if he was up to thirteen internal Australian flights in six weeks. But every time he and his family got off the plane it was like a coronation. He was one of Australia's premier acts. The Sugar Man was thankful as he wondered about American audiences. As he traveled from one concert site to the next Rodriguez often spent part of every night walking the streets of the local town. He had that curiosity about the blue collar, working class Australian.

The Sugar Man's social conscience was demonstrated when he suggested a concert at a local prison. At first the authorities were flummoxed but on serious consideration they realized it was a wonderful idea. He appeared in concert at Melbourne's Pentridge Prison.

During the 1979 Australian tour Rodriguez realized he had a legion of fans and he was active in record store signings to help his product sell. As he recorded a live album for local release, he envisioned a commercial future. The one-year licensing deal for the live album is one indication of the increased business sophistication Rodriguez brought to his career. There was a considerable sum of money from the 1979 tour. Konny left her position in the Wayne State University library. She remained at home as a full time mother when Regan arrived. Then the household budget had more money as Eva joined the military.

When Rodriguez returned for the 1981 Australian tour, Zev Eizik was once again the force behind a lucrative set of concerts. The fifteen shows in ten cities went off flawlessly as Eizik demonstrated his professionalism. This tour included his appearance at the Tanelorn Music Festival, which created even better publicity than the 1979 shows. The Sugar Man made it obvious he could play large venues.

The tragedy of the two Australian tours is Stephen "Sugar" Segerman had no idea that Rodriguez was popular outside of South Africa. Or maybe he knew about Australia but didn't want to contradict the myths he sold to Malik Bendjelloul.

Eight

Stephen 'Sugar' Segerman and Craig Bartholomew-Strydom are the Ones Who Rescue Rodriguez from Obscurity

"People were burning draft cards, protesting the war, assassinations and riots."

Rodriguez on U. S. politics

"Some editors are failed writers, but so are most writers."

T. S. Eliot

"We see how Stephen 'Sugar' Segerman built his career on the bodies of betrayed friends."

A South African Acquaintance

As **Searching For Sugar Man** opens the first scene shows Stephen "Sugar" Segerman driving his car down Cape Town's majestic Chapman's Peak singing along with Rodriguez' "Sugar Man."

Segerman turns to the camera and describes how he got his nickname. No one in the army could pronounce Segerman, so he became "Sugar." He is a friendly, photogenic pitchman for the story. He is also the person who rescued Rodriguez from obscurity.

Segerman's obsessive-compulsive mania for Rodriguez led him to emphasize all aspects of the Sugar Man's life. The nickname "Sugar" is the ultimate tribute to Rodriguez.

When Segerman met Rodriguez he emphasized his nickname "Sugar." This began his often-disingenuous relationship with Rodriguez. From the first time he heard the lilting vocals in **Cold Fact**, the singer known as Sixto Rodriguez fascinated Segerman. What happened to him? That question took on a manic direction. Segerman spent almost thirty years figuring out the riddle of what happened to the Sugar Man. His obsession bordered on paranoia as he imagined the world failing to recognize his idol's talent.

He also believes he invented the story. The truth is more complex. Segerman didn't know the record distributors had a complex database listing every world act. Rodriguez was in that database. There was plenty of information on Rodriguez. If you stopped three young people in Sydney, Australia, two could readily sing a line from "Sugar Man." He wasn't the mysterious figure Segerman spent forty years searching for as he praised one song "Sugar Man." As one of the Segerman's close friends told me: "He had almost an unhealthy mania for Sixto Rodriguez. We humored him." Then things really got crazy in August 2017 when Segerman advertised he was ready to go on tour with in-depth lectures about the Sugar Man "for a fee." That fee was four thousand dollars, plus hotel, plus meals, plus traveling expenses. As one of Segerman's friends said: "As far as I know this is not possible as Segerman is no longer in Rodriguez' inner circle. How could he possibly deliver speeches that have 'an inside view' when he is on the outside?" This person suggested for all of the Segerman's knowledge, which is formidable, he has not kept up with the on line or computer generated information on the Sugar Man. He knows a version of the story. It is the one he created. He is still selling it.

By the early 1990s computers catalogued every album. When Segerman initially told his story, he acted like had no knowledge of why or how the Sugar Man fell out of the record world. He made it his goal to find Rodriguez. He did. He brought him in concert to South Africa. He did in 1998 for six sold out local shows.

Then Sixto Rodriguez vanished from the international stage until 2012.There is a back-story. Rodriguez' career slowly gained steam from 2007 until 2011 before **Searching For Sugar Man** became an award winning documentary. To understand how and why Rodriguez achieved international stardom, it is necessary to consider Stephen "Sugar" Segerman's partnership with the talented writer Craig Bartholomew-Strydom. Together they put the pieces in place concerning Rodriguez' career.

Keep in mind Stephen "Sugar" Segerman is a great guy. He is also a blustering egomaniac. His sense of self-importance eventually strained his relationship with Rodriguez and his family. That said the Sugar Man's story would have been difficult without Segerman.

The Confusing Questions Surrounding Segerman's Story

There are some questions surrounding Segerman's version of the story. How could he not be aware of Rodriguez' Australian tours? They were well publicized. The London music magazines, which Sugar read voraciously, reported as early as 2006 Rodriguez' had a cult following. **The New Musical Express** and **Melody Maker** commented on the difficulty of finding the albums.

In London the Berwick Street record shops were filled with his fans. They searched for his out of print vinyl masterpieces, the rare 45 singles, and the Australian and South African imports. The drama built up around the mysterious and elusive Sixto Rodriguez was transported to London.

In the age of the Internet the buzz on Rodriguez was minimal. It was the record geeks living in their parent's basement that discovered **Cold Fact**. Segerman spun the story. Australians have gone out of their way to point to the confusing questions surrounding Segerman's tale of a lost mythical artist. It tarnishes his legacy. Fact checking is not Segerman's forte. Perhaps Segerman's biggest critic was a respected London journalist, Peter Bradshaw, who asked many penetrating questions.

How and Why Peter Bradshaw Exposed Segerman

Peter Bradshaw, writing in the **London Guardian**, observed: "A rudimentary Internet search shows Rodriguez' musical career did not vanish the way the film implies....the film has skated round some facts...exaggerated the mystery, to make a better and more emotional story."

After Bradshaw skewers Segerman for haughty proprietary attitudes, he comments: "**Cold Fact** was a popular album in the late 70s in my high school in Australia." The charge is clear. Segerman created the myths, exploited Rodriguez' talent and turned himself into a star via **Searching For Sugar Man**. Then he wanted to march Rodriguez around like a creative puppet. The Sugar Man got rid of him. Perhaps Bradshaw's conclusion explains the myth and reality behind the documentary. For that the fans can be thankful.

That said Segerman is still central to the story. Initially, he was the single most important force behind the story. He has a defined proprietary interest. As he should!

When Segerman talks about the lyrical magic, and the musical brilliance of Rodriguez, the mystery deepens. In **Cold Fact** you hear the words of a true believer.

If you didn't know who Rodriguez was or how his music sounded, you were intrigued by the award-winning documentary. I have written about rock and roll music for five decades. I had never heard of Sixto Rodriguez. I had no idea how **Cold Fact** sounded. That is until I sat through fifteen screenings of **Searching For Sugar Man**. The minute I heard Rodriguez' lilting vocal on "Sugar Man," I was hooked. The story told me more about the record business than I wanted to know. I also had a hero. It was Stephen "Sugar" Segerman. Without him the Oscar winning documentary, the marvelous music, and the commercial resurgence of Sixto Rodriguez would have been impossible. But I wondered how well and how accurately Segerman told the story? I soon found out. He could tell it well. His accuracy, however, remains in question.

When asked if he remembers the first time he heard "Sugar Man," Segerman reflectively said: "Of course, I remember the first time I heard Rodriguez, like everybody." He seemed offended by the question. You learn as you watch him. He is a pompous ass. But he is loveable.

Like many South Africans, he never forgot the new words that Rodriguez taught him. He learned "anti-establishment" from listening to Rodriguez. He learned about class differences. He learned how people became prejudiced and ethnically judgmental. He learned about the dark side of the record business. He coyly recalls he learned about political protest. He became aware of social-economic differences. All this sounds strange. Or does it? He had to learn some of the terms in law school. Or was he spinning a good story? He was like some South Africans who believed Rodriguez taught a new form of politics. That says it all about Segerman. Sophistication! I don't think so. But when he met fledgling filmmaker Malik Bendjelloul he spun the Sixto Rodriguez tale with skill and creative insight.

Meeting Malik Bendjelloul

In 2006 Malik Bendjelloul wandered into Stephen "Sugar" Segerman's Cape Town Mabu Vinyl store. This encounter changed their lives. After Bendjelloul filmed their initial meeting, he came back a year later to continue the story. It took another five years to complete **Searching For Sugar Man**.

How effective was Segerman's explanation of Rodriguez? He was like a pitchman selling a product. Segerman convinced Bendjelloul to move into the small cottage behind his house. They worked on the story for months. This strange beginning was unwittingly the road to the Academy Award's and an Oscar.

When Malik Bendjelloul recalled the first time he heard the Sixto Rodriguez story, he couldn't believe the pathos, the complexity and the contrasting styles of Detroit and Cape Town as Rodriguez' music played in Mabu Vinyl. It was a cathartic moment of triumph for Segerman.

What is important about Segerman? He had a number of goals in his search for the Sugar Man. Segerman's mission was to secure Rodriguez' royalties. He convinced Bendjelloul that illegal taping and bootlegging provided the impetus for Rodriguez' South African fame. It also cost the Sugar Man a great deal of money. When the documentary was shot, Bendjelloul ambushed Clarence Avant on film. The African American record executive looked guilty of not knowing where the royalties were deposited. One assumes that Avant was guilty of not paying royalties. Nothing is further from the truth. A number of people told me his company, Avant Garde Productions, is a model of music industry propriety. The company funded an album, they promoted an album and they collected royalties on two albums **Cold Fact** and **Coming From Reality**. Neither sold. There was little in the way of royalties from Rodriguez' two albums. It wasn't until Matt Sullivan's Light In The Attic and the documentary brought Rodriguez back that Avant was able to pay royalties. He did. He paid royalties twice a year to 2015. After that the royalty flow slowed. There was still a yearly payment. Always on time! Everyone associated with Avant speaks to his honesty, his integrity and his fairness. He is not the shady character **Searching For Sugar Man** portrays.

The hand of Stephen "Sugar" Segerman is in the background to Malik Bendjelloul ambushing Avant on camera. Segerman doesn't understand the American record industry. All he saw was the sales of South African albums. Those sales didn't come close to covering the money Avant lost on the two Rodriguez albums. Segerman made these judgments without knowing much about Avant. That is a tragedy. Others like Matt Sullivan and Steve Rowland speak glowingly of the label head. He is a giant in the record business. He is a respected figure. He is also an honest man.

The duplicity Segerman demonstrates was illustrated when he talked in a praiseworthy manner about Avant. But that is Segerman's way. He is like the wind. He changes his view with prevailing opinions to curry favors with the powers. Segerman will do anything for fame.

In sharp contrast, Steve Rowland never tells the story beyond the limits of the material. The same cannot be said for Segerman. This is the reason Clarence Avant was victimized in the documentary. Segerman told Malik Bendjelloul time and time again Avant cheated the Sugar Man out of his royalties. He had no evidence concerning Avant's business practices. Avant is a good guy. He is a solid businessman. He is not a crook. The duplicity in Segerman's character allegedly suggests his concern with making royalties a key to the story. Sad!

Steve Rowland: "I have been paid regularly without fail the proper royalties each year for producing **Coming From Reality** and I receive a check for the songs I produced on **Searching For Sugar Man**. Others may have complaints about royalties. I have been paid regularly."

When Steve Rowland talks about fairness, he was a ringside observer to Rodriguez' story. Segerman came in late. He twisted the truth. Rowland says Clarence Avant is a good guy. He is happy with Matt Sullivan and Light In The Attic's re-releases of **Cold Fact** and **Coming From Reality**. Rowland is overjoyed Rodriguez is receiving royalties. Segerman is too busy talking about himself to comment.

There is no evidence Avant did anything illegal. In the documentary, he became visibly angry when Malik Bendjelloul asked where the royalties were paid. Avant said he didn't know anything about royalties. This is Segerman's major concern. He believes in justice for Rodriguez. That justice takes the form of economic compensation. Now Rodriguez has placed him on the sidelines. He is too vocal.

It is Rodriguez' concern with justice that impressed Segerman. At times the documentary takes too much credit for Rodriguez' music helping to end apartheid. It was important. But the impact of "The Establishment Blues" must be kept in perspective. The leadership of Nelson Mandela, the role of native South African music, and the force of international pressures, combined with Rodriguez' political songs, to create a culturally free South Africa. Rodriguez' music was important but not as dominant as Segerman suggests. An examination of South African politics shows his importance to the larger picture.

South African Politics and Rodriguez

In South Africa some critics suggest the political movement to end apartheid was fueled by Rodriguez' music. Apartheid excluded black South Africans from the mainstream. Other critics contend Rodriguez wasn't a part of the anti-apartheid movement. This viewpoint is nonsense. He was one of many whites opposed to the oppressive political system. Rodriguez' words and music bounced off the streets into the small clubs, the political dens and the centers of media protest. He was as much a part of anti-apartheid, as anyone living in South Africa.

Stephen "Sugar" Segerman and Craig Bartholomew-Strydom were typical of white South Africans opposed to apartheid. They didn't know how to frame their comments or oppose the system. You could be fined, go to jail and taken from public scrutiny for improper political comments. The Sugar Man's music provided hope for a democratic society. Segerman said: "We didn't understand anti-establishment until we heard Rodriguez' music."

Apartheid in South African lasted from 1948 until 1994. By that time, Rodriguez' **Cold Fact** and **Coming From Realty** albums were twenty plus years old. Segerman was forty years old. He must have felt relief. He could listen to the Sex Pistols without fear of recrimination. He may have felt funny listening to Sid Vicious at forty, but he was free from government reprisals. He also began the serious part of his quest to find Rodriguez. If it hadn't been for political change, Segerman would not have had the freedom to continue the search for the Sugar Man.

When Nelson Mandela was released from prison on February 11, 1990, he toured the world. He began "the long walk" to end the brutal and oppressive apartheid system holding black South Africa back politically and economically. Apartheid prevented white South Africans from fully exploring intellectual themes, and the repressive system virtually enslaved the native population. This is where Rodriguez filled the void. No one intellectually inclined was happy with apartheid.

For Stephen "Sugar" Segerman and Craig Bartholomew-Strydom, apartheid's end meant they could indulge their fascination in all types of music. While Rodriguez was the soundtrack to their lives, they had the time, the freedom and the money to pursue their quest to find the Sugar Man.

Stephen "Sugar" Segerman: "Rodriguez became something of a rebel icon....We all bought his records." The quest for political and social change took a leap forward due to Rodriguez. But it was a native South African movement, led by Nelson Mandela, that ended the corruption and brutal oppression of the Dutch colonists. When the colonial South African apartheid state began in 1652 no one envisioned a Mexican-American singer from Detroit fueling a portion of the march to freedom.

From 1990 to 1994, South Africa went through a transition where black majority rule triumphed. This provided new freedoms for musicians, writers and intellectuals. The young, white citizens were better off as wages, working conditions, job availability; educational facilities, movies and music liberated the local psyche.

There was intellectual controversy in the realm of popular music. Paul Simon and South African musicians including Ladysmith Black Mambazo and Ray Phiri created an internationally popular form of South African music. Simon's album **Graceland**, released in August 1986, was his seventh solo album. The album went platinum. It became the biggest South African seller since Michael Jackson's **Thriller**. In 1987 **Graceland** was awarded album of the year. The following year it won for record of the year.

Artists United Against Apartheid criticized Simon's album. They argued he exploited South African musical talent. It was a contentious time. Eventually, some critics praised Simon for encouraging world acceptance for such South African musicians as Hugh Masakela, Miriam Makeba and Ladysmith Black Mambazo.

For more than two decades Rodriguez listened to Simon and Garfunkel and other pop sounds. While **Graceland** was a mid-1980s Simon hit, two decades earlier the Sugar Man was aware of and listened to Simon's early solo material and the mellifluous harmonies of Simon and Garfunkel.

Rodriguez listened intensely to Simon's **Graceland.** In an interview with **The New Yorker**, Rodriguez told Edward Douglas he listened to Paul Simon's "I Am A Rock." The Sugar Man also said he listened to Simon's August 1965 album **The Paul Simon Songbook**. When Simon toured Europe in the summer of 1965, he was still an up and coming solo act. When he returned to the U. S., Simon cut **The Sound of Silence**, which was Simon and Garfunkel's breakthrough LP. It also included "I Am A Rock." Those close to Rodriguez told me he was mesmerized by Simon's solo sound, as well as the Simon and Garfunkel hits. He was a fan. There was an influence.

This indicated Rodriguez listened to commercial songs. He wasn't a hippie songwriter. He was a seasoned composer with a commercial touch. He was working toward a hit record. No one recognized it. While Rodriguez' material is nothing like Simon and Garfunkel's, the story suggests he was working on his commercial possibilities.

When Edward Douglas asked Rodriguez about his future. He was happy to discuss his career revival. By 1972, he was done as a recording artist. He explained to Douglas: "The genre of the protest song was something I chose to do as a means to express those ideas." Then Rodriguez paused in the interview and talked politics. This exchange demonstrated how the Sugar Man wove social themes, political malfeasance and a demand for changing the system into lyrical beauty. But was his music influential in South Africa? It was!

There was no controversy surrounding Rodriguez' music. He was influential. There is no question musical groups and individual artists marched in South Africa to freedom to the beat of the Sugar Man's music. There were many South African bands ready to end the odious apartheid system.

Rodriguez' music was the stuff of revolution. "I Wonder," was used to question the racist policies of South African President Frederik Willem de Klerk, who was forced in 1990 to begin negotiations to end apartheid. Rodriguez' **Cold Fact** contained songs that voiced stringent opposition to apartheid. "Crucify Your Mind" educated every young South African how to phrase words and implement policies challenging apartheid.

When Rodriguez wrote: "How many times can you wake up in this comic book and plant flowers," he unwittingly commented on the lack of protest early on among young white South Africans. This changed when South African bands employed Rodriguez' lyrics to challenge the political establishment.

As a political force, the Sugar Man was subtle, understated and wise. This is why his message resonated to all ages and classes. He was a cultural healer.

Rodriguez as A Cultural Healer

What impact did Rodriguez' music have upon South Africa? He was responsible for liberating the minds of South Africans. In the Afrikaans communities his lyrics opened the door to a wider view of the world. There was an intense cultural revolution for white South Africans, as they listened to Rodriguez' lyrics. The outside world came alive in a panoply of new visions and directions.

When the South African government introduced loyalty programs to keep the races separate, it was Rodriguez' lyrics which showed another way to achieve racial balance. When television came to South Africa in 1976 the outside world and its influences inundated the society. Rodriguez' music ran counter to established thought patterns as his images slowly seeped into the mainstream of South African society. Marthe Muller of South African Women in Dialogue said: "Rodriguez's music was calibrated to our pain." The lyrics allowed for words to challenge government edicts. When Rodriguez talked about the system, South Africans listened. He remarked there should be more women running for political office.

Women remain a strong influence in the Rodriguez story. He is a feminist. While in South Africa, Rodriguez lent his voice to many liberal political concerns. The feminist movement was a latecomer to South African society. Rodriguez gave his approval for support of women's issues on stage, and he donated a portion of his concert fees to battered women's shelters.

The notion of being anti-establishment was introduced by Rodriguez; he criticized every area of government dysfunction. When Rodriguez wrote: "Garbage ain't collected, women ain't protected. Politicians using people, they've been abusing, the mafia's getting bigger, like pollution in the river," he hit a chord with virtually every white South African even though he described Detroit.

Rodriguez' passion for visual imagery had a dramatic impact upon white South Africans. There was a dignity and humanity to Rodriguez. His music cut through racial strife.

Stephen "Sugar" Segerman to the Rescue

Stephen "Sugar" Segerman is a former jeweler who became a partner in a Cape Town record store. He also studied law. His employment resume is at best spotty. He is as a friend said: "a dilettante with a social conscience. He comes from a privileged background." His parents lived in the politically left Johannesburg suburb Emmarentia. Segerman grew up Jewish, upper class, economically privileged, and he was extremely intellectual. From an early age he was a voracious reader. His intellect was demonstrated when he was selected as one of South Africa's quiz kids. Personally, he was prickly. His life as a young man was at the Synagogue and the local candy store. He was interested in music and the arts. Segerman was a well-rounded, bright kid growing up in Bernard and Joyce Segerman's home.

He was much like Little Lord Fauntleroy with a privileged background and every advantage in a society bent upon racial injustice. Fortunately, he was liberal and enlightened. He was never a force for apartheid. He was a staunch opponent of this brutal system.

Segerman was upset the repressive South African apartheid government separated the native population from the more recent Dutch immigrants He never said a word. It was too dangerous. While South Africa was a multi-racial society, the Dutch minority controlled politics, the cultural life and the radio and television content. There was institutionalized racism. Some of Rodriguez' songs were banned for liberal content and inappropriate words. In this atmosphere, Segerman developed a curiosity about things outside South Africa.

When he discovered Elvis Presley, Cliff Richards, the Rolling Stones and the Beatles, he was a teenager with a penchant for new music. He had an early fifteen minutes of fame when he was a South African quiz kid. In 1954 the first non-government controlled radio station went on the air, SABC. He remains one of South Africa's longest lasting Quiz Kids. By all accounts, Segerman is a brilliant individual with an inquisitive mind. His formidable intellect quickly translated to punk music, the blues, forms of protest music, and he developed a collector's treasure. He stores his rare vinyl, CDs, pictures, assorted memorabilia and other rock and roll rarities in the Blue Trommel room. This is a collector's dream that can be toured by making an appointment at Mabu Vinyl.

From 1972, when he discovered Rodriguez, until he began writing reviews for the **SA Digest**, Segerman built his knowledge of the industry and how music was recorded, distributed and publicized. He was only seventeen years old, about to turn eighteen, when the record-collecting bug hit. He began to analyze where records were pressed. He learned Rodriguez' **Cold Fact** had a South African pressing. He looked up the musicians. There weren't any listed on the album. He learned the producer's names, Mike Theodore and Dennis Coffey. He began researching who was responsible for the LP. He learned about Clarence Avant, Harry Balk and he discovered names like Jesus Rodriguez and Sixth Prince. None of this made sense to the inquisitive young man. He was at work daily pushing a pencil in a military office with dreams of a life outside the confines of the military and the strict, repressive South African society. By the time he finished his university education in 1977-1978, he moved into a nine-person commune in the Johannesburg suburb of Parktown. Music still lurked in his soul. He had no interest in a nine to five job. The dilettante in his soul prompted Segerman to take the easy way out.

After university, Segerman worked in his father's jewelry business. He married. He began a family. The vinyl disease was still in place. He collected records. He also continued his infatuation with Sixto Rodriguez. He knew the Sugar Man was probably dead. At least those were the rumors. He also knew Rodriguez' music was the national anthem to a generation of freedom loving South Africans. The drive to end apartheid was an African political movement bringing Nelson Mandela to power and ending the brutal and repressive racial policies that made black South Africans second-class citizens. As a Jew, Segerman experienced discrimination, notably from his high school principal, when he wanted to audition for the Quiz Kids. He became an unrequited liberal who fought for the underdog.

Like most record collectors, once Segerman found that there was no information on Rodriguez, he became obsessed with finding the lost singer. "Rodriguez's music was for us like what Jimi Hendrix and the Doors were for the guys in Vietnam," Segerman concluded.

As Segerman observed: "In the 1970s, if you walked into a random white, liberal, middle class household that had a turntable and a pile of records...you would always see **Abbey Road** by the Beatles, **Bridge Over Troubled Water** by Simon and Garfunkel and **Cold Fact** by Rodriguez."

When Sugar moved his family to Cape Town, it provided the backdrop for the final stage of the Sixto Rodriguez story. Unbeknownst to Segerman and his friends they were about to find the Sugar Man.

When Craig Bartholomew-Strydom and Stephen "Sugar" Segerman met for the first time at a Cape Town coffee shop, they were instantly on the same page. After this meeting Craig returned to Johannesburg. He began the laborious process of posting notes on his apartment wall with clues to all of the Sugar Man's songs. In **Searching For Sugar Man** there is a sequence where Craig points to his detective work. It was Bartholomew-Strydom who did the legwork. He was the brain. He was the co-conspirator. He was also the unrequited intellectual. He was also the writer.

Craig Bartholomew-Strydom: The Co-Conspirator

Craig Bartholomew-Strydom is a journalist. He had the same fixations as Segerman concerning Rodriguez. For a time he lived in Baltimore Maryland. This U. S. community is nowhere near Detroit. This didn't discourage him from spending the better part of two decades searching for Rodriguez. By the time Bartholomew-Strydom found the Sugar Man, he was forty-eight years old.

While growing up in South Africa, Bartholomew-Strydom listened to Rodriguez' music. He also imbibed the myths associated with his career. Like Segerman, it bothered him no one knew anything about Rodriguez. This didn't seem possible. After all everything was on the Internet. As a journalist, Bartholomew-Strydom had questions. What happened to the royalties? Why weren't the records reissued? Why was there no information on the singer known as Sixto Rodriguez? Why were there so many labels outside the U. S. issuing Rodriguez' albums? Why wasn't anyone in America interested in his music?

Bartholomew-Strydom focused on the lyrics: "The little man gets shafted, songs and moneys drafted...." He thought a great deal about the music. This intensified his search for Rodriguez. It was in the lyrics Bartholomew-Strydom believed the Rodriguez riddle would be solved.

He teamed up with Segerman who, along with Alec McCrindle in 1997, created a website, the Great Rodriguez Hunt. The story suddenly had a new beginning and a specific direction.

They wanted to find out how he died. A milk carton was put up on the website. The website posed a question: "Does anyone know of Rodriguez' whereabouts?" In time one of Rodriguez's daughters, Eva, placed a message on the chat board. The search for Rodriguez was over. But that was just the beginning of the story. No one knew anything about Rodriguez. Who was he? Where did he live? Did he have a family? All those questions were answered. There were surprises. "This is a story that keeps having happy endings," Segerman remarked.

The Increased Role of Craig Bartholomew-Strydom with Segerman by His Side

Craig Bartholomew-Strydom is the hidden secret weapon in the Rodriguez story. He lived in Baltimore Maryland for much of the time Stephen "Sugar" Segerman was searching for Rodriguez. Craig also understands American rock and roll. He is an excellent writer. Unlike Segerman, he is not a dilettante.

While living in Baltimore, he began to research and write the story that became the script for **Searching For Sugar Man**. It is Bartholomew-Strydom's contributions to the script, which makes the documentary so touching. His words combined with South Africa's majestic landscape paints a picture of hope. The dilapidated, decaying Detroit city view is in sharp contrast to Cape Town's beautiful landscape, lush foliage and balmy weather.

When the Oscar was announced for **Searching For Sugar Man**, Bartholomew-Strydom was in Hollywood. He watched with pride as filmmaker Malik Bendjelloul accepted the award. He was asked why Rodriguez was not present, Bartholomew-Strydom said: "He didn't want to take any of the credit himself. That says everything about the man and his story that you want to know."

Segerman and Bartholomew-Strydom Sitting for an Interview

In the aftermath of **Searching For Sugar Man's** successes, the 85th Academy Awards presented the best Oscar documentary award to Simon Chinn and Malik Bendjelloul. Just before the Oscar was presented, Stephen "Sugar" Segerman and Craig Bartholomew-Strydom sat down for an interview with a South African TV program, Top Billing. The host, Jo-Ann, presented quite an interesting look at the Rodriguez phenomenon.

She reported when Segerman came to Cape Town with his wife and family looking for economic opportunity, he found it when he purchased an interest in a record store, Mabu Vinyl. This is the premier record store in Cape Town. The movie has made Rodriguez famous, it has done little to change Segerman's daily life. He is still a businessman. Although he is one who attended the 85th Annual Academy Awards.

When Craig Bartholomew-Strydom came into the store, they talked at length about finding Rodriguez. It was 1997. It had been twenty-six years since **Coming From Reality** was issued. They pointed out the search took some time. They used the library, encyclopedias, music magazines and the telephone with no luck. Then after their website went up, they connected with Rodriguez' daughter, Eva Alice Rodriguez, and this put them in touch with Sixto Rodriguez living in a working class section of Detroit on Avery Street.

This was due to a faux milk cartoon with a drawing of the Sugar Man. The slogan on the milk carton stated: "**WANTED**." This led to Eva's call stating her father was well, and he was living a tranquil life. After Segerman and Bartholomew-Strydom recovered from the shock of finding Rodriguez the story took on new twists and turns.

Regan and Eva became allies in the film that would make Rodriguez a household word. The article in the South African **Mail** and **Guardian** on February 20, 1998 with an eye-catching headline, told one all they needed to know about the Sugar Man. The headline read: "Fact: Rodriguez Lives." The Sugar Man's mystery ended. Then from 2001 to 2011 he emerged as a cult artist. The decade long journey to **Searching For Sugar Man** became another mythical tale.

"For me this was the end of the search," Segerman remarked. He didn't realize this was the beginning of a new journey. The next year Rodriguez undertook a dramatic South African concert tour. He was back from the dead. When Rodriguez appeared on the South African TV Show, Top Billing, he talked about how exhilarating the 1998 concerts were for him. When he was asked if he was angry about losing his royalties. "I think the issue about the back royalties will be taken care of," Rodriguez said. Since that statement there have been three major lawsuits. The royalty issue remains unresolved. Rumor has it all lawsuits were settled. Further rumors are Rodriguez won all three lawsuits.

Once Segerman found Rodriguez, he talked to him on the telephone; Segerman said he couldn't have imagined the story would continue. It did. Segerman was responsible, with Craig Bartholomew-Strydom, for bringing Rodriguez in concert to South Africa. These shows were filmed. They provided a great deal of the drama in **Searching For Sugar Man**.

Rodriguez' Impact on Segerman

For Segerman certain Rodriguez songs bring him back to his youth. Segerman said: "If I put on 'Crucify Your Mind' I get that Fuck, I'm in the army feeling…." He still remembers that night on September 15, 1997 when his home phone rang. Segerman was astonished. It was Rodriguez on the line. When asked about his reaction, Segerman commented: "I mostly just told him how massive he was in South Africa. I told him that if he came here, he wouldn't believe how popular he was." On Rodriguez' part there was reticence. He had been disappointed too many times. Segerman persisted. Rodriguez came to South Africa for the concerts. The rest is history.

In January 2012, when Segerman accompanied the director, Malik Bendjelloul, to the opening night of the Sundance Film Festival, he had Rodriguez with him. It was a dream that started in the 1970s when a young South African soldier listened to "I Wonder" and "Sugar Man." Without Segerman's obsessive-compulsive drive to find Rodriguez, the story might have been one of lost opportunity and forgotten music. Segerman made sure that didn't happen.

On attending the Sundance Festival, Segerman said: "It was just a magical night. There was snow everywhere. It was a trip." No one from the 1960s could have said it better. "I'm happy to be part of the story, but truly, this is about Rodriguez. It couldn't have happened to a nicer person. He's a mensch. He's a gentleman. You can't swear in front of him," Segerman observed. He still remembers the day they connected with Rodriguez.

"I came to work and Alec McCrindle said you are not going to believe this," Segerman continued. "Rodriguez called." Then he questioned his friend about the call. McCrindle continued to tell Segerman the search was over. They had found Rodriguez. That night Rodriguez called Sugar. The story took still another turn. It was a turn that would lead to international acclaim, sold out concerts and finally a flood of royalties.

Segerman believed his quest had ended. He found Rodriguez. He had, along with Bartholomew-Strydom, solved one of rock and roll's greatest mysteries. Or was it a mystery? More obviously it was a good story taking on mythic proportions in **Searching For Sugar Man**.

The Coming From Reality Album and Its Impact Upon Segerman

Coming From Reality had a special impact upon Segerman. It appears he didn't know about the album's scarcity until he met a young American girl, Ronit Molko, on the beach at Camps Bay. She was looking for **Cold Fact**. Then one of her friends began talking about **Coming From Reality**. Segerman may not have heard of this album. Then he had an epiphany. Why couldn't anyone find and purchase Rodriguez' records in Los Angeles? No one had heard of it. It was out of print. It was at this time he began searching for what he termed: "The missing Rodriguez album." That LP turned out to be **Coming From Reality**. This created another avenue for Segerman to pursue Rodriguez.

This young girl piqued Segerman's brain to the point where he was determined to find out everything he could about the Sugar Man. The obsessive-compulsive collector set a goal. Segerman would search out the Sugar Man's music. He would find out about his life. He would find him. He did all that in a twenty plus years search sparked by a second album, **Coming From Reality**.

The quest for **Coming From Reality** proved to be a moment of defeat. After searching every record store he could find, as well as thrift and second hand shops, Segerman gave up the quest. One day he wandered over to his friend Andre Bakkes' house. He lamented his futile search for **Coming From Reality**. Bakkes smiled. He went into another room and came out with a mint copy of Rodriguez' second album. It was the official South African release. This intensified Segerman's interest. The business side of the Rodriguez story also intrigued him. He added up the royalties the Sugar Man should have received. He was astonished at the lost royalties.

Coming From Reality was released in South Africa in 1972. It was an A & M-Sussex (SXBS 7012) release. The A & M label, on the top of the record, had a square black and silver Sussex logo. Steve Rowland's name was prominent on the bottom of the vinyl album. The operative wisdom was Rowland's hit making prowess would cross the album over into the commercial mainstream. There is one other strange credit on the album: "Impresario Clarence Avant."

The A & M version of **Coming From Reality** sold moderately in South Africa. It went out of print. Segerman was told a re-release of **Coming From Reality** was in the works. The problem is the South African record company didn't have the original tapes. Company executives didn't have a copy of the album. They weren't sure where to go and what to do. When the LP finally was released it was on the Sussex label. When the record company received the pristine album, they called Segerman and asked him to write the liner notes. He enlisted Bakkes' help.

There are phrases from Segerman's 1976 liner notes that were a portent of things to come: "There were no concrete cold facts about the artist known as Rodriguez. It is not known if he is alive or dead. Any musicologist detectives out there?" These words of wisdom brought Craig Bartholomew-Strydom into the story.

The first step in the rediscovery process was finding the Sugar Man and bringing him to South Africa. They did for the triumphant 1998 tour. It could have ended there. It didn't. Segerman, Bartholomew-Strydom, Andre Bakkes and a host of other Rodrigologists continued their quest to reignite the Sugar Man's career. It would not end with six South African concerts in 1998. They wanted him to achieve international stardom. They wanted his songs re-released. They wanted recognition for his superlative songwriting. No one believed they would achieve these goals. They accomplished all of them.

The Final Steps in Finding Rodriguez

After Segerman persuaded his workmate, Alec McCrindle, at the tech company where he worked, Intekom, to put up a Website, the stage was set in April 1997 to launch the Website: "The Great Rodriguez Hunt." This was the final step to discovering the Sugar Man. It also brought the dank Detroit streets into the story.

When Craig interviewed the best-known American expatriate musician living and working in South Africa, he found the expatriate American singer, Shawn Phillips, had no knowledge of Sixto Rodriguez. After a ninety-minute interview with Phillips, Craig hit another dead end. Then he had an idea. He would follow the money.

With diligence Craig went to PolyGram. He asked about Rodriguez. They knew nothing. They weren't sure why RPM distributed the two albums. PolyGram was flummoxed at Bartholomew-Strydom's questions. Why was he asking them? The search continued. It led to Mike Theodore. He was the co-producer of the first album **Cold Fact**. That is when Bartholomew-Strydom found out Rodriguez was alive and living near Detroit's Cass Corridor in Woodbridge. It was a shock and a revelation. The stage was set for the contact to bring the Sugar Man to South Africa for the 1998 concert tour.

In the midst of the chaos of finding Sixto Rodriguez, Craig married his long time Baltimore girlfriend Philippa Strydom. Now things heated up. They prepared to bring Sixto Rodriguez to Cape Town for his first South African tour. Unwittingly, this was the initial step in the international resurgence.

The South African duo was an odd couple. Segerman is an in your face fan-businessman. He is loud mouthed and searching for personal fame. In sharp contrast, Bartholomew-Strydom is quiet, self effacing and reflective. He had no interest in fame. This was not lost on Sixto Rodriguez. In time the Sugar Man turned away from Segerman's mania for the spotlight. His abusive personality was a sharp contrast to Bartholomew-Strydom's quiet pessimism.

The Segerman-Bartholomew-Strydom team achieved amazing results. Their search will never be duplicated. One of the ironies is Rodriguez was well and alive performing in Australia. He continued to play the gutbucket Detroit clubs. He wrote. He raised a family. He had a career as a political activist. He pursued his education. He lived a normal life. When Malik Bendjelloul entered the picture, the filmmaker laid this out for the viewer. It is one of the most interesting stories in the annals of rock music. It will never be repeated.

Nine

The South African Comeback 1998

"He's really alive! These were the words on more than one nostalgic fan's lips as a crowd of over 2000 listened to Rodriguez's first ever-live performance in South Africa - and his first appearance on stage in 18 years. The 'Sugar Man' enthralled from the first, instantly recognizable, notes of 'I Wonder' through to the much requested and long-awaited 'The Establishment Blues."

Afrikaans newspaper Die Burger March 7, 1998

"Dead men don't tour."

Konny Rodriguez

"There have been so many rumors and urban legends all these years. Stories that he was dead, blind and imprisoned have all proven to be false."

Stephen "Sugar" Segerman

Once the search for Sixto Rodriguez ended, Stephen "Sugar" Segerman convinced him to tour South Africa. The Sugar Man was reticent. It took some time. Segerman persisted. The performer who was more popular than Elvis, the Beatles or the Rolling Stones was ready to appear for the first time in a country where he was a superstar. There was general skepticism. Was this the real Rodriguez? Was this a scam? Was this a hoax? The story sounded too good to be true. It wasn't!

The press, record industry magnates and hard-core music aficionados were skeptical. Rumors and urban myths were quickly put to rest with a series of stunning performances in which Rodriguez casually sauntered on stage to thunderous applause. He was relaxed. It looked like he had been doing this his entire life. He had. But his performances were in Motor City gutbucket bars.

The logic of someone dying in a fire on stage or of a drug overdose and then returning from the dead was a tale too good to be true. He was alive. Myth continued to triumph reality. Then the rumors grew into epic proportions. Drugs, alcohol, prison sentences, killing his wife and a host of other stories were bandied about as Sixto Rodriguez and his family prepared to land in Cape Town.

RODRIGUEZ
SOUTH AFRICA
1998

Then another rumor swept South Africa. A local Rodriguez impersonator would front the back up band Big Sky. The sense of mystery deepened. Who was responsible? The blame lies in the music business. The manner in which it manipulated publicity for Rodriguez' concert appearances guaranteed success.

The South African musical direction was dominated by a particularly inoffensive soft, syrupy pop sound with the hand of London producer Mickey Most directing the insipid local hits. This was all done with the approval of the apartheid government. By the time Rodriguez appeared in 1998 that had changed.

The State of the Music Business in South Africa 1998

When Sixto Rodriguez toured South Africa in 1998 the country had a record industry in commercial growth. For years the white dominated government controlled what music was played on radio stations, what was sold in the shops, as the local authorities monitored the content. The government impeded the growth of local musicians and only flim flam pop producers like Britain's Mickey Most could sell their pop schlock.

The South African record labels lacked funds for promotion, and the black-white divide that ended with apartheid didn't heal the problems in the record business. Angus Kerr, the owner of Tropical Sweat Studios observed: "The South African record industry waned over the years to a state of indifference." Kerr lamented the lack of support for local artists. Why is this important? By the time Rodriguez appeared, for his triumphant 1998 concert tour, the locals were looking to crown a South African icon. They crowned the Sugar Man even though he wasn't a South African. He felt like one. His records sold like he was a native son. When he visited he felt at home. It was heart warming.

Is This the Real Rodriguez?

In February 1998 there was an air of excitement over publicity surrounding Rodriguez' appearance. His music took over the airwaves. Radio Good Hope played a portion of "I Wonder," as listeners were told repeatedly of Rodriguez' impending concerts. The **Cape Times** and the **Star** featured stories on the Sugar Man. A South African living in America, Selwyn Miller, telephoned Marketing Director, Steve Harris, of Polygram, informing him Rodriguez was on his way. He was ready for stardom, it arrived in due time!

Rodriguez almost didn't make it to South Africa. He had his doubts. He was reticent to travel half way around the world for an unknown audience. He was glad he did. He wasn't disappointed. The question when Rodriguez walked into the room was: "What happened to the royalties?" There was no answer. The cold trail to the royalties continues to the present day. It is not a pretty story.

The search for Rodriguez' royalties were aided by conversations with record executives like Steve Harris. Others in the South African record industry, notably Robbie Mann and Terry Fairweather, had knowledge of where the royalties were sent. They have never discussed the subject. They are reticent to talk about it. But at this point they were simply happy the Sugar Man arrived for a series of concerts.

Stephen "Sugar" Segerman is a smart person. He insisted, as did the promoter, Rodriguez bring his family to South Africa. This helped to ease his initial reticence. Segerman convinced him to come to South Africa with his soft sell. Rodriguez does not intuitively trust people. He has been burned too many times.

Although he had never performed in South Africa, Rodriguez' music was released by Polygram and RPM Records. When Matt Mann, Robbie's father, founded RPM in South Africa, the label was instrumental in releasing Rodriguez' material for three decades.

Craig Bartholomew-Strydom Interviews Rodriguez

When Craig Bartholomew-Strydom telephoned Rodriguez, there was a meeting of the minds. The noise in the background distracted Bartholomew-Strydom. He didn't realize the Sugar Man was sitting on a bar stool at the Motor City Brewing Company. The noise emanated from a group of beer drinkers who had no clue, as to Rodriguez' South African celebrity. The jovial atmosphere prompted the Sugar Man to take charge. He did most of the talking. This is not characteristic of Rodriguez. It is a means of disguising his shy, private nature. Rodriguez at times seemed to be interviewing Craig. They talked at length like old friends.

Bartholomew-Strydom realized the Sugar Man was not an easy interview. He was suspicious. He was reticent. Craig made a list of questions he believed would make Rodriguez comfortable. When this interview appeared in the **Mail And Guardian** on February 20, 1998 fans in South Africa and the U. K. learned not only that Rodriguez was alive, he was still an aspiring musician. He had been working in Detroit clubs sporadically since the 1970s. He never mentioned this to Bartholomew-Strydom.

When the interview began Rodriguez asked: "So, tell me about yourself?" As Bartholomew-Strydom remarked he smiled: "I was born in Kimberley, a very dry and dusty mining town with a mentality to match, and literally hours after my last school exam, I got the hell out." Rodriguez took over the interview. He asked a number of questions. Finally, Bartholomew-Strydom said: "Hey! Who's doing this interview?"

Maybe Rodriguez was nervous. He said that the story he was born five blocks from downtown Detroit is an urban legend. "I like to tell people that I was born on Michigan Avenue, five blocks from the centre of Detroit," Rodriguez said.

Bartholomew-Strydom: "In 'A Most Disgusting Song' you say you've played faggot bars, hooker bars, motorcycle funerals, opera houses, concert halls and even half-way houses. Are you still playing?"

Surprisingly, Rodriguez commented he was back working with Mike Theodore. He didn't elaborate. He was obviously in the recording studio. It sounded like he was making new music. Then Rodriguez startled Bartholomew-Strydom by talking about another artist. It was typical Sixto Rodriguez. He was uncomfortable talking about himself. He disdained praise.

When they discussed Pat Metheny, Rodriguez remarked he listened to Metheny's "I Dream With Mexico." He generally liked his recordings. "I've heard the piece" Rodriguez continued. "Overlapping guitars. In my opinion, the guitar is central in popular music. Guitars have evolved, changed shape, become electrified. It is one of the most unifying language tools in the world. I'd be lost without one." While he was out of the limelight Rodriguez listened to Billy Joel, James Taylor and Hank Williams. Then Bartholomew-Strydom asked him: "How is your guitar proficiency?"

Rodriguez said it was about the time he dropped out of high school that he began playing the guitar. "It altered my life," Rodriguez said. Then he talked about a summer he spent with a group of Native Americans. "It was a great summer. We went swimming in Grand Bend and to pow-wows [a magical Indian ceremony] throughout Michigan. As far back as 1974 I was involved in powwows at the Wayne State University Campus," Rodriguez continued. "The Native American culture is a vibrant and natural culture."

Bartholomew-Strydom: "In your music you mention names like Jane S. Piddy, Molly MacDonald and Willie Thompson. Who are they?"

Rodriguez: "These people are fictional. I tapped on the writer's poetic license giving them names and shapes. Almost as a caricature works for the visual artist." The interview with Rodriguez saw

Bartholomew-Strydom elicit more material from the Sugar Man than previous journalists. Not only was he happy about coming to perform in South African, he was in a talkative mood.

Rodriguez and His Family on the Way to South Africa

In February 1998 Detroit experienced its usual brutal winter. Snow! Sleet! A lack of city services! The employment outlook was bleak due to the auto industries imminent collapse and a town led by corrupt politicians with little regard for the blue-collar worker. After laboring for more than twenty-five years in menial, home repair, building demolition and handyman work, Rodriguez, his wife and his daughters were flying on a twenty-four hour trek to South Africa.

It was an amazing time. There was no haggling over concert guarantees, the contract included first class accommodations, time for sightseeing and while he didn't have a band or a guitar the concert promoter agreed to find anything the Sugar Man needed. There were no impediments to his upcoming shows.

Once Rodriguez' family landed everything was in order. All the contractual obligations were fulfilled. He would soon thank Segerman, Bartholomew-Strydom and everyone involved in the 1998 shows.

As they settled into a comfortable Camps Bay townhouse, Rodriguez was concerned about the backing band. He needn't have worried. They had played his songs for decades.

Walking on Stage in South Africa: Would it Happen?

When Rodriguez walked on stage for his first South African concert there was disbelief. This famous singer was back from the dead. He was the folk rock icon that gave birth to a sense of freedom, and the notion the government needed to change its apartheid policies. Rodriguez' music for almost thirty years was the national anthem to free white South African thoughts.

The myth of Rodriguez' death on stage by shooting himself or by a drug overdose had little to do with reality, and there was much more creative myth making. The myths surrounding Rodriguez were so pervasive South African journalists remained skeptical. The public was intrigued. The publicity surrounding his return evoked a mystical Jesus coming from afar. The reality is the 1998 concerts were triumphs. Why didn't they translate to the American music scene? That remains an unanswered mystery.

When advertisements for Rodriguez' appearances were placed on every South African billboard, coffee shop, bar or telephone pole, there was a great deal of skepticism. Was he still alive? As the Sugar Man's wife, Konny Rodriguez, said: "Dead men don't tour." There was also a journalistic blitz sending an aura of intrigue throughout the country. Rodriguez' elusive South African image was one of mystery and intrigue. That was about to come to an end.

The first South African show was an unqualified success. There were a few things the fans missed. The Sugar Man had forgotten the lyrics to "A Most Disgusting Song." It had been seventeen years since he recorded or played the tune. Rodriguez was nervous. After he received photocopies of the lyrics, he relaxed. In typical Sugar Man mode, he began thinking of his stage show. He wasn't an amateur. The years playing in and around Detroit created a professional demeanor the Sugar Man could count on in his South African concerts. It was as if he had never been off stage. As his daughter, Eva, said in **Searching For Sugar Man** it seemed natural for him to saunter on stage and entertain an appreciative crowd. He had been training for it all his life. He was now, as he said, a solid fifty-six. He mesmerized the 1998 South African audiences.

There was no reason for Rodriguez to worry. From the early morning, when Cape Town's Bellville Velodrome opened, the people who had lined up for hours rushed into the arena. There was a festive air. The Sugar Man was coming. No one wanted to miss it. To add to the excitement, Rodriguez' back up band, Big Sky, was a major South African concert draw.

When he came out of obscurity in South Africa, Rodriguez had raised three daughters. They were on their own. His life was a quiet and a peaceful one. He lived in Detroit in the house where he settled years earlier. He led a simple life. He read. He wrote. He thought about the key political issues. He continued to go out to clubs to see new music. He read **Billboard**, the local rock magazine **Creem,** and when Dennis Loren founded **Record Profile Magazine**; he bought and read it religiously. He performed locally, if sporadically.

Preparing for Rodriguez

The preparations for Rodriguez' triumphant visit to South Africa took a great deal of time. On February 11, 1998 a jubilant Stephen "Sugar" Segerman telephoned Craig Bartholomew-Strydom to announce: "Rodriguez is coming." Then signs went up all over Cape Town.

On February 12, Radio Good Hope began blitzing the airwaves with the announcement Rodriguez was on his way. The radio station blasted out brief snippets of "I Wonder." Was he the real Rodriguez? That was the question. The answer was soon to come.

Main Event Management brought in corporate sponsors to help defray the cost. No one was sure Rodriguez would draw a substantial audience considering the myths and legends attached to his career.

The publicity surrounding Rodriguez' appearances began with a press release: "The mystery that will be solved is: What ever happened to Rodriguez, the artist who recorded the cult album **Cold Fact**?"

The 1998 South African Tour Dates

Rodriguez' March 1998 welcome to South Africa tour is the stuff of legend. He was presumed dead. There were no facts to quote Stephen "Sugar" Segerman, "about the artist known as Rodriguez." Yet, he was in South Africa playing to adoring crowds. The March 6-7: Velodrome, Bellville, Cape Town appearance provided a set list for the tour. There were some minor variations, but Rodriguez gave his fans the songs they desired.

The Set List for the 1998 Tour with Minor Variations

- I Wonder
- Only Good For Conversation
- Can't Get Away
- Crucify Your Mind
- Jane S. Piddy
- To Whom It May Concern
- Like Janis
- Inner City Blues
- Street Boy
- Halfway Up The Stairs
- I Think Of You
- Rich Folks Hoax
- Climb Up On My Music
- **Encores:**
- Sugar Man
- Establishment Blues
- Forget It

March 9-10: Standard Bank Arena, Johannesburg: Getting Ready for the Tour

The Johannesburg audience varied in age as applause from those in their mid-twenties to senior citizens rang from the auditorium rafters. The Standard Bank Arena is an indoor stadium seating five thousand. Rodriguez sold it out within a day of the concert announcement.

The joy of Rodriguez' fans suggests the intimacy of his shows. He was not only welcomed, it was as if he came back from the dead. There was a festive mood for the opening Rodriguez shows. There was a small ceremony backstage after the initial Standard Bank Arena concert. Rodriguez was presented with a South African platinum record for sales of **Cold Fact** in excess of 50,000 albums. The Sugar Man was overwhelmed. He didn't care about the money. Recognition was another matter. Rodriguez' daughters made a comparison to the Cinderella story. His family loved the recognition.

On March 9-10, 1998 when Rodriguez appeared at the Standard Bank Arena in Johannesburg the crowd exceeded the available seating. This five thousand-seat auditorium had room for another 1200 chairs. As the arena was made ready, Eva Rodriguez filmed the arena. It was empty. There was no need to worry as more than six thousand fans stormed into the Standard Bank Arena. They were eager to see the performer who defined the counterculture and civil rights for black and white South Africans.

This concert, as well as the others, paved the way for reintroducing Sixto Rodriguez. The problem was product. There was nothing new in the stores. Sony quickly taped the shows for release. They had to obtain the rights to the songs. This was easily done. The result was the album, **Live Fact**. The familiar songs were done in a new and innovative manner. Sony distributed the album guaranteeing a wide placement and the payment of a fair royalty. Long before **Searching For Sugar Man's** success, Sony was paying the Sugar Man. The problem was **Live Fact** was available only in a limited market.

The spoken introduction by Tony Blewitt is a nice touch. Blewitt was one of the premier FM radio personalities, and he was a TV presenter. **Live Fact** was released in the stores on June 12, 1998. Sony Music South Africa released it on the Columbia label. Clarence Avant provided the licensing. The royalty money allegedly was sent to his company Avant Garde Productions. There were so many different labels, so many side deals and confusing contracts some of the money didn't arrive directly at Avant Garde. It was difficult, if not impossible, to track the royalties. It does cloud the issue.

"As far as I am concerned young man, Rodriguez never happened," Avant remarked to Malik Bendjelloul in **Searching For Sugar Man**. This seems a strange comment in light of **Live Fact** and its licensing. But, again, there are no concrete cold facts of Avant's duplicity. **Live Fact** became a collector's item due to the release of a cassette version. There were some differences in the songs, the most notably being "To Whom It May Concern."

Sixto Rodriguez was finally a rock and roll icon. The seventeen live songs featured key tunes from his first two albums. The South African musicians who backed him notably guitarist, Willem Moller, played his material for decades. Moller could cover Rodriguez' tunes in his sleep. It was a dream come true for Moller and his fellow musicians. They came of age playing "I Wonder" and "The Establishment Blues." Now it was time to back the great man on stage. They didn't disappoint.

March 11: Carousel, Pretoria

In the Carousel Ballroom, a tent like structure just outside of Pretoria, Rodriguez took the stage to the astonishment of the audience. Many people believed he was dead. This was perhaps nothing more than a scam. It wasn't. For an hour and a half Rodriguez performed to an audience that had loved his music for more than twenty-five years.

March 13: Village Green, Durban

Musicians
Sixto Rodriguez: Vocals, acoustic guitar
Willem Möller: Electric Guitar
Russel Taylor: Keyboards
Reuben Samuels: Drums, percussion
Graeme Currie: Electric bass, acoustic bass
Tonia Selley: Background vocals, percussion

One wonders what Rodriguez thought when he walked off the plane in South Africa and saw his name on posters tacked to telephone polls. He rode in a limousine to a condo before he began his South African tour. His shock and awe at his fame was evident. He was the same old Rodriguez. It didn't faze him. He took the adulation as a chance to perform. Rodriguez sees patience as a virtue. He is not a star struck performer. The existential nature of Rodriguez' personality is a safety guard against fame's excesses.

When the critics compare Rodriguez to Bob Dylan, Cat Stevens, Leonard Cohen and Nick Drake, they miss the point. Rodriguez strikes a personal chord with the listener. There is a bond. Stephen "Sugar" Segerman is a perfect example of the fan that would not let the music die. And thankfully for everyone, Segerman found Rodriguez and the rest, as we say, is history.

Rodriguez' South African tour was highlighted in a television documentary, "Dead Men Don't Tour," which played on South Africa's SABC 4 television on July 5, 2001. The documentary combined the songs from his concerts with interviews. Rodriguez' three daughters, as well as comments by Segerman and Bartholomew-Strydom, highlight his humanity, his musical genius and his humility. It was a homecoming for a person who had never been in South Africa. Yet, to the country, he was like a long lost son. America ignored Rodriguez' talent. South Africans embraced it.

The rumor mill ran rampant. When the lyrics were recalled to "Forget It," the notion persisted Rodriguez committed suicide. Critics used the words: "Thanks for your time, and you can thank me for mine, and after that's said, forget it!" Some critics suggest these were his last words spoken live on stage. The most egregious notion was he murdered his wife, and he was now in a Michigan penitentiary. There was concern fading eyesight prompted Rodriguez to use his lyrics "open the window and listen to the news" to express his health concerns. It was the reference to drugs in the **Cold Fact** album that led to speculation of death by an overdose. None of these rumors were true. It was Segerman and his journalistic cohort, Craig Bartholomew-Strydom, that wouldn't let the Rodriguez myths die.

Rodriguez' road to Cape Town began in 1970 with the release of **Cold Fact.** It sold so well in South Africa a local record company released his second album **Coming from Reality**. When he sang: "The Mayor hides the crime rate ... the public forgets the vote date," it indicated his political direction. This suggested why he was a perennial candidate for public office. While running for public office, raising a family and working on his music, he had a full life. He didn't need fame and fortune. It arrived.

Why Big Sky Made the 1998 South African Concerts Triumphant

When a legend returns it is often hit or miss. From the moment the Sugar Man walked out on stage March 6, 1998, at the Bellville Velodrome, he had the crowd in the palm of his hand. The show was tight; the musical backing by Big Sky was perfect as the crowd cheered and South African fans beamed with pleasure.

Why was Big Sky the perfect band to back the Sugar Man? They were skilled musicians without pretension. When guitarist Steve Louw founded the group in 1990 he was looking to play his Gibson guitar to appreciative audiences. Their debut album **Waiting For The Dawn** and the follow up **Horizon** made Big Sky a South African fan favorite. After a long string of Top Ten hits, they were honored as the 1996 FNB Music Award for Best Rock Act. Prior to backing Rodriguez in the 1998 shows they recorded their third album **Going Down With Mr. Green**. Why is this important? Big Sky was a seasoned, top-flight rock band. They could play anything including Rodriguez' material. They would back the Sugar Man with skill and precision. As the concert promoters, the fans and those who would make his acquaintance said to the press: "There is no reason to worry. We have it covered," Louw said.

But there was reason to worry. The Sugar Man was nervous. When he walked out of the wings onto the stage the burst of photoflashes caused Rodriguez to smile. He looked out over the crowd. Everyone was standing and cheering. It was a portent of good things to come. Nerves were still a factor. Graeme Currie walked over and slowly bent to Rodriguez' ear muttering, "break a leg." The Sugar Man smiled. Currie told him the crowd was there to see him. That comment pulled Rodriguez out of his bout of nerves. The concert began, and it exceeded everyone's expectations.

Tonia Seeley realized there was a serious error. No one was taping the show. While Rodriguez' daughter, Eva, had a small movie camera, this historic concert was not being taped for commercial use. Tonia quickly called Georgina Parkin, who worked for the production company in charge of the Rodriguez tour, and they taped the Sugar Man's historic inaugural South African concerts. A contract was drawn up, and Zev Eizik took it to the Rodriguez family. They signed off on it. There was also an agreement to film the remaining concerts. Why is this important? Without these agreements, Malik Bendjelloul would not have had the concert footage for these iconic

Sugar Man performances. The ambiance of Rodriguez' performing genius, and the onstage magic that was the 1998 South African tour was forever caught on film. It was another fourteen years before the South African TV film was essential to the documentary.

When Seeley produced her 1998 TV documentary, **Dead Men Don't Tour**, it was a blueprint for Malik Bendjelloul's **Searching For Sugar Man**. The South African shows featured encores in which Rodriguez appeared like he didn't want to leave the stage. He was a seasoned music professional who relished his late in life stardom. But the clock was ticking. He would be an international star fourteen years later thanks to **Searching For Sugar Man**.

One of the South African promoters was Swedish. He put together a brief Swedish tour of three cities to break Rodriguez in the country. This tour was a rough one. After many setbacks, the Sugar Man finally performed in Sweden. It was a blockbuster series of shows.

Rodriguez's Swedish Tour 1998

I JUST CAME BACK FROM A 3-DAY TOUR IN SWEDEN WITH RODRIGUEZ... MY ROLE WAS TO PLAY KEYBOARDS. THE SOUTH AFRICAN BAND (*BIG SKY*) WAS BOOKED TO DO THE TOUR BUT A WEEK AGO RODRIGUEZ SAID HE MIGHT NOT BE ABLE TO COME...SO THE BAND'S TICKETS WERE CANCELLED...THEN RODRIGUEZ SUDDENLY COULD MAKE IT...AND THEN IT WAS TOO LATE TO GET THE TICKETS BACK...ALL THE CONNECTIONS WERE FULLY BOOKED!

- MATTIAS BYLUND, SWEDEN, 16TH JUNE 1998

The brief three day tour of Sweden in 1998 was the first indication that Rodriguez' music was making a mark outside of South Africa or Australia. When Rodriguez' Swedish appearances took place, there was little knowledge about his music. There were five concerts booked in three days in Stockholm, Gothenburg and Malmo. This created the first signs of local interest in the Sugar Man.

There was some early confusion when the Swedish tour was planned. For some unexplainable reason, Rodriguez wasn't sure he could make it. He had throat issues. After medical treatment, he was ready for Sweden. Big Sky was the band backing him. They had their tickets cancelled. He used four Swedish musicians who filled in admirably. Mattias Bylund described his group that backed up the Sugar Man as "Blues Brothers type music."

When the Swedish backup band showed up to rehearse with Rodriguez they had very little idea how to play his music. "We didn't listen to the lyrics the same way over here, but I liked the songs a lot," Mattias Bylund remarked.

The interest in Rodriguez' music was evident after the first Swedish show. Swedish national television broadcast a short musical segment prior to his first Stockholm show. This national television exposure was highlighted by Rodriguez' versions of "I Wonder" and "Climb Up On My Music." While the Swedish musicians claimed no one knew his music, the reception was warm and appreciative. Once the locals heard "Sugar Man" and "Forget It," they embraced his lyrics. There were some highlights that popularized his appearance. A lengthy and beautifully crafted show at the trendy Stockholm celebrity Sky Bar brought the press out in mass to praise the Sugar Man. The presence of major local celebrities made Rodriguez' appearance a legendary one. He charmed the Swedes.

The midnight show in Stockholm's Sky Bar received extraordinary press. The Sky Bar is located on the 9th floor of the Royal Viking Hotel with a magnificent view of Stockholm's skyline. It was not Rodriguez' usual venue. The audience was not a typical rock and roll crowd but one of celebrities. But the Sugar Man loved the venue. He spent time talking to the people. There was a VIP table where he sat with drinks. He reveled in the acclaim.

He established a cult Swedish audience. The press turned the show into a well-publicized media event. There was also an outdoor concert earlier in the day in Stockholm. While it rained the audience sang along to "Sugar Man" and "I Wonder." The reason that the locals could sing along was due to constant airplay on Swedish radio. The show in Gothenburg, the following day, was the best of the tour. It was a club date. The intimate feel necessary to listening to Rodriguez wafted through the air as a celebrity filled audience clapped with rapturous approval.

Rodriguez ended the Swedish tour with a show in Malmo. The reception led to his records selling in large numbers in Sweden. What is intriguing is no matter where Rodriguez performed a market for his music quickly developed.

The Swedish Tour 1998 Itinerary

June 12
Morning: TV4 show
Evening: Rolambshovsparken, Stockholm
Midnight: Spy Bar, Stockholm
June 13
Afternoon: Götaplatsen, Gothenburg (with Paul Young and Staffan Hellstrand) This was a free concert that drew an enormous crowd. It was also a benefit supporting an organization Ecological Measures For The North Sea.
Evening: Park Lane, Gothenburg
June 14
Mölleplatsen, Malmö
Musicians
Sixto Rodriguez: Vocals, Acoustic guitar

Olle Junholm: Guitar
Kenneth Holmström: Bass
Mattias Bylund: Keyboards
Magnus Sjölander: Drums

The Set List

I Wonder
Only Good For Conversation
Can't Get Away
Inner City Blues
Street Boy
I Think Of You
Climb Up On My Music
Sugar Man
Forget It

Sixto Rodriguez: Vocals, Acoustic guitar
Olle Junholm: Guitar
Kenneth Holmström: Bass
Mattias Bylund: Keyboards
Magnus Sjölander: Drums

The Swedish tour is a good example of how quickly Rodriguez' music picks up an audience. He now had a presence in Sweden. The irony is a young Swedish filmmaker, Malik Bendjelloul, would soon bring Rodriguez back from obscurity. That wouldn't occur for another fourteen years.

The Swedish tour was a surprise. His popularity was helped by TV appearances and positive concert reviews. There was also a great deal of favorable publicity over a free concert where Rodriguez performed to help save the Baltic Sea from pollution.

The fans attending Rodriguez' Swedish tour were surprised he had autographed copies of **Live Fact**. He gave some CDs away. He sold a few to interested spectators.

The Third Rodriguez CD in the Midst of Rediscovery and Why it Wasn't a Third Album

Then it was back to South Africa. Rodriguez anticipated the release of his third CD after discussion with Sony Music South Africa. The notion of a third Rodriguez album was a scam. There was no third album. The repacking of his two albums, three previously unreleased songs and assorted live songs created the so-called third album. But the press couldn't resist describing a third Rodriguez album. Myth triumphs reality!

The business dealings behind this remain a mystery. The demand for new Rodriguez material came at a time when he did not have new songs. Nor did any of the labels have material in the can. The various record companies discussed a live album. Rodriguez had commercial possibilities. They just didn't know how to merchandize him. Nothing had changed since 1971 when **Coming From Reality** was released to tepid sales.

The mirrors and smoke used to describe Rodriguez' third album was complete nonsense. There was no third album. But this didn't prevent the industry from promising and promoting a mysterious third album. **After the Fact** was released in 1976. It was a vinyl release only in South Africa. Some said the third album was the 1981 Australian Blue Goose release **Alive**. This album consisted of live recordings from Australia with the three added tracks. Then Sony and Columbia announced a third album. The purported third album, Sony and Columbia gratuitously publicized, was **Live Fact**. The point is there was no third album. Past material was cobbled together. It was an amateur show centering on a mythical third album.

The Blues Room Concerts, June 1998: A Bump in the Road

The June 16 through 18 1998 Blues Room concerts solidified Rodriguez' legendary reputation. On June 16 the State of the Nation Concert to celebrate Youth Day at the Standard Bank Arena featured the South African band Just Jinger. Rodriguez attended this show as a spectator. The Sugar Man went to the dressing room and thanked Just Jinger for covering his material. When Rodriguez sauntered out on stage to wave to the crowd there was pandemonium. He didn't sing, but he received a standing ovation. Then the Sugar Man was driven to the Blues Room for a brief show.

When Rodriguez arrived for the Blues Room concerts in Rivonia, it was to publicize his new CD. Bands, like Just Jinger, celebrated his songs and helped with the publicity. Not Surprisingly, Just Jinger, one of South Africa's premier bands, recorded a live version of "Sugar Man." Just Jinger remarked: "Rodriguez was one of our inspirations."

People chatting up each other in the Blues Room made so much noise it drowned out the Sugar Man's music. It was an event that at times ignored Rodriguez. One commentator observed: "It was more social and less about Rodriguez." It was a bar and not a concert hall. This is one reason there was a disparity of interest.

The Blues Room shows were designed to publicize and sell his new South African CD. A large number of industry people and entertainment insiders attended. This made for a difficult show. For the real Rodriguez fans it didn't matter. He performed with zest. When the Blues Room shows concluded, Rodriguez thanked everyone. He returned to obscurity. While living in Detroit, he was now in his late fifties, and he was still doing home construction and demolition work. This is hard labor. It is not easy on the body. As Rodriguez approached sixty years of age, he believed his brief time in the limelight was over. He didn't realize that the South African audiences and a young Swedish kid would change his destiny in the next decade.

Tracy Croucamp, who covered the Blues Room shows, remarked: "Rodriguez thanks us for stepping out to see him, but some didn't even have the courtesy to applaud him." He was back. He could have cared less about the society types who were there to be seen. After all that is what he writes his songs about.

Ten

Rodriguez on Rodriguez: How This Helps the Biographer

"In 1973 I left the music scene....
but didn't leave music, in the sense that
I've kept up with everything...."

Rodriguez

"It's too late to go backwards.
Forward is the whole deal."

Rodriguez

"These fragments I have shored against my ruins."

T. S. Eliot

"Detroit is a symphony but I'm only one
small musician in a grand orchestra."

Sixto Rodriguez

"I am no more keen about a biography than I am about reserving a plot for myself."

Saul Bellow

By the mid-1970s Rodriguez was settled comfortable on Avery Street in a Detroit neighborhood with two story homes, cracked sidewalks, large beautifully foliaged trees, children running around, college students walking by with backpacks and a feeling of community revival. The Sugar Man still walks the Woodbridge area with a guitar slung over his back. Due to diminished eyesight, his companion, Bonnie, or his daughter, Regan, accompanies him. He is the same Sixto Rodriguez who was a presence in the neighborhood before fame and fortune arrived with **Searching For Sugar Man**.

As he wanders down the Cass Corridor, he will stop in the Cass Café for something to eat or the Old Miami for a drink. The Sugar Man is well known on the Detroit streets. He is the urban philosopher friendly to everyone.

Rodriguez is a street philosopher. He reflects Detroit's history. But he is a private person. When asked about his loss of privacy, Rodriguez told Edward Douglas: "I enjoy my privacy and everybody's got a personal private life but we're all public people, but I think I like to step away from this so I try to protect that as much as possible. That's why I'm reluctant to be in the film." This convoluted explanation goes a long way toward explaining Rodriguez' ambivalence toward his late in life stardom. In a number of 2012 interviews, the Sugar Man talked about his education. It was the end of his recording career that drove Rodriguez back to Wayne State University to complete his degree in philosophy. When he graduated with honors at thirty-nine, his professors recommended a PhD program. The Sugar Man opted to continue his musical journey.

His sporadic time studying in the honors college at Wayne State was important to his creativity. When he attended WSU, he temporarily forgot about the music business. He preferred life on Avery Street to the outside world. He didn't forget about the music business. He took a sabbatical from it.

Life on Avery Street After Leaving the Music Business

Sometime after leaving the entertainment industry, he purchased his home on Avery Street. According to tax records he paid $750 for an old wood and brick structure. He purchased the Avery Street home to raise his three daughters. It was a perfect location. It is also a comfortable two story, solid house with a long, steep stairway. The warmth of the neighborhood and its proximity to Wayne State University, with its libraries and museums, provided all Rodriguez needed emotionally and intellectually. Since fame and fortune arrived in 2012, he has remodeled some of the interior, rebuilt the front steps and there is a new fence as you face the house on the right side. Rodriguez remains true to his personal vision. He lives simply without frills.

The Avery Street neighborhood is quiet. Perfect for the creative artist. Considering the violence and upheaval Detroit experienced in the previous decade it was the perfect hideout for Sixto Rodriguez. He would stay there until his 1998 South African comeback. Then, after the accolades in Cape Town, he once again returned to obscurity in Detroit. He loved life without fame and celebrity.

The Nomadic Rodriguez: The Urban Poet

To people in and around Detroit, Rodriguez was viewed as a nomad. He was a colorful character walking the streets with a guitar strapped to his back. He never said where he lived. He didn't tell people he had a family. Sixto Rodriguez was a private person. He was a man of mystery.

He was urban born and raised in the city. He believed in the warmth and vitality of the streets. The small clubs, the decrepit neighborhoods, the seedy bars and the blue-collar student shops in and around Wayne State fueled his writing. He was an urban poet in search of musical redemption.

One day Rodriguez was walking down the Cass Corridor. He stopped near the Old Miami in front of a vacant lot. He looked at the empty beer cans, the broken wine bottles and the scattered debris. He walked into the vacant lot. He saw a rusted rake. He picked it up. He spent two hours raking the debris into a neat pile. This simple act defines Sixto Rodriguez.

Rodriguez loves Detroit's isolation. He lives in an academic cocoon with Wayne State University nearby, and the bars, restaurants and coffee shops provide material for his songs. As he worked in home demolition and repair with Detroit spiraling for decades into economic chaos, he had more work than he could handle. When he became an overnight sensation, after forty years, **Rolling Stone** published ten things his fans needed to know about the Sugar Man.

Rodriguez Explains His Life in Brief

The details of Rodriguez' life remain shrouded in controversy. That is there are some family factors that have not been verified. He had brothers. There is no record of those who are alive or if there was a sister. His parents are presented in a sketchy way. The best source for Rodriguez life comes from interviews where he lets his guard down. One of the best is with Rob Hughes. The Sugar Man provides some gems about his past.

Sixto Rodriguez: "I took a B. A. in philosophy. I became a social worker, I worked on a building site and got into politics. I always saw politics as a mechanism from where you can affect change."

When Rodriguez talked about his reemergence he traced it to David Holmes featuring "Sugar Man" on his mix album **Come Get It, I Got It**. Rodriguez recalled Holmes tracked him down and brought him in the studio with a thirty-piece orchestra to lay down the "Sugar Man" vocals on the album **David Holmes Presents The Free Association**. The reason Rodriguez liked what Holmes did is it brought the Sugar Man to prominence in the U. K. and Europe. He had a career before Malik Bendjelloul tracked him down and completed the documentary. Rodriguez believes the story was ready for Malik.

The lack of bitterness in Rodriguez' life attests to his humanity. In August 2012, when asked about the intrusion of fame in his life, Rodriguez said: "It's like a whirlwind. I can hardly believe it. We're going to be appearing on the David Letterman Show, the Newport Folk Festival and dates in New York and elsewhere. It all feels wonderful, it's a lot to take in. So far I've seen the film thirty five times! Had I given up on ever making it? I think I probably had. Put it this way, I was too disappointed to be disappointed. But now we've been four times to South Africa and four times to Australia and I'm finally breaking into the American market." That said it all Sixto Rodriguez had arrived in the music business. It was about time.

Rolling Stone's 10 Things You Don't Know About Rodriguez Revisited

In March 2013, in the midst of the acclaim for **Searching For Sugar Man**, Andy Greene, writing in **Rolling Stone**, listed ten things the public didn't now about the Sugar Man.

The list is not revealing or for that matter surprising. It does sum up the story in a well-rounded manner. **Rolling Stone** pointed out Australia was as much a key to Rodriguez' success as South Africa. Australia's importance is it was the first time the Sugar Man played large concert halls or for that matter any concert hall. He was a bar or small club performer. Australia broadened his in concert persona. When he was in Australia **Billboard** commented: "The man seemed almost embarrassed on stage. He spoke no more than a dozen lines throughout each show." He was shy. The public was just learning about this character trait in 1979. It still persists.

There are other insights from Australia. Rodriguez said of his 1979 tour: "I thought it was the highlight of my career." Fast-forward to the 1998 South African shows and **Rolling Stone** claimed he retired after the six shows that made him a performing icon in the country. He returned to Detroit. He continued to work in the home demolition business while performing sporadically in local clubs.

Rolling Stone pointed to the large sums of money he made since the release of **Searching For Sugar Man**. He gave most of it away. His daughter, Regan, married and has children. She is now Regan Barachkov, and she lives on E. Drahner Road in Oxford, Michigan. His other daughters Eva and Sandra have full family lives. Eva is retired from the military and raising her son who is ready for college. Sandra is pursuing a songwriting and performing career. Eva recently moved back to Detroit. She purchased a home in the Woodbridge area. In the decade before **Searching For Sugar Man** hit the big screen, Rodriguez began a slow but steady rise to cult status. He was working on cult stardom from 2005 when the London press recognized his albums and his concerts.

Regan's husband Peter Muir Barachkov is a general contractor, an intelligent, handsome guy with a penchant for hard work. He is the perfect husband for Regan. He is often on tour with the kids. Like Regan he is private and family oriented. The Sugar Man depends upon his family as glaucoma has taken away much of his eyesight. There is more to Rodriguez than music.

One of **Rolling Stone's** interesting points is Rodriguez is patriotic. He hoped to volunteer for the draft to fight in Vietnam in the 1970s. He failed the physical. They also highlighted his obsession with privacy when filmmaker Malik Bendjelloul told **Rolling Stone** "You shouldn't get your hopes up about an interview." The concern for the Sugar Man's privacy was evident. It took numerous visits before Rodriguez agreed to sit down for a brief interview. But the Swedish filmmaker persisted.

Malik Bendjelloul: "I went to Detroit every year for four years. He didn't agree to be interviewed until my third visit. I think he only changed his mind because he felt sorry for us. He saw how hard we were working and was like, 'I think I better help these guys."

The **Rolling Stone** article was the first to detail his health problems. But they have made too much of it. He has glaucoma. The rest of his body is like a piece of steel. They missed a key element of his musical interests. That is the cover song. He has an encyclopedic knowledge of old tunes. He can perform them on the spot. Rodriguez commented: "I like to do covers of my own songs." What he means is he performs his signature songs in different ways.

Rolling Stone concludes by speculating on the ubiquitous third album. Will it take place? Who knows! The interviews ten points in **Rolling Stone** suggest Rodriguez is a complex person. He is also moody, paranoid and creative. He is a contrarian individual. He is a writer defined by the Motor City. His writing and speaking about Detroit brought him an audience that sees his lyrics continually defined by the Motor City.

Lyrics Continually Defined by the Motor City

As things got tougher economically, as the Motor City headed toward bankruptcy, and as people fled to the suburbs, Rodriguez watched his city slowly dissolve into bankruptcy. He walked the streets to chronicle the misery and despair that defined Detroit. His writing depended upon urban blight. Rodriguez' rebellious voice and nonchalant hippie demeanor attracted followers. He didn't have to be famous to have people listening to his every word. He was the nomadic Socrates.

Living on Detroit's Avery Street without central heating or air-conditioning didn't bother Rodriguez. He fed his wood stove in the winter. He moved his bed closer to the stove. A fan and open windows made the summers manageable. It was the way of an artist. While living in a large, primitive home without a telephone, a computer and a modern kitchen, Rodriguez could read and write. He could also raise his children. As his daughter, Eva, recalled in **Searching For Sugar Man,** the art museum and the library became the family day care.

The Working Detroit Rodriguez: Changing the System

When Rodriguez left the music business, he renovated houses. He also taught. He was employed for a brief time as a social worker. He found a job in a steel mill rewarding, and, for a brief time, he was employed in a packing plant. In the midst of raising three daughters, he dabbled in the music scene. He kept in touch with Detroit's city issues. It was a rich and full life. He had no regrets. It wasn't until he performed in South Africa that anyone was interested in his songwriting.

In March 1998 in Cape Town Rodriguez was asked what inspired him to write his songs: "My inspiration comes from the environment and personal angst...each song is written to a theme." That statement echoed Steve Rowland. He had the same mantra.

There is much more to Rodriguez. He spent a great deal of time pursuing his education. He is well read, philosophical and quietly studious. His degree in philosophy is one indication of his political bent. It is a liberal one. He ran for public office many times. This suggests his political activism. Rodriguez describes himself as a "musical political." He ran twice to be Detroit Mayor with the first campaign in 1981 receiving 1,446 votes and the second in 1993 totaling 170 votes. He also was on the ballot three times for a City Council slot, once with 168 other candidates. His name was misspelled on the ballot. He was not successful in any election. He generally received less than a thousand votes. It was his statements, his policy ideas, and his plans for the future that drove his political interest. He wanted to make a difference. He registered as a Democrat. His friends told me he was an independent. He also was on the ballot for a Michigan State Senate seat. Despite his electoral failures, he continues to be political. He was a success on the issues. "I saw some things I thought people should be made aware of," Rodriguez continued. "But I was unable to do that with my music." He has separated his musical life from his political world.

Rodriguez' political activism has not gone unnoticed. After the success of **Searching For Sugar Man**, the Michigan State Legislature passed Senate Resolution No. 22 commemorating Rodriguez' political voice and the documentary **Searching For Sugar Man.** The Detroit Senator Coleman A. Young, II introduced the resolution praising Rodriguez. In 2000 Rodriguez was a candidate for a seat in the Michigan House of Representatives for District 7. In the August 8, 2000 Democratic primary he polled seven hundred and twenty eight votes. They were mostly from Detroit.

On life, Rodriguez has a philosophy; it is a Zen like approach suggesting he waits patiently for recognition. It came forty-one years after **Coming From Reality** was released. But it was the soundtrack to the documentary that brought fame and fortune.

As Fame Approaches Rodriguez Reflects

As Sony Legacy prepared to release the **Searching For Sugar Man** soundtrack, Rodriguez reflected on the reasons for his success forty years after the fact. "My father's night would usually end with a couple of drinks and a few songs. I would listen to his heart breaking songs. He loved music, and I picked it up through him." How did this impact the Sugar Man? He never gave up on his musical dreams.

As he talked about his early career, Rodriguez described it as one made through introductions. He talked of meeting Detroit producer Harry Balk, and how this led to a contract with Impact Records. It was while working with Balk that Rodriguez developed the technique of using his classical guitar with an electric pick and playing his riffs through an Ampeg bass amp. It gave his music an echo with a fuzzy sound. He used this technique when he recorded "Crucify Your Mind."

He discussed the impact of the Bob Seger System, the MC 5 and Iggy Pop and the Stooges upon his music. From day one, Rodriguez praised his Motor City upbringing and the manner in which it shaped his art. He reflects the gritty, down home atmosphere that is Detroit.

There were also obscure influences. Nolan Strong and the Diablo's' "The Wind" had an impact upon the romantic tone of Rodriguez' songwriting. When Steve Rowland began producing **Coming From Reality**, he saw this side of Rodriguez' musical persona.

Rodriguez' Interview with a London Jackass Journalist

Three years before **Searching For Sugar Man** was released, a London reporter asked Rodriguez what his story meant. "My story isn't a rags to riches story," Rodriguez continued: "It's rags to rags and I'm glad about that. Where other people live in an artificial world, I feel I live in the real world. And nothing beats reality."

The exchange with this reporter, James Delingpole, was a strange one. The **London Telegraph** writer argued with Rodriguez' daughter, Regan, over taking a picture. There is a private side to the Sugar Man. It surfaces from time to time. There is also a paranoia that keeps him away from jackasses like Delingpole. It didn't work this time. He had to do the interview. It got worse. The London based journalist was so full of himself it might as well have been about Delingpole as he continually knotted his ascot, acting like Little Lord Fauntleroy, and he sipped his tea with a delicate finger swinging in the air. Rodriguez looked amused. He remained polite. The Sugar Man must have felt blessed about his poor eyesight. He didn't have to look at this pathetic wanker.

Delingpole suggested Rodriguez was not forthcoming because of "some medication." It is moments like this, which makes Rodriguez, think of going back to carrying refrigerators on his back down three flights of stairs in a Detroit tenement. That job was better than facing a pompous, jackass disguised as a journalist.

After acting like a complete wanker, Delingpole proceeded to tell Rodriguez how much he enjoyed listening to his music. He said it was much like Love's **Forever Changes**. It wasn't hard to tell why Rodriguez was speechless. He was doing an interview where the writer for the **London Telegraph** was asking and answering the questions.

When asked about his guitar playing, Rodriguez said: "I have a sloppy style of playing guitar. A percussive style. Unique in fact." Then he showed Delingpole that he was missing half a finger. Maybe that was the finger he wanted to give the journalist. He was too polite for that.

Rodriguez' Political Activism Shines Through in 2009: Delingpole's Politics Cause His Ire

There were some interesting comments from the Delingpole interview. Rodriguez mentioned he brought a member of the Chicano Brown Berets on stage while in Los Angeles on a promotional tour. It was a political move. He explained to Delingpole his long-standing Detroit political activism. The journalist yawned. He wasn't interested in substantive matters.

While hanging out in Los Angeles, Rodriguez spent time with Mexican American political activist, David Sanchez, This took place when he promoted an early single. The Sugar Man seemed to say it was a mistake, and it was one of the things derailing his early career.

After this inquisitional interview, Rodriguez played the Green Man Festival in Wales on August 23, 2009. He was one of eighty-nine artists to perform in this three-day festival. He continued to attract the attention of the British press.

It wasn't just the British media that came to see Rodriguez. His hotel was filled with well-wishers from South Africa. It was the Fall of 2009, and the triumphs of **Searching For Sugar Man** were still a few years away. But he did have a career.

The interest in Rodriguez prompted the London press to follow his every move. Rodriguez' daughter, Regan, did her best to get him to sit down for interviews. He doesn't like to talk to the press. He did talk for a bit to the media but it was reluctantly.

James Delingpole was the wrong person to interview Sixto Rodriguez. Why? He is a London based right wing journalist who has written novels and political books displaying little or no understanding of working class people-i. e. Rodriguez. Delingpole tells people he is a "libertarian conservative." He bored Rodriguez by telling him global warming didn't exist. He also told Rodriguez in London he was a person who was discriminated against because he was a white journalist. There was a dead silence. Rodriguez wondered what the hell was going on?

The Sugar Man drank his glass of wine. He smiled. Rodriguez wondered if the media publicity was worth listening to this journalist. Not surprisingly, when Breitbart came to London he went to work for this alt-right racist organization. Sixto Rodriguez showed Delingpole nothing but respect. His kindness was not returned. One wonders if the decline recently in media interviews is a result of the nightmares from this raving conservative English journalist?

Matt Sullivan Realizes Rodriguez' Commercial Potential Despite Delingpole

Matt Sullivan realized Rodriguez' commercial potential. As a result, Light In The Attic developed a cult market for **Cold Fact**. The publicity from LITA spurred steady record sales. Maybe Delingpole should be thanked. His article is filled with quotes never repeated elsewhere. After the nasty interview with Delingpole, Rodriguez was happy to escape the clutches of the London paparazzi.

LITA not only booked Rodriguez in some excellent venues, they continued to publicize his material in a worldwide market. They were a successful boutique record label with a growing reputation for brilliant reissues. This prompted the media to belatedly recognize the Sugar Man's unique songs and continued performing talent. It was his art that attracted people. That is the art of writing songs.

In a conversation with Craig Bartholomew-Strydom, Rodriguez remarked: "Art is in all of us. We all have a talent. It is up to us to listen and draw within ourselves and pull out the words, the form or some creative action."

To Rodriguez songwriting is an art form. He has the ability to present word pictures of Detroit's underbelly, to lecture his listeners on the Mafia, or to provide images of everyday people. The blue-collar worker and the lost soul populate the Sugar Man's world.

He told Bartholomew-Strydom, he had strong views on alcohol and marijuana. "Clearly alcohol is a much more destructive substance. Weed is a natural substance. Less harmful and helpful in some cases," Rodriguez concluded. During this interview, Rodriguez emphasized he loved Detroit and would live there forever. He also made it clear he was a life time advocate for legalizing marijuana. The Sugar Man and his family were upset when **Rolling Stone** reporters spent more time describing, "stoking the magic dragon" than talking about his lyrical brilliance. There is an element of paranoia to the Sugar Man.

In **Searching For Sugar Man** the idea Rodriguez didn't appear in clubs, and he was completely out of the performing picture is an erroneous one. He performed sporadically from 1975 until he returned triumphantly to South Africa in 1998. Then after a few years in relative obscurity Light In The Attic re-released his two albums in 2008-2009. He was back on the performing circuit. This brought him into the small clubs, and he attracted devoted college audiences. The media discovered him earlier. From 2005 through 2009 the London press covered Rodriguez' intimate pubs concerts and festival appearances with regularity. He had a strong U. K. media presence. He was far from the obscure performer pictured in **Searching For Sugar Man**. His club dates drew increasingly larger audiences.

In the documentary there is a segment where Rodriguez is described as a homeless drifter. This is of course cinematic license. The Sugar Man has always been a responsible tax-paying citizen with a penchant for fine clothing. The real Sixto Rodriguez is a mainstream political activist who went to work every day and showed tremendous family responsibility. The hippie musician described in **Searching For Sugar Man** is Rodriguez' other persona. The best way to understand the man is to listen to what he has to say about his life and how it changed after the documentaries success.

Rodriguez on Sugar Man and Other Influences

In **Searching For the Sugar Man**, Rodriguez remarked: "Who would have thought that his thing has exposed me to a larger, larger audience?" When asked about his loss of privacy, he said: "I have such an ordinary life but that's not the case now."

"I like language, words," Rodriguez continued. "And I think the survival skills I've developed over the years have added a lot to my perspective." He paused: "I see protest music as a vehicle." He observed Neil Young's "Ohio" and Barry McGuire's "Eve of Destruction" were key songs influencing his writing. He has a penchant for composing commercial hits. The public finally recognized his word magic.

When asked if he gave up construction work or the demolition jobs he had over the years. Rodriguez commented: "Well you never throw away your work clothes."

On his recent success, he remarked: "This thing is like a monsoon." He continued: "There have already been rewards just from the opportunity to do all this. I guess we all want to get there right away, but I believe it's never too early, never too late."

On the themes to his songs, Rodriguez said: "My inspiration comes from the environment and personal angst...each song is written to a theme…." Then the Sugar Man came close to defining his act. "I've always concentrated on social issues, because I've always found it easiest to write about things that upset me. But I can (and have) explored the boy-girl theme in music and I enjoy writing ballads too."

The numerous comparisons to Bob Dylan make the Sugar Man nervous. Effusive praise is not a Rodriguez trait.

"Let's be clear," says Rodriguez, coolly dressed in black from head to foot, save for a blood red tie. "Bob Dylan has written more than 500 songs. I've written 30 — but the comparison is sweet, thanks a lot."

When asked if he was political, Rodriguez replied that he was "a musical political…I don't see how anybody…is not political."

On his return to South Africa in 1998, Rodriguez observed: "Well it was, it was epic." When a reporter asked him if he felt any pangs of regret, Rodriguez said: "Well, no, not in that sense…hate is too strong an emotion to waste on someone you don't like." After he was asked a number of times about fame, he replied: "Well fame is fleeting…." He did observe his life is different now that fame and fortune came his way.

The years of obscurity were ones Rodriguez embraced. "I stopped chasing the music dream in 1974," Rodriguez said. He was sitting in a Manhattan hotel room after appearing on Imus In The Morning when he made this ironic comment. He performed "Sugar Man" on the Imus show with an acoustic guitar. Imus asked him about his life before fame. Rodriguez responded: "I did a lot of heavy lifting-construction, demolition, that kind of thing. Dusty, dirty work."

When Imus talked to Rodriguez, he was broadcasting from his ranch in New Mexico. Imus enjoyed the music. He asked Rodriguez how much guitar he played over the years? Rodriguez let his host know in addition to playing the guitar he kept up with the music business. "I don't sing, I do vocals, Sinatra sings," Rodriguez remarked to Imus. "Not to patronize you but you are wonderful," Imus concluded.

The Imus in the Morning show was the top rated New York talk show on the Fox Business News channel, and the jump in record sales was an obvious result. At the end of "Sugar Man" Imus asked: "After you made those albums and you didn't go anywhere did you still play the guitar?" He told Imus he practiced the guitar daily.

Sixto Rodriguez: "Oh yes, all the time, practice, practice. Stay in tune…I always practiced. I read the trades. Use the library a lot. The Thesaurus…those kind of tools."

Charming New York at Tribeca

New York audiences are notoriously fickle. They are also incessantly critical. It is tough to charm New York. Rodriguez did. He did so by being himself. The Tribeca Film Festival was filled with gnarly, pompous, self-important writers. No one escaped Rodriguez' incipient charm. When asked: "How has the music changed?" Rodriguez thought for a moment and replied: "Formulas. They always put a girl's voice at the end of the song. It's a formula and it works. My stuff is straight-out."

When Rodriguez took the stage at the Tribeca Festival on April 24, 2012 New York instantly fell in love with the Sugar Man. He performed "Cold Fact" after **Searching For Sugar Man** finished its premier showing. The Sugar Man's soft voice and barely audible acoustic guitar had the audience unusually quiet. Soon there was soft and then louder clapping. Rodriguez' voice got louder, he smiled, and everyone was on the Sugar Man's page. It was a sweet moment.

When asked if he was surprised by the documentary, Rodriguez observed: "It's very abrupt, and the thing is, we didn't know he was gonna win these awards and maybe we wouldn't be here. I just want to mention the Voltaire thing, the pen is mightier than the sword. Now I think the camera is even mightier than the pen." Touché!

As he reflected on his early years, Rodriguez commented: "I was too disappointed to be disappointed….In the music business, there's a lot of criticism and rejection. If you embrace it, you'll be better off when the adjustment comes." Success can destroy a person. So can failure. Rodriguez is immune to both success and failure. He is an existential philosopher disguised as a songwriter. That explanation in itself explains a great deal about the man.

When Rodriguez was approached by Malik Bendjelloul to cooperate for a documentary, he was wary and suspicious. "I was skeptical about the whole idea," Rodriguez said. "I resisted. In the music industry there's a lot of casualties because of that kind of attention." There was no way to tell Bendjelloul no. Eventually, Rodriguez cooperated. He remarked: "Malik has done quite a remarkable thing. I'm a lucky man." So is the audience.

Rodriguez on Radio Airplay

Cold Fact never received radio airplay. "A lot of the radio stations wouldn't touch me, because of the nature of the songs," Rodriguez continued. "I would never get played in the Bible Belt…I wasn't trying to be controversial, it was just the way people spoke."

The teen hops were not his favorite venues. Rodriguez ignored the disc jockey radio interviews, the American Bandstand type dance shows, the hookers, the drugs and the music business bullshit didn't appeal to him. The attitude of key record executives didn't sit well with him. He told Harry Balk, when he was with Impact Records, he would not appear on the teen marketing circuit. Lip-syncing was not his thing. He told Balk to find him adult listeners. Harry dropped him from the label.

It was writing that interested the Sugar Man. While he wanted to perform, it was composing lyrics that influenced his daily life. He wanted more than a teen audience. Like most record executives, Harry Balk was incensed. He told Rodriguez he called the shots not the artist.

Harry Balk: "Rodriguez was a difficult character. I dropped Little Willie John when I go tired of bailing him out of jail. Every time I flew to the South and took him from the clutches of the law I vowed no more Little Willie. He made me a lot of money. I put up with it. I dropped Rodriguez after listening to his political bullshit. He wanted to tell me who his audience was and that was unacceptable. He always had some woman who took care of him. It wasn't for me. I cut him loose. He never made me a dime. He had a vision I didn't understand. He had this dope-smoking sidekick that drove me crazy. I did like his women."

What Balk didn't appreciate is the Sugar Man had a message. Rodriguez didn't care about the money, the teen showcases or the industry nonsense. He was a serious songwriter. Harry thought that was bullshit. He was wrong. Harry told me Rodriguez would ignore his audience. He wondered if they were listening? For Harry it was all about the money.

When he wrote "Forget It," the song reflected the lack of attentive audiences. Like many artists, he wanted recognition. As the racial strife, the high levels of unemployment and the lack of a fulfilled dream ruined Detroit; Rodriguez went to work and raised a family.

Rodriguez Looks Back and Talk of a Third Album

There are no regrets for Rodriguez. At least none he exhibits publicly. When asked what it was like to find fame four decades later, he said: "I guess it feels as good as it would have felt if I was a success earlier."

In an interview with **Uncut's** Michael Bonner, Rodriguez was unusually candid. He said success later in life was a mixed blessing. He hoped to record a third album. He also remarked: "My career was a mess." He discussed a return to the recording studio.

The third Rodriguez album was in the talking stages during **Searching For Sugar Man's** early success. In 2013, as Steve Rowland and David Holmes talked to Rodriguez about his new songs, preparations were being made for a third LP. The problem was Rodriguez was booked in concert almost continually.

Rowland wants Rodriguez to come to Palm Springs where they can work without distraction. His touring commitments are steady. Other producers, like David Holmes, believe a sparse-live Johnny Cash type Rick Rubin LP would be perfect. On the question of new material, Matt Sullivan pointed out Rodriguez has written new songs. He says he has heard them. "He just needs to find the time to put it out," Sullivan said. It has been a long way from the 160 seat Joe's Pub in New York to the Barclay Center in Brooklyn. The only person unconcerned is Rodriguez.

The newfound fame has done little to change him. He loves hanging out backstage and talking to the band. He is the one who goes and gets the drinks. He loves being back in the mix. He doesn't care if he is a star. He is in his milieu.

When **Searching For Sugar Man** became an Oscar winning documentary, Rodriguez was asked about the early days. He had a great deal to reflect upon as he told various interviewers he was influenced by listening to Charlie Christian's electric guitar. "I'm a self taught musician," Rodriguez told Jeff Niesel. "I used folk music...the protest song...where I can describe social issues and the conditions of the people on the streets."

He also commented he met Dennis Coffey and Mike Theodore in 1969. "They came to a show and checked me out, and I was the first product on Sussex," Rodriguez said.

Rodriguez on the Bob Dylan Comparison

When he is described as "the Chicano Bob Dylan," Rodriguez squirms uncomfortably. He sees himself differently. He never compares his writing to Dylan's. Or for that matter to any other songwriter! He is a solitary voice with a literary bent.

Sixto Rodriguez: "In the 60s and 70s, a protest song was a genre in music. And so I chose that to describe the things that were in my environment. You have Syria and Darfur. You have government oppression. You have police brutality. The issues are still there."

Rodriguez readily admits he knew nothing about South Africa when Stephen "Sugar" Segerman contacted him. "I did discover what the parallels were, in relation to the Vietnam War protests here," Rodriguez said. A South African soldier told Rodriguez: "We made love to your music, and we made war to your music." He was surprised by this comment.

Journalists have weighed in on the Rodriguez-Dylan comparison. The **London Telegraph's** David Gritten observed: "His body of work is too slim to justify comparisons with Bob Dylan, but his songs, rooted in folk and blues, are poetic, intimate and passionate." The die-hard Rodriguez fan would argue his thirty songs stand as a monument to his talent.

The comparison to Dylan is best explained by Malik Bendjelloul "He's a shy, mysterious guy. Just like Bob." Well-said Malik!

"Be gentle with your anger," Rodriguez remarked to a reporter in Milwaukee. "He conquers who conquers himself."

No one cared about his thoughts, ideas or philosophy until **Searching For Sugar Man** won an Oscar. Then the world fell in love with Rodriguez. It doesn't matter how long fame and fortune lasts, Rodriguez will continue to be the same person. There is no altering the perception and direction of the Sugar Man.

Looking back on his success, Rodriguez is happy to have a forum for his music. His friend, Stephen "Sugar" Segerman, summed up the phenomenon: "Things like this just aren't supposed to happen in real life." Segerman theorized Rodriguez' "proper audience is Americans, not South Africans or Australians." Thanks to Segerman and others the Sugar Man now has an international audience. "This is a story that keeps having happy endings," Segerman concluded.

Segerman's attention to detail helped to bring Sixto Rodriguez back to the mainstream. It was a forty-year journey and Sugar deserves much of the credit. The journey was not an easy one. The result was recognition for a talent that was ignored.

The best way to understand Rodriguez is through his lyrics. When he recorded "Cause," with Steve Rowland, the producer was emotional in the studio. Steve had never heard nor had he recorded such a poignant song. He smiled. He thought he would have many chances to make other Rodriguez records. It didn't happen. When Rowland finished the mixing for **Coming From Reality**, he believed he had produced the artist who would bring him increased recognition. Steve didn't need credibility. He produced hundreds of hit records. There was a connection to Sixto Rodriguez he didn't have with other artists. The lyrics were ones Rowland never forgot.

"While the rain drank champagne. My Estonian Archangel came and got me wasted. Cause the sweetest kiss I ever got is the one I've never tasted," Rodriguez wrote. He was writing about his life. Rowland allowed the Sugar Man complete studio freedom. But another album wasn't commissioned. Now the rumor is forty-six years later Rodriguez will employ and select the musicians, and he will pay for the album. He will own the master tapes. He picked this up watching Van Morrison when he performed with him at a festival. Whether or not Steve Rowland is the producer is unknown. They have talked. Rodriguez has mentioned Rowland as a suitable and potential producer. A bartender at the Motor City Brewing Company overheard the Sugar Man remarking, "Steve Rowland is the only producer I would consider for another album."

I asked Steve: "Are you ready to produce Rodriguez' third album?"

He replied: "I don't talk personally about Rodriguez. If you want to know ask him." I got the idea. Rodriguez on Rodriguez is the best source. The lyrical beauty and musical brilliance that is Sixto Rodriguez is a key to the personal Sugar Man. To understand him it is necessary to analyze his revealing interviews. They tell more about where he has been, what he has done and why he is a private, cautious, individual with strong suspicions about the music business.

The Most Revealing Early Rodriguez Interview

There are a number of reflective interviews. The best ones took place before **Searching For Sugar Man** catapulted Rodriguez to fame and fortune. In 2009, Rodriguez played a show in Black Mountain North Carolina and a local journalist, Fred Mills, sat down for a casual conversation that turned into an insightful interview. The documentary's fame was three years away. The Sugar Man was unusually relaxed and candid. The Mills-Rodriguez conversation took place in early January 2009 as Rodriguez played Black Mountain's Grey Eagle Club.

Fred Mills asked interesting questions. He brought forth unique perspectives. During the interview Rodriguez referred to Mills as "Sir" or "Mr. Mills." This is not a new insight into the Sugar Man's personality. This is how he addresses people.

Mills asked: "How are you preparing for this tour?"

Rodriguez: "See, we're all working at it, so I think it's in the air, you know? Busy at our craft. Yeah, I practiced with a drummer last night and we went through a lot of material. The other day I practiced with this other guy too — so I'm getting ready. I'm having a great time with this. It's totally — it's a great time for me, and the thing is, it doesn't happen every week, so I'm serious at it. I gotta take this chance. It's like Eminem says, you get just one opportunity, so don't blow it." [*laughs*]

Fred Mills: "Even though you can get back together with groups of musicians when you return to their towns or regions, do you ever wish you had a permanent touring band to play with?"

Rodriguez: "Well, my style is that I'm a musical slut! [*laughs*] I do it like this because that's how I am. Cheap drinks and all! But yeah, I have to do it like this — air flights [and expenses], all that. And I enjoy meeting new musicians too. But once I could guarantee a band, then we're in. But right now this is how I'm doing it. And I'm going to do the European tour – Amsterdam, Dublin, Rome, Paris, London — with a Swedish band. I've worked with them and I'm lucky that I have. So if we all just hang in tight and close, I think something can happen. And I hope they all hold with me. I'm out there, you know? I got my amp in the wind. So that's the way this is going for me. I'm not a band; I'm a single, a solo."

Fred Mills: "You've been through this whole rediscovery thing three times now: first in Australia and New Zealand, then South Africa, and now America. Does this create any anxiety for you — does it turn your world upside down each time it happens?"

Rodriquez: "I'm as nervous as a clock, so I reach for the rum or the brandy. But yeah, you do get nervous; you're reading me just right. So I have a 'cheer.' And then when I see them after the show, the fans and the fan base and the band, we'll go out and party. Of course, last time we partied until four in the morning, so I'm cutting down the parties on *this* tour! Just an hour. Because it gets intense.

We're going to get up [each morning] at 11 a.m. and then out of that city. It's getting so very busy."

Fred Mills: "Onstage you don't betray any nervousness. In fact, you appear pretty relaxed...."

Sixto Rodriguez: "That's just the way I perform. I have my eyes closed, I'm listening to the band, and trying to remember my lyrics and trying to find the microphone. So in a way, I'm almost in a trance when I'm up there. I'm getting better at it — better at ending songs and stuff like that. But I don't want to be so manicured and sharp that it loses something. You know what I mean? So right now, you're watching me as I develop. The thing is, you have to prepare, and be prepared. So that's the other thing, why I'm practicing [at home], so when we hook up we'll knock it out."

Fred Mills: "Let me ask you a few things about **Coming From Reality.** It's as strong as **Cold Fact**, but in a totally different way, with a completely different sound for most of the songs. How did it come about that you shipped all the way off to London to do the album?"

Rodriguez: "Well, the guy who ran my label, Clarence Avant, I thought it was him who was the hero of my career. But it actually turns out to be another guy, Neil Bogart, from Buddah Records. [Buddah distributed Rodriguez' record label, Sussex.] He wrote a letter to Clarence and said that this guy in London wants to record the second album, a guy named Steve Rowland. So it was like, I dunno, inner city meets Hollywood! [*laughs*] I mean, he's full production, one of these guys right at home [in the studio].

One thing about *Coming From Reality* that people might catch, for example: we have a Stradivarius on those tunes, a full violin section, cello and viola. So it's a major kind of difference and approach [from *Cold Fact*]. I just worked with the rhythm section on *Cold Fact,* but I went over to London — and there they are! The strings; Chris Spedding is on guitar; bongos [by Tony Carr of Magna Carta and Donovan's band]; and the drummer is imitating a lot of different styles."

The notion Sixto Rodriguez didn't have success until **Searching For Sugarman** is one of many myths continuing to plague his career. The list of 2009 tour shows goes a long way toward establishing his small venue draw.

Rodriguez – 2009 Tour Dates
Wed, May 13 Rock and Roll Hotel Washington DC *
Thu, May 14 Johnny Brenda's Philadelphia PA *
Fri, May 15 Bowery Ballroom New York NY *
Mon, Jun 22 Richard's On Richards Cabaret Vancouver BC
Tue, Jun 23 The Triple Door Seattle WA
Wed, Jun 24 Doug Fir Lounge Portland OR
Fri, Jun 26 Slim's San Francisco CA
Sat, Jun 27 El Rey Theatre Los Angeles CA
Fri, May 29 Paradiso Amsterdam Netherlands
Sat, May 30 Whelans Dublin Ireland
Mon, Jun 1 Nouveau Casino Paris France
Wed, Jun 3 Circolo Degli Artisti Rome Italy
Sat, Jun 6 Barbican London UK
Sun, Jul 12 Les Ardentes Festival Liege Belgium

- **w/ The War on Drugs**

The Problem of Writing a Rodriguez Biography and How to Solve It

Rodriguez' natural reticence in talking with the press, discussing his life and cooperating with a project on his music made it difficult for Malik Bendjelloul to complete **Searching For Sugar Man**. He did. How? He had Regan Rodriguez' cooperation. The Sugar Man's other two daughters, Eva and Sandra, were instrumental in forming a complete picture of their father. After attending a dozen Rodriguez concerts, I put together fifteen observations that helped in writing the second of my three volumes on the Sugar Man. The following list consists of contradictions, personal traits, observations, reminiscences and idiosyncrasies explaining Sixto Rodriguez. I have physically pursued the story in order to understand the man. That is I have visited his home, many concert venues and I have interviewed more than a hundred people in Detroit, Los Angeles, Seattle, Portland, San Francisco, Phoenix and I was backstage before a concert with Steve Rowland, Sixto Rodriguez and his daughters Regan and Sandra at the Luckman Center at California State University, Los Angeles. Here is what I have learned.

1.) He is an uneven concert performer. His shows are either average or well done. The irony is the fans don't care. They are seeing the legend. That is enough. It is also enough for Rodriguez. There is a mutual love fest at his concerts. He is overall a brilliant performer who at times is sabotaged by age, people around him (think Stephen "Sugar" Segerman), and simple things like the sound system or a promoter who is over the top. In other words the concert business is often perilous to Rodriguez' psyche.
2.) I have gone to the majority of the musical, literary, coffee, college places that influenced the Sugar Man's career. If you sit in the Old Miami you understand a seedy bar atmosphere where you satisfied the customers or else they beat the hell out of you. A visit to the bar or a table to eat in the Cass Café tells one all they need to know about the hospitality, and student life around Wayne State University. How it impacts Rodriguez is an amazing story. The Motor Brewing Company didn't come along until Rodriguez was almost finished raising his family. His career remained in obscurity. If you sit at the bar and talk to a bartender or the owner the real Sixto Rodriguez emerges. He is much like the Sugar Man in the documentary. He remains humble, thoughtful, and he has a private under the radar personality.

3.) After finding Rodriguez' house in Detroit on Avery Street, it is easy to understand his penchant for speaking out supporting the blue collar working person. He is one of them. There is an anarchist collective near his Avery Street residence. It tells one all they need to know about the young people in the area. Nearby the cluster of what were once rich people's homes gives the area a feeling for its distinguished, wealthy historical past. Now these homes are merely upper class residences. But they highlight the class and income divides that permeates the Sugar Man's music and Detroit. It is not just the birthplace. It is also the small or often trivial coffee shop giving character to his intellect, his songs and his life.

4.) Richard Holmes' "footstep" principles is used in this book. That is a method that has the obscure people, the often hidden folks or those who have observations escaping the mainstream press. These people offer a fresh perspective. There are hidden stories, unknown facts and warm anecdotes suggesting the Sugar Man's rich and full life.

5.) By following Rodriguez on the concert trail I developed a picture of him backstage. He likes to relax. He prefers to have family around. But he runs the show. He hires a professional tour manager. There is a comfortable and well-equipped tour bus and the musicians, the tour manager and the roadies stay in first class hotels. There is a firm, carefully planned touring schedule. Sixto Rodriguez is a pro. It has not always been this way.

6.) Since Rodriguez is a child of the 1960s, it is imperative to understand how and why that decade influenced him. It continues to shape his persona. By following his footsteps through the decade it is apparent in his songwriting, his lifestyle and his values that his lyrics emanate from the dream to change society into a peaceful place.

7.) Rodriguez' mind is another matter. It is presumptuous of me to think I can inhabit it. So here goes I am presumptuous. When Konny Rodriguez mentioned in numerous interviews she didn't believe in divorce, she still loved the Sugar Man, she punctuated her comments with the statement: "I simply can't live with the man." That insight tells one all they need to know about Rodriguez. He is personally quirky, introspective, suspicious and private. Since 2012 he has been a rock star in a fish bowl. That is the contradiction of his present life.
8.) To place Sixto Rodriguez in the pantheon of rock and roll history is not an easy task. He is an outsider. To understand him I interviewed or read the press of those associated with Rodriguez notably Matt Sullivan, Steve Rowland, Dennis Coffey, Mike Theodore, Richard Niles, Regan, Sandra and Eva Rodriguez, Stephen "Sugar" Segerman, Harry Balk, Craig Bartholomew-Strydom, Malik Bendjelloul and a host of studio, industry and press people close to the Sugar Man. When people in the music business start out as outsider success often brings an insiders role.
9.) Analyzing the top level or management personalities in the rock and roll music world is another means of placing Rodriguez' life and body of work in perspective. Clarence Avant, Simon Chinn, Freddy Bienstock, Harry Balk, Neil Bogart, Jack Baverstock and a host of other industry insiders tells one a dark, deep and often frustrating story of who cheated the Sugar Man, who helped Rodriguez and who muddied the waters with convoluted facts and imprecise financial-personal statements. The biographer must never accept interviews at face value but through the interviews one can deduce who did and who did not help Rodriguez' career. When corporate interests, like Sony Legacy, came to his aid after **Searching For Sugar Man**, he was treated

equitably. Many of his friends recounted the sordid manner he was treated in his early career.

10.) Since I am a professionally trained historian I decided to attempt to deal with historical recovery. When I finished my PhD at the University of Arizona my major professor told me; "No biography is ever definitive. No life ever ends." Then I was told historical recovery is a life long process that leads to new facts. The past changes as new interpretations, new ways of looking at facts, and new information adds to our knowledge. In the case of Sixto Rodriguez the royalty controversy, the reasons for poor album sales and the machinations of the music business are paramount to the story. An index of historical change is necessary to understand a biographical subject. Would we remember Sixto Rodriguez so fondly if he hadn't been the hero in **Searching For Sugar Man**? Probably not!

11.) History is visionary. Sixto Rodriguez' life offers an insight into this process. He went from a forgotten singer-songwriter into a cultural icon. This was due to the popularity of **Searching For Sugar Man**. Why is Rodriguez so loved? The answer lies in the values of our culture and the romance of redemption.

12.) Would Rodriguez' rise as a popular culture figure be so important if his words, phrases and ideas had not taken on an intellectual tone? Probably not! The role of words and music is one that causes us to judge some singer-songwriters at a higher place while others languish in obscurity. Rodriguez' lyrical magic falls into the higher plain of literary achievement. He observes and analyzes with the wisdom of a philosopher what he sees in his surroundings.

13.) Sixto Rodriguez might have been a forgotten musician who recorded two albums if it were not for Stephen "Sugar" Segerman, Craig Bartholomew-Strydom, Mad Andy Harrod,

Brian Currin and a host of other South African's too numerous to recount. They had the sole purpose of keeping Rodriguez' music alive.

14.) The obsessive compulsives, some of whom I have already named, are important to the story but one stands out. That is Malik Bendjelloul who spent half a decade filming the Rodriguez story. That story was one where Steve Rowland acted as a midwife to the Oscar winning documentary.

15.) Biography is important in highlighting the trends, the direction and the future path of society. Few people provide more insight into how and why we use myth to overcome reality. That is the nature of biographical subjects. How does one understand Sixto Rodriguez? It is easy. Remember the following. He is humble. He is thoughtful. He is brilliant. He is a figure virtually unknown for forty years. He is a cultural icon. In his convoluted way he defines how popular culture evolves and changes our perception.

The biographer's task is to place Rodriguez in the center of our culture. Then the biographer interprets how and why he emerged as an icon. It is a story of redemption, overcoming myth to create reality, and the tale is one that tells us as much a reflection of ourselves as it does about the Sugar Man.

Steve Rowland on Rodriguez

Steve Rowland is the closest person to Rodriguez, intellectually other than his family, since fame and fortune took away his privacy. They talk from time to time. There are rumors Rowland could produce a third album. It is at this point only a rumor. Rowland will not comment.

Stave Rowland: "I just think Rodriguez is a wonderful human being. I admire his tenacity. He is his own person. He is one of the few artists I have the most respect for everything he has done and will do in the future. Some of his songs like 'Cause,' 'I Wonder,' 'Crucify Your Mind' and 'Like Janis' are to me great."

How well do you think he has handled stardom?

Steve Rowland: "He is just as humble as ever and he is the same person today as when he started out. It must be hard for him physically. He has worked construction. He has glaucoma. All that opulence and stardom is something he has no interest in."

A Reflective Rodriguez in 2017

In April 2017 the Sugar Man talked of taking his music to the people. He told Gary Graff: "We've got a full load." He meant touring was satisfying. As he prepared for a tour of Canada and the U. S. West Coast, he said: "Its always great to start a tour and to end it. My tours are staggered so I can get some rest time and that's also great. It's the beginning and end of something."

When asked about new material Rodriguez is coy and reflective. He said most reporters ask questions that are inappropriate. "Have you written any books lately? That kind of thing," Rodriguez said of recent inquiries. "I think this whole industry and the world and the art form and the trade has changed so much. Music is an art form, and it's a business and an industry I'm learning to understand. And it's even morphing into something. There's enough for everybody, of all kinds." In his convoluted manner the Sugar Man echoed his frustration with fame. The few years of interviews after the success of **Searching For Sugar Man** are a window into the creative genius that is Sixto Rodriguez.

The constant questions have pushed the Sugar Man away from interviews and into a more reflective personal space. He loves to use words to point to the absurdity of journalistic questions. "The things you need for success," Rodriguez continued. "You need a passport. You need a bank account. You need a good vocabulary, one that includes politeness. And you have to have a pair of sunglasses. Keep it real."

The Joy and Frustration of Writing About Rodriguez

The joy of writing about Sixto Rodriguez is balanced with the frustration one experiences following the Sugar Man's life. He is quiet. He is unassuming. He is family oriented. He is an unrequited intellectual. He is an existentialist. He lives a counterculture lifestyle long after computers, the Internet, Facebook, Instagram, Twitter and entertainment style news, devoid of content, has taken our minds off serious subjects. He doesn't fit into this world. That is the beauty of his story.

This is the second book on the Sugar Man. It is an investigation to celebrate his brilliance. In my previous music biographies of Elvis Presley, Chuck Berry, Van Morrison, Paul McCartney, the Beatles and Del Shannon there was more material than I could master. For the three books I am completing on the Sugar Man, I have talked to everyone around him. Like Gay Talese I found the soundmen, the back up band members, the bar flies in the Detroit drinking scene, those in the Motor City coffee shops, the music business moguls, the small people in the entertainment industry and the myriad of individuals passing through his life provided a window into Rodriguez' world.

What did I find in this second volume? The gifted, subtle, social-political criticism that is the Sugar Man stands out. There is a self-indulgent sense to Rodriguez. He wants to do everything his way. He is irascible in a mild way. He doesn't suffer fools very well. He is unfailingly polite and seldom displays anger.

Steve Rowland asked me why the strong attraction to Rodriguez' music, his career and his life? I did find the Sugar Man's tale a once in a lifetime story. I also found myth and reality didn't mesh. I searched for the reality. There is so much to the real story three books and the 1300 plus pages were needed to flush out the story.

Someone asked me: "Why write three books on a singer who had a brief moment in the sun with the Oscar winning **Searching For Sugar Man** and then will tour until he dies?" I replied: "Why not!" That is what a biographer does. The Sugar Man's story continues. He is in a position to live out his years with a new album, a series of concerts and a future influencing his singer-songwriter legend. The story doesn't end, it continues to the final summation of his enormous talent. Stay tuned!

Eleven

Rodriguez' Songs: Lyrical Beauty and Musical Brilliance

"And you claim you got something going
Something you call unique.
But I've seen your self-pity showing
As the tears rolled down your cheeks."

Sixto Rodriguez Crucify Your Mind

When I have fears that I may cease to be / Before my pen has glean'd my teeming brain ..."

John Keats

There are many themes in Rodriguez' songs. It is in the use of names he excels. While names are an important part of his creative process, the lyrical beauty associated with these names impacts his music. His songwriting reflects what he observes.

"Jane S. Piddy" and "Like Janis" are examples of how well Rodriguez writes. He weaves personal anecdotes into these folk-rock pop masterpieces. In "Like Janis," Rodriguez starts off by writing:

"Now you sit there thinking " and the song involves into a personal tale. Not surprisingly, he is not reflecting on Janis Joplin. He is writing about a Janis that was part of his Detroit life. He described a momentary love interest. His many love interests could fill a large suitcase.

Rodriguez' songs excel in the use of language. He can take an everyday occurrence and compose a song that provides an insight into a problem, a person or an event.

There are numerous examples of seemingly insignificant incidents turning into poignant songs. "Forget It" is about a romance that went sour. Or perhaps it was influenced by the indifference of the audience at the Sewer By The Sea.

Steve Rowland: "Rodriguez' songs come from his personal experiences. He used them to craft some of the most brilliant, romantic lyrical songs that I have ever heard."

When a reporter asked Rodriguez if things would have gone better for him if his music was discovered early in his life, he replied: "Not necessarily." Rodriguez is elusive with the press. He is not interested in dissecting or interpreting his songs.

When **Esquire** named Rodriguez' "I Wonder" the song of the month for August 2012, his lyrics were accorded the respect they deserved. This was another reason not to discuss the content. It was personal.

Once **Searching For The Sugar Man** came out, record collectors began looking for his rare records. These songs include a version of "Inner City Blues" (live on a Paris street) as well as a cover version of Frank Sinatra's "I'm Gonna Live Till I Die" (live at The Triple Door in Seattle).

Light In The Attic wrote of Rodriguez in a press release:

"WE ARE CELEBRATING RECORD STORE DAY 2010 WITH THIS 7" RELEASE OF TWO LIVE PERFORMANCES FROM RODRIGUEZ TAPED DURING HIS 2009 TOUR. THE A SIDE FEATURES A RECORDING

OF 'INNER CITY BLUES' PERFORMED ON THE STREETS OF PARIS AND RECORDED BY L'EXPRESS. THE B-SIDE IS A COVER OF FRANK SINATRA'S 'I'M GONNA LIVE TILL I DIE' RECORDED DURING HIS DATE AT THE TRIPLE DOOR IN SEATTLE."

This publicity broadside was a reference to a show Rodriguez was part of at Seattle's Triple Door to celebrate Light In The Attic's anniversary and its eclectic roster. It was the perfect venue for Rodriguez with its intimate setting.

The Music and What It Means

Some critics view **Cold Fact** as a lost psychedelic masterpiece. It has poetic images that fit into that genre. It also has a set of lyrics describing the Sugar Man's nemesis, that is the drug dealer in the neighborhood. What makes the music intriguing is the use of language. In "Crucify Your Mind," Rodriguez talks at length about a Dylanesque world. As Rodriguez completes an album that is an unrecognized cult classic, he was unaware people in South Africa were marching in the streets to his lyrics demanding freedom from apartheid. His music is the background to the South African revolution. **Cold Fact** is full of tales of drugs, forlorn love, and songs reflecting the gritty streets in and around Detroit.

Steve Rowland: "I never thought **Cold Fact** was a psychedelic album. It was a selection of brilliantly written songs, they were deeply emotional and well performed."

The album sank without a trace. Some of Rodriguez's idiosyncratic behavior, like performing at an industry showcase with his back to the audience, hurt the promotion. Mike Theodore remembers how he would only play at "hooker bars, inner city dives, and biker bars." When the follow-up, 1971's **Coming From Reality**, also tanked, Rodriguez called an end to his recording career.

The tide began to turn in 1996, when journalist Craig Bartholomew set out to get to the bottom of the mystery. Stephen "Sugar" Segerman had been on the hunt for more than twenty-five years. The two of them formed an unlikely team. One owned a record store and the other was a writer, as well as a full time worker in the day. Unlike Segerman who was a rich, spoiled dilettante, Craig was a blue-collar guy on the hunt for the Sugar Man. But they had one thing in common. They loved Rodriguez' music. They also had great respect for the man.

After many dead ends, they found Rodriguez alive, well, free and perfectly sane. This ended years of speculation about his death. Rodriguez himself had no idea about his South African fame. **Cold Fact** had gone multi-platinum. Although Rodriguez hadn't received as much as a Rand in royalties, in 1998 he began a triumphant South African tour.

Rodriguez was still largely unknown in the northern hemisphere until 2002, when David Holmes listened to "Sugar Man," **Cold Fact's** extra-terrestrial lead track. The DJ discovered the album in a New York record store. He included it on his **Come Get It, I Got It** compilation. He re-recorded the song with Rodriguez for his Free Association project a year later.

Light In The Attic brought **Cold Fact** to CD. There's an entirely new audience, who can finally find out why Rodriguez is talked about in the same respected tones as the Doors, Love and Jimi Hendrix.

The lyrical beauty and musical brilliance was there for the general public. A few people discovered it. There were those in South Africa who couldn't get enough of Rodriguez. He had to hang up his construction clothes to head back to South Africa in September 2001 for a month long tour. It was almost interrupted when the terrorist attacks in New York on 9-11 turned attention away from music and into the political arena. Rodriguez left New York a few days before the 9-11 attacks.

Explaining Rodriguez' Lyrical Brilliance: Why and How He Developed It

Everyone agrees Sixto Rodriguez is a brilliant songwriter. He gives one a view into his life inside Detroit. There is a continual history lesson. His songs are much like an autobiographical novel or perhaps a fictionalized memoir.

Lyrical beauty often obscures meaning. In "Sugar Man" he writes of purchasing drugs from a street corner dealer. The lyrics suggest the moral dilemma of dealing with a drug dealer:

"Sugar Man
Won't ya hurry
Coz I'm tired of these scenes
For a blue coin
Won't… bring back
All those colors to my dreams."

Do these simple lyrics reveal the inner Sugar Man? Is this an example of Rodriguez' neglected Catholicism? Is this front and center in "Sugar Man?" There are moral tones to many of Rodriguez' songs. A good example is another stanza from "Sugar Man."

"Met a false friend
On a lonely, dusty road
Lost my heart
When I found it
It had turned to dead, black coal."

As a non-practicing Catholic, Rodriguez reflected on how his will was weakened by the lure of drugs, the nightlife, the musical world, the Cass Corridor nightspots, the coffee shops, the eateries and the intellectual morass that was so much a part of his early youth. He wrote about it with a lyrical beauty seldom seen in someone not yet thirty. As he grew older, Rodriguez' writing in **Coming From Reality** had a softer, somber, more mature tone. They were songs with a pop, commercial touch.

As he reflected on his songs in 2009, in an interview with the **Chicago Tribune's** Greg Kot, he summed up his songwriting. It combined lyrical beauty with a sense of the present. He also talked politics.

Sixto Rodriguez: "The current economic situation keeps people in classes, so when you hear a song like 'Cause' it applies. I'm surfacing in a unique space for a lot of reasons. But people created these problems, and people can fix them. I don't know if my music is going to help at all, but those are the things that have always been in my music. I only wrote about 29, 30 songs, but they still seem to hit people. That means a lot."

The onset of fame and fortune pushed the Sugar Man into explaining the background of his life. He is no longer comfortable talking about how he feels about his long time in obscurity. He has no interest in dissecting his songs. He writes new songs. He performs fifty to sixty days a year. He spends time with his family. He spends his money on family and friends. Rodriguez is happy, well-adjusted and enjoying fame and fortune. He doesn't want to talk about it.

Twelve

South African Tour 2001 and Live Fact

**"And I'll forget about the girl that said no
Then I'll tell who I want where to go
And I'll forget about your lies and deceit
And your attempts to be discreet."**

Sixto Rodriguez "I'll Slip Away."

**"Sugar man, won't you hurry. Cos
I'm tired of these scenes."**

Sixto Rodriguez "Sugar Man."

"Rodriguez lives the kind of life he sings about. He is against the establishment, suffers hangovers now and again and takes little notice of bureaucracy and schedules."

Zev Eizik

The 2001 Return to South Africa and the Big Town Playboys

In September 2001, Rodriguez returned to South Africa for sixteen triumphant sold out concerts. He remained a hot concert item. For these appearances the London based Big Town Playboys, featuring vocal blues stylist Big Joe Louis, arrived to back him. They also played their own brand of classic rock, rhythm and blue and traditional blues blended with original songs.

The Big Town Playboys are a six-piece London band featuring a rhythm and blues revival sound with Louis' classic vocals. They also perform original songs. Their earlier lead singer, Mike Sanchez, is one of the U. K. best vocalists never to achieve mainstream stardom. He is a classic rocker with a rockabilly touch, and he remains an original talent. He continues to tour and record with his band. When Sanchez left the band in 1999, he embarked on a successful in-concert solo career. The Big Town Playboys brought in Big Joe Louis. They never missed a beat. They were the perfect backing group.

As they backed Rodriguez, the Big Town Playboys released their seventh album **Western World**. They previously toured with Eric Clapton and Jeff Beck. They remain one of the U. K.'s best rhythm and blues aggregations.

The Big Town Playboy's musical roots allowed Rodriguez to insert a rock and roll medley that included covers of Little Richard's "Good Golly Miss Molly" and "Lucille" into his shows. The Playboys also were able to render Rodriguez' version of Midnight Oil's "Redneck Wonderland" into a crowd-pleasing concert favorite with a new twist.

Rodriguez had wide musical tastes. This allowed him to work up songs by the Box Tops, Jackie DeShannon, the Righteous Brothers and a Joe Cocker-Ray Charles inspired "Unchain My Heart." These songs surprised onlookers. This was a new Rodriguez who came in with classic songs. He had a renewed commitment to his rock and roll roots.

The Big Town Playboys and Rodriguez were like oil and water. The Playboys hit the stage with a precise set list, a formula performance and the clothes and stage mannerisms of a polished stage act. Rodriguez didn't like a set list. He preferred to tell the band what he would play next. He loved to improvise on many songs. It was not a formula for in concert happiness with the Big Town Playboys, but the shows were generally excellent ones. The backstage conflict and turmoil was constant. Somehow everyone got through it.

The September 2001 Concerts

On September 17, 2001 Rodriguez appeared at the Whale Hall, Hartenbos, Mossel Bay. Thanks to the fans and Brian Currin's website there is a clear picture of not only Rodriguez' music but his concert influences. At the sound check, Rodriguez went into a brief version of a Roy Hamilton inspired "Unchained Melody." His set included a medley featuring Bill Haley's "Shake Rattle and Roll," Bob Dylan's "Subterranean Homesick Blues" and Elvis Presley's "Hound Dog." Later in the set another medley featured Midnight Oil's "Redneck Wonderland" and brief excerpts from the Box Tops "The Letter" as well as Ray Charles' "Unchain My Heart." When he came out for an encore, Rodriguez performed a cover of Jackie DeShannon's "What the World Needs Now Is Love." He said the song was to honor the victims of 9-11. He also performed a cover version of Vanessa Williams' "Save The Best Till Last." The seventeen-song set ended with "Forget It."

This was the new Rodriguez. He set the tone for the next decade and a half of mixing old songs, from a wide variety of genres, into his originals. He didn't want to play only the numbers his fans knew.

Rodriguez looked to expand his concert repertoire. He thanked the Big Town Playboys for their indulgence, their carefully crafted backing and their willingness to improvise. Rodriguez did recognize the Big Town Playboys skill in concert. It simply wasn't the way he wanted to craft his shows. But he was praiseworthy of the band. He was never critical.

Eva Rodriguez on Her Father's New Fame: The 3rd LP Question Persists

"At his discovery in the 90s, he was around fifty at the time," his daughter Eva Rodriguez continued. "Can he still play? Can he still perform? Yeah!" She said that he could still perform with skill. He has for more than twenty years. Now in his seventies, Rodriguez remains a vibrant in-concert performer. Eva talked at length about a possible third album. This subject continued to intrigue his followers. She ended her comments stating he was happy to perform for his new fans.

One of the myths associated with Rodriguez is he vanished from public sight in 1972. This is not even close to the truth. The truth is more complicated. He continued to perform where and when he could find a venue. In clubs like the Old Miami, Ann Arbor's Mr. Flood's Party and a host of hooker, biker, college fraternity parties, the raucous college bars, coffee shops and private parties, Rodriguez quietly and without fanfare honed his performing skills. He also wrote songs. None of which he was happy with, and he read and thought about current events. When and if a third album is recorded it will have a forty-year gestation period. By 2017 word was out the Sugar Man had nine songs he could lay down in the studio. But he had talked about a third album for half a decade.

In January 2013 Rodriguez told **Rolling Stone** he was exploring a third album with Steve Rowland acting as the producer. "He told me to send him a couple of tapes, I'm going to do that," Rodriguez said. Steve is still waiting for the tapes. There was also talk of bringing David Holmes in to remix some of the songs.

The problem with a third LP is Rodriguez' touring schedule. He is back on the road. This complicates the songwriting and recording process. When **Rolling Stone** interviewed Rodriguez in January 2013, he talked about going into the studio. By the summer of 2014 it hadn't happened. After his performance at the California State University Luckman Hall, Rodriguez talked in his dressing room with Steve Rowland. I observed their discussion. Steve said he had musicians. Rodriguez appeared interested. They talked in hushed tones! The topic of a third album came up. Steve and Rodriguez were deep in discussion. There was no solution.

After the Luckman Center show Rowland drove back to Palm Springs. The Sugar Man, his family, the crew and the musicians headed to downtown Los Angeles to relax at the Ace Hotel. This is Los Angeles' hip hotel for musicians. It is pricey but worth it for the comfort. Regan did everything she could to make her father comfortable. This is one reason he is an excellent performer. After the show food and drink flowed and the sense of pleasing a tough Los Angeles audience gave the Sugar Man a reason to smile.

Why The 2001 South African Tour: What Did It Mean?

Sixto Rodriguez' popularity in South Africa continued while he was in Detroit rehabbing homes and preparing to turn sixty. His body was slowly wearing out from overwork. He continued to live in Woodbridge in his two-story home. His daughter, Regan, occupied the upstairs while the Sugar Man lived comfortably downstairs. He wasn't sure he wanted to tour.

When tour promoters describe Rodriguez as a person who "takes little notice of bureaucracy and schedules," they unwittingly expose a dilemma. He is mercurial. He is unpredictable. He does not adhere to a set list. He has periodic stage fright. It has eased. He does show up on time for his concerts. He controls his songs with a passion after forty plus years of neglect. He does it his way. But he never does in an overbearing manner.

In 2001 the second Rodriguez South African tour was an uneven one. But it continued his legend. He discovered his friend, Stephen "Sugar" Segerman, was a rank amateur with an agenda. He was arranging a portion of the tour. He did a terrible job. The South African dilettante believed he invented the story. That led to internal dissension, strong disagreements and eventually Segerman was shunted into a role outside Rodriguez' inner circle.

Why The Second South African Tour Left Rodriguez Wondering

The second South African tour in 2001 did not go well for many reasons. Zev Eizik did what he could to salvage many of the tour dates. Stephen "Sugar" Segerman had good intentions. He had no training in touring logistics. Everyone I interviewed for the book said he was the fly in the ointment. He wanted control. He saw himself as the Sugar Man's protector. He was slowly impeding a career on the rise.

There was something of a tug of war among South African producers to bring the Sugar Man back for another tour. Stephen "Sugar" Segerman and David Marks made Rodriguez an offer to promote the tour. He decided to have Zev Eizik and Magnus Erickson finalize his second set of South African shows. They were respected and seasoned professionals with U.K., South African and Australian concert promotion experience.

Segerman was still a friend. But he wasn't a concert promoter. He was a super fan. Rodriguez didn't trust his career to a rank amateur. For some reason Segerman was on the 2001 tour. Why? He was

Rodriguez' friend. Segerman's diffident personality and abrasive manner was a problem. Even worse his mania for control left many cold. In sharp contrast, Eizik operated with efficiency and excellent box office results. He was a smooth, business like person. Eizik was a talented promoter with a plan.

For a few years Rodriguez worked easily with Eizik. There were no apparent problems. Then in October 2007 he filed a contract suit against Eizik and his corporation alleging fiscal irregularities. There is no record what the dispute was over and why the suit took place. It was adjudicated. In 2007 when Rodriguez sued Eizik in an Eastern Michigan Court, it appears he may alleged contract infringement. This lawsuit suggested Rodriguez' newfound business sophistication.

There was no loss of friendship between Segerman and Rodriguez. The South African understood he was not a manager or a concert promoter. Segerman had difficulty accepting his diminished role. His ego got in the way of his good sense. It was a tumultuous time. Segerman attempted to manipulate behind the scenes. The Sugar Man was now a businessman. Segerman refused to recognize Rodriguez had taken over his business duties with skill and aplomb.

The idea of a record storeowner promoting his concerts did not ring true as Segerman was more interested in promoting Mabu Vinyl and his daughter's singing career than he was in securing Rodriguez equitable contracts. Rodriguez had been through this many times. He quietly took over and moved Segerman into the background.

In time Segerman's attitude strained the relationship. The diffident, pompous Segerman never understood his egregious behavior was offensive. After all he told Rodriguez he was a former South African quiz kid. That meant he was the smartest guy on the block. The Sugar Man smiled. He never mentioned his philosophy degree was with honors. There were two egos. One was outsized-Segerman. The other one was in check-Rodriguez.'

Segerman in Detroit with Dead Men Don't Tour

In August 2001, Segerman showed up at Rodriguez' Woodbridge home with a copy of the South African TV show "Dead Men Don't Tour." He was invited in the house, and they all went upstairs to watch the documentary in Regan's living space. It was a special moment for Rodriguez. He was finally getting the respect he deserved. He appreciated Segerman's interest.

Why would Segerman show up in Detroit a month before the Sugar Man left for his second South African tour? Control! The mania to manage Rodriguez made Segerman a pest with an impediment to mainstream success.

As Segerman and Rodriguez watched the documentary one of Regan's friends couldn't believe the South African TV show. Few people in and around Wayne State University, the Cass Corridor and Woodbridge knew of the Sugar Man's South African fame. After they watched the TV show a second time, the group wandered out for dinner. After a night of rest, Rodriguez provided Segerman with a Detroit tour. Sugar met some of Sixto's friends, they went to Sandra's home and Rodriguez' two wives, Rayma and Konny, were part of the tour. The two wives were friendly with each other. There was no conflict in Rodriguez' world. Life was good for the Sugar Man.

After his Detroit visit, Segerman flew home. He told Rodriguez he would meet him at the airport to make sure he and his family was comfortable for the second tour. As Segerman and Rodriguez hugged upon Sugar's departure for Cape Town, there was no doubt they were close friends. But for Rodriguez there was an uneasy feeling. He had been disappointed too many times to allow a rank amateur to influence his career. It was a conflicting moment.

There is a level of uncertainty and insecurity to Rodriguez' life. He told close friends in Detroit his friendship with Segerman was a lifelong one. He would never forget the dedication, the solid friendship and the integrity that Segerman displayed promoting his career. That attitude would soon be put to the ultimate test.

The Personal Journey of Stephen “Sugar” Segerman on the 2001 Tour

In the Rodriguez story too many people believe they are responsible for his success. Everyone wants the credit. They develop a protective mindset. In the present day, his daughter, Regan, who manages him, is the primary minder. She is the gatekeeper. She knows what he wants. She is also a consummate professional. She’s the only one who can manage his career. She is the only one with experience.

When promoters brought Rodriguez to South Africa in 2001 they made a series of mistakes. The reason? The tour was poorly planned, amateurish in nature and there were too many highbrow accoutrements. That is high-end hotels, fancy dinners and isolation from his legion of fans. This prevented Rodriguez from enjoying the concerts and the fans. They had no idea about Rodriguez’ penchant for blue collar, working class folks. He was uneasy with five star hotels. The hangers on became a problem. He had minders who kept track of him. He likes to walk the streets alone. Now he couldn’t go out in public in South Africa. He was a mega celebrity. Something was wrong. Rodriguez vowed to solve the mess.

Everyone interviewed for this book said that Rodriguez and Segerman had a love-hate relationship. The Sugar Man was loyal to his South African friend. He liked having him around when Sixto’s family was not in the mix. As Rodriguez complained about Segerman he was, in a sense, a security blanket for the singer’s shy nature. It was complicated.

The concert promoters alleged Stephen “Sugar” Segerman had a negative impact upon the Sugar Man. Rodriguez has a level of personal insecurity that needs to be addressed. For a time he felt comfortable with Segerman despite his bluster and over the top behavior.

They loved to hang out and as Segerman reflected to a friend from South Africa they loved "stoking the magic dragon." The point is without Segerman, Rodriguez was uncomfortable with the luxurious trappings during the 2001 South African tour. This accounts for a small number of uneven performances. The Sugar Man's mercurial behavior resulted from the good hearted, but misguided, attempts of local promoters to provide him with world-class treatment. It was a strange twist from earlier times. He was adjusting to his initial taste of fame. Fortune was on its way.

During this tour, Rodriguez was relaxed when he sat in Segerman's home in Oranjezicht, which is a Cape Town suburb. There is no doubt that the 2001 South African tour did not go well at times. At other times he was brilliant.

The Musical Background to Rodriguez South African 2001 Tour

There was an immense amount of drama associated with Rodriguez' September 2001 tour. The terrorist attack on New York's World Trade Center reverberated around the world. Rodriguez was deeply affected by the terrorist action.

Zev Eizik and Magnus Erickson hired an events company, Authentic Ideas, to coordinate the day-to-day tour events. When Segerman showed up to meet Rodriguez, he connected with Nancy Hillary. She was co-coordinating the events to promote the tour. She and Segerman didn't hit it off. A member of the staff at Authentic Ideas thought Segerman was pompous, officious, controlling and full of himself. He told me "Segerman was an amateur constantly underfoot."

Segerman and Hillary fought over mundane details. Other arguments over important details could be heard in frequent shouting matches. This did not sit well with Rodriguez. During the 2001 tour Hillary made it clear Segerman was a bore, an unrequited wanker and a person with little knowledge of promotion in the music business.

When Segerman left the tour, there was a collective sigh of relief. There was a blow up at the Orient Express Hotel where Hillary and Segerman shouted at each other. The South African thought if he left so would Rodriguez. That was not the case.

Nancy Hillary and Rodriguez bonded. The reason? She was a political activist. Her concern was fighting crime in South Africa. They talked. Rodriguez explained the mean streets of Detroit. Hillary talked of signing a petition to fight crime. Hillary evolved into a heavyweight music management mogul. She now works in Sydney Australia. When she met with and directed Rodriguez' 2001 South African tour she was managing tours at the top of her craft. From 1996 to 2010 she was one of South Africa's artist management pros. She worked closely with Rodriguez and since that time she has coordinated tours for Celine Dion, Julio Iglesias, the Hollies, George Benson and Deep Purple among others. She helped to set up the promotional events for Rodriguez. That part of the tour was successful.

The relationship with Nancy Hillary offers an insight into the personal Rodriguez. He is a good judge of character. With Hillary he saw a person without ego. He saw a professional. He saw a person who did her job 24/7. He realized that as a music agent she had few peers. How accurate was the Sugar Man's evaluation? It was spot on. Hillary is currently director of All Things Entertainment in Sydney Australia. The company is a music agency specializing in management. In South Africa she was in the early stages of her career and Hillary made the 2001 tour a modest success when it could have been a complete disaster. As Stephen "Sugar" Segerman ran around telling everyone how brilliant he was and how great his daughter was as an opening act performer, Hillary asked: "Why was Segerman's daughter an opening act?" Hillary quietly and professionally set up key events.

When Rodriguez was to arrive there was a promotional meal planned at the Four Seasons Westcliff Hotel restaurant pool deck. He would get off the plane and take a limousine to the hotel as the media was filled with food and booze. The Orient Express Hotel chain that owns the Four Seasons Westcliff Hotel has a reputation for style and opulence that was not in character with Rodriguez' music. The pool restaurant overlooks elephants in the nearby zoo. It boasts one of the most spectacular views of the city.

As the assembled journalists, hangers on and assorted VIPs, arrived for the welcome to Johannesburg luncheon for Rodriguez, he was still in New York. He missed his flight. The Sugar Man was wandering around JFK International Airport. Erickson grabbed a phone and called New York. He convinced JFK International to page Rodriguez. They did. He came on the line. He was put on a loud speaker in Johannesburg booming over the terrace of the hotel. It was a surrealistic moment. The Sugar Man smiled. He loved attending a cocktail reception by phone.

The Press Release on Rodriguez' 2001 Arrival in Johannesburg

The irony of this tour is it was brilliant in spots, lackluster at other times and there were a few low points. Overall it was successful with glitches. One of the unsung heroes in his popularity was the work of Authentic Ideas. This agency not only publicized his South African success, but the company framed his future. He was an act with more than a past. With Nancy Hillary in charge the Sixto Rodriguez story marched ahead suggesting a renewal and rebirth. The press release, compiled by Jane Ranger, indicates how and why he continued to evolve as a brilliant entertainer.

> **With close on ten gigs under his belt, Rodriguez and The Big Town Playboys have been wowing audiences around the**

country. Rodriguez has eased into his shows with The Big Town Playboys and with his easygoing nature and friendliness; crowds have really taken to him.

Not many people actually believed the man himself was coming to South Africa. There have been rumours since Rodriguez's last tour to SA, that he was dead. Obviously this is not true. However, fans in Pietersburg were convinced that a cover band would be playing his hits while Vanderbijlpark fans thought a local nightclub were throwing a Rodriguez theme party. Bloemfontein fans were so excited they threatened to stab the venue owner if Rodriguez wasn't actually there! Rodriguez is well, alive and performing somewhere near you!

Rodriguez has taken time out after every show to meet his fans and sign their posters, CDs, t-shirts and homemade flags. Nothing has been too much for him and fans have had countless opportunities to meet the man after his shows. Rodriguez has made the effort with each and every person he meets. Whether he's checking out of hotels or taking three hours to do autographs, Rodriguez has had no disappointed fans.

Rodriguez has dedicated the last two songs of each of his shows to his fellow countrymen in America. Although deeply worried about the situation in his country, Rodriguez has promised to fulfill his obligations for the rest of his tour in South Africa before heading back to the US.

Rodriguez has displayed great pride and almost surprise at the reaction he has received from many fans! Not surprising taking into consideration that he never knew, up until a few years ago, what a fan base he had and what a rock icon he is in South Africa! Fans have been very supportive of Rodriguez and he has been overwhelmed by the response he has received, especially the “I Love You” banners at his shows! The crowds singing along have drowned most of his songs out!

Rodriguez has been performing at smaller more intimate venues on this tour, in comparison with his last sell-out tour where he performed in huge stadiums. He wanted fans to experience his music live, something they so seldom have the chance to do and also give fans that missed his shows first time round, an opportunity to see him live. Rodriguez requested to perform in smaller venues this time around so he could get up close and personal with his fans. He wanted the opportunity to meet his fans from all over the country. Rodriguez has visited places such as Pietersburg, Vanderbijlpark and Mossel Bay on his nationwide tour. This tour encompasses 16 dates countrywide; one of the longest tours by an international artist. Rodriguez has opened most of his shows with his hit ‘I Wonder’ which has got the crowds going right from the start! The ‘Sugarman’ himself is delighting audiences countrywide!

Catch Rodriguez in Port Elizabeth on September 18 and 19, The Strand on September 20, Cape Town on September 21 and 22, East London on September 26 and Durban on September 27 and 28. Doors open at all venues at 7pm with the shows starting at 8.30pm. There will be seating available at the Port Elizabeth, Strand, Cape Town, East London venues. Rodriguez will then be available for autographs after the shows. There are limited tickets available through Ticketweb and tickets will be available at the gates. However it is advisable, to avoid disappointment, to get your tickets early!

Gauteng fans need not despair if they missed Rodriguez the first time round! He will be performing his final performance at Woodstock 3 on September 29. Fans can come

to Woodstock 3 for the day for R120, available at the gate, where Rodriguez will perform on the Musica stage at 5pm. A great place to end a great tour!

- Compiled by Jane Ranger for Authentic Ideas (PTY) LTD, 17 September 2001.

9-11: Rodriguez Stuck in New York, the Cocktail Party He Never Attended

With Rodriguez on the phone from New York, Erickson asked him to sing a few lines from "I Wonder." The Sugar Man was flummoxed. What the hell was going on?

What Erickson accomplished was brilliant. The press not only realized Rodriguez was returning for a second set of South African shows, they praised the cocktail party as an innovative and a lavish introduction to the second Sugar Man tour. Nancy Hillary was in the background making sure the press minions had plenty to eat and drink.

The irony is this over the top media event was as far away from Rodriguez' personality as one could imagine. A few weeks earlier he came home every day covered in dust, filthy and tired from back-breaking labor. Now he was headed to a Five Star hotel in the beautiful South African landscape. It was surreal.

It was two days after the abortive cocktail-publicity party that Rodriguez finally arrived in his suite at the Four Seasons Westcliff Hotel. The lavish suite must have caused Rodriguez to ponder his past. He lived in a house without central heating or air conditioning.

Once he arrived at the Five Star hotel, Rodriguez walked down to the Johannesburg zoo. It was beautiful. He walked back and had a meal at the Cellar Door where the hotel pairs wine and food in an elegant manner. This was a far cry from his Detroit digs. But it was what was happening in America that impacted Rodriguez.

The 9-11 attacks had a profound impact upon the Sugar Man. He is first and foremost a political activist. He needed to make sense of the brutal attacks in New York and the plane crash into the Pentagon. South Africa was not the ideal place for political news. Apartheid ended a decade earlier. But the local news was still difficult to assess. He talked about the attacks in his concerts. His political activism, although a quiet one, impressed those close to Rodriguez. He was first and foremost a patriot.

"I think the 9-11 attacks brought a sense of renewed commitment to politics for the Sugar Man," one South African label owner confided.

Back To South Africa, September 2001

The September 2001 South African tour offers a window inside the Rodriguez phenomenon. The sixteen concert dates, with the Big Town Playboys, was a skilled marketing campaign to sell the recently released **Live Fact** album. He remained unknown in America. He was a star in Australia. His daughters had grown up. Sandra and Eva had families. Regan came of age, and she was dating.

A number of people close to Rodriguez remarked he didn't like playing the cavernous stadiums or even the mid-sized arenas. As a result the 2001 tour was booked into smaller or more intimate venues. This made for personalized shows designed to add to Rodriguez' legacy. It did little for his pocket book.

The South African tours in 1998 and 2001 were amongst Rodriguez' favorites. After **Searching For Sugar Man** became a phenomenon, he had trouble going out in public. In South Africa he could not as easily walk the streets. Fame had intruded upon his personal space.

Rodriguez' 2001 South African Tour

September 7-8: Carnival City, Brakpan
September 9: Bandu Inn, Pretoria
September 12: Pintoberg Theater, Pietersberg
September 14: AFP Hall, Vanderbijipark
September 15: Callie Human, Bloemfontein
September 17: Whale Hall, Paardekraalweg, Hartenbos, Mossel Bay
September 18-19: PE Tech Theater, MMM Loubser Auditorium, Port Elizabeth
September 20: Strand Hall, Strand
September 21-22: 3 Arts, Plumstead Cape Town
September 26: Orient Theater, East London
September 27-28: BarGo, Durban
September 29: Woodstock 3, Heidelberg Kloof

The Early Concerts and Rodriguez

Rodriguez began his tour at the Carnival City Big Top Arena in Brakpan. This is a world-class venue with a high-end casino, a marvelous sound system, as well as spectacular seating. The Casino provided Five Star lodging and Michelin star award dining. The gourmet restaurant was not Rodriguez' style. He brought in a big spending crowd. This made him nervous. He worried about being too commercial. His music sold in platinum numbers. His concerts continued to sell out. His press was positive.

Then the shows moved to the Bandu Inn in Pretoria were there was once again a world class resort atmosphere. This made Rodriguez feel like he was on a vacation. As he walked out on stage, the sun was setting. The perfect weather caused the blue sky to radiate. Rodriguez looked up. He told a band member he felt blessed. Recognition was sweet after years in obscurity.

The Bandu Inn has a capacity of perhaps four hundred. It was sold out. There were so many people outside waiting to get in; there was strict crowd control. Rodriguez was still the hottest ticket in South Africa. No one in America had a clue.

During this trip to South Africa the myths behind Rodriguez' career slowly gave way to reality. His music was established. Now he was a performing icon. The mystery ended. Rodriguez was real. The media asked: "Will Rodriguez' Concert Magic Last?" The answer was an unrequited "Yes."

The Tenor and Tone of the Tour

The first three concerts went off magically with loud bursts of applause. The capacity crowds and excellent press coverage welcomed the Sugar Man back to South Africa. Then the tour settled into Pietersburg, where a rumor started a cover band was going to play his songs. Someone intensified the rumor Rodriguez would not appear. The rumor mill was fueled by arcane journalism. Rodriguez remarked: "Pietersburg was cold. The building was cold. They tell me their stories. The soldiers tell me their stories (about when they first heard his songs). I hear all that stuff, everything. I try and sign autographs for them." Rodriguez was happy with the zeal of the adoring Pietersburg audience. He continued on with the tour signing autographs for hours after each show. One autograph period lasted for three hours. He never said no to his South African fans.

There was no pretension. There was a great deal of concern from Rodriguez for his fans. He was humbled as young and old fans alike stood in line for hours for an autograph or a picture. He made sure no one was disappointed.

The tour with the Big Town Playboys at times did not go well. There were times when Rodriguez drank too much, stoked on the magic dragon too many times or was simply exhausted. There were times when the Big Town Playboys had trouble with the Sugar Man's set changes. They were a precision band. They didn't like last minute changes or on the spot innovation. The Sugar Man was an eclectic performer. He had differences with the band. His laid back attitude, Zen like countenance, and his musical, literary direction didn't fit with the Big Town Playboys. Rodriguez was like a jazz hipster or a beatnik passing in the night.

Rodriguez was much like the French poet, Baudelaire, who was the cursed poet doomed by bad luck. In the Sugar Man's case the bad luck turned into gold. He was the star of the show. This did not sit well with the Big Town Playboys. Rodriguez and the Big Town Playboys were two groups who passed in the night and didn't connect.

The Big Town Playboys Walk Off Stage as Rodriguez Shows Up with a Snootful

After two weeks of shows, Rodriguez appeared at the 3 Arts Theater in Cape Town with too much to drink. He wasn't used to the road. With Stephen "Sugar" Segerman in the audience, Rodriguez stumbled through his set. Some fans told me Segerman was a bad influence. He loved to hang out with the Sugar Man. Their personality excesses allegedly led to a rip roaring drunken adventure.

People left disgusted. He slurred his words. He complained to the band they weren't backing him properly. Then after half an hour of attempting to back the Sugar Man the Big Town Playboys walked off stage in protest. It was a tense moment. Segerman made it worse by berating the Big Town Playboys. One of the band members said: "This amateur asshole was someone we tolerated." Rodriguez was embarrassed. "I almost punched out that foul mouthed bald headed bastard," another member of the Big Town Playboys remarked of Segerman.

The Big Town Playboys are a professional musical group. Craig Bartholomew-Strydom and Stephen "Sugar" Segerman's book describes the group as "session musicians..." This insipid comment ignores their popularity in the U. K. It also disparages their professionalism. It is also an inaccurate description of a highly professional band. The Big Town Playboy's have strong album sales, sold out concerts, and they have had wonderful press for more than two decades. Stephen "Sugar" Segerman was a rank amateur posing as a music manager. These errors carry over into their book. Amateurs are amateurs. That is a concrete cold fact.

What the Bartholomew-Strydom-Segerman book misses is in 2001 the Big Town Playboys had released seven stellar albums including one with Jeff Beck celebrating Gene Vincent's music. When they were booked to back Rodriguez, there was some confusion. They believed they were the headline act. This misunderstanding was due to Segerman's amateurish approach to the tour. He pissed everyone off including Rodriguez. The Big Town Playboys vowed never to work with Rodriguez or Segerman again. Segerman vowed to protect the Sugar Man. He did in his book with Craig Bartholomew-Strydom, as they created myths that didn't square with reality.

As Rodriguez and the Big Town Playboys fought like adolescents, the Sugar Man's **Cold Fact** album charted at number four on the South African LP chart.

Misrepresenting the Big Town Playboys: Is This the Pattern?

The misuse of rock and roll history in the Bartholomew-Strydom-Segerman book is staggering. The most egregious example of their inability to research anything other than Rodriguez comes in their description of the Big Town Playboys. They write: "The Playboys were session musicians under the leadership of the band's bass player, an on-and-off bassist for Van Morrison. (p. 182) Wrong! Ricky Cool founded the Playboys with Andy Silvester in 1984 as a band influenced by Little Walter and Amos Milburn. Their debut album in 1985 **Playboy Boogie** remains a collectible. They are a seasoned band playing more than a thousand shows by 1998.

Things get worse in the author's description of the band. "Erickson who managed Van Morrison's European tours, which was how he came to put the band together...." This is another misuse of facts and a lack of understanding of the basic history of rock and roll history.

When Rodriguez showed up to practice with the Big Town Playboys he had a guitar without strings. The Sugar Man didn't want to put in an hour practice session, so the guitar was his foil. The Playboys offered him a guitar. An argument broke out. Their version is "things were slightly frosty between the band and Rodriguez." (p. 183) They know what happened. They didn't write about it. The Big Town Playboys complained the Sugar Man wasn't prepared for the tour. They don't want to anger him and his family. As a result the book is a classic statement in hagiography. Myth never triumphs reality. In the process they disrespect the story. They denigrate the memory of Malik Bendjelloul. They make claims that bear no resemblance to reality.

Bartholomew-Strydom-Segerman Promoting Hagiography

Craig Bartholomew-Strydom and Stephen "Sugar" Segerman's **Sugar Man: The Life, Death And Resurrection of Sixto Rodriguez** suggests the Big Town Playboys were not an appropriate backing band. This is utter nonsense. The author's demonstrate their inability to research a group that produced two excellent vocalists Mike Sanchez and Big Joe Louis. This is a tragedy. The Big Town Playboys remain a premier headlining group. But if you are stuck in Cape Town without access to the outside world, you don't realize the Big Town Playboy's professionalism. Or if you are a hagiographer defending the Sugar Man you spin the story.

One of the problems with the Bartholomew-Strydom-Segerman book is a tendency toward hagiography. They are fans. They are not professional historians or biographers. They inform you they are telling the true story and everyone else is wrong. I perceived excessive hagiography. That is unfortunate. We can forgive their transgressions and lack of professionalism. They have told a wonderful, if psychopathic tale, in their well-written book. But it is far from the truth.

The truth is the Big Town Playboys remain one of the premier U. K. classic rock-blues bands. They are a professional group with a large U. K. and international following. They have a body of material released on a variety of record labels. They count Ace Records founder Roger Armstrong amongst their fans.

From 1985 to 2004 the Big Town Playboys recorded nine excellent commercial chart oriented albums. They also backed Jeff Beck on his **Crazy Legs** album in 1993. This album paid tribute to Gene Vincent's music. A number of their songs have appeared on soundtracks for films including **The Pope Must Die**. The Big Town Playboys are musically tight, professional, and they were eager to back the Sugar Man. It happened some nights. It didn't happen other nights.

A small part of the South African press, three years after Rodriguez' comeback, continued to speculate on his career. There were only two failed concerts in 2001. The abortive shows at Strand Hall and the 3 Arts appearance were rough ones. The local press castigated Rodriguez' lackluster performance. Those who attended these shows loved them. This is a testament to his fans enduring passion. It is also an insight into how the press and fans differ in their view of Rodriguez' performances.

Craig Bartholomew-Strydom wrote the 2001 Rodriguez concerts failed because there was a no-smoking ban in South Africa preventing the Sugar Man's fans from lighting a joint. Bartholomew-Strydom wrote: "Without cigarette smoke to mask the smell, people were reluctant to light up a joint, as one does at a Rodriguez concert, which seemed to have a negative effect on the crowd in the auditorium. Ultimately, the concert fell a little flat." (p. 183) This is, of course, a ridiculous and juvenile comment. The Big Town Playboys lead singer, Big Joe Louis, remarked the Sugar Man didn't want to practice. He didn't seem to care about a tight show. This was remedied for the last four concerts as Rodriguez recovered from a bout of nerves.

At one show a member of the Big Town Playboys wondered what was going on with the Sugar Man. He didn't bring along his guitar. He forgot it. When he recovered the guitar the Big Town Playboys noticed the Sugar Man's guitar didn't have strings. The Big Town Playboys were outraged. Rodriguez asked one of the audiences if the show was better without the band. The crowd cheered. They never forgot it. But one thing the differences did was to make the last few shows among the tightest of the tour.

The Big Town Playboys

BIG JOE LOUIS: VOCALS, ACOUSTIC GUITAR
IAN JENNINGS: DOUBLE BASS
MARK MORGAN: DRUMS
WEST WESTON: PIANO AND HARP
DAVE WILSON: GUITAR
NICK LUNT: BARITONE SAX
LEE BADAU: TENOR SAX

There was an American patriotic side to Rodriguez during this tour. He performed a medley of hits including Jackie De Shannon's "What The World Needs Now Is Love," which he dedicated to the victims of the September 11, 2001 attack on New York's World Trade Center. He was clearly the same Rodriguez. That is a civil rights oriented person. He is a patriotic American. This was evident in comments during the second South African tour about the 9-11 tragedy.

He opened most shows with “I Wonder.” This song not only a crowd pleaser, it was also a song that everyone knew. The crowd sang along.

Conclusions on the 2001 South African Tour

The 2001 South African tour was a portent of things to come. At times the Sugar Man is brilliant in concert. At other times he is excellent. He cares about performing but he is in his mid-seventies. Some nights it doesn’t happen. Regan has learned to pace the shows so Rodriguez remains fresh. The number of back up bands around the world is another problem. Some bands are excellent, while others are average to inadequate. In 2001 none of this mattered, Rodriguez was not an international star.

When he broke through to worldwide stardom in 2012, the Sugar Man was able to perform cover songs. He sporadically covered 1950s-1960s classic rock, blues and doo-wop selections in concert.

Before he was an international star, Rodriguez had trouble with extended tours. He is private. He likes to write. He hangs out with average people. In the middle of the 2001 South African tour, Rodriguez secretly checked into a small hotel in the Cape Town suburb of Sea Point. He was tired of people. He was tired of security. He needed some down time.

One question hung in the air from the 2001 South African tour. It was the money question. No figures exist but rumors persist that not all the concert fees were paid. Rodriguez has never commented. No one in South Africa mentioned the concert fees. The question remains unanswered. There was a 2007 lawsuit Rodriguez filed in an Eastern Michigan court against the concert promoter, Zev Eizik, but there is no information on the outcome of this legal action. Was it pertinent to the 2001 tour? Who knows!

There were other problems. Rodriguez' records were no longer pressed in South Africa. His 2001 performances prompted a slight decline in local CD sales. It didn't matter! Overall the 2001 tour was a resounding success with the reviewers, if a bit of a soap opera. One thing is certain. Rodriguez loves South Africa and nearby Namibia. Three years later he combined a visit with his eldest daughter, Eva, with some concerts in the beautiful, picturesque Namibia.

Relaxing in South Africa 2001

Rodriguez is an interesting interview. He is polite. He is often formal. He is often elusive. In 2001 he sat down at the Po-Na-Na-Souk Bar in the upstairs balcony, Heritage Square on Shortmarket Street in Cape Town, he was relaxed. Before the interview began, Rodriguez reminisced about Ray Charles and B. B. King: "What I do like is Ray Charles and B. B. King…." What did he mean? He talked at length about their vocal styles. The Sugar Man made it clear he studied how vocals were used to mesmerize the audience. Then he went on to suggest he couldn't play the guitar like King. But who can?

During this interview for the 2001 South African trip, Rodriguez reflected on what inspires him. He lumped writers, musicians and performers together and talked about what he does as an "art form." He commented: "There's no blueprint for success in music." He also reflected that it was difficult to have a global music presence. He now has it.

A Few Economic Concerns from the South African Shows

There is one caveat from the 2001 tour that stuck in the Sugar Man's mind. Despite the worshipful countenance of the South Africans there was a problem with money during the 1998 tour and Rodriguez and his family worried about this taking place once again. The reason that the Sugar Man was late for the fancy press conference was due to his monetary concerns. He wanted to be paid in advance. He negotiated with Eizik and Erickson for advance payment and during this process his airline ticket didn't arrive. This was the reason he was late for the cocktail party welcoming him back to South Africa.

Eizik blamed FedEx, Segerman and a lack of coordination with Detroit on the problems. Lurking in the background his chief fan, who called himself Sugar, lusted for fame and this would impact Rodriguez when he returned to South Africa in 2004. He was experiencing the same problems he had years earlier with Harry Balk and Clarence Avant. He was not about to go through these career scenes again.

Why is this important? There were those who said Rodriguez wasn't reliable. This was nonsense. He was by 2001 a responsible businessman. He had enough training being screwed by pros in the business. He lived to perform. He also had money during the tour handing out bills to young kids who virtually mobbed him. The second South African tour was a learning experience and it was obvious the Sugar Man had control of the business end of his career. Stephen "Sugar" Segerman was the only person who didn't understand the fiscal sophistication of Rodriguez and his family. There would be a blow up in the future and Segerman would be banned from Rodriguez' inner circle. That blow up came in 2004 when Rodriguez appeared in Namibia.

Thirteen

Rodriguez in Namibia and The Garden Route, 2004

"Rodriguez was in top form and played three lengthy sets which included many of the best known songs off Cold Fact."

Stephen "Sugar" Segerman commenting on the 2004 shows.

"Rodriguez today still sells gold in South Africa-only in the last five years he sold another gold disc...."

Malik Bendjelloul.

What is the Garden Route? It is a popular coastal stretch on South Africa's southeastern coast. This scenic area is replete with game preserves and beautiful beaches. It has a majestic coastline. This pristine setting is a haven for environmentalists. It is one of the most beautiful scenic routes in the world. The one hundred fifty mile area is one Rodriguez loved. He quickly became a local advocate for the environment. He joined one of the organizations committed to preserving the environment. While touring South Africa, he donated a portion of his earnings to environmental causes. He kept this as quiet as possible. The publicity shy Rodriguez wasn't interested in praise. His only goal was preservation. He wasn't interested in publicity. The excessive praise caused the Sugar Man to withdraw. It wasn't a problem. The Garden Route treated him like he was a native.

The Garden Route is a holiday paradise spanning Cape Town to Port Elizabeth. The spectacular coastline is set alongside rugged mountain ranges and a coastal forest provides a cool breeze. The one hundred eighty six mile coastline is home to secluded lagoons, white sand beaches and striking gorges. It is set off by the Garden Route National Park with lakes, lagoons and forests. There are ten Wilderness preserves. Beauty is everywhere.

The South African landscape had a special draw for Rodriguez. There is an ecological side to his personality. His daughter, Eva, lived for a time in the Namibia area. She raised her child amidst the scenic beauty. The Sugar Man frequently visited her family. The peace and tranquility of the South African coast is a perfect match for Rodriguez' personality. He is a thinker who remains close to nature.

When he performed in Namibia concert guarantees were not a concern. He was paid handsomely. He was there to visit his daughter, his new grandchild and to enjoy the scenic beauty. He couldn't wait to experience the Garden Route.

What is the Garden Route?

The Garden Route is South Africa's answer to ecological purity. It has a mild climate with warm summers and tourist friendly winters. The locals pay close attention to preserving wildlife. It was not uncommon to see Rodriguez walking, talking and working with environmentalists.

The area is calm and laid back. It is much like parts of America in the 1960s. That made it home to the Sugar Man. Surfing along the Garden Route is virtually a religion. Rodriguez visits here often. He loves it. His daughter, Eva, was married to the South African bodyguard from the 1998 tour. She lived in the Wilderness area. At forty-nine Eva Alice Rodriguez found peace of mind, as she studied to become and passed the tests to be a traditional healer. Her spiritual awareness of nature, and her close ties to her father made his visits special.

The Garden Route defines Rodriguez' life. It is an area celebrating diversity and scenic beauty. He still loves the countryside, as does his family. Fame may intrude upon privacy, but it also provides new adventures.

How Did Searching for Sugar Man Play in Namibia?

Searching For Sugar Man had a dramatic impact upon Namibia. The locals viewed him as the secret rock star supporting their drive for independence. When he studied Namibia's independence movement, he observed there was no need for a revolution. The system would crumble from oppression, greed and bigotry.

The Namibian War of Independence took place in 1990 long before Rodriguez appeared in South Africa. But his music also fueled that independence movement. When the Namibian Independence Day celebration took place at the Windhoek Sports Stadium on March 21, 1990 the Sugar Man's music was in the hearts and minds of the locals. It would be fourteen years before he toured there but the affection for his music, and the thanks for his inspiration rang out in every corner of this newly established country.

Rodriguez in Namibia: 2004 and the Contrast to Detroit's Fourth of July Taste Test

When he left for Namibia in the summer of 2004 Rodriguez told friends he celebrated how Namibia embraced its freedoms. He loved the idea of these newfound freedoms. In 2004, when Rodriguez performed in Namibia, there were continual changes taking place. Namibia shares a boundary with Angola and Zambia. Namibia is an African word meaning: "Land of the Brave." The radio stations played Rodriguez' music with the same fervor as in South Africa. His fans have the same attachment to **Cold Fact** and **Coming From Reality**.

When Rodriguez flew into Windhoek in Namibia on July 10 it was his sixty-second birthday. The Namibia Rodriguez show was a benefit for the Cheetah National Arts Commission. Not surprisingly, Rodriguez belonged to the Cheetah Foundation. He also donated a substantial portion of his concert fee to the organization. Money is not one of Rodriguez' concerns. His daughter, Eva, was with him at the show.

Since Rodriguez had free time he traveled to Cape Town to see his friend Stephen "Sugar. Segerman. He surprised Sugar when he walked in unannounced at Mabu Vinyl and greeted everyone warmly. When a local reporter interviewed Rodriguez, he remarked: "I hope to play to South Africans, and also to communicate to America what it sounds like on this side of the globe. I feel like Marco Polo...."

Rodriguez' first concert on Friday August 13 was at Mossel Bay. It was much like a coronation as the crowd erupted after every song. The Garden Route Casino draws a young, free spending crowd. Rodriguez' reception showed he had an audience that was younger, proportionally better educated and with free spending habits. His popularity continued to grow as did album sales.

The concert on July 15 at Otjiwarongo was in a small sized venue. There is a natural beauty to Otjiwarongo. It is a town of 70,000. The name is an African word for where fat cattle graze. The primary attraction is its game preserve. The Otjibama Lodge is an Afro Colonial lodge catering to white tourists and South Africans. It was a segregated country club. Rodriguez broke the color barrier. The area is heavily populated with German speaking people. In the past it was one of the worst areas for civil liberties. Despite this history, Rodriguez was welcomed with open arms. The locals told him they were changing their formerly Neanderthal racial policies. He remains a catalyst for social change even in ethnically challenged areas.

The appearances in Namibia were successful ones. They continued to build Rodriguez' brand outside the U. S. It wasn't that way back home. The Motor City had no idea it had a famous son.

Detroit's 4th Street Fair Centers Rodriguez

When he returned to Detroit, Rodriguez was once again just another anonymous Motor City resident. He was happy to be back in Detroit. Everything Rodriguez represented resulted from his hometown. He was active in community celebrations. He continued to pursue liberal politics. He worked for political change.

When Rodriguez attended the 4th Street Fair, he was happy to celebrate with friends. Detroit defined his soul and persona. Rodriguez got back to enjoying the 4th Street Fair. He performed an impromptu set of songs. Perhaps a hundred people witnessed this little concert. Rodriguez smiled. He performed to thousands in South Africa but no one in the Motor City knew about it. He doesn't like talking about his career. He does like the small clubs. One of his daughters said he lived for the small out of the way gin mills. He always preferred the small audiences as they applauded with vigor showing their appreciation.

Rodriguez is now a financial supporter of the 4th Street Fair. This is a community event celebrating working class people and diversity. For years he helped to organize and put on the 4th Street Fair. He still shows up in his work clothes to set up and clean up during the event. Humility remains his calling card.

As Detroiters walk down Forest between Trumbull and Third they often see Rodriguez wandering up the street with a guitar on his back. He remains a neighborhood regular. No one pays him extra attention. He wouldn't have it any other way. He met a passerby and Rodriguez remarked: "I'm a walker. I don't' drive."

The Rodriguez Tribute Band and The Real Rodriguez

During the 2004 South African tour, Rodriguez attended a show outside Knysna by a Rodriguez tribute band. The group, known as Garden Root, performs Rodriguez' songs. He showed up to thank the band for keeping his music alive. When Rodriguez and his young South African grandson attended one of their concerts everyone remarked on his generosity complimenting the band. Someone asked him if he was one of the South African Rodriguez impersonators. He smiled. When he said he was the real Sixto Rodriguez there was speculation. The Sugar Man loved it.

"I'm supporting the musicians who support me," Rodriguez continued, "but they're doing it better than me."

An astonished Garden Root lead singer, Jono Lumley, remarked: "Meeting the icon of my musical career. It's just incredible. He even called me 'Sir.'" That is Sixto Rodriguez. The band also included Graeme Sindall, lead guitar and vocals, Heath Sindall, drums and Neil Lord bass. Eventually, they backed Rodriguez on a mini-Garden Route tour.

Rodriguez on the Garden Route

When he played the Garden Route, Rodriguez felt a kinship with the area. He flew there and the pilot invited him into the cockpit. He regularly visited the Wilderness area. He connected not only with his fans, but the locals who had not previously heard his music. They welcomed him. He was humbled and honored. South Africans could not get enough of Rodriguez. The Garden Route established a solid fan base persisting to the present day.

While Rodriguez was in Namibia, he celebrated his sixty-second birthday. He was with his daughter, Eva and it was a tranquil time. He loved the peace and contentment. The sale of his records, CDs and tapes continued to fly off the shelf. What was puzzling in 2004 was the lack of concern, or for that matter connection, from record labels for new material. He was selling a great deal of product in South Africa and Australia. The major labels didn't take note. He also had a well-developed cult audience in London. There was a continual buzz about the two albums. Everyone wondered why **Cold Fact** and **Coming From Reality** hadn't been re-released. The growing cult status in London contributed to the demand for Rodriguez' music.

When he went on the Namibia tour in 2004 it was his seventh international tour. He began performing internationally since 1979 when he toured Australia. Still Rodriguez wasn't a well-known international star. It was puzzling to those who championed his music.

Fourteen

London in 2005-2006 and on to Australia 2007

"I've played every kind of gig there is to play now…"

Rodriguez

"Those of you who were lucky enough to see Rodriguez play on his first visit to South Africa can…share a goosebump or two with those of us ex-pats who have had to wait for him to finally appear on stage in London."

John Samson, October 10, 2005

"206 Productions, Sugar Music and PT Music are proud to announce that Rodriguez will be launching his new CD compilation, 'Sugarman: The Best of Rodriguez' with a series of live concerts in Cape Town and London…."

Josh Georgiou

While performing in London in 2005-2006, and in Australia in 2007, Rodriguez unwittingly laid the groundwork for a cult presence on the Indie music scene. The London and Australian press praised his talent, his concerts, and they created a new level of appreciation for his songs. Suddenly "Sugar Man," "I Wonder," "Cold Fact" and "Crucify Your Mind" were memorialized in the mainstream press. The mystery of Sixto Rodriguez continued. The cult status built slowly but surely.

After the 1998 concerts in South Africa, Rodriguez continued to sporadically perform in the U. K. and Australia. South Africans working in London helped to keep the Rodriguez story alive. There were also record collectors who discovered **Cold Fact** and **Coming From Reality**. The London music magazines, the **New Musical Express** and **Melody Maker,** periodically mentioned Sixto Rodriguez. South African promoters were also interested in booking London shows.

Where was the London Rodriguez Phenomenon Centered?

The London Rodriguez phenomenon centered in the raucous clubs in trendy Camden Town. The search for his records extended to Central London. There on Berwick Street South African collectors frequented local record shops. Berwick Street with its half dozen record stores stocked Rodriguez' material. Much of it was bootlegged and again the royalties question was not addressed.

In London there were a large number of South African expatriates who searched for new Rodriguez records. It was only natural for the Sugar Man to perform in the U. K. In 2005 and 2006 he appeared in small concert venues, as well as doing publicity to launch his re-release material. The crowds were raucous. Was it the raucous pub atmosphere or was it Rodriguez' music?

In Camden Town the Shaka Zulu restaurant was home to Rodriguez's fans. It is a Namibian restaurant favored by South

Africans. The favorite drink, Mataku, is a watermelon wine popular in Namibia. The South African Chenin Blanc is the popular wine. But it is around conversations on rugby, soccer and Rodriguez' music that sets Shaka Zulu apart from other restaurants and pubs. Why was Rodriguez a favored conversation piece?

The obvious answer is Rodriguez had a dedicated cult following. Since 1998, when he resurfaced in South Africa, there was renewed interest in his concerts, his records and his life. The only people who didn't get it were the record companies.

One of the supreme ironies is he went back to demolition and construction in Detroit, despite his South African success. He returned once again to an anonymous Detroit lifestyle.

Segerman and Josh Georgiou Bring Rodriguez to London, 2005

For almost a decade, Rodriguez was a London cult figure. The number of South African's working in the U. K. lived in and around London. Many were in the middle of the trendy Camden Town area where the Jazz Café often featured South African musicians. Someone said Oval Road in Camden Town was a Cape Town suburb. This joke was one demonstrating the number of South African expatriates flooding the clubs. There were also South African nightclubs popularizing the Sugar Man's music.

There was one South African who operated as a promoter, a record scout, an A & R person, a nightclub owner and a promoter in London and in the Johannesburg clubs.

His name was Josh Georgiou. He was a South African nightclub owner who operated the 206 on Louis Botha Avenue in Orange Grove. In this Johannesburg suburb, Georgiou worked as an A & R talent scout for Sony. He helped to sign the Springbok Nude Girls who became one of South Africa's legendary 1990s rock groups. He was also an aspiring dj who had his eye out for new talent. He recycled old talent. He was intent on making his mark in the music business.

The 206 night club was the first multiracial music venue in Johannesburg. It was a small club on a not so busy street in Orange Grove. The Louis Botha address was perfect as once you pass the entrance a loud musical atmosphere and a dance floor bar hit you in the fact. The variety of music was vast and free of restrictions. One South African told me Georgiou's club was the first to expose South African's to hip hop. Georgiou and Freeman were more than hipsters. They invented a multicultural entertainment industry. It still thrives.

During his lengthy and acclaimed career Georgiou managed jazz musician Hugh Masakela. Since 1999 Georgiou had a presence in London. He was responsible for the import of a number of South African musical styles to the U.K. He inaugurated Kwaito Nights in Brighton. Kwaito is a musical direction that began in Georgiou's hometown, Johannesburg, during the 1990s. It is a variation of house music using African sounds and samples. One producer labeled it "slowed down garage music." It was popular amongst South Africa's black youth. Georgiou's role was to take it to the U. K., thereby creating a demand for his services. He quickly went into promotion and booking acts. He helped to bring Rodriguez to the center of the London music scene.

Once he established his nightclub and talent scout credentials, Georgiou expanded his musical empire. His partner, Alan Freeman, was a likeminded entrepreneur. Georgiou and Freeman were the ultimate hipsters. They were also good business people. In South Africa there was nothing hipper than Sixto Rodriguez. Since 1998 the Sugar Man's return to the South African concert stage accelerated his legend. Despite the abortive 2001 concerts, Rodriguez was still a hot commercial item. They signed on to promote Rodriguez' 2005 shows.

The problem, as Rodriguez found out, was Segerman. He was a rank amateur amidst professional concert promoters. Josh Georgiou saved the day. When he promoted Rodriguez' club appearances in

London it was with a view to the future. Georgiou is a shrewd judge of performing talent! He realized Rodriguez would be a strong draw at the Kentish Town Forum because of its intimate atmosphere and trendy reputation. Georgiou knew the benefit of a strong press. He was the reason for the incredible reception in London newspapers and music magazines. The entire time he had Stephen "Sugar" Segerman looking over his shoulder. It drove him crazy.

He kept Segerman in check. The imperious South African took time away from promotion. Despite Rodriguez' cult popularity, there was constant tension. Segerman's mercurial temperament was a concern. Georgiou asked Segerman to take a secondary role. Brimming with confidence, Segerman allegedly said: "Absolutely not." It didn't turn out that way. The London and South African 2005 concerts were a roller coaster ride of uneven shows. Some were excellent performances while others were average. But the crowds didn't care they loved Rodriguez. The Sugar Man was a cult star. He had a strong box office appeal. His records sold well. He was mesmerizing in concert. But arrangements had to be precise to capture his concert magic.

Josh Georgiou's Production and Management Magic

The Sugar Man was lucky to have Georgiou in his corner. Georgiou was experienced in all aspects of concert promotion. He had a sense of which clubs the Sugar Man could conquer. If there is a quiet force working behind the scenes to establish Rodriguez' legend it was Georgiou. He was a hero.

What Georgiou accomplished was incredible. He convinced Rian Malan to write the Sugar Man's story in an October 2005 issue of the **London Telegraph**, Malan described the two lives Rodriguez led as "bizarre." It would take another seven years before the world caught up with the Sugar Man.

Georgiou also arranged for South African expatriate, John Samson, to write an October 2005 press release for the London shows. Samson's 2012 book, **Cold Fiction**, is a tribute to the Sugar Man. His writing exudes the rare qualities making Rodriguez a cult star. Samson's twelve short stories provide brilliant insights into Rodriguez' songwriting genius.

Rian Malan 10 Quotes on The Sugar Man or by Rodriguez

1. BUT IN SOUTH AFRICA RODRIGUEZ IS A STAR OF SUCH MAGNITUDE THAT HE HAS MINDERS TO KEEP HIS FANS CALM."

2. "SOMEONE AT SOUTH AFRICA'S GALLO RECORDS TOOK A LIKING TO COLD FACT,

HIS FAILED DEBUT ALBUM, AND ARRANGED SOME RELATED LOCAL RELEASES."

3. "FOR JO'BURGS HIPPIES, RODRIGUEZ WAS A REVELATION-A LONG HAIRED CHICANO FORM THE MEANEST STREETS, SINGING SONGS OF LOVE, DRUGS AND IMPENDING REVOLUTION IN A RUINED AMERICAN CITY.

4. "RUMOUR HAS IT THAT HE JOINED A LEFT WING TERRORIST GROUP AND GONE INTO HIDING."

5. "RODRIGUEZ IS A WIRY LITTLE GUY IN BLACK, BEMUSED BY THE CARDS LIFE HAS DEALT HIM. 'I'M LUCKY,' HE SAYS. IT'S OKAY THAT SUCCESS HAS COME LATER TO ME, BECAUSE I NMIGHT AVE BURNED UP IF IT HAD HAPPENED EARLIER."

6. "IF LAST WEEK'S WARM UP GIG IN CAPE TOWN IS ANYTHING TO GO BY, THE'RE IN THERE WITH A CHANCE. THE AUDIENCE CONSISTED LARGELY OF TWENTY SOMETHINGS...."

7.. HE LOOKED TERRIFIED, AND PROCEEDED TO SCREW UP HIS FIRST FEW SONGS, SINGING OFF-MIKE AND SOEMTIMES FORGETTING TH WORDS. IT DIDN'T MATTER. THE CROW SANG FOR HIM. THEY KNEW EVERY WORD."

8."IF THE GODS OF ROCK AND ROLL MADE A SERIOUS MISTAKE BACK IN 1969, AND RODRIGUEZ IS WHAT WE IMAGINED HIM TO BE: AN AUTENTIC AMERICAN ICON."

9. "I MIGHT HAVE BURNED UP EARLIER IF IT HAD HAPPENED EARLIER," RODRIGUEZ TALKING TO MALAN.

10. "HE TELL'S ME HE'S WORKING ON DEMOLITION SITES THESE DAYS, AND STILL LIVING WITHOUT A CAR, PHONE OR TV." MALAN TALKING TO RODRIGUEZ

MORE RODRIGUEZ RECORD RELEASES IN SOUTH AFRICA

In August and September 2005 **Cold Fact** and a best of Rodriguez album were released in South Africa with distribution in the U. K. PT Music released the most anticipated album **Sugarman-The Best of Rodriguez**. It was a compilation of past material. The release of this material prompted a number of prestigious London music venues to inquire about booking the Sugar Man. Josh Georgiou had the knowledge and the connections to make it happen.

While in school, Georgiou knew Stephen "Sugar" Segerman. They weren't close friends. Segerman was a nerd! Georgiou a hipster! One day Georgiou called Segerman and asked if he could arrange a London-South Africa series of Rodriguez concerts. Sugar said: "Yes of course." It was tough for Georgiou to deal with Segerman. "Sugar" was pompous and entitled. Georgiou envisioned a chance to make a lot of money, and he wanted to pay Rodriguez. Segerman was demanding. Georgiou couldn't figure out why.

By late August 2005 the South African company, 206 Productions, which Georgiou and Freeman established, worked with Sugar Music, which Segerman formed and PT Music, which was a legitimate record label, to make the shows special. They were extremely intimate performances. That is they were in small venues, which Rodriguez preferred, and where Segerman wanted to publicize and sell Rodriguez' music. Consequently, the Cape Town concerts were limited to 250 tickets, thereby providing Rodriguez with a venue prefect for his music. It wasn't designed for his pocketbook.

The problem was concert costs, promotional fees, travel costs and lodging for the artist, the band's fees and a host of other fiscal concerns created a small profit line. No one was making much money. There was little money left for Rodriguez. It was like working for a friendly Harry Balk.

Segerman hoped to make his mark producing London Rodriguez shows. He had little experience in these venues. He knew very little about the London music scene. He had few contacts in the U. K. Terry Fairweather of PT Music was the only person in this drama with London based experience. He would prove instrumental in setting up the tour and whatever limited success took place was due to PT Music and Fairweather's astute judgment and experience as well as the Georgiou-Freeman team. Whatever went wrong was due to Segerman.

Stephen "Sugar" Segerman Formed Sugar Music and What It Meant to The Sugar Man

Sixto Rodriguez is loyal to his friends to a fault. He has always appreciated Stephen "Sugar" Segerman's advice and his unfailing friendship. But there is another side to Rodriguez. He is an excellent businessman. He is a brilliant person. Those characteristics didn't serve him well during the 2005 London shows. While Rodriguez didn't approve of Segerman's lack of professionalism, his haughty demeanor and his pushy, abrasive personality, he vowed not to embarrass his friend. When Josh Georgiou inquired about booking Rodriguez, Segerman set up a management agency. To curry favor with Rodriguez he called it Sugar Music, in partnership with Brian Currin. The idea was a positive one. The outcome was a negative one. Rodriguez was irritated.

After setting up Sugar Music, Segerman had Rodriguez stay in his guesthouse and the backup band, the Blue Coins, practiced with him. Rodriguez doesn't like staying in other people's homes. He has a defined sense of personal freedom. He had to suffer through Segerman's inane and often irritating conversations. The pauses between Segerman's comments and waving his middle finger in the air when someone disagreed with him irritated Rodriguez.

But Rodriguez did like the band. They put together a tight set. Then his daughter, Eva, and her bodyguard-husband, Juan, arrived to take over the management duties. The Sugar Man felt like he was released from a friendly prison.

Things were complicated. Eva pointed out the hotels on the tour were inadequate. Her father didn't complain. Eva thought Sugar was taking advantage of her father. She pointed out the backstage was a disaster. No food. No beverages. No comforts. Eva asked: "What the hell was going on?" Things were not going well. Then Clem Leech came along to rescue the Sugar Man. He helped to make the shows minimally successful. Sugar Music was a disaster. It was amateur hour. But Rodriguez was calm, rationale and he didn't care. Eva was unhappy. Clem Leech was the hero.

Clem Leech: The Only Person Who Knew What He Was Doing During The 2005 London Shows and Rian Malan Explains It

The 2005 South Africa and London shows were at times averagely produced and the hotels, concert fees and logistics were inadequate. It was one amateur decision after another, but Rodriguez believed his friends had his best interests at heart. They did. They just didn't know what they were doing. At times the concerts were brilliant, but it was a strange mixture of success with periodic defeats.

Who is Clem Leech? He founded TouchSky Media to promote entertainment and sports activity in South Africa. Not surprisingly TouchSky Media was founded in 2004 and cut its corporate teeth making Rodriguez' shows a success. The London office at 4 River Bank was instrumental in the radio, TV and newspaper publicity building a strong U. K. base for Rodriguez. Leech is an Internet and mobile publicity pioneer. Rodriguez had a landslide of positive publicity.

It didn't matter to the fans. They loved the shows. This is a recurring theme in viewing the Sugar Man's life. But the 2005 shows were almost a failure. They weren't. There was positive press due to 206 Productions. Clem Leech loved the Sugar Man's music. He went out of his way to promote his stardom for a performer he believed should be an international star.

Clem Leech worked for 206 Productions in public relations. He was a high level concert professional ready to go out on his own. He was also a Rodriguez fan. While Segerman was huffing and puffing about how important he was to the locals, Leech carefully cultivated two of London's outstanding music journalists, one of whom had South African origins. The avalanche of publicity brought Rodriquez into the London media mainstream.

It was a South African, Rian Malan, writing for the **London Telegraph**, who effusively publicized Rodriguez' forthcoming shows, thereby accelerating his London career. There was no need to convince Malan. He said the Sugar Man was a future star. It is hard to believe at sixty-three Rodriguez was considered a future prime time performer. Malan had followed the Sugar Man since 1998 when he broke out in South Africa.

Of all the journalists who have written about Rodriguez, Malan is the best. He grew up in a pro-apartheid South African family. He quickly abandoned any pretense of racial hostility. He was an unrequited liberal. He immigrated for a time to the U.S. where he was a staff writer for **New West Magazine**, a senior writer for the **Los Angeles Herald-Tribune** and he eventually wrote for **Rolling Stone**. He is also a musician with a major label CD on Sony. Why is all this important?

Rian Malan is significant as the first London journalist to review the scope and direction of the Sugar Man's emerging talent. He understood the brilliance of the music. It is hard to believe Rodriguez, now in his early sixties, was on the verge of a career resurrection. During the 2005 London shows, Malan crafted the Sugar Man's story with the skill of a novelist.

This is not surprising as Malan's memoir **My Traitor's Heart** explored South Africa's race relations through a prominent murder. He reflected on past South African history and its apartheid stigma. What set Malan's book apart from others is one of his relatives, Daniel Françoise Malan was an architect of the apartheid doctrine. His views on race relations allowed Malan to write about Rodriguez with an understanding that few journalists possessed. He denounced apartheid. Rodriguez' influence was paramount.

Rian Malan is one of the heroes of the Rodriguez story. Why? He is an unlikely hero. He is a journalist who traces South African music with a tenacity, an in-depth knowledge and a view of how Rodriguez' music fit into the South African and London music scenes. In a 2000 **Rolling Stone** article, Malan traced the origins of the song "The Lion Sleeps Tonight" and one of his themes is the songwriter, Solomon Linda, never received a penny in royalties. He tied this in to the Sugar Man's story.

When Malan's story came out on Rodriguez he labeled the Sugar Man "The Lord Lucan of rock and roll." This was a reference to a charismatic London 7th Earl of Lucan who disappeared for more than forty years. It is a great simile but does it apply to Rodriguez? It does. Rodriguez also came back after forty years. The similarities end there.

Alexis Petridis: The Journalist Who Got It Right Seven Years Before Stardom

Alexis Petridis was another London journalist who praised the Sugar Man's music. He interviewed Rodriguez before he was re-discovered. It was seven years before **Searching For Sugar Man** thrust the mantle of fame on Rodriguez. Petridis found him a star. In an article in the **London Guardian,** he labeled the Sugar Man "the singer who came back from the dead." With Stephen "Sugar" Segerman interrupting every few minutes, Rodriguez spun his story for the veteran music journalist. Petridis was flummoxed. He was amazed at the Sugar Man's persistence and talent. The London journalists turned an otherwise uninspiring set of Rodriguez shows into the first step toward the Sugar Man's legacy.

The interview with Rodriguez took place in early October 2005 when Rodriguez, who was staying with Segerman in Cape Town, talked with Petridis on the phone. After this interview, Rodriguez flew from Cape Town into London. Rodriguez was eager to meet his wife flying in from Detroit. Without family and Detroit friends, he was ill at ease. Segerman never stopped talking. Those around him treated Rodriguez like a God. He was homesick, frustrated and uncomfortable. But, as always, he put on a smiling face. His impeccable manners prevented even close South African friends from realizing the true nature of his pain. Soon Konny arrived and everything was fine.

As the Sugar Man waited at London's Heathrow Airport for his wife, Konny, to arrive, he fondly recalled the London **Guardian** and **Telegraph** articles. He saw the Malan and Petridis articles as excellent publicity. He knew he was on his way to becoming a cult artist.

Why did Alexis Petridis get it right? The reason is a simple one. He is an English journalist who is the pop critic for the **London Guardian**. He knew the inner workings of the rock and roll world. He also knew how to describe talent. From 2005 to 2012 Petridis won the "Record Reviews Writer Of The Year" award each year. He did everything he could to describe Sixto Rodriguez as the next big star. No one believed him. That is until it happened. Petridis told anyone who would listen that in small, intimate venues there was no one more mesmerizing than the Sugar Man.

The London Shows Benefit from the Venue

The London shows were helped by contact with a former South African, David Broido, who was a bass player living in London. He suggested to Georgiou and Freeman they book Rodriguez into the Kentish Town Forum. They never asked him: "Why this venue?" The answer was Broido could walk from his low-end apartment. The early planning for a series of South African and London concerts was sketchy at best. No one seemed in charge. But the Sugar Man took it seriously. While in South Africa preparing for the London concerts, Rodriguez experienced a feeling of weariness.

Sugar arranged warm up concerts in South Africa prior to flying to London for two shows at the Kentish Town Forum. The sojourn in Cape Town provided Rodriguez with time to polish his act. It showed. When the English welcomed the Sugar Man to London, he was ready to put down some great shows. He did. The only real problems were inadequate sound systems, imprecise scheduling and raucous pub crowds drowning out the music. Rodriguez survived!

Despite the excellent pre-concert reviews, the publicity generated by 206 Productions, and the lukewarm help of Stephen "Sugar" Segerman, there was not enough interest for two sell out shows at the Kentish Town Forum.

The English Welcome Rodriguez

The English are always an important source in recognizing musical genius. It took some time for Rodriguez to establish a cult following in the U. K. In the decade from 1996 to 2005 he was recognized as a neglected musical genius. Such prestigious London based magazines, as **Q**, **Mojo**, **Melody Maker and** the **New Musical Express** extolled his talent. The London media loved his music. They didn't always have the full story. His London club shows went a long way toward widening his audience. He was brilliant.

The English fascination with Rodriguez was due in part to his South African releases. The London record stores on Berwick Street stocked the South African label, PT Music. This is an independent South African label that previously released **Cold Fact** and **Coming From Reality**. They also re-released, **The Best of Rodriguez**, which featured seventeen songs from the two studio albums plus three songs that were not on these LPs.

The Best of Rodriguez had a long shelf life. In 1982, RPM issued it as an LP and also in a cassette version. It had the same track listing as a 1977 Australian album **At His Best**. Then a 1996 reissue was a much-improved product due to re-mastering. There were seventeen songs, as opposed to eleven on the previous issues.

Stephen "Sugar" Segerman provided the best in-depth review of **The Best of Rodriguez**. Segerman wrote: "During November 1996 the third in the trilogy of Rodriguez LPs 'The Best of Rodriguez' will be released in South Africa on CD for the first time." Segerman pointed out how rare and unavailable Rodriguez' material was outside South Africa. He wrote: "These three LPs have been almost totally unknown and unavailable anywhere else in the world." Segerman suggested South Africans lived in "a multitude of adopted countries." Segerman, paused like Socrates, and proclaimed: "Who Rodriguez was or is remains a mystery with even the record companies still religiously paying royalties to an unknown source." Intellectual horseshit is appealing. Or is it appalling? He had no knowledge of where the money was paid, but he was pontificating. Segerman did everyone a disservice when he suggested Clarence Avant was hiding out to escape paying royalties. This was a guess on Segerman's part. He had no inside knowledge.

Segerman wanted to take credit for everything surrounding the Rodriguez phenomenon. What is never mentioned is Steve Rowland living in Palm Springs was the catalyst to Malik Bendjelloul finishing the documentary. As Segerman extolled Rodriguez' performing genius, he received too much credit for the Sugar Man's story. He should have butted out of Rodriguez' career in areas where he had no expertise. That is not Segerman's mantra.

Preparing for the London Shows in South Africa

The primary reason for the return to South Africa's concert stage was to support and publicize the September 2005 release of Rodriguez' **Sugarman: The Best Of Rodriguez**. The copious and well-written liner notes by Stephen "Sugar" Segerman not only helped popularize the CD, but second generation interest in Rodriguez' career surfaced. This wasn't a Rodriguez tour per se. Rather it was spreading the word about his recorded material. He was selling his product.

Rodriguez took the time in South Africa to perfect the musical set list for his London appearances. Rodriguez was a professional. He was determined to give his best performances. He did so with a series of South African promotional concerts in small venues. These shows established his concert brilliance. He recovered from the abortive 2001 tour. The set list for these shows was an extensive one. The songs included covers of Bob Dylan's "Like A Rolling Stone," Etta James' "At Last" and a Frank Sinatra inspired "I'm Going To Live." The remaining seventeen songs were vintage Rodriguez. He usually opened with "I Wonder" and closed with "Forget It."

The South African shows provided a chance to visit with his oldest daughter, Eva, her husband, Juan, and his grandchild Ethan. It was the type of family reunion that made Rodriguez unbelievable in concert. Family and close friends bring out the best in the Sugar Man.

Then disaster struck. Eva and Juan attempted to take over the management duties. They clashed with Segerman. He was, according to one source, "a complete asshole." Things got out of hand. One musician told me: "It was a clusterfuck."

Rodriguez is all about family. He simply felt more comfortable with Eva overseeing the South African-London 2005 shows. As one musician told me: "Segerman was more interested in getting his picture taken with the Sugar Man than doing the necessary planning and leg work for his shows." Eva felt there were those who were taking advantage of her father.

The good news is the small band backing the Sugar Man was superb. This turned out to be a blessing. At times Rodriguez is uneven in concert. The Blue Coins were a professional group with a performing flair. They were the perfect back up group. They added a great deal to Rodriguez' shows.

The Blue Coins and Perfect Backing

The group for these performances, the Blue Coins, was composed of Sean Ou Tim, drums, Sascha Sonnbichler, guitar and David Broido, bass. The Blue Coins were Rodriguez aficionados. They were very familiar with his music. While not as accomplished as the Big Town Playboys or Big Sky, they were a backup band allowing Rodriguez' frail vocals to dominate the South African shows. The reviews were ecstatic.

On September 29 and October 2 the band performed in South Africa at Cape Town's Armchair Theater, Observatory in preparation for the London concerts. On October 1, Rodriguez signed his latest release at the CD Wherehouse, V & A Waterfront while performing in a brief free concert. That night he appeared at the Dorp Street Theater in Stellenbosch. The next day he was back at the Independent Armchair Theater, and then after eleven days off he finished the South African warm up tour in Johannesburg. In the warm up to the Dorp Street concert, Segerman's daughter, Natalia, was practicing for a solo set with her guitar. She opened the show with six songs.

There were complaints from everyone about Segerman's daughter dominating the spotlight. Sugar simply smiled. Backstage prior to the show, Segerman hollered at Rodriguez' grandson telling him to "shut up." Eva and her husband Juan were incensed. The atmosphere was taut and tense. Segerman didn't get it. He had overstepped his boundaries.

The irony is when the Sugar Man came on stage following Natalia, he was angry. He remained mellow, quiet and composed. The only way to settle the tense atmosphere was to deliver a magnificent show. He did. Segerman was impervious to the hard feelings. He stood at the side of the stage like a pompous major domo overlooking his people. It was time for Rodriguez and his family to get rid of this egomaniacal personality.

When Rodriguez and the Three Coins arrived at the CD Wherehouse, Segerman asked if there was a place to smoke. The manager led them to a back room. The joints came out and everyone got mellow. Then the air conditioning system blew the smoke out into the theater. The CD Wherehouse manager came screaming into the small room and everyone ran outside. This was another indication of Segerman's amateurish management. Rodriguez was furious with him.

The Independent Armchair Theater highlighted one of the miserable failures Segerman orchestrated. It was a grungy, always dirty, student theater with a penchant for insignificant acts. Segerman couldn't have selected a worse venue. The good news is the 250 tickets sold out immediately. The crowd was curious about the Sugar Man. Fortunately, Eva stepped in to bring sanity and professionalism to this amateur hour production. She watched with mirthful laughter as Stephen "Sugar" Segerman ran around signing autographs and getting his picture taken with schoolgirls. Eva simply shook her head. She had watched her dad go down this road in the early 1970s.

The irony is the hot, sticky, smelly Independent Armchair Theater provided Rodriguez with proof positive Segerman was a rank amateur. The Sugar Man and Eva sat in a small, damp room before the show with rats darting out of the wall and live electrical wires placed carelessly around the room. It was at this point the Sugar Man realized his daughter, Eva, and later his daughter, Regan, could manage his career more effectively. He could trust his family. No one else earned this moniker. It was seven years before **Searching For Sugar Man's** resounding success. Much of the success of the South African dates resulted from Eva's last minute interaction with the media and the students. She had her father's best interests at heart. The conflict over his future prompted Rodriguez to buckle down. The result was one of his strongest shows.

His performance at the Bassline Theater was a crowd pleaser. Some thought that it was the tour's best performance. The Bassline Theater, founded in 1994, presented comedy as well as rock music seven nights a week to a rabid local audience. Rodriguez had capacity crowds. It was a high-end entertainment palace. Rodriguez loved the club. Its technologically advanced sound system provided vocal elegance. He stunned the crowd with his show. These were tune-up dates in preparation for his two London shows.

The Singer Who Came Back from the Dead Redux

In 2005, in the midst of his brief U. K. tour, the **London Observer** labeled Rodriguez "the singer who came back from the dead." The reason is a 1996 letter in **Q** magazine asking for information on Rodriguez. Alexis Petridis wrote: "No one in Britain had heard of Rodriguez in the first place, onstage suicide or not. How times change." By 2005 the London press was all over the Sugar Man's story. High-end music producer, David Holmes, who composed the soundtrack to the hit movie remake of Ocean's 11, said: "I'd never heard anything quite like it. It was quite surprising to me to see how many people don't know it."

David Holmes is one of the unsung heroes of **Searching For Sugar Man**. He was born in Van Morrison's Belfast. For a time he was a hairdresser, a chef and he operated a nightclub. He was a disc jockey and musical producer with a keen eye to musical trends. He became one of the Sugar Man's advocates long before it was fashionable. He was ready to do what he could for the Sugar Man's fledgling career.

Why is David Holmes a hero in the Rodriguez tale? The answer is a simple one. He discovered the song "Sugar Man." He was obsessed by it. He included Rodriguez' song on a sample mix album released in the 1990s, **Come Get It, I Got It**. The result was to slowly build the Sugar Man's cult status.

Then the **London Observer** got on the phone to Rodriguez. The October 2005 interview with Alexis Petridis indicated David Holmes was an early catalyst to interest in the Sugar Man. Petridis wanted to know how a sixty three year old construction worker became a South African legend? Rodriguez said: "When I started out, a real heavy cat in the music business world told me it was going to take me ten years to get there." The reporter wondered how he could be so popular without airplay.

The October 7-8, 2005 Kentish Town Shows: What They Meant

The October 7-8 London Kentish Town shows were triumphs despite Segerman's amateur tactics. The uncertainty about a sixty three year old singer coming back from the dead continued to intrigue the press. The shows opened with a set by Laurie Levine, a singer-songwriter, and her partner Jim Neversink. They were South African musicians with diverse styles blending country, rock, oldies and punk into a commercial package.

The Kentish Town Forum shows were a turning point in Rodriguez' career. There was little, if any, knowledge of the Sugar

Man's music from the general London fan. This led to a promotional blitz creating interest in the Detroit singer. Rodriguez rose to the occasion with a stunning show. There was one moment that almost ruined the first night's performance. After "A Most Disgusting Song" concluded Stephen "Sugar" Segerman waddled out on stage with a glass of wine. He smiled to the crowd. He handed the wine to Rodriguez. Someone in the audience hollered: "Who the fuck is that?" There was derisive laughter. Then the Sugar Man held up the glass of wine. He smiled at the audience. After a silent toast he performing a cover of "I'm Going To Live Until I Die" as the Kentish Town Forum audience burst into rapturous applause. Not even Segerman could torpedo the show. His time as a Rodriguez confidant was nearing an end.

Rodriguez: South Africa and London Tour 2005

SET LIST

1. I Wonder
2. Only Good For Conversation
3. Can't Get Away
4. Crucify Your Mind
5. Like Janis
6. To Whom It May Concern
7. You'd Like To Admit It
8. Inner City Blues
9. Street Boy
10. Like A Rolling Stone [Bob Dylan]
11. Jane S Piddy
12. A Most Disgusting Song
13. I'm Going To Live [Judy Garland or Frank Sinatra]

14. At Last [Etta James]
15. I Think Of You
16. Rich Folks Hoax
17. Climb Up On My Music
18. Sugar Man
19. Establishment Blues
20. Forget It

Who is Justin Cohen?

Justin Cohen came along to the Kentish Town Forum to watch the show with his friends and talk with Sixto Rodriguez. He was a fledgling filmmaker whose student film in 2002 was shown on South African television. Cohen's film **Looking For Jesus**, took its title from Craig Bartholomew-Strydom's article on the Sugar Man. This film intensified public interest in Rodriguez's music.

Looking For Jesus is a strange piece of film. It was completed in two parts. You Tube has both works. It is a fictionalized drama where a character playing Craig Bartholomew-Strydom searches for the Sugar Man. He finds him in Detroit and sits on the front steps of his home while Rodriguez sings "Cause." What is the importance of **Looking For Jesus?** It continued Stephen "Sugar" Segerman's infatuation with a film about Sixto Rodriguez. The film may have helped Malik Bendjelloul to begin the documentary.

The Cohen film is a good one. It suffers from the heavy hand of Stephen "Sugar" Segerman who is listed as the executive producer. The script and cinematography by Cohen is first rate for a student film. The twenty-eight minutes of film, completed in 2002, is a tribute to Rodriguez' music. Whether or not it influenced Malik Bendjelloul is unknown, but **Looking For Jesus** is a valuable addition to the Sugar Man's lore.

Justin Cohen's video is not only a tribute to Rodriguez, it is a sensitive look at the conditions surrounding the music industry. The opening is in an automobile not unlike that of **Searching For Sugar Man**. "Rodriguez wherever you are South Africa is listening," a voice remarks. Then they talk about people who disappear for a reason.

As "I Wonder" plays there is a person looking at record albums from the early 1970s. There is an eerie sense of the Sugar Man's mystery. An unknown record shopper pulls out Segerman's liner notes and reads from them.

Then the young kid, who is supposed to be Craig Bartholomew-Strydom, finds Rodriguez' **Cold Fact** album in his bedroom. It was apparently his dad's copy. A look online on a computer is shown in a search for the Sugar Man while "Climb Up On My Music" plays in the background. The rest of part one of **Looking for Jesus** deals with the search for the mystical Jesus who is Sixto Rodriguez! The two-part student film is a masterpiece deserving more views on You Tube.

Segerman and Rodriguez Get Into a Tiff in London

The love-hate relationship between Rodriguez and Segerman intensified by 2005. It threatened his impending shows. It diminished their relationship, and clouded the future. He was a sixty three year old singer trying to find his way back into the music business. 206 Productions was at wits end with Rodriguez and Segerman. They didn't agree on anything. The only thing they mutually accepted was there was enough of the magic dragon to smoke while in London. There was!

Rodriguez had a vision. He told Segerman he saw his daughter, Eva, returning to bring sanity to the 2005 London concert mess. The Sugar Man worked hard on his music. Segerman wanted to party. Rodriguez realized he had a chance at a career. He took the London shows seriously. Segerman wanted to sign autographs and be a star. It was a partnership not long for the books.

Segerman wanted to tell Rodriguez which songs to perform and which ones to neglect. Segerman insisted the Sugar Man exclude cover songs from his concerts. That was another bone of contention. The irony is their differences prompted Rodriguez to deliver well-paced, carefully crafted shows. Although the audiences weren't capacity ones, they cheered the Sugar Man's every move.

A well-known London entertainer told me Segerman attempted to upstage Rodriguez. A South African in the audience had a negative reaction. Segerman simply couldn't stop stirring the pot. Or smoking it!

Wilmer Selkirk: "That bald headed son of a bitch from South Africa came out on stage with a glass of wine. He smiled at the crowd. It was like this egomaniacal bastard was telling the Sugar Man here is your glass of wine for performing so well. What an asshole!"

Rodriguez on the Little Britain TV Show with Matt Lucas

There was another caveat to the 2005 London shows. Rodriguez was booked on a BBC radio and TV show "Little Britain" hosted by the comedy star Matt Lucas. The show featured a panel discussing various subjects and usually there was a musical guest. When it got around to Rodriguez he performed "The Establishment Blues." The panel asked if it was from his new album. When Rodriguez said it was from a 1970 release there was a stunned silence.

The reaction in London was immediate. People wanted to know more about the Sugar Man. He also appeared on BBC Radio 4 answering questions and performing. No one realized that Rodriguez' popularity had been building since 1996. He wasn't a household name. His music made slow inroads in the U.K. He was now officially a cult artist. No one expected mainstream success. Not even Rodriguez.

The Decade that Formed the U. K. Rodriguez Cult: 1996-2006

What is striking about the London concerts is the time and energy Rodriguez' supporters devoted reestablishing his career. For a decade the London press was intrigued with the Rodriguez story. In 1996 a letter to **Q** magazine requested information on Rodriguez. It was a line from the song "Forget It" that interested journalists.

After Rodriguez performed for two nights at the London Forum, also known as the Kentish Town Forum, there was an increased buzz about his music. This magnificent building, built in 1934, was for a time an art deco movie theater. It was the perfect venue for Rodriguez with its intimate feel and soft acoustic sound. As he walked out on stage to rapturous applause, the bass line to "I Wonder" dominated his entrance. With his dark shades, black hat and stylish clothes, Rodriguez looked younger and his cool street hip persona had the girls swooning. He was now sixty-five years old. He still cut a dashing figure.

The songs from **Cold Fact** received the loudest applause. The audience loved his cover of Bob Dylan's "Like A Rolling Stone." There were so many sing along lines it was often difficult to hear Rodriguez. He just smiled. The crowd was with him every step of the way.

The two live London shows were career altering ones. There was a buzz among the critics as Rodriguez delivered strong shows. It looked like Rodriguez might suddenly have a career. It didn't happen. It wasn't because he didn't try. The obsessive, if small, fan base kept after the critics. As he prepared to return to London the following year, Rodriguez was a viable underground cult figure.

Back to London: 2006

The making of Rodriguez' legend continued in London. There was a steady demand for his first two albums. The problem was Rodriguez' material was not available.

During a cold, blustery late November 2006 evening Rodriguez was back in London to perform at the Shepherd's Bush Empire Theater. This theater has a two thousand-seat capacity, which makes it perfect for a Rodriguez concert. This show was filled with Australian and South African expatriates. The tickets sold briskly weeks in advance of his appearance. The balcony was full of cameras. The audience sang along with the songs.

The press reacted positively to the 2005-2006 London shows. **Time Out** wrote: "Remarkable and slyly subversive." This is a brilliant comment based on the duality of Rodriguez' political songs combined with the Steve Rowland produced romantic tunes on **Coming From Reality**. The **London Guardian** proclaimed Rodriguez is "pitched somewhere between Bob Dylan and Love." The **London Daily Telegraph** observed: "An authentic American icon."

It was the 2006 London publicity that demonstrated the English were once again in the vanguard of the movement to recognize Rodriguez' talent. The English press picked up on Rodriguez. Their interest was a key in reviving his career.

On to Australia in 2007

Searching For Sugar Man led many to believe Rodriguez was in the creative and concert wilderness since the early 1970s. Nothing is further from the truth. When he arrived in Australia for the Byron Blues Festival in April 2007, it was more like a coronation than a concert. He was a star down under since 1979 and twenty-eight years later he was still filling stadiums.

The Byron Bay Blues Festival included Bo Diddley, Taj Mahal, Tony Joe White, Bela Fleck and the Flecktones, Bonnie Raitt and Ben Harper and the Innocent Criminals.

After his Byron Blues Festival appearance, Rodriguez went to the signing tent where his fans lined up. The line for autographs was long and Rodriguez signed everything and anything. He was also given copies of his Australian LPs by a fan. The Australian tours indicated his fan base increased since his first tour down under in 1979. Even when he was the opening act for Midnight Oil, his fans arrived in droves.

There is one thing Sixto Rodriguez dislikes. This is personal conflict. He is also adamant no one can take advantage of him or direct his career. This personality trait brought Rodriguez and Segerman to loggerheads.

Fifteen

The Sugar Man and Sugar are at Loggerheads: Then Light in the Attic Rescues Segerman

"A false view of what has happened in the past makes it harder to see what might occur in the future."

Michael Lewis

"He didn't really have a manger, just people who helped him out and introduced him to people, because he was pretty shy. I'm not sure we even knew it was the same guy when we saw him at The Sewer. It didn't really matter because he sounded so different. The way it happened in the movie is really what it was like."

Mike Theodore

From 2005 to 2006 Stephen "Sugar" Segerman was Rodriguez' self-appointed manager. It was not an easy relationship. Sugar talked down to Rodriguez. He attempted to make decisions for him.

They were not smart ones. He envisioned himself as Colonel Tom Parker managing Elvis Presley. It was a relationship fraught with tension, indecision, amateur contracts, and disputes over hotels and concert perks. He never had the logistics to make for smooth public appearances. One South African told me he had the feeling Segerman had many of the same traits as those who derailed Rodriguez' early career. Sugar was an honest man, not a criminal, but he was an inept businessman with a penchant for self-aggrandizement.

What Segerman Did and Didn't Do for The Sugar Man

After the 2005 London shows, Rodriguez began rethinking his relationship to Segerman. He was a friend. He was a fan. He fancied himself a manager. He wasn't. The abortive 2005 London shows, and the short South African concerts prior to the U. K. shows were not to Rodriguez' liking. The bookings were in venues the Sugar Man felt uncomfortable with in concert. Segerman's sense of self-importance left a bitter after taste.

Segerman's imperious attitude made Rodriguez yearn for his family. The incident that set the Sugar Man off took place when his wife Konny landed at London's Heathrow Airport. He had read or knew of the contents in stories in the **London Guardian** and the **London Telegraph**. The positive stories by Rian Malan and Alexis Petridis were too personal. There was too much inside information. The Sugar Man believed the bald headed South African had gone behind his back with anecdotes that should remain private. Rodriguez attempted to warn Segerman. Rodriguez said privacy was his main concern. Sugar smiled. He ignored Rodriguez. He was in charge.

The Sugar Man disliked Segerman's reference to Team Rodriguez. There were numerous distractions hurting the concerts. Rodriguez ignored Segerman's constantly critical remarks, and his inane suggestions. At the last show at the Kentish Forum, Rodriguez was in fine form. He delivered his best show in years. He did so by ignoring Segerman. It was time to make some changes.

Firing Segerman the Day After the Kentish Town Forum Shows

On October 9, 2005 Rodriguez called for a meeting in a conference room in his London hotel. When 206 Productions announced the gathering, no one realized it was the Sugar Man who orchestrated it. The meeting was to talk about the possibility of Rodriguez performing in one more concert in Johannesburg prior to returning to Detroit.

The hotel provided coffee, tea, biscuits and the atmosphere was festive. Then Rodriguez asked: "Is there anyone in the room who should not be in attendance?" There were puzzled looks. What did he mean? It meant Rodriguez was taking charge of his career. He had been too many times in the hands of amateurs, music sharks or those who had their own agenda.

The first thing Rodriguez did was to tell Segerman he was fired. Sugar's baldheaded body jiggled with rage. He couldn't believe it. Segerman asked himself what the hell was going on? Hadn't he done enough for Rodriguez? He was no longer in the inner circle. The partners at 206 Productions were confused. Rodriguez thanked Georgiou and Freeman for their excellent work. He had high praise for Clem Leech and everyone else. He singled out Segerman. He let his South African friend know he had crossed a line. That was it. They were friends but no longer concert partners. Segerman never understood why. One of the principals at the meeting told me: "Segerman doesn't understand he didn't invent the story." Rodriguez took control of his career. To this day, with his daughter Regan, he is carefully planning, directing and taking his music into a direction that allows him to maximize his talent.

As Segerman left the hotel meeting room, he was not only embarrassed, he was angry. What Sugar didn't realize is that since 1998 he had overstepped his boundaries. He infringed on Rodriguez' life. He never listened to the Sugar Man's suggestions. Booking agents, club owners, promoters and media types complained about Segerman. Was he impossible? He was!

The next day Rodriguez and Segerman flew back to Johannesburg. They sat next to each other on the plane. Neither said a word. It was an uncomfortable flight. It was the end to a disastrous trip.

How Segerman Got Back into The Sugar Man's Good Graces

The differences between Rodriguez and Segerman simmered for a time. After they were apart, the Sugar Man forgave his South African friend for an amateur tour of South Africa and a few London concerts of minimal financial success. How did Segerman get back in Rodriguez' good graces? The answer is a simple one. He helped to pave the way for Light In The Attic to re-release **Cold Fact** and **Coming From Reality**.

When Matt Sullivan, the head of Light In The Attic, looked for Rodriguez, he contacted Segerman. In a February 7, 2006 e-mail Sullivan introduced himself, his label, and his hopes to release Rodriguez' albums. He stressed he paid royalties. Light In the Attic was more than a boutique label releasing long forgotten records. It was headed by a hungry group of record entrepreneurs who understood guerrilla marketing and how and why vinyl, collectible 45s and special reissues were creeping into the record market. LITA was in advance of the reissue trends. They were finding long forgotten artists and reissuing their vinyl masterpieces. The sales through alternate marketing indicated LITA's marketing genius. They were a young and hungry group of businessmen. They looked like they didn't shave and loved buying records at the Goodwill. The corporate heads at LITA had an appearance that fooled everyone. They weren't record geeks. They were competent professionals. When Sullivan asked about Rodriguez the dialogue began for the reissues.

Sullivan wondered if the Sugar Man would allow reissues? He knew the difficulty in finding copies of **Cold Fact**. Would Rodriguez be as difficult? He wasn't.

The answer was quick and forthcoming from Segerman. He thanked Sullivan for the e-mail. He mentioned he had just seen the Last Poets reissue. He was impressed. Segerman said he had been working with Rodriguez for a decade. This was, of course, stretching the truth. He failed to mention their recent falling out. Segerman saw this as a means of getting back in the Sugar Man's good graces. He did.

Unbeknownst to Rodriguez, Segerman gave Sullivan too much personal information. Suddenly Rodriguez saw the same behavior in Segerman's well-intentioned amateur career advice. One of the surprising points behind the e-mails between Sullivan and Segerman was the mention of film directors interested in the Sugar Man's story. Although Malik Bendjelloul wasn't the first to plan a documentary, he and others were sidetracked by lack of interest from Rodriguez. There were other concerns. He was concerned about the problem of raising production funds and the difficulty of selling a feature on an obscure Mexican-American folk singer early on hampered the project. The problems seemed insurmountable. There were other stylistic concerns. The bleak Detroit atmosphere was not a selling point. The genius of Malik Bendjelloul is he used the dank, dark Detroit backdrop to contrast it with the sunny bucolic South African landscape.

The Willemiek Kluijfhout Interlude

Sixto Rodriguez was opposed to any and all documentaries. At a concert, when Dutch filmmaker Willemiek Kluijfhout attempted to film a Rodriguez documentary, she asked for the Sugar Man's permission. He said: "No." He threatened to walk off stage if he saw her at one of his concerts. He didn't like her. He didn't want to be filmed. She had talked to Malik Bendjelloul. Rodriguez did not want to be bothered.

The Willemiek Kluijfhout interlude tells one a great deal about Rodriguez. When she met the Sugar Man, Kluijfhout was in her thirties and an up and coming filmmaker. She was more experienced and better known than Malik Bendjelloul. She would make her name in 2012, the same year as **Searching For Sugar Man**, with the documentary at the Berlin Film Festival **L'Amour Des Moules**, which in translation is "Mussels In Love." This film views the world through the eyes of the mussels who make love, multiply and are stressed. It is stylish and amusing.

Why did Rodriguez turn down Kluijfhout's overtures while accepting, somewhat reluctantly, Bendjelloul's film? The answer tells one all they need to know about Rodriguez. Her look into his life would feature wives, the Australian stardom and his penchant for things intellectual. Malik in sharp contrast made his documentary focus upon the music, an elusive family and the nasty folks in the music business. That approach won the Sugar Man's cooperation.

Not only had Kluijfhout studied philosophy at the University of Amsterdam, she attempted to impress upon Rodriguez the importance of his existential personality. He wasn't buying it. He did not want to be the documentary's centerpiece. He was also too busy with plans for the reissues of his two long lost albums.

Matt Sullivan's Perseverance Pays Off

After these exchanges Sullivan worked with Segerman and then Clarence Avant for two years to secure the rights to re-release **Cold Fact** and **Coming From Reality**. Along the way Segerman did everything possible to help Rodriguez achieve reissue success. The problem was not Sullivan or Segerman. It was Rodriguez. He had been burnt too many times. He was cautious. Segerman was acting like one of the old style Hollywood record magnates with a cigar. But Segerman was important to the reissues. He opened the door for Sullivan. Then Rodriguez took over the negotiations. He executed a proper and fair contract.

Why was Matt Sullivan the winner in the Rodriguez reissue sweepstakes? The answer is a simple one. He was a young man with an up and coming record company. He was passionate about the artists and their releases. He was also an honest person. He paid royalties. His knowledge of the concert business, his in-depth record store experience and his plans to break the Sugar Man as an Indie cult favorite brought Rodriguez into the American market. Sullivan was so unlike Clarence Avant that the Sugar Man was comfortable with a second shot at the mainstream. Matt Sullivan persevered from day one. That caught Rodriguez' attention. He was not a wanker like Segerman.

Long before Rodriguez' success, Light In The Attic sent the Sugar Man cords of wood at Christmas. That meant as much to Rodriguez as royalties.

There was the problem of past legal and illegal Rodriguez records issued by a variety of labels and complicit bootleggers. The large number of Rodriguez reissues is a convoluted and difficult story. How does one interpret it? There are some simple explanations. There was a lot of money made from album sales. None of it went to Rodriguez. Where did it go? Who knows? To this day there is no adequate explanation. There are some devils lurking in the shadowy area of the royalty game.

There is one man with a dominant shadow. This is Neil Bogart. He may be the grinch who stole the royalties. But now that he is dead and buried. We will never know. He does cast a long shadow over the story.

The Story of the Sussex Reissues: The Shadow of Neil Bogart

An IRS lien bankrupted Sussex. The original distributor Neil Bogart and Buddah Records no longer was in the mix. CBS Records paid off the debt Sussex owed to the IRS. Avant continued to administer the label's catalogue. Eventually, Sony-BMG owned the master tapes for both Rodriguez albums. This meant when Matt Sullivan and LITA got the licensing rights to reprint in the U.S., Rodriguez was finally guaranteed royalties. They paid twice a year. The Sugar Man couldn't believe it.

On August 19, 2008 **Cold Fact** was released to universal praise. Matt Sullivan's LITA was a boutique label with a sterling reputation. To promote **Cold Fact** they secured the Sugar Man quality club appearances. The road to overnight stardom took four more years but LITA was with him all the way.

Light In The Attic packaged **Cold Fact** beautifully. The vinyl release was an even more expensive package and a Canadian dj, Kevin "Sipreano" Howes, provided in depth, beautifully written liner notes.

A year after **Cold Fact's** release, Matt Sullivan wrote an effusive letter of praise to Stephen "Sugar" Segerman in South Africa concerning the positive reception for Rodriguez in concert. His shows in San Francisco and Los Angeles were not only well received; Light In The Attic put together an eight-piece band with three horns for the Los Angeles show and a ten-piece aggregation in San Francisco. The Sugar Man never sounded better. Sullivan had high hopes for Rodriguez' music reaching a larger audience. Sullivan said the shows brought him to tears.

During this tour Rodriguez performed a free show at the Amoeba Record store in San Francisco at the end of Haight Street next to a McDonald's. He looked and across the street at Golden Gate Park. The sight of Rodriguez eating in McDonald's was one his cult legion of followers loved. The Sugar Man remained a symbol of humility three years before international stardom.

Matt Sullivan's Seminal Role in The Sugar Man's Story

Matt Sullivan is the unsung hero of **Searching For Sugar Man**. His label, Light In The Attic, not only reissued **Cold Fact** and **Coming From Reality,** they booked the Sugar Man for almost five years building a cult following. There were a number of important LITA bookings creating a slow, but sure, buzz for his music.

On July 26, 2008. Rodriguez performed in Montauk, New York with Malik Bendjelloul in attendance. Steve Rowland was invited. He sent his regrets. He was occupied with his book signings and reissues of his previously produced materials. The forty plus year career retrospective Rowland experienced was a welcome blessing. He wasn't always happy with the renewed interest in his various projects. He was tired of people. He was not interested in the mainstream music business. The Sugar Man had the same feelings as he went through a path to rediscovery.

The irony is Rowland and Rodriguez roared back into the musical mainstream at the same time. They have always had somewhat parallel lives and the bookings Rodriguez fulfilled were similar to the book signings Rowland was engaged in around the U. K. But the Montauk concert was important to the Sugar Man. It was a venue of significance and a test of his enduring creative powers on stage.

Why was the Montauk concert significant? It is an upscale resort in the Hampton's east of New York. It is home to a high-end crowd with close ties to the media. Sullivan was aware of the need to break the Sugar Man in 2008 to a wider audience. The record geeks living in their parent's basemen brought him to the public's attention. Now it was time for mainstream stardom. Rodriguez showed up with his daughter, Regan, at the resort. He remarked how happy he was with his re-released albums.

The American press took little notice of the 2008 concert. The **London Guardian** assigned Stevie Chick to interview the Sugar Man about his first headlining concert in America since his debut **Cold Fact** album. She observed: "It's the unflinching honesty of Cold Fact's songs that speaks to his new, young audiences." That said it all. Then the Sugar Man answered her questions in a lengthy interview drawing more interest from the London record geeks than their American counterparts.

He was talking to reporter, Stevie Chick, of the **London Guardian**, and he was unusually open and candid about his future. He praised his daughters for believing in him. He singled out Regan for her computer expertise, which helped to attract an Indie audience to the Sugar Man's music.

Sixto Rodriguez: "It's all due to my daughter Regan. I don't have her understanding of the new technology, and that's what's changed in my career. It was through the Internet that they found me and resurrected me."

Sullivan and LITA brought Rodriguez into the small clubs; the mid-level concert stages and the young audiences embraced his music more than thirty years after releasing **Cold Fact**.

Light In The Attic booked Rodriguez into San Francisco's Great American Music Hall. This is a retro nightspot near the Mitchell Brothers porno theater located in a neighborhood of hookers, transvestites and low life's. As the Sugar Man walked into this beautiful art deco showcase, he smiled. He was home. At least it felt that way. The Fresh and Only's, a local band, backed him with a recently hired horn section. Every preparation was made to achieve the brilliance of Rodriguez in concert while making his vinyl re-releases and his CDs available in a wide variety of stores and the on line marketing was so strong LITA had a hit. This was three years before **Searching For Sugar Man**. When the documentary came out the profits were an avalanche and LITA moved its corporate offices to Los Angeles. Soon they would have college interns working in their office, the mainstream media came calling and the number of re-releases and new artists coming out of LITA made their catalogue grow in a disproportionate manner.

From 2009 through 2011 LITA continued booking, publicizing and bringing Rodriguez into the music business mainstream. In the process young bands like the Fresh And Onlys, independent labels like Merge and a ground swell of college audiences slowly built his brand. Matt Sullivan told anyone who listened Rodriguez was a good human being. Perhaps the best he had ever dealt with in the music business. He was also one hell of songwriter and performer.

By 2009 the sporadic concerts booked by LITA turned into mini-tours. Ironically, Rodriguez was a bigger draw in New York and Washington D. C. than he was in Detroit. Europe beckoned. In May and June 2009 a European tour included France, Belgium, Italy and London. He received royalties from LITA. The concert guarantees were more than fair. At this point, thanks to Sullivan and LITA, the Sugar Man believed he had reached the high point of his career. He was in for a big surprise. International stardom and an Oscar were just a few years away.

Sixteen

Steve Rowland Enters the Entertainment Witness Protection Program

"I produced hundreds of hit records. No artist was more talented than Sixto Rodriguez. He was easily the best."

Steve Rowland

On September 21, 2007 Steve Rowland left London and returned to the United States. He had successfully produced a wide range of musical acts including Jerry Lee Lewis, the Cure, the Thompson Twins, P. J. Proby, Sarah Brightman, Peter Frampton, the Pretty Things and the Herd. His productions made him a respected and much sought after producer. His rock group, the Family Dogg, was a cult band. The reissue labels were after him for the rights to re-release their material.

There are many traits to describe Rowland. He is precise, analytical and careful to a fault. He would not allow just anyone to release his material. The Family Dogg was his band. He created it. He selected the songs. He paid for the record production. He was the producer.

In the midst of working with Rodriguez and other acts Steve's Family Dogg concept took off in Europe and the U. K. Steve said if you mixed the sound of the Mamas and Papas with that of the Fifth Dimension you would have a mega hit making group. It worked.

The U. K. and European success of the Family Dogg continued after Rowland finished recording **Coming From Realty**. Building on the success of the 1969 Family Dogg debut album **A Way of Life**, which featured a number six U. K. chart hit with the title track, Rowland's concept of an English Mamas and Papas appeared destined for stardom. Then things fell apart. Albert Hammond left the group. He sued Rowland. The suit was dropped. Hammond was angry. There was no evidence that Rowland withheld royalties. The Family Dogg was in disarray. After reorganization the new name was Steve Rowland and the Family Dogg. Steve was ready to record a new album.

In this incarnation the group recorded six of Rodriguez' songs before breaking up in 1975 after covering Randy Edelman's, "Uptown, Uptempo Woman" which peaked at twenty five in September 1976 on the U.K. charts.

Steve Rowland: "I paid for forty tracks all the production money in the studio. Everything! The first single was a hit. It didn't even pay for what it cost to make it. The other tracks recovered my costs. None of the companies sent me any royalty statements. Therefore, I didn't have the money to pay anyone. Albert thought I did. He sued me. They dropped the case it never went to court. I simply didn't have the money the individuals owed me."

People Have Said I am Difficult But Precise

In 2014, Cherry Red Records released **The View From Rowland's Head**. It was a compilation of fifty-one tracks with bonus cuts from the Rowland produced Pancho and Cisco records, the Steve and

Albert 45s and four solo cuts by Ireen Sheer. Amongst rock and roll aficionados the Family Dogg material is blessed with support from members of Led Zeppelin.

When the CD was released Steve Rowland went ballistic. In reissuing the tracks a demo of "Moonshine Mary" was used not the original featuring Pam "Zooey" Quinn.

I asked Steve: Why does this matter? I liked the vocal on "Moonshine Mary." It was perfect. There was a long silence. Steve looked at me like I was nuts.

Steve Rowland: "No, you have it wrong. We were preparing the song for Zooey. Albert, Mike and I went into the studio to get the track ready for Zooey. I put my voice down to give her a guide. She learned the track. She recorded it and it was beautiful."

I asked Steve: "Why is this important? It sounds fine to me?"

Steve Rowland: "My voice on the demo was to show Zooey how the song should proceed. Her voice was brilliant. My voice left a great deal to be desired."

What did you do to correct this error?

Steve Rowland: "I called Cherry Red and told them the problem. They said they would correct it. They didn't."

Why is one song important?

Steve Rowland: "It ruined the fucking album. I am not looking for the glory. I want a proper album. I don't think they knew the quality of Zooey's vocal."

How did the people at Cherry Red react to your request?

Steve Rowland: "People have said I am difficult but precise."

Really!

There is no doubt Rowland is difficult and precise. But there is a silver lining. Without his attention to detail, his devotion to allowing the artists he produced to find their way with their music and his ability to take talented as well as non-talented artists to the charts tells one all they need to know about his record productions.

Steve Moves on to Another Direction

Steve has moved on. He is developing a TV series Hollywood Heat. This TV show, based on 1950s Hollywood, came together and occupied much of Steve's day. His daily two hours in the gym makes him physically and mentally fit. He has other ideas and projects.

By the time Rowland arrived and settled in Palm Springs, he was looking forward to a new and relaxed life. The California sunshine, the proximity to Beverly Hills, and his contacts in the entertainment business made for a full life. Steve thought he was going to retire. He believed he had entered the Entertainment Witness Protection Program. He relaxed for five years and then all hell broke loose. His book **Hollywood Heat** was a steady seller, he began a ten-year development of the book for a TV series. Once **Searching For Sugar Man** turned into an Oscar documentary, Steve was as busy as ever. The changes in his life can be traced to 2007; it was the seminal year in what would be a fourth career. Rowland had already been a television and movie actor, a singer in various bands, a record producer and now he was back in the midst of a television series focused on the American screen dealing with gangsters, tinseltown and the aura of the nostalgic 1950s. Character and content define Rowland.

2007: Rowland's Seminal Year, Hollywood Heat and Retirement, Maybe! Maybe Not!

In many respects 2007 was a seminal year in Steve's life. His memoir on Hollywood in the 1950s was set for release the next year. His London life was winding down.

During this period Steve joked about entering the Entertainment Witness Protection Program. He meant he wanted to be left alone. He was in a continual creative mood. He had his fill of people. Palm Springs California offered a respite from the trendy, snobbish, pompous London intellectual climate and stagnant music business. He was two hours away from Hollywood's entertainment capital. He had the isolation, the access to musicians as well as to recording studios and to the Hollywood movie-television industry defining his time in California. He also had great weather after forty years of damp London and pompous critics. He settled quietly in Palm Springs.

Steve's 2008 book **Hollywood Heat: Untold Stories of 1950s Hollywood** sold out in the U. K. Then seven years later it was re-published. During that time Hollywood movie executives and a variety of entertainment figures in the U. K. and U. S. urged Rowland to commission a screenplay for a proposed television series. Rowland went one step further. He formed an LLC, and his production company planned and completed the script. He quietly took his vast knowledge of the mob, the movie producers, the actors and the hangers on who destroy celebrities into the TV mainstream. Rowland knew the business. He would do it his way. That way was one with a top scriptwriter, a high level agent and a corporate structure to protect his intellectual property rights.

Like Rodriguez he had been cheated out of big money by industry tycoons. That was no longer tolerated. He took the necessary steps to make sure his material was protected.

His production company brought in a top Hollywood scriptwriter, contacted leading actors, brought together the music of the 1950s to provide a soundtrack for an insider's view of the movie industry. Rowland had a positive feeling about the project. The nefarious deeds of the Mafia are central to the series. This piqued the interest of those who produced the Sopranos. They saw the grit and authenticity in Rowland's project.

Rowland wanted to create his series without someone looking over his shoulder. In London he worked forty-years as an independent producer. He had the autonomy to finish record albums without outside interference. He realized selling a television series and writing for cable TV would take a great deal of time and effort. He hired the requisite staff to pitch and sell the TV series.

He was tired of the snobby attitudes and imperious nature of the suits running the record business. It was time for a change. Welcome to Palm Springs!

In 2007 Rowland and Rodriguez Crossed Paths But Didn't Notice It

In 2007 Rowland finalized his move to Palm Springs California. Ironically, Rodriguez was taking his first steps toward mainstream success. Both of them were continuing their creative march. Soon their paths would cross. They had always worked in a parallel universe and 2007 was no exception.

Rowland had a cache of new music. He also had a backlog of demos that could be leased to major record companies. Rowland kept up with the trades, as did Rodriguez. Then just as Steve thought he was done with the music business, he found out Sixto Rodriguez lurked on the commercial horizon. Steve wondered how in the hell was this happening? How could he be back? He had never made it. This is when Rowland learned Matt Sullivan and Light In the Attic was reissuing the Sugar Man's two long neglected albums. As the London press provided a roadmap to Rodriguez' growing popularity, Rowland took notice. He smiled. He was happy for the Sugar Man.

Then one day quite by accident Steve picked up a copy of **Mojo: The Collection**. This November 2007 book consisted mainly of record reviews; it was almost a thousand pages in length. Rowland could read about any album on the music scene he may have missed. He was surprised to find a reference to Sixto Rodriguez' popularity in Australia. He wondered where Rodriguez was, and why he had never entered the commercial mainstream?

The irony is the Sugar Man performed in Rotterdam in 2007 when a young U. K. musician Paolo Nutini discovered his music. Nutini quickly began promoting Rodriguez' sound. After he read about Rodriguez in **Mojo: The Collection**, Rowland went about cleaning up his affairs in London. He thought a lot about Rodriguez.

Steve marveled at Light In the Attic, a Seattle based reissue label, that was in the process of re-releasing **Cold Fact**. They would follow it with **Coming From Reality**. The stars were aligned to have Rowland and Rodriguez come together much like they had in 1970-1971.

Getting out of London proved to be a bigger task than Rowland expected. He had gone broke some years earlier. He recovered financially. His social life was a full one. He continually connected with friends. It was wearing him out. He was seventy years old, but he had the energy of a thirty year old. Where do you go after forty years of producing hit records in London? The answer was Palm Springs.

As Rowland prepared to leave London for Palm Springs he thought of the many visits with his parents. What did he like about the sunny California climate? It was lifestyle. He looked forward to escaping the dreary London weather and the snippy music industry types who screamed "cred" daily.

He returned to Palm Springs for half a dozen visits before moving permanently to the California oasis city. Rowland likes to watch foreign films at Palm Springs' art movie theaters. He loves the wide variety of ethnic restaurants. The bookstores provide the literature he reads, the Indian Casinos presents the major musical arts he enjoys, and he is an avid fan of the local theater groups. Steve is not a nighttime guy. The days of the clubs and parties are behind him. He is not a drinker and smoker. He will have a cocktail before dinner. That's it. But the ladies aren't safe. He is still out and about with a well-rounded social life. That is a given in Palm Springs where there are more places to eat, drink and party than one can imagine.

Steve Rowland: "I envisioned escaping the assholes in London. I had done my forty years. It was time for some California sunshine."

His lifelong friend, Budd Albright, lived in Palm Springs where he still dabbles in movies and television. Budd was effectively retired.

He was also a source of inspiration when Steve talked about a proposed television series. Budd was a good sounding board for Steve's ideas. He is also an excellent writer.

After looking around Palm Springs, Rowland settled on a beautiful single story home down a private street. His lush backyard, his enclosed entertaining rooms, his stylized pool, and the tranquility of Palm Springs was a perfect fit.

He was thinking about another book. His earlier volume, recalling the golden days of Hollywood, was written in the style of the 1950s writers Mickey Spillane and Raymond Chandler. He told people he might retire. But retirement was an unrealistic goal. Steve had a number of projects to finish.

After moving into his Palm Spring home, he put his nineteen gold records on the wall. He has more memorabilia and signed celebrity photos than can fit into the house. The bathroom has signed pictures of every major Hollywood star from the 1950s into the early 1960s. There are other signed photos throughout the house as well as multi-colored posters from the various movies Rowland starred in during two decades in the industry. The Palm Springs home is a monument to his success. But it is not a museum. He is still a working entertainment figure. He also has extensive artwork for the Family Dogg albums in his den. The Palm Springs house is a paean to Rowland's enormous intellect and creative spirit.

The Family Dogg was amongst Rowland's most creative projects. They were the band featuring his lead vocals, the music of Sixto Rodriguez as well as the Steve and Albert original 45s. In the U. K. Bell Records released the Steve and Albert 45 "Follow the Bouncing Ball" backed with "I Don't Wanna Go To Sleep Again" providing Steve and Albert Hammond with a gimmicky pop 45. "The Bouncing Ball" was a 1920s cartoon where the song was sung, and the lyrics appeared on half the movie screen. This pop, bubble gum song was one European radio and the pirate radio stations loved. Steve and

Albert debuted the song on Top Of The Pops. They also performed it on a British TV children's show with Steve in a red shirt and Albert in a green shirt. At the song's conclusion they throw balls into the audience. They looked uncomfortable. It is a moment in Rowland's career displaying his varied talents. In New Zealand a May 1970 45 on Polydor sold better than the U. K. release.

"Follow The Bouncing Ball" has a strange history. The U. K. record impresario, record collector, radio host and all around critic John Peel selected "Follow The Bouncing Ball" as one of the 100 worst records of all time. This was in 1992. The song played in a TV movie in August 1992 featuring Peel with a video clip of Steve and Albert performing the song. Steve laughed all the way to the bank.

It was **The Family Dogg** that made Rowland's name. The group was a chart hit aggregation in Europe and the U. K. He has other solo music projects, some of which may soon see the light of day.

He also has frequent lunches with his old friend, Shel Talmy, who lives in Los Angeles. Talmy, who produced the Kinks and the Who, among others, is at times a sounding board for Rowland's ideas. At least once a month Steve is in and around Hollywood's movie and music industry. He is far from retired.

When **Searching For Sugar Man** was in its early planning stages, Steve wondered what had happened to the greatest songwriter he recorded? He soon found out. He received a phone call from a young Swedish documentary filmmaker, Malik Bendjelloul, who was making a short film on the Sugar Man.

While putting his affairs together in London, Steve had no idea a major documentary on the Sugar Man was in the planning stages. He knew of other top flight documentary filmmakers who looked at the story and, for one reason or another, passed on it. He had fond memories of Rodriguez. He had lost track of him. He wondered how he was doing. This changed when he received a phone call as he prepared to resettle in Palm Springs.

Malik Bendjelloul Calls

As Steve prepared to leave London, he received a phone call from a young Swedish filmmaker who identified himself as Malik Bendjelloul. "He had a very pleasant voice on the phone," Steve continued. "He asked if I was the producer of **Coming From Reality**." Rowland told him he was the producer.

They talked about Rodriguez. Steve said: "What happened to Rodriguez?" Bendjelloul said they found him. He explained the documentary. It was in the planning stage. He would eventually call it **Searching For Sugar Man**. They talked about an interview. Malik said he had many questions about Rodriguez. Bendjelloul said he hoped to discover the mysteries of **Coming From Reality**. Rowland was impressed. The young man's questions and pervasive knowledge intrigued him. Steve told the filmmaker he was leaving for Palm Springs. Bendjelloul took his contact numbers.

Steve Rowland: "I figured it was another guy with a failed idea, it will never happen. Then I thought about the kid's passion. He sounded knowledgeable and excited. I thought that might be enough to complete the Sixto Rodriguez story."

Steve settled into Palm Springs. He wanted to be left alone and enjoy the sun. He wanted to live quietly. It was September 21, 2007 when he flew out of London on United Airlines. His friend, Budd Albright, told Steve he should move to Palm Springs. He took Rowland around Palm Springs. The luxurious homes, the gourmet restaurants, the remnants of the music business and the proximity of Hollywood made relocating to Palm Spring an easy decision. When he saw Johnny Rivers driving his red Ferrari, Nancy Sinatra walking down the luxurious El Paseo shopping district or Trini Lopez driving fast in a high end Mercedes, he knew there was some glamour to Palm Springs. Steve wanted a calm life, not glamour. But what the hell a little glamour didn't hurt.

After looking at thirty-six homes, he found his Shangri La. It is a beautiful home with an eclectic feel. His home has an Asian room, the tile is historic Southern California Spanish, the bedroom is European and the walls are filled with tasteful art and cinema-art memorabilia. Victor Harrigan was the architect. The house sits off South Palm Canyon Drive. The home is next to the mountains. It offers a quiet retreat.

The calm, relaxing life Rowland hoped for didn't materialize. When Malik called Steve it was about two months after he moved to Palm Springs. Bendjelloul finally showed up in 2008 to interview Rowland. Then Steve went to London for his book launch. When he returned Malik called again and showed up with cinematographer Camille Skagerstrom in tow. During the first visit Camille filmed Rowland's home as he talked about Rodriguez. He told Steve that he would be in touch for further interviews.

Then six weeks later Malik returned. He had an idea to film Rowland using the front gate as a prop to highlight his property and the mystery surrounding the Sugar Man. The highlight of the visit resulted in Steve sitting pensively in his front room. He played "Cause" to show how and why Rodriguez left Clarence Avant's Sussex label. He was dropped without warning prior to a major holiday.

Steve Rowland: "Cause' was the last song Rodriguez recorded. Sussex Records released him two weeks before Christmas. Sad!" The memory of these types of record business moves was enough to have Rowland think about entering the Entertainment Witness Protection Program.

Rowland in the Entertainment Witness Protection Program

As Rowland settled in Palm Springs he believed he was through with show business. He needed a break. He wanted to relax. The bullshit of the music business wore him down. Unfortunately, Steve's identity was discovered quickly. He began receiving phone calls and e-mails about all the various musical acts he produced in London for forty years.

Once the reissue labels Ace, Cherry Red, Rhino, Bear Family, BR Music and Repertoire began re-releasing records for the retro markets his productions were in demand. The royalties flowed steadily. They provided money for a rainy day. Steve realized there was no hope of retiring. The good news is he could call the shots. He licensed only what he felt appropriate.

Then all hell broke loose. When the documentary **Searching For Sugar** was released there was a demand for speakers who could describe the documentary. Enter Steve Rowland. He grew up in the industry and he knew every facet of the movie business. Steve discussed the movie at the Palm Spring's art theater Palme d'Or and also at the Camelot. Then he was off to Los Angeles where he participated in five Question and Answer sessions about the documentary. The audience at Hollywood's Arclight gave Rowland a standing ovation.

Steve was close to the beach, Hollywood and his old social friends. He loves the area. He is far enough away from Hollywood's bullshit so as not to be influenced by it. But when he wants Hollywood, he hops into his dark metallic grey BMW puts on his ray ban sunglasses and heads to Sunset Boulevard. You can take the kid out of Hollywood but you can't take Hollywood out of the kid. Steve also found love when he moved to Palm Springs.

Judy Lewis Returns and Steve is Happy

In 2009, his high school girl friend, Judy Lewis, came back into Rowland's life. Although they attended different high schools, she was his first girl friend. She was fourteen, and he was fifteen. "Judy snuck out of the house and her mother, Loretta Young, said that she forbade her to go out with me." Rowland continued: "When her mother caught her she was forbidden to ever see me again." Why did this take place? Steve had a group of hip friends and Loretta Young viewed them as hoodlums in training. This wasn't the case.

She visibly became angry when one of the servants told Loretta she had seen Judy getting into Steve's car. All of this came to light years later when Judy told Steve how Loretta Young viewed young Rowland in a negative light.

When she came back into his life, he was happy. They met at Norm's Restaurant on La Cienega. They planned to get married in 2011. They sent out the invitations for a Christmas wedding. They planned an Alaskan Cruise and a life together. They were set to do lectures on their books. Steve's **Hollywood Heat: Untold Stories** and Judy's **Uncommon Knowledge** were popular entertainment books. Judy's book was about her mother Loretta Young and her father Clark Gable. They had a romance hidden from the public. Judy was the illegitimate daughter of Clark Gable. Then Judy died of a brain tumor. "We were skiing at Heavenly Valley in Lake Tahoe, we came home to Palm Springs. She got up one morning and said that she couldn't see out of her left eye," Rowland said. Then seven months later Judy died. Steve still mourns her.

Steve Rowland: "That is why I love **Searching For Sugar Man**. It is about grief. I thought my life was coming to an end when Judy died. After all the years without each other, we finally got back together. We were really happy. It was not to be."

When Malik Bendjelloul came into Rowland's life he never expressed his private grief. This is one of Steve's traits. He is intensely private. Just like Sixto Rodriguez.

Things Changed When Malik Bendjelloul Came into Rowland's Life

Steve Rowland's friendship with Malik Bendjelloul changed his life. He never had a son. Malik was as close to a son as Steve could hope for as they had similar interests, instincts and often agreed on something before it was completed. From the time Malik first showed up in Palm Springs, they kept in close touch by e-mail and phone.

What did Rowland see in Bendjelloul? He saw a person much like himself. Malik was passionate about the Rodriguez project. He also worked with the same care and precision as Rowland. They had another thing in common. They were both intrepid storytellers. Like Rowland, Bendjelloul had a way of creating a film. He had a clear and defined beginning, a middle portion telling the story and an ending validating the reason for the film. This is why **Searching For Sugar Man** won an Oscar. Rowland produced his hit records using the same formula. When Bendjelloul passed away, Rowland was devastated. He had many fond memories that eased the pain.

Remebering Malik Bendjelloul

In October 2013, Steve met Malik in New York. He was with his girl friend, Brittany Huckabee. They talked about doing a television series based on Steve's book. The project already had serious interest from a number of cable television channels.

Steve Rowland: "I told him I was thinking about doing a television series inspired by my book. We talked about it. He was interested in working with me. I thought that he was extremely talented and a great guy." Rowland continued. "For me he was easy to get along with and he always had excellent ideas about cinematography."

When Steve recalled Camille Skagerstrom he remembered she also had an enhanced sense of vision. "They lit the scene inside my house to show the type of house I have," Rowland remarked. This set the stage for the eerie sense of doom Steve described when Rodriguez was released from his contract two weeks before Christmas. This scene provided the documentary with a heightened sense of suspense and created the mysterious drama that is the Sugar Man's story.

Steve Rowland embraces the film industry, television, the record business and his show business career. When he relocated to Palm Springs I told him he was entering the Entertainment Witness

Protection Program. I was wrong. He was simply changing his place of residence. He had two other loves of his life pass away when his father, Roy, and his mother, Ruth, died. His parents lived into their nineties. They left him with fond memories of family life. He had seen too many show business types die young; too many who had not enjoyed their lives. The list of drug and alcohol tragedies went on forever. This was a daily lesson.

How does one describe the many faces of Steve Rowland? He is a multi-faceted talent with an insider's knowledge of the movie industry, the music business and he was early on a Hollywood gossip magazine writer. He was particularly adept in dealing with the media.

Rowland is much more than a handsome face on camera talking about producing Rodriguez' **Coming From Reality**. He is a contemplative philosopher on the record industry. He also knew something about the pressures of show business, the lure of fame and fortune and the highs and the lows of media exposure. For a time he simply wanted to be left alone. That is true to the present day. The problem is Steve remains creative. He needs outlets for his creativity.

His television series in progress is an example of his never-ending creativity. The Hollywood mobster series set in the 1950s for American television is one where the scripts, the music, the setting and the actors need to fit into the picture's theme. That is Steve Rowland. He is the consummate professional with a creative mind that continues to churn out new material.

Steve Rowland: "The star of the series is Hollywood in the 1950s with the gangsters Mickey Cohen and Louis Dragna. The other part is the glamour and the beautiful ladies."

As he works in Palm Springs on his television series, Rowland remains much in demand. When German filmmakers arrived at his house to film a segment for a documentary on his father, he was the perfect host. With Rowland it is not about him. It is about the cinema, as he refers to it after forty years living in London, it is about continuing to produce cutting edge music, it is about writing scripts, dialogue and creative fiction and non-fiction that has been so much a part of his rich and productive life. Steve Rowland told me he entered the "Entertainment Witness Protection Program." He did so in jest. There is nothing retiring about Rowland.

I asked Steve: "How did nepotism affect you?

Steve Rowland: "It is basically resentment. People thought I had made it in the shade. My father told me I had to work for everything if I wanted to accomplish anything. Nepotism almost derailed my career. I worked doubly hard to accomplish my goals. You don't just give up your dream. Nepotism is one of the reasons I concentrated on music. I made it there without anyone knowing about my Hollywood background."

Steve's dad, Roy, was a top director and his uncle, Louis B Mayer, was a major producer. This put temporary roadblocks into his career path. He overcame these obstacles in an acting career with roles in major films, a bevy of recurring television appearances and along the way he established a reputation as a solid show business journalist with his column "The View From Rowland's Head." Steve was much like Sixto Rodriguez he had to fight for everything he accomplished. He was given nothing in the entertainment world and from time to time the connection to his father made it difficult to succeed. He did despite these obstacles.

Steve Rowland: "My father was against me becoming an actor. He said it was not a secure profession. That he would not help. However, he said if you want to pursue it you are going to have to work doubly hard."

Initially, Steve may not have known what his father meant. He soon found out.

It is in the audition tales that Steve explains his love-hate relationship with the movie industry. The various auditions provide the reason he left acting for a legendary music-producing career.

When Steve showed up for an appointment where he was age appropriate, he did a good job in the audition and he had the necessary experience for the role. The director often asked if he was Roy Rowland's son. When Steve said: "Yes." The director said: "Next." That was the end of the audition.

When he left Hollywood in May 1963 he had a multi movie deal in Spain. It was there he hooked up with a Madrid band, Los Flaps, and his singing and eventual producing career took precedence over movie roles. To this day Steve is angry over nepotism. It helped some actors. For Steve Rowland it was a force he overcame on the path to a legendary producing career.

Steve Rowland is a complex and creative individual. He hasn't mellowed with age. The exacting standards he set for his early writing for fan magazines, his study of and dedication to acting, his forty years of record production and his book **Hollywood Heat** were all done in the same exacting style. He wants it right. If you don't get it right. Look out Steve is in your face. This is why he is accomplished in so many fields. That said, once you are in his social milieu, he is easy going, never demanding and he has a sympathetic ear for his friends.

Seventeen

Rodriguez: Fame, the Malik Bendjelloul Mystery and the Biographer

"You either live under a rock or you walk in the sunshine."

Sixto Rodriguez

"How much of you is repetition?"

Sixto Rodriguez

"What you live is better than what you write."

Goethe

The rock and roll marketplace is unforgiving. For some artists fame is a once in a lifetime occurrence. For others it is the balm of daily life. For every Bob Dylan there is a P. F. Sloan. Some endure and some are lost in the rock and roll scrap heap. Sixto Rodriguez' early failure was neither enduring nor accepted as a part of his daily life. He didn't initially achieve fame. He lived an isolated, unconventional existential life. He read. He wrote. He continued to educate himself on the music business.

Sixto Rodriguez was like many musicians playing where he could and continuing to chase the music dream into early middle age. Then fame arrived like a hurricane. The initial hand clapping, the cries of joy for the music and the tumultuous applause stunned the Sugar Man. It was January 2012, and he was now, as he said, "a solid seventy." He joked it was time to use his "senior advantage." He joked about success. But there was no sugar coating the surprise.

Fame came unexpectedly on his doorstep forty-one years after the release of **Coming From Reality**. It was welcomed. How well was Rodriguez prepared for international stardom? He was ready. His daughters have commented numerous times to close friends that he lives to perform.

When he appears in concert, now in his mid-seventies, the Sugar Man is fit, well dressed and he has a command of his music. He needs help getting on and off the stage, due to glaucoma, but this doesn't impede the shows. He is ready to entertain. This is part of his existential nature. Nothing bothers him. He has lived through hell. Heaven is now part of the deal. He tours when he feels like it. He gives his money away. As Rodriguez told a friend in the Motor City Brewing Company: "Fame ain't no big thing." Or is it!

Rodriguez stumbled into the music business almost by accident. Had it not been for the constant prodding of his then late 1960s girl friend, Rainy M. Moore, he might have played small Detroit clubs to the present day. With his dashing good looks, his cool clothes, his hip language, his intellectual persona and his musical genius the Sixto Rodriguez story might have played out in local bars like the Old Miami or the college bars like Mr. Flood's Party. Instead his career is performing on the David Letterman Show, appearing in concert at London's Royal Albert Hall and exciting the rabid French fans at the Olympia in Paris. These performing arenas, as well as dozens of other high-end venues, and every major festival brought Rodriguez to an international audience. The days of driving to Ann Arbor to play Mr. Flood's Party or driving a few miles to a local Detroit bar are over.

Malik Bendjelloul: Myth Becomes Reality

On May 13, 2014 I was touring Europe on a vacation with my wife Carolyn. I had finished volume one of my three Sixto Rodriguez books. I was hard at work on this book. I e-mailed Steve Rowland daily. Steve was devastated. Malik Bendjelloul had committed suicide. I had never interviewed him. I had some brief contact with him through e-mails. Steve Rowland kept in constant touch with the young filmmaker. I thought long and hard about how Malik Bendjelloul persevered and made an Oscar winning documentary. This was despite long odds and what seemed to be incalculable fiscal difficulties. Malik beat the system only to take his own life. Why? Who knows! It is a tragic tale.

What was Bendjelloul's significance to the Rodriguez story? In the first volume I sketched out Malik's life, his meeting with Stephen "Sugar" Segerman, and his eventual triumph in completing **Searching For Sugar Man**. Without meeting him and only interacting with people he knew, I believed I got to know Malik Bendjelloul. Over many hours of conversation with Steve Rowland, Malik emerged as a creative filmmaker that left us too soon.

There was humility, humanity and a cinematic genius to Malik Bendjelloul. The beauty of South Africa and its wonderful people influenced much of what he accomplished in **Searching For Sugar Man**. As Yale psychologist Paul Bloom observed: "People do help others in ways that don't benefit themselves." That is the essence of Steve Rowland, Paolo Nutini, Mike Theodore, Dennis Coffey, Matt Sullivan and David Holmes. They came to Bendjelloul's aid time and time again. Their beneficent attitudes are in sharp contrast to Stephen "Sugar" Segerman's egomaniacal attempts to slip into the music business limelight. Kudos to Rodriguez for banishing this pretender into a well deserved exile. In the beginning Segerman pitched the story.

Bendjelloul's Cinematic Genius: South Africa Influenced It

The first step to understanding how Bendjelloul's cinematic genius was translated into **Searching For Sugar Man** is to analyze his friendship with and input of Stephen "Sugar" Segerman. The scenario begins when Malik wrote to Segerman on September 15, 2006 explaining he was a Korba TV employee in Stockholm, and how he hoped to work on a Rodriguez documentary.

Bendjelloul arrived in Cape Town. It was early December 2006. They talked at length about the project. Malik was impressed with a London newspaper article on Rodriguez. He told Segerman he wanted to know more about the Sugar Man.

The two new friends took a ride in Segerman's car. They went up Tafelberg Road with Bendjelloul admiring the beautiful South African landscape. Cape Town looked to Bendjelloul like an urban fairyland. The contrasting beauty of the sea and the vegetation brought a calm feeling to the usual hyper Swede.

They parked and left Segerman's Opel to marvel at the city view. When Bendjelloul went back to his hotel, he made notes. He saw the stark contrast between Cape Town and Detroit. He would use it to highlight the sublime nature of the Rodriguez story.

The story continued on for a number of years. Then in early January 2008 Malik e-mailed Steve Rowland.

January 4, 2008
Dear Steve,

My name is Malik Bendjelloul and I'm a Swedish documentary filmmaker. We are working on a documentary film about

Rodriguez and would very much like to make an interview with you. Later this spring we're going to travel all over the world to meet all the people involved in the story, and your part is of course very, very interesting. Would we have time to meet you?

Yours sincerely
Malik Bendjelloul
________________January 18, 2008
SVT - National Swedish Television
Oxenstiernsgatan 26
105 10 Stockholm
Sweden
phone + 46 73 817 92 95

This e-mail to Rowland was the major turning point in developing **Searching For Sugar Man**. Malik was struggling with the ways of the music business and the documentary film field. He needed a mentor. Rowland became that mentor.

Why Malik's e-mail was a Turning Point

This e-mail was the turning point in the road to completing the Oscar winning documentary. Malik also secured a noted cinematographer Camille Skagerstrom. Thanks to Steve's funding ideas, experience in filmmaking and moral support, the project got off the ground. For the next four years they worked in earnest. One of the keys to the documentary was securing an interview with former Sussex Record head Clarence Avant. Rowland provided some insights into how to approach the legendary record man. It worked. He came on board. It was when Bendjelloul sat down with Avant he knew his film would be a major one. He told close friends this was the beginning of his "confidence period."

Malik skyped and e-mailed Rowland his concerns about how to open the documentary. It took some time for the young Swedish director to make up his mind. Steve encouraged Malik to think independently. It was his project, Rowland said time and time again. He warned Bendjelloul not to let others take the credit for his work.

As Bendjelloul, Segerman and Skagerstrom worked out the early scenes, Malik heard from Clarence Avant. He agreed to an interview. He offered to pick them up at the Los Angeles International Airport. He took them to lunch prior to the filming. Avant said he heard Rodriguez was big in South Africa. In the next breath he wondered why he hadn't received royalties from the South African record companies? Clarence asked for a means of contacting the Sugar Man. This erased questions of Avant cheating Rodriguez.

Here is the smoking gun. Segerman continued urging Malik to attack Avant on camera concerning past royalties. He did! It made the film. The problem is it wasn't the truth.

There was a great deal left out of my first book on the Rodriguez story. Bendjelloul was a shy, but quirky, young kid. He was driven. He became obsessed with the Sixto Rodriguez story. Unlike Stephen "Sugar" Segerman, he never used Rodriguez to search for his fame. He won fame for his hard work on the documentary.

The Malik Bendjelloul Mystery: Can it be Solved?

The Malik Bendjelloul mystery remains unsolved. There are some hints how and why he took a dark road ending his life. How did he get there? That is the question. Here are some random ideas. Fear of failure! Pressure! Unexecuted expectations! The inability to find a worthwhile second project! These are some of the concerns that drove Bendjelloul to an early grave according to people in Sweden and the U. S.

Malik Bendjelloul is a victim of the Sixto Rodriguez story. He committed suicide after feeling inadequate, underappreciated and maligned by those who were his friends, colleagues, benefactors and supporters. It is a deep and dark story. How does one analyze it? The how and why a person commits suicide is a speculative question. It is as much a guess as it is an examination of the external evidence.

After the adulation for **Searching For Sugar Man** died down, Bendjelloul looked for new projects. He was offered feature films, a few documentary projects, television shows and a number of high level commercials. None met his expectations. What went wrong? There is a blueprint for explaining what went wrong.

The Malik Bendjelloul tragedy begins with the making of **Searching For Sugar Man**. In the six plus frustrating years he spent conceptualizing, formatting, scripting, filming and financing the Oscar winning documentary, he was often alone, depressed, paranoid and out of sorts. Self-doubt gave way to personal loathing and a well-developed feeling of inadequacy.

As Bendjelloul spent one thousand plus hours editing the documentary he e-mailed Steve Rowland regularly. From Palm Springs, Rowland offered advice and friendship. It was an unpleasant and frustrating time for Malik. But Steve, like other close friends, had no idea the degree of Bendjelloul's depression.

What kept Bendjelloul alive? It was the story. He was obsessed with the Sugar Man's tale of redemption. He didn't realize he would provide final redemption for Rodriguez and a path to international stardom. He worked early on without funds, without a distributor, without encouragement and without hope for completion of the project. How did he overcome his doubts? The answer is a simple one. Stephen "Sugar" Segerman came along to add depth to the story. Then the Rodriguez family, slowly but surely, warmed to the project. He traveled to Detroit meeting Rodriguez and his family. They took Malik in and literally made him a part of the family. Steve Rowland continued to mentor Malik from Palm Springs. Simon Chinn, Sony Legacy and a host of people in their realm brought **Searching For**

Sugar Man to the Sundance Film Festival. Success took place quickly. Bendjelloul was an acclaimed director with youthful good looks and what seemed to be an unlimited future.

The February 24, 2013 85th Academy Award ceremony was the beginning of Bendjelloul's downward spiral. After he experienced the accolades, the cascading fame and the joy of accomplishment, he looked to his future. That look was an immediate disaster. He hoped to make a feature film. No one stepped up to fund it. At least not the feature film he envisioned. He had offers. He didn't like the story line or the finances. He couldn't find a worthwhile project that met his standards.

When his suicide was announced, a close friend, Bobo Ericzen, remarked: "If you spoke five words to Malik, you fell in love with him. He had a tremendous personal aura."

Bendjelloul Had Difficulty with Fame: What About Rodriguez?

Malik Bendjelloul's whirlwind ride to fame and fortune led to an early death. What about Sixto Rodriguez? How did he handle fame? The contrast between the two tells one a great deal about the story, and why fame kills.

The fame game began in January 2012, when the Sugar Man attended the Sundance Film Festival. For a time he played with celebrity. That said he withdrew from the fame game by 2017. Rodriguez never asked for fame. He refuses to embrace it.

The attendant problems created by fame didn't go away. Rodriguez' business interests were difficult ones. He had many opportunities, and he knew that only those that fit into his expertise could be exercised. But he had trouble sifting through business deals because of the sycophants, the wannabes, the industry insiders, the potential managers, the quick buck shysters with shady projects, as well as the Hollywood insiders were promising Rodriguez stardom. In 2016-2017, it became virtually impossible to secure a Sixto Rodriguez interview. The press lost interest in the tale. His story had been told. Cinderella was back performing at the ball. It was apparent Rodriguez could tour in small or large venues, perform when and where he wanted. His life took on an increasingly predictable pace. It was exactly the way he liked it.

Sitting Home in Front of the Fire and Walking the Cass Corridor

There is no mystery to Sixto Rodriguez. He loves to sit at home in front of his wood-burning stove in the winter. He loves nothing more than being at home feeding wood into a roaring fire. Despite his fame and fortune, Light In the Attic sends him a chord of wood every winter. The summer is another story. The Sugar Man walks the streets when the stifling heat permits. He has a life in and around the Cass Corridor. Age has slowed his walking. He is out visiting friends, eating at local restaurants and attending cultural-political events. Fame has not caused him to vanish from the public eye. At least not in Detroit. As Professor M. L. Liebler commented, he has a life in the Cass Corridor.

Privacy is and will always be Rodriguez' mantra. In 1986 he was walking through Hart Plaza carrying his guitar. He was dressed in a stylish suit. His expensive shoes glowed. He had on a gold plated watch (it was actually a Timex) and his guitar was slung over his back. A local fan snapped a picture. Rodriguez demanded the film. The fan refused. Then twenty-one years later in 2017, he asked a fan not to snap a picture. The fan agreed. What is the point of these stories? Sixto Rodriguez is a rock star. He was born to play this role. In 2017 he was no different than he was thirty years earlier. He still sits at home in front of his wood burning fire and walks the Cass Corridor. He still doesn't like his picture taken without his permission.

The Biographer Takes a Look at Fame and Fortune

After spending five plus years on the Sixto Rodriguez story, Steve Rowland asked me: "What have you learned about his elusive life?" Great question! Now for the answer! I learned Detroit defined his talent.

As I wandered through the Cass Corridor, I drank beer at the Motor City Brewing Company with their wonderful pizza and ate the world's best barbecue. The next stop was another beer at the Old Miami; I would then wander over for a late night meal at the Cass Café. In the afternoon I would sit at the Cass Café bar. Late at night I would wander in once again, and they saved me at seat at the Cass Cafe bar. I was treated like a regular. They told me they were going to name a drink after me. I assumed they were kidding. Everyone I talked to loved the fact I was writing a book on Sixto Rodriguez. He deserved it. So I decided to write three books. I hope the bar fly crowd at the Cass Cafe are still with me. Then, as the bars closed, I was satiated with food and drink. I walked down Avery Street to stare at the Sugar Man's house. I figured out what was going on. He was private. I had to remember that when I am on his block on Avery Street. Life was the same for him in many ways since fame and fortune. He does have some problems maintaining his privacy. He does have money. That is a change. He doesn't live his life much differently than he did prior to **Searching For Sugar Man**.

On the trail of Sixto Rodriguez I found lovely people and made some life long friends. I have tried to step inside Rodriguez' life. This has made me uncomfortable. I have left out much of the personal material I discovered in more than one hundred interviews.

Empathy is a word describing the Sugar Man. What is empathy? It is helping strangers. It is seeing the world through the life of others. It is doing good deeds for neer do wells, along with family and friends. When Rodriguez purchased a new car for his first wife, when he gave a generous sum for a family member to purchase a home, or when he tipped three hundred dollars to a college student he heard couldn't afford tuition, he demonstrated his empathy

On one of my trips to Detroit I cradled a take out coffee from the Cass Cafe, I walked past the Motor City Brewing Company and I walked down Avery Street toward the Anarchist Collective. Rodriguez came down the steep cement steps from his house. He was holding onto his partner, Bonnie, and they walked toward the Motor City Brewing Company. I said: "Hi." Rodriguez smiled and gave me the peace sign. It was surreal. Then it was off to the Anarchist Collective for interviews. I thought it was strange in **Searching For Sugar Man** they didn't have Rodriguez walking in his neighborhood. It is a blue-collar bastion of working class pride.

The tale of the Sugar Man is not just about his music. It is a broader and more inclusive tale of the record business, the fans that obsess (even the biographer) and the role his music plays in popular culture. It is the changes in popular culture, the rise of the Internet, the independent record labels like Light In The Attic, the young record gurus like Matt Sullivan and the continued importance of the troubadour tradition that keeps Rodriguez' star shining brightly.

Why Searching for Sugar Man III?

The third book on Sixto Rodriguez will define his place in the pantheon of musical giants. Or more accurately it will examine in copious detail how Matt Sullivan and his record label, Light In The Attic, brought Rodriguez' music from a small, cult audience into a booming, mainstream cultural phenomenon. When Sullivan's label re-released **Cold Fact** and **Coming From Reality** they promoted him with a ferocity Clarence Avant and Sussex Records could only imagine. The concerts LITA booked, the attendant publicity, and the Sugar Man's persona set the stage for **Searching For Sugar Man's** success.

Matt Sullivan is like Steve Rowland's son. He doesn't like publicity. He doesn't like being in the limelight. He doesn't like praise. He deserves it. He set the table for Rodriguez' incipient success.

There are many industry insiders important to the Rodriguez history. One is the former Casablanca chief, Neil Bogart, who had an impact on why **Cold Fact** didn't find commercial success. Bogart was so busy putting his disco acts and the Casablanca label in place he ignored his distribution deal with Sussex Records. Rodriguez was the victim of disco and Bogart.

Another is his daughter, Regan Rodriguez, who is the ballast and the front person for his recent career. She is unfailingly loyal. She has excellent judgment. She has an honesty and integrity not found amongst those in the music business. She is a seasoned professional.

John Sinclair, the poet, radical political and marijuana advocate, is another positive influence upon the Sugar Man. As Sinclair commutes between New Orleans, Detroit and Amsterdam the pot-smoking guru remains close to Rodriguez. Sinclair is one of the brightest, if non-mainstream, critics of the American way of life. He is amongst Rodriguez' closest friends.

Steve Rowland remains in close touch with Rodriguez concerning a third album. In 2013 Rowland was the musical director for two New York shows. They have a common view of the music business. The Sixto Rodriguez story is less about the man and his enormous talent and more about why and how the record industry eats its own. It is not a pleasant tale.

Since 2012 it is rumored he has written songs, planned the direction of his concert career, fiddled in a dilettantes manner with a third album, and he has a plan for his future. Now in his mid-seventies Rodriguez has crafted a niche in the concert marketplace. He still has the drive for a third album. He has reached out repeatedly to Steve Rowland with plans to finalize new songs.

Joyce Carol Oates once described biography as dominated by pathography. What is pathography? According to Oates, it is a form of biography demeaning and deflating its subject by emphasizing the low points of the subject's life. It is those low points that make the Sixto Rodriguez story unique. To understand the Sugar Man it is necessary to follow in his footsteps.

Footsteps: Following The Sugar Man

When I talked to people close to the Sixto Rodriguez story, I realized it was less about the Sugar Man and more about the people close to him. It was also about the storied influence of the Motor City, the plight of the working poor who Rodriguez has embraced and defended, the music business and the assortment of criminals, drug addicts, thieves, unbalanced narcissists, money grubbing record producers, sleazy promoters, groupies, hangers on, wannabes, hookers, star fuckers and other assorted assholes. Someone asked me: "You have so many people in your book. You have so many themes. You have so many influences. How in the hell did this ever come together?" When I pointed out the three books were more than about Sixto Rodriguez, the person said: "Oh!"

The many friendships, wives, children, relatives, dope smoking buddies, casual Wayne State acquaintances and music industry figures who came through his life didn't change him. This is the story. He has a solid, loving family. He is also a bit paranoid and distrustful of record executives, filmmakers, and journalists, booking agents, lawyers and biographers. You have to be persistent, trustworthy and a counterculture devotee to hang with the Sugar Man.

Rodriguez is educated, a world traveler, a poet, a community activist and a blue-collar construction guy. You put all this together and come up with the following conclusion. The Sugar Man is a free spirit, a private counterculture icon, a contrarian and a devoted family man.

Not surprisingly, women play an important role in his life. His two wives helped develop an intellectual awareness of feminist needs long before it was fashionable. His three daughters nurtured his mind, his consciousness and his approach to life.

Hesitation, missteps, false starts, dead ends and record industry malevolence didn't derail his career. Why? There is a simple answer. Rodriguez never took his eyes off the prize. There is the question of his elusive personality. There is a romantic and tragic side to Rodriguez. Se**arching For Sugar Man** is a story too good to be true. The reality of Rodriguez' long term Australian fame, his two marriages, his talent as a performer, his mercurial independence, and his "I could give a shit" attitude is not a part of the Oscar winning documentary.

To understand Rodriguez, it is necessary to live in his world. It is not a conventional one. There is a romantic and tragic sense to the story. The meaning and events in his life coalesce to form the story. Rodriguez continues to fascinate as he eases into his mid-seventies.

Rodriguez' Backstory Continues in Detroit

The back-story continues to be Detroit. It is the main influence in Rodriguez' life. It defines his existence, his sense of self worth, his future and his past. Detroit is much like an unforgiving mistress cajoling, haunting and inspiring. In Rodriguez' world the dank, dark streets that engulf the Motor City are his muse.

What is missing in a study of Rodriguez' life? The writing process is one the Sugar Man has never discussed. When does he write? What inspires him? Does he have a muse other than Detroit? These are questions he will hopefully address. As the **Huffington Post's** Kia Makarechi observed: "Sugar Man is remarkable because it conjures an overwhelming unique sense of hope. It's a tale of talent being recognized, of humility's triumph."

No one was more astonished at the wealth and fame resulting from the Oscar winning documentary **Searching For Sugar Man** than Rodriguez. That said there was no change in his daily life at home in the Cass Corridor. His family benefitted from the money. His daughter Sandra went to Florida in the winter to escape the Motor City, another daughter Regan moved to a toney Detroit suburb. She now has two children, a husband and a career directing Rodriguez' enterprises. Eva was around from time to time. Then she relocated to the Cass Corridor. She now lives near her father.

Eva Rodriguez' Accomplishments

Eva is very successful. She was married to James Koller and later to Juan Introna. She has lived in Junction City, Kansas and Dorado, Puerto Rico while pursuing a highly successful military career. She is a retired U. S. Army pilot, and she is a spiritual healer, an author and a dedicated community activist.

Eva Rodriguez: "My parents did tough things to keep going and raise three kids." Despite the hardscrabble existence in her early life, Eva was a superior student, hard working and career oriented. There is a series on "fly girls" and her accomplishments dominate the video. By 1986 she was a combat nurse working in South Korea. She was also among the first female Army pilots. From 1988 to 1990 she served in Germany as an official military pilot. She was also a military adviser in Honduras, Guatemala and Belize. She was a humanitarian worker in El Salvador, Nicaragua and Belize. After serving in the Persian Gulf War and flying in supplies through the war zones from Iraq to Saudi Arabia and Kuwait, she thought of retirement. When she entered the military in 1981, her educational achievements led to a storied career. By 2001 the prospects of retirement looked good. She wasn't ready for retirement. Eva's high-level education, her skills and her training in multiple fields made her too valuable to the U. S. Army. She re-upped.

The decade before she considered retirement Eva's career was one milestone after another. Eva worked as a nurse in Kansas for four years. Then she traveled for a year to Egypt acting as an official peacekeeper. After she returned to Kansas, Eva discovered her father was a South African rock star. By that time it was 1998, and she had almost twenty years in the military. Then in 1999 she had a son. Her life changed. She said being a soldier and mother didn't work. She wanted to be a full time mother. The family atmosphere that was so important took over, and she began to think of life changes.

Eva Rodriguez: "I was a soldier by day and a mom by night. But once you become a mom your mind-set changes. For the first time I had something to live for."

She thought of concluding her military career as she followed her father to South Africa for the 1998 concerts.

There was a major change in Eva's life. When she was given orders to fly a Black Hawk helicopter in the midst of a Columbia drug raid, she realized the Army and being a mom were incompatible. She remained in the army until 2001. The raid in Columbia changed her mind.

Eva Rodriguez: "As a woman, the effects after a war are very hard. Everyone admires you as a hero, but you don't feel like one. Twenty years was enough, so I took early retirement."

She married in South Africa and lived for a time there. She also became a licensed spiritual healer. She wrote a book **The Circle Of Love**, which showed children how nature and a sense of spiritual forces enriches life. As a healer and successful author she is on the road to another career. This one has a humanitarian tone.

Rodriguez' family is intact. That is all that mattered. They are happy, healthy, emotionally and psychologically well-adjusted, fiscally independent and enjoying life. That had been Rodriguez' goal since the 1960s. Now he has achieved it. Fame and fortune were incidental. He simply didn't care about money. It was still about the music.

Thoughts of a Sympathetic Biographer: Rowland and Rodriguz are Alike, No Question!

Steve Rowland and Sixto Rodriguez agree on practically everything. Have they talked about how and why they agree on most subjects? Steve said: "No." They spent some years in decline. They came roaring back to commercial prominence. Both are prickly. That said they are decent, loyal, heart felt personalities who have never thrown their friends or their families under the bus. They are not sour or ill tempered. There are no complaints about a lack of respect. They are hard working, quiet and private. Neither likes the limelight. They are difficult to get to know. They don't take people into their confidences easily. They are wary of strangers, con artists and those who feed off celebrity.

Their private lives remain exemplary. There is no sign of drug or alcohol abuse in either Rowland or Rodriguez. They are simply normal, quiet people. Why is this important? Their work is their craft. They spend time with family and friends. They are so normal those close to them comment they are boring. They are controlled achievers leaving an artistic legacy.

Thinking About Malik Bendjelloul

The year before **Searching For Sugar Man: Sixto Rodriguez' Mythical Climb To Rock and Roll Fame and Fortune** was finished, I was in New York as was Malik Bendjelloul. He was living with his girl friend. She had no idea he was depressed.

His girlfriend, Brittany Huckabee, is a filmmaker. Her documentary, **Sexy Baby**, premiered at the Tribeca Film Festival. She provided Malik with a knowledgeable ear to bend. She was a continual inspiration as well as a stabilizing force. They met at the Tribeca Film Festival. They were inseparable until his untimely suicide.

He found one excellent story when he discovered South African conservationist Lawrence Anthony who was attempting to rescue animals from the Baghdad zoo. Peters labeled, the Elephant Whisperer, saved animals from the Baghdad zoo in the midst of continual war. There were many other projects Bendjelloul talked about hoping to reignite his creative senses. He loved jazz. He discussed an Ornette Coleman movie. Malik had actors interested in his various projects. Phillip Seymour Hoffman met with him to discuss a proposed movie a few months before Hoffman's heroin fueled death.

When word arrived Bendjelloul committed suicide, while vacationing in Stockholm, there was shock. His girl friend, Brittany, had been with him daily since he moved to New York. Simon Chinn talked to him regularly on the phone. He had no idea what caused the suicide. Neither did anyone else. The unexpected death left everyone bewildered. To understand Malik's humanity and his devotion to **Searching For Sugar Man** one only needs to examine his thoughts about Sixto Rodriguez.

Quotes About Rodriguez by Malik Bendjelloul

1. **"I WAS ALMOST AFRAID TO LISTEN TO THE MUSIC BECAUSE I THOUGHT, IT CAN'T BE AS GOOD AS THEY SAY. BUT IT WAS." MALIK BENDJELLOUL, THE FILM DIRECTOR OF SEARCHING FOR SUGAR MAN TO THE HUFFINGTON POST.**
2. **"IT WAS LIKE, THIS IS THE BEST STORY I'VE EVER HEARD IN MY LIFE OR THAT I'M EVER GOING TO HEAR. I WAS LIKE, NO WAY. IT WAS A BEAUTIFUL STORY." MALIK BENDJELLOUL**

3. **“I DON’T EVEN WANT TO LISTEN TO IT BECAUSE... WHAT IF IT’S BAD? I PLAYED IT TO A DYLAN FAN AND HE SAID: ‘THIS IS BETTER THAN BOB DYLAN.” MALIK BENDJELLOUL**
4. **“I REALIZED THIS IS NEVER GOING TO HAPPEN AGAIN IN THE HISTORY OF THE WORLD.” HE CONTINUED. “IT’S A TRUE CINDERELLA STORY. IT’S BETTER THAN CINDERELLA BECAUSE CINDERELLA DIDN’T HAVE AS GOOD A SOUNDTRACK.” MALIK BENDJELLOUL**
5. **“I SPENT FIVE YEARS ON THE PROJECT, INSTEAD OF MY USUAL FOUR WEEKS.” MALIK BENDJELLOUL**
6. **“A LOT OF PEOPLE THOUGHT HE WAS GOING TO BE THE NEXT BOB DYLAN. “ MALIK BENDJELLOUL**
7. **“RODRIGUEZ IS DETROIT IN A WAY.” MALIK BENDJELLOUL**
8. **“YOU WEREN’T AWARE OF SOMETHING THAT WOULD HAVE CHANGED YOUR LIFE FOREVER.” REMARK OF FILM MAKER MALIK BENJELLOUL TO RODRIGUEZ IN SEARCHING FOR SUGAR MAN**

On May 14, 2014, the press reported Malik Bendjelloul threw himself in front of a subway train in downtown Stockholm. It was in one of the busiest shopping areas in Sweden. The suicide took everyone by surprise. The tall charismatic young Swede with the soft, mellow voice was moving on to new projects. He met with Simon Chinn in New York on April 17, 2014. They discussed his next film. He told Chinn he hoped to return to the documentary forum. They had lunch. They laughed. They parted with a handshake. They agreed to meet once more for breakfast in a week in London. On April 25, 2014 Chinn and Bendjelloul met in London for breakfast. They talked about his future. He returned to Stockholm. In twenty days Malik was dead.

The celebrity news outlets sent reporters to Stockholm. The **Hollywood Reporter** spent so much time on the story the reader knew what Malik had for breakfast each morning, but they had no clue as to the suicide. The hurt they caused his friends and family can't be measured. No one was more distraught than Sixto Rodriguez. He owed his mainstream stardom to the filmmaker. Equally shocked in his Palm Springs home, Steve Rowland didn't do much for almost a month. He was hit so hard by Malik's passing he refused to discuss it. To this day he won't talk to me about it.

When I talked to Detroit producer Harry Balk before he passed away, he looked at me and asked: "Why three volumes on Sixto Rodriguez? This was in 2012 when I began this project. I outlined what I thought the story should contain. I told Harry I hadn't written a word only an outline. When I wrote the biography of Del Shannon, I spent a great deal of time with Harry. He is a brilliant producer, a consummate businessman, and he has an eagle eye when it comes to musical talent. I didn't talk to him the last few years of his life when he was in a care home. He left me with some thoughts about Sixto Rodriguez.

The life of the average person is what makes American history. This is precisely the Sixto Rodriguez story. There is a choreographed dance to the Sugar Man's life. When producer Steve Rowland described how slowly and what great skill it took to produce a hit record, he said it was like a movie. When I asked Steve what he meant, he described an elaborate three-step process by which he introduced the song, he developed a solid story line and the song evolved into a climatic ending. Anyone who has listened to his productions, particularly Rodriguez' album **Coming From Reality**, is familiar with his producing technique. I asked Steve: "Do you see Rodriguez' life much like how you produced a song?"

Steve Rowland: "Absolutely."

Eighteen

Why Steve Rowland is the Force Behind Searching for Sugar Man: Myths Created by Stephen "Sugar" Segerman

"I've produced a lot of big name artists with big hits, like Peter Frampton and Jerry Lee Lewis, but I've never worked with anyone as talented as Rodriguez."

Steve Rowland

"I never understood why he didn't become a big star, so to see him rise like a phoenix from the ashes, it's just as inexplicable, but it makes me really, really happy...he's a wonderful, humble person, and he really deserves it."

Steve Rowland

"My task which I am trying to achieve, is by the power of the written word to make you hear, to make you feel...."

Joseph Conrad

Steve Rowland produced Rodriguez' second album **Coming From Reality**. After he listened to it, Malik Bendjelloul researched the London based producer. He was not surprised to learn Steve grew up in the film industry. He was intrigued legendary film producer Louis B. Mayer was his uncle. When Malik discovered Rowland made five films in Spain in the 1960s he researched and watched many of these films. He was struck by the wide range of Rowland's background. Malik decided to film Steve, but he was determined to find what secrets in the film industry he possessed and to get his input into the documentary.

This set the stage for five years of e-mails and skype calls. Steve became a co-conspirator. When I asked Rowland about his influence. He replied: "All the credit goes to Malik. I gave him my opinion. I did not have a big impact on the documentary."

This is typical Steve Rowland. He does not like to take credit for anything but his projects. After examining the e-mails, listening to descriptions of some of the skype calls, Rowland had an enormous cutting edge impact upon **Searching For Sugar Man**.

He had a pronounced influence upon the planning, the process and the completion of Malik Bendjelloul's documentary. Most people didn't realize the years of e-mails and skype calls between Rowland and Bendjelloul were a path to completing the project.

After viewing hundreds of e-mails between Steve and Malik Bendjelloul there is no doubt Rowland is an unsung creative force behind the documentary. He was the tutor, the psychological ballast and the day-to-day guide to Bendjelloul's cascading creativity. Without Rowland's diligent counsel, **Searching For Sugar Man** would not have been completed.

Segerman was the key figure early in the story. For the first few years he was the creative angel, the cheerleader, the person who provided housing for Malik Bendjelloul when he visited Cape Town, and he dealt with Matt Sullivan on the early discussions for Light In The Attic to release **Cold Fact** and **Coming From Reality**.

In 2007 Segerman convinced Malik Bendjelloul to pursue a full-length documentary. He did! In January 2012 **Searching For Sugar Man** premiered to great acclaim at the Sundance Film Festival. It was in the years 2007 to 2009 Segerman's influence was prominent. Then in January 2009 Bendjelloul increased his weekly e-mail to Steve Rowland. That ended Segerman's seminal role. This is the extent of his influence. Segerman was important in the first couple of years of planning. Why did Segerman continue to take credit for a project he influenced but had little input on the final product? He wanted control. He diligently pursued fame. He wanted wealth. There is no wonder Rodriguez had to cast him away from the kingdom.

Rowland's Personality: He Will not Take Credit

Steve Rowland doesn't like to do interviews. He doesn't like to talk about his accomplishments as an actor, a singer, a producer or a writer. He prefers to do the work. He lets his product do the talking. This has created problems. His contributions are in so many fields they are often overlooked. He is not thought of as a punk rock founder. Yet, he discovered the Cure. He nursed their early music. He brought the Cure into the record business. He is not demonstrative about his discoveries.

One of the untold tales in **Searching For Sugar Man** is Rowland's influence upon the documentary. He was a paramount contributor to the story. Throughout the filming Steve advised Malik weekly. When **Searching For Sugar Man** was in an embryo stage of production, Rowland made a storyboard. This was a road map to producing the documentary through a series of illustrations and statements indicating the key points and the important scenes. The sound effects, the dialogue, and the placing of the music were in Rowland's comprehensive storyboard. He provided Bendjelloul with a road map to production success.

When they planned **Searching For Sugar Man**, there was no doubt in Rowland's mind they were working on an Oscar winning documentary. He wondered how fame would impact the story? When fame arrived it altered the lives of Segerman and Bartholomew-Strydom. It did little to change Rowland or Rodriguez. But fame did have an impact.

Where Were Segerman and Rowland When Fame Hit?

When fame and fortune made Rodriguez an international star, his life changed. He lost his privacy. He was constantly in the limelight. In sharp contrast, Steve Rowland quietly continued his Palm Springs daily routine and his lifelong friendship with Rodriguez. How did Rowland impact the story and the resurgence in Rodriguez' career?

There would not have been **Searching For Sugar Man** had it not been for Rowland's continual exchange of e-mails and skype calls with Bendjelloul. He was the person who nursed and advised Malik as the documentary slowly rolled to final fruition. When I began this book, I realized after reading the e-mail exchanges how important Steve was to the finished product. When I ran this chapter by my critic without including the e-mails between Bendjelloul and Rowland, he had one word for it: "Horseshit!" Then Steve graciously said I could select from and use any of the e-mails between he and Malik. I expected Steve to select the e-mails. He didn't. "You have carte blanche to use what you want," Steve continued. "I want this story told the right way." I selected 2008 and 2014 as the key years. From 2009 to 2013 there were more phone calls than e-mails. Steve graciously shared some of the phone messages. The e-mails demonstrate the enormous influence Rowland had upon the Oscar winning documentary. He has resisted until now telling his side of the story.

Of all the people who have talked with and approached Rodriguez, after **Searching For Sugar Man's** success, Rowland is the only one, outside of the Sugar Man's family, to play it straight. Steve doesn't tell Rodriguez he is the next big thing. He tells him the truth! That is a mantra for his personal relationship. He listens to Steve. He calls him from time to time. How much he follows his suggestions no one knows. But it is a solid friendship built on mutual respect.

Steve Rowland: "Rodriguez is the best songwriter, the best recording artist, the best person I have dealt with in the music business."

The Malik Bendjelloul e mails and Steve Talks to the Filmmaker About The Sugar Man

The constant flow of e-mails between Rowland and the filmmaker helped to focus and direct the documentary. Rowland's suggestions kept Bendjelloul's spirits high. The hundreds of skype calls and Steve's weekly opinions on the latest film clips were important to the documentaries progress. As Bendjelloul filmed, he sent Steve the rough cuts. Then they talked on the phone. There were also numerous e-mail suggestions on how to frame the story. Rowland believed it was a mystery that had to be explained slowly with compassion.

What did these e-mails do for **Searching For Sugar Man**? When Bendjelloul began e-mailing Rowland, it was on January 18, 2008 from SVT-National Swedish Television. Every indication was Malik wasn't sure he would continue the project. He had many reservations. Steve answered all of Malik's questions. He made it clear the obstacles to finishing the documentary could be overcome. Malik talked of completing a twenty to thirty minute film. Rowland convinced him a feature length documentary would tell the story with precision, detail and insight. He emphasized to Malik it must be a tribute to Sixto Rodriguez' brilliant writing and charismatic performing. Steve said the sharp contrast in Detroit's gritty streets with Cape Town's sunny climate were keys to the projects cinematic beauty.

Early on there were problems. Malik had reservations about the information Stephen "Sugar" Segerman presented. Malik loved the South African for his dedication to the Rodriguez story. He was concerned Segerman called himself "Sugar." He did so to identify with Rodriguez and to place himself deeper into the story than he deserved. This was a dangerous omen. Bendjelloul kept Segerman in the mix while privately concerned that the South African turned out to be much too much of the story. It was after all a Rodriguez biography. Segerman didn't seem to understand it was not about him. But, like Rowland, Bendjelloul suffered fools in silence. There were some positive accomplishments the South African brought to the documentary.

It is because of Segerman's pervasive influence Matt Sullivan and Light In The Attic reissued the two albums that made Rodriguez a cult star on the college and the Indie club circuit.

Rather than coming from total obscurity, as **Searching For Sugar Man** suggested, Rodriguez had cult star status in the U. S. and the London clubs while continuing to perform in South Africa and Australia. Segerman convinced Bendjelloul to leave these events out of the documentary. This was a smart decision as the mystery of the Sugar Man's demise, his eventual rediscovery and his path to stardom would have not appeared as mysterious if all the facts of his life were on the table.

Rodriguez constantly dealt with Segerman's overbearing behavior. The Sugar Man overcame the boorish behavior of his South African friend. Bendjelloul also ignored Segerman's incipient meddling. Since 2008 Rodriguez has distanced himself from Segerman. The series of London concert fiascos from 2005 to 2007 placed Rodriguez into a position where he had to get rid of Segerman. The Sugar Man watched, as his career slowly built, while Segerman's advice derailed his slow comeback. Over time the Sugar Man became so angry he wouldn't let Segerman backstage when he came to South Africa. In 2009 Segerman sat in the audience as the Sugar Man completed a triumphant South African tour.

Searching For Sugar Man does Rodriguez a disservice. How? It has too much of Segerman and too little of Rodriguez. But without Segerman there might not have been a documentary. That is the dual tragedy of this brilliant story.

When I contacted a South African record label executive, he said Segerman meant well. He also said he couldn't separate himself from the story. He thought he was the story. He was a great guy with a penchant for "extravagance and ego oriented manipulation," an RPM record executive commented. I wasn't sure what that meant. I nodded like I understood. I didn't. We agreed on one thing. Segerman was instrumental in developing the story.

There are five points to consider in Rowland's influence upon **Searching For Sugar Man**. These points suggest the reasons for Bendjelloul's eventual success. This material is collated from e-mails between Steve and Malik. The five points are taken from more than a hundred e-mails.

First: Steve helped Malik frame the story. Bendjelloul had completed a few promotional films. He had no idea how he was going to focus the film. He called Steve because he had a film background. "He wanted to know if he was doing the right thing," Rowland remarked. Steve told him to consider the mystery associated with the Sugar Man. "I said you have a great situation here, you told me about all of these conspiracy theories about him shooting himself. I would start it out with a blank screen with the very things you are telling me," Steve said. Rowland emphasized a sense of a dark and mysterious past made for audience appeal.

Steve Rowland: "I wrote out some suggestions and sent them to him as a way to approach the film. He called me a week later. He said: 'Thanks.' He was going to start the film with the trip up Chapman Peak with Segerman talking about how he discovered Rodriguez."

Second: Rowland was important for suggesting how and where to place the music. "When you finally put him on screen and the music behind him you need is like a flower awakening in the sun,"

Steve said. Bendjelloul used "Sandrevan Lullaby-Lifestyles" to make this point. Bendjelloul said his favorite Rodriguez song was "Cause." Rowland agreed. This led to the scene in the movie where Rowland comments on "Cause's" heart-breaking nature. It was a poignant moment in the documentary. Steve sitting in his house shook his head and talked about Rodriguez being fired two weeks before Christmas. The look of disappointment, frustration and resignation on Steve's face told it all. No one needed an explanation. The record business was a cruel mistress.

Third: Malik confided in Steve he was conflicted about framing his film. He was continually unsure how to present the documentary. This prompted Steve to create a way to begin the film. It was rather simple. A blank screen would come on and the mysteries of Sixto Rodriguez would be explained. It was a roadmap to viewing the documentary. The e-mails and skype calls acted as a sort of storyboard that examined every nook and cranny of Sixto Rodriguez's life and career.

Steve Rowland: "Malik called up on skype. He said: 'I want to play you what I have shot so far.' He wanted to know what I thought of it. He wasn't sure the best way to present it. He confided in me because I grew up in the business. He asked me certain things. I gave him my opinion. He asked me: 'What do you think is the best way to present the story?' I told him."

Rowland in e-mails and phone conversations kept Bendjelloul's spirits alive. How? He made suggestions on securing funding. The main question was how to bring the documentary into the commercial mainstream? Bendjelloul asked Steve many questions about the film business. When Steve asked why the continual questions on the film business? Malik said: "You were brought up in the film business and you know it inside out."

Steve Rowland: "He also talked to my girl friend, Judy Lewis, who was in a Broadway play. She produced an afternoon television show. Her mother was Loretta Young and her father Clark Gable. She was born in the business and pursued an extremely successful career as an actress-producer. Malik listened to her. She loved the story."

Steve Rowland: "She said to Malik on skype, 'Oh I love this, it is Oscar material.' She was positive that the documentary would be a hit."

At the time Rowland and Lewis were preparing to marry. She had been Steve's high school sweetheart. She died of cancer in 2011.

Fourth: "I told Malik how I would present the documentary," Steve said. When Rowland was asked to verify a fact, the identity of a person or what he thought the sequence was in the story, he gave Bendjelloul his honest opinion. He never sugar coated the facts. "I told Malik whatever I say it is only my opinion," Steve said. When I talked to South African record executives, some promoters and a few club owners, they complained Segerman slanted the story. He saw himself as the hero. Rowland in sharp contrast simply told the truth.

Fifth: "Malik was fortunate that Simon Chinn came in as the overall producer," Rowland said. Steve reminded Bendjelloul the people around him had agendas. "I told him to watch for those people who suddenly appear from under a rock. This is what destroys many young filmmakers." Malik survived to win an Oscar. "Malik was a very talented and sensitive guy, give him the credit," Rowland concluded.

After **Searching For Sugar Man** was completed Rowland and Bendjelloul explored the idea of a creative partnership. As late as 2013 they talked in New York with Manny Elias and Richard Niles, who Rowland brought to the Rodriguez shows, about a proposed television series.

Steve Rowland: "He showed interest in my television series. I was well along with the proposed series, Malik had my book, and I told him when you are finished with this I am trying to develop a television series based on my book **Hollywood Heat**. I was hoping we could collaborate."

It was Bendjelloul's untimely death that ended this potential partnership. But to the end Steve was in touch. He was a constant source of and support for the young filmmaker.

The Road to e-mailing Steve Rowland: How He Became a Quiet Co-Collaborator

One day when I was working with Steve Rowland, I noticed as he opened a computer file he had an entire section devoted to e-mails from Malik Bendjelloul. The e-mails began in January 2008, and they didn't conclude until shortly before Malik's tragic suicide. These e-mails provide a road map to how Bendjelloul created, filmed and financed the documentary. They also suggest Rowland's input in the project.

As Malik began his initial full-length feature, he was unusually well prepared. While working in Swedish television he learned a great deal about animation. In **Searching For Sugar Man** animation was not only effective in highlighting Rodriguez' career, it was cost effective. He also learned the importance of pacing and placing his subject into a favorable context.

Malik Bendjelloul: "I came to realize that a good story is irresistible in a way that few other things can be." What this translates to is Rodriguez didn't want to cooperate. That was a good thing. Malik reasoned too much of the Sugar Man would doom the documentary. He needed to remain an elusive, mysterious, romantic figure. His talking appearance in the documentary where he drinks a glass of water displays his calm demeanor, shy nature and regal bearing. It is also a display of why he was reticent to participate in the film.

Malik Bendjelloul: "The searching became an additional part of work in itself." Malik learned the Sugar Man's tale from reading a London newspaper. Then he went to Cape Town to talk with Stephen

"Sugar" Segerman. Once again Segerman uses myth to overcome reality. He erroneously suggests he told Bendjelloul the Sugar Man's story as he wandered into Mabu Vinyl.

The time line for the documentaries early preparation began in 2005 when Bendjelloul read Alexis Petridis' article on Rodriguez. As he read Petridis,' "The Singer Who Came Back From The Dead," in the **London Guardian**, October 5, 2005, Bendjelloul discovered the story of a lifetime. Here is one of many myths Segerman perpetuated. He stated he told Bendjelloul the Rodriguez' story in depth. The reality is that after reading Petridis' article Bendjelloul knew a great deal about the Sugar Man. He recognized the bankable nature of the musical tale. Malik quickly visited Cape Town walking into Mabu Vinyl to make Segerman's acquaintance. He told close friends initially Segerman put him off. He warmed to him when the bellicose Cape Town Rodriguez fan made it known he wanted the Sugar Man's legacy on film. Bendjelloul agreed.

Rowland urged Bendjelloul to look at what he termed the cinematic quality of the story. When Steve talked about the television series he was working on concerning Hollywood in the 1950s, he impressed Bendjelloul with small items such as how Detroit buildings would appear on film. When Malik visited the Motor City, he skyped Rowland about the unique landscape. He had never seen anything like it. Detroit looked like a war zone. It was the perfect compliment to Cape Town's beauty.

Bendjelloul had a great deal of experience in Swedish television. He was adept at urban scenes that evoked a mysterious aura. But he had concerns. He was uncertain how to make a feature film. By Christmas 2007 he had talked with and lived with Stephen "Sugar" Segerman. He was wary of Segerman's continual attempts to frame the story. But Bendjelloul needed Segerman.

When Bendjelloul e-mailed Segerman on September 15, 2006, he discovered Matt Sullivan from Light In The Attic had been in touch seven months earlier looking to release the Sugar Man's albums. There were a number of people interested in Rodriguez. There were other filmmakers that saw this beautiful story. It had box office gold written all over it. The Rodriguez family declined a number of previous offers.

Other Filmmakers Looking at Sixto Rodriguez

One of the ironies of the Sixto Rodriguez story was the interest of filmmakers prior to Bendjelloul's film. A Canadian filmmaker, Alan Zweig, looked at the U. K.'s obsessive record collectors. Zweig's 2000 documentary "Vinyl" highlights the nerdy and obsessive record collectors. He calls them the "wax nerds." "They are pictured as lonely people with little purpose in life. From this documentary, Zweig discovered the Rodriguez story. In 2003 Australian TV highlighted a grouchy collector, Joe Bussard, whose goal was to find every obscure blues country, hillbilly, blues 78s and any other form of roots music. This had nothing to do with the Sugar Man, but Bussard's story interested documentary filmmakers.

A young Malik Bendjelloul discovered the world of obscure, rare and collectible records through the Zweig documentary. His interest was piqued. When Malik heard the Sixto Rodriguez story he flashed back on not just the records but also the independent record store. The geeks living in their parent's basement had an impact upon the fledgling Swedish filmmaker.

In 2008 a documentary, "I Need That Record," appeared as Malik began his film. This film dealt with the decline and possible end of the independent record store. A brief section of the video alluded to obscure artists piquing Bendjelloul's interest. The record collector's obsession prompted Bendjelloul to remember how those who listened to **Cold Fact** described it as a virtual religious experience.

While this film dealt with the disappearing hip, Indie record store, it identified a possible audience for **Searching For Sugar Man**. This is the only rock music film featuring comments from radical political philosopher Noam Chomsky. He remarks unrestrained corporate capitalism is killing the small record shop. These films set the stage for what Malik Bendjelloul was working toward. How many of these documentaries he viewed is unknown. What is known is he was familiar with Alan Zweig's work. Bendjelloul also used footage from the South African hour-long television show "Dead Men Don't Tour" in **Searching For Sugar Man**.

That TV show "Dead Men Don't Tour" was the last minute contribution of a musician playing behind the Sugar Man. Her name was Tonia Selley. She realized this history moment would be lost. She quickly put together a professional crew to film the 1998 shows. On You Tube these films provide a marvelous insight into Rodriguez' mesmerizing South African shows. When the hour-long film "Dead Men Don't Tour" appeared on South African television it was a hit. The filmmakers looked at this television special hoping to persuade Rodriguez to cooperate in a documentary. This overture fell upon deaf ears.

Tonia Selley is a hidden factor in **Searching For Sugar Man**. She is shown as a back up musician on the 1998 South African tour. She was a former punk musician. But she is also a skillful film editor. She worked on the 2008 Indie South African film **Visa/Vie**. It is a poignant story of a French-Moroccan émigré working illegally in Cape Town. Rumor has it she provided Bendjelloul with tips on how to proceed with the Rodriguez story.

Selley remains a multi talented performer. A 2011 You Tube video of Selley displays her unique talent performing "How Much" with Willem Moller on guitar as she continues her musical journey. The point is a number of Independent filmmakers and musicians surrounded Bendjelloul as he worked on his documentary.

The Flood of Offers After Searching for Sugar Man, 2012

Since 2012 the flood of projects presented to the Sugar Man attest to his commercial appeal. Johnny Depp inquired about optioning the story for a Hollywood film. Depp would star as the Sugar Man. Alex Baldwin had interest in pursuing a television series. Phil Schaaf, who directed the award winning documentary **Don't Quit: The Joe Roth Story**, approached Rodriguez with a Broadway musical. Hollywood director Phillip Noyce was filming a feature film, **Mary And Martha**, with Hillary Swank in South Africa in 2013, when he dropped into Mabu Vinyl. He asked Segerman to meet Rodriguez and his family. The family turned down these offers.

What is the most intriguing of these commercial projects? The most appealing one is a script from a well-known San Francisco writer with a series of options including Broadway destined music in the mold of Hamilton. There is also an urban Opera built on Rodriguez' songs. It remains a unique story. When international television came calling, they proposed shows on his life, his music and his impact upon the industry. They were turned down. A number of movie studios, scriptwriters and high level stars, like Tom Cruise, have approached the Rodriguez family. Why would they turn down these proposals? The answer is a simple one. He is not concerned with monetary rewards. His legacy is intact with two albums and an Oscar winning documentary. Privacy triumphs corporate capitalism.

Rodriguez' Existentialism and Its Impact

Rodriguez is first and foremost an existentialist. What did the Rodriguez family conclude concerning Bendjelloul? They saw honesty, commitment, integrity and an angelic appearance. One conclusion is from 2008 onward Rodriguez watched closely as the documentary progressed toward completion.

Like everyone the Sugar Man came to admire and respect Bendjelloul. As he watched the young filmmaker work, he had a sense of his mission. The documentaries planning stages built slowly, faltered and burst into a commercial phenomenon. It is a complicated story set in different stages. Rowland was there at every interval.

How does Rodriguez' existentialism impact the story? As a creative artist Rodriguez operates in a fluctuating world of security and insecurity. The result is isolation, a constant need for privacy and a suspicion of all things surrounding his creative endeavors. The mood of the Sugar Man's life is dictated by the grim reality that is Detroit. He is a natural storyteller. Without the support and assistance of his daughter, Regan, his stories might have remained on the kitchen table in his Avery Street home. Now the world listens to his poetic images. His daughters encourage his endeavors in various ways. But it is Regan who is at the forefront of this creativity. Her use of the Internet and the careful publicity for his songwriting and performing created the path to international stardom. She is the hero bringing her father to the musical-literary forefront.

The Early Stages of Planning: Regan is the Hero

In 2007 the planning stages for **Searching For Sugar Man** brought the story into a rough form. The road to production began unevenly. By June 2007 Malik was back in Sweden. He wrote Segerman and talked of his plans for making a feature documentary. Prior to that time, he was thinking of a short feature. The story had too many twists and too many turns. He saw the Oscar possibilities. No one said anything about a Hollywood Oscar. The first person to do so was Steve Rowland. In January 2008 he encouraged Bendjelloul to think along Oscar lines. It was a boost to his waning confidence. He had limited funding. Rowland suggested other funding options. They talked for more than two years about funding.

I asked Steve: "Weren't you a key factor in funding?"

Steve replied angrily: "How many times have I told you 'No.' What is it about 'No' you don't understand? I didn't know Simon Chinn. I didn't talk to Simon Chinn. I didn't meet him until **Searching For Sugar Man** became a box office success." I guess I did understand. I still think Steve had more impact on funding than he recalls. The funding Malik received in Sweden benefitted from Rowland's knowledge. Swedish sources told me Rowland educated Malik on his approach to the money people.

Bendjelloul received funding from Swedish prime time television. But a host of obstacles emerged. This is where Steve Rowland's influence is paramount. From January 2008 through December 2011, when the final preparation was completed for the Sundance Film Festival, Rowland and Bendjelloul were in touch weekly. A sample of hundreds of e-mails is included to demonstrate why Rowland was the final cog in the **Searching For Sugar Man** production team.

Steve doesn't take credit for funding. He should. His suggestions paved the way through the fiscal jungle and alerted the money people to Rodriguez' commercial potential.

Steve Rowland: "Malik had a great film, I did everything I could to help him focus it and bring in the right feeling. I am so proud of him. All credit to Malik."

Rodriguez was shy. His daughters were in charge. He was skeptical of the project. Bendjelloul leaned on Rowland for ways to frame the story. He also asked Steve for suggestions to influence the Rodriguez family. It would take four years of backbreaking production work, a constant search for funds and, at times, frustrating dealings with Rodriguez and his family to complete the film.

Malik had an irresistible story line. The problem was not Malik Bendjelloul. He had a script. He had a vision. He had a commercial window into the bankrupt, corrupt world of rock and roll music. The forgotten, ill treated singer from Detroit, who was a major star in South Africa and Australia, was too good a story to ignore. If only he could convince Sixto Rodriguez. Bendjelloul didn't need to, as the Sugar Man's youngest daughter, Regan, pushed the creative documentary forward toward an Oscar.

Regan Rodriguez, despite her youth, shared Bendjelloul's artistic vision. They grew very close during the filming. She was the hero keeping the family in the mix. This was a difficult task. Her shy and talented father had little interest in a cinematic masterpiece on his life. He had heard the story of his talent too many times. He was now entering his golden years. He was determined to enjoy what time he had left. Stardom was not an option.

The Problem is Sixto Rodriguez: Shy and Talented

Before he approached the family, Bendjelloul looked long and hard at the Sugar Man's story. He realized Rodriguez was shy, private, paranoid and suspicious of anyone in the entertainment field. He was a mysterious figure somewhat removed from a traditional middle class lifestyle. A young kid from Sweden would have little success convincing Rodriguez to grace a documentary that no one would view.

But Malik had a plan. He was a writer. Rodriguez was a writer. For more than a month, Bendjelloul crafted one copy after another of the same letter. According to a close friend, at SVT TV in Stockholm, Malik joked he was writing a letter that felt like a novel. But he was sure of himself. The story moved him.

In his letter Malik pointed out he was a professional working for Swedish television. He remarked he had been in South Africa interviewing and talking to Stephen "Sugar" Segerman. Malik didn't realize that revelation was one that almost prompted the family to ban him from their Avery Street residence. They didn't! He touched a chord with Regan. She saw what the story would do for her father's long dormant career.

Why did the Rodriguez family consider the letter? The answer is a simple one. The word "Australia." When Malik sent the letter he mentioned Rodriguez' Australian popularity. This piqued Regan Rodriguez' curiosity. She saw the audience down under as a permanent one. Regan wrote to Malik and let him know the family would be on board for the proposed documentary. She had her reservations. She didn't share those with Bendjelloul. Her father had been disappointed too many times. She didn't want him hurt once again. The balancing act to completing **Searching For Sugar Man** was navigated with precision by Regan.

Why Stephen "Sugar" Segerman Skewed the Documentary Before it was Filmed

In the early stages of planning Stephen "Sugar" Segerman recognized the hostility and hatred journalists have concerning music moguls. He urged Malik to ask Clarence Avant tough questions and exploit the evils of the music industry. Why is this important?

Segerman wanted drama. Even if the drama was contrary to the facts. In the end it was detrimental to the documentary. Segerman viewed it as a tension filled atmosphere-drawing people to the film. He had read about the American Congressional hearings into payola. He didn't understand Dick Clark's alleged criminal duplication and the villains in the music industry were too sophisticated for his comprehension. Segerman didn't understand American rock and roll history and this caused him to miscast the Sugar Man in most scenarios. He is an impressionistic observer who speaks before he knows a subject.

He was well aware of the South African ban on suggestive lyrics prior to the end of apartheid. He thought he was a brilliant music historian. He saw Avant as the devil. That was a mistake. He torpedoed much of the story.

What was wrong with Segerman's approach? He knew that Avant paid for the two Sussex albums. The former Sussex Record chief also funded two Rodriguez recording sessions with Mike Theodore after his albums faltered commercially. Segerman knew Avant paid for the recording of the three songs Light In The Attic included on **Coming From Reality**. Segerman did everything in his power to disparage Avant. That is one of the tragedies of the Rodriguez story.

There was nothing malevolent in Segerman's attitude. He wanted the best for Rodriguez. He urged Bendjelloul to continue to rant and rave about lost money. He did. This was to the detriment of Clarence Avant one of most respected figures in the music industry. Avant was ambushed on camera.

In their book Craig Bartholomew-Strydom and Stephen "Sugar" Segerman write: "Sugar suggested Malik not ask Avant directly about any missing royalties." (p.252) There is no doubt this is not what happened. Bendjelloul seemed tasked to find the lost sums of money. What neither Bendjelloul or Segerman realized is that the pressing plants in South Africa sent their product to a distributor and then the money trail ended. There appeared to be no records of albums sold. No one received a royalty statement. It was the record business in the early 1970s and the artist was told to make his or her money in concert. The artist's simply weren't paid. This infuriated the South African. Segerman intensified the royalty question without evidence or knowledge of the ways of the industry. He was a well-meaning amateur who in time would hurt Rodriguez' comeback career.

Segerman incited everyone he met concerning Rodriguez' royalties. He was crazed to have the Sugar Man treated fairly. Somewhere in this scenario there needed to be an adult. That individual turned out to be Regan Rodriguez. She is the hero in the early stages of **Searching For Sugar Man**. She would continue to be that hero. Until the documentary was completed, Regan was there every step of the way. Her father would not be disappointed this time.

Why is Regan Rodriguez the Hero in Searching for Sugar Man?

Regan Rodriguez facilitated the completion of **Searching For Sugar Man**. When Malik sent her a letter proposing the documentary, she responded enthusiastically. This is where Rowland comes in. He was a silent adviser who quietly showed Malik how to approach the family, frame the documentary, place the music and overcome the thorny issue of how to deal with privacy concerns. Steve also explained how to pitch the product to industry money people. Rowland had a calming influence upon Bendjelloul. He was like a father that had an encyclopedic knowledge of the business. Steve had a secret weapon. The Sugar Man was a long time political advocate. Malik caught on and he became a quick study in American politics. Soon Bendjelloul and Rodriguez discussed politics. That opened the door to the documentary.

When Rowland and Rodriguez worked on **Coming From Reality**, they often talked politics. Rowland let Bendjelloul know the importance of activist politics. This helped break down barriers. Rodriguez' reticence about appearing in **Searching For Sugar Man** eventually evaporated and he was on board.

Thanks to Steve Rowland, Bendjelloul discovered the importance of the 1998 South African television show Tonia Selley directed, "Dead Men Don't Tour." At the same time he was in touch with Craig Bartholomew-Strydom who led Malik to Mark "Marty" Rathbun's half hour radio show on CBC Canada. This program was an early blueprint for the documentary. When the Rathbun show aired, it featured interviews with Bartholomew-Strydom. There was a sense the Sugar Man's story could be told. But a feature documentary was not on the radar. It would be in a few years.

What was the Rathbun show? Mark Rathbun, a free lance Canadian journalist, was one of the early people interested in a Sixto Rodriguez documentary. It was 2008 when Rathbun met

Craig Bartholomew-Strydom. He was transfixed with the Sugar Man's story. He produced a half hour radio show on Rodriguez' life and music. It didn't go anywhere, but the implication was clear. It was a once in a generation tale of redemption. It would take a professional to bring it to the general public. Bendjelloul was that professional.

What is important about the Rathbun radio show? It was his unadulterated praise for Rodriguez. In 2013 he wrote: "If you have not already seen the Oscar winning documentary on this extraordinary fellow, **Searching For Sugar Man**, I highly recommend it. You might learn a little something about walking the walk and the Tao." Poetic and spot on.

Rathbun was able to corral Craig Bartholomew-Strydom and bring him into the studio. The result was not only Canadian interest in the Sugar Man but other filmmakers looked at the story. The Rodriguez family held firm. Bendjelloul was the only one they let in the family fold. That turned out to be a smart decision.

After Rodriguez and his family turned down the other interested filmmakers they agreed, if somewhat reluctantly, to work with Malik Bendjelloul. One of the documentary filmmakers first tasks was to find Steve Rowland. The rest is history. Rowland does not like taking any credit for his role in **Searching For Sugar Man**. Much of what I have written about his advice to and influence upon Bendjelloul, he disagrees with but those close to the story confirm my conclusions. By examining the e-mails between Rowland and Bendjelloul they provide a window into Malik's creative genius. "All credit goes to Malik," Steve Rowland said.

The early e-mails between Rowland and Bendjelloul are a unique window into a creative partnership. Both are shy. Both are private. Both are hard working. Both have a quirky, unique creative bent. They quickly formed a common bond around the Sugar Man's story.

The Rowland-Bemdjelloul 2008 e-mails and Searching for Sugar Man: What is the Influence?

January 4, 2008
Dear Steve,

My name is Malik Bendjelloul and I'm a Swedish documentary filmmaker. We are working on a documentary film about Rodriguez and would very much like to make an interview with you. Later this spring we're going to travel all over the world to meet all the people involved in the story, and your part is of course very, very interesting. Would you have time to meet with me?

Yours sincerely
Malik Bendjelloul
_________________January 18, 2008
SVT - National Swedish Television
Oxenstiernsgatan 26
105 10 Stockholm
Sweden
phone + 46 73 817 92 95

• • •

Steve Rowland: "I said absolutely if it is about Rodriguez. Then I saw a phone number and I called and e-mailed him. I was really excited someone wanted to do something on Rodriguez. I didn't know about the conspiracy theories, his popularity in South Africa and his rising career."

The following e-mails are a selection from more than two hundred I was able to read. They tell the story of a friendship and how Malik and Steve worked daily to bring Rodriguez into the musical mainstream. The e-mails tell one not only of their friendship but how and why **Searching For Sugar Man** came together as an Oscar winning documentary.

From: Malik Bendjelloul <malik.bendjelloul@svt.se>
Subject: Sv: Re: Rodriguez documentary
Date: January 19, 2008 at 10:46:37 AM PST
To: Steve Rowland <stever@familydogg.com>

Dear Steve,

Thank you so much! We're very grateful!

We'll keep in touch concerning if London or Palm Springs would be the best location. Do you by any chance have any photos from the Rodriguez sessions or know anyone who might have?

Really looking forward to meet you!

All the best!
Malik

Rowland reached into his archives and put together a group of Rodriguez' pictures demonstrating the mystery and inherent star power of the long forgotten singer-songwriter.

Dear Malik—

Thank you for contacting me regarding Rodriguez.

I most definitely would be more than happy to participate in helping you with your proposed documentary. I'll give you whatever time you need.

I will be in London in May, but I'm not sure of the exact dates as yet.

I live in Palm Springs, California. You can contact me on: 001-760-327—.

I'll look forward to hearing from you.

Regards,

Steve Rowland

On Feb 26, 2008, at 2:06 PM, Malik Bendjelloul wrote:

> >>
> >>
> >> Hi Steve!
> >>
> >> Hope you're very good!
> >>
> >> The Rodriguez documentary is evolving and we now got some dates
> >> that we would like to check with you. We're planning to be in

> >> California in the beginning of May and wonder if it would be a
> >> good idea to come to Palm Springs somewhere around the 7 and 8 of
> >> May to meet you. Or is that when you're in London?
> >>
> >>
> >> All the best!
> >> Malik

As they e-mailed and talked on skype, Steve was asked numerous questions. Bendjelloul's primary questions centered on financing as he continually talked with Rowland about the necessity of convincing the money people. He had the story. He had filmed it. Without fiscal support, travel funds, money for the editing process and the final pitch for the documentary it would have been an impossible task.

The First Steps in Securing Financing for Searching for Sugar Man

In February 2008 the first steps to secure financial backing for **Searching For Sugar Man** took place when Stockholm based producer Hjalmar Palmgren contacted Stockholm's Hysteria Films. He asked if they had received the script. They had! There was good news! Malla Grapengiesser, a producer, read the script and she liked it. Hysteria signed on as a co-producer. Then she heard Rodriguez' albums. She loved the music. Hysteria Films was on board as the first producer for **Searching For Sugar Man**.

For much of February and March 2008 Bendjelloul planned the documentary. He was ready to begin filming. He wrote to Steve and later skyped him on the opening scenes. They spent an inordinate amount of time setting the opening scenes. The planning was over, the script was in embryo development and Bendjelloul and Camille Skagerstrom were ready to begin filming in Cape Town.

> >>

On Apr 5, 2008, at 8:41 AM, Malik Bendjelloul wrote:

> >> Dear Steve,
> >>
> >> On Monday we'll fly to Cape Town to start shooting the Rodriguez
> >> documentary. We'll be filming for a couple of weeks and the ideal
> >> would be to meet you on Monday May 5 (exactly one month from
> >> today!). Would that work out with you? We are very much looking
> >> forward to meet you!
> >>
> >> All the best
> >> Malik

For the next month as Rowland and Bendjelloul e-mailed and frequently skyped to discuss the early filming, they talked about a wide variety of subjects. The one thing they had in common was to set the documentaries tone so it treated Rodriguez as a brilliant artist. Respect for the man was a subtheme.

As the daily rushes were sent to Rowland, he was ecstatic. The Swedish kid was a pro. Steve made notes and dissected the early filming. He saw the story line unfolding with the sense of drama that was the mystery surrounding Sixto Rodriguez.

Steve loved Camilla Skagerstrom's cinematography. He encouraged Malik to film as much as possible with her. Malik said he would, but he did point out she was on loan. Malik filmed some of the scenes in Searching For Sugar Man before Skagerstrom landed in South

Africa. This was because of a lack of funding. When Skagerstrom arrived in Cape Town in the middle of April 2008, Malik had shot some exterior scenes. They quickly redid the earlier scenes.

When Malik set up the initial filming, he asked Steve for daily input. Rowland suggested they divide the time up with at least two weeks in Cape Town and the same amount in Detroit. Malik agreed. He also set up his Palm Springs visit.

> >>
> >>On Apr 6, 2008, at 11:53 PM, Malik Bendjelloul wrote:
> >> Perfect! That's great! Thanks a lot!
> >>
> >> We'll land in Palm Springs 1 am - in the middle of the night, - on
> >> May 5 and the flight to Detroit, to met Rodriguez, departs 4 pm on
> >> May 6. So maybe like 1 pm on May 5 would be ideal...?
> >>
> >> It's going to be a very cinematic film so the first thing we would
> >> like to find is a really nice location for the interview.
> >> Something visually interesting. Do you know any good place?
> >>
> >> How much time do you think you'll have to spend with us?
> >>
> >> We're a small crew, just two persons, me and Camilla, the girl who
> >> shoots the film.
> >>
> >> And by the way, do you know any hotels or bed & breakfasts close

> >> to you where you think it would be a good place to stay?
> >>
> >> All the best!
> >> Malik

When Steve researched Skagerstrom's cinematography, he realized she was a prize-winning talent. He told Bendjelloul this boded well for the documentaries future.

Steve Rowland: "She was terrific. I said come to my house we can do it here. I am right beneath the mountains." Bendjelloul was intrigued by Palm Springs. When he saw Steve's house, Malik said: "This is perfect." He couldn't believe the beauty of the physical setting as the sun bounced off the mountains, the palm trees shimmered in the light wind and the swimming pools and golf courses seemed to go on forever. Malik made the decision to feature Rowland and Palm Springs early in the documentary. The sheer physical beauty of the area combined with Rowland's eloquent memory of Rodriguez caught the viewer's attention. It was a cathartic moment in the documentary.

Early Rushes for Searching for Sugar Man

On April 8, 2008 Malik Bendjelloul arrived in Cape Town to begin shooting the documentary. For the next four months Malik endured Stephen "Sugar" Segerman's constant suggestions. As filming began there was a mild buzz for the Light In The Attic re-release of **Cold Fact**. It sold sell from the day it was released. That day didn't take place until August 18, 2008, but LITA sent out early promotional copies to key journalists. The early reviews prompted Bendjelloul to intensify his work on the documentary. The **Cold Fact** release garnered a praiseworthy London press.

Matt Sullivan believed in **Cold Fact**. He had never heard such sterling songwriting and he hatched a plan to continue to blitz the Indie crowd on Rodriguez' coming stardom.

On August 8, 2008 a review by Graeme Thomson, in the **London Guardian**, stated: "The career of Sixto Rodriguez has until now amounted to somewhat less than a scrawled footnote in music history." Thomson went on to praise the album and predict big things for the Sugar Man. The London Rodriguez cult was in its early stages. Malik read the review in the **London Guardian**. The story continued to intrigue Malik. How to frame it? That was the question. He continually asked Steve his opinion on framing.

Steve Rowland: "Malik spoke to me on numerous occasions. He asked for my thoughts on the direction of the film. I said in my opinion this is how I would see the film proceed."

The commercial buzz over the re-release of **Cold Fact** inspired Malik to work at breakneck speed. Malik saw in London the crescendo of positive reviews in the usually cranky London press. As he worked from morning to late in the night, he needed constant input into what he was doing. This led to daily skype calls with Rowland. It was a time of coming together for the documentary.

For the next month, Malik and Steve talked about the direction of the documentary. They frequently spoke of the importance of the Sugar Man's mystery. They discussed his integrity, honesty and Rodriguez' achievements. Steve was ecstatic working with Bendjelloul. Eventually, Malik had seven weeks of film. Now came the problem of focusing the material.

Rowland re-connected with Rodriguez. He wrote Malik concerning how happy he was to be back in touch with the Sugar Man. Steve quickly thanked Malik.

> >>June1, 2008, at 11:58 AM, Malik Bendjelloul wrote:

Hi Steve!

> >>

> >> Back in Stockholm after seven weeks on the road!

> >>

> >> It was really truly amazing to meet you! You were extremely kind
> >> and a delight in front of the camera. One of the best interviews
> >> in a collection of fifteen, all very good interviews. I showed
> >> Rodriguez some of the interviews, including yours, and he was
> >> really moved, the last night we were in Detroit he brought all his
> >> family over, his ex-wife and children and grand children and he
> >> showed the interviews to them. They never heard those things about
> >> him, and they were sometimes almost brought into tears in emotion.
> >> He has a lot of new songs written, songs as good as the old stuff,
> >> I heard some small excerpts, and I'm sure that if we kindly ask
> >> him he would be prepared to go into a studio again....
> >>
> >> I'm now going to edit together a small trailer of the material and
> >> on July 9 I'll go to Italy, to a pitch forum, and meet some money-
> >> guys. Many people I've spoken to has said like, well, if the film
> >> doesn't win an Oscar it's surely not because the story isn't good
> >> enough. It's really true, it's one of the greatest stories in rock
> >> history.

> >>
> >> Just one question; when did you say you were going to go to
> >> England? We are going to England anyway to interview a guy called
> >> John Samson who released a fictional book of twelve short stories
> >> inspired by each of the songs on Cold Fact and just thought that
> >> maybe we should do some shooting with you at the place where
> >> Coming from Reality was recorded. Do you know if it still exists?
> >> You said it used to be a swimming hall, didn't you?
> >> How is everything going with the book? Good I hope!!
> >>
> >> All the best
> >> Malik

From: stever@familydogg.com
> >> Subject: Re: Stockholm calling!
> >> Date: Tue, 3 Jun 2008 08:26:03 -0700
> >> To: malikbendjelloul@hotmail.com
> >>
> >> Dear Malik—
> >>
> >> Once again thank you for the compliments on my interview. I really
> >> appreciate it.
> >>
> >> It was terrific speaking with Rodriguez after all these years. He
> >> sounded exactly as he did all those years ago.

> >> I'm really happy to hear that at last he is about to attain the
> >> success that he deserves. He is truly a wonderfully talented man.
> >> I hope that his success spreads throughout the entire world. I
> >> wish him all the best.
> >>
> >> I will be landing in England on July 1st and staying through until
> >> the first or second week in August. I'll be staying with my ex and
> >> her family in Barons Court, London. That is very near Hammersmith.
> >> You'll be able to contact me on; 0207-381—— (Sally Farmiloe's
> >> home phone) 07956-564—(my mobile).
> >>
> >> I'll look forward to hearing from you while I'm in London. Please
> >> do get in touch.
> >> I'll also have my computer with me. You have my e-mail.
> >>
> >> I wish you good luck with the moneymen. I can't see how you can
> >> fail in raising the money needed to make a sensational film.
> >>
> >> All the very best to you and Camilla.
> >>
> >> Kindest Regards,
> >>
> >> Steve

When he arranged for the first session to film Steve Rowland, Bendjelloul had Oscar aspirations. Steve encouraged this type of thinking. It seemed premature. It wasn't. Since he knew very little about Palm Springs, Bendjelloul depended upon Rowland for a perspective. When Malik arrived at Rowland's home, it was a spectacular Palm Springs day. The California sun was setting perfectly in the sky framed by the beautiful mountains and the shimmering heat endemic to Palm Springs. This prompted the cinematographer to comment on the unique landscape. Camilla Skagerstrom's camera caught the local beauty as she shot the stylish people, the magnificent homes and the cultural artifacts unique to the California desert. Palm Springs was once the home to Frank Sinatra and the Rat Pack. It had a mystique that transfixed the Swedes.

Filming Steve Rowland in Palm Springs

Palm Springs was an inspiration for Bendjelloul. He spent hours talking to Steve about the landscape, the contrasts with Cape Town and Detroit, and he envisioned an atmospheric aspect to the documentary. Bendjelloul accomplished a great deal in Palm Springs. Now it was time for Malik to return home for the laborious editing process.

When Steve and Malik made plans to meet for the original filming they were both busy. This led to an avalanche of e-mail's. Malik was busy planning the film schedule. He also worked side jobs to keep alive financially. Steve was busy preparing to return to London for the launch of his book **Hollywood Heat**.

Malik skyped Steve and said he loved the scenes he shot in Palm Springs. He wanted to shoot more of the local glamour, and they set up a time for Steve to do a second filming. It was in this filming that Malik shot Steve opening the gate and taking out the early Rodriguez pictures that so dramatically highlighted the Sugar Man's mystery.

Steve Rowland: "I didn't know Malik was showing the rushes for **Searching Man** to the family. It was great. He showed it to the money men and I knew he would get backers."

Rowland advised Bendjelloul on how to cope with the English. Steve didn't want to suggest the English often were privileged and pompous. He had heard the word "cred" from not only other producers, but from the music papers who supposedly employed knowledgeable music critics. How did Rowland react to this inane and disrespectful commentary?

Steve "I just ignored it. I know who I am."

I asked Steve: "When you talked with Malik did you recommend that he approach Simon Chinn as a producer because of his success with "Man On Wire?"

Steve Rowland: "We never talked about Simon Chinn. I didn't mention it. I knew his brother in London when he had the rock group the Sweet. But Malik and I talked general finance. I didn't meet and talk to Simon until **Searching For Sugar Man's** publicity brought me to Los Angeles. We had a nice talk."

As Rowland advised Bendjelloul on how to place Rodriguez' music in the documentary, he was glad to be away from London. He was tired of the hip, trendy, phony attitudes and the over use of the word "cred." Steve had credibility in a wall full of gold and platinum records in his Palm Springs home. He had over a dozen movie posters hanging in his home with his name front and center. Malik was impressed. Steve said very little about his acting career. That was behind him. Bendjelloul Googled his films and they spent time talking about how one makes a movie.

There were so many times that trendy music people said he had little credibility. Rowland could barely stand to hear the four-letter word they used-"cred." Steve suggested to Malik how to navigate the U. K. entertainment world. He told Malik whether you were talking to musicians or film people, you had to know the terrain. Steve explained it in detail. Bendjelloul listened intently. He had no trouble negotiating with the London based fiscal moguls.

> >>
On Jun 12, 2008, at 11:58 AM, Malik Bendjelloul wrote:
> >>
> >> Dear Steve,
> >>
> >> Perfect. I understand it's impossible to know already now, we'll
> >> hope everything will work out.
> >>
> >> The project is going just wonderful. It's such a pleasure to work
> >> with, the story is really one of the greatest stories I heard in
> >> my life and everyone in the film are so helpful and kind and
> >> really want to tell the story. It's seems like Rodriguez have put
> >> eternal, sweet memories in everyone he ever worked with. Mike
> >> Theodore said that he didn't think it was as good as Dylan. It was
> >> better.
> >> And also - so far it seems like it will be quite easy to get it
> >> financed, it's really one of those stories that are too good to be
> >> true, and people seem to understand that.

> >>
> >> I completely missed that you were instrumental in discovering and
> >> signing The Cure! Good job!!!
> >>
> >> All the best
> >> Malik

Malik skyped Steve and they talked at length about other musicians. Then the conversation invariably centered on the styles of music that were commercial and how to produce a hit. Malik applied this information to the documentary. Malik was educating himself beyond Rodriguez' music.

From: stever@familydogg.com
Subject: Re: Stockholm calling!
Date: Thu, 12 Jun 2008 10:25:41 -0700
To: malikbendjelloul@hotmail.com

Dear Malik—

Thanks for the compliments regarding the book. However, I must tell you that "Hollywood Heat" is written in an entirely different style. Those stories on my website are, for the most part copies from my original fan magazine columns that appeared in the late fifties. I've had some of these stories printed in my book as they originally appeared at the time. There is some similarity in style, however. Adding the fan magazine stories give the book more credibility.

At the moment the days you've picked are OK. I have to see the lay of the land when I get to London. I have no idea at this time what my schedule will be, but I'm sure that it can all be organized to fit everything in.

By the way, how are things going with the project?

Regards & cheers,

Steve
> >>
On Jul 19, 2008, at 8:48 AM, Malik Bendjelloul wrote:
> >>
> >> Dear Steve,
> >>
> >> Hope you're well!
> >>
> >> I just talked to Regan, Rodriguez' daughter. Next Saturday, July
> >> 26, Rodriguez will do his first gig ever in the United States, in
> >> Montauk, New York.
> >> It has been decided very quickly, and I know it's a very quite
> >> notice.
> >> But both me and the Rodriguez family would love to have you there!
> >> And I could arrange flight tickets if you would be able to come.
> >> It would be such a great pleasure, having
> >> you reuniting after 37 years!
> >>
> >> All the best!
> >> Malik

From: stever@familydogg.com
> >> Subject: Re: Stockholm calling!
> >> Date: Sat, 19 Jul 2008 20:21:42 -07–
> >> To: malikbendjelloul@hotmail.com
> >>
> >>
> >> Dear Malik—
> >>
> >> I'd love to be in attendance at Rodriguez's first gig in the US.
> >> Unfortunately I have a friend visiting me here in Palm Springs at
> >> the moment and It wouldn't be right if I just took off. Also I've
> >> already booked my flight for London leaving on the 29th of this
> >> month. They're expecting me to be there to help with my book's
> >> promotion.
> >> By the way my book, Hollywood Heat is on amazon.co.uk. Check it
> >> out if you'd like. Go to books then film. It's there to see.
> >>
> >> Thank you so much for inviting me to attend the gig. I would love
> >> to be there to see what I know will be a great positive reaction.
> >> I will however, be there in spirit.
> >> Please give my apologies to Rodriguez and family. I'm sure that
> >> there will be a next time very soon. Whenever that is I'll
> >> definitely try my best to be there.
> >>

> >> I'll be in London for the entire month of August. You can contact
> >> me at the numbers that I've given you.
> >>
> >> Once again I'm terribly sorry that I won't be able to be with all
> >> of you. However, I know that the Rodriguez gig will be a huge
> >> success.
> >> Please let me know the outcome.
> >>
> >> All the very best to you and especially to Rodriguez.
> >>
> >> Go for it.
> >>
> >> Steve

From: stever@familydogg.com
Subject: Re: Stockholm calling! Date: Wed, 23 Jul 2008 09:45:42 -0700
To: malikbendjelloul@hotmail.com

Yeah Malik—They may have rebuilt CTS studios somewhere else in and around London. I'm really not sure. However, I'm certain that you can find out.

Lansdowne in itself is a very cool place to record. I had many hit records out of there.

The guy that was in charge of CTS as well as Lansdowne is Adrian Kerridge. He knows me. If you by chance are able to get in touch with him do mention my name. It might help.

After checking the website I see that indeed CTS was rebuilt and is in Watford, an easy place to get to. Adrian

Kerridge is still in control. call and speak to him. Good luck.

Cheers, Steve

> >>
> >>**From:** Malik Bendjelloul <malikbendjelloul@hotmail.com>
Subject: RE: Stockholm calling!
Date: July 28, 2008 at 6:46:01 AM PDT
To: Steve Rowland <stever@familydogg.com>

Dear Steve,

The gig was great! Two sets, 45 min each, outside in a nice place in Montauk. Fantastic!

This is Adrian's answer about the studio:

"I would be delighted to help you but we sold off the studios and property some two years ago it is now being redeveloped as a rather large residence. We still have the very large room at Watford for big orchestral projects."

"Then it wouldn't be possible to do something inside, would it? Are there any other places in London where you have memories connected to Rodriguez, do you think?" All the best!
Malik

Malik Bendjelloul e-mailed Rowland on July 23: "The idea would be to film in the actual place the record was recorded. "Do you think that would be possible?," Malik asked Steve via Skype. The idea of filming where **Coming From Reality** was recorded was an intriguing one. Malik asked Steve and others if the aura in the studio created the wisdom of Rodriguez lyrics? I asked Steve: "Is this true?" He looked at me like I was nuts. He replied: "Listen to the album. You are a rock journalist. You are a Professor. You figure it out." I didn't tell Steve I am Professor Emeritus. That is retired. I am still trying to figure it out.

During July 2008 Steve spent a great deal of time describing to Malik how and why Lansdowne Studio in Holland Park was important to the story. Bendjelloul attempted to film in Lansdowne to evoke a sense of how Rowland and Rodriguez worked. Finally, after a great deal of time spent attempting to pave the way for Bendjelloul to film in Lansdowne Studio, Steve e-mailed his opinions to Bendjelloul. Lansdowne had closed down. It was now an apartment house.

Steve Rowland: "What happened is that Adrian Kerridge left Lansdowne. The studio was brilliant. He was a wonderful guy. I tried to get Malik into what was left of the studio."

The 2008 e-mails demonstrated how Steve Rowland encouraged, guided, gave advice to and alerted Malik Bendjelloul to the dangers of the music-film business. He was a constant source of encouragement to the young Swedish filmmaker who was completing his first full-length feature. Steve knew the dangers of the business. He was part coach, part cheerleader, part professor and a full time friend.

Steve and Malik Talk 2008-2013: What is the Outcome?

From 2008 through 2013 Steve and Malik talked at length via skype. The e-mails slowed to a snail's pace. Rowland's main contribution was to fill Malik in on music history, and the changes in the record business necessary to facilitate completing the documentary.

When Malik traveled to Italy in the summer of 2009 seeking funding, he talked to Rowland about how to approach the financial types. At this stage of the project Malik titled the documentary **The Only One Who Didn't Know**. That was a working title that soon gave way to **Searching For Sugar Man**.

By 2009 the early rushes drew rave reviews from Rowland. I asked Steve: "Weren't you the key to much of Malik's early planning?" Angrily Steve responded: "No." He bristles when asked that question. I didn't ask again. Rowland did agree that by 2009 Matt Sullivan was making Rodriguez a bankable act. He pointed to the September 2008 Joe's Pub appearance in New York as a turning point. "Remember Malik did everything right," Rowland continued. "It was a slow but steady building career."

The avalanche of publicity, the key club bookings, the record store appearances and a strong and positive press made Rodriguez bankable on the Indie circuit. The Joe's Pub booking in New York was the first step to limited fame.

The Joe's Pub Gig and The Sugar Man is Back as a Cult Hero

The slow building Rodriguez phenomenon took on a new life in September 2008 when he appeared at New York's Joe's Pub. The one hundred sixty-seat venues was the perfect place for Matt Sullivan and Light In The Attic to publicize the re-release of the Sugar Man's two albums.

When Matt Sullivan booked the Rodriguez show in New York at Joe's Pub, he planned and executed a media blitz. There was an interview on WNYC, which is New York's first and still premier public radio station. Joe's Pub is an outstanding dinner venue. It attracts a high-end entertainment audience. After the show the Sugar Man hung out and had dinner with the crowd. It was Rodriguez' first New York show. Why was it important?

The September 2008 Joe's Pub show was an early turning point in Rodriguez' career. When Jonny-Leather reviewed the appearance for the New York press the conclusion was "not everyone can rise to fame as quickly or as easily as someone like Vampire Weekend." With that stilted prose and obtuse verbiage the writer concluded: "a little bit of luck goes a long way." Like many New Yorkers Jonny-Leather concluded: "It's taken a very, very long time, but Sixto Rodriguez is finally beginning to receive the attention he deserves for writing one of the finest albums of its time." There was no writer with better hip credentials than Jonny-Leather. His is hip. He is well read. That was the assessment of **Cold Fact**. The next year the re-release of **Coming From Reality** drew similar rave reviews.

The Joe's Pub gig was a wonderful experience for the Sugar Man. When he ended the show with a cover of Etta James' "At Last," Rodriguez made his point. It was September 2008, he was on the verge of a cult career. At least it was the minor league big time. But Joe's Pub is a major league venue.

There were some highlights to the Joe's Pub show. With a gray sport coat and an easy singing style, Rodriguez performed a slow, version of "Crucify Your Mind" with his guitar blending into the vocals. You could hear a pin drop. A fan sitting in the front row shot a video of the song displaying the ambiance that is New York's East Village and the Sugar Man's extraordinary talent.

That night at Joe's Pub, Rodriguez walked out and ate dinner with the patrons. New York was in love with the Sugar Man. His fans filmed the performance with their cell phones. He was all over the Internet three years before **Searching For Sugar Man**. At Joe's Pub someone asked him what he thought of **Cold Fact**. Rodriguez replied: "It's very stark. If you overproduce, you lose something."

The cornpone humor Rodriguez exhibited between songs at Joe's Pub won the usually critical New York audience over as he remarked: "Do you want to know the secret to life?" The crowd quieted. It was like a religious revival. Rodriguez said: "You breathe in, then you breathe out. In and out." The crowd erupted with laughter and raucous applause.

Matt Sullivan and Light In The Attic worked the New York media to produce an avalanche of praise. Rodriguez was out on the road. This ultimately helped the documentary.

By 2009 Bendjelloul recognized Rodriguez' emergence as a cult artist. As Light In The Attic stewarded him around the U. S., the Sugar Man returned for another South African tour. Bendjelloul cut back on the filming. He was working on the final product. As Rodriguez distanced himself from Stephen "Sugar" Segerman, so did Bendjelloul. He needed space and less input from the South African. He came to rely heavily on Rowland. The late night skype calls provided a step-by-step training ground with Rowland smoothing out the film's rough edges. But, as Steve said: "Malik did the work. He was brilliant. I was proud. All credit to him."

From 2009 through 2013 Rowland and Bendjelloul spent most of their time skyping.

Steve Rowland: "He would skype me about his successes. He wanted me to go to Sundance, I didn't tell him I had severe arthritis. Everybody has something. I was in pain."

Rowland Bendjelloul e-mails 2013-2014

Steve Rowland: "When I saw him on October 13, 2013 in New York, we discussed my TV series. He said: 'Don't worry I will be in L A in January and February.' When I didn't hear from him I sent an e-mail three months later."

As 2013 ended the documentary won an Oscar, the theater sales were strong, the DVD was selling well and the soundtrack charted on **Billboard**. The DVD Blue Ray release added a second life to **Searching For Sugar Man**. After more than thirty awards for documentary excellence it didn't appear that there were more vistas to conquer. There were! The e-mails continued in the years after **Searching For Sugar Man** took the world by storm. The Sixto Rodriguez story was an international phenomenon. The Sugar Man's two albums, the soundtrack and the DVD racked up huge sales.

By 2014 Malik Bendjelloul's e-mails were not as focused. He was frantically attempting to find a new project. The sales of this documentary, the praise and the attendant financial rewards should have made Bendjelloul happy. That wasn't the case.

When the DVD was released in early 2013 it brought **Cold Fact** back to the **Billboard** Top 200. **Rolling Stone** noted the continued popularity of the Rodriguez story. Many other publications labeled it a story that wouldn't go away. During 2013 and into early 2014 the e-mails continued and Bendjelloul was increasingly elusive. He was still friendly with Rowland but there was something going on. Steve had no idea.

From: stever@familydogg.com
Subject: Where are you??
Date: Tue, 28 Jan 2014 12:32:26 -0800
To: malikbendjelloul@hotmail.com

Hey Malik—

I just returned from London where it rained every day. After a week there I was longing for the Palm Springs sunshine. I don't know how I lived there for 40 years without getting depressed. I must have got used to it.

Where are you right now? I would really love to meet up. There's a great deal that I'd love to discuss.

I hope that things are booming for you. You certainly deserve it.

Take care. Say hello to your lovely lady for me.

As ever,

Steve

From: stever@familydogg.com
Subject: Re: Where are you??
Date: Thu, 30 Jan 2014 12:40:28 -0800
To: malikbendjelloul@hotmail.com

Hi Malik—

ABSOLUTELY!
Great mention of Sugar Man in that article. Wow, Martin Scorsese must have thought your film had it all.
Terrific !

Let me know the best time for us to Skype each other.

Cheers,

Steve

Steve Rowland
stever@familydogg.com

Malik answered Steve immediately. As he commuted between New York and Stockholm, Bendjelloul was the picture of good health and confidence. He was after all an Oscar winner who at thirty-six defied the odds to take Hollywood's most prestigious award home. With his tousled brown hair, his infectious smile, his lean athletic body, he seemed to have the world by the tail. Nothing was further from the truth. It was preposterous and out of character, **The**

Hollywood Reporter observed, of Malik's suicide. Simon Chinn, the co-producer chided the media for making a circus out of his death. But in February no one knew that on May 13, 2014 that young Malik would throw himself from a metro platform in the center of Stockholm to an unthinkable death. There are no hints of this in his e-mails.

On Jan 30, 2014, at 11:28 AM, Malik Bendjelloul <malikbendjelloul@ hotmail.com> wrote:

Hey Steve!

Good to hear that you're safely back in the Californian desert! England has some serious weather issues. I don't know why they're still living there, all those British people. I guess it's just old habit.

Would be great to catch up! I'm in New York and up for a Skype anytime!

Btw, did you see this article in Variety?

http://variety.com/interstitial/?ref=http%3A%2F%2Fv arseseiety.com%2F2013%2Ffilm%2Ffeatures%2Fvariety-creative-impact-award-in-acting-jonah-hill-1200977051%2F

Pretty cool! Let's Skype soon!

Cheers,
Malik

The article in **Variety** that Bendjelloul referred to included future directors to watch, and this angered Bendjelloul. Malik, for whatever reason, was not on the list. He never said he felt disrespected. He was. Clearly, Bendjelloul was feeling pressure from his success. He was going through periods of euphoria followed by bouts of depression. He increasingly regimented his life. Every morning he had the same thing for breakfast. He walked in a redundant circle in his apartment each morning. He obsessed over the lack of a new project. Steve never saw any of this behavior. Nor did anyone else.

By the end of January 2014 the two years of success for **Searching For Sugar Man** prompted Rowland to attempt to buoy Bendjelloul's spirits. He told him regularly there were great opportunities coming his way. They talked frequently of collaborating. There was no comment from Malik. Rowland, like everyone else, had no idea of the depths of personal self-doubt swirling in the Swede's psyche. But he had one desire. That was to work on a Hollywood project.

The character driven spontaneity of Steve's 1950s Hollywood gangster show intrigued Malik. He realized it was more than just an exploitive look at tineseltown. Steve's series **Hollywood Heat** was about the flawed characters inhabiting Hollywood. Malik loved its gritty, authentic base.

The flawed characters in Steve's scripts and the gangsters who populated the landscape intrigued Bendjelloul. He wondered. Was Steve one of those flawed individuals? He didn't seem like it. Then again! Malik went to the Margaret Herrick Library in Beverly Hills to find out more about Steve's father, Roy Rowland, and to research the industry. Since the 1990s the Herrick Library was known as the Library of The Motion Picture Academy. It was close enough to Clarence Avant's home for Malik to find it. Malik realized nepotism almost destroyed Steve's budding film career. The constant demands for "cred" from the pompous London based music producers were hurdles Rowland overcame in his legendary career. There was a lesson here for Malik. Never lose sight of your dreams. Never stop pursuing your goal. Work hard. Stay focused. Bendjelloul did on the way to an Oscar.

Malik realized Steve Rowland seldom talked about his accomplishments, his years growing up and driving around town with James Dean. Malik always paid attention to Steve. Now he would soak in whatever wisdom he had in the post fame stage as **Searching For Sugar Man** was a mammoth box office hit. Malik couldn't get Rowland's flawed, larger than life characters out of his psyche. It was a story he would spend some time analyzing. Maybe he and Steve could work together on it.

From: stever@familydogg.com
Subject: Re: Where are you??
Date: Mon, 3 Feb 2014 15:02:58 -0800
To: malikbendjelloul@hotmail.com

Hey Malik—

Tomorrow is good. Remember that you're three hours ahead time wise.
Mid-day your time is the best time to catch me in.
Looking forward to speaking with you.

As ever,

Steve

Steve Rowland
stever@familydogg.com

On Feb 3, 2014, at 6:04 AM, Malik Bendjelloul <malikbendjelloul@hotmail.com> wrote:

Maybe later today? Or tomorrow if you prefer?

Cheers,
Malik

There are hundreds of e-mails between Steve and Malik. What do they suggest? Many things! Steve was a constant source of inspiration. Malik asked for his advice. Steve freely gave it. When Malik asked questions about the industry, Steve did his best to guide him through the creative process and the fiscal jungle. Steve worried these forces destroyed so many artists. It could do the same to Bendjelloul. For that reason he was careful and precise with his advice. The e-mails speak for themselves. The closeness of the two filmmakers was important to completing the project. The Oscar winning result was due to their collaboration.

Steve Rowland: Sitting in Palm Springs in 2017 Thinking of Malik Bendjelloul, Searching for Sugar Man and Coming From Reality

In May 2017 Steve Rowland sat down in his Palm Springs home and talked about Malik Bendjelloul's, **Searching For Sugar Man**. He also reflected on how and why he produced **Coming From Reality**. Bendjelloul was unsure how to begin his project. Steve had written a storyboard. I asked him about it. He told me it wasn't a storyboard. I stood corrected. The poster board Steve used contained suggestions to bring out the mystery in the Rodriguez story. Steve believed the Sugar Man's mysterious life, combined with his literary songwriting, drove the intense drama that was the Sixto Rodriguez story.

Steve Rowland: "I talked with Malik at length about the opening of the movie. He went over all the stories. He told me he was having trouble with the opening."

Over skype Bendjelloul discussed the opening scene showing Stephen "Sugar" Segerman driving his car on Chapman's Peak Drive. Neither Bendjelloul nor Rowland believed this was the most exciting way to begin the film. Segerman badgered Bendjelloul to open the film in Cape Town at Chapman's Peak for its majestic beauty. He also wanted moviegoers to know his South African nickname "Sugar." That was the first myth to crush reality. Segerman had only used the nickname "Sugar" for the last few years. Segerman went on telling a tall tale that no one could pronounce his name in the army, so they called him "Sugar." Craig Bartholomew-Strydom, Segerman's close friend and co-author, alleges this is not true. But Segerman's input in the documentary remained an important contribution.

Malik told close Swedish friends he would include the film's opening as a thank you to Segerman. He lamented he regretted that decision. Segerman's blustery, imperious behavior embarrassed the director. That said, Rowland liked the opening scene. He urged Malik to keep it in the documentary. He did! Then Malik asked Steve to analyze the direction the documentary should take.

Steve Rowland: "I said a lot of these documentaries start out with a black screen, and I suggested writing on a black screen about Sixto Rodriguez the artist who made two albums in 1970-1971. What happened to him? He became the most popular artist in South Africa bigger than Elvis, the Beatles or the Rolling Stones. The man has remained a mystery."

As Steve visualized the film opening with a black screen, he had a sense of the mystery. Malik told him the story line, Steve thought about it for a long time. He spent a great deal of time on an opening to enhance audience interest. Steve outlined the mysteries of how Rodriguez supposedly died. The mysteries of his career are important to understanding the documentary, Steve emphasized.

Rodriguez was "a man of mystery." He also talked of the "conspiracies surrounding the Sugar Man."

As Steve wrote on a blank screen, he continually rewrote and outlined how he believed the film might progress. Steve told Malik many times his thoughts were only suggestions. He suggested the young filmmaker be his own man. He told Bendjelloul to leave space open for "other ideas." Steve sent the elaborate opening to Bendjelloul. He emphasized there have been many mysterious theories about Rodriguez. These tales create a sense of mystery, suspense and viewer interest. Rowland told Bendjelloul when you leave a space in the storyboard for additions it helps the film to emphasize the circumstances behind the Sugar Man's literary-musical style.

Steve Rowland: "My suggestions were simply my own ideas. It was Malik's film. He did a marvelous job and all credit to him."

Cape Town and Segerman's Horseshit Meter

After shooting in South Africa, Malik and cinematographer Camilla Skagerstrom celebrated Cape Town's scenic beauty with a local tour and scenic shots of the coastline. There were some difficulties. Their host attempted to take over the documentary. Bendjelloul was uncomfortable. Stephen "Sugar" Segerman wanted to have more input than Bendjelloul desired. It turned into a bit of a standoff. Bendjelloul never complained to Rowland about Segerman. There were subtle signs of Malik's discontent. Steve sensed the project slowing down. He continued to give Malik advice from the feature films he made.

Rowland's inner knowledge of the movie industry led Bendjelloul to Simon Chinn in London who was the final piece in the funding area. Steve's relationship with those in the business gave Malik a calling card or a means of meeting and discussing his project with the top money people.

In December 2009 Malik told Rowland the documentary was like a long distance race. He wasn't sure he could finish it. They continued to talk at length about how to cast the story. This conversation went on for two years. He emphasized to Malik to listen to suggestions with care. "You are enormously talented, Malik, go with your gut feelings," Rowland continued. "All credit goes to Malik. It is a magnificent film."

As the first year of filming ended there was a problem. Rodriguez was running cold on the documentary. The Sugar Man was tired of listening about the project. He was concerned about his privacy. He was certain nothing would come of this endeavor. He had been disappointed too many times. His daughter, Regan, was the savior in this period. She kept the family and Malik pointed toward completing the documentary. By the time Malik arrived in Cape Town for a second round of filming in February 2010 he was running out of money. His enthusiasm remained infectious. He held skype calls with Steve Rowland. He was swimming in a morose of hard work.

In February 2010 Bendjelloul got off the plane in Cape Town with a Swedish friend, Daniel Hager, and he continued to skype Steve Rowland in Palm Springs. They talked at length about the best way to continue **Searching For Sugar Man's** creative process. Malik had his fill of Segerman. He told "Sugar" he needed privacy. Malik made reservations at a small bed and breakfast on Cape Town's Buitengracht Street. Segerman arrived as soon as Malik checked in. Bendjelloul complained to close friends that "Sugar" had an agenda. He was driving the filmmaker crazy. The pompous South African believed he was the story. This intensified Bendjelloul's skype calls to Rowland. He needed sage advice. Steve presented it while reminding Malik it was his film.

Segerman wanted the Swedish filmmaker to experience Chapman's Peak Drive and its majestic view. Malik reluctantly went along with Segerman's suggestion to open the documentary. In retrospect, it was a great opening as "Sugar" was right about the majestic view of the South African coast. But, as Rowland told Bendjelloul, follow it with Detroit's stark images. He did! The result was an Oscar.

When Segerman suggested dialogue, Malik humored him. The dialogue that Sugar offered was gratuitous concerning Rodriguez. Malik listened. Then he did it his way. In his twice-weekly skypes with Rowland, Bendjelloul reported on the progress of each day's filming. Steve continued to tell him that he was completing an "Oscar project." Malik told a number of close friends that Rowland was his "psychological angel."

When Segerman's friend Craig Bartholomew-Strydom wrote **Sugar Man: The Life, Death and Resurrection of Sixto Rodriguez**, Segerman confessed he did not receive his nickname from Rodriguez' "Sugar Man." It was an out and out lie. Bartholomew-Strydom wrote: "This small distortion of how Stephen became Sugar was to the ends of truth." (p. 274) This convoluted explanation alleges some of the film's dialogue had a loose relationship with the truth. I am not sure what this means. Distortion is distortion. Myth is not reality.

It gets worse. Bartholomew-Strydom wrote: "He would also take certain speeches or chunks of dialogue said by one person and asks someone else to relay the very same story, in order to spread the representation of that particular player in the film." (p. 274). This alteration of facts was the beginning of Segerman spinning the story. The fake dialogue or misuse of quotes tells one all they need to know about Segerman's integrity. He would say his intensity. Or as his best friend Bartholomew-Strydom suggests there is a lack of veracity.

Not only did Segerman twist the truth, he borrowed material from Craig Bartholomew-Strydom without detailing his sources. When he suggested dialogue for the documentary to Bendjelloul, Segerman lifted material directly from an article Craig published in **Directions** magazine. When Bendjelloul used Segerman's truncated version of the Sugar Man's story there was hell to pay. Everyone close to the story was angry. Segerman's perennial lust for fame, and his desire to control the story gave it fictional overtones. Bartholomew-Strydom observed: "Needless to say this caused resentment among the sticklers for truth." (p. 275)

When he was filming in South Africa, Bendjelloul skyped Steve Rowland even more frequently with questions on how to proceed. They talked at length. The constant pressure for financial support threatened the documentary. It was at this point that Malik began using a $1.99 Iphone app to film some of the sequences. This Iphone device is known as the 8mm Vintage Camera. The scenes shot on this inexpensive device didn't differ in quality from what Malik shot on expensive eight mm film. Malik worried this footage would not look right. Steve saw the rushes. He said it was fine.

Rowland told him to look for authenticity. He found the South African skyline filmed with the Iphone app to have an irresistible visual appeal. There was no getting rid of Segerman in the early Cape Town filming. He was obsessed with his place in the story.

When the Academy Awards took place on March 7, 2010, Segerman e-mailed Bendjelloul: "While watching the Oscars this morning….I realized that there now exists the possibility that something I am involved in could possibly be in next year's Oscar ceremony." Malik was frightened. He wasn't sure he could trust Segerman to honestly tell the story.

When Malik returned to Stockholm to edit the early takes, he did so in his home. He also edited at Stockholm's SVT studio. He needed to talk to Steve Rowland. He believed it was necessary to slant the story slightly away from South Africa. There remained the need for increased funding, the pressure to place the story in a proper perspective, and the constant e-mails from Rodriguez' family on the progress of the film caused Bendjelloul a great deal of concern.

An early trailer for the film was sent to a number of industry insiders. He used this long trailer to approach film festivals. He also traveled to Copenhagen and Sheffield England in search of funding. He also met with Willemiek Kluijfhout and they discussed the embryo

Searching For Sugar Man. She had abandoned her quest to make a Rodriguez movie, but she was open and full of excellent suggestions. She told Malik it was the story of a lifetime. She encouraged him.

Rowland and Bendjelloul: Editing the Documentary

Steve Rowland: "He would do his editing in his house, he would call or skype me and send me a DVD of what he had completed, Judy Lewis was here and she helped. It was not disagreeing with him it was trying to add to what he was doing. Judy said when she saw the first rushes this is Oscar bound. When I met with him in New York in 2013 we talked about the series, and he was interested in seeing what I was doing."

After Malik read Steve's book, he thought a great deal about the subject matter. It had the sense of drama, the edgy characters, the sunny California lifestyle, the criminal, the corrupt police, the drama of Hollywood and a personal intimacy necessary to a hit TV show. He was interested. He decided to share his feelings with Rowland.

Malik Bendjelloul: "I understand what you are trying to do I would like to at least talk about it," Malik continued. "I love the old Hollywood stories."

It is difficult to get Rowland to talk about his help in formatting **Searching For Sugar Man**. He is uncomfortable taking credit. He told me time and time again it was "Malik's film, give him the credit." The lengthy e-mails, the skype calls and the general partnership that developed paved the road to completion for the Oscar winning documentary. "I have told you one hundred times it is Malik's film," Rowland said with exasperation. After five years I finally got Steve's message.

How Stephen "Sugar" Segerman Created Myths of Searching for Sugar Man: How The e-mails Showed Steve Rowland's Influence and the Real Story

One of the problems writing about Sixto Rodriguez is the veracity of the material. When Stephen "Sugar" Segerman and Craig Bartholomew-Strydom finished their book, they employed the phrase: "true story." This was used time and time again to describe their biography. What is the importance of **Sugar Man: The Life, Death And Resurrection of Sixto Rodriguez**?

It is an excellent piece of work. The writing is superb. The tale is told from their viewpoint. There is a great deal of new material on Rodriguez and his family. That is the good news. The bad news is hoary clichés, a lack of knowledge about the conditions in the music business, the quagmire of contracts and the historical direction of American rock and roll fail to find their way into the book. Bartholomew-Strydom and Segerman combine arrogance that they were right because they had physically pursued their subject through the vineyards of biographical knowledge. The problem is they attempted to develop the story in a manner that fit their preconceived notions. That is a tragedy disparaging the Sugar Man and lessening his importance.

There are jurisdictional fights over who owns the story. The details on personal behavior, particularly the statement to enjoy a Rodriguez concert you need to smoke a joint, reeks of duplicitous arrogance and pompous ineptitude. This compromises their book. It reeks of juvenile reporting, imprecise research, and hagiography. Other than that the book is fine.

The problem with the Segerman-Bartholomew-Strydom book is their notion it is the "only true story." The unmitigated arrogance of this statement speaks for itself. This pompous attitude not only degrades Sixto Rodriguez, it takes away from an otherwise brilliant story of rediscovery and redemption.

There are some constants in the Sixto Rodriguez story. That is there are ten indisputable truths. First, Rodriguez and his family are the close, warm, loving people in the documentary. Second, the Sugar Man is a calm, relaxed, quiet, private individual with a defined lifestyle. Third, he is a dedicated political activist. Fourth, he is a scholar, an existentialist and a thoughtful intellectual. Fifth, he is a dedicated songwriter. He understands the craft. He has mastered the craft. He pursues the craft. Sixth, while he is a quiet individual with excellent integrity, past problems with record labels makes him at times a difficult character. Rodriguez is in charge of his career. He finalizes all decisions. He is blind from glaucoma and his daughters read and discuss the current business proposals. He has turned down the majority of these propositions He has learned from past mistakes. Seventh, he is writing new songs with nine completed as this book goes to press. He is working diligently on a third album. Eighth, he has given away the majority of his money earned since 2012 to his family. A great deal of his money is directed toward charitable-political needs. Ninth, he continues to develop his philosophical base with more verbal messages than written ones. He remains a force for peace, love and change in the American way of life. Tenth, he remains wary of people. Some describe him as paranoid and this is an exaggeration as he is concerned about his legacy. He has this in common with Steve Rowland. They worry the force and focus of history will not record their legacy.

Steve Rowland and the Real Story Behind Searching for Sugar Man

What is the real story behind **Searching For Sugar Man**? The story is Malik Bendjelloul was responsible for the film entirely. He negotiated with Clarence Avant, who graciously gave permission to use the music. This approval came despite the brutal interview where Avant was ambushed on camera. That was Segerman's doing. He was obsessed with Rodriguez' back royalties. Bendjelloul quietly worked with an editor and illustrator. He continued to pay close attention to the cinematography. Steve Rowland hovered in the background dispensing knowledge and psychological support. Steve's main contribution was helping Bendjelloul understand Sixto Rodriguez and focusing the film.

After three trips to Detroit, Malik convinced Rodriguez to appear on camera. The Sugar Man was not an easy sell. But he was essential to the project. Along the way Rowland emphasized the contrasting story line urging Malik to build to a spectacular ending much like a feature film.

The American political scene was one Malik didn't understand. When a rough copy of **Searching For Sugar Man** was shown to a U. S. executive there was concern about a clip in which Rodriguez talked of running for political office. That scene was cut from the film. Steve educated Malik on the intricacies of the U. S. political scene, and how and why the Sugar Man was a well-known activist. Steve also helped Malik understand the subtle nuances of American politics. This built a window into Rodriguez' life. Malik also avoided the attempts by some to make the Sugar Man appear like a wide-eyed political radical. He wasn't. He was portrayed in **Searching For Sugar Man** as a sage political force in his early life. This was as accurate as it got and Rodriguez briefly appeared in the film. The dignity with which he was treated was important to the finished product.

There were numerous movie business minefields. Rowland helped to secure final funding. The years that Steve spent watching his father make movies, the time he acted and the business end of the industry were points of wisdom he departed to Bendjelloul. He wanted the best for Rodriguez and success for Bendjelloul.

Steve Rowland's heretofore unrecognized role in **Searching For Sugar Man** suggests the layers of planning, hard work and commitment to the project that led to Malik Bendjelloul's Oscar. In the end it was Cinderella coming to the ball forty years after the fact.

Nineteen

Sixto Rodriguez and the Troubadour Tradition

"There are no guarantees in music, and I knew that from the beginning. I think it's better if these heartbreaks happen to you early than when you're later in your years. I think it's better that you get the bumps early."

Sixto Rodriguez

"I saw some things I thought people should be made aware of, but I was unable to do that with my music."

Sixto Rodriguez

"It's getting busy, and I'm not worthy. But I'm going for it. Rock 'n' Roll is a crazy world, and it's how things work out you can't predict."

Sixto Rodriguez

"Rodriguez is an appealing, unpretentious singer who seems to want nothing more than to deliver the song and get out of his own way."

Sasha Frere-Jones, The New Yorker

What is the point of Sixto Rodriguez' career? Is he simply a forgotten singer with two neglected albums who was rediscovered? Or is there a deeper story? The tale is one that operates in the deep recesses of the troubadour tradition. That is he writes songs to highlight Detroit's increasing police brutality, to expose political corruption, to argue for honest government, to fight for the blue collar working person, to demand rights for women, and along the way the Sugar Man follows the troubadour tradition by demanding social-political change in song. Through these tunes there is a message suggesting a path to an improved quality of life. He also argues for a sense of fairness in a world of corporate corruption and egotistical politicians.

There are dangers to being a troubadour. Some succeed. Others fail. Some go off the deep end. The troubadours who are remembered often have few hit songs. Woody Guthrie's hits were prescient after his death. Phil Ochs had an impact and spiraled into self-destruction. Drugs got some artists notably Tim Buckley, Karen Dalton and Fred Neil. Others retired to the country like James Taylor, where he found a compromise between creativity and commercial success.

Unlike Bob Dylan there was no pressure to write the next influential song for Sixto Rodriguez. He wrote from the heart. The rock music marketplace didn't dictate his songs. He wove tales of suburbia, broken romances and betrayal. His pocketbook attests to his lack of fiscal success. He didn't care. Art triumphed commercial reality. He knew his songs had a lasting impact. He wasn't sure if he would ever have a commercial legacy. When he toured Australia in 1979 and again in 1981, he believed he had begun and ended his troubadour legacy. Rodriguez has not recorded a new released tune since 1971. When he suddenly burst on the scene in 2012, via **Searching For Sugar Man**, all the media could talk about was a third album. That discussion is still in the air.

Rodriguez did not have songs released to the mass market. Why? Neil Bogart torpedoed his two albums. Sussex Records went bankrupt. Clarence Avant wouldn't allow re-release of his material until Light In The Attic's Matt Sullivan dogged Avant for two years. The Sugar Man was a public troubadour without an audience. Sullivan made sure his anonymity ended when he re-released **Cold Fact** in 2008 and followed with **Coming From Reality** in 2009. These album releases set up early concerts making Rodriguez an Indie cult favorite. He was back as a performer by 2009. The best was yet to come.

The primary characteristic of the troubadour is a devil may care mentality. That describes Sixto Rodriguez' attitude. It is all about his music. Nothing else matters! Money is never a concern. It is about the lyrics, the art, the presentation and the drive for cultural change.

The Rodriguez Shows in Australia in 1979 and Portending The Future: The Message is the Key Not the Glitz

Sixto Rodriguez refuses to compromise. Why is this important? As a troubadour, with a message, there was no glitz to his shows. The glitz is in the lyrics. This is the way Rodriguez approaches his craft. He is led out onto the stage. His advanced glaucoma precludes walking out by himself. After his partner, Bonnie, or one of his daughters, Regan or Sandra, helps him find the microphone, he puts on his hat, he adjusts his sunglasses and he begins his show. There is usually not a set list. He will perform as many as five covers and the requisite and required album songs including "Sugar Man," "Forget It," "The

Establishment Blues," "It Started Out So Nice," "Crucify Your Mind" and "Climb Up On My Music."

When he talks about how and why he writes, Rodriguez remarks: "I tapped into the writer's poetic license." This is a reference to the lyrics and imagery in "Jane S. Piddy." It goes a long way toward explaining his songwriting genius. As far as song content is concerned Rodriguez observed: "Knowledge in itself is nothing. It's what you do with that information."

Class struggle is and will always be one of the Sugar Man's primary motivations. It is the reason he puts pen to paper. When he wrote "Cause" Rodriguez was concerned the song would reflect on him. It didn't. It became a tune Rodriguez embraced in **Searching For Sugar Man**. He predicted the demise of his recording career.

The Lack of Pompous Bullshit: The Rodriguez Credo

One of the hallmarks of Sixto Rodriguez' career is his utter disdain for bullshit. While the Sugar Man lives on the edge of the hippie 1960s subculture, he is a deep thinker, an introspective writer and a virulent critic of America's political crimes. He will go to the most obscure political meeting, like he did recently to oppose water rate hikes. He addressed the Detroit Water Board. He described those living on fixed incomes as not being able to afford utility increases. He had been one of those folks for more than forty years. He still cared. He is fighting for the little person every day of his life.

It is easy to romanticize Rodriguez' flaws and to elevate the mythology **Searching For Sugar Man** created. His shows are an example of the Troubadour's mantra. There is no personal glamour to the Sugar Man on stage. His shows are tinged with reality. There is a sense of retribution on the silver screen when **Searching For Sugar Man** is shown. Rodriguez is uncomfortable with celebrity.

There is a notion music brings out the societal rejects. This is, of course, academic hocus pocus practiced by the likes of Greil Marcus. The Sugar Man worked hard to earn an honors B. A. in philosophy. Rodriguez is more like Leonard Cohen. He has a songwriting vision he has never abandoned.

Steve Rowland: "I see Rodriguez as a Leonard Cohen type performer and writer. Bob Dylan was a real protester. Rodriguez is a poet. He understands people and relationships."

Rodriguez writes with a realism combined with a harsh reality. There are songs with a sense of salvation. He is the troubadour with a minimal message. In "Cause'" he sings: "My heart's become a crooked hotel full of rumors." That says it all about lost love.

Detroit's image makes his songs personal. When he sings: "But it's I who pays the rent for these fingered-face out of tuners," he laments the difficulty of making a living while playing in bars where no one cares. He is a troubadour. He sings on and on. Eventually, the crowd gets it.

The environment is increasingly a favorite topic. "The environment just shook," Rodriguez remarked to the **Chicago Tribune's** Greg Kot. Then the Sugar Man laments the decline of environmental controls, the rise of utility prices and the persistence of the Trump administration ending governmental regulation. He can work in the political marketplace quietly and without fanfare.

When he reflects on politics. He explains why he reacts to politicians. He says: "What makes us political is your home turf, your family, your life space. We just got rid of a Mayor who ended up in jail." That said it all. Integrity! Morality! Honesty! Perseverance! These are traits Sixto Rodriguez brings to the table. "The current economic situation keeps people in classes, so when you hear a song like 'Cause' it applies," Rodriguez concluded. For years Steve Rowland has delivered the same message about the Sugar Man. Finally, people are listening.

Rodriguez Embraces the Troubadour Tradition, 2009: Speaking to Greg Kot

Long before he made the improbable rise to stardom, due to the surging power of **Searching For Sugar Man**, Rodriguez spoke of his musical role. When Greg Kot of the **Chicago Tribune** asked Rodriguez about his role as a troubadour in 2009, he had specific thoughts. This was three years before fame and fortune.

The message Rodriguez imparted to Kot was simple. The journalist entitled his May 2009 **Chicago Tribune** article "The Long, Crazy Trail of Sixto Rodriguez." Kot wrote: "Rock 'n' roll is full of lost albums and unrecognized masters." This comment paid tribute to Rodriguez' perseverance. Matt Sullivan was lurking in the background. He was orchestrating the press for the Friday night concert at Chicago's Schubas club. Kot was more than just a musical journalist. His radio show "Sound Opinions" on WBEZ-FM was another means of publicizing the Sugar Man.

When Kot asked if his career was back on track, Rodriguez said: "I'm at the top of the line, man. I mean, things are happening." Kot remarked Rodriguez appeared like an extremely happy man reaching his goal. He was back.

The Kot interview described musical influences Rodriguez had not previously identified. "I loved Jimmy Reed, the chord changes, the lyrics," Rodriguez continued. "I started writing lyrics and got away from the boy-girl thing pretty early." That said it all. Harry Balk attempted to persuade Rodriguez to write pop ditties for a teen market in 1967. The Sugar Man refused. He had a broader vision. He spoke of his vision to Kot who ended the **Chicago Tribune** article with Rodriguez' observations.

Sixto Rodriguez: "The current economic situation keeps people in classes, so when you hear a song like 'Cause' it applies. I'm surfacing in a unique space for a lot of reasons. But people created these problems, and people can fix them. I don't know if my music is going to help at all, but those are the things that have always been in my music. I only wrote about 29, 30 songs, but they still seem to hit people. That means a lot."

The troubadour tradition is not one designed to achieve riches. The artist travels frequently, often plays low paying clubs, there is an up and down interest in the artist and there are few lucrative recording contracts. Since 2012 the Sugar Man experienced a steady increase in income. He is now quite well to do. As most of the figures about his personal wealth are private, Rodriguez' fortune is derived from many sources. By 2015 there were reliable figures on his earnings. His net worth was pegged at approximately a million dollars. The next year it allegedly doubled. None of these fiscal figures are official ones; they are estimates by financial professionals.

In 2011-2012 it is estimated Rodriguez' CDs earned $63,593, in 2012-2013 $78,431, by 2013-2014 the sum increased to $102,302 and in 2015-2016 it was estimated he earned $117,647. These figures are unofficial. If he is worth a million dollars where does the rest of the money come from and why does the money remain a mystery.

There are some monetary figures that are verified. From **Searching For Sugar Man's** popularity **Cold Fact** netted him $174,825, **Coming From Reality** $142,045, **Rodriguez Alive** $108,225 and **Live Fact** $81,169. There were ancillary rights of $63,131, which makes the total earnings for the Sugar Man's music $638,686 thanks to the popularity of the award winning documentary. The amount of money from endorsements is not a matter of public record. One indication is that the Sugar Man has endorsements outside of the U. S. But, again, there is only a statistic he brings in almost thirty thousand dollars a year in some form of endorsements.

There is no question the money is flowing into the family coffers. It is dependent upon touring, as well as record and memorabilia sales. After more than forty years the royalty train is rolling. Rodriguez and his family enjoy the fruits of his musical brilliance. It is about time.

Have Small Decisions Shaped Rodriguez' Life?

Do small decisions shape a troubadour's life? They do! The 1960s was a time defining the Sugar Man's troubadour persona. His recounting of Detroit's hard times is a feature of his lyrics. He never found rewarding employment. He opted for a contrarian lifestyle. His parents, his brothers, and one wonders if he had any sisters, all of these people remain a murky configuration in his life. The nine to five world was not to his liking. He worked for brief times as a teacher, a social worker and he had other professional employment. He preferred the blue collar, hardscrabble life as a construction worker. There is little evidence how these brief employment endeavors impacted his life. One can only suspect it was bureaucracy that drove the Sugar Man to rehabbing homes with blue-collar workers.

Did his decision to give up his early music career to raise his daughters result from the hard times his mother and father experienced? There is no doubt that influenced him. He spent a brief time in an orphanage. He didn't want his daughters to go through the same ordeal.

The whereabouts of his brothers remains a private matter. He has never spoken about it. They are somewhere in his private universe. Or are they? He doesn't talk about personal matters unless it is in song.

What is it that drives the Sugar Man's songwriting? It is reading. It is existential thought. It is observation. It is a tribute to a voracious intellectual curiosity. Rodriguez is more like an insightful novelist than a rock musician. His writing is the story of his mind. It is a swirling cacophony of brilliant insights into a civilization receding into the pit of barbarism. Rodriguez was born to write and perform to an ever-growing audience.

The Rodriguez story is a fascinating musical mystery for the ages. His rediscovery came when he was performing right under our noses. Malik Bendjelloul's documentary brought a troubadour to the mainstream. There is no bitterness or a sense of a missed opportunity. That tells one all they need to know about the man.

The Troubadour Tradition in 2009: Brad Wheeler's Criticism

On July 3, 2009 Rodriguez performed a Friday night set at the Toronto Harbourfront Centre during the Hot Spot Festival featuring King Sunny Ade and Nigerian Afrobeat performer Femi Kuti. A **Toronto Globe and Mail** reporter, Brad Wheeler, chastised those who told the story Rodriguez was killed on stage or perhaps died of a drug overdose. The Canadian journalist pointed out in 2009 the fake South African stories were still being told. He wondered why? Wheeler alleged Segerman was promoting fake news. No one cared. No one listened when the documentary arrived to the critic's acclaim. Rodriguez' story was too good to question.

Like many media types Wheeler proclaimed Rodriguez a star. It was July 2009. It was two and a half years before **Searching For Sugar Man** created "Rodriguez mania." The headline to Wheeler's article told it all: "Sixto Rodriguez Isn't Dead, He's On Tour." Later, Wheeler was even more critical of Segerman.

Brad Wheeler: "It is a testament to the utter evaporation of the troubadour Sixto Rodriguez that documentary which chronicles his 1998 concert jaunt of South Africa is called 'Dead Men Don't Tour.' And that title is true-you need only to show up at Harbourfront Centre tomorrow evening to verify that the long-lost topical singer-songwriter is completely non deceased."

What documentary was Wheeler referring to and why? It wasn't **Searching For Sugar Man**. That documentary would not be released until January 2012. It was 2009, and there was already an hour-long documentary on the Sugar Man. This hour long show on South African TV "Dead Men Don't Tour" followed Rodriguez' triumphant 1998 South African tour. Sometime during this period Malik

Bendjelloul discovered there were others who worked along documentary lines. When Malik discovered the Tonia Seeley documentary, he found in-concert gold footage. It helped him understand Rodriguez' unique talent and expanding popularity.

How did Brad Wheeler unwittingly become a publicity cog in the Sugar Man's machine? The answer is a simple one. The press asked: "Who is behind the Sugar Man?" Wheeler was enthralled by the Sugar Man's stage show. He was an act as good as any on the festival circuit. The **Toronto Globe And Mail** reporter urged everyone to find his re-released albums. It was 2009 and Matt Sullivan orchestrated an early cult career for the Sugar Man.

Wheeler praised Light In The Attic for releasing **Cold Fact**. He urged Toronto's psych-folk crowd to turn out for the show. He believed Rodriguez was not only a troubadour; he continued to entertain with new and fresh songs. This boded well for the future.

Matt Sullivan quietly orchestrated excellent press coverage. He told anyone who would listen the Sugar Man was the next big thing. He also talked of the power of the folk troubadour.

The troubadour is a storyteller who sees America's future. That is a description of the Sugar Man and his lyrical magic. He is able to notice the world around him and interpret it. He finds images of beauty interspersed with stoned visions of an America seeking its way. He sees political turmoil. He sees greed. He sees clusters of truth amidst a sea of hypocrisy. When the Sugar Man walks the gritty Detroit streets he is able to find inspiration in unlikely places. That is what troubadours do in a world beset with political conflict, economic injustice and violent visions.

How Did Fame Alter the Troubadour Tradition?

When Sixto Rodriguez walked on a Southern California stage at the El Rey Theater in late September 2012, he had experienced eight months of heady stardom. He was feted by an industry that had ignored him for forty years. But no one described him as a Mexican-American artist. That is until he walked into the El Rey Theater. In the midst of praise for **Searching For Sugar Man** the **Los Angeles Times** critic, Ernest Hardy, described him as "the Mexican American singer-songwriter who released two critically praised but commercially stillborn albums in the early 70s...." The El Rey show turned into what Hardy claimed was a "near religious event." He was right. Rediscovery after forty years was sweet. When Rodriguez sauntered out on stage he was continuing the troubadour tradition.

Steve Rowland drove from Palm Springs to the El Rey Theatre to reunite with Rodriguez. It was as if they had never been apart. It was a warm Saturday night on June 27, 2009 when Rowland and his friend Sondra drive into Los Angeles. Matt Sullivan greeted Rowland warmly. Steve was impressed. Light In The Attic aggressively promoted the re-release of **Cold Fact.** The critics raved about an album that sounded fresh.

Matt Sullivan's influence was in the counterculture press as they praised Rodriguez. The reason for LITA's success was in your face promotion, the release of a tenth anniversary 7 inch series 45 featuring Rodriguez' "I'll Slip Away" performed by Charles Bradley & The Menahan Street Band and the original "Sugar Man" on the b-side. It was promotional brilliance as Rodriguez evolved into an Indie icon. Sullivan carefully planned promotional materials. Vinyl versions of **Cold Fact** were given away at Los Angeles radio stations.

He was now singing his songs, telling his stories and joking with rapt audiences. The days of performing for loud college students near the University of Michigan at Mr. Flood's Party were over. He was no longer a bard in the wilderness. Fame hasn't altered his adherence to the troubadour tradition. He performs in the same manner as when he mesmerized University of Michigan students. Now he was at the Hollywood Bowl or the Royal Albert Hall. Times change! Rodriguez doesn't. The troubadour tradition remains in his soul.

Some critics carp about the shows. Other reviewers love his concerts. His fans never waver. The story is a simple one. A good guy, who is humble and a brilliant songwriter, comes back from obscurity to stardom. It is a tale for the ages. Redemption! Rediscovery! Feel good tales! True talent wins out! This is balanced with Rodriguez' natural humility. It is a rare combination.

The troubadour is a teacher highlighting the need for compassion, reforming the system and creating a positive view of the world. This is what the Sugar Man does on stage and in his private life. He has never tired of sending his message out through song and in media interviews.

The rambling folk guitar wordsmiths were an inspiration to the Sugar Man. But he also blended the blues, rock and roll oldies and old fashioned pop music into his act. He is an itinerant singer-songwriter from the past. He appeals to a deep thinking cultural past.

When Rodriguez was profiled on CBS's 60 Minutes, they called him "a troubadour." He realized he was finally at center stage. It had been a long time coming. Rodriguez vowed to enjoy the ride. He has!

The 60 Minutes spot went viral. It has had a huge viewership on 60 Minutes Overtime and the result is a curiosity about Sixto Rodriguez that is extraordinary. What is the untold story? One of the many mysteries remaining is where he fits into the American political tradition.

Twenty

Rodriguez and the American Political Tradition

"I describe myself as a musical political. There's a lot of issues that Detroit has, and so I stay interested."

Sixto Rodriguez

"The Mayor hides the crime rate. Councilwoman hesitates. Public gets irate but forget the vote date. Weatherman complaining predicted sun, it's raining. Everyone's protesting."

Sixto Rodriguez

"Nothing beats reality, so I decided to go back to work, though I never really left music. I took a BA in Philosophy, I became a social worker, I worked on a building site and got into politics. I always saw politics as a mechanism from where you can affect change. It took me ten years to get my four-year degree, then I ran for office. I actually ran for

Mayor, for City Council, for State Representative in Michigan and I also ran for my life! You know what I mean? I didn't have the political pull of the big guys, so you just do what you can do."

Sixto Rodriguez

"I disapprove of what you say, but I will defend to the death your right to say it."

Evelyn Beatrice Hall, The Friends of Voltaire, 1906

As the 2017 Detroit Mayoralty election loomed there were thirty-seven candidates filing to lead the Motor City. Among those was the name of a perennial political dissenter and a voice of the blue-collar worker Sixto Rodriguez. "There's a lot of issues that Detroit has, and so I stay interested," Rodriguez remarked to WDET-FM (101.9). This late March 2017 interview with a Detroit radio station was an indication the Sugar Man's political activism hadn't slowed. He was still a beacon for reform in the Motor City.

WDET-FM welcomed the Sugar Man regularly. The Sugar Man's favorite disc jockey, Stephen Henderson, put him on the air as soon as he walked into the studio. These interviews had gone on for more than two years. In early April 2015 Rodriguez walked in for an interview. He would do that for the next two and a half years. He periodically sat down and put on a pair of WDET headphones. The April visit was to explain his creative journey. In 2017 he toyed with the idea of running for Mayor. He made it clear he was too busy. One of the more interesting WDET programs was when the Sugar Man talked of his career and his hopes for Detroit. He had friendly exchanges with Congressman Dan Kildee on the people's needs. Kildee, a Democrat in the U. S. House of Representative, is a popular figure in the Flint Township. He has been a consistent voice to solving the local water problem. Michael Moore and Sixto Rodriguez are Kildee Democrats. They love his politics. So Rodriguez was gentle with his criticism. There were rumors of Kildee running for government in 2018. He declined the bid to draft him as Michigan's next governor. For Detroit no one has a stronger voice than Rodriguez. Kildee complimented the Sugar Man on his political advocacy.

In late March 2017 Rodriguez took over the mike at WDET to emphasize his newfound wealth and fame had not altered his politics. "I'm interested in what happens to Detroit and all its residents who've paid their dues already," Rodriguez said. When asked if would run for Mayor, he said: "Sometimes the people who are the underdogs need a candidate who everybody knows. Power to the people, you know." That said it all. But he didn't run. He was a voice for a new future.

The Detroit of 2017 is a city moving forward recovering from economic blight, inept political leadership and destructive partisan politics. Now cranes hover all over the city. They are rebuilding the infrastructure. The downtown shows signs of revitalization, Rodriguez' neighborhood, the Cass Corridor, remains a bastion of student activism, left over counterculture dreams and a liberal enclave. But that is today. What about the 1960s?

How the 1960s Impacted Rodriguez' Political Activism

As Dennis Coffey remarked in **Searching For Sugar Man:** "Detroit is a hard place." But it was a formative influence upon Rodriguez' developing political consciousness. You see it in his songs. You see it in his daily life. You see it in his concern for the blue-collar worker. When students were tear gassed in the streets Rodriguez was outraged. But he differed from his fellow political left cohorts. He had a program for change. When the Detroit City Council met, he was there to make constructive, workable suggestions. The Sugar Man's message was government officials must take responsibility for their actions. He did it with class, intelligence and without conflict. He was a peacemaker and a policy advocate. He was never a wide-eyed radical. He was a person who reflected his education with well thought out political ideas. This seemed to fly in the face of the contemporary political ideology. The Detroit riots had a lasting impact.

When the 1967 Detroit riots broke out, Rodriguez was in his mid-twenties. He wasn't a wide-eyed college student; he was a young man with a daughter and family responsibility. He also had a 45 record released on Harry Balk's Impact label and a songwriting career influenced by the violence and intimidation from the Detroit police.

When he looks back after half a century, he sees the garbage in the street, the inept politicians, the broken dreams of a past generation and a racial atmosphere polluting the mind. He is frustrated. He remains politically dedicated to restoring Detroit to its past glory.

When the riots broke out one of Rodriguez' friends told me he stood in front of the Big B Liquor Store uncertain of the future. In the irony of all ironies today there is a portrait series of large graphics hanging above this liquor store honoring those who are heroes in Detroit's comeback. The portraits are of the unemployed, there are images of urban rioting and the presence of political incompetence from the politicos who ignored the people and doomed the Motor City. One of those large portraits is of Sixto Rodriguez. He couldn't do much to stop the devastation. But fifty years later he is remembered as an urban pioneer. The paintings are a hidden history of the struggles of the Motor City. He is a hero to the blue-collar working class.

The number of and the intensity of his 1960s protests are events lost to history. Those I interviewed remarked he was on the front line of most demonstrations. He also hung out with a rising political radical, John Sinclair, who was instrumental in shaping and reinforcing many of the Sugar Man's political beliefs.

Unlike many 1960s protesters, Rodriguez advocated working through the system. He said political change was a civic duty. This is the reason he ran continually for public office. He always believed in the potential for a people's democracy. He also had a penchant for dissecting issues. He wasn't a wide-eyed, unthinking radical.

John Sinclair: Detroit's Political Angel: The 1960S and Beyond

Rodriguez is not known for having a political guru. John Sinclair is the closest person in Detroit to influence the Sugar Man's political activism. Who is Sinclair? He is a poet, and in his spare time he managed the MC5. In 1968, while working in the rock music business, Sinclair founded the White Panthers. The next year he was arrested for possession of marijuana. He was sentenced to ten years in prison. Before going to jail, he spent many afternoons and evenings with Rodriguez in local coffee shops. They shared a love for the magic dragon and radical politics.

John Sinclair's prison sentence was an egregious miscarriage of justice. He was targeted for his political activism and his demands to legalize marijuana. The militant and anti-racist White Panthers, which he founded, was enough to scare the authorities who equated Sinclair's group with the Black Panthers. After his arrest and conviction for possessing marijuana, he sued the U.S. government for illegal domestic surveillance. He won the case. He served a little more than two years in prison and when he was released he resumed his friendship with Sixto Rodriguez.

Although he was a 1960s activist, Sinclair spent parts of 1969 to late 1971 in jail for violating marijuana laws. The legal issues surrounding Sinclair's case intrigued Rodriguez. The courts became the focus of the "Free John Sinclair Movement." As marijuana-wafted daily over the Wayne State University campus, there were rallies, petitions and pressures to decriminalize the weed. The irony is the case drew so much attention for Michigan's aggressive prosecution and the subsequent excessive jail sentence the Michigan legislature responded by passing the Controlled Substance Act of 1971. This law classified marijuana as a distinct type of substance and this law reduced penalties for its sales and possession. On December 13, 1971 Sinclair was released from jail and it was during the watershed years of the 1970s that he and Rodriguez talked about what happened to the counterculture dream. Prior to being incarcerated in 1968 Sinclair was friendly with the Sugar Man and they shared many similar political positions. The friendship continues.

John Sinclair's notoriety increased when ex-Beatle John Lennon include a song on his 1972 album **Some Time In New York** dealing with Sinclair's legal problems. The three minute and twenty-eight second song not surprisingly called "John Sinclair" publicized Sinclair's legal difficulties. At this time Sinclair was hiding out at Detroit's Artists' Workshop. It was a strange moment in American history as Lennon wrote: "It ain't fair John Sinclair. In the stir for breathing air. Won't you care for John Sinclair?" Sinclair was pleased but he hid out in his small Detroit apartment. The Sugar Man was a frequent visitor.

When Rodriguez visited the Artists' Workshop at 4863 John Lodge in Detroit, he talked to Sinclair who lived upstairs in the building in a small apartment. After his arrest, Sinclair became a subject of counterculture politics. Abbie Hoffman jumped on stage during The Who's Woodstock performance to protest Sinclair's excessive jail sentence. As everyone turned on, tuned in and screamed for the music, Hoffman asked the crowd to support Sinclair's release.

What was Sinclair's influence upon the Sugar Man? Rodriguez told a friend he loved tilting at political windmills. Sinclair spurred him to run for public office. He had no illusions about being elected. His mantra was his message.

In a 2012 interview with Rob Hughes, Rodriguez claimed he didn't spend a lot of time hanging out with John Sinclair or the

MC5. This is because by the late 1960s Sinclair went to jail and they were together more often in the 1970s as the counterculture dreams faded into disco.

He said he did get to know the local scene. According to the Sugar Man's friends, he and Sinclair were on the same political wavelength. In October 2013 at the Barclay Center in Brooklyn, Sinclair opened for him. For some unexplainable reason, he didn't mention this long friendship with Malik Bendjelloul. There is no mention of Sinclair in **Searching For Sugar Man**. What Rodriguez did mention were his broad musical roots. These roots have been chronicled in a major compendium of Detroit music by a Wayne State University professor, M. L. Liebler. The complicated and diverse Motor City music scene is a vivid reminder of the multiple influences on Rodriguez' music. The essays pointing to what influenced Rodriguez come from Los Angeles based critic and Jerry Rubin biographer, Pat Thomas, who ties the extraordinary Motor City diversity to Rodriguez' literary songwriting genius.

In M. L. Liebler's extraordinary collection of essays on Detroit, **Heaven Was Detroit: From Jazz To Hip Hop And Beyond**, this almost five hundred page book paints a picture of a vibrant Motor City music scene influencing all aspects of Rodriguez' music. There is one essay that deserves special attention. Pat Thomas's "Rarities of The Revolution: Archie Shepp, the MC5, and John Sinclair" is an in depth look at how Sinclair used Archie Shepp's jazz sound as an inspiration for his 1966 revolutionary poems. The twenty four year old Sixto Rodriguez was impressed with Sinclair's message. But, according to Thomas, it was more than just jazz. The music reviews Sinclair wrote and the vibrant local music magazine scene intensified his radical politics. In San Francisco and Berkeley music melded with politics. It also did so if in a less recognized form in the Motor City.

Like most revolutionary music movements there were artists who had little public recognition. Thomas describes a musical collective, the Tribe, which shaped local African American culture with songs as far from Motown as one could imagine. "The time is now for revolution," the Tribe wrote. Pat Thomas shows how and why the Motor City was a complex musical-political community influencing Sixto Rodriguez.

Pat Thomas argues Motown pop and punk coalesced in Rodriguez' music to form the essence of his message. The hint of radicalism Thomas' writing exudes postulates how and why the Sugar Man's politics leaned increasingly to the hard left. He had nowhere else to go in the 1970s as the Village People and K. C. And the Sunshine Band embarrassed rock and roll music.

There were other changes in the 1960s influencing Rodriguez. The shift from peaceful protests to more aggressive demands for the government to withdraw from Vietnam shifted the Sugar Man's songwriting increasingly to protest themes. He saw it was necessary to use ones beliefs in song form. Hence, "The Establishment Blues."

The civil rights movement was a catalyst influencing Rodriguez' early songwriting. He quickly evolved into a more romantic, pop direction. When asked what the 1960s did for his songwriting? Rodriguez told **Uncut:** "The troubles in the city, the riots in Detroit… those were the things….Let's see, we had the Vietnam War, which is the backdrop, the students were burning their draft cards resisting the draft,….The students were moving to Canada….All these things were happening." Then Rodriguez pointed out the 196 killings in Mississippi prompted him to write "The Establishment Blues" long before he recorded it.

Sixto Rodriguez: "There was this lady called Viola Liuzzo. She was a Detroit lady, a white lady from the suburbs, and she went down to help a voter registration and she was killed in Alabama, in 65…. Detroit has supplied some of these issues, from the northern cities to down south. They might be obscure people but they certainly were of the 1970s." This comment suggests one early inspiration for Rodriguez' songwriting.

What Nursed Rodriguez' Political Leanings?

Labor union protests and challenging the corporate power structure increased the intensity of the Sugar Man's political activism. It was after he returned from the triumphant South African concerts in 1998 he shifted to more of a neighborhood political activist.

The Sugar Man's blue-collar employment confirmed his need to speak out. He saw a need for economic equality. He worked for a time in some of Detroit's most exploitive factories. At the falling down decrepit Dodge Main Chrysler plant, Rodriguez saw first hand worker misery. He worked there briefly on the assembly line. He was also employed at the Dodge Main plant, which was a dirty, poorly managed sixty- seven-acre factory located on the Detroit-Hamtramck border. It was akin to slavery. Poor wages, inadequate working conditions, a lack of benefits, and the increasingly stifling bureaucracy forced Rodriguez to other work. For a time he was employed at the Eldon Avenue Gear and Axle plant which was the most dangerous place to work in Detroit. Somewhere along the line Rodriguez lost his middle finger in an industrial accident. The last stop was demolition work. After inhaling dust, carrying refrigerators down two flights of stairs on his back and absorbing grime, Rodriguez went home each day exhausted. He was a committed union activist because of his employment experiences. The times changed. So did Rodriguez' political terrain. He narrowed it. He was primarily a community activist.

Education and Political Activism in the 1970s Onward: Changing Political Terrain and Cold Fact Never Dies

When **Cold Fact** was released in 1970 Rodriguez had a chance to share his political message. He saw the failure of radical politics and the counterculture dream. The 1960s were a lesson in political futility. He went into a furtive writing mode. He was lost in Richard M.

Nixon's America. It was a time of political mediocrity. Rodriguez decried the state of affairs in his lyrical poetry. Unfortunately, no one was listening! By 1971 his songwriting led to a batch of new tunes that made up **Coming From Reality**. That album fared no better than **Cold Fact**.

Rodriguez abandoned all pretensions of pursuing a music career. He settled into a happy, normal family life. He simply left the music business. It was time for a real life. At the exact time of this self-imposed exile from his career, United Artists released **Cold Fact** in South Africa. The vinyl release in South Africa began a strange trail for **Cold Fact**. The embryo South African record business saw A & M release a cassette in 1973. The following year **Cold Fact** came out and the locals were surprised to learn it was on United Artists. That appears to be the last legal release of Rodriguez' first album. **Cold Fact** never died. In one form or another it was sold, traded and copied. How did all this influence the Sugar Man? It didn't. He had no idea. Education and political activism became his focus.

It was the summer of 1974 and the thirty-two year old family man was back at Wayne State University working diligently toward a philosophy degree. He had no idea the album was released in South Africa and selling in Australia. He was done with the music business.

Rodriguez was one of the organizers of a Native-American Pow Wow in Detroit. He persuaded a Wayne State University student organization to sponsor the event. In addition to highlighting the art and culture of Detroit, the Native American Pow Wow dealt with health issues. Rodriguez referred to the "invisible minority" he saw in Native American cultural events. In nearby Oakland there were ten thousand Native Americans and Wayne County had almost twenty thousand residents. It was a sizeable population. The Sugar Man wanted them represented in government.

Rodriguez and his older brother also met with the Detroit Mayor Coleman Young to discuss multicultural and civil rights issues. The

Motor City was undergoing change. Rodriguez was in the vanguard of a political movement empowering minorities and blue collar, working class people.

Why 1974 was a Watershed Political Summer

The 1974 summer spurred another round of political activism for the Sugar Man. He was concerned his community work was failing. He had a dim view of the Mayor. He decided to run for state office. Rodriguez was increasingly frustrated with his reform attempts in the Motor City. Could the state pick up his message? Rodriguez organized a campaign to sit in the Michigan House of Representatives. He campaigned for this seat in the 21st District. He lost to David S. Holmes an African American Democrat with a long history of party activism. Holmes was the candidate of the United Auto Worker's, and he was a well-known civil rights activist. Rodriguez didn't have a chance against this seasoned Democrat. Holmes campaigned with the slogan: "The champion of the people." He was also a close friend and ally of Mayor Coleman Young. These factors brought him victory.

Rodriguez believed his reform mandate failed. He increasingly became more active in the Cass Corridor. He was now a neighborhood activist. But in the mid-1970s there was a different Sixto Rodriguez. He was young. He was confident civil rights would triumph. It had been two decades since Brown v. The Board of Education desegregated the schools and it had been a decade since the Civil Rights Act of 1964 paved the way for African American inclusion in the political process.

Rodriguez was enthralled by these changes. He confessed much later his youthful optimism gave way to a cynicism and pessimism. The point is the 1960s formed the Sugar Man's intellectual persona. He also read the literature of the 1960s becoming familiar with

Ralph Ellison's **Invisible Man** about an African American whose color renders him invisible. Rodriguez modeled his writing on Ellison's approach with its emphasis on subjects such as black Nationalism, Marxism, identity, racial policies and an existential vision of American with a Kafka informed absurdity. Ellison may have been an informative influence upon the Sugar Man. He has never said. But his writing reflects the Ellison demeanor.

The mid-1970s was a time of African American civil right activism. Rodriguez was squarely in the forefront of this movement. He also advocated multi-culturalism. He emerged as a leader in the Mexican American political community. He had close ties to Cesar Chavez and the United Farm Workers of California. In the summer of 1975, Rodriguez attended a United Farm Workers of California rally in Detroit Clark's Park. This well attended community event featured a rousing speech by Cesar Chavez urging a Michigan wide boycott of California grapes.

Rodriguez' Political Expertise: The Cass Corridor

For half a dozen years Rodriguez was recognized for his political expertise and his leadership in the Cass Corridor. The police targeted him for his tirades against oppressive law enforcement. He would not back down on the question of police misconduct. They eventually backed him down by beating the hell out of him.

Rodriguez' political activism was highlighted in a city sponsored pamphlet **Detroit: A Young Guide To The City**. It was essentially a tourist's guide. The free giveaway had stories of the ethnically diverse Motor City. Sixto Rodriguez was featured as a prominent Mexican American political activist. No mention was made of his music. There is a picture of the Sugar Man standing in the middle of an urban agricultural farm. Detroit has the largest number of urban farms in the U. S. The Sugar Man is shown speaking with a group of young children. He is described as a person working for change.

The grassroots political activism Rodriguez practiced was a portent of things to come. Unbeknownst to Rodriguez, the FBI was lurking around the Wayne State University campus. I put in a Freedom of Information request for Sixto Rodriguez. I was told there was not a file on him. On the other hand John Sinclair's FBI file has extensive information on the Sugar Man's political activity, as well as his lengthy friendship with Rodriguez. The Sugar Man was on the FBI's radar in Sinclair's file.

Rodriguez' persistent political activism led to a confrontation. On October 17, 1975, he arrived on the WSU campus. He walked over to the newspaper office. He asked to speak to the **South End** editor. He inquired: "Would you like to publish a story on police brutality?" They agreed to do the story. The issue of police misconduct in the Cass Corridor was not the first story on this subject. At the time the Sugar Man was an upper division student in the Monteith honors college. In 1979 Monteith closed, but he continued his degree progress over the next few years. This explains Rodriguez' 1981 graduation.

From day one Monteith College fit into the Sugar Man's psyche. There were no long, boring lectures with hundreds of students. The honors college depended upon small colloquiums. The students meet in small seminars. They wrote papers, discussed their work and engaged in give and take discussions with the professors. The Monteith College was designed to strengthen the intellect. It was a philosophical approach to education. It is also one in which there were no clear answers. As an existentialist, this was a school forming the Sugar Man's future intellectual persona.

Wayne State University is a blue collar, working-class college with a top ten-labor studies department. The history professors in labor studies were among the most radical, respected and forward thinking of any faculty on campus. They influenced the Sugar Man's labor oriented politics. Rodriguez was vocal about police misconduct. Soon he experienced it personally.

On October 22, 1975 the **South End**, a local WSU student newspaper, reported Sixto Rodriguez was going to court to file charges against the Motor City police for a beating in the police station. A picture of Rodriguez displayed a bruised face with ugly blue welts, a half shut eye and marks on his head. The beating Rodriguez experienced allegedly took place in the 4th Precinct Detroit Police Station. He had four broken cheekbones and four stitches hid some of the damage to his face. Sgt Robert Meyers, the Detroit Precinct Commander, said that Rodriguez slipped. The Sugar Man claimed his feet were kicked out from under him.

Why was Rodriguez arrested? It resulted after a phone call from a convenience store. The owner complained Rodriguez came into the store and asked for change for five dollars to give his daughters lunch money. The owner said no. Rodriguez insisted on change. They hollered at each other. The police were called.

Rodriguez' daughters, Eva, 12 and Sandra, 10, witnessed this miscarriage of justice. The police report identified Robert Scott, the owner of the small convenience store, as the complaining party. Scott not only called the police, he pulled a shotgun on the Sugar Man. When the press showed up, Scott told them he would sue. To make matters worse the police were talking about a felony charge against Rodriguez.

The Sugar Man hired a lawyer, Alan L. Kaufman, who was a voice of reason. He pointed out Rodriguez was the aggrieved party. The case was dropped. The Detroit justice system prompted Rodriguez to continue to fight against police brutality. The Sugar Man increasingly concentrated on his private life after this abortive incident.

Personal Changes in Rodriguez in the 1970s

Sometime in 1975-1976 Rodriguez purchased his home on Avery Street in the Woodbridge area. He settled in to raise Eva and Sandra. On May 30, 1979, Regan, was born completing the family.

Throughout the later part of the 1970s, Rodriguez played where and when he could find a venue to spin his folk-psych songs. They came out in droves to see him. No one expected mainstream stardom. He was also a frequent concert attendee. On July 29, 1979, he was in the audience when the Detroit Blues Review presented a free concert on a Sunday down by the river featuring Little Mac Collins, Mr. Bo, Jesse Wiliams, Little Junior, Eddie Burns and Chicago Pete. The Sugar Man loved the blues.

In the Fall of 1980, Rodriguez ran for Detroit Mayor. He didn't win. He knew he had no chance of being elected. Why did he run? The Motor City was in a precipitous decline. The combination of racial tensions, fiscal missteps and a weak Mayor in Coleman Young did little to suggest the Motor City had a bright future. Detroit was a one trick pony. They had an auto industry. That was it. The auto industry was in a downward spiral. Racial tensions prompted white and African American workers to refuse to work side by side. There was a flight to the suburbs. There was little hope for Detroit's future.

Rodriguez reflected Detroit's influence. This was obvious when he wrote "Inner City Blues." "The Inner City birthed me. The local pusher nursed me. Cousins make it in the street. They marry every trick they meet." Rodriguez wrote these lines decade earlier and he told a close friend nothing had changed. The 1980s simply reflected the previous two decades. Community activism remained Rodriguez' direction.

In **Searching For Sugar Man** there is a scene where Regan pulls out a box of Rodriguez memorabilia. She displays a series of election brochures from the Fall of 1989 when Rodriguez ran for a seat on the Detroit City Council. His name was spelled incorrectly on the ballot. She explained he had been a candidate for various city and state political offices: State Representative (twice), City Council (three times), Mayor (twice) and one attempt for the State Senate. She looked as frustrated as her father.

The Transition in Rodriguez' Life

The 1970s and 1980s were a transition period for Rodriguez. He shifted his attitudes away from the larger picture of anti-war protest to the streets of Detroit. He spent more time educating himself on local affairs. His two failed attempts to secure a seat on the Detroit City Council is testimony to his local politics. He saw the futility of attempting to influence the big picture.

From 1970 to 2000 Rodriguez promoted a biracial, working class coalition of young people advocating women's rights, drug treatment plans, safe community streets, policing the police and responsible city spending. He was a relentless urban reformer.

It had been less than two years since Rodriguez' triumphant 1998 South African concert tour. His career was once again dormant. The Sugar Man was a Bill Clinton supporter. The 1990s was a time of heady optimism for Rodriguez. He had visions of a better America. The Clinton years were important to him. He saw progress economically. In matters of race relations, he was happy progress was evident. He was a fan of the first lady Hillary Clinton. For decades he advocated changes in the workplace for women in terms of job placement, equal pay and equitable working conditions. The softening of attitudes on marijuana intrigued the Sugar Man. He supported legalizing marijuana since the 1960s.

The frightening specter of George W. Bush in the White House spurred the Sugar Man's political concerns. He stepped away from the Cass Corridor to run for a larger office. His campaign began securing signatures, funding and a sophisticated set of campaign offices were organized for a seat in the Michigan House of Representatives.

In the Michigan House of Representatives election for District 7 in the August 7, 2000 Democratic Primary Rodriguez polled seven hundred twenty eight votes to finish third behind the party nominee Hansen Clarke. The Sugar Man's campaign emphasized community issues. He campaigned primarily in the Cass Corridor.

The horror story of the Bush years was followed by what Rodriguez viewed as the progress of Barack Obama's presidency. Rodriguez was an avid Obama supporter. He believed the progress under President Bill Clinton made America great again. He didn't realize this slogan of making America great again would lead to the election of the singularly least qualified candidate in American history, Donald J. Trump.

Rodriguez Reflects on His Political Career in 2017: Home Loan-School Crusades

When he reflected on his political career in 2017, Rodriguez told Detroit radio station WDET 101.9 FM: "I've run for mayor of Detroit. I've run for City Council of Detroit. I've run for state representative of Michigan, and I've also run for my life. I'm political as a person. I do music too."

That said it all. But what are the issues? By 2017, approaching seventy-five, the Sugar Man scaled down his political positions. He was concerned over city and state funding for neighborhoods. He was alarmed, if privately, about the future of a Trump dominated America.

A key issue in 2017 Rodriguez dealt with was affordable housing. The large number of cash housing sales in Detroit made it difficult for young people in the Cass Corridor to afford an apartment. It was increasingly difficult to purchase a home. Rents increased rapidly as did housing costs. The Sugar Man took on the housing issue.

Rodriguez' politics are sophisticated. He began campaigning against redlining. What is redlining? During the Great Depression, the federal government produced maps to assist banks and other financial institutions to qualify buyers for home loans. These guidelines helped to create a lending system excluding African American and Mexican American purchasers. Rodriguez is a critic of redlining.

The Sugar Man's other concerns center around the Detroit school system. He said the public schools now have an irreversible debt issue, the low salaries hurt teacher-hiring policies, a morale problem made for low-test scores and future funding remained uncertain. "I'm interested in what happens to Detroit," Rodriguez continued, "and all its residents who've paid their dues already." That said it all!

Then in April 2017 a Rodriguez spokesman said he was not running for Mayor. He was supporting Dr. Bob a chiropractor operating out of a psychedelic painted office. The Sugar Man was still concerned, but he had no time to run for political office. The Psychedelic Shack is the place for Dr. Bob's business. But it is hardly the typical campaign place to elect a Mayor. But then again that is the Sugar Man's mantra. He is a musical political not a politician.

The tenacious political attitudes defining the Sugar Man have not changed since the 1960s.

Rodriguez Reflects on His Political Career

In August 2012, Rodriguez sat down for an interview with Dave Segal for the Detroit paper, **The Stranger**. His reflections on his political aspirations provide a rare insight into his thinking concerning the American political tradition.

Sixto Rodriguez: "I've run for office eight times, from mayor of Detroit to State Representative of Michigan and City Council of Detroit. To get to the ballot, you have to petition for the needed signatures. The most votes I've ever received…was for city council. I received 7,000 votes. The cutoff was 30,000, so I'm voting Obama in this coming election. I don't feel like I'm being represented by a governor's son, with that Teflon kind of look."

This convoluted explanation tells one a great deal about the Sugar Man. He is a serious political thinker. He is now a neighborhood or ward politician. Then four years later in 2013, Rodriguez lent his support to Raquel Castaneda-Lope, a Latina, who was elected to the Detroit City Council from District 6. She is the first Latino to sit on the Council. He appeared at one of her campaign events and lent his name, as well as his financial support, to her bid for public office.

While touring Australia Rodriguez talked politics. In a November 2016 interview with Rip Nicholson, the Sugar Man reflected on the U. S. presidential election a few days before voting took place. He said he was voting Hillary Clinton. Then the Sugar Man analyzed American politics.

Sixto Rodriguez: "You see a lot of hypocrisy and political adolescence today, and these are serious matters that go well beyond the reach of a billionaire. But, (Trump's) the best they've got in the Republican Party at the moment, and that's a shame…."

As he talked about the future, he was concerned with the plight of the blue collar, working class. The factory worker, the day laborer, the itinerant or casual worker and those searching for employment are never far from his mind. Then he returned to the 2016 presidential election.

Sixto Rodriguez: "Whoever is going to be the Commander-in-Chief of this country, it's going to be an important position. I think of the two candidates, I am voting for the younger person Hillary Clinton, and the reason is that she is more of a statesman…."

Because of his experiences performing in South Africa, Australia and the U. K., Rodriguez displayed a global political conscience. "You bring up the economic status. Well, I travel the world now and I've been to Australia six times and my synopsis of the world is that there's enough for everyone and in fact there's too much for anyone. America is a leader and they have to show that leadership...."

Rodriguez in the Age of Trump: What are His Thoughts?

In January 2017, Donald J. Trump was sworn in as the 45th President of the United States. During Trump's first hundred days, the Sugar Man was quiet about his future political directions. He was shocked at the rise of the Trump presidency.

The good news is Rodriguez is considering another run for political office. He has had little time with touring, songwriting, visiting with his grand children, and spending a great deal of quality time with his extended family. He will surface again in the political arena.

As a man of simple means, Rodriguez is not an in your face musical political. But if you listen to "Can't Get Away," he tells the story of what our nation is going through under the Trump oligarchy. He watches as the poor get poorer and the middle class recedes slowly before ultimately vanishing. It is not a pleasant sight for the Sugar Man.

The best description of Rodriguez' involvement in the political arena comes from his oldest daughter Eva. When he was discovered alive and well in Detroit, by the cadre of South African's searching for him, Eva sent a series of e-mail to the website looking for her father. In her messages she pointed out her father was educated, hard working and above all else politically involved. Eva extolled the integrity, the humanity and the commitment to social justice that is Sixto Rodriguez. She also suggested he might be left along. He wasn't. The rest is history.

Twenty-One

How Matt Sullivan made Rodriguez a Cult Star: The 2009 West Coast Tour

"Nothing beats reality, so I decided to go back to work, though I never really left music. I took a BA in Philosophy, I became a social worker, I worked on a building site and got into politics. I always saw politics as a mechanism from where you can affect change. It took me ten years to get my four-year degree, and then I ran for office. I actually ran for Mayor, for City Council, for State Representative in Michigan and I also ran for my life! You know what I mean? I didn't have the political pull of the big guys, so you just do what you can do."

Rodriguez in conversation with Rob Hughes.

"And at the end of all our exploring.
Will be to arrive where we started. And
know the place for the first time."

T. S. Eliot, Four Quarters.

Matt Sullivan is one of the unheralded heroes in the Sixto Rodriguez story. He not only contacted Stephen "Sugar" Segerman to inquire about reissuing the Sugar Man's two long forgotten LPs, he contacted the producers, Dennis Coffey, Mike Theodore and Steve Rowland, and he commissioned a writer with deep knowledge to provide copious liner notes for both albums. Sullivan provided the first comprehensive examination of Rodriguez' life and a re-mastered set of CDs celebrating the vision of his neglected genius.

Light In the Attic set up promotional concerts for Rodriguez. This eventually led to early media appearances on the David Letterman Show and the Tonight Show among others.

What is not apparent to the casual observer is from June 2009 until **Searching For Sugar Man** triumphantly debuted at the Sundance Film Festival; Sullivan was promoting Rodriguez night and day. It is important to examine how Sullivan and his label, Light In The Attic, made him a cult star by late 2011. In June 2009, Rodriguez flew into the Seattle-Tacoma Airport for concerts in Seattle, Portland, Vancouver, San Francisco and Los Angeles. It was a mini-tour establishing the Sugar Man's slowly rising career. He was on the commercial radar.

When the Sugar Man emerged from the plane, he walked into the Sea-Tac terminal in a stylish black jacket that looked like it came from the Beatles' 1964 U. S. tour. It had gold piping. Rodriguez smiled. He proudly announced it came from a Detroit thrift store. The cost? Five bucks! Sullivan drove Rodriguez to Ballard. This is a quaint Swedish-Norwegian area that was once home to fishermen. It is now home to hipsters, alternative music clubs and millennial businesses. Rodriguez was scheduled to rehearse for a mini-West Coast with the San Francisco band the Fresh and Onlys.

Rodriguez was brought to a rehearsal where he met the horn section for a late afternoon jam. J-Maa Catering provided the food. The menu of roasted chicken, ricotta olive toasts, salad, zucchini and a desert of maple syrup tres leches poached with rhubarb and wild strawberries made the mellow crowd downright comfortable.

There was more to the night than dinner and rehearsal. The Sugar Man met the Light In The Attic staff. He bonded with public relations guru Ever Kipp. The opening band for the first promotional concert, Arthur and Yu, were at the dinner. A feeling of kinship quickly developed. While practicing Rodriguez surprised everyone with a brief version of "The Tennessee Waltz." It was a portent of things to come.

Ever Kipp is one of the unsung heroes in the Sixto Rodriguez story. His Seattle based media firm, Tiny Human, is a boutique public relations company founded in 2009 to promote artists like the Sugar Man. He worked in New York and arrived in Seattle to toil for the Indie label Barsuk Records. It didn't take long for Kipp to establish his legendary publicity credentials. Death Cab For Cutie and Rufus Wainwright among others depended upon his deft publicity skills. One only has to look at what he has done for Lee Hazlewood to realize how lucky Rodriguez was to have this promotional guru in his corner. The Sugar Man realized this and let Kipp know he appreciated everything.

The next day Rodriguez stood in front of the LITA office on Aurora Avenue. The hookers had gone home, the seedy nature of the area looks a bit better in the daylight and the promotional photos of the Sugar Man in the office were highly professional ones. Then the entourage drove to Canada to a Vancouver club to begin the mini-West Coast tour. No one knew what to expect.

The Rodriguez phenomena built slowly from this humble beginning. Then two and a half years later it burst into a major commercial phenomenon with the screening of **Searching For Sugar Man**.

Before they arrived in Vancouver the Rodriguez party stopped at a small record store in Bellingham Washington. It is the home of Western Washington University. It is the most accomplished small college in the state. Many successful graduates have been turned out as well as many excellent writers. (I am a graduate.) The Bellingham store, Avalon Records, is home to the earliest Rodriguez cult. Sullivan had trouble-pulling Rodriguez out of the store. He wanted to stay on and talk about Pacific Northwest music. The Sugar Man loves the Sonics.

When they arrived at the upscale Vancouver club, Richard's on Richards, the San Francisco backing band the Fresh and Onlys were ready for the night's show. They were set up on stage. Rodriguez met Kevin "Sipreano" Howes who wrote the in-depth, superb liner notes for **Cold Fact.** After a short sound check, they headed to Zulu Records. Once again this is a bastion of Rodriguez mania. Again they had to almost kidnap him to get the Sugar Man out of the record store.

They adjourned for a snack as Rodriquez consumed two bowls of soup. The rest of the entourage ate delicious sandwiches, energy bars and tacos. After some much needed rest, the band and Rodriguez walked out on the Richard's at Richards stage at eleven in the evening. The sixty-six year old Rodriguez appeared eager to perform as did the band. The crowd loved the show. The sales at the merchandise table exceeded expectations. Rather than stay overnight in Vancouver, the entourage piled into a van full of burger wrappers, stale tacos and coffee cups. Some four hours later they pulled into Seattle. It was almost five in the morning. It was a rough day, but it set the stage to build the Rodriguez cult.

By the third day of Rodriguez' West Coast tour the Sugar Man was ready for the major event. He would appear at Seattle's Triple Door. What is the Triple door? It is an upscale club with fine food, a state of the art sound system and a reputation for bringing the Emerald City fine entertainment.

Matt Sullivan had some surprises. In addition to two shows at this plush venue, he arranged for a special concert over Seattle radio station KEXP. Demonstrating his business expertise, Sullivan set up VIP seating. This was a special concert for charity. He had patrons donate over $500 to charity. This three in the afternoon show not only benefitted charity, it created a defined window into the Sugar Man's music.

The evening shows went well and everyone loved the cover of a Frank Sinatra inspired "I'm Gonna Live Till I Die." The night was spent celebrating and feeling good about the crowd's reception. After three standing ovations, the Sugar Man was elated.

Then the next afternoon it was off to Portland. As the Fresh and Onlys crowded into their van with their music equipment and took off for Portland, Rodriguez followed in a car with Marc Capelle, the Fresh and Onlys trumpet player/keyboardist. Sullivan drove, but before leaving Seattle, he had a surprise. Before cruising onto Interstate 5, they stopped for the Emerald Cities best tacos at the food truck known as Rancho Bravo Tacos in Seattle's Wallingford district. Then it was off to Highway I-5 to Portland. Coffee and donuts were picked up on the way.

When they arrived at Portland's Doug Fir Lounge, Rodriquez loved it. The rooms where the band slept were a few feet off stage. It was perfect to practice, crash or people watch. After a quick sound check Rodriguez and Sullivan headed over to Jackpot Records for another signing and more fan appreciation. Not surprisingly, two South African's were first in line. Then it was back to the Doug Fir Lounge to sit in the room one hundred feet from the stage.

By eleven after a set from the Fresh and Onlys, Rodriguez took the stage opening with "Inner City Blues." Sometimes the crowd loved Rodriguez' covers other times they scream "no covers."

But there was something that set these shows apart. Sullivan hired a horn section allowing the Sugar Man to display another side of his performing genius. The horn section allowed Rodriguez to put his own brand on Bob Dylan's "Like A Rolling Stone." The patrons stood and cheered.

Why was Sullivan important to the birth of the "cult of Rodriguez?" The answer is a simple one. He is able to appeal to the media. The morning after the Portland show, Rodriguez continued with his media blitz. Courtesy of Matt Sullivan! He did two telephone interviews with Toronto media outlets, as he was scheduled to leave shortly for Canada. Then they met with disc jockey Jeff Rosenberg of Portland's alternative KBOO, which is at 90.7 FM, and it is a non-profit community station where the Sugar Man felt at ease. With the media interviews behind them, Rodriguez and Sullivan drove to Yreka California.

On the way to Yreka, Sullivan and his entourage stopped for food and drink in Eugene. Once again Sullivan displays a genius in promoting Rodriguez' material by visiting premier local record stores. It is the home to the University of Oregon Ducks. Eugene is a typical college town. It has bookstores and cheap eateries. There is a quaint skid row on Railroad Avenue and, of course, the requisite collector's record store. At the House of Records, Rodriguez meets Fred and Martha and they begin talking music. It is hard to get the Sugar Man out of the store. This is a recurrent theme. Hunger pangs rescue the group. When they leave Eugene, Sullivan and Rodriguez talk politics. When they tire, they talk music.

Finally, at eight in the evening, they pull into the sleepy town of Yreka. Everyone is famished. They find a place to eat. At Grandma's House a dinner of breaded veal cutlets for the Sugar Man and a chicken salad sandwich for Sullivan ends a brutal day. They are exhausted. The Fresh and Onlys drove from Portland to San Francisco with no more than stops for gas and tacos. They live in San Francisco.

On the drive to San Francisco, Sullivan and Rodriguez speculate on how and why Michael Jackson died. They trade conspiracy theories. They talk about the doctor who provided the addictive medicine. They talk about the magic dragon. Then from time to time they veer into political conspiracy theories. The Zapruder film on John F. Kennedy's assassination is a frequent Rodriguez conspiracy topic. It is only a year into President Barack Obama's leadership. They both feel good about America's future.

After six days with the Sugar Man, Sullivan arrives in San Francisco. The Rodriguez show, the previous year, was at the Great American Music Hall. This is a special venue. This art deco theater is in a seedy area full of hookers, drugs and near the Mitchell Brothers porno theater. For years it was Van Morrison's favored venue when he lived in Marin County. It is a funky, intimate theater with a balcony that allows people to walk around and watch the band on the stage. But this venue was booked. Sullivan was able to secure a night at Boz Scaggs club Slim's. Located in an industrial area of San Francisco, Slim's for almost three decades, is the club of choice for touring bands seeking an intimate place to perform.

With Sullivan in charge there is a defined set list. For the Slim's show the set list included: "Inner City Blues," "I Wonder," "To Whom It May Concern," "Crucify Your Mind," "Only Good For Conversation," "Sugar Man," "Rich Folks Hoax," "Like Janis," "I Think of You," "The Establishment Blues," "You'd Like To Admit It," "Climb Up On My Music" and "Forget It." After the thirteen song set, Rodriguez left the Slim's stage to rapturous applause He returned with three encores closing with "Jane S. Piddy." The horns and accompaniment of the Fresh and Onlys had the critics raving. It was 2009. Matt Sullivan brought Rodriguez to cult stardom.

While in San Francisco Sullivan and Rodriguez stayed in the Phoenix Hotel. This is a trendy, super hip 1950s era hotel in the tenderloin. The idea of a boutique hotel amongst the drug addicts, the hookers, the homeless and the hip tourists appealed to Sullivan and Rodriguez. The Phoenix Hotel is the type of contradiction that explains San Francisco. It is a Joie de Vivre hotel, which means in plain English it is expensive. It has a complimentary happy hour. It is also trendy and hip. The location at 601 Eddy Street is just a few blocks from the San Francisco Cable Car. It is not like the place where Sullivan and Rodriguez stayed in Yreka.

The Slim's show is an example of how fame hampers an artist. He could walk around and talk to this fans as they stood waiting for the show. He signed albums. He signed pictures. He had his picture taken with fans. It was a love fest. Then eight years later all this changed. He now plays larger venues. He has a managed schedule. One wonders if Rodriguez believes fame and fortune is worth the tedious, backbreaking schedule.

In 2017, it was impossible for the Sugar Man to wander out into the crowd after a show. There are minders, there is a tour manager, there is a tour bus and there is a hard-core schedule. This is how it is in 2017. Fortunately, under Matt Sullivan's expert guidance all of the pitfalls of stardom were avoided in 2009. It was simply a different time. One wonders if Rodriguez has written songs comparing the two periods in his career?

In 2009, under Matt Sullivan's tutelage, Rodriguez spent time with his fans signing autographs, taking pictures and talking music. The Slim's show was magical and a late night stop at Pronto Pizza continued the convivial mood. There was one show left. It was in Los Angeles. The Sugar Man looked forward to connecting with Steve Rowland.

The legendary El Rey Theater is the last stop on the tour. The drive from San Francisco to Los Angeles is a grueling six-hour test of endurance and stamina. The three in the afternoon sound check looms as they barrel down Interstate Highway 5. Then miraculously they spot an oasis. It is the Kettelman City. There is a mammoth and delicious place to eat. It is the In And Out Burger. They stopped for multiple burgers and fries. As Rodriguez sits at a round table in the California San Joaquin Valley sunshine, the mouth-watering cheeseburgers, the fries and the large coke blended into the local landscape. It is warm. The people are friendly. They sat outside talking for an hour. Not even Seattle's Dick's Drive In can compare to an In and Out Burger and its french fries.

When they reach the El Rey, Rodriguez, Sullivan and the band weren't prepared for the reception. It is the afternoon, and there are already people milling outside the art deco El Rey Theater. The press is buzzing around. The alternative newspaper, the **LA Weekly**, is ready to do a story. They sent two reporters, a photographer and a young girl who looks like a movie star to interview the Sugar Man. KCSB is another community radio station located at the University of California, Santa Barbara This alternative UC radio station played Rodriguez frequently and they answered questions for more than hundred interviews. It is after all hip Los Angeles.

The **LA Weekly** is one of two El Rey sponsors. The other, KCSB, shows up to interview the Sugar Man. Then it is off to Fairfax Avenue and the legendary Canter's Deli for dinner. They sat in a booth the waitress said Frank Zappa occupied decades earlier.

Rodriguez's wife, Konny, arrives in Los Angeles for the gig. She is ready to see the show. There is another surprise, Steve Rowland shows up with his friend, Sondra, to lend support. It is the first time since 1971, when **Coming From Reality** was produced, that the two friends reconnected. Rowland and Rodriguez talked in person and in great detail. It was tough to get them apart.

Steve Rowland: "Rodriguez thought Sondra was my wife. I thanked him but I said 'No.' She is a friend."

There were many people in the El Rey dressing room. Steve couldn't have an in-depth conversation with Rodriguez because of the activity of those around him. Finally, Steve went out front to watch the show.

The 2009 mini-West Coast tour ends. It is a resounding success. What is the point? Rodriguez was back as a cult artist. **Searching For Sugar Man** created the commercial whirlwind sending Rodriguez into hiding or at least seclusion. Stephen "Sugar" Segerman spun the story ignoring the obvious evidence Matt Sullivan and Light In The Attic brought Rodriguez back from oblivion three years before the documentary exploded on the big screen. The myths and realities of the search for the Sugar Man tell one a great deal about the egregious, pompous statements that Segerman made to convolute the story and twist the facts.

There is no question Matt Sullivan not only made Rodriguez a cult star, he believed in his music, the man and the story. When Malik Bendjelloul came along to film **Searching For Sugar Man**, Matt paved the way for the documentary. Why he wasn't featured prominently remains a mystery. Perhaps that is the point. His comments might detract from the mysterious tales of Rodriguez shooting himself on stage, dying of a drug overdose or simply vanishing into the hinterlands. None of this was true. It did make for sensational press. Sometimes popular culture is beyond the realm of reality. That was the case with small segments of the Sixto Rodriguez story. There is no question the pervasive images of Detroit and Cape Town and the romantic view of Rodriguez' comeback in South Africa make the documentary a tour de force Cinderella tale. Perhaps if Sullivan had appeared and had a speaking part in **Searching For Sugar Man**, he would have lessened the romantic impact of the tale. That would not have been good box office. Then again!

Twenty-Two

Myths and Realities in The Rodriguez Story: The Lost Facts Disrespect Sixto Rodriguez

"I like to say I do covers of my own songs."

Sixto Rodriguez when asked about why he uses backup bands.

"It has that combination of obscurity of quality."

David Holmes describing Cold Fact

"America is not so much a nightmare as a non-dream. The American dream is precisely a move to wipe the dream out of existence."

- William S. Burroughs

"It started out with butterflies on a velvet afternoon."

Sixto Rodriguez

**"Emancipate yourself from mental slavery,
none but ourselves can free our mind".**

ROBERT NESTA "BOB" MARLEY,

The myths and realities of the Sixto Rodriguez story are largely the product of Stephen "Sugar" Segerman's fertile mind. He is aided by a bevy of London based journalists and, as Joseph Campbell observed in **The Power of Myth**: "People say that what we're all seeking is a meaning for life. I don't think that's what we're really seeking. I think that what we're seeking is an experience of being alive, so that our life experiences on the purely physical plane will have resonances with our own innermost being and reality, so that we actually feel the rapture of being alive."

How does this impact the Rodriguez story? It reinforces facts, opinions and information contrary to the prevailing truth. It is important to analyze those who have twisted the tale for personal, journalistic or fiscal reasons.

Rolling Stone Lists 10 Things No One Knew About Rodriguez

In March 2013, in the aftermath of the Oscar for **Searching For Sugar Man**, Rolling Stone's Andy Greene headlined: "Ten Things You Didn't Know About the Star of Searching For Sugar Man."

Greene pointed to his Australian popularity. He wrote how frenetically the Aussies embraced the Sugar Man. There was no mention of this in the documentary. Midnight Oil drummer, Rob Hirst, was mystified about how anyone could not find Rodriguez. The band found him every time they toured America. They also found his daughters. The Australian concert promoter, Michael Coppel said: "He played to 15,000 people in Sydney...."

The **Rolling Stone** article alluded to Rodriguez making money in Australia and later after the 1998 Australian tour he went back to the construction business for only a brief time. When the documentary came out in 2012 there was no mention of a cult decade long career prior to **Searching For Sugar Man**. He wasn't rich. He was making a living. But Rodriguez didn't achieve bookings at Coachella or the Glastonbury Festival until the documentary, success.

There are some minor changes in his life **Rolling Stone** discovered. He had no computer, no television, no air conditioning, no central heating, no toaster, no microwave, no electric toothbrush and no conveniences. His daughter Regan talked him into a cell phone. That is not a contradiction. It is the existential way of the Sugar Man.

The **Rolling Stone** article hinted at Rodriguez' patriotism. This seems like an oxymoron for a former hippie to be patriotic. Everyone I interviewed told me the Sugar Man had an "intelligent patriotism." In the age of Donald J. Trump this is a compliment. How did Rodriguez define patriotism? He said he would volunteer to fight in Vietnam. He failed the physical. He said he would fight until his last breath for government reform. He has done so running multiple times for public office. These are the political concerns the Sugar Man carried in his life.

Can Rodriguez Still Perform?

After the documentaries whirlwind success, the question of whether Rodriguez could still perform was asked? No one realized he had been on the road since 2005 and prior to that played where and when he could find a gig. Because he played regularly in South Africa, London and Australia he had a large number of musicians who loved to back him in concert. They were invariably talented and seasoned performers and from the day **Searching For Sugar Man** was released the Sugar Man was a concert favorite.

Rodriguez' use of backup bands led to comparisons with how the late Chuck Berry toured the last forty years of his performing life. Berry's concerts were often dreadful. This is not the case with the Sugar Man. It hasn't hurt Rodriguez' performances. Unlike Berry, the Sugar Man loves to perform. He rarely gives a poor show. He has an extraordinary ability to reach his audience. In conversation with Andy Greene, Rodriguez recalled how and why he likes to use various bands from around the world.

Sixto Rodriguez: "I have a dozen bands all over the world. That's no exaggeration." When he was asked about the quality of his shows, the Midnight Oil drummer Hurst took over the question stating: "We'll rehearse for a few hours when he comes into town. He doesn't like to rehearse so we'll be flying by the seat of our pants...." Hirst's comment perfectly describes the Sugar Man's approach to the concert stage. He remains the ultimate existentialist. But, unlike Rickie Lee Jones, he can cover his songs effectively bringing out the poignant meaning of his lyrical beauty.

The Singer Who Came Back from the Dead: Once Again

The Sixto Rodriguez story is driven by the notion he came back from the dead. This is, of course, total nonsense. The two best explanations of this phenomenon are Rodriguez' second wife, Konny, uttering the comment when they arrived in Cape Town in 1998: "Dead Men Don't Tour." A television special using that theme was shown on South African TV. The British journalist, Alexis Petridis, writing in the **London Guardian**, discussed the idea at length. It is a romantic notion contrary to the facts. He was developing a cult career when the Petridis article appeared in October 2005. Petridis anticipated how and why **Searching For Sugar Man** tugged at the heartstrings of the worldwide audiences making Rodriguez an international cult superstar.

When Petridis interviewed Rodriguez in 2005 there were elements inspiring the documentary. The influence of DJ, producer, writer, performer, mix artist and all around musical genius David Holmes was highlighted. Why Holmes wasn't in the documentary is a mystery. It is Holmes who alerted those in the music business to the Sugar Man's incipient genius. He deserves recognition.

One of the ironies of the Petridis interview is it was completed via phone while Rodriguez was in Cape Town. There were some insights from the Sugar Man. He talked about how and why Detroit music people liked his songs and came to see him at gutbucket bars like the Sewer By The Sea. He discussed Neil Bogart without naming him. It appears Bogart was instrumental in convincing Avant to sign Rodriguez. It was an insightful, deep interview sensing Rodriguez had a future. Those around him saw his brilliance. It was another seven years before the world woke up to the Sixto Rodriguez story.

True Story or The Making of a Myth?

Bill Cody writing in **Coming Soon** asked: Why was the Sugar Man in the documentary only for a few minutes? He also charged big parts of the story were left out. Cody said the Sugar Man's impact upon South African civil rights was overblown. You can trace all this back to Stephen "Sugar" Segerman the pied piper of hagiography. When this article was published in January 2013 no one paid attention. Cody's thesis is one person in South Africa tilted the story, fabricated its direction and twisted the facts. Guess who?

The Cody article charges Stephen "Sugar:" Segerman misrepresented the facts. I don't believe Segerman purposely skewed the story, but he missed many key points. Segerman's psychological makeup prompted him to create a mea culpa scenario that didn't fit the story. There was no intended malevolence. This twisting of a marvelous story in the end disrespected Sixto Rodriguez. Why did Segerman head in this interpretive direction?

Bill Cody: "Perhaps the story was so compelling they didn't want to spoil it."

Segerman is a record storeowner who has no idea about the history of the music industry. He is a well-meaning amateur. He has a comprehensive computer system listing all in print and out of print albums. He seems never to have looked at it. There were a number of comprehensive record databases in place by 1982. They evolved into sophisticated record-artist search devices by 1990. I interviewed more than a dozen hard-core Rodriguez fans that ordered his material from Australia due to Internet connections. Even his bootleg releases were found on the Internet. Segerman had no idea about Rodriguez' popularity down under. He has never said anything about the lost facts.

When Segerman and his cohort Brian Currin put up a website looking for the Sugar Man, they must have had some idea he was alive. Then again! If they were rank amateurs or story manipulators one could understand, but they were serious and knowledgeable fans. Or were they? Now Segerman advertises talks he will give on Rodriguez for four thousand dollars a pop. Maybe he will answer these questions. Then again!

Peter Bradshaw, writing in the **London Guardian**, noted the discrepancies between **Searching For Sugar Man** and the actual events in Rodriguez' life. It was Bradshaw who suggested Rodriguez had a career before Malik Bendjelloul's Oscar winning documentary. His arguments were dismissed, but he was right on the mark. Segerman did his best to keep Bradshaw's ideas in the background.

The direction of Bradshaw's 2012 review is he argued the documentary opens up the history of racial abuse in South African visa via race relations, government injustice, hindered freedoms and a rock music industry suffering from Mickey Most's pop slop productions. Then he asks: "Where is the intrigue? That mystery centers on Rodriguez' quirky personality. The mystery that is Sixto Rodriguez, Bradshaw argues, is what makes the documentary fascinating. But the question of why Rodriguez was so big in South Africa is never satisfactorily answered.

Bradshaw concluded: "Searching For Sugar Man is an interesting footnote to a species of secret or denied cultural history: the history of South Africa's white liberal class." Bradshaw suggests Segerman's connection to Rodriguez is peripheral. He sees Segerman as an entitled wanker riding on other people's coattails.

Segerman proved he wasn't fair-minded. He purposely ignored key parts of the story. He inflated other aspects of the tale. He blew enough smoke up the presses ass to cause a fire. That is Segerman's mantra. It is also Rodriguez' dilemma.

When does myth replace reality? This happens when you place the personal Rodriguez into a preconceived box. He is a scholar. He is a thinker. He is a great writer. He also has a philosophy education that no one has examined. He has read and knows what the great writers argue and opine in looking to the future.

A Myth is Replaced by Reality

The reality is Rodriguez quotes Voltaire more often than Bob Dylan. That tells one a great deal about the Sugar Man. The real Sixto Rodriguez is not a complex person. When the glare of fame interrupted his previously private life; the Sugar Man told Larushka-Zadeh: "It's important I can retreat back to my own private world." She wondered who wrote the story he committed suicide on stage or perhaps died of a drug overdose. The Sugar Man laughed. He continued to describe himself in this candid July 2012 London interview for the **Metro**. "I'm yours," Rodriguez remarked to Larushka-Zadeh. In time the Sugar Man would end the media circus. In the aftermath of the documentary and a well-deserved Oscar, he basked in the attention that eluded him for forty plus years.

When he talked with Larushka-Zadeh, his image influenced her attitudes and descriptions. She described the Sugar Man as "dressed from head to toe in black, his military-jacket giving him a faint Michael Jackson air, Rodriguez's presence seems to hover somewhere behind his sunglasses." This is how Rodriguez influences journalists; he is a visual version of rock star imagery. She found him thoughtful. When Larushka-Zadeh asked about politics, Rodriguez commented: "My work is more to me than just music. In the 1960s and 1970s I thought there was going to be a revolution but now I don't think that is necessary."

The real Sixto Rodriguez is nothing like the visionary Jesus character in **Searching For Sugar Man**. If that is the case there is a mystery. Who is the real Sugar Man? That is the question. The answer is a complex one. He is moody, irascible, creative, and difficult at times. He is prone to heavy reading, quiet socializing and social-political activism in a city that has gone through hell. At other times he is jovial, convivial and sincere. He is kind to a fault. He never hurts anyone's feelings. He has a sense of humanity second to none. This is the real Sixto Rodriguez. He is a well-adjusted self-described musical-political walking quietly along the Cass Corridor toward Wayne State University or the Motor City Brewing Company. There is no mystery. He is a bright person who suddenly became an international music icon.

During the first year of **Searching For Sugar Man's** hysteria, Rodriguez spoke freely and eloquently about fame and fortune. As he sat down with the **Washington Post's** David Malitz, Sixto Rodriguez highlighted how important his real life was in sharp contrast to the myths in **Searching For Sugar Man**.

As he sat in his Georgetown hotel room, Rodriguez gazed at a poster of **Searching For Sugar Man**. It was a picture of him with blurbs of praise and a group of four-star logos from renowned film festivals. He basked in the glow. If somewhat nervously and with great hesitation, he sat down with the **Washington Post** to answer questions. He is visibly nervous. When he is asked about the guitar in the picture, the Sugar Man smiles and tells David Malitz that it is a picture aided by Photoshop. It is late July 2012 when this interview takes place.

Malitz writes of the documentary: "It doesn't need even the slightest assistance in mythmaking." He remarks being treated with respect is something new for Rodriguez. As he talked with the **Washington Post** and other publications, the subject of new songs and a third album persisted. Then five years later nothing had changed. The rumors, the innuendo, the hopes for a new product are still in the air. But now people wondered! Did Rodriguez have new songs? Could he still write?

Could The Sugar Man Still Write? Yes He Could!

By the spring of 2017 Rodriguez had seven or nine new songs, depending upon your source. They were written in his unique style. He has heard the rumors. Could he still write? He didn't need to prove he had the skill to compose. He did. At the proper moment the world would hear his new songs. That is when he was ready.

The irascible, dope smoking Detroit poet, John Sinclair, arrived from Amsterdam in late April 2017 to buoy the Sugar Man's spirits. They talked in depth about new songs. They performed a few songs after Sinclair read some poems late the night of April 22, 2017 at Detroit's Old Miami. It was only fitting amongst the cigarette smoke, the smell of disinfectant and stale beer they should relive their early songs and poetry. They are grey hairs but you would never know it by the brief midnight show. Reality triumphed myth that night. Those who paid the twenty-dollar cover charge had a rare insight into two of Detroit's premier poetic-musical iconoclasts.

That night at the Old Miami led to an intense, private, political discussion about Trump's America. It centered on the dangers of old white guys running the country. As Sinclair and Rodriguez talked of their hopes for America, they were depressed. The country had fallen down a right wing rat hole. The two former 1960s radicals lent their voices to support change, but they believed the system could collapse. They saw Trump as the precursor to the most drastic changes coming in American democracy.

The passion and energy for a musical life never left Rodriguez. The creative fuel still burns musically in his mid-seventies soul. This is evident in his laid back, but brilliant, concerts. There is a clarity and simplicity to the Sugar Man's life. That is the reason he still writes with panache and rare insight.

His life is rich in detail and critical analysis. But make no mistake Rodriguez is a complex and at times a difficult person. That is the nature of an insightful writer.

The Segerman-Bartholomew-Strydom Myths

In 2015 Craig Bartholomew-Strydom wrote **Sugar Man: The Life, Death And Resurrection of Sixto Rodriguez**, published by Bantam Books in South Africa and Australia, in a blaze of media publicity. It is a good book. It did take some time for it to come out in the U. S. It is well researched. It presents new material. It has a pro-Rodriguez viewpoint. It tells the truth from the author's viewpoints. Bartholomew-Strydom tells the story with accuracy, verve and a sense of the overall picture. He also has critical remarks about his friend Stephen "Sugar" Segerman. In particular Bartholomew-Strydom told the truth about how Segerman became obnoxious, controlling and diffident. He also speculated why Rodriguez distanced himself from the South African. The claim that Segerman brought Rodriguez back to concert and recording fame is one he tells daily. Bartholomew-Strydom disagrees. He does it with a sense of what is best for the Sugar Man. There is a back-story. Segerman takes too much credit for everything. As this book has shown, Rodriguez was a cult Indie star by 2009 and had Sony Legacy, Simon Chinn and Passion Pictures not pulled out the publicity stops Rodriguez would still have been the story of the year. But not the international legend he became in the years after **Searching For Sugar Man** stormed the box office. Segerman takes much of the credit. He had nothing to do with neither the documentary's success nor Rodriguez emerging as a mainstream act. In fact, as this book suggests, his amateur tactics almost destroyed Rodriguez' fledgling career. Bartholomew-Strydom does a good job detailing many of the problems.

It is in examining and describing the American influence upon the Sugar Man that Segerman skews the story. He simply doesn't understand American history. He has no in-depth knowledge of the U. S. music industry, the educational system at the university level, and he lacks the expertise to analyze the social-economic-political changes driving American popular culture. The most egregious mistakes involve those swirling around Clarence Avant. The former Sussex Record chief should be recognized for what he did to further Rodriguez' career despite the royalties controversy.

Harry Balk: A Giant in Detroit and a Good Guy

There are so many myths perpetuated in the Bartholomew-Strydom book, it is necessary to address the key ones. He writes: "Avant was, in truth, an impresario. Rodriguez's only impresario." (p. 251) This is, of course, complete nonsense. Harry Balk was an impresario with Impact records. He produced Rodriguez. He had a label friendly contract which allowed him to share in the Sugar Man's songwriting, publishing and mechanical royalties. Later, after fame and fortune, Harry's daughter was allegedly the mastermind behind a lawsuit alleging Rodriguez had defrauded Balk's publishing company. The outcome of that legal action has never been made public. Balk released a Rodriguez single that didn't bring a profit. Harry didn't publicize it. Balk took songwriting credit. It might sell in the future. There were no royalties. Balk was the ultimate music business insider. He was not a criminal. He simply presented a one sided recording agreement and young singers signed the contract. There was no coercion. You want a hit record kid, sign with Harry. They did. They got the glory. They got the drugs. They got the girls and the good times. Harry got most of the money. This was the way it was done in the music business. Balk was not the exception as a music industry tycoon; he was the typical music mogul.

The respect for Harry Balk in the music community is second to none. He was one of the prime movers in the Detroit record scene and he was responsible for Del Shannon's early hits "Runaway" and "Hats Off To Larry" whose original title "Hats Off To Harry" indicated his close relationship with Shannon. The dozen people interviewed about Balk's Detroit music empire had nothing but good things to say about him. Harry was not only the ultimate urban hipster; he gave many acts a chance to grace the national stage.

The list of acts Balk brought to national fame include Little Willie John, Johnny and the Hurricanes, Rare Earth and when he was hired by Motown he single handedly made Marvin Gaye's "What's Going On" a monster hit. Balk was in the forefront of the music business for four decades. The lack of respect, the failure to recognize Balk's contribution to the music business and his impresario credentials are a part of the Craig Bartholomew-Strydom and Stephen "Sugar" Segerman volume as they fail to understand him.

Harry Balk was not only a Detroit music pioneer, he was typical of the times. He made Little Willie John a star. He worked with a local band, the Sunliners, and he turned them into the mega-hit band Rare Earth. Del Shannon had hits with Harry, he left when his contract was up and he returned to have more hits with Balk. Dennis Coffey was a session musician. Harry single handedly took him to the top of the charts. Johnny and the Hurricanes were a rock band playing high school dances. Balk took them numerous times into the Top 40 with their instrumental hits. The Royal Tones were a local Detroit band featuring Dennis Coffey, George Katsakis and Bob Babbitt and Harry took them to the top of the Detroit music scene. Other acts he worked with or reconfigured included R. Dean Taylor, Kiki Dee and Meat Loaf. Harry Balk was Mr. Detroit rock and roll.

In the Bartholomew-Strydom book there are many misrepresentations of Balk's role in the story. Whey they claim Balk believed in Rodriguez they fail to show how and why he was a part of the Detroit scene. Why did Balk believe in Rodriguez? They never explain it. His lengthy work in the clubs is ignored. The manner in which the Sugar Man educated himself in the way of the business helped him. This is treated in a cursory manner. "Harry Balk proving his belief in the young Rodriguez's abilities put together some seasoned musicians...." (P. 1-2) This simply isn't true. Harry used the same musicians. Maybe they were seasoned. Maybe they weren't seasoned. What Harry did was to throw out an exploratory single. If it caught on with radio airplay, Balk went to step two which was local promotion with an intensity making it a Detroit hit so he could lease it to a major label.

Harry Balk's role in the Detroit music scene rivaled Berry Gordy's. In Bartholomew-Strydom's view Harry was a part time worker who found it difficult to garner employment. This is the ultimate sign of disrespect for Detroit's most brilliant independent record producer of the 1960s and 1970s. Bartholomew-Strydom writes: "Balk, now out of work, sought and found employment with Berry Gordy at Motown." (p. 111) My book **Stranger In Town: The Mysterious Life of Del Shannon** has a chapter on Balk that tells the real story. Gordy came to Balk with an offer of a Vice-Presidency with a carte blanche agreement to produce what he wanted, how he wanted and when he wanted. Balk didn't need the job. Motown was fading and they needed Harry. To minimize Balk's role is a failure to understand the Detroit music scene and where the Sugar Man's career fit into the Motor City.

The sin of omission is what dooms **Sugar Man: The Life, Death And Resurrection Of Sixto Rodriguez**. It is a book that says virtually nothing about Rodriguez and everything about themselves. The material on the lack of royalties, the stardom from 2005 as a cult artist, the inability to describe his politics, the exaggeration of their role and the disdain for other viewpoints spells doom for their insipid volume. None of the key points are covered in depth. Myth ruled the day.

The Myth and Legend of the Impresario in The Sugar Man's 's Story: Why Does It Matter?

The Bartholomew-Strydom-Segerman tome has a strange premise concerning impresarios. They discuss at length the Impresario in Rodriguez's career. They don't know anything about the so-called impresarios. They should have used the term manager. An impresario is an Italian word for a person who finances, plays, concerts and operas. These were not the people associated with Rodriguez. But, once again, Bartholomew-Strydom and Segerman know little, if anything, about how the U. S. rock and roll world operates. -Every person associated with the Sugar Man looked to make money. They were all impresarios. No one was in it as a hobby. Well maybe except for Bartholomew-Strydom and Segerman describing how close they were to filmmaker Malik Bendjelloul. Their prose verges on the border of being preposterous. Hagiography rules the day.

The impresario, this is Bartholomew-Strydom's term, was not friendly to the artist. There is no sugar coating the ruthless behavior, the disregard for contracts and the gangster infested nature of the music business. But there is also no evidence Harry Balk or Clarence Avant cheated Rodriguez.

The role of the so-called impresario was to promote, cultivate and advance Rodriguez' career. This didn't happen. When Mike Theodore, the producer of **Cold Fact**, was asked about the Sugar Man's lack of success he didn't blame it on Avant. So who is to blame?

The evidence is clear Rodriguez is a contrarian. He wouldn't do the required interviews. He wouldn't schmooze with the Dick Clark's who controlled airplay; he wasn't interested in the brain dead industry people like Neil Bogart. He required solitude. These traits did not spell stardom. He didn't mesh with the industry types. This changed by the time **Searching For Sugar Man** was in production. The e-mails between Rowland and Bendjelloul attest to those changes in the Sugar Man's demeanor.

The most egregious charge in their book is "Rodriguez and Avant had had a falling out after recording **Coming From Reality**." (p. 252). This was not the case. Avant paid for two more recording sessions realizing he might reap zero dollars. He loved the Sugar Man's music. To this day Avant has only good things to say about Rodriguez.

The level of inside misinformation dished out by Bartholomew-Strydom's prose reaches heights of absurdity. Segerman suggests Bill Clinton approached the Israeli-Australian-South African-London promoter Zev Eizik concerning Rodriguez's career when the former president visited Israel. Fake news is what one Rodriguez insider told me when I mentioned this piece of uncorroborated information. Bartholomew-Strydom wrote: "Sugar had it on good authority that when former president Bill Clinton visited Israel, he contacted Zev Eizik for his good friend Clarence's instructions." The idea that former President Clinton was a gofer for Clarence Avant is ridiculous. This sounds good. There are problems. Avant supported Barack Obama for president in 2008, and not Hillary Clinton. Another problem is Clinton and Avant have appeared at political fundraisers together. They have talked. They have taken a picture together. There is no evidence they talked about Sixto Rodriguez. Or for that matter that they knew each other. A political fundraiser is when you give money to have your picture taken with a famous American politician. There is not a shred of evidence to support their preposterous claims.

There is Reality for Rodriguez at Montieth Honors College: But Not in Their Book

The picture of student life at Wayne State University and Rodriguez' admission to the Montieth Honors College bears little resemblance to reality. Bartholomew-Strydom writes: "First university, then kids. But nothing Rodriguez ever did was straightforward or the way society would have had him do it." (p. 150). This comment demonstrates a lack of understanding about the American educational system. Does this matter? Is there a correlation to learning? What is the point? Bartholomew-Strydom analyzes Monteith's educational direction. He misses the freedom it allowed the Sugar Man's intellectual development. It also is an indication of how little they understood Rodriguez' intellect, his college experiences or the U. S. music scene.

When students enter the Monteith Honors College, they do so by invitation. You cannot register for it. You have to be pre-selected. The purpose of the honors college is to foster independent, creative thought. They did this with the Sugar Man. Monteith College placed Rodriguez in an intellectual environment conductive to his songwriting mantra. His philosophy professors taught him to think, deduce and write with skill. When Bartholomew-Strydom writes of the faculty using first names he demonstrates a complete lack of knowledge concerning the American educational system. "A minority of students-perhaps ten to twenty percent-hung around the student center and faculty offices." (p. 151) This is the type of filler detracting from the story. The manner in which Wayne State University fostered the Sugar Man's enormous intellectual growth is the key ingredient in his writing. The South African's failed to recognize Monteith's nurturing of his prose. It gets worse as they show little, if any, understanding of the special academic process Rodriguez experienced at Wayne State University.

Here is the real story of Monteith College and Sixto Rodriguez. The honors segment of Wayne State University founded in 1959 was for twenty years designed to recognize diversity in thought, writing and the approach to academic life. Inclusion in the Monteith community is by invitation. A number of professors must recognize a student and recommend their admission into this select academic community. His education prepared the Sugar Man for his career as a "musical-political."

It is common knowledge Rodriguez frenetically wrote, honed his performing craft, raised his family and continued to read the trades in the 1970s and 1980s. When Midnight Oil appeared in Detroit they were amazed at the Sugar Man's knowledge of the industry. He wasn't a star. But he was far from the recluse who vanished. He also performed sporadically all over the Detroit area. The aura and mystery of the Sugar Man was still in the air. The two South Africans were inventing a story that did exist. They didn't describe it accurately. Even their beginning comments are suspect.

The Script for Searching for Sugar Man: Segerman is Essential or Is He? He Is!

Bartholomew-Strydom and Segerman wrote: "Malik in the meantime scripted a first draft…and emailed it to Sugar." (p. 254) In a way this is accurate. What it fails to mention is Steve Rowland's input. They talked to Rowland. They simply didn't get the full story of his contributions to **Searching For Sugar Man**. Why? They didn't ask. They failed to mention how Steve guided the documentary and while their contribution is paramount they refuse to recognize others. This ego-incinerating tactic challenges their credibility and diminishes their contribution to **Searching For Sugar Man**. Ego destroys common sense and alters the tale.

Their book claims Bendjelloul said: "It was a documentary, it was impossible to write an actual script." What they leave out is Rowland's blackboard, or what Steve calls a storyboard or a simple blank large board, with a complete sequencing of the opening of the documentary. The positioning of the music, and the sense of mystery and drama Steve suggested went a long way to forming **Searching For Sugar Man**. The music became the focal point of the documentary thanks to Rowland's advice. In some respects Bendjelloul was flying by the seat of his pants. But Segerman also helped a great deal when he sent Malik two boxes of Sugar Man memorabilia. This was essential to visualize the story.

Segerman had very little input into the script. He was important to the film's more dramatic sequences. He provided old footage of Kruger National Park, D. F. Malan Airport in Cape Town and a cable car running up and down Table Mountain. In doing so he created a sense of South Africa's scenic landscape.

When cinematographer Camille Skagerstrom landed a week later, she was stunned by opportunities for visual beauty. Here is where things got weird. Rather than spend time filming and highlighting Cape Town's easy life style, the quality of the surroundings and the civilized nature of the locals, Segerman insisted they film the inside of his house. He is proud of his record collection. Malik confided to Steve Rowland that he was uneasy with this direction. Since Segerman was essential to the story, Malik went along with it. If reluctantly! There were some unique scenes shot in Mabu Vinyl. It created a sense of Rodriguez' popularity in South Africa.

While Segerman was a gadfly to the early filming of **Searching For Sugar Man**, Malik had to rely on Steve Rowland for the nitty gritty day-to-day filming knowledge. Steve educated Malik on the some of the vagaries of the film business. He doesn't like to talk about it, but the e-mails are conclusive proof of his expertise.

Why was Rowland ignored or minimized in **Sugar Man: The Life, Death And Resurrection of Sixto Rodriguez**? The answer is a simple one. Further interviews with Rowland would have compromised the myth of Rodriguez they were selling in their book.

Identifying the Myths the South African's Perpetuated: The Story was so Strong it Didn't Ruin it, But the Truth?

The problem with the South African's book is the exclusion of material. What is excluded? As we have seen the influence of Australia, the impact of the U. S. record industry, the differences with the various South African and Australian record companies, the mercurial and at times abrasive behavior by Rodriguez, the failure to adequately describe Matt Sullivan and Light In the Attic's role in making the Sugar Man an Indie star from 2008 to 2011 and the continual emphasis on Stephen "Sugar" Segerman's role, even after Rodriguez banished him from the inner circle. These facts distort the story. It is the same ultimate act of disrespect toward Rodriguez.

There is virtual hero worship in Bartholomew-Strydom's description of Segerman. "To step into Stephen Segerman's music room is to step into his mind," Bartholomew-Strydom continues. "Nothing is ever thrown away. It is all absorbed twice. Once into his brain through the senses, the second time into his sphere as a possession." What it shows is the search for Jesus led Bartholomew-Strydom to confuse the Jesus character. I hate to tell him it is not Segerman.

The Myth of Rodriguez and the People Around Him

It is clear they do not understand the Sugar Man. In their book Bartholomew-Strydom quotes a letter from Bendjelloul. "Rodriguez is not the easiest guy to be friends with. Someone told me something that might be true. Rodriguez likes new people and to make new acquaintances but the closer you think you get to him, he'll react the opposite way." What this quote demonstrates is the South African definition of friendship is much wider and less inconclusive than that in the U. S. Segerman agreed with Malik. He suggested he would act as the go between in the event of any difference. Once again this was pure self-interest on Segerman's part.

What was Rodriguez' nature? He is a reflective intellectual. He needs time to think, write and consider his place in the universe. That is what the existentialist intellectual does. He is not interested in placing his karma in the forefront.

The strain in the Rodriguez-Segerman friendship intensified in 2005 during the abortive London shows. When the Sugar Man arrived in South Africa in 2009 he didn't invite Segerman to his performances.

Segerman manipulated the Sixto Rodriguez story for his own ends. He created many myths. He is incapable of separating myth from reality. When Craig Bartholomew-Strydom completed the book on Rodriguez, Segerman's boorish behavior demonstrated the dilettante in his soul. This is one reason Rodriguez got rid of him. The story was more complicated than the documentary suggests. Their book purposely ignored many of Steve Rowland's insightful and penetrating comments. They interviewed him. They were aware of the e-mails between Rowland and Bendjelloul. They didn't use any of these e-mails because it contradicted the mythical tale of Sixto Rodriguez.

Rodriguez Has the Last Word: "My Career... It's Been a Mess"

It is fitting for Sixto Rodriguez to have the last word. In February 2013 he sat down for an interview with a British journalist Tom Pinnock. Some months later in July 2013, the interview was published as the Sugar Man was lauded for the documentary, the Oscar and his triumphant concerts. It was a heady time. The **Uncut** interview took place in the swirl of publicity as the Academy Awards presented **Searching For Sugar Man** an Oscar for best documentary.

As he ruminated about his career, the Sugar Man displayed his usual panache. When asked what he liked the most about stardom, Rodriguez replied: "I enjoy room service." Not surprisingly, some of the myths associated with the Sugar Man are the product of his interviews. Rodriguez said: "I didn't do any music. I was never on the circuit...I stayed pretty much out of it...." That was the truth. The Sugar Man failed to mention he diligently pursued his craft. He did perform for years in small venues in and around the Motor City. He may not have had much to show for it, but he was developing into a consummate professional.

When the **Uncut** reporter asked: "How does it feel to find fame four decades later?" Rodriguez responded: "I guess it feels as good as it would have felt if I was a success earlier." Then he paused to think about it adding: "But now because it's so many times over the success that anybody could dream of, global success, I think that's what changes the picture. In the 1970s, I wouldn't have reached any part of the audience I reach now, with technology, and through the film."

In the **Uncut** interview Rodriguez lamented his busy concert schedule. This caused the delay for a third album. He has written new songs. Matt Sullivan, of Light In The Attic, remarked he had heard some of the tunes. There are seven or nine new Sugar Man tunes in various states of completion. How and why they fit into the marketplace is the question. Neither Rodriguez nor Rowland are retro types. The rumor is Rodriguez' new songs are fresh and lyrically inspiring. The exact nature of the new songs remains a mystery.

Matt Sullivan pointed out LITA sold twenty thousand copies of **Cold Fact** and 15,000 copies of **Coming From Reality** prior to the documentary. Then all hell broke loose. **Searching For Sugar Man** made it difficult, but not impossible, to keep the record stores supplied. On line sales were so brisk LITA hired extra employees to keep up with the demand.

There were problems with Rodriguez. He doesn't like to rehearse. When he played New York's Joe's Pub in 2008, which seats one hundred sixty people, he wanted to perform covers and hang out. The big time was four years away.

Wymond Miles: "The first time I met him we had a rehearsal space rented here in the city, we had horn players, a percussionist this whole big nine piece band we built around us for him. We had this big group there, and everyone else had to go and really he didn't even want to play his songs. We'd play them a couple of times. We'd get half way through 'Crucify Your Mind' and he would just applaud and say, 'It's going to be great.' He isn't really interested in rehearsals...."

As Miles practiced with Rodriguez, he noted he loves to play other people's songs. When they were rehearsing for the Portland Doug Fir Lounge show, the band spent three hours playing "everything from Marvin Gaye to contemporary pop things."

How does Rodriguez see his career? "I always wanted to make something of myself through music," Rodriguez continued. "In music, I think if I put another thing out and it has value, I've achieved. If it can make them dance and sing, it's good, I can feel that."

Is Visual Reality the Right Way to Go?

Malik Bendjelloul used the visual beauty that is South Africa. But there were only white faces in the documentary. There was a discussion of apartheid but only in a minimalist way. **Searching For Sugar Man** didn't examine how black South Africans were influenced by Rodriguez' political lyrics. There are few clips of South Africa emphasizing its misery and poverty. The bleak nature of Detroit comes through much better in the documentary.

While Cape Town is warm, sunny, visually stunning and the living standard is one of the best in the world, there are still racial questions. What does this have to do with Rodriguez? Plenty! He was as much a barometer for women's rights, the crusade for environmental change and freedom for musicians as he was for his opposition to apartheid. He was a liberal political crusader who didn't get his due.

Searching For Sugar Man minimized Rodriguez' radical Mexican American political roots. His support for Cesar Chavez and the United Farm Workers is ignored. This side of the Sugar Man was left out of the documentary. He was a constant political critic with a platform for change. The Sugar Man was an advocate for Native American rights long before it was a trendy liberal position. The documentary failed to give full credence to Rodriguez' political activism.

Film is a medium allowing for atmospheric scenes. In the case of **Searching For Sugar Man**, Rodriguez walked through Detroit neighborhoods where he had little connection. He was filmed walking in some of the Motor Cities most dreadful areas. It was atmospheric. He is a blue-collar worker with an attachment to the values of the working person. He has the intellectual credentials for political reform. The use of visual beauty from Cape Town distorted what Rodriguez stands for and how he lives. It did provide for an atmospheric setting making the story a true Cinderella drama.

The gritty, down home literary types who liked to stoke the magic dragon around Wayne State University created the intellectual aura populating the Sugar Man's songs. He was an urban philosopher celebrating existential thought.

The self-imposed Detroit exile, after **Coming From Reality** failed to sell, continued his intellectual growth. The problem is we have not heard the new songs. That will happen when the third album is released.

Several of the characters in Rodriguez' songs are barely disguised versions of close friends. In "Heikki's Suburbia Bus Tour" Rodriguez writes of visiting the suburbs to laugh at the squares. His daughter, Eva, wrote a short description of the song.

Eva Rodriguez: "In the sixties, there were these people called hippies. It can be said that a long hair, dark skin, free thinking musician, like Rodriguez could have been labeled one....In my youth I recall hearing about how 'rich folks' (those living in the suburbs) would come down to the inner city of Detroit to actually see these 'oddities' in their natural environment. Maybe even take a picture or two. This happened to be my neighborhood....Rodriguez had a very good friend named Heikki. I remember a large man with long blond/brown hair. He had a very nice home, a wife named Linda and two huge bullmastiff dogs. despite stereotypes, Heikki was mathematician from 'Estonia'....Anyway someone made fun of Rodriguez' friend. Protective of Heikki's feelings, Rodriguez organized what I consider to be a peaceful form of retaliation. A bus was chartered full of hippies, four gallons of wine, etc. The group went to Grosse Point, Michigan and surrounding areas where they visited suburban malls...." As Eva pointed out the Sugar Man organized a tour for the hippies to stare at the straights and take their pictures. It was hilarious to turn the tables on middle class conformity.

In real life he is Heikki Kansa. Some like Heikki are described accurately and in great detail. Women, racism and corrupt politics come directly out of the Detroit experience. Rodriguez highlights his opposition to the impediments that face many Americans. But women are a key part of his political mantra. His partnerships with women fuel his songwriting. He also examines the psychosexual components of racism.

One of the contradictions in Rodriguez' life is his contrarian, critical, anti-middle class writing and public statements. He detests the boring and well-adjusted suburban types. This provides an interesting contrast with his long-term marital and monogamous lifestyle.

There is a cinematic quality to Rodriguez' songs. It was there before his experience working with Steve Rowland while recording **Coming From Reality**. Rowland enhanced this quality in the Sugar Man's songs.

To Avoid Hagiography: Another Side of The Sugar Man

The biographer shuns his duty if he praises his or her subject while ignoring the warts, the grumpy moments, the betrayals and the need for a perceptive critical analysis. These traits are essential to an honest book. The Segerman-Bartholomew-Strydom volume is a brilliant book, but it fails to dig deep into Rodriguez' soul and psyche. They write as unabashed fans with excessive hagiography. There is little honesty to this tome.

It is not easy to understand Sixto Rodriguez. He is private. He is principled. As Malik Bendjelloul observed you never get to know the real Sugar Man. He puts a wall up. He is mercurial. This explains why there may never be a third album.

His decisions concerning his career and music have not always been wise ones. He had limited knowledge of music contracts. This led to an unfair and invariably one-sided contract with Harry Balk at Impact Records and Clarence Avant had Rodriguez sign a contract typical of the times. The contract that didn't initially pay royalties with Clarence Avant's Sussex label that failed to produce royalties. Since that time the Sugar Man has refused to sign a recording contract. He did allow a Hi Fi store in Australia to release a 2014 set of live concert songs. This CD **Rodriguez Rocks: Live in Australia** is a wonderful piece of music that is poorly produced. The sound is great on some cuts, adequate on others and on some cuts the volume is too low. What is the point? The point is quality control. This is why Regan Rodriguez is important to her father. She insists on quality control.

At times Rodriguez' work rate has been astonishing while at other times he works at a slower pace. This is the way of the artist. Complexity explains the Sugar Man. Unlike many creative artists, there are no skeletons in Rodriguez' personality. He is a good guy. What you see is what you get.

Twenty-Three

Rodriguez and the Poetry of Pop: How Coming From Reality Defined Pop Poetry

"The true paradises are the paradises that we have lost."

Marcel Proust

"He speaks in a breathy whisper with a lilting quality, often in long rambling chunks of free association."

Corey Hall on Sixto Rodriguez

"When the mysterious songwriter poet started his touring in 2010, Rodriguez even graded such musical landmarks as the Commodore Ballroom and Zulu Records."

David LaCroix

What is the poetry of pop? Why is it important? When Bob Dylan won the Nobel Prize in Literature his award highlighted the poetry of protest. Or was it really the poetry of pop? Dylan's Nobel Prize in Literature legitimized folk-rock-pop songwriting. Again it was the wide popular appeal of his music bringing Dylan the Nobel Prize. He isn't a pop singer, but the poetry of pop wafts through his songs.

What is the poetry of pop? It is the soundtrack of our lives. Each generation depends upon pop music. It is a vehicle to define the direction of American popular culture. There is one persistent question. What was Rodriguez' path in songwriting? For Rodriguez his lyrics criticize the negative impact of the suburbs, the malevolence of government, and songs he describes are important to generational values. It is a form of poetry defining a time in history. When Steve Rowland produced **Coming From Reality**, he provided an interpretive window into the early 1970s.

Poetry is not a chosen medium of young rock music fans. How is it possible to consider pop music a form of poetry? If you examine Sixto Rodriguez' lyrics, they are more than simple boy girl songs. Although the Sugar Man confesses to writing mundane boy girl themes, he also writes literary songs. Does his audience realize he channels Samuel Taylor Coleridge's **Rime of The Ancient Marine**? Probably not! Does it matter? Is there a literary legitimacy to **Coming From Reality**? Does Rodriguez have a mentor, a prototype or a facilitator? He does! It may well be Van Morrison. When you listen to the Belfast Cowboy's "Into The Music," it is like a window into Rodriguez' songwriting. He captures moods, ideas and images others miss.

Rodriguez is a chronicler, a moralist, a healer, a Shaman and a social critic. He is a subtle, if stringent, critic of capitalism. "Rich Folks Hoax" is an observation on what has gone wrong in American life. "Street Boy" and "Sugar Man" attempt to understand the modern drift to suburbanization, and the lure of the streets.

How and Why Rodriguez' Poetry Emerges: T. S. Eliot Beware

The image of T. S. Eliot's "The Waste Land" is not the poetry of rock and roll. Or is it? Rodriguez' lyrical language is replete with rhythm, rhyme and metaphor much like Eliot's work. Unlike more pretentious rock artists, Rodriguez does not announce his poetry in song form. It is up to the listener to interpret it.

Greil Marcus in his seminal book on pop music, **Lipstick Traces: A Secret History Of The Twentieth Century**, argued in 1975 the Sex Pistols gave music a new direction as Johnny Rotten and his band mates connected with the Dadaists, perhaps a fringe group of anarchists and the result is not a youthful rebellion but the birth of a new aspect of music culture. Marcus's book, published by Harvard University Press, is a necessary corrective to rock and roll history. For the Sixto Rodriguez story Marcus suggests its musical connections are derived from unseen or unknown influences. Those influences for the Sugar Man emanate from poetry and literature. What is the Sugar Man doing when he writes lyrics like those in "The Establishment Blues?" Rodriguez writes: "The pope digs population, freedom from taxation….?" He makes it clear where he stands politically. Detroit is the backdrop to his lyrics as suggested by "Adultery plays the kitchen, bigot cops non-fiction. The little man gets shafted, songs and monies drafted." That says it all in one song. But is it pop poetry? Perhaps it is rock philosophy.

The list of subjects Rodriguez covered, analyzed and interpreted include:

- Political instability
- Relationship struggles
- Violence against women
- Mafia increasing
- Environmental pollution
- Gun control
- Lack of women working
- Marriage instability
- Smoking and health
- Taxation rules

- Drink driving
- Prostitution
- Adultery and cheating
- WWII and the east
- Public psychology

He can write of serious themes in a pop vein. Few songwriters have had as many varied themes in their tunes. Perhaps Rodriguez is much like F. Scott Fitzgerald.

How Rodriguez was Like F. Scott Fitzgerald

The Sugar Man is a talented writer. He composes at his kitchen table or in a coffee shop with clarity, insight and charm. The ascetic beauty of his writing is lost in the folk-rock milieu. This type of prose is not considered poetry. It is! His songs continue to be current forty plus years after he recorded them. That is the poetry of pop. Like F. Scott Fitzgerald, he doesn't have a magnetic personality. Like Fitzgerald he is concerned with his art and his life style. Like Fitzgerald, the Sugar Man found fame a mixed blessing. He lived life as "a dream," as did Fitzgerald. He has also had an uneven marital life, like Fitzgerald. He has coped with spouses who don't understand his lifestyle, and often his girlfriends don't share his view of the world. His writing genius wasn't one that came initially with monetary rewards.

From day one Rodriguez believed in his art. He worked hard. He spent years rewriting, rethinking and recasting his observations. When Fitzgerald's **The Stories of F. Scott Fitzgerald**, appeared in 1951, it provided a link to Rodriguez. Fitzgerald rewrote, rethought and reinterpreted his observations. Rodriguez followed the same path to maturity and his late in life successes. It is the path Roseanne Cash took that defined her pop poetry. She is an earlier version of the Sugar Man.

How Roseanne Cash Defines the Poetry of Pop: In a Rodriguez Sense

"I often lament that true songwriting will end up as an arcane folk art," Rosanne Cash observed. When Cash said she: "devoted my entire adult life to the pursuit if that beauty," she meant a lyrical songwriting form akin to poetry.

What does this have to do with Sixto Rodriguez? Plenty! Like the Sugar Man she struggled in New York to write pop, and lyrically brilliant songs. Critics who identified her with her father, Johnny Cash, held her back from popular acclaim and concert success. They derided her songs because of her famous family. It took her almost forty years to overcome the stigma of being a member of the Cash clan. Like Rodriguez, she has had to prove herself every day and she loves the poetry of pop.

The poetics of pop song lyrics is not a subject most people consider important for **The New Yorker** crowd. Imagine Rodriguez' surprise when he was featured in **The New Yorker**. No one made pop song lyrics more poetic than Sixto Rodriguez. His songs on **Coming From Reality** evoke a sense of a mature Dylan. How does the pop lyric translate to poetry? It is in his performances. When Rodriguez takes the stage "Crucify Your Mind" evokes the sense of poetry that is in his lyrical soul. Through the poetry of pop we can see in "The Establishment Blues" how the 1967 Detroit riots and hundreds of other conflicts were interpreted by artists like Crosby, Stills, Nash and Young when they stand before thousands singing "Ohio," the Kent State tragedy comes alive. Rodriguez is a part of this school of songwriting. Pop and political go hand in hand.

Roseanne Cash commented the poetry of pop is never appreciated. It doesn't fit into the intellectual milieu surrounding pop music. She is committed to fighting for the pop intellectual writer, as is Sixto Rodriguez.

Why is the New Yorker Aboard the Rodriguez Star Train?

The New Yorker is the benchmark for trendy intellectuals and those who define popular culture. Why is there a story on Sixto Rodriguez in this esteemed literary magazine? Sasha Frere-Jones spent July 2012 looking at the Sugar Man's phenomenon. What did she find? The answers might surprise you.

Sasha Frere-Jones wrote: "Crate diggers dream of finding that record." That record was **Cold Fact**. The documentary is described as "a boy's childhood dream." That is true. There are some devils, some evil monsters and some crass assholes in the mix. **The New Yorker** article doesn't find them. Instead the focus is, as it should be, among the good guys.

David Holmes is the first good guy. When he heard "Sugar Man," he began the process of introducing Rodriguez to the Indie crowd. The story is, as the author suggests, "a juicy, freaky detective tale with a big payoff." But is it the truth? Frere-Jones never addressed this question. Rodriguez is described as "the shadowy street poet." This is exactly what **Searching For Sugar Man** suggested. **The New Yorker** developed the myths Stephen "Sugar" Segerman explored and that is a tragedy. Myth triumphs reality!

Frere-Jones got it right. The Sugar Man "is an appealing, unpretentious singer who seems to want nothing more than to deliver the song and get out of his own way." This is an excellent description of Rodriguez' unique talent. **The New Yorker** pointed out the story is not about money. It is about culture, talent, original songs, and a mystery in need of a solution.

The New Yorker provided the fascination with, the respect for, and the adulation necessary to recognizing the Sugar Man's legacy. When Rodriguez is summarized the conclusion is: "They talked about him in the same breath as those rock gods in South Africa."

Who are the rock gods? They are the Beatles, Elvis Presley and the Rolling Stones. This is the ultimate sign of respect.

Sixto Rodriguez and Steve Rowland Define the Poetry of Pop

When Sixto Rodriguez walked into the Lansdowne recording studio to work with Steve Rowland, he carried a small, black briefcase with cassette tapes. The tapes contained rough mixes of his songs for **Coming From Reality**. This marked a shift in the Sugar Man's career. He was on his way to making a softer, more mainstream pop album with **Coming From Reality**. The bells and whistle from **Cold Fact** were left to another time. He wanted pop hits. Rowland wanted a hit record. They talked about it.

The mix of pop music and serious poetry is a subject for the professor's in the Ivory Tower. But the pairing of producer Steve Rowland and Detroit counterculture bard Sixto Rodriguez produced the ultimate pop poetry.

What did Rodriguez learn from Rowland? Steve makes his musical productions much like a movie with a strong, intricate and often mysterious beginning. This is following by a building sense of drama and a whirlwind conclusion with an intense dramatic conclusion. At the end of a Steve Rowland produced song there is a belief you have been told a serious, interesting and provocative story. Your energy is drained by the emotional experience. Steve's productions are a wellspring of pop, intellectual poetry. What about the comparisons to Bob Dylan? Are they valid? You bet! They are in many ways!

Is There a Comparison to Bob Dylan?

Rowland emphasized Rodriguez' writing when he produced **Coming From Reality**. There is a question critics frequently pose. Was the album superior song wise to anyone working in rock music? As Mike

Theodore said when asked why Rodriguez wasn't a star. He said it was "apples and oranges." What he meant is there were too many variables to analyze why the Sugar Man fell under the radar. But the comparison to Bob Dylan remains to the present day.

It was 1971. It was simply a matter of time before the hits climbed the charts. This was what Rodriguez believed, but it didn't happen. Steve emphasized his poetic approach. The problem is Rodriguez didn't write lyrics for commercial purposes. He didn't even think about it. Style is an artistic pattern in Rodriguez' creative mantra. But he never thinks about commercial possibilities when writing. In concert his soft, lilting voice evokes images of lost love, betrayal, ennui and incipient egoism. The creative process is one where the boundaries between poetry and song lyrics didn't mesh until October 2016 when the Swedish Academy awarded Bob Dylan the Nobel Prize in Literature. The Nobel Committee stated that Dylan "created new poetic expressions within the great American song tradition." How does Dylan compare to Rodriguez?

To the unwashed it would appear ludicrous to compare someone who has written less than thirty songs with the Shakespeare of the rock world. Dylan has written in excess of five hundred songs. Yet, there is a valid means of contrasting the two artists. Take Rodriguez' signature song "Sugar Man." If you examine how it has gone all over the place, you will notice the manner in which the Sugar Man writes like Dylan. Remember that Ken Boothe, a Jamaican singer, Nas, a hip hop performer, The Smoke, an English cult band, David Holmes, a producer-dj genius, remix producer-etc and pop artists like Susan Cowsill embraced Rodriguez' music. This certainly doesn't make him Dylan. Or does it? You tell me!

When you analyze Rodriguez' lyrics they are not unlike the poetry of William Blake or Robert Frost. What makes rock music poetry? It is how the lyrics stand the test of time. Rodriguez recorded two albums in 1970-1971. No one cared. In 2017 the lyrics are discussed, analyzed and repeated. They have stood the test of time. Why? The answer is a simple one. The language is poetic and the allure is pop. Understanding it is a reflection the songs stand the test of time.

Like Bob Dylan, Joni Mitchell, Leonard Cohen and Lou Reed, the Sugar Man is a poet with an intellectual pedigree. His honors degree in philosophy highlights his lyrical brilliance. He has done everything to torpedo his career. He appeared in **Searching For Sugar Man** for a few minutes. This heightened the mysterious sense of the long neglected, but talented, singer walking the dark Detroit streets. But the reasons for falling under the commercial radar are ones associated with the music business. He would not perform at teen dances nor would he lip synch his songs on TV dance parties. He abhorred the music industry. The music business has little to do with intellectual fervor. How is Rodriguez different? The difference is the Sugar Man is well read, introspective and shy about his intellectual rigor.

The shy and elusive Rodriguez is not open to explaining what his songs mean. Nor is he interested in speculating on why he writes them. He has given some hints. When he was asked about the Phil Ochs' tradition he supposedly embraces, the Sugar Man responds: "He was political." That said the Sugar Man continued to observe, in an interview with Corey Hall of Detroit's **Metro Times**, that American politics was filled with conspiracies and unexplainable events. He views Ochs' death as a political assassination. That is the personal Rodriguez. It is also the political Sugar Man.

Twenty-Four

How David Holmes, Paolo Nutini, Matt Sullivan and Steve Rowland Spent Ten Years Bringing The Sugar Man Back

**"Cinderella? As opposed to Sleeping Beauty?
I knew where I was – and I like my family,"**

Rodriguez says, before letting out a hearty laugh in conversation with Billboard's Phil Gallo.

**"For the first time my name said
out loud means nothing."**

Marguerite Duras

**"The biographer is the shadow of
the tombstone in the garden."**

Saul Bellow

**"Be curious, observe attentively
and indulge fantasy."**

Leonardo Da Vinci

The road to stardom was long and convoluted for Sixto Rodriguez. The operative wisdom is the South African's Stephen "Sugar" Segerman and Craig Bartholomew-Strydom brought him back to prominence. They did. Or did they? As Rodriguez performed in South Africa to adoring crowds in 1998, he quickly vanished once again into obscurity. Rodriguez accepted the accolades of a country where he had been a star since the 1970s. There were others in the story as important, but they were not a part of the Oscar winning **Searching For Sugar Man**.

After the accolades for Rodriguez' brilliant and unexpected rise to mega-stardom died down, the real story emerged. It didn't detract from the Sugar Man. He was the unknown singer-songwriter who came back from the dead to international stardom. But he wasn't dead. He was performing from the 1970s into 2012 when the documentary ended his calm, relaxed life.

When he returned to Australia in 2016 for another tour, Iain Shedden observed: "Sixto Rodriguez is a man of simple means, even if, at seventy-three he is reaping considerable financial rewards after decades in the rock 'n' roll wilderness." In conversations with Shedden he said the Sugar Man was a difficult interview. He was circumspect and closed to many questions.

When Shedden interviewed Rodriguez he broke one of the Sugar Man's cardinal rules. He talked at length about his private life. Shedden wrote of Rodriguez: "His manner is warm and friendly, perhaps aided by the fact he likes to chill out by 'smoking a lot of weed' he's an old school rock star, which is also the feel and style of his music." This is one reason the interviews have slowed since 2016. Tales of dope smoking drive the Sugar Man and his family into hiding. They are paranoid concerning the media.

When Shedden finished his 2016 interview Rodriguez said: "I don't mind the way it went. You can't fix that kind of stuff. You can't really go back in time and change things. I'm a lucky kid in a lot of ways. I've seen a lot of the world over the past few years. I've got a couple of good years, I think, including in Australia." Then

Rodriguez performed six Australia shows in November-December 2016.

The decade before stardom there were people bringing the Sugar Man back to prominence.

The People Who Brought Rodriguez to Stardom

One of the obvious conclusions is Stephen "Sugar" Segerman and Craig Bartholomew-Strydom didn't bring the Sugar Man back from recording obscurity to international stardom. They alerted the key players to the story. They remained in the background telling tall tales; talking about a music industry they didn't understand. They blew smoke up everyone's ass about their importance. The truth is more complicated. Matt Sullivan, Paolo Nutini and David Holmes brought the Sugar Man's music to an appreciative Indie audience. Eventually an international crowd emerged to crown Rodriguez the come back kid. If a somewhat old comeback kid. What happened? It is simple. In the decade before **Searching For Sugar** David Holmes brought the Sugar Man to the hip-hop, remix, dj, Indie cult audience. Paolo Nutini took his good looks, his winning concert appeal and his message about Rodriguez' songwriting genius to a wide variety of audiences.

Although not directly interacting with the Indie music scene, Steve Rowland worked with Malik Bendjelloul on the real story. Rowland also spent a great deal of time telling the press to take a close look at Rodriguez' songs.

Bendjelloul Told the Real Story: His Four Helpers Contributed to the Truth

The real story is the one told in Malik Bendjelloul's documentary **Searching For Sugar Man**. Steve Rowland hovered quietly in the wings providing advice. Matt Sullivan and LITA regularly brought the Sugar Man to increased public recognition. Paolo Nutini and David Holmes gave him credibility with a young, hip, highly sophisticated audience. By the time **Searching For Sugar Man** was released Rodriguez had been back on the road with two moderate selling CDs. He was a cult star.

In the decade prior to Bendjelloul's Oscar winning film a group of disparate souls, who loved the Sugar Man, plotted to bring him to international stardom. David Holmes, a dj/remix producer, Paolo Nutini a U. K. pop star, Matt Sullivan, co-founder of Light In The Attic and Steve Rowland the producer of **Coming From Reality** worked independently of each other in the decade prior to **Searching For Sugar Man's** success. But, in retrospect, it appeared as if they worked in tandem. From 2002 until January 2012, when the documentary was hailed for its brilliance, the four music industry insiders talked of Rodriguez' songwriting-performance genius, they framed his story of being forgotten and rediscovered. His incipient talent blossomed. A look at each of their contributions suggests they were important to his impending stardom.

Who is David Holmes?

In 2002, the road to bringing Rodriguez to concert prominence began with David Holmes. Who is David Holmes? He is a Belfast born Northern Irish dj/remix producer who placed "Sugar Man" on a mixtape catching the attention of Light In The Attic chief Matt Sullivan. They both sought out Rodriguez. This began a decade long climb to fame and fortune. It took two years for Sullivan to find an American vinyl album and an Australian CD of **Cold Fact**. He listened and became a stone fan. He attempted to contact Clarence Avant to license a reissue. For a few years there was no response. Avant wasn't interested in a small, boutique label re-releasing Rodriguez.

Sullivan was determined to release **Cold Fact**. He personally guaranteed a fair royalty. Clarence Avant wouldn't give him the time of day. Sullivan decided to take commando action. He crashed a Seattle wedding to talk to Avant. The record mogul recognized Sullivan's passion. He signed an agreement for **Cold Fact** and **Coming From Reality** to be re-released. Sullivan didn't just re-release them; he spent a fortune on re-mastering, commissioning copious liner notes, special vinyl editions and cassesete tapes. Then he began a marketing campaign to let the world know of the Sugar Man's enormous talent.

The August 2008 release of **Cold Fact** began a journey that Sullivan enhanced with a series of small club bookings. In 2009 Rodriguez appeared before cheering Indie audiences. The idea of a man in his mid-sixties selling out Indie clubs seemed preposterous. It happened. An international star at seventy seemed a long shot. It happened. All thanks to Matt Sullivan and LITA.

Paolo Nutini and Rodriguez: Student and Mentor

Along the way Paolo Nutini came into the mix. Who is Paolo Nutini? He is a Scottish singer whose hit "Last Request" brought him stardom in 2006. He is also a huge Rodriguez fan. He performed with him in Detroit where they covered "Last Request." The Sugar Man loves the song and often features it in his live shows. It was 2008 when Nutini began extolling Rodriguez' musical genius. In a 2012 interview with Mickey McMongle, Nutini observed: "The man is incredible, he really has heart. Everything about his music is amazing and really speaks to me."

Unlike the hangers on, the Johnny come lately types and those who blow smoke up Rodriguez' ass, Nutini is a solid friend. Rodriguez sent him a present. It was a DVD in which the Sugar Man was on a train looking out the window covering Nutini's "Last Request." It was a special moment for the Scottish singer.

Paolo Nutini: "The beauty of it is the mystery of the man, in his own movie it takes about 50 minutes for him to appear."

In concert, Nutini's versions of "Forget It" and "Inner City Blues" brings the audience to its feet. He always gives the Sugar Man a strong endorsement as he introduces these tunes. Nutini spent the years from 2006 through 2011 telling the world about Sixto Rodriguez. Then **Searching For Sugar Man** demonstrated Nutini's vision.

Their friendship began long before Rodriguez achieved fame and fortune. In 2007 Nutini joined Rodriguez on stage on September 30, 2007 at St. Andrews Hall in Detroit for a rousing rendition of "Sugar Man."

Rodriguez returned the favor. At the Iron Horse in Northampton, Massachusetts, Rodriguez covered "Last Request" on September 2, 2012.

Matt Sullivan: An Indie Start in 2009

Matt Sullivan is now an old guy. He is in his late thirties or perhaps early forties. He still looks like a record geek in a thrift store searching for a rare Jimi Hendrix record. Almost single handedly, Sullivan brought Rodriguez back releasing his two albums. He also provided a series of promotional appearances and carefully crafted mini-tours. In 2009 he broke Rodriguez in the American market. Prior to that from 2005 to 2009 the Sugar Man had a London following as well as fame in South Africa and Australia.

Unlike the industry people who dealt with Rodriguez, Sullivan was a fan and a reputable businessman. In many ways it is the businessman's hat that is the important one. That is what brought Sixto Rodriguez to commercial prominence. There is one event that is the key to Rodriguez' fame. That is the LITA 2009 West Coast Rodriguez tour.

He set up a 2009 West Coast tour. The personal side of this trip tells one why the Sugar Man and LITA had a relationship unique to the music business. By examining the personal, not the musical, side of this tour it is obvious Rodriguez' humanity, cooperative nature, love for his fans and the rabid need to make his music mainstream trained him for the grueling stardom from 2012 on that would force him to sit with two or three people in a small room offstage to escape the throngs waiting to meet him. After **Searching For Sugar Man** turned his cult stardom into a mainstream frenzy everyone wanted a piece of him. He couldn't leisurely sign autographs and chat with the fans. Times had changed. There was too much pandemonium. The 2009 West Coast tour offers a window into a singer who has a close relationship with those promoting his career, and the venues that welcomed him. The fans couldn't get enough of his signature songs. He couldn't get enough of his fans. It was a mutual love fest.

In late June 2009 Matt Sullivan and his Light In The Attic crew began a West Coast Rodriguez tour making him a cult star. After playing Seattle, Portland and Vancouver B. C., Rodriguez headed to San Francisco and Los Angeles with Sullivan in a rickety van with empty donut shop bags, greasy taco wrappers and assorted fast food burger boxes. What is important about this tour? As we have seen in chapter twenty-one it reignited the Sugar Man's career in the Indie circuit.

There were commercial reasons for promoting the Sugar Man but Sullivan went far beyond the record label owner looking for a profit. Sullivan was searching for an artist. He found a treasure. Like everyone else who met and spent time with the Sugar Man, his humility, his generosity, and his enormous talent awed Sullivan. An under the radar artist who showed no visible signs of emotional trauma or hostility, Rodriguez is now a super star.

The Real Story is Not the Segerman Tale

If there is a grinch in **Searching For Sugar Man** it is Stephen "Sugar" Segerman. He now advertises for a four thousand dollar fee he will deliver a speech on Rodriguez and answer questions. When Segerman announced his talk on the Sugar Man he said it was: "An informative and inspiring motivational talk abut the Rodriguez phenomenon." His friend, Brian Currin, handles the bookings.

The point is Segerman is attempting to make a buck from the Sugar Man's story. That is fine, but he has made his money. It is time to butt out. The real story needs to be told which includes Australia, London and the U. S. But don't expect Segerman to give up his entitled role any time soon. He might have to get a life.

There is no way to diminish Rodriguez' story, his talent, his ultimate rewards and his existential life. The only regret is to view those around him who want to benefit from his tale. That is a sad fact.

Epilogue

"What you do to yourself, you do to the world,
What you do to the world, you do to yourself."

BUDDHIST PROVERB

"Australians are very vocal people. Very much so!
And the audience generates a lot of the action."

SIXTO RODRIGUEZ, 2016

"Less is more."

MIES VAN DER ROHE

'The greater your achievements,' the narrator of *More Die of Heartbreak* (1987) tells us, the less satisfactory your personal and domestic life will be.... The private life is almost always a bouquet of sores with a garnish of trivialities or downright trash."

SAUL BELLOW

"Never say you know the last word abut any human heart."

Henry James

The Sixto Rodriguez story is more than a tale of redemption for a down and out singer who became an international star due to **Searching For Sugar Man**. It is also a story that will never be retold. The Internet and instant communication will make it difficult to find a future Rodriguez. This is the tale of a phenomenon. While I have not attempted to invade Rodriguez' privacy, there are some personal influences shaping his character, his music and his elusive personality. His family, a myriad assortment of friends, Detroit's gritty streets, his up and down history, the bucolic influence of South Africa, the various record companies that did and didn't treat him fairly, his songwriting and publishing royalty controversy and Rodriguez' prodigious intellect combine to form this story. It is one hell of a story.

Had it not been for the Oscar winning **Searching For Sugar Man**, there might not have been the hurricane of fame Rodriguez experienced since 2012. When asked about how the Rodriguez story came to the screen, Malik Bendjelloul remarked he needed to get "the right people to believe in the project." He did!

Malik Bendjelloul: "That was the hardest thing. I thought it was evident that the story was good – had it been conceived by a screenwriter you would have thought that it was too much, too unbelievable to make sense. I thought that the fact that this really happened – and the way it happened – would be enough to attract investors. But in the end the story attracted everyone except the investors. Maybe it was because I was a new director. I was so passionate about it that I didn't receive a salary for three years, I just worked on the movie, but there was a point where I had to find a proper job and I thought I would have to give up."

How did Rodriguez' family receive **Searching For Sugar Man**? The Sugar Man's daughter, Regan, gave the answer. They loved it.

Regan Rodriguez: "**Searching For Sugar Man** is a testament to my father's unbelievable story. My whole life, I watched my dad defend himself and try to stake his ground as a musician. Finally, I get to see him up there. The authentic artist, as opposed to a carefully crafted commercial character, makes it! That is so satisfying - I can't even explain how good it feels. I could not be more thankful that this all came together and worked out so well. The whole thing is a real rock-n-roll dream come true."

This quote from Regan suggests why she is wary of strangers. When I was backstage with Rodriguez and Steve Rowland at the Luckman Center at California State University, Los Angeles, I asked her: "Where did you stay in San Francisco last night?" They had performed there the previous night. I knew their hotel. She didn't answer. She smiled. She was polite. She was paranoid. She thought I was after something more than writing a simple biography. I was simply trying to be friendly. Nothing malevolent on her part. It was their past. It haunted them. Don't trust the wannabes, the strangers and the hangers on. The filmmaker completing **Searching For Sugar Man** had an important insight into the Sugar Man and his family.

Malik Bendjelloul: "They have a paranoia from their past. I don't understand it."

It is not difficult to understand. After forty year of neglect, the Sugar Man and his family were wary of strangers.

This is one of the reasons a third album has not taken place. There are too many cooks in the kitchen. A third Rodriguez album is unlikely. He hasn't finished the nine songs he is working on. The atmosphere is cluttered with fame, fortune and a clouded, if successful, future. Rodriguez runs the show. His daughters are the gatekeepers.

Why was the documentary successful? On the surface it appears as a story that had little public interest. On the screen the tale is a heart warming one of overcoming incredible odds to become a major concert attraction and in the process an internationally acclaimed musician.

Why and How Searching for Sugar Man Impacted the Story: His Mysterious Daily Life

It is the care and diligence to detail that made the documentary successful. That same detail is used by Regan Rodriguez to guide her father's career and to make sure the creative isolation, the commercial lows and the disrespect from the industry never again occurs.

Little is known about the Sugar Man's daily life. That is intentional. He was private before fame and fortune. He is even more private now that he is a public figure. One wonders if he is like Descartes and Balzac who worked at night and slept in the day. In the brief interview in **Searching For Sugar Man**, he doesn't appear to favor the daylight hours. He is creative. He is calm.

Some hints about Rodriguez' life in 2017 took place when he talked briefly with the **Ottawa Sun**. The Sugar Man pointed out he had more offers to perform in concert, more opportunities to record, write for the movies, compose an autobiography and the various projects filled his daily schedule. He had too much on his plate. He remained a working class, blue-collar person. He told Lynn Saxberg: "I'm a worker, but I think that all workers get an idea of what to do to get free." Rodriguez paused thoughtfully and he continued. "Any kind of bondage, even economic bondage, is slavery. You gotta get free and I'm working on that. I'm doing well now." That said it all. Rodriguez has a daily life ignoring fame and fortune.

When Saxberg asked him about his flourishing half a decade career, Rodriguez said: "You can't be unconscious in this racket, this business, this art form, this industry, of the passing of so many notables. They're dropping like flies before my eyes." Rodriguez pauses and reflectively looks out the window. He has a tear in his eye. He is remembering Glen Campbell, Leonard Cohen and Steely Dan's Walter Becker who passed recently at Rodriguez' age.

As a political person, Rodriguez is universally quiet and circumspect about the presidency of Donald J. Trump. He is now a Detroit neighborhood activist. But he has a dim view of the Trump oligarchy. In a strange comment the Sugar Man alluded to Mother Nature taking care of the current malevolence in American government. When he refers to "Mother Nature" in the next quote he suggests environmental change will erase the Trump presidency.

Sixto Rodriguez: "She's the one that works to change ways, and that's what will take care of the presidency."

In a warm September 17, 2017 night in Ottawa he told the Canadian reporter about his life and the future. It is a fitting description of his present day contentment and success.

Sixto Rodriguez: "We have fun and that's a prerequisite for me. I'm rehearsed, but not scripted. I know when it's not right. You want to have good songs. I can't play if it's not in tune." Then he walked out onto the City Stage to appear in the City Folk Festival in Lansdowne Park in Ottawa. The irony caused Rodriguez to smile as he performed songs from **Coming From Reality**. He recorded the album at London's Lansdowne Studio and now almost fifty years later he was performing them in Lansdowne Park.

Regan Rodriguez' Key Role: Why and How She Created Touring Success

Regan Rodriguez is the daughter who has had the most to do with the documentary. This doesn't mean Eva and Sandra aren't important. They are. They continue to support their father. Regan was the catalyst to bringing Malik Bendjelloul into the family. She allowed him into the inner circle. She was also instrumental in convincing her father to tour from 2005 through 2011. Regan realized he was developing a cult audience. She was confident this would sell the

Light In The Attic reissue CDs. Although she supported Bendjelloul and approved of the early stages of **Searching For Sugar Man**, she saw the road to cult stardom. She traveled it with her father for half a decade prior to the documentary.

After allowing Bendjelloul to film her in-depth, she asked him to take her out of the documentary. It was a strange request. She told Malik she was "stiff" on camera. Malik urged her to wait for the final product. He assured her she was an integral part of the story. Then the South African, Stephen "Sugar" Segerman, allegedly said featuring two of the daughters would cause the gossipmongers to wonder if there was something wrong in the Rodriguez family. There wasn't. Segerman attempted to take credit for the inclusion of all three girls appearing in **Searching For Sugar Man**. It was never an issue. He made it one in his book. When Bendjelloul talked with Rowland about the daughters there was never a question they wouldn't be in the documentary.

Bendjelloul convinced the Rodriguez family there needed to be a view, if only a brief one, into their inner life. He asked Regan for family memorabilia. She pulled out the box of political materials, which was used in the filming of the documentary. It was a poignant moment. Regan was on the second floor of the house where she resided and the brief clip in **Searching For Sugar Man** helped to understand the frustration and eventual success that was the Sugar Man's. She is the antidote to Segerman's constant prattling about the story.

Segerman wrote to Bendjelloul complaining that neither Regan nor Rodriguez looked good on camera. Why did he do this? Only he can answer that question. This behavior was typical of the South African. Malik humored him. He was privately horrified by Segerman's blunt conclusions. The South African may have told people he had the Sugar Man's interests at heart but his private letters, e-mails and phone calls indicated he thought the story was about him. That is the tragedy of Segerman's role.

It was in the use of facts on American rock and roll that the South African failed the litmus test. One example of this took place when he identified Arthur Lee and Love as a San Francisco band. This was only one of many mistakes, misstatements and glitches. Malik was kind. He never mentioned Sugar's egregious misuse of the material.

When Rowland and Bendjelloul talked, Steve's girl friend, Judy Lewis, came on the line telling Malik he was headed for an Oscar. Judy was an actor, a producer, a director, and an award-winning writer. She was the daughter of Loretta Young and Clark Gabel. She had a show business lineage bordering on royalty. Soon Steve and Judy were in daily contact with Bendjelloul.

It was during this period that Simon Chinn came on board as a financial backer. On May 1, 2011 Malik talked at length with Steve Rowland when they finalized the fiscal strategy guaranteeing that **Searching For Sugar Man** would be completed prior to Christmas 2011 and be ready for the film festival circuit. Despite Segerman's amateurish attempts to influence the story, the documentary was ready for prime time.

In the irony of all ironies, Rowland's discussions of where and how to obtain financing helped to pave the way for the young filmmaker to figure out whom to approach. This led Bendjelloul to London. This may have led unwittingly to Simon Chinn's office. It is another mystery of the Sugar Man's story. Steve said he didn't help with the financing part other than to give Bendjelloul advice. The credit for the financing, Steve suggested, is totally Bendjelloul's. In the e-mails between the two there were many tips on how to finance the documentary. Steve's refuses to take any credit for the financing. This is typical Steve Rowland. He gets cranky when I ask him about financing or anything personal about Rodriguez.

The High and Low Points of Rodriguez' Story

There are highs and lows in the story. That said there is a lesson to his re-emergence in the music world. This lesson centers on a small record label, Matt Sullivan's Light In The Attic, the shadowy world of record promotion, think Neil Bogart and Harry Balk, the royalties and business end of the story, think Clarence Avant and Harry Balk, and the manner in which artists like Sixto Rodriguez influence the direction of popular culture, think appearances on the David Letterman Show and the Tonight Show, think press outlets **The Hollywood Reporter**, **60 Minutes** as well as a host of other media sources.

The road map to this story began with the two South Africans, Stephen "Sugar" Segerman and Craig Bartholomew-Strydom. They brought the Sugar Man back to prominence in South Africa in 1998. They wrote an excellent book about their exploits after the Oscar winning **Searching For Sugar Man** took the story global.

The book by Craig Bartholomew-Strydom and Stephen "Sugar" Segerman is a tour de force of the inside story. What bothers me is that lack of personal Sixto Rodriguez insights. It appears they hardly talked to the Sugar Man. As I interviewed people in and around Detroit, I was told Rodriguez was uncomfortable with the documentary and their book. He had enough of Segerman to last him a lifetime. I was surprised in his book Bartholomew-Strydom took a dim view of Segerman. What happened to the friendship?

What makes the Rodriguez story unique? It is he never relied on behind the scenes songwriters or producers. His music is his own. His producers Dennis Coffey, Mike Theodore and Steve Rowland gave Rodriguez carte blanche studio freedoms. This is one reason the albums are brilliant. He also survived the multiple evils of the major labels, the industry insiders and the hangers on who destroy many artists. Despite his success forty years later, Rodriguez is not comfortable with fame. He has no problem with fortune. He can give the money away. He remains the same person. Humble. Intellectual. Eccentric. Private. It took the industry a long time to catch on to the value of Rodriguez' songwriting. Hopefully, a third album will continue to celebrate his unique talent.

Sundance, The Sugar Man and the Protest Song

The Sundance Film Festival recognized the depth and breadth of the story. They provided the initial stage to launch the Sugar Man. There are so many good guys in the story it is heart warming. Dennis Coffey and Mike Theodore weighed in on the brilliance of the **Cold Fact** album. Steve Rowland gave his blessing to the soft, and pop hit sounds in **Coming From Reality**. Even those, like Harry Balk, who took advantage of Rodriguez, praised his talent.

There is one part of Rodriguez' career that was almost lost in the shuffle. That is his ability to write protest songs. He displayed a window into American politics, the crucial issues of a society bent upon minimizing the middle class, and he was equally at home with themes of mobster infested corruption in a society heading toward imminent change.

Most recording artists don't gave satisfying answers as to why they write. What vision do they see in their music? Rodriguez is the exception. In his music he sees a microcosmic reflection of what is right and what is wrong in American life. While he is introspective, he doesn't give answers appearing pompous or self-serving. If anything, Rodriguez is too humble.

For an artist without a hit record, there has been a great deal written about him. Much of what we know about him is mythical. Perhaps the best way to look for the real Sixto Rodriguez is to examine his world. It is the bastion of a blue-collar union worker. His message examines a repressive government and laws restricting personal freedoms. The real Sixto Rodriguez is a blue-collar person with an enormous writing and performing talent.

Much of Rodriguez' life from 1974 to 1998 makes for dull reading. He has left no public correspondence. He has written less than thirty published songs. Despite all this, Rodriguez remains an intellectual icon and a brilliant public figure.

Once Again the Question of Royalties

The question of royalties continually rears its ugly head. When film critic Roger Ebert called Rodriguez "a secular saint," he hit upon the crux of the royalties argument. He makes it appear Rodriguez had little interest in royalties. No one cares more about equitable royalty statements than Sixto Rodriguez. It was wonderful to romanticize the story and remark he doesn't care. It just doesn't happen to be the truth.

Rodriguez wrote in "Rich Folks Hoax:" "The priest is preaching from a shallow grave. He counts his money. Then he paints you saved. Talking to the young folks. Young folks share the same jokes." That tells it all in lyrical form.

Stephen "Sugar" Segerman, who acts as an unofficial publicist for Rodriguez, sees things changing. Segerman said: "Rodriguez has created a whole new consciousness about robbing an artist."

Robbie Mann, of RPM Records, said he believed his South African label sold at least a half million copies of Rodriguez' records. Other labels heads suggest that in the last few years he has sold in excess of 250,000 CDs. Still there are no reported royalties for the Sugar Man from South African sources.

In June 2014 the **London Guardian** reported Harry Balk's Gomba music sued Interior Music guru Clarence Avant for "fraudulently collecting Rodriguez' royalties." Balk had a five-year contract with Rodriguez due to expire in the summer of 1971. By that time Avant's Sussex label recorded two Rodriguez albums. Harry sued alleging fraud. Harry's contract gave him a share of the songwriting royalties. He didn't write a word. So Rodriguez used the songwriting names Jesus Rodriguez and Sixth Prince. Balk's company, Gomba Music, argued Clarence Avant "stole Rodriguez's music." It is complete nonsense. In the first book in a chapter on the royalties I concluded a compromise or private solution was concluded on the royalty issue. The sealed agreement would tell us the whole story.

Then the rocket scientists in the music business turned their venom on the Sugar Man stating he is "accused of breaching warranties and representations, plus a failure to cooperate." This is ludicrous. Rodriguez was not paid a penny in royalties. As the Sugar Man said: "It's the music business." So I guess the story is he didn't cooperate with the record heads and the nefarious labels who didn't pay him. The **Guardian** stated his attorney hadn't responded. Gee, I wonder why? He didn't get paid. Is he supposed to respond? As we go to press the issues remain unresolved. At least for the general public, allegedly someone cut a deal, Harry Balk passed away, and Clarence Avant is operating out of his home. Rodriguez' pre-**Searching For Sugar Man** money is tilting in the wind.

The Sixto Rodriguez Legacy

Cold Fact and **Coming From Reality** began the Sixto Rodriguez legacy. His career as a writer was formed by the first album and intensified by the second release. His roots go deep and wide in American classic rock and blues. His writing expresses the soil of human thought and its ultimate expressions. What caused Rodriguez' writing to be so deep and meaningful? The answer is a simple one. He reads deeply in serious literature. He also had a formal education beyond high school. His B. A. in philosophy from the Wayne State Honors College tells one all they need to know about his philosophical base as well as his intellect. You were invited into the honors college. It is for special students who achieve academically. It is also for non-traditional thinkers and contrarians.

There were other influences. By studying Eastern philosophy, occultism and mysticism, Rodriguez established a base for his songwriting. There is an Oriental philosopher's tone to Rodriguez' writing. He is also a fundamentally religious man. He lacks the strict dogma and contradictions of religion.

By blending Hindu philosophy with the idealism of the New England Transcendentalists, Rodriguez' songs are uniquely American. He also embraces Nietzsche's dismissal of conventional religion and morality. He found his own inner path to happiness. His humor and daunting satirical comments fly in the face of convention. He displays a wisdom highlighting his feelings. It is Rodriguez' unique voice and lyrical brilliance that comes out of this milieu.

The critics label Rodriguez a Shaman. They have a point. His writing reflects the influence of his friends, his wives, his children and his surroundings. He presents an oral history of his family and those around him with biting satire and humorous overtones.

Rodriguez' songwriting polarized critics. They either loved it or hated it. Then along came the **Searching for Sugar Man**. The triumphs of his writing were lauded as new and innovative. This is a compliment forty years after the fact. By revealing himself there is an honesty and integrity to Rodriguez' writing. The hackles of convention and tradition are cast aside in Rodriguez' lyrical beauty.

It is Rodriguez' love of words and his ability to place his thoughts in lyrical form that makes him special. The conventional documentary evidence for intelligent rock and roll lyrics begins and ends with Bob Dylan. This is unfortunate. Since Dylan has to use Robert Hunter as a co-writer, his biting edge has vanished. Now Dylan songs are like Socrates meets Chuck Berry. That is they are obtuse, convoluted and confused. Sixto Rodriguez has written only thirty songs but they are all masterpieces. He never accepted the industry dictum to write as much as possible. He writes what he wants, when he wants and how he wants. That is the beauty of Sixto Rodriguez. He remains his own man. His talent is his to share with his fans. To his credit, he believes the music business can go to hell. That is why everyone loves him.

Rodriguez writes for love of the word. He is a writer who has a direction and themes that are unwavering. There is an innate creativity to Rodriguez. The sensitivity in his writing reflects a similar sensitivity in his life. Rodriguez remain a modest, humble talented person who cares for others, he still has a social-political conscience.

Myth and Reality Revisited in The Sugar Man

The Sixto Rodriguez story has played out. He is no longer a mythical legend. The tales of suicide, burning himself up on stage in a club, a death by drug overdose and other mysterious events are just that myth. The reality is he remains a strong in concert performer. He is by all accounts, from those close to him, still able to write well. He has money. He has fame. He has international acclaim. That's it. He is happy. Or is he?

The reality is this is not a positive development for the Sugar Man. He is basically shy. He is a loner. He is an existential thinker. He is family oriented. He is loyal to those around him. He is a person who continues to grow. Fame makes him nervous. But at seventy-five what is left? That is the question! Only the Sugar Man can answer it.

One wonders if the burden of fame will push this shy, somewhat reclusive, writer back into the obscurity that was his life for forty years. It doesn't appear that will happen. Rodriguez embraces the stardom. He has a financial freedom he never previously experienced. He is eager for new challenges.

The Elusive Sixto Rodriguez

Despite fame and fortune Sixto Rodriguez remains pleasantly elusive. He lives in the same house he purchased at an auction in the 1970s. He still feeds his wood stove in winter. He sweats out the summer Detroit heat. The difference is a steady source of money and international recognition for his beautifully written songs. He can perform when and where he desires. He remains elusive. The Sugar Man doesn't want to share his family, his friends and his life with the public. That is now a difficult task. He is a celebrity. It is a mixed blessing.

In the right circumstances, Rodriguez remains approachable. It is his management team, not the Sugar Man that lessened the media appearances. This is a smart move as the mystery behind Rodriguez' career is important to maintaining the myth and ignoring the reality.

There is another side to the Rodriguez story. It has nothing to do with the Sugar Man. That is Detroit's influence. It was a metropolis divided by race and social class issues. As the Motor City auto industry went in precipitous decline the pension system vanished. Urban decay set in and destroyed key parts of the city. Some of the streets are deserted. Others look like a bombed out war zone. Urban bankruptcy hovered over the Motor City as it slowly crept back to a position of economic and social stability. This is the backdrop to Rodriguez' songs.

Now Detroit has urban gardens. Quicken Loans is attempting to bring downtown business back. Rodriguez walks the Cass Corridor amazed at the positive changes. It is a fertile time for Rodriguez to observe the Motor City in his beautiful and poignant lyrics.

Rodriguez is Through Giving Interviews: But for Australia Anything

By the summer of 2017 the wear and tear of touring, the pressure to record a third album and the tedium of stardom changed Rodriguez. He was reluctant to do interviews. He had appeared on numerous radio and television shows. He had done everything Sony asked to promote **Searching For Sugar Man**. He was tired. He was also seventy-five and finally experiencing the financial gain of rock 'n' roll stardom. One of the myths of the documentary was he was lost and forgotten in the musical jungle. That is simply not true. He writes to perform. As we have seen from 2005 to 2011 he appeared regularly in concert. He also completed international tours in South Africa, Australia, London and Paris.

Rodriguez was done with the press. In depth interviews declined. He had given the same interviews, answered the inane questions and smiled for photos. Then Iain Shedden, a Sydney music writer, called and requested an interview. The Sugar Man agreed. All things Australian appealed to him.

The Shedden interview, which appeared in the **Australian** in July 2016, displayed the relaxed, convivial side of the Sugar Man. The interview began with Rodriguez talking about remodeling his house. Well it was not exactly a remodel. He said some cosmetic changes and some creature comforts were added. This is the usual humble Rodriguez. It was a housing makeover. The Avery Street home now was more comfortable.

Sixto Rodriguez: "You might not recognize the place now." Then he went on to discuss how he did most of the work. "I'll be happy to show it off when it's done," he concluded. This interview was a prelude to Rodriguez' November and December 2016 Australian tour. "It was Australia that helped me out," Rodriguez continued. "But South Africa really generated an audience."

Rodriguez was frustrated with the press. The Australian fans didn't receive the proper credit for keeping his career alive prior to South African stardom. Shedden was impressed. Then Rodriguez explains: "I didn't write the film. I didn't have anything to do with the making of the film....It's an independent art form." What did Rodriguez mean? He believed the documentary had a message. It was to look beneath the film for a deeper meaning. This is how the Sugar Man views the world. He sees and writes about things others miss. This is the mind of the existentialist.

Then the Sugar Man discussed the royalty issue. "It's my version of the Led Zeppelin deal," he said with a sardonic smile. What did he mean by "my version" of the Led Zeppelin deal? This is an obvious reference to the problems Led Zeppelin had collecting their royalties from their manager and the record label. The comparison for Rodriguez was one that told the world he would manage his career and his money. The old days of villains in the music industry stealing from him were in the past. When asked about the years in the musical wilderness, he said: "I don't mind the way it went. You can't fix that kind of stuff. You can't really go back in time and change things. I'm a lucky kid in a lot of ways. I've seen a lot of the world over the past few years. I've got a couple more good years, I think, including Australia." Then Rodriguez hung up the phone. Now we know how he has spent his money. He has a home telephone and a cell phone. That is progress. That is the Sugar Man.

Easing Into 2017: Rodriguez and Rowland Continue on Their Creative Paths

By early 2017 Sixto Rodriguez continued to perform. His daughters planned his concert schedule carefully. There was plenty of rest between shows. It had been almost six years since **Searching For Sugar Man** became a commercial phenomenon. Everyone's life changed. Rodriguez was now a wealthy man. Regan was married with two children. Sandra had a happy and healthy family and a budding career as a songwriter and performer. The Sugar Man's oldest daughter, Eva, was retired from the U. S. military raising a son who is ready for college. She moved home to Detroit and lives in the Woodbridge area.

Race, Detroit and the Early 1970S: His Life Reconsidered

The question of race is never far from rock and roll biography. Most writers ignore the subject. In the case of Sixto Rodriguez race is front and center to the story. When Harry Balk told the Sugar Man that Mexican American singers couldn't be teen idols, Harry was not being racist. Or was he? I know Harry and there is not a racist bone in his body. He told Rodriguez the simple truth. As Balk chomped on a cigar with his pork pie hat, cool nightclub clothes and personable manner, he gave the Sugar Man some advice.

Harry Balk: "You are a talented, good looking guy who needs to play teen dances, appear on the TV dance shows lip synching your record and talk to the fanzines. I told this to Del Shannon and Johnny and the Hurricanes. They took my advice. Listen to me kid I have been doing this for years."

Rodriguez wouldn't go along with Balk. The question of race was on Rodriguez' mind. When Harry said Question Mark and the Mysterians were all the Mexican rockers Detroit needed, the Sugar Man took exception to this comment. He never said a word to the press. His close friends say he was angry.

Race, Detroit and Rodriguez is the question. It is also the answer. As the Sugar Man grew up an African American middle class emerged in the Motor City due to a thriving auto industry. There was a legendary record label, Motown, and in 1973 an African American Mayor, Coleman A. Young, was elected. Things looked rosy for the Motor City only to decline into urban bankruptcy.

When the Detroit police beat Rodriguez, he put his protestations in song. Then corruption, mismanagement of city funds, the intrusions of state and federal officials in Detroit politics and the decline of the local economy forced him into rehabbing homes.

What did race contribute to the Sugar Man's art? The importance of the underdog, the strength of the working person, the search for justice and the all-encompassing passion of the intellectual drove Rodriguez' creativity. The Sugar Man witnessed separate and unequal in America. He writes about it with a fervid passion. Institutionalized racism didn't detail his career; it provided the focus for a lyrical beauty that defines America in his songs.

In the contentious political age we live in Sixto Rodriguez is a breath of fresh air. He is an entertainer, a family man, a political icon and a person who sees the absurdities of the American condition. While the facts on Rodriguez' life are elusive, they are out there. Surprisingly, for those who want on an inside view, he is a normal family man with one hell of a musical talent.

The difficult task is to discover the intricate details of Rodriguez' life. He is on the road as many as seventy- days a year depending upon his health. The public loves his shows. He is in a position to perform when and where he pleases. He is writing new songs. He is in the recording studio. The Sixto Rodriguez story is far from over.

What should one remember about Rodriguez? If nothing else his sensitive use of language sets him apart from those who write in the rock and roll idiom. He reports on the people and events around him with a rare sensitivity. His illuminating portraits of the American blue-collar worker, the frustrated politico, the music moguls and family life make him an observer with a conscience providing rare insights into the American condition.

The Problems, Perils, Pitfalls of Success and the Man

After five years of unrequited stardom, Sixto Rodriguez discovered the perils of rock and roll stardom. The pitfalls of stardom necessitated changes in his life. Privacy is an increasing concern. Management problems, while minimal, occupy much of the Sugar Man's attention. The conniving ways of the music business make Rodriguez inherently suspicious of people with new projects and business offers. He is by all accounts a good businessman. He has the scars from forty years of being in the creative wilderness. He suffers his personal indignities with grace and good humor.

The handsome and virile young Rodriguez of 1971 aged gracefully. In 2017 the ladies were still screaming: "We love you." The Sugar Man's subtle intelligence and elegance on stage is an indication of his maturity and growth in spite of fame. The pitfalls of success have been minimized. He retains a personality transfixing women. The words Rodriguez uses to craft his songs displays his intellectual genius.

What did Rodriguez accomplish? He cemented his legacy by seizing control of his product. He explained his career to the press in numerous in-depth interviews. Then he shunned the media. This isn't a contradiction. This is simply Sixto Rodriguez. To uninformed outsiders, he appears quirky, paranoid and suspicious. To those who are close friends, they tell the tale of a private, compassionate person who never abandons his friends.

Edmund Wilson and Art from a Wound and Fame

In 1941 Edmund Wilson wrote a widely quoted essay "The Wound And The Bow" in which he postulated all art comes from a wound. Rodriguez' songs fit into this category. He remains a working class hero. His feet are the ground and his head in a philosophy book. The wounds of everyday life generated his lyrical magic.

Fame might be as destructive as failure. It has impacted Rodriguez' life but not noticeably. He retains the core values and the lifestyle that made him just another blue collar, working class Detroit denizen.

Where did the title "Searching For Sugar Man" come from for the documentary? As Craig Bartholomew-Strydom suggests in his book: "The Only One Who Didn't Know" was an early working title. **Searching For Sugar Man** was a title Simon Chinn, Sony Legacy and other investors came to believe created the best publicity for documentary success.

Searching for Sugar Man: What Does It Mean?

In 2012 when **Searching For Sugar Man** cascaded across the silver screen it was a runaway hit. Sixto Rodriguez received the acclaim for his musical genius. The story of redemption, success and the fairy tale quality of an obscure Detroit folk singer becoming an international star was the feel good story of the year. Like many such tales it was as much based in fiction as in fact. That is part of the mystery. Where does one separate fact from fiction?

Rodriguez' lyrical magic, his performing genius and how his story exposed a music industry that abused its own is a real tale still played out daily. The Sugar Man and his family are the heroes. The record industry heroes include Sussex label owner Clarence Avant, Matt Sullivan of Light In The Attic, and producers Steve Rowland, David Holmes, Mike Theodore and Dennis Coffey, writer Craig Bartholomew-Strydom and director Malik Bendjelloul.

There is substance to Sixto Rodriguez' life. He is a brilliant songwriter. He is a charismatic performer. He is a contrarian. He is a contradiction. That is the beauty of the Sugar Man. There is shallowness to the media. Rodriguez has ignored it.

What is Missing in a Rodriguez Biography?

The Sixto Rodriguez story has played out in film, in biographical studies, on television and on college campuses. His genius is debated in the realm of popular culture. Is anything missing in a

Rodriguez biography? The man is missing. Not the musical man. Not the entertainment man. Not the philosopher. What is missing is the ethnic lineage be it Mexican American or Native American. How does this polyglot ethnic heritage influence the Sugar Man? No one knows.

How did cultural influences shape Rodriguez? His life is one of tolerance, forgiveness, abstractions and politically driven thoughts. His Mexican American heritage, his dad's brutal treatment in the Detroit industrial plants, and the constant threat of political brutality on the Detroit streets shaped his Latino heritage. He has never discussed it except in song.

There are references to Indian pow-wows and other political events. There is no concrete evidence his ethnicity influenced him. Unlike Goethe, who wrote 12,000 letters in his life, there is no evidence Rodriguez has written a letter. Why is this important? It is because the only hints to his life are in song. His interviews, his public statements, his education and his family comments never tell the tale of Mexican American and Native American concerns.

Another missing component is the intellectual biography Rodriguez deserves. He is educated, well read, and he is thoughtful on a wide variety of subjects. Yet, we have no idea what he reads. What are his literary concerns? We know his politics. His liberalism is a big part of his daily life. The rest is a mystery.

Scenes from a Hard Life Turned to Fame and Fortune

The traditional path to success was not one Rodriguez took. This is not surprising considering his hardscrabble life. It is the times that doomed the Sugar Man in the 1970s music business. The revolutionary politics of the 1960s gave birth to his songwriting brilliance. The disco mania of the 1970s and jackass record executives like Neil Bogart and Harry Balk that doomed his success.

The riveting one of a kind tale that is the Sugar Man's story is pursued. His working class background, his impeccable manners, his shy but vulnerable nature, his serious and thoughtful side, his mania to help the blue-collar working class and his ethnic heritage define a singer-songwriter and a champion of the blue collar, long forgotten worker.

While other writers wax poetic, Rodriguez does so from personal experience. The Sugar Man's songs have a wisdom, a complexity and a maturity uncommon to rock music. He is a stoic, existentialist refusing to talk about or interpret his songs. They are what they are. Listen to them. He does this with a keen eye. Rodriguez' songs capture the intricacies and contradictions of American life.

If the literati who write about rock and roll had accorded the Sugar Man an exalted place in the pantheon of reviews would it have made a difference? Probably not! Greil Marcus's overwrought prose, Dave Marsh's beautifully crafted sentences or the deep insights of Ed Ward could have helped his career. Rodriguez experienced none of these major writers. That is in itself is a good thing. His music matured like a fine wine.

There is a tendency to romanticize Rodriguez' life. That is a mistake. He has lived a hardscrabble existence. He is tough. He is driven. The conflicts in his personality come from having too much responsibility early in life.

As Rodriguez grew up in the 1950s, he lived in an age of repressed sexuality. He was twenty-two when the Beatles arrived on the Ed Sullivan Show. He was "drowning" in middle class conformity. It was off to work and Wayne State University. In some respects the 1950s formed the Sugar Man's character and reaction to the stultifying intellectual mediocrity of his youth. He never gave in to the suburban malaise terrifying America in the late 1950s and early 1960s. He began crafting songs. He was a blue-collar poet in a white-collar world. A decade later in 1970-1971 he committed his poetry in song form in two marvelous albums.

The Unknowable Sixto Rodriguez

Sixto Rodriguez is a songwriter and performer with an extraordinary connection to his audience. His fans turn up at concerts with an atmosphere bordering on a love fest. The Sugar Man's connection to his audience is through his songs. They don't know him. No one, except for his immediate family, knows Rodriguez. Why is the unknowable Rodriguez important?

His sophisticated intellect and defined art appeals to a wide fan base. It is impossible to approach Rodriguez. He is not an open book. It is an intimacy with him on his own terms that defines the Sugar Man. He is uncompromising. This explains the twists and turns in his almost fifty year pursuit of hit records. He hasn't had any hits. He is a cult artist with an international audience. Rodriguez is an earthy character who doesn't want a biographer, who doesn't want it known he stokes the magic dragon and he doesn't want his private life analyzed. The Sugar Man is not a straightforward subject open to scrutiny, but in his life the elements of American popular culture coalesce. The result is his songwriting is a window into our societal malaise. The biographical material on his life tells us a great deal about the music industry.

The fans and critics have a disparity of views abut the Sugar Man. The audience accepts his genius. His intimate pop songs in **Coming From Reality** are a stark contrast to his brilliant language in **Cold Fact**. His compositional gifts are filled with dark images of political wrongdoing that are contrasted with bright, personal songs reflecting his bohemian life. The perils and pleasures of love is a recurrent theme in Rodriguez' songs. He is vulnerable. He has survived the jackasses in the music industry who disrespected, disparaged and ignored his material.

When Virginia Woolf wrote: "Is it not anyone who has lived a life, left a record of that life, worthy of biography-the failures as well as the successes, the humble as well as the illustrious." In her convoluted prose Woolf unwittingly describes Sixto Rodriguez. Stay tuned. The wisdom of the Sugar Man continues.

There is a shadowiness to Rodriguez' life. Perhaps that is part of the charm. He is the poet for everyman. He is not Bob Dylan, but he stands on his own as a songwriter with a disdain for the music industry. Recently, in Target I heard "Sugar Man" wafting out of the sound system as a group of ladies placed twenty bags of candy on the counter. As "Sugar Man" played one lady turned to the other, she said: "Who is that singing?" The other lady said: "It's Wayne Newton I just love his voice." Rodriguez still has anonymity.

Sixto Rodriguez was always searching for new ways to express his creative side. He never wanted to be categorized. He was never predictable. That is part of his charm. That is part of the legend.

The Sugar Man's songs are part of a grander mosaic visible only to his creative sense. The lyrics reveal an invisible part of the creator's mind. Artists are generally not humble people. They are larger than life. They live in a thin, unhappy space between arrogance and self-hatred. Sixto Rodriguez escaped this type of life because he doesn't brag, he is not full of himself, he respects the songwriting process and he follows his art.

Left to Right: Bobby Rey, Steve Rowland and Budd Albright At The Guys And Dolls Club, Hollywood

Budd Albright, Steve Rowland: A Picture For Opening Night At The Doll House

Budd Albright 1957 Performing in Hollywood

Appendix I

Quotations of Stephen "Sugar" Segerman

1. "TRYING TO EXPLAIN HOW INGRAINED RODRIGUEZ WAS IN OUR LIVES, THE MOVIE SEEMS TO OVERSTATE IT BUT YOU COULD MAKE A THREE-HOUR MOVIE AND STILL NOT CONVINCE PEOPLE OF HOW IMPORTANT THIS GUY WAS TO US." SEGERMAN IN CONVERSATION WITH FRONT ROW REVIEWS, JULY 15, 2012.
2. "SUNDANCE WAS SUCH A TRIP! I'M NOT A MOVIE PERSON AT ALL; THIS WAS ALL NEW TO ME. I'VE BEEN WORKING ON THIS WITH MALIK FOR ABOUT FIVE YEARS; THREE YEARS WAS ACTUALLY MAKING THE MOVIE. HE'S BEEN TO SOUTH AFRICA A FEW TIMES. WE SHOT A TRAILER, ABOUT ONE AND A HALF MINUTES, THAT WON AT A FESTIVAL WHERE YOU PITCH YOUR DOCUMENTARIES. SO IT'S TAKEN A LONG TIME. WE NEVER REALLY KNEW WHAT WE WERE GOING TO DO WITH IT, BUT WE ALWAYS HAD SUNDANCE IN MIND – MALIK REALLY WANTED TO GO TO SUNDANCE. SO WHEN WE SENT IT TO THEM, WE GOT AN EMAIL BACK SAYING THAT WE WERE THE OPENING FILM. THAT WAS A LIFE-CHANGING MOMENT. I

COULDN'T BELIEVE THAT – NOT THAT THEY'D ACCEPTED IT BUT THAT THEY WERE OPENING THE FESTIVAL WITH IT. WE KEPT HEARING FROM THEM HOW MUCH THEY LIKED IT, HOW THEY WERE PUNTING IT, AND WE WERE JUST AMAZED. THEY FLEW US ALL THERE, EVERYBODY WAS AT SUNDANCE: SANDRA, RODRIGUEZ'S DAUGHTER, AND REGAN, HIS YOUNGEST (EVA WAS STILL IN SOUTH AFRICA), CRAIG, MALIK, ME, RODRIGUEZ WAS THERE – WE WERE KIND OF LIKE THIS ENTOURAGE. WE WENT AROUND TO ABOUT SIX OR SEVEN SCREENINGS OF THE FILM, AND WE'D SNEAK RODRIGUEZ INTO THE MOVIE HOUSE, SO NO ONE KNEW HE WAS THERE." SEGERMAN IN CONVERSATION WITH FRONT ROW REVIEWS, JULY 12, 2012.

3. "THE POINT IS, ANYONE WHO WANTED TO CONTACT OR FIND OUT ANYTHING ABOUT RODRIGUEZ HAD TO COME TO US. THERE HAVE BEEN A LOT OF TOURS. HE'S COME TO SOUTH AFRICA MANY TIMES, WE TOOK HIM TO LONDON IN 2005 AND 2008 – HE PLAYED KENTISH TOWN FORUM – SO THERE'S BEEN A LOT OF PUBLICITY. MATT SULLIVAN FROM LIGHT IN THE ATTIC RECORDS, NICE LITTLE INDIE LABEL, CAME TO US THROUGH THE WEBSITE LOOKING TO RELEASE RODRIGUEZ IN AMERICA. THERE'VE BEEN TWO BEAUTIFUL RELEASES IN AMERICA ON CD. SO WE ARE THE FILTER BECAUSE WE'RE IN CONTACT WITH THE FAMILY. NOT WITH RODRIGUEZ – IN FACT HE PULLED HIS PHONE OUT OF THE WALL ONCE BECAUSE HIS NUMBER GOT OUT AND EVERYONE WAS CALLING. HE'S A VERY PRIVATE GUY. SO WE PASS ON WHAT'S IMPORTANT AND WE DON'T WHAT ISN'T." SEGERMAN IN CONVERSATION WITH FRONT ROW REVIEWS, JULY 12, 2012.

4. "OVER THE YEARS, SINCE WE FOUND HIM, I'VE STAYED IN CONTACT WITH HIM. I SPOKE TO HIM THAT FIRST NIGHT THE WAY I TELL IT IN THE FILM, THAT LITERALLY HAPPENED. THEN HE CAME TO SOUTH AFRICA AND I TOOK ALEX MCCRINDLE, WHO DEVELOPED THE WEBSITE WITH ME. WE WERE DRIVING DOWN CAMPS BAY DRIVE AND RODRIGUEZ WAS STAYING IN A LITTLE TOWNHOUSE/HOTEL THING AT THE BOTTOM OF CAMPS BAY. FOR ME IT WAS WEIRD, BECAUSE THIS WHOLE THING HAD STARTED ON CAMPS BAY BEACH AND NOW I WAS DRIVING BACK INTO CAMPS BAY TO MEET THIS INCREDIBLE HUMAN BEING. IN THE MOVIE THERE'S THIS SHOT – WHERE WILLEM SAYS, "WHAT IF HE'S JUST SOME GUY?" – AND RODRIGUEZ IS JUST STANDING THERE, AT THE TOP OF THE STAIRS, IN THIS BEIGE SUIT. AND THAT'S HOW I'LL ALWAYS REMEMBER HIM. THE BAND WAS THERE, (RODRIGUEZ'S MIDDLE DAUGHTER) EVA WAS THERE... WE ALL MET THAT FIRST NIGHT HE WAS IN CAPE TOWN." SEGERMAN IN CONVERSATION WITH FRONT ROW REVIEWS, JULY 12, 2012.
5. "RODRIGUEZ IS AS RESERVED, CONTEMPLATIVE, PHILOSOPHICAL, ENIGMATIC, AND DEEP-THINKING AS HE COMES ACROSS IN THE FILM." SEGERMAN IN CONVERSATION WITH SPLING.CO.ZA http://www.spling.co.za/movie-news/interview-stephen-sugar-segerman-on-searching-for-sugar-man
6. "RODRIGUEZ BECAME SOMETHING OF A REBEL ICON ..... WE ALL BOUGHT HIS RECORDS. EVERYBODY I KNEW HAD HIS RECORDS. 'I WONDER' THAT WAS THE BIG SONG THAT EVERYONE WAS SINGING. THERE HE WAS ON THE RECORD COVER – SORT OF A HIPPIE WITH SHADES. BUT NOBODY KNEW

ANYTHING ABOUT HIM. HE WAS A MYSTERY, UNLIKE OTHER ARTISTS THAT YOU COULD READ ABOUT. NOBODY KNEW ANYTHING ABOUT RODRIGUEZ – HE WAS A MYSTERY." http://mondoweiss.net/2013/06/revolution-original-apartheid/#sthash.RMn88ZT5.dpuf

7. "NEW VINYL IS A BIT PRICEY." IN CONVERSATION WITH SUE SEGAR 2014.
8. "IT IS MUCH MORE EXPENSIVE TO BUY A VINYL RECORD THAN TO DIGITALLY DOWNLOAD AN ALBUM." IN CONVERSATION WITH SUE SEGAR 2014.
9. "MABU VINYL IS MY SHOP, MY LIVELIHOOD, MY PASSION, WHICH AFTER ELEVEN YEARS, HAS REAPED THE BENEFIT OF THE RESURGENCE OF VINYL, PLUS THE WONDERFUL PUBLICITY THE RODRIGUEZ MOVIE BROUGHT US. SEGERMAN IN CONVERSATION WITH SUE SEGAR, 2014.
10. "MY FEELING, AFTER ALL THAT HAS HAPPENED, IS OF ABIDING CONTENTMENT AND HAPPINESS THAT THIS HAS ALL WORKED OUT SO WELL, AND THAT I AM ABLE TO BE PART OF IT." SEGERMAN IN CONVERSATION WITH SUE SEGAR, 2014.
11. THIS IS PROBABLY ONE OF THE MOST VIRAL MOVIES OF THE CENTURY." SEGERMAN ON SEARCHING FOR SUGAR MAN. SEGERMAN TO SUE SEGAR, 2014.
12. "WE KEEP THE REALLY VALUABLE STUFF THERE... IN BLUE TRUNKS. THE HIP REDORD GUYS KNOW IF THEY WANT TO BUY SOMETHING REALLY SPECIAL, IT IS WHERE THEY COME. IT'S KIND OF BY APPOINTMENT ONLY." SEGERMAN TO SUE SEGAR, 2014.
13. "WHAT I'VE LEARNT IS IF ANYBODY TAKES THE TROUBLE TO COME AND INTRODUCE THEMSELVES TO YOU, YOU MUST GIVE THEM FIVE OR TEN MINUTES." SEGERMAN TO SUE SEGAR, 2014.

14. **"I AM COMPLETELY AWARE THE LIMELIGHT EVENTUALLY MOVES ON." SEGERMAN ON HIS FAME IN CONVERSATION WITH SUE SEGAR, 2014.**
15. **"I DON'T KNOW WHAT I DID TO DESERVE THIS...I'M SPEECHLESS...IT'S BEEN A WONDERFUL JOURNEY." SEGERMAN ON HIS FAME IN CONVERSATION WITH SUE SEGAR, 2014**

Appendix II

Quotations of Brian Currin

1. "WE JUST KEPT THINKING THIS WAS THE LAST THING THAT WAS GOING TO HAPPEN...AND HERE WE ARE. IT'S BEEN, LIKE, 15 YEARS OR SOMETHING. IT WAS A THRILL JUST TO RELEASE THE CD AND SEE MY NAME IN THE LINER NOTES. BUT AS FAR AS WE WERE CONCERNED HE WAS DEAD." CURRIN IN COVERSATION WITH FRONT ROW REVIEWS, JULY 15, 2012.
2. "GROWING UP IN THE 70'S IN SOUTH AFRICA, I LISTENED TO THE RADIO ALL THE TIME (WE ONLY GOT TV IN ABOUT 1976!)." CURRIN, FEBRUARY 5, 2017 https://briancurrin.wordpress.com
3. "CAN'T REMEMBER WHEN EXACTLY I FIRST HEARD 'COLD FACT'. FOR ME HIS MUSIC JUST ALWAYS SEEMED TO HAVE BEEN THERE. A NUMBER OF THE MIXTAPES FROM MY TEENAGE YEARS SHOW 'SUGAR MAN', 'RICH FOLKS HOAX' AND 'I WONDER' AS BEING FROM 1973/74 WHEN I WAS ABOUT 14/15." BRIAN CURRIN, SEPTEMBER 1, 2012.

4. "IN 1997, STEPHEN "SUGAR" SEGERMAN SET UP A WEBSITE, CALLED 'THE GREAT RODRIGUEZ HUNT', WITH THE INTENTION OF FINDING ANY INFORMATION ABOUT THE MYSTERIOUS U. S. MUSICIAN OF 'COLD FACT' FAME. IN THE SAME YEAR BRIAN CURRIN ESTABLISHED 'CLIMB UP ON MY MUSIC', A TRIBUTE SITE TO THE LIFE AND WORKS OF RODRIGUEZ." http://paper.li/sugar_man/1343195168#/
5. BRIAN CURRIN WROTE SHORT DESCRIPTIONS FOR SOME OF THE SONGS ON SUGARMAN: THE BEST OF RODRIGUEZ IN TANDEM WITH SEGERMAN.
6. CURRIN'S CLIMB UP ON MY MOUNTAIN WEBSITE WAS AN IMPORTANT FORCE IN ESTABLISHING A MODERN TONE TO SOUTH AFRICAN ROCK AND ROLL MUSIC.
7. BRIAN CURRIN, ALONG WITH SEGERMAN, ESTABLISHED THE SOUTH AFRICAN DIGEST AND WERE PARTICULARLY INFLUENTIAL ON THE FIRST ISSUE. THIS WAS ANOTHER STEP TO MODERNIZING SA ROCK AND ROLL.
8. BRIAN CURRIN HAS WRITTEN A MARVELOUS PIECE "RODRIGUEZ AND HIS PLACE IN THE STORY OF ROCK," WHICH IS ON THE SUGARMAN.ORG THE OFFFICAL RODRIGUEZ WEBSITE, REPLETE WITH A PICTURE OF THE SUGAR MAN STANDING WITH CURRIN. IN THIS INTERESTING POST CURRIN DISCUSSES A MIX TAPE OF HITS IN 1973-1974 IN WHICH RODRIGUEZ DOMINATES LOCAL SOUTH AFRICAN CHART HITS, REALLY BEFORE THEIR WERE CHARTS, AND THEN CURRIN DISCUSSES HOW HE DISCOVERED THE INTERNET IN 1996. HE WAS SURPRISED; THERE WAS NO INFORMATION ON RODRIGUEZ. LIKE SEGERMAN HE INTENSIFIED HIS SEARCH TO FIND OUT WHO THE SUGAR MAN WAS AND WHY HE WAS IGNORED IN

THE HISTORY OF ROCK AND ROLL. BRIAN CURRIN IS ANOTHER HERO IS IN THE SEARCH FOR AND THE REDISCOVERY OF SIXTO RODRIGUEZ.

9. CURRIN'S CLIMB UP ON MY MUSIC WEBSITE WAS EVENTUALLY MERGED WITH STEPHEN "SUGAR" SEGERMAN'S WEBSITE TO PRODUCE SUGARMAN.ORG
10. IN THE SA ROCK DIGEST BRIAN CURRIN WROTE EFFUSIVELY ABOUT JOSH GEORGIOU ANDHIS PLACE IN THE SOUTH AFRICAN ROCK MUSIC INDUSTRY. THIS PAVED THE WAY FOR SEGERMAN TO WORK WITH GEORGIOU'S 206 PRODUCTION COMPANY ON THE LONDON RODRIGUEZ SHOWS IN THE 2005-2007 ERA.
11. IN SOUTH AFRICA BRIAN CURRIN IS KNOWN AS THE PERSON WHO MAINTAINS THE FACTS, THE IDEAS AND THE CONCEPTS DEFINING SIXTO RODRIGUEZ. HE IS ALSO THE PERSON WHO OPERATES SUGARMAN.ORG WHICH CONTINUES TO MAINTAIN THE BEST INFORMATION ON RODRIGUEZ.
12. CRAIG BARTHOLOMEW-STRYDOM REPORTS CURRIN NOW WORKS FOR MABU VINYL. "PART OF HIS DAILY ROUTINE IS TO SHIELD SUGAR FROM CURIOUS TOURISTS WHO HAVE MADE MABU VINYL A PORT OF CALL." (P. 344) THIS CURIOUS COMMENT TELLS ONE MORE ABOUT SEGERMAN'S EGO THAN IT DOES ABOUT MABU VINYL.
13. FOR BRIAN CURRIN'S PLAYLIST FROM 1969 TO 1978 SEE LET THE MUSIC PLAY https://www.mixcloud.com/briancurrin/vagabond-rock-show-19-february-2017/ THIS PROVIDES AN INSIGHT INTO HIS MUSICAL TASTES.
14. IN 1987 HE FOUNDED THE NATIONAL DIRECTORATE OF LAWYERS FOR HUMAN RIGHTS.

15. **IN 1994 SOUTH AFRICAN PRESIDENT NELSON MANDELA NAMED CURRIN TO THE TRUTH AND RECONCILIATION COMMISSION SUGGESTING HIS LAW DEGREE, HIS KNOWLEDGE OF SOUTH AFRICAN HISTORY AND HIS INTEGRITY MAKE HIM A HISTORY MOVER.**
16. **CURRIN HAS A SPECIALTY IN LABOR LAW AND INDUSTRIAL RELATIONS.**
17. **TODAY CURRIN IS A CONSULTANT IN RISK AND CONFLICT MANAGEMENT. HE IS A PROFESSIOAL MEDIATOR AND PEACE PROCESS FACILITATOR.**

Appendix III

Quotations of or About Craig Bartholomew-Strydom

1. **"AN OBSTACLE IS AN INSPIRATION." CRAIG QUOTES IN REEL LIFE WISDOM http://www.reellifewisdom.com/taxonomy/term/3638/0**
2. **"AFTER RUMORS CIRCULATED REGARDING HIS MYSTERIOUS DEATH, TWO SUPER-FANS STEPHEN 'SUGAR' SEGERMAN AND CRAIG BARTHOLOMEW STRYDOM SET OUT TO DISCOVER THE TRUTH. *SEARCHING FOR SUGAR MAN* IS A WONDERFUL TESTAMENT TO THE POWER OF MUSIC AND ART TO INSPIRE US ALL." http://www.beliefnet.com/entertainment/galleries/changing-the-world-inspiring-award-winning-documentaries.aspx?p=5**
3. **"A ROCKSTAR WINEMAKER WITH WINE INSPIRED BY SIXTO RODRIGUEZ. WINEMAKER CHARLES SMITH ON WINE, MUSIC SEATTLE MAGAZINE" THIS IS A POST ON CHARLES SMITH A SEATTLE WASHINGTON WINEMAKER INSPIRED BY RODRIGUEZ.**
4. **"SEARCHING FOR SUGAR MAN IS A 2012 SWEDISH–BRITISH DOCUMENTARY FILM OF A SOUTH AFRICAN**

CULTURAL PHENOMENON DIRECTED AND WRITTEN BY MALIK BENDJELLOUL WHICH DETAILS THE EFFORTS OF TWO CAPE TOWN FANS IN THE LATE 1990S, STEPHEN "SUGAR" SEGERMAN AND CRAIG BARTHOLOMEW STRYDOM, TO FIND OUT WHETHER THE RUMOURED DEATH OF AMERICAN MUSICIAN SIXTO RODRIGUEZ WAS TRUE, AND IF NOT, TO DISCOVER WHAT HAD BECOME OF HIM. RODRIGUEZ'S MUSIC, WHICH HAD NEVER ACHIEVED SUCCESS IN THE UNITED STATES, HAD BECOME VERY POPULAR IN SOUTH AFRICA ALTHOUGH LITTLE WAS KNOWN ABOUT HIM IN THAT COUNTRY." A WIKIPEDIA DESCRIPTION OF BARTHOLMEW-STRYDOM'S ROLE IN THE DOCUMENTARY.

Appendix IV

Rodriguez v. Eizik et al

The Following Information is that of a Law Suit Filed by Sxito Rodriguez in 2007 Against Zev Eizik and His Corporation and Others Involved in The Sugar Man's Career

Rodriquez v. Eizik et al
Plaintiff: Sixto Rodriquez
Defendant: Zev Eizik, Zev Eizik Corporation and Hangar 11, Limited
Case Number: 2:2007cv14150
Filed: October 1, 2007
Court: Michigan Eastern District Court
Office: Detroit Office
County: Wayne
Presiding Judge: Bernard A Friedman
Referring Judge: Mona K Majzoub
Nature of Suit: Contract: Other
Cause of Action: No cause code entered
Jury Demanded By: None

Appendix V

Sixto Rodriguez on You Tube

1977: RODRIGUZ-AT HIS BEST. THIS IS A COMPILATION ALBUM RELEASED ORIGINALLY IN AUSTRALIA BY THE BLUE GOOSE LABEL. THIS RECORD WAS BOOTLEGGED AND FOUND ITS WAY TO SOUTH AFRICA WHERE EVENTUALLY OVER THE YEARS IT SOLD PLATINUM. https://www.youtube.com/watch?v=bzLvIPEFaKo

1979: THE RODRIGUEZ LIVE ALBUM RECORDED AT SYDNEY'S REGENT THEATER HAS BEEN POSTED ON YOU TUBE, THE ENTIRE ALBUM ON JANUARY 19, 2013. DON'T MISS LISTENING TO THIS RARE ALBUM. THE SONGS ON THIS ALBUM WERE RECORDED LIVE AT THE REGENT THEATER, SYDNEY, AUSTRALIA, MARCH 17-18, 1979. SEE THE NEXT ENTRY.

1981: RODRIGUEZ ALIVE (RARE ALBUM) 1979 SYDNEY AUSTRALIA https://www.youtube.com/watch?v=Ga5aR0MwWOs THIS IS AN ABSOLUTE MUST FOR ANY SUGAR MAN FAN AS IT IS 40 MINUTES OF GREAT LIVE VERSIONS OF HIS KEY SONGS.

1998: "I WONDER" IS PERFORMED LIVE IN SOUTH AFRICA.

1998: THE SOUTH AFRICAN TELEVISION SPECIAL ON RODRIGUEZ "DEAD MEN DON'T TOUR" IS ON YOU TUBE IN ITS ENTIRETY. TONIA MOLLER (SELLEY) PUT THIS TOGETHER AND IT WAS BROADCAST ON SABC TV 3 AT 9:30 PM ON JULY 5, 2001. THIS IS AS GOOD AS THE AWARD WINNING DOCUMENTARY.

2007: "SUGAR AMAN" IS PERFORMED AT THE ST. ANDREWS HALL IN DETROIT WITH PAOLO NUTINI JOINING RODRIGUEZ ON STAGE.

NOVEMBER 23, 2008: "I WONDER" IS PERFORMED AT SAN FRANCISCO'S AMOEBA RECORD STORE TO A PACKED AUDIENCE. LIGHT IN THE ATTIC SPONSORED THE SHOW.

JUNE 2, 2009: "CRUCIFY YOUR MIND" (STREET SESSION) PARIS. THERE IS ALSO A VERSION OF "INNER CITY BLUES" FROM PARIS.

JUNE 23, 2009; RODRIGUEZ AT SEATTLE'S TRIPLE DOOR PERFORMING "TO WHOM IT MAY CONCERN." THERE IS ALSO A VERSION OF "CAN'T GET AWAY" WHICH WAS BROADCAST LIVE ON KEXP. THE HORN SECTION MATT SULLLIVAN BROUGHT IN MAKE THESE RECORDINGS BRILLIANT ONES. HE ALSO PERFORMED "INNER CITY BLUES" WHICH WAS ALSO BROADCAST ON KEXP.

APRIL 11, 2010: FROM THE FACTORY THEATER SHOW IN SYDNEY AUSTRALIA THERE ARE SOME SONGS THAT COME AND GO ON YOU TUBE.

DECEMBER 14, 2011: BEFORE FAME A RELAXED RODRIGUEZ IS FEATURED ON THE PAM ROSSI SHOW FROM THE UNIVERSITY OF DETROIT MEDIA CAFÉ WHERE HE PERFORMS A COVER OF PAOLO NUTINI'S "LAST REQUEST."

APRIL 25 2012: RODRIGUEZ PERFORMS"CRUCIFY YOUR MIND" AT JOE'S PUB IN NEW YORK CITY.

JULY 28, 2012: A VERSION OF "LIKE JANIS" CAN BE VIEWED FROM THE NEWPORT FOLK FESTIVAL.

SEPTEMBER 2, 2012: RODRIGUEZ PERFORMS A COVER OF PAOLO NUTINI'S "LAST REQUEST" AT THE IRON HORSE MUSIC HOUSE IN NORTHAMPTON, MA.

SEPTEMBER 27, 2012: A SOUND CHECK PRIOR TO A SHOW AT SAN DIEGO'S CASBAH CLUB FFEATURES THE SUGAR MAN PRACTICING ON LITTLE RICHARD'S "GOOD GOLLY MISS MOLLY" AND THE FLAMINGOS "I HAVE ONLY HAVE EYES FOR YOU."

NOVEMBER 2012: "CRUCIFY YOUR MIND" WITH A 25 PIECE STRING SECTION ON LATE NIGHT WITH DAVID LETTERMAN

2012: A COVER OF "LA VIE EN ROSE" BY RODRIGUEZ LIVE IN PARIS. EDITH PIAF WOULD LOVE THIS VERSION. https://www.youtube.com/watch?v=V_ePfMIlHko

2102: FROM AN UNNAMED VENUE RODRIGUEZ PERFORMS A COVER OF AN ELVIS PRESLEY INSPIRED "BLUE SUEDE SHOES" FOLLOWED BY"FORGET IT." THIS IS A MARVELOUS TEN-MINUTE VIDEO WITH A GREAT DEAL OF RODRIGUEZ DIALOGUE. https://www.youtube.com/watch?v=vrGnwxu93jg

NOVEMBER 13, 2012: THE JOOLS HOLLAND SHOW FEATURES RODRIGUEZ PERFORMING "SUGAR MAN." HE WEARS A SEDATE BUT STYLISH COAT AND A WHITE SHIRT. AFTER ALL IT IS LONDON.

NOVEMBER 2012: "LIKE A ROLLING STONE"

FEBRUARY 9, 2013: RODRIGUEZ PERFORMS "SUGAR MAN" AT THE GRAND WEST ARENA IN CAPE TOWN.

"2013: "I WONDER"AND "SUGAR MAN" AT JAZZ A VIENNE.

MARCH 13, 2013: A VERSION OF "YOU'D LIKE TO ADMIT IT" LIVE FROM LONDON IS FOUR PLUS MINUTES OF THE SUGAR MAN'S BEST ON STAGE PERFORMANCE. THERE IS ALSO A YOU TUBE VIDEO OF THE CROWD SINGING ALONG AS PEOPLE WHO POST SONGS FROM THE SHOW BITCH ABOUT THE SING A LONG. THEY CAN'T HEAR THE SUGAR MAN.

MARCH 24, 3013: RODRIGUEZ AND THE BREAK PERFORM "CAN'T GET AWAY."

MARCH 28, 2013: RODRIGUEZ IS FEATURED IN THE JAMBALAYA TENT AT THE BLUESFEST IN BRYON BAY, NEW SOUTH WALES.

2013: FROM THE AUSTRALIAN TOUR THERE IS A MARVELOUS VERSION OF A FRANK SINATRA INSPIRED "I'M GONNA LIVE UNTIL I DIE."

JUNE 3, 2013: "CAN'T GET AWAY" PERFORMED IN PARIS AT THE SOLD OUT FIRST SHOW AT THE ZENITH.

July 2013: RODRIGUEZ COVERS JERRY LEE LEWIS'S "WHOLE LOT OF SHAKIN' GOING ON." IT IS FROM A CLIP AT THE TOULOUSE FRANCE CONCERT. THEN HE GOES INTO "RICH FOLKS HOAX. https://www.youtube.com/watch?time_continue=188&v=oCTyvaP_STA

JULY 2013: THERE ARE NUMEROUS YOU TUBE VIDEOS OF RODRIGUEZ PERFORMING AT GLASTONBURY WITH "CRUCIFY YOUR MIND" AND "SUGAR MAN" AMONG THE MOST POPULAR SONGS PERFORMED.

JULY 2013: RODRIGUEZ AT THE GLASTONBURY FESTIVAL. THIS IS A SIXTY MINUTE SET FEATURING HIS SONGS AND COVERS OF LITTLE RICHARD'S 'LUCILLE," A ROY HAMILTON INSPIRED "UNCHAINED MELODY," LOU RAWLS' "DEAD END STREET," A VERSION OF "LOVE ME OR LEAVE ME" AND THE FLAMINGOS "I ONLY HAVE EYES FOR YOU." THERE ARE EIGHT OF HIS SONGS IN THE SET. A GREAT VIEWING OF A RODRIGUEZ SET AT A MAJOR FESTIVAL WITH WONDERUFL SOUND AND TOP FLIGHT VISUALS.

OCTOBER 10, 2013: A RADIO CITY MUSICAL HALL NEW YORK SHOW A THREE-MINUTE VERSION OF "I WONDER, AND A REMARKABLE " "SUGAR MAN."

OCTOBER 11, 2013: THIS IS A GREAT CLIP OF RODRIGUEZ COVERING LITTLE RICHARD'S "GOOD GOLLY MISS MOLLY" AND JERRY LEE LEWIS' "WHOLE LOT OF SHAKIN' GOING ON." IT IS LIVE FROM THE RADIO CITY MUSIC HALL IN NEW YORK.

NOVEMBER 11, 2013: "SUGAR MAN" PERFORMED LIVE ON WITH JOOLS HOLLAND, LONDON.

MARCH 21, 2014: IN BOLOGNA ITALY RODRIGUEZ PERFORMS "SUGAR MAN" TO A RAPT AUDIENCE. THERE IS ALSO A SEPARATE CLIP OF "I WONDER."

MARCH 22, 2014: RODRIGUEZ IS IN MILAN AND A MARVELOUS CLIP OF "I WONDER" FROM THE LOCAL AUDITORIUM IS A GEM.

SEPTEMBER 3, 2014: RODRIGUEZ LIVE IN BOURNEMOUTH IS A LOOK AT THE BEGINNING OF HIS EUROPEAN TOUR. THIS IS A TOUR DE FORCE OF GREAT VIDEO. THERE IS A TERRIFIC VERSION OF "CRUCIFY YOUR MIND" ON THIS YOU TUBE VIDEO.

OCTOBER 2014: A CLIP FROM AUSTRALIA OF A COVER OF THE FLAMINGOS "I ONLY HAVE EYES FOR YOU" IS A MARVELOUS VERSION. THERE IS ALSO A COVER OF A LITLE WILLIE JOHN INSPIRED "FEVER" FROM THE BRISBANE AUSTRALIA SHOW IN 2014. ALSO A VERSION OF "I THINK OF YOU" FROM THIS TOUR. "I'M GONNA LIVE UNTIL I DIE" IS ALSO FEATURED FROM THE 2014 AUSTRALIAN TOUR.

MAY 7 2015; THE ROYAL ALBERT HALL SHOW HAS ONLY ONE SONG ON THIS VIEWING. A VERSION OF THE JEFFERSON AIRPLANE'S 'SOMEBODY TO LOVE" IS A WONDERFUL LOOK AT THE SUGAR MAN'S DIVERSITY.

JUNE 26, 2015: RODRIGUEZ IS FEATURED LIVE AT THE FOX THEATER IN ATLANTA, GEORGIA PERFORMING "INNER CITY BLUES."

JANUARY 22, 2016: RODRIGUEZ PERFORMING THE JEFFERSON AIRPLANE'S "SOMEBODY TO LOVE" AT THE

CARRE AMSTERDAM. EVERYBODY HAD A HIGH TIME. RUMOR IS JOHN SINCLAIR WAS BACKSTAGE.

2016: "I WONDER" PERFORMED IN SOUTH AFRICA IS POSTED IN FEBRUARY ON YOU TUBE IN A SMALL, NON CONERT SETTING. RODRIGUEZ IS WEARING A WHITE HAT, A SPORT COAT AND PEOPLE ARE WALKING IN FRONT OF HIM AS HE SINGS INTO A MICROPHONE WITH A SOLO GUITAR. THERE IS NO BACKUP BAND.

JULY 22, 2016: "I THINK OF YOU," "LIKE JANIS," "FORGET IT" AND "CRUCIFY YOUR MIND" ARE FEATURED FROM A SHOW IN LONDON AT THE LONDON PALLADIUM. THESE SONGS ARE ON SEPARATE YOU TUBE VIDEOS.

AUGUST 31, 2016: "I THINK OF YOU" IS FROM A SHOW AT THE JUBILEE AUDIITORIUM IN CALGARY, ALBERTA, CANADA.

NOVEMBER 25, 2016: "SUGAR MAN" LIVE IN MELBOURNE

Appendix VI

Key People and Events on the Coming From Reality Album

1.) ADVICE TO SMOKEY ROBINSON: THIS IS A SONG THAT RODRIGUEZ WROTE BUT NEVER RECORDED. IT WAS RECORDED AND RELEASED BY STEVE ROWLAND'S FAMILY DOGG GROUP IN 1972. THE LYRICS SAID THAT ROBINSON LEFT THE AFTER HOURS CLUB AND "AN ANGRY AGENT THERE CLAIMED I'D INJURED HIS PRIDE." GREAT LYRICS. IT IS ALSO A BRILLIANT OBSERVATION ON FAME AND FORTUNE. SMOKEY ROBINSON SELDOM TALKED TO REAL PEOPLE. RODRIGUEZ WAS REAL. SMOKEY RAN AWAY IN A FUROR AND HE IGNORED RODRIGUEZ' COMMENTS. HE ALSO DIDN'T LEARN ANYTHING FROM THE SUGAR MAN'S OBSERVATIONS.

2.) AFTER THE FACT: THIS IS THE TITLE OF THE SOUTH AFRICAN RELEASE OF THE COMING FROM REALITY ALBUM. THIS WAS A REISSUE OF COMING FROM RELAITY BUT THE RECORD LABEL A AND M INDULGED IN ECONOMIC SKULLDUGGERY. THE REASON FOR RETITLING COMING FROM REALITY

WAS TO MAKE IT APPEAR LIKE A NEW ALBUM. ANOTHER REASON WAS TO SUGGEST IT WAS RELATED SOMEHOW TO COLD FACT. THIS IS ALSO THE SOUTH AFRICAN LP THAT PIQUED STEPHEN "SUGAR" SEGERMAN'S INTEREST IN FINDING RODRIGUEZ IN 1994.

3.) CLARENCE AVANT: THE HEAD OF SUSSEX RECORDS WHO ISSUED COLD FACT AND COMING FROM REALITY. A HIT RECORD BY BILL WITHERS "LEAN ON ME" DERAILED ANY ATTEMPTS BY THE ENIGMATIC AVANT TO PROMOTE THE RODRIGUEZ MATERIAL. IT IS ALLEGED THAT RODRIGUEZ DIDN'T RECEIVE ANY ROYALTIES FROM THE LABEL. AVANT CLAIMS THAT THE RECORDS DIDN'T SELL AND HE DIDN'T RECEIVE ANY ROYALTIES. SOUTH AFRICAN AND AUTSTRALIAN RECORD LABEL HEADS DISAGREE. LABEL HEADS IN AUSTRALIA AND SOUTH AFRICA CLAIM THEY SENT ROYALTIES TO AVANT. HE ALSO OWNED SOME OF THE COPYRIGHTS AND THE LICENSING. THE LABEL WENT BANKRUPT IN THE MID-1970S AND THE IRS SEIZED AND SOLD THE ASSETS. HE IS A PIONEERING AFRICAN AMERICAN BUSINESSMAN AND AVANT IS WIDELY RESPECTED AMONG HIS MUSICAL PEERS. HE WAS ALSO RESPONSIBLE FOR ORGANIZING, FUNDING AND WORKING WITH MINORITY BUSINESS INTERESTS IN THE AFRICAN AMERICAN COMMUNITY. HE ALSO BUILT A PEPSI COLA BOTTLING PLANT IN SOUTH AFRICA. AVANT IS TIED CLOSELY TO LIBERAL DEMOCRATIC POLITICS AND PRESIDENT BARACK OBAMA APPOINTED HIS DAUGHTER AS AN AMERICAN AMBASSADOR. NEITHER RODRIGUEZ NOR STEVE ROWLAND HAS RECEIVED A STATEMENT FROM

SUSSEX. STEVE ROWLAND: "TO THIS DAY I HAVE NOT RECIVED ROYALTIES." ROWLAND'S QUOTE IS ABOUT SUSSEX RECORDS. SINCE SEARCHING FOR SUGAR MAN STEVE HAS BEEN PAID BY AVANT.

4.) AVANTE GARDE ENTERPRISES: THIS IS A COMPANY THAT LICENSES RODRIGUEZ' MATERIAL. THIS COMPANY IS LOCATED AT 369 DOHENY DRIVE IN BEVERLY HILLS, CALIFORNIA. IT IS A COMPANY OWNED AND OPERATED BY CLARENCE AVANT. THE COMPANY PHONE NUMBER IS 310-247-1714.

5.) JACK BAVERSTOCK: HE WAS THE HEAD OF FONTANA RECORDS. WHEN ROWLAND WENT THERE TO BE INTERVIEWED FOR A SINGING CONTRACT, HE WOUND UP AS AN ACCLAIMED PRODUCER. ROWLAND HAS SAID REPEATEDLY THAT HE OWES HIS RECORD-PRODUCING CAREER TO BAVERSTOCK. IT WAS THE FONTANA RECORD CHIEF WHO GAVE HIM HIS START. WITHOUT BAVERSTOCK THERE WOULD NOT HAVE BEEN A COMING FROM REALITY ALBUM. BEFORE COMING FROM REALITY ROWLAND HAD MANY HITS AND THIS IS THE REASON BAVERSTOCK WENT TO BAT FOR STEVE PRODUCING RODRIGUEZ.

6.) COMING FROM REALITY: THIS IS RODRIGUEZ' SECOND ALBUM PRODUCED BY STEVE ROWLAND IN LONDON. THERE ARE SEVEN DIFFERENT COVERS FOR THE LP AND IT HAS BEEN RELEASED SIX TIMES SINCE THE ORIGINAL 1971 RELEASE. THE 2009 RELEASE BY LIGHT IN THE ATTIC CONTAINED THREE BONUS TRACKS "CAN'T GET AWAY," "STREET BOY" AND "I'LL SLIP AWAY." WHEN THE ORIGINAL ALBUM WAS RELEASED THE NOVEMBER 6, 1971 BILLBOARD AWARDED THE LP A "SPECIAL MERIT PICK." MIKE THEODORE RECORDED THE THREE

BONUS SONGS AND CLARENCE AVANT PAID ALL THE PRODUCTION COSTS.

7.) JIMMY HOROWITZ: HE WAS THE VIOLINIST ON "SANDREVAN LULLABY-LIFESTYLES." HE ALSO ARRANGED THREE OF THE ALBUM TRACKS INCLUDING "IT STARTED OUT SO NICE."

8.) INTERIOR MUSIC GROUP: THIS COMPANY LICENSED THE USA 2009 REISSUE OF COMING FROM REALITY ON LIGHT IN THE ATTIC. NOT SURPRISINGLY CLARENCE AVANT OWNS INTERIOR MUSIC. IN 2014 AVANT SUED RODRIGUEZ ALLEGING THAT HE WAS NOT FORTHRIGHT IN HIS DEALINGS WITH INTERIOR MUSIC. THE TIMING OF THE LAW SUIT PERPLEXED MOST MUSIC EXECUTIVES AS IT WAS NOT FILED UNTIL RODRIGUEZ BEGAN EARNING LARGE SUMS OF MONEY.

9.) I THINK OF YOU: THIS SONG IS FROM THE COMING FROM REALITY ALBUM. THE LYRICS ARE MORE LIKE A FRANK SINATRA TUNE AS THE BEAUTIFUL GUITAR WORK BY CHRIS SPEDDING LEADS INTO RODRIGUEZ' ROMANTIC BALLAD VOICE.

10.) LANSDOWNE STUDIOS: THIS LONDON STUDIO WAS FOR THIRTY DAYS THE HOME TO RODRIGUEZ RECORDING COMING FROM REALITY.

11.) LYRIC SHEET: THERE WAS A LYRIC SHEET INCLUDED WITH THE ORIGINAL RELEASE OF THE AMERICAN VERSION OF COMING FROM REALITY. IN AUSTRALIA A LYRIC SHEET WAS PUT TOGETHER FOR THE MEDIA. THE LYRIC SHEET INTENDED FOR SOUTH AFRICAN'S WHO OFTEN MADE MISTAKES IN TRANSLATING THE WORDS. THIS IS STRANGE AS THEY SPOKE ENGLISH AND ONE WONDERS WHY THE WORDS WERE NOT TRANSLATED CORRECTLY. THE REASON IS A SIMPLE

ONE. THE PERSON MAKING THE TRANSLATION ERRORS DIDN'T HAVE KNOWLEDGE OF RODRIGUEZ, HIS MUSIC OR AMERICAN HISTORY. THE LYRICS WERE CORRECTED BY 2002.

12.) RPM: THIS IS THE COMPANY IN SOUTH AFRICA THAT LICENSED AND DISTRIBUTED THE COMING FROM REALITY REISSUE WITH AUTHORIZATION FROM SUSSEX SOUND OF SUCCESS. IT IS THE LARGEST INDEPENDENT RECORD LABEL IN SOUTH AFRICA.

13.) SANDREVAN LULLABY-LIFESTYLES: THIS SURREALISTIC SONG STARTS OUT AS AN INSTRUMENTAL AND THEN IT CONTAINS AN INSIGHTFUL LOOK AT AMERICAN SOCIETY IN THE LIFESTYLES PORTION. IT IS CALLED SANDREVAN LULALABY AS IT INCORPORATES HIS DAUGHTER'S NAMES. IT IS A LONG SONG AT SIX MINUTES AND THIRTY FIVE SECONDS BUT UPON RELEASE IN 1996 IT WAS A FIVE MINUTE AND FIVE SECOND SONG AND THIS REMIX WAS ALSO INCLUDED ON THE 2005 REISSUE. THE GUITAR VIOLIN DUET IS THE STUFF OF MUSICAL GENIUS. RODRIGUEZ REMARKED THAT A STRADIVARIUS VIOLIN WAS USED DURING THE RECORDING. RODRIGUEZ PRACTICED THE SONG FOR HIS 1998 SOUTH AFRICAN TOUR BUT HE DIDN'T PERFORM IT IN CONCERT.

14.) MILTON SINCOFF: HE WAS THE DIRECTOR OF CREATIVE PACKAGING AND MERCHANDISING ON THE COMING FROM REALITY ALBUM.

15.) CHRIS SPEDDING: HE PROVIDED THE EXQUISITE GUITAR SOUNDS ON THE COMING FROM REALITY ALBUM.

16.) ANDREW STEELE: HE WAS ONE OF THE DRUMMERS ON THE COMING FROM REALITY ALBUM.

17.) IT WAS WHILE HE WAS IN THE CARLIN MUSIC PUBLISHING HOUSE THAT ROWLAND SAW COLD FACT, PICKED IT UP, LISTENED TO IT AND TOOK IT HOME. THIS LED TO ROWLAND PRODUCING COMING FROM REALITY.

18.) "WE RECORDED HIS VOCALS AND HIS GUITAR AND THEN ADDED THE MUSIC LATER." STEVE ROWLAND

19.) "I FELT THE VIBE OF THE ALBUM WAS LIKE A SINGLE." STEVE ROWLAND.

20.) "I DIDN'T SEE RODRIGUEZ AS A SINGLES OR 45 ARTIST." STEVE ROWLAND

Appendix VII

Awards for Searching for Sugar Man

- *Searching for Sugar Man* won the Best Documentary category at the 85th Academy Awards.[18] Rodriguez declined to attend the award ceremony, as he did not want to overshadow the filmmakers' achievement if he came up on stage with them. Upon accepting his award, Chinn remarked on such generosity, "That just about says everything about that man and his story that you want to know." However, Malik Bendjelloul also said on stage, "Thanks to one of the greatest singers ever, Rodriguez."
- The film also won the Best Documentary category at the 66th British Academy Film Awards on 10 February 2013.
- The Directors Guild of America awarded the DGA Award for best documentary on 2 February 2013.
- The Writers Guild of America awarded the WGA Award for best documentary.
- The Producers Guild of America awarded the PGA Award for best documentary.
- The American Cinema Editors awarded the ACE Eddie Award for best documentary.

- It won the Guldbagge Award for Best Documentary at the 48th Guldbagge Awards.
- It won The National Board of Review in New York on 5 December 2012.
- The International Documentary Association (IDA) awarded *Searching for Sugar Man* Best Feature and Best Music at the 28th Annual IDA Documentary Awards on 7 December 2012 at the Directors Guild of America building, Los Angeles, California.
- It also won Best Documentary during Critics' Choice Awards – *Searching for Sugar Man*
- The film won the Cinema for Peace Most Valuable Documentary of the Year Award.
- *Searching for Sugar Man* won the Special Jury Prize and the Audience Award for best international documentary at the Sundance Film Festival. The film also won the Audience Award at the Los Angeles Film Festival, the Audience Award at the Durban International Film Festival, the Audience Award at the Melbourne Film Festival, 2nd place Winner Audience Award at the Tribeca Film Festival and the Grand Jury Prize at the Moscow International Film Festival.
- At the International Documentary Film Festival Amsterdam held in November 2012, *Searching for Sugar Man* won both the Audience and the Best Music Documentary awards.
- Doha Tribeca Film Festival (DTFF) *Searching for Sugar Man* was awarded $50,000 (US) where the film shared the "Best of the Fest" audience award with the Chinese feature film *Full Circle.*
- Best Film—Días de Cine Awards
- Best Film—In-Edit Festival in Santiago de Chile
- The Cinema Eye Honors for Nonfiction Filmmaking has nominated *Searching for Sugar Man* for five awards, tying with *The Imposter* for the most nominations. Winners of the 6th

Annual Cinema Eye Honors will be announced on 9 January 2013 as Cinema Eye returns for a third year to New York City's Museum of the Moving Image in Astoria, Queens, New York.

- Nonfiction Feature Filmmaking—Malik Bendjelloul and Simon Chinn
- Production—Simon Chinn
- Graphic Design and Animation—Oskar Gullstrand, Arvid Steen
- Debut Feature Film—Malik Bendjelloul
- Audience Choice Prize—Malik Bendjelloul

The film was also the recipient of the Australian Film Critics Association award for Best Documentary of 2012, beating locally produced musical documentary *All the Way Through Evening.*

Appendix VIII

Those Who Love The Sugar Man's Music or Have Been Influenced by It

1. **DAVE MATTHEWS IS A SOUTH AFRICAN WHO IS ONE OF AMERICA'S PREMIER ROCK ACTS. HE HAS COVERED "SUGAR MAN" IN CONCERT AND MENTIONS HIS LOVE FOR RODRIGUEZ' MUSIC IN PERIODIC INTERVIEWS.**
2. **DAVID HOLMES IS INSTRUMENTAL TO THE SUGAR MAN'S STORY. HE SAMPLED HIS MUSIC. HE BROUGHT HIM INTO THE STUDIO. HE PUBLICICIZED RODRIGUEZ' MATERIAL. HIS 2002 REMIX OF "SUGAR MAN" BEGAN THE RODRIGUEZ U. K. CULT.**
3. **PAOLO NUTINI: LIKE MANY OTHER PERFORMERS THE SONG "SUGAR MAN" INTRIGUED HIM AND HE BECAME A RODRIGUEZ FAN AFTER HEARING IT. HE HAS PERFORMED ON STAGE WITH RODRIGUEZ. HE IS ONE OF THE MOST ACTIVE EXTOLLING AND PROMOTING RODRIGUEZ' LONG UNRECOGNIZED TALENT.**
4. **MIDNIGHT OIL: THE AUSTRALIAN MEGA HIT GROUP CALLS THE SUGAR MAN "THE GODFATHER POLITICALLY" TO THEIR MUSIC.**

5. **STEVE ROWLAND: HE RECORDED SIX OF THE SUGAR MAN'S SONGS WITH HIS GROUP THE FAMILY DOGG.**
6. **SUSAN COWSILL: SHE RECORDED ONE OF RODRIGUEZ' SONGS AND SAID HE WAS AN INFLUENCE ON HER SOLO CAREER.**

Appendix IX

Steve Rowland's Quotes on Coming From Reality

1. **"I WAS IN ONE OF THE EXECUTIVES OFFICES AND I SAW THE ALBUM. I SAID 'WHAT'S THIS?' THEY SAID SOME GUY LIKE BOB DYLAN. I PLAYED A COUPLE OF TRACKS....IT GOT ME GOING ON THE ROAD TO PRODUCING RODRIGUEZ."**
2. **"HE WAS SUCH A PRO. WE DID EVERYING IN ONE OF TWO TAKES."**
3. **"ALL OF HIS SONGS REFER TO THINGS THAT HAPPENED IN HIS LIFE."**
4. **"I THINK OF YOU.' IT WAS A ROMANTIC SIDE COMING OUT. IF YOU LISTEN TO HIS LYRICS NOT THE ONES LIKE 'THE ESTABLISHMENT BLUES,' THEY ARE ABOUT PERSONAL RELATIONSHIPS."**
5. **"I FEEL THAT HE IS ONE OF THE BEST SONGWRITERS OF HIS GENERATION."**
6. **"MY GOAL WAS TO FEATURE HIS VOICE....PRODUCTION WISE LESS IS MORE."**
7. **"IT WS THE BEST STUDIO IN LONDON BECAUSE IT HAD NATURAL ACOUSTICS. IT HAD A SWIMMING**

POOL IN THE BASEMENT. THEY TOOK IT OUT AND THAT MADE THE SOUND." COMMENTING ON LANSDOWNE STUDIO.

8. "YOU CAN HEAR IT ON THAT ALBUM." ROWLAND COMMENTING ON THE ECHO SOUND AT LANSDOWNE STUDIO ON COMING FROM REALITY AND HOW IT IMPACTED THE ALBUM.
9. "CAUSE' IS MY FILM SONG." WHY? "HE WAS VERY PARALLEL TO WHAT WAS GOING ON IN HIS LIFE AT THE TIME. HE WAS DROPPED FROM SUSSEX TWO WEEKS BEFORE CHRISTMAS."
10. "THERE AREN'T ANY WEAKNESSES IN COMING FROM REALITY. IT CAN BE PERCEIVED THAT THE SONGS WEREN'T AS STRONG AS THE SONGS ON COLD FACT. THEY WERE MORE ROMANTIC AND PERSONAL SONGS."
11. "WE HAD NO COOPERATION FROM ANYBODY CONNECTED WITH COMING FROM REALITY. I COMPARE IT TO THE CHRISTMAS HOLIDAY. ONCE THE ALBUM WAS OVER EVERYONE MOVED ON TO SOMETHING ELSE. NO PROMOTION."
12. "RODRIGUEZ WAS A PLEASURE TO WORK WITH. I CAN'T SAY THAT ABOUT ALL THE RECORDS I MADE."
13. "I HAVE SUCH RESPECT FOR RODRIGUEZ AS A HUMAN BEING."
14. "I HAD A GIRL FRIEND NAMED JANIS. HE WROTE ABOUT HER JUST LIKE I REMEMBER HER."

Appendix X

Malik Bendjelloul Quotations

1. **"YOU NEVER KNOW RODRIGUEZ BETTER THAN THE FIRST DAY YOU MEET HIM."**
2. **"THERE'S NOWHERE LIKE DETROIT; IT'S A MODERN NECROPOLIS; ALL THESE ART DECO MASTERPIECES CRUMBLING AWAY."**
3. **"I DON'T THINK 'SEARCHING FOR SUGAR MAN'S' A MUSIC DOCUMENTARY ANY MORE THAN 'THE SOCIAL NETWORK' IS ABOUT COMPUTERS. IT JUST HAPPENS TO HAVE THE BEST SOUNDTRACK EVER."**
4. **"I DON'T LIKE MUSIC DOCUMENTARIES, USUALLY. THERE'S NOTHING TO REALLY SAY. WHAT CAN YOU SAY ABOUT MUSIC? NORMALLY, YOU CAN'T SAY TOO MUCH. THERE ARE A FEW REALLY GOOD ONES, BUT THE MAJORITY ARE BORING...."**
5. **"IF YOU'RE AN ARTIST, YOU'RE AN ARTIST; THAT'S THE ONLY WAY I CAN EXPLAIN IT."**
6. **"MOST MUSIC CAREERS SLOWLY BUT SURELY GO DOWN."**

7. "THERE ARE FEW REALLY FANTASTIC STORIES LEFT AND THAT KIND OF GIVES YOU INSPIRATION TO FIND NEW ONES."
8. "THE PERFECT STORY IS ONE YOU CAN TELL IN THREE MINUTES, AND EVERY SINGLE SENTENCE IS INTERESTING."
9. "THE KIDS GROWING UP IN THE APARTHIED ERA WERE SO RESTRICTED AND AGNRY-IF THEY SPOKE OUT AGAINS APARTHEID THEY WERE THROWN IN JAIL."
10. "MY SPECIALITY IS TWO THINGS: MUSIC OR REALLY STRANGE STORIES."
11. "IN SOUTH AFRICA IT WAS AS IF THE BEATLES HAD BEEN FOUR FACELESS MEN WITHOUT NAMES. RODRIGUEZ WAS AT LEAST AS FAMOUS THERE AS THE ROLLING STONES AND YET NOT EVEN THE RECORD LABEL KNEW WHERE HE WAS." MALIK BENDJELLOUL IN CONVERSATION WITH ROB HUGHES. FOR THIS ARTICLE SEE IT AT: http://www.folkworks.org/index.php?option=com_content&task=view&id=40560
12. "THE GREATEST STORY I EVER HEARD IN MY LIFE."
13. "A MAN WHO LIVES HIS WHOLE LIFE AS A CONSTRUCTION WORKER, DOING REALLY HARD WORK IN DETROIT, UNAWARE THAT IN ANOTHER PART OF THE WORLD, HE'S MORE FAMOUS THAN ELVIS PRESLET."
14. "SUCCESS IS NOT ONLY ONE THING. IT'S NOT ONLY HAVING A NICE HOUSE IN BEVERLY HILLS AND DRIVING A NICE MERCEDES."
15. "I THINK MUSIC DOCS COULD TURN OFF SOME PEOPLE."

Bibliographical Sources

See Howard A. DeWitt, **Searching For Sugar Man: Sixto Rodriguez' Mythical Climb To Rock N Roll Fame and Fortune** (Scottsdale, 2015) for the first album and Rodriguez' rise to prominence after forty plus years in the music business. For Rodriguez' career in Australia see Glenn A. Baker, **Rodriguez Alive**, the sleeve notes to the album.

The problem with Rodriguez' career is he was on two small, independent record labels. The first one with Harry Balk was the Impact label and then Clarence Avant's Sussex imprint signed the Sugar Man to a three record contract. After making two of those albums he was released. For the history and impact of independent labels see John Broven, **Record Makers and Breakers: Voices of the Independent Rock 'N' Roll Pioneers** (Urban, 2009). Broven does an excellent, if brief, analysis of Balk's influence upon the Detroit record scene.

The Joe's Pub appearance in New York in late 2008 was an early indication of Rodriguez' potential star power. For this show see, Jonny-Leather, "At Last: Sixto Rodriguez' First Ever New York Performance," **New York Press**, September 4, 2008 http://www.nypress.com/at-last-sixto-rodriguez-first-ever-new-york-performance/ Also for the Joe's Pub gig see Saul Austerlitz, "This Singing Sensation Was Nearly 40 Years In The Making," **Boston**

Globe, September 21, 2008 http://archive.boston.com/ae/music/articles/2008/09/21/this_singing_sensation_was_nearly_40_years_in_the_making/

For some of Rodriguez' musical influences see Edward Douglas, "Interview: The Award-Winning Doc Searching for the Sugar Man," **Comingsoon.net**, July 25, 2012, http://www.comingsoon.net/news/movienews.php?id=92699 Also see Sasha Frere Jones, "Cold Facts," **The New Yorker**, August 3, 2012 for one of the best reviews of **Searching For Sugar Man**. For an excellent review by a critic who didn't view the documentary until four years after its release see, Joel Epstein, "Searching For Detroit And Los Angeles," **Huffington Post**, February 9, 2016 http://www.huffingtonpost.com/joel-epstein/searching-for-detroit–lo_b_9196132.html For a positive view of Detroit see Herb Boyd, **Black Detroit: A People's History of Self Determination** (New York, 2017) which is a book of key tales or important stories considering how and why African American contributions shaped the city. See Yvonne Teh, "Film Review: Searching For Sugar Man," **South China Morning Post**, April 24, 2013 for an interesting perspective on the documentary. http://www.scmp.com/magazines/48hrs/article/1218454/film-review-searching-sugar-man

Andrew Pulver, "Searching For Sugar Man Wins Best Documentary Oscar," **London Guardian**, February 25, 2013.

Poppy Harlow, "Sixto Rodriguez Becomes Superstar, Doesn't Know It For 30 Years," **KASDK.com** August 15, 2012 www.ksdk.com/news/article/333230/28/Sixto-Rodriguez-becomes-superstar-couldn't-know-for-30-years Also see the beautifully written article by Tony Karon, "Sixto Rodriguez, Secret Rock Star Behind Searching for Sugar Man," **Time Entertainment**, August 21, 2012.

On **Searching For Sugar Man**, also see, Rabbi Herb Cohen, "A Rabbinic Take on 'Searching For Sugar Man," **The Huffington Post**, July 6, 2013, Beth J. Harpaz, "Sugar Man's Star Meets Adoring New York Crowd," **The Huffington Post**, June 8, 2013, and Penelope Andrew, "A Myth Is Replaced By A Miracle In New Doc, Searching for Sugar Man, Resurrecting Work Of Elusive Musician Sixto Rodriguez," **The Huffington Post**, October 13, 2012.

There are a number of reviews calling into question the documentaries accuracy, see Peter Bradshaw, "Searching For Sugar Man-Review," **The London Guardian**, July 26, 2012 https://www.theguardian.com/film/2012/jul/26/searching-for-sugar-man-review

For Konny Rodriguez' reaction to the Oscar nomination and his appearance on the Tonight Show with Jay Leno, see, Eric Lacy, "Oscar-Nominated 'Searching For Sugar Man' Star Rodriguez, A Detroit Native To Appear On NBC's Tonight Show With Jay Leno," www.mlive.com/entertainment/detroit/index.ssf/201 Also see more of the comments of Rodriguez second wife Konny in Eric Lacy, "Wife of Oscar-Nominated 'Searching For Sugar Man' Star Rodriguez Says He'll Stay in $50 Detroit Home," **Mlife**, January 11, 2013, http://www.mlive.com/entertainment/detroit/index.ssf/2013/01/wife_of_oscar-nominated_search.html

On the Oscar's see Anne Thompson, **The $11 Billion Year: From Sundance to the Oscars, An Inside Look At The Changing Hollywood System** (New York, 2014).

On Detroit, see, for example, Charlie LeDuff, **Detroit: An American Autopsy** (New York, 2013); Scott Martelle, **Detroit: A Biography** (Chicago, 2012) and Mark Binelli, **Detroit City Is The Place To Be: The Afterlife Of An American Metropolis** (New York, 2012).

Michael Phillips, "An Improbably Happy Ending For Rodriguez," **The Chicago Tribune**, August 1, 2012 is an excellent article on how the documentary **Searching for Sugar Man**, changed Sixto Rodriguez' life. For a contrary view see Bill Cody, "Searching For Sugar Man'-True Story Or The Making Of A Myth?" January 21, 2013 http://www.ropeofsilicon.com/searching-for-sugar-man-true-story-or-the-making-of-a-myth/

Also, see the well-written, cogently argued and wonderfully researched article on Rodriguez by, Guy Blackman, "The Cold Fact Is

He's Hot Again," http://www.theage.com.au/news/entertainment/music/hes-hot again/2008/09/25/1222217392243.htmlN] Also see David Malitz, "Searching For 'Sugar Man' Documentary Rediscovers Sixto Rodriguez," **The Washington Post**, July 26, 2012. For Rodriguez' reflections and in-depth comments with song analysis of the **Cold Fact** album in a telephone interview see, "Rodriguez: Return of the Sugar Man," http://www.socialstereotype.com/_/Features/Entries/2008/8/11_RODRIGUEZ.html

Also see Giselle Defares, "The Myth of Sugar Man Sixto Rodriguez," **Crixeo: Where Life And Art Intersect**, http://www.crixeo.com/sugar-man/ for a comparison with other obscure artists.

See "At 70, Detroiter Rodriguez Couldn't Be Happier About His Unlikely Success,"http://blog.sugarman.org/2012/11/02/at-70-detroiter-rodriguez-couldn't-be-happier-about-his-unlikely-new-fame-music-detroit-free-press-freep-com/]

Also see Richard Pithouse, 'The Resurrection of Sixto Rodriguez," **The South African Civil Society Information Service**, January 23, 2013 http://www.sacsis.org.za/site/article/1550

For Rodriquez' show at the Los Angele El Rey Theater see Ernest Hardy, "Sugar Man's Rodriguez Plays Los Angeles," **Los Angeles Times**, September 29, 2012.

Also see George Varga, "Truth Stranger Than Fiction For Rodriguez,' **U-T San Diego**, September 22, 2012 for San Diego's Casbah Club show. On Rodriguez politics see Corey Hall, "Free Associating With Sixto Rodriguez," **Metro Times** August 8, 2012 http://metrotimes.com/screens/free-associating-with-sixto-rodriguez-1.1355607

On the bursting Rodriguez phenomenon see, Larry Rohter, "A Real-Life Fairy Tale, Long In The Making And Set to Old Tunes," **The New York Times**, July 20, 2012 http://www.nytimes.com/2012/07/22/movies/a-film-spotlights-the-musician rodriguez.html?smid=fb-share&_r=0, and the equally insightful article by Rachel Dodes, "A Rock 'n' Roll Mystery," **The Wall Street**

Journal, July 20, 2012 http://online.wsj.com/article_email/SB10001424052702303754904577533272231687922-lMyQjAxMTAyMDIwMDEyNDAyWj.html?mod=wsj_valetleft_email Manhola Dargis, "Rock Musician Shrouded In Mystery Of What Might Have Been: Malik Bendjelloul's 'Searching For Sugar Man," **The New York Times**, July 27, 2012 http://www.nytimes.com/2012/07/27/movies/malik-bendjellouls-searching-for-sugar-man.html is an excellent piece.

On Craig Bartholomew-Strydom see, Mary Carole McCauley, "Ex-Baltimorean Went 'Searching For Sugar Man," **The Baltimore Sun**, April 27, 2012 http://articles.baltimoresun.com/2012-08-27/entertainment/bs-ae-sugarman-film-20120824_1_strydom-royalty-checks-music-industry

See James Delingpole, "Sixto Rodriguez Interview: The Rock 'n' Roll Lord Lucan," **London Telegraph,** August 11, 2009 for a view of Rodriguez before the documentary. This is an article that talks with Malik Bendjelloul who is in the process of making **Searching For Sugar Man**. Also see the candid interview, Irene Lacher, "The Sunday Conversation: Malik Bendjelloul," **Los Angeles Times**, February 23, 2013 http://www.latimes.com/entertainment/envelope/moviesnow/la-et-ca-mn-malik-bendjelloul-conversation-20130224,0,5383393.story

The best Rodriguez interview prior t the fame and fortune of **Searching For Sugar Man** is Fred Mills, "Return To Sugar Man: Rodriguez," **Blurt http://blurtonline.com/feature/returning-sugar-man-rodriguez/** This is a 2009 interview published some years later in a small magazine with Rodriguez relaxed, open and candid in his thoughts.

Harry Balk graciously sat down for a series of interviews, which set the record straight about his involvement with the music industry in general and Del Shannon in particular. Then I came upon the Sixto Rodriguez story and realized that Harry Balk was an unrecognized hero as he was the first person to discover, record and place Rodriguez with Dennis Coffey and Mike Theodore. Interviews with Ike Turner added a great deal to this period of rock music history.

Dan Bourgoise, the world's best copyright and song publishing guru at Bug Music, filled in many spots in the story from his long association with key figures in the music industry. Dennis DeWitt, "Harry Balk Interview," **And The Music Plays On: Del Shannon Magazine**, issue 4, summer, 1995, pp. 4-12 is an important starting point for Balk's career. His article is the best work done on Balk to date with great research and excellent writing.

On Australia see Stevie Chick, "Detroit's Comeback King," **The London Guardian**, August 7, 2008 www.guardian.co.uk/music/2008/aug/08/popandrock3 Also see Iain Shedden, "For Sugar Man Sixto Rodriguez, The Search Is Over," **The Australian**, July 6, 2016 http://www.theaustralian.com.au/arts/music/for-sugar-man-sixto-rodriguez-the-search-is-over/news-story/270932363e9aa312c8dc177037156781 An interview with the late Iain Shedden in the summer of 2016 filled many gaps in the Australian side of the story. Shedden was a drummer with a rock and roll career and he relocated from Sydney to London in 1992.

See Adrian Mack, "Rodriguez Shows His Human Side," **Straight.com**, October 12, 2012 for his Vancouver, British Columbia appearance. A brilliant article demonstrating that Rodriguez was a Canadian star and a Vancouver B.C. favorite by 2010 is David LaCroix, "Vancouver Is Sweet On The Sugarman," **Vancouver Weekly**, August 11, 2017 http://vancouverweekly.com/vancouver-is-sweet-on-sugarman-58037-2/ What LaCroix suggests is since 2010 the Rodriguez cult exploded into a mainstream audience with a continual love fest. He played Vancouver's Orpheum Theater on May 8, 2017 and this larger venue was necessary as Rodriguez sold out every time he appeared. His four previous Vancouver shows resulted in not only a positive press but also the persistent theme the Sugar Man does not display anger for his years in the wilderness.

Howard A. DeWitt, **Chuck Berry: Rock N Roll Music** (2nd Ed., Ann Arbor, 1985) provided background material. On the early 1960s see Howard A. DeWitt, **The Beatles: Untold Tales** (Fremont, 1985) for some essays on the early 1960s influencing Del Shannon's career. Also see, Howard A. DeWitt, **Paul McCartney: From Liverpool To Let It Be** (Fremont, 1992) for an examination of the London media.

On the role of Johnny and the Hurricanes in Harry Balk's career, see, for example, Bill Millar, "Blowin' Up A Storm," **Melody Maker**, number 54 (March 24, 1979), p. 42: Bill Millar, "Johnny & The Hurricanes," **Goldmine**, number 57 February, 1981), pp. 10-11. For Little Willie Johnson see, for example, Lou Holscher, "Little Willie John—Fact or Fiction," **Goldmine**, number 72 (May, 1982), p. 189, Bill Millar, "Free At Last," **The History of Rock**, number 17 (1982), 336-337, Steve Propes, "Little Willie John: King of Detroit Soul Music," **Goldmine**, number 171 (February 13, 1987), p. 22.

On the royalty controversy between Del Shannon and Embee Productions see Bob Fisher, "Writs and Royalties," **And The Music Plays On**, number 1, (Fall, 1994), p. 16. On Rodriguez' royalties see Jeff Karoub and Michelle Faul, "Rodriguez Searching For SA Royalties," **Mail And Guardian**, February 23, 2013 http://mg.co.za/article/2013-02-23-rodriguez-searching-for-sa-royalties The best article on Rodriguez' lost royalties is David Kronemyser, "What Likely Happened To Royalties For Sugar Man: A Tale of Record Business Chicanery?", Also see, Michael Hogan, "Rodriguez, 'Searching For Sugar Man Star, Talks Protest Songs and Politics on HuffPost Live," **The Huffington Post**, August 16, 2012. Also, see, Eriq Gardner, "Searching For Sugar Man: Star's Amazing Journey Erupts Into A Lawsuit," **The Hollywood Reporter**, May 2, 2014. Also see Brian McCollum, "Sixto Rodriguez Pursues Review Of Contracts, Sales In Search of Royalties," **Detroit Free Press**, May 17, 2013 and for a strong local Detroit concert by the Sugar Man, see Brian McCollum, "Sixto Rodriguez Takes Detroit Stage To Enchant Hometown Crowd," **Detroit Free Press**, May 19, 2013. Also see the excellent article by David Kronemyer, "What Likely Happened To The Royalties For The 'Sugar Man," **Medium.com**, November 10, 2013 https://medium.

com/@davidkronemyer/what-likely-happened-to-the-royalties-for-sugar-man-d45d9371f800#.63b1o0c39 Also see Joel Freimark, "Searching For Sugarman Star Being Sued 40 Years Later," **Death And Taxes Magazine.com**, May 29, 2014 http://www.deathandtaxes-mag.com/221906/searching-for-sugarman-star-being-sued-40-years-later/

For a summary of the royalty question and why it continues to drag on see, Sean Michaels, "Four Decades On, Searching For Sugar Man Singer Dragged Into Legal Battle Over His 1970s Recordings," **The London Guardian**, May 30, 2104 https://www.theguardian.com/music/2014/may/30/rodriguez-accused-misrepresentation-searching-for-sugar-man

Extensive interviews with Jimmy McCracklin, John Lee Hooker, Solomon Burke, Charles Brown, Bob Geddins, Guitar Mac and Lowell Fulson helped to fill in material on the African American acts from Detroit and Balk's New York experiences.

For Rodriguez' literary side and his comparisons to John Donne see, for example, John Hayward, editor, **John Donne: A Selection of His Poetry** (London, 1950).

On Rodriguez in concert see, Sarfraz Manzoor, "Sixto Rodriguez, The Round House Review," **London Telegraph**, November 15, 2012. On William Blake, see, for example, William Blake, **The Poems of William Blake** (London, 2011). For Bob Dylan's literary side see the brilliant book by Michael Gray, **Song And Dance Man III: The Art of Bob Dylan** (London, 2000) chapter 2. This book is indebted to Gray's brilliant analysis. See David Gritten, "Sixto Rodriguez: On The Trail of the Bob Dylan of Detroit," **London Telegraph**, June 14, 2012. For the return of the Sugar Man see the **Detroit Free Press** from the summer of 2012 to the summer of 2015.

See Jada Yuan, "Sundance: The Electrifying Search For Sugar Man," www.vulture.com/2012/01/sundance-the-electrifying-search-for-sugar-man.html for early reaction to the documentary. See the beautifully written, fact laden and cogently argued piece by a sports writer, Wright Thompson, "Searching For Sugar Man," www.grantland.com/story/_/id/7874744/acclaimed-new-documentary-goes-hunting-lost-dylan The role of his new found fame is detailed in Dave Hokstra, "Rediscovered By Film, Rodriguez Asks, 'How do I Process All This?" **Chicago Sun Times**, September 20, 2012.

On the Woodbridge section of Detroit where Rodriguez lives see, for example, Jim Zemke, "Woodbridge Pub Plants The Seeds of Community in Detroit," http://www.modeldmedia.com/features/MSHDA201306-1.aspx Also see Laarushka Ivan-Zadeh, "Sixto Rodriguez: It's Important I Can Retreat Back To My Own Private World," **Metro**, July 26, 2012 http://metro.co.uk/2012/07/26/sixto-rodriguez-its-important-i-can-retreat-back-to-my-own-private-world-511015/ This London writer described the essence of the Sugar Man in depth with compassion and detail.

On Jim Geary and the Woodbridge Pub see, "Jim Geary," May 22, 2013 http://www.uixdetroit.com/people/jimgeary.aspx

See Roger Ebert, "Searching For Sugar Man," **The Chicago Sun Times**, August 8, 2012 for a major article praising the documentary. For the Sheffield Festival see Vivian Norris, "What A Wonderful World: Documentary Is Alive And Well For Now," **The Huffington Post**, June 16, 2012. http://metro.co.uk/2012/07/26/sixto-rodriguez-its-important-i-can-retreat-back-to-my-own-private-world-511015/

For David Holmes's cover of "Sugar Man," see Ben Thompson, "Success Is Sweet For the Sugar Man," **London Telegraph**, August 28, 2003.

On the 2005-2006 London appearances see Alexis Petridis, "The Singer Who Came Back From The Dead," **London Guardian**, October 5, 2005. Also see "Rodriguez-the Music, London 2005-London 2006" at www.sugarman.org/london2005.html For a jaded view of the Sugar Man phenomenon suggesting it is all about marketing, see Amber Hudson and Luke Sklar, "Everything Is Marketing-Live Your Sixto Rodriguez," www.sklarwilton.com/resourfes-centre

For the role of Matt Sullivan and Light In The Attic on Rodriguez' career see, Joe Williams, "Label Owner Matt Sullivan Explains Why Cold Fact First Bombed And What Made Him Search For Rodriguez," **Seattle Weekly**, October 12, 2012 http://blogs.seattleweekly.com/reverb/2012/10/matt_sullivan_rodriguez_i_wond.php Also see, Joe Williams, "Tell Me About That Song: Rodriguez's 'I Wonder," **Seattle Weekly News**, October 9, 2012 http://archive.seattleweekly.com/music/872525-129/music

See Jonathan Zwickel, "Seattle Label Revives Rodriguez's Career Four Decades Later," **Seattle Times**, June 21, 2009 for early comments by Rodriguez on his career.

Also see Pete Bland, "As Myth of Rodriguez Has Blown Up, Label That Found 'Sugar Man' A Little Lost In The Shuffle," **Columbia Daily Tribune**, September 27, 2012 http://www.columbiatribune.com/arts_life/after_hours/as-myth-of-rodriguez-has-blown-up-label-that-found/article_f5b4afc9-8713-5ac4-200f0878bd8e.html#.UQm5lmDN5WM

On Detroit's Palmer Woods, see Christina Rogers, "Detroit Classics, Priced to Move," **The Wall Street Journal**, January 18, 2013, M 1, 6. On the Detroit reaction to his re-emergence see Ben Edmonds, "40 Years Later, Rodriguez Takes His Show On The Road," **Detroit Free Press**, January 30, 2012. For a local Detroit concert see, Gary Graff, "Concert Review: Rodriguez Delivers A Sweet 'Sugar Man' Homecoming At The Crofoot," **The Oakland Press**, November 3, 2012. Also see Barney Hoskyns, editor, J. Poet, "The Rock's Backpages Flashback: Rodriguez Comes In From The Cold," http://music.yahoo.com/blogs/rocks-backpages/rock-backpages-flashback-rodriguez-comes-cold-161611729.html

See the insightful article by Stephen "Sugar" Segerman, "Rodriguez-Cult or Crap? The Cold Facts," http://sugarman.org/rodriguez/cult.html ? Also see Caryn Dolley, "The Man Who Searched For Sugar Man: Film Reels In Fame For Vinyl Store," **The Cape**

Times, January 14, 2013, p. 3 and the provocative article by Iris Mann, "Ravages, Rape, Rodriguez And Real Estate," **Jewish Journal.com**, June 13, 2013 http://www.jewishjournal.com/summer_sneaks/article/ravages_rape_rodriguez_and_real_estate_2012061

Olivia Snaije, "France Is Sweet On Sugar Man," **The New York Times**, January 25, 2013 for Rodriguez' French audience. Also see, Hannah Berk, "Mystery Singer Sixto Rodriguez Catches The Spotlight at Last, First In South Africa, Then In America," **The Urban League: The Urban School of San Francisco**, October 17, 2012 http://www.urbanlegendnews.org/arts/2012/10/17/mystery-man-sixto-rodriguez-catches-the-spotlight-at-last-first-in-south-africa-then-in-america/

For a candidate interview after a year of success Rodriguez reflects see Tom Pinnock, "Rodriguez: My Career…It's Been A Mess," **Uncut**, July 2013 http://www.uncut.co.uk/features/rodriguez-my-career-its-been-a-mess-68557

Also see Alasdair Morton, "The Return Of The Sugar Man, **Facebook/tnt magazine** http://sixtorodriguez.files.wordpress.com/2012/08/tnt-magazine-rodriguez-feature-mb-quotes.pdf for an excellent interview. See Belinda Luscombe, "10 Questions for Sixto Rodriguez," **Time**, January 28, 2013, p. 56 for some interesting trivia. See Sean Michaels, "Rodriguez Set To Return to Studio After 42 Year Absence," **London Guardian**, January 30, 2013 http://www.guardian.co.uk/music/2013/jan/30/rodriguez-returns-studio-after-42-years

For Rodriguez' second chance see Kristina Puga, "Rodriguez, A Music Legend In South Africa, Gets A Second Chance At Fame," **NBCLATINO**, August 14, 2012 http://nbclatino.com/2012/08/14/rodriguez-a-music-legend-in-south-africa-gets-a-second-chance-at-fame/ and Julie Hinds, "Searching For Sugar Man Gives Overlooked Icon His Due," **Detroit Free Press**, July 29, 2012. Edd Hurt, "Rodriguez Embraces Newfound Fame Through The Doc Searching

For Sugar Man," **Nashville Scene, http://www.nashvillescene.com/nashville/rediscovered-singer-songwriter-sixto-rodriguez-embraces-newfound-fame-through-the-doc-searching-for-sugar-man/Content?oid=3036007**

The best description of the singer-songwriter is Bob Stanley, **Yeah, Yeah, Yeah: The Story of Modern Pop** (London, 2013), pp. 407-415.

One of Rodriguez' most revealing interviews is with Andy Markowitz, "Talking To Sugar Man: A Few Words With Rodriguez," **Musicfilmweb**, June 19, 2012 http://www.musicfilmweb.com/2012/06/rodriguez-music-documentary-sheffield-docfest/

See Anthony Kaufman, "Truth Profiteer: Producer Simon Chinn Makes Good With Docs," **The Wall Street Journal**, July 26, 2012. Andrew Watt, "Rodriguez's Sweet Surprise," February 11, 2013 contains some excellent quotes on his successes http://www.theage.com.au/entertainment/music/rodriguezs-sweet-surprise-20130210-2e6fd.html Also see the comments on Stephen "Sugar" Segerman in Andrew Watt, "International Man Of Mystery," **The Sydney Morning Herald**, March 1, 2013 http://www.smh.com.au/entertainment/music/international-man-of-mystery-20130228-2f6vm.html See the Segerman interview where he explains his view of Rodriguez. "Seeking Out Sugar, Who Searched For Sugar Man, **Front Row Reviews**, July 15, 2012 http://www.frontrowreviews.co.uk/interviews/seeking-out-sugar-who-searched-for-sugar-man/17740

Ken Shane, "The Popdose Interview: Sixto Rodriguez," **Popdose.com**, January 11, 2013 http://popdose.com/the-popdose-interview-sixto-rodriguez/ is a revealing interview.

For the New York Highline Ballroom show see, Dino Perrucci, "Resurrecting Sugar Man: Rodriguez Comes Alive In Solo New York Show," **Rolling Stone.com**, September 4, 2012 http://www.rollingstone.com/music/blogs/alternate-take/resurrecting-sugar-man-rodriguez-comes-alive-in-solo-new-york-show-20120904

For the Cleveland appearances at Cleveland's Beachland Ballroom, see Jeff Niesel, "Sugar Man's Second Calling," **Cleveland Scene Magazine**, October 31, 2012 http://www.clevescene.com/cleveland/sugar-mans-second-coming/Content?oid=3085140

Also see, "Rodriguez Resurfaces With Tour Behind Searching For Sugar Man," **Sound Spike**, August 23, 2012 http://www.soundspike.com/story/4696/rodriguez-resurfaces-with-tour-behind-searching-for-sugar-man/ The first Beachland show is reviewed in Michael Galluci, "Concert Review-Rodriguez At The Beachland Ballroom, 4-24," **Scene Magazine**, April 27, 2009 http://www.clevescene.com/c-notes/archives/2009/04/27/concert-review-rodriguez-at-the-beachland-ballroom-424

Brian Howard, "Rodriguez Concert Raises The Question: What If," **Philly.com**, October 30, 2012 http://articles.philly.com/2012-10-30/news/34818514_1_1970-s-cold-fact-sugar-man-monkey is an interesting look at his career. See James Reed, "Searching For Sugar Man: Cult Musician Rodriguez," **The Boston Globe**, August 4, 2012 for a review of the documentary.

For the 23 minute interview see Scott Feinberg, "Finding 'Sugar Man': Rodriguez Reflects On A Crazy Year With A Hollywood Ending," **The Hollywood Reporter**, February 13, 2013 http://www.hollywoodreporter.com/race/finding-sugar-man-rodriguez-reflects-422022

On Dennis Coffey see his well written memoir, Dennis Coffey, **Guitars, Bars And Motown Superstars** (Ann Arbor, 2004) and Benjamin Michael Solis, "A Cuppa Joe With Motown's Dennis Coffey," **The Washtenaw Voice**, March 2011 http://www.washtenawvoice.com/2011/03/a-cuppa-joe-with-motowns-dennis-coffey/ Also see, Allan Slutsky, **Standing In The Shadow of Motown: The Life And Music of Legendary Bassist James Jamerson** (Detroit, 1989). Also see the documentaries **Standing In the Shadows of Motown** and **Radio Revolution: The Rise And Fall of The Big 8**. A brilliant book connecting Motown to more relevant Detroit political issues is Suzanne

E.. Smith, **Dancing In the Street; Motown And The Cultural Politics of Detroit** (Cambridge, 20001). Also see, Jack Ryan, **Recollections The Detroit Years: The Motown Sound By The People Who Made It** (Whitmore Lake, 2012) and Gerald Posner, **Motown: Music, Money, Sex And Power** (New York, 2005). Nelson George's **Where Did Our Love Go? The Rise of Fall Of The Motown Sound** (Urbana, 2007) suggests some factors that apply to Sixto Rodriguez' career.

For a review that chides Malik Bendjelloul for leaving out the Australian part of Rodriguez' career, see Paul Byrnes, "Rodriguez Found, But Take This Sweet Story With A Grain of Salt," **The Sydney Morning Herald**, October 4, 2012. Byrnes criticizes **Searching For Sugar Man** for leaving out the Australian connection. Byrnes also talks about the rumor that there is a pot of money in Sydney waiting for Rodriguez.

On winning the Oscar for best documentary see, Mark Olsen, "Oscars 2013: 'Searching For Sugar Man' Wins Best Documentary," **Los Angeles Times**, February 25, 2013; Julie Hinds, "Searching For Sugar Man' Wins Oscar, Putting Detroit-Themed Documentary In Worldwide Spotlight," **Detroit Free Press**, February 25, 2013.

The notion of rediscovering Rodriguez and the mystery behind the story is a theme in Rebecca Davis, "Resurrecting Rodriguez," **Daily Maverick**, August 3, 2012 http://www.dailymaverick.co.za/article/2012-08-03-resurrecting-rodriguez A marvelous article on Rodriguez' influence on South Africans is Barbara Nussbaum, "Sugar Man's Medicine For Salty Wounds: The Oscar Goes To A Cultural Healer," **The Huffington Post**, March 1, 2013 http://www.huffington-post.com/barbara-nussbaum/searching-for-sugar-man_b_2790787.html Also see Regina Weinreich, "Searching For Sugar Man At Guild Hall: Alec Baldwin, Honorary Chairman of the Board," **The Huffington Post**, July 7, 2012 http://www.huffingtonpost.com/regina-weinreich/searching-for-sugar-man-a_b_1656310.html For a critical look at **Searching For Sugar Man** that asks questions about the wives, see, Daniel Menaker, "Searching For Searching For Sugar

Man, August 5, 2012, **The Huffington Post**, http://www.huffingtonpost.com/daniel-menaker/searching-for-sugar-man_b_1744704.html Menace concludes that it is not a documentary but a docudrama.

See "Rodriguez Has Been Found," **Grammy.com**, January 10, 2013 for an interview prior to the Oscar's http://www.grammy.com/news/rodriguez-has-been-found

On Rodriguez' fame see Andy Greene, "Life After Sugar Man," **Rolling Stone**, April 11, 2013, pp. 20, 22. This is a particularly good article as Greene and Rodriguez walk and talk. It is one of the few later articles where Rodriguez management hasn't shut down his opinions. Also see Andy Greene, "Rodriguez: 10 Things You Don't Know About The 'Searching For Sugar Man' Star," **Rolling Stone**, March 28, 2013.

See Ruben Blades, "Whose Success?" **The New York Times Book Review**, April 7, 2013, p. 6 for the letter suggesting that label president's, like Columbia's Clive Davis, did little, if anything, to help an artist achieve success.

For Rodriguez' success see Michael Bonner, "The Sweet Taste of Success," **Uncut**, July 2013, pp. 46-50. On the abortive 2013 Mayor run for Rodriguez see David Sands, "Rodriguez For Detroit Mayor: Searching For Sugar Man Folk Star Begins Political Campaign," **The Huffington Post**, March 21, 2013 http://www.huffingtonpost.com/2013/03/21/sixto-rodriguez-mayor-detroit_n_2918080.html

To understand Steve Rowland's early music career see the Earl Palmer biography, Tony Scherman, **Backbeat: Earl Palmer's Story** (New York, 2000). Also see Mark Worth, "Cause It's The Greatest Last Song Ever Recorded," July 6, 2014, http://sugarman.org/rod-whatsnew.html This article is an unusually perceptive look at "Cause." See Chris Cabin, "Searching For Sugar Man," **Slate Magazine**, April 28, 2012 http://www.slantmagazine.com/film/review/searching-for-sugar-man for a comment on "Cause."

For Rowland's early reaction to **Searching For Sugar Man** see, Brian Blueskye, "Behind Sugar Man: Meet Palm Springs' Steve Rowland-Actor, Singer and Legendary Record Producer," **CV Independent**, http://www.cvindependent.com/index.php/en-US/music/music-news-and-features/item/2207-behind-sugar-man-meet-palm-springs-steve-rowland-actor-singer-and-legendary-record-producer

Anna Hartford, "Sugar Rush: Letter From Cape Town," **The Paris Review**, February 26, 2013 is a brilliant look at the Rodriguez phenomenon in South Africa in early 2013. A brilliant piece of writing on how and why South Africa embraces Rodriguez and how fame and fortune may have blunted the message.

On the chances for a third album see, Nathan Rabin, "Searching For Sugar Man: Comeback Kid Rodriguez Meets With Producers To Discuss Potential New Album," January 29, 2013 http://www.avclub.com/article/emsearching-for-sugar-manem-comeback-kid-rodriguez-91751 For an article that is more fiction than fact on the Sugar Man and his proposed third album that has not materialized, see, Kia Makarechi, "Searching For Sugar Man' Star Rodriguez May Record New Album," **Huffington Post**, January 30, 2013 http://www.huffingtonpost.com/2013/01/30/searching-for-sugar-man-rodriguez-album_n_2582039.html

On Neil Bogart see, Larry Harris, Curt Gooch and Jeff Suhs, **A Party Every Day: The Inside Story of Casablanca Records** (New York, 2009) and Frederic Dannen, **Hit Men: Power Brokers And Fast Money In Music Business** (New York, 1990).

For Clarence Avant's relationship to Soul Train see Nelson George, **The Hippest Trip In America: Soul Train And The Evolution of Culture & Style** (New York, 2014), pp. 59-62. George's excellent book gets some of the facts wrong. He claims Rodriguez sold 30,000 LPs when in fact it was closer to 500,000. He also credits the film's editing with making Avant look bad. The truth is Avant's statements were broadcast verbatim. It was Avant who made himself look like a predator. But George did point out the respect, the business savvy and the sixty plus year career in show business for Avant.

For a view of Rodriguez before the documentary and his place in South Africa, see Rian Malan, "Bizarre Is A Word For It," **London Telegraph**, October 6, 2005 http://www.telegraph.co.uk/culture/music/rockandjazzmusic/3647008/Bizarre-is-a-word-fo

Brian Currin, "Rodriguez And His Place In The Story of Rock," September 1, 2012 http://blog.sugarman.org/2012/09/01/rodriguez-and-his-place-in-the-story-of-rock/ is an unusually perceptive analysis of the Sugar Man and where he fits in the broader scope of rock and roll.

Also see the excellent review by Gervase de Wilde, "Rodriguez At The Union Chapel, Islington, Review," **London Telegraph**, December 10, 2009 http://www.telegraph.co.uk/culture/music/live-music-reviews/6780523/Rodriguez-at-the-Union-Chapel-Islington-review.html

For a brilliant examination of what Rodriguez meant to South Africa, see Richard Pithouse, "The Resurrection of Sixto Rodriguez," http://sacsis.org.za/site/article/1550 Pithouse is a Professor at Rhodes University and he fits Rodriguez' music and influence into the mainstream of South African history. Also see, Edward Douglas, "Interview: The Award-Winning Doc Searching For Sugar Man," **Comingsoon.net**, July 25, 2012 http://www.comingsoon.net/movies/features/92699-interview-the-award-winning-doc-searching-for-sugar-man

The influence that Soul Train may have had on Rodriguez is seen in Nelson George, **The Hippest Trip In America** (New York, 2014) and Questlove, **Soul Train: The Music, Dance and Style of a Generation** (New York, 2014). For some of the criminal elements in the music business and how they carried over into Rodriguez' day see, Joel Selvin, **Here Comes The Night: The Dark Soul of Bert Berns And the Dirty Business of Rhythm and Blues** (New York, 2014).

On Malik Bendjelloul's tragic death see Rodriguez' reaction, Bob Gendron, "Rodriguez Pays Tribute To Director Bendjelloul," **Chicago Tribune**, May 15, 2014. Also see, Kory Grow, "Searching For Sugar Man Director Malik Bendjelloul Dead At 36," **Rolling Stones**, May 14, 2014, Bruce Weber, "Malik Bendjelloul Oscar Winner For 'Sugar' Man Film, Dies At 36, **New York Times**, May 13, 2014, Mark Olson, "Oscar Winning 'Sugar Man' Director Malik Bendjelloul Dies At 36," **Los Angeles Times**, May 13, 2014 and Xan Brooks, "Searching For Sugar Man Director Malik Bendjelloul Dies Aged 36," **London Guardian**, May 14, 2014.

For a brilliant in depth report with information from Stockholm on the tragic death, see Scott Johnson, "Oscar To Suicide In One Year: Tracing The 'Searching For Sugar Man' Director's Tragic Final Days," **The Hollywood Reporter**, June 11, 2014 http://www.hollywoodreporter.com/news/searching-sugarman-director-dead-thr-710882 Also see, Anthony Andrew, "Searching For Malik Bendjelloul-A Tragedy Revisited," **The London Guardian**, July 13, 2014.

On the dangers of success, the fame and fortune syndrome for Rodriguez, see George Palathingal, "Life Not So Sweet For 'Sugar Man' Sixto Rodriguez," May 29, 2013http://www.smh.com.au/entertainment/music/life-not-so-sweet-for-sugar-man-sixto-rodriguez-20140529-zrroy.html#ixzz33OX56blU

The 2013 concerts had widely divergent reviews. See Charles R. Cross, "Concert Review: Rodriguez Charming But Disjointed and Flat," **The Seattle Times**, April 26, 2013. By 2014 the reviews were still excellent ones. See Roy Trakin, "Searching For Sugar Man': There is Sixto Rodriguez Today?" **Billboard**, June 12, 2014 http://www.billboard.com/articles/news/6114238/searching-for-sugar-man-where-is-sixto-rodriguez-today For the November 2012 Rodriguez show at Usher Hall in Edinburg, Scotland, see, Graeme Thomson, "The Spirit of Sugar Man Wins Through On A Night of Occasional Brilliance," **The Arts Desk**, November 26, 2012 http://www.theartsdesk.com/new-music/rodriguez-usher-hall-edinburgh

Steven Mirkin, "Rodriguez Turns In Erratic Set At The Greek," **Orange County Register**, June 3, 2014, reviews the Los Angeles Greek Theater Show in depth with positive and negative comments. The negative outweighs the positive as he believes it was a weak show.

See Glen Baker's description of **Rodriguez Alive** on **Sugarman. Org: The Official Rodriguez Website http://sugarman.org/alive. html**

On the Clarence Avant law suit against Rodriguez see Keith Allen, "Searching For Sugar Man Royalty Mystery May Be Solved," **The Hollywood Reporter**, May 4, 2014 http://guardianlv.com/2014/05/searching-for-sugar-man-royalty-mystery-may-be-solved/

Also see the curious facts behind the Clarence Avant lawsuit in Kathleen Flynn, "Sixto Rodriguez Named In Lawsuit By Music Company," May 29, 2014http://www.nola.com/music/index.ssf/2014/05/rodriguez_named_in_lawsuit_by.html

For an in-depth look at Rodriguez' Edinburgh show in 2013 see Phyllis Stephen, "Solid At 70-Sixto Rodriguez At The Usher Hall," **The Edinburgh Reporter**, http://www.theedinburghreporter.co.uk/2012/11/solid-at-70-sixto-rodriguez-at-the-usher-hall/

For life after the Academy Award winning documentary, see the radio broadcast on Detroit's WDET. FM and short Internet comments by, Stephen Henderson, "Sixto Rodriguez On Life After 'Sugarman," WDET.com April 10, 2015 http://wdet.org/posts/2015/04/10/80189-sixto-rodriguez-on-life-after-sugarman/ Rodriguez appears on this broadcast.

The early Rodriguez story didn't attract much media attention for the best story on the Sugar Man prior to the fame and fortune of the documentary see Greg Kot, "The Long, Crazy Trail of Sixto Rodriguez," **Chicago Tribune**, May 8, 2009 http://articles.chicagotribune.com/2009-05-08/entertainment/0905060201_1_chris-spedding-south-africa-rock-n-roll

Detroit is a city with a rich and varied music history. This book suggests how and why the Motor City is important to Sixto Rodriguez' career. For a look at Detroit's expansive music history see, M. L. Liebler, editor, forward by Dave Marsh, **Heaven Was Detroit: From Jazz To Hip-Hop And Beyond** (Detroit, 2016). The essays from this book helpful to this volume are Marsha Music, "John Lee Hooker and Joe Von Battle: No Magic, Just Men," pp. 67-69, John Sinclair, "Motor City Blues Through the Ages," pp. 92-97, S. R. Boland, "Fortune Records For Truly Great Music," pp. 98-112, Joel Martin, "Two Detroit Music Icons and Two Classic Theaters: Artie Fields and Harry Balk," pp. 129-131, Gary Graff, "The Story of Hitsville: Motown Days," pp. 142-156, Melba Joyce Boyd, "Waiting For Smokey Robinson," pp. 168-176, Pat Thomas, "The Revolution Will Be Recorded," pp. 197-200, Susan Whitall, "Detroit, My Detroit," pp. 215-218, Howard A. DeWitt, "Who Is The Sugar Man?" pp. 299-305 and Pat Thomas, "Rarities of The Revolution: Archie Shepp, The MC5 and John Sinclair," pp.423-425.

One of Rodriguez' friends is featured in the Detroit press. See, for example, Michael Jackson, "The Brewer: John Linardos," **Detroit Metro Times**, June 10, 2105, http://www.metrotimes.com/detroit/the-brewer-john-linardos/Content?oid=2349244

For the influence of the Detroit streets on the Sugar Man see the 600-page book of fiction, short stories and images of the streets M. L. Liebler, editor, **Working Words: Punching The Clock And Kicking Out The Jams** (Coffee House Press, 2010). This is an important book to understand the symbolic power of Detroit's streets. Liebler's poetry, short stories, anthology contributions and his political activism helped me understand Detroit and its role in Rodriguez' life. There is no one who has a better feel for the Detroit streets than Professor Liebler.

For other important works on Detroit via photos, see, for example, Michael Arnaud, **Detroit: The Dream Is Now: The Design, Art, and Resurgence of An American City** (Arnaud, 2017) and Andrew Moore, **Andrew Moore: Detroit Disassembled** (Akron, 2010). For lost Motor City landmarks see, Cheri Gay, **Lost Detroit** (Pavilion,

2013). David Maraniss, **Once In A Great City: A Detroit Story** (New York, 2015) tells the story of the Motor City's boom years.

For the Sugar Man's eldest daughter, her accomplishments, her lifestyle, her time living in Namibia see, "Thoroughly Unconventional Eva Rodriguez," **Georgia Herald http://www.georgeherald.com/news/News/General/25764/Thoroughly-unconventional-Eva-Rodriguez** The article is important for shedding light on Eva's brilliance and her connection to her father's intellectual mantra.

The 2016 Australian tour is discussed in an interview, see Arne Sjostedt, "Sugar Man Rodriguez Heads Back to Australia," **The Sydney Morning Herald**, July 14, 2016 http://www.smh.com.au/entertainment/music/sugar-man-rodriguez-heads-back-to-australia-20160609-gpfq9q.html

An aspect of Rodriguez's success is in his relationship to the South African music industry. To understand how and why, see, for example, William Murray deVilliers, "Aspects of The South African Music Industry: An Analytical Perspective," M. A. Thesis, University of Pretoria, 2006. Perhaps the most interesting part of DeVilliers thesis is a section on record piracy. South Africa ranked eighth in the world in piracy. This explains why some many copies of **Cold Fact** were sold without royalties.

To understand how and why Sixto Rodriguez emerged as a cult artist see, for example, Phil Gallo, "Cult Singer Rodriguez Risen In New Film 'Sugar Man," **Billboard**, July 29, 2012 http://www.billboard.com/articles/news/480733/cult-singer-rodriguez-risen-in-new-film-sugar-man and Sarah Jane Griffiths, "Discovering Sugar Man Rodriguez," **BBC News**, July 26, 2012, http://www.bbc.com/news/entertainment-arts-1897489

In 2016-2017 there were few Rodriguez interviews. For a brief one where he reflects on his success, see Gary Graff, "Rodriguez At The Crofoot, Things To Know," **Pontiac Daily Tribune**, April 21, 2017.

http://www.dailytribune.com/arts-and-entertainment/20170421/rodriguez-at-the-crofoot-3-things-to-know

See Allan Winkler, **To Everything There Is A Season: Pete Seeger And The Power of Song** (New York, 2011) for some arguments paralleling the Sixto Rodriguez story. Also see David Dunaway, **How Can I Keep From Singing: Pete Seeger** (New York, 1990).

The importance of the music industry to Rodriguez career is a subtheme to the three volumes on the Sugar Man. There is an extensive literature on the music business. There are some books that stand out and apply to the Sugar Man. See, for example, Clive Davis, **The Soundtrack To My Life** (New York, 2013) in which he apologies for music insiders who have ruined the industry. He is one of them. Also see, Frederic Dannen, **Hit Men: Power Brokers And Fast Money Inside The Music Business** (New York, 1990) and Jory Farr, **Moguls and Madmen: The Pursuit of Power In Popular Music** (New York, 1994) for the nefarious deeds of the record industry. The Dannen volume chronicles the record business from Morris Levy to Walter Yetnikoff, the president of CBS Records and the book caused many CEO's and other moguls in the music business to complain. They should not have said a word as Dannen got it right. They were a bunch of crooks, lacking ethics and integrity. The record business went from small time crooks to labels hiring shrewd lawyers to offer a contract that would result in very little money. Some artists, like Van Morrison, fought this and others like Sixto Rodriguez faded into obscurity.

See Brad Wheeler, "Sixto Rodriguez Isn't Dead, He's On Tour," **The Globe And Mail**, July 1 2009 for the story of how and why he was popular three full and complete years before **Searching For Sugar** Man brought fame and fortune to a performer that was long overdue.

http://www.theglobeandmail.com/arts/music/sixto-rodriguez-isnt-dead-hes-on-tour/article4279566/

A 2016 interview with an Australian journalist is particularly revealing, see, Iain Shedden, "For Sugar Man Sixto Rodriguez, The

Search Is Over," **The Weekend Australian**, July 6, 2016. This is a telephone interview that Shedden conducted when it appeared that Rodriguez no longer was giving in-depth interviews. Adam Bradley, **The Poetry Of Pop** (New Haven, 2017) is a brilliant examination of how popular songs evoke a sense of poetry. Bradley is an English professor at the University of Colorado. He is adept at linking pop lyrics to pop culture. Also see Michael Robbins, **Equipment For Living: On Poetry And Pop Music** (New York, 2017) for the argument poetry and pop music is essential to daily life. Bradley, a Harvard PhD, and Robbins, a University of Chicago PhD, work in the academic world. They have come up with a means of locking poetry and pop music into the modern world. No one fits better into this stilted scenario than Sixto Rodriguez. The relationship between words and music is an important aspect of the direction Bradley and Robbins take in their attempt to analyze why and how pop music is important. Who examines Detroit and Rodriguez as well as the myths and realities of **Searching for Sugar Man**? This is a brilliant piece of analysis by Professor Cole who is in the Department of History, Western Illinois University, see, Peter Cole, "Searching For Detroit," **Safundi: The Journal Of South African And American Studies** (volume 14, 2013, Issue 4) http://www.tandfonline.com/doi/abs/10.1080/17533171.2013.841063?src=recsys&journalCode=rsaf20 The Cole article is important for his analysis of why Malik Bendjelloul did not feature people of color in South Africa and he intimates without mentioning his name that Stephen "Sugar" Segerman had too big on impact upon the story. The result was myth and stereotyping bested reality.

There are very few rock and roll manuscript collections. But some do exist. See, for example, The John and Leni Sinclair Papers 1957-1999, Bentley Historical Library, University of Michigan and the University of California, Berkeley has extensive collections. See, for example, Free Speech Movement Records, Bancroft Library. This is four boxes, five cartons and two oversize boxes of leaflets, letters, petitions, bumper stickers, buttons, long playing records and notebooks. http://www.oac.cdlib.org/findaid/ark:/13030/kt3m3n99kp/ These materials are important to understanding Sixto Rodriguez' political development and that of his friend John Sinclair. There is also extensive literature written by Sinclair, see, for example, John Sinclair, **It's All Good: A John Sinclair Reader** (Head Press, 2009) and John Sinclair, **Guitar Army: Rock And Revolution With The MC5 and The White Panther Party** (Process, 2007). For a review of Sinclair's legal problems, see the DVD Frank Bach, **20 to Life: Life And Times of John Sinclair** (2007).

For an academic examination of Rodriguez see Bryan D. Palmer, "Sugar Man's Sweet Kiss: the Artist Former, and Now Again, Known as Rodriguez," **Marxism and Historical Practice: Interventions And Appreciations**, volume II (Boston, 2015). Also see, Howard A. DeWitt, "Sixto Rodriguez: The Sugar Man Returns," **Blue Suede News**, number 99, Winter 2012-2013, pp. 21-27. For Steve Rowland see, Howard A. DeWitt and Ken Burke, "Steve Rowland: Actor, Rocker and Internationally Acclaimed Producer, Part One," **Blue Suede News**, number 113, Fall, 2017, pp. 20-25. The two articles began my journey to the three books on Sixto Rodriguez. A brilliant academic look at the theoretical relationship in lyrical form between Bob Dylan and the Sugar Man is an intriguing article by Shirsho Dasgupta, "Climb Up On My Music: Tracing Bob Dylan's Influence In The Lyrics of Sixto Rodriguez," http://www.academia.edu/32883277/Climb_Up_On_My_Music_Tracing_Bob_Dylans_influence_on_the_lyrics_of_Sixto_Rodriguez Professor Dasgupta teaches in the Department of English at Jadavpur University in Kolkata, India and he has a view of the Sugar man that needs to be examined.

For recent comment his life see, Lynn Saxbert, "CityFolk Preview: Rodriguez's Life After Sugar Man," **Ottawa Star**, September 15, 2017 http://ottawasun.com/2017/09/15/cityfolk-preview-rodriguezs-life-after-sugar-man/wcm/cfc62516-46ad-46aa-8ece-f7f2baf853f7

Acknowledgements

This book is the second adventure or volume in the Sixto Rodriguez tale. There are many people who contributed to this project. The primary ones include Steve Rowland, Harry Balk, a very brief conversation with Matt Sullivan, Budd Albright, Richard Niles, Mike Theodore, Dennis Coffey, Matt Lucas and a host of people who preferred to be anonymous sources.

For almost five years Steve Rowland answered multiple questions At times they were the same question. He did so with good humor and infinite patience. I appreciate the time he took and the material he allowed me to view. This book would have been impossible without him. I am sure I didn't get it right. That is my joke to Steve as he is unusually precise about the truth. He wants the story told accurately.

The Detroit Public Library was like a second home during three Detroit trips. The staff was unusually kind and efficient.

My thanks to my wonderful and supportive brother and sister in law, Ken and Barb Marich, for their sane and intelligent choice of wine and food as well as their social-political wisdom My brothers Dennis and Duane DeWitt listened to me in the past, and they offered their opinions. Thanks to Mike Levy, Ed Hackney, Ron Brock, Dennis Siler, Paul Perry, Claude Amerson, Dr. Richard Bailey, John and Cindy Milliken and the McDonald's-Panera-Starbuck's-Coffee

Bean crews for listening to me and serving me too much coffee. Pat Thomas fielded long distance phone calls with skill, patience and understanding. He also gave me a deeper understanding of the story. Although previously mentioned Steve Rowland spent hundreds of hours recalling his Rodriguez experiences. Pat Brown listened to my ideas on her Scottsdale visits. Jackie and Joe Hladik provided inspiration, critical remarks and wine.

The Hladik's with care and precision critiqued the manuscript, and they made it a better book. They spent hundreds of hours asking questions, correcting grammatical errors, arguing for better syntax and making excellent content corrections. All errors reside with the author. Matt and Barbara Lucas added to the material on Detroit and Matt's illustrious career parallels that of the Sugar Man.

Marc and Gaby Magg Bristol are good friends and they publish my ranting on rock and roll music in **Blue Suede News**. Thank you Marc and Gaby for not only being critical editors but good friends. They have edited my rock, blues, country and rockabilly articles for almost thirty years. Thanks for being such good friends. Neil Skok, Steve Marinnuci, David L. Page, Jim McCue and Fred Hopkins are friends who have advised me on this and other projects.

Brian Young who operates the Del Shannon Appreciation Society is a good friend, listener and astute critic.

The staff of the Chicago Public Library, the University of California, Los Angeles Library, the newspaper room at the University of California, Berkeley and the UCB Bancroft Library provided newspaper and periodical materials. The Detroit Public Library was a major source.

Ken Burke, one of America's premier rock writers, fielded my late at night and early in the morning phone calls, as did Professor B. Lee Cooper who remains America's premier rock scholar in tandem with Burke.

Photographer Scott Amonson was responsible for the post-processed photos and I thank him for a job well done.

About the Author

Howard A. DeWitt is Professor Emeritus of History at Ohlone College, Fremont, California. He received his B. A. from Western Washington State University, the M. A. from the University of Oregon and a PhD from the University of Arizona. He also studied at the University of Paris, Sorbonne and the City University in Rome. Professor DeWitt is the author of twenty-seven books and has published over 200 articles and more than 200 reviews in a wide variety of popular and scholarly magazines.

DeWitt has also been a member of a number of organizations to promote the study of history. The most prestigious is the Organization of American Historians where he was a reviewer for a decade.

For more forty-five years he has taught full and part time at a number of U. S. colleges. He is best known for teaching two college level courses in the History of Rock and Roll music. He continued to teach the History of Rock and Roll music on the Internet until 2011. Among people he brought to class were Bo Diddley, Mike Bloomfield, Jimmy McCracklin, Paul Butterfield, George Palmerton, Ron Peterson, Neil Skok and Pee Wee Thomas. In a distinguished academic career, he has also taught at the University of California, Davis, the University of Arizona, Cochise College and Chabot College. In addition to these teaching assignments, Professor DeWitt is a regular speaker at the Popular Culture Association annual convention and at the National Social Science Association meetings. He has delivered a number of addresses to the Organization of American Historians.

He wrote the first book on Chuck Berry, which was published by Pierian Press under the title **Chuck Berry: Rock N Roll Music** in 1985. DeWitt's earlier brief biography, **Van Morrison: The Mystic's Music**, published in 1983, received universally excellent reviews. On the English side of the music business DeWitt's, **The Beatles: Untold Tales**, originally published in 1985, was picked up by the Kendall Hunt Publishing Company in the 1990s and is used regularly in a wide variety of college courses on the history of rock music. Kendall Hunt also published **Stranger in Town: The Musical Life of Del Shannon** with co-author Dennis M. DeWitt in 2001. In 1993 **Paul McCartney: From Liverpool To Let It Be** concentrated on the Beatle years. He also co-authored **Jailhouse Rock: The Bootleg Records of Elvis Presley** with Lee Cotten in 1983.

Professor DeWitt's many awards in the field of history include founding the Cochise County Historical Society and his scholarship has been recognized by a number of state and local government organizations. DeWitt's book, **Sun Elvis: Presley In The 1950s**, published by Popular Culture Ink. was a finalist for the Deems-ASCAP Award for the best academic rock and roll book. His first book on Sixto Rodriguez was] a finalist for a Michigan Notable Book Award.

In his research for any and all of his books, Professor DeWitt employs the Gay Talese method interviewed everyone around and connected to his project

Professor DeWitt is a renaissance scholar who publishes in a wide variety of outlets that are both academic and popular. He is one of the few college professors who bridge the gap between scholarly and popular publications. His articles and reviews have appeared in **Blue Suede News, DISCoveries, Rock 'N' Blues News**, the **Journal of Popular Culture**, the **Journal of American History, California History**, the **Southern California Quarterly**, the **Pacific Historian, Amerasia**, the **Western Pennsylvania Historical Magazine**, the **Annals**

of Iowa, the **Journal of the West**, **Arizona and the West,** the **North Beach Review**, **Ohio History**, the **Oregon Historical Quarterly**, the **Community College Social Science Quarterly**, **Montana: The Magazine of the West**, **Record Profile Magazine**, **Audio Trader**, the **Seattle Post-Intelligencer** and **Juke Box Digest**.

For forty plus years DeWitt has combined popular and academic writing. He has been nominated for numerous writing awards. His reviews are combined with articles to form a body of scholarship and popular writing that is frequently footnoted in major works. As a political scientist, Professor DeWitt authored three books that questioned American foreign policy and its direction. In the Philippines, DeWitt is recognized as one of the foremost biographers of their political leader Jose Rizal. His three books on Filipino farm workers remain the standard in the field. He was a featured speaker in 1996 in Manila at the Philippine Centennial.

During his high school and college years, DeWitt promoted dances in and around Seattle, Washington. Such groups as Little Bill and the Bluenotes, Ron Holden and the Playboys, the Frantics, the Wailers and George Palmerton and the Night People among others played at such Seattle venues as the Eagle's Auditorium and Dick Parker's Ballroom.

Howard and his wife Carolyn have two grown children. Darin is a Professor of Political Science at California State University, Long Beach and Melanie is a Special Education teacher with two children Natalia and Katarina. They both live in Los Angeles. Howard's wife of forty-seven plus years, Carolyn, is an educator, an artist and she continues to raise Howard. She is presently retired and vacationing around the world. The DeWitt's live in Scottsdale, Arizona. That is when they are not in Paris looking for art, books and music. Howard is working on a book on Portugal' Secrets, That is a year or two away.

His book on the president **Obama's Detractor's: In The Right Wing Nut House** is a marvelous look at the radical right and the tragedy of Fox TV News, right wing book authors and political kooks like Laura Ingraham and Ann Coulter. It was also the reason that some of his friends in Scottsdale and Saddlebrooke no longer talk to him about politics. His novels **Stone Murder** and **Salvador Dali Murder** feature a San Francisco P.I. Trevor Blake III and a gay mobster Don Gino Landry, and much of the story line will evolve around crimes that DeWitt witnessed while working four years and two days as an agent with the Bureau of Alcohol, Tobacco and Firearms. He was a street agent for the BATF and his tales of those years are in manuscript waiting for publication. He was also a key figure in the BATF Union.

Meeting Hitler: A Tragicomedy, published in 2016 was a best seller with excellent reviews. In 2017 **Sicily's Secrets: The Mafia, Pizza and Hating Rome** was a number one best seller for travel books on Amazon. DeWitt is working on a like-minded book on Portugal. His next book is **Trump Against The World: A Foreign Policy Bully-Disaster At Home, Democracy In Peril**, which is scheduled for 2018 publication.

Any corrections or additions to this or the subsequent volumes that will follow this study can be sent to Horizon Books, P. O. Box 4342, Scottsdale, Arizona 85258. DeWitt can be reached via e-mail at Howard217@aol.com

Made in the USA
Lexington, KY
05 December 2017